SERVICE MANAGEMENT

An Integrated Approach

Third Edition

Service Management

An Integrated Approach

Edited by

Paul Gemmel

Bart Van Looy

Roland Van Dierdonck

PEARSON

Harlow, England • London • New York • Boston • San Francisco • Toronto • Sydney
Auckland • Singapore • Hong Kong • Tokyo • Seoul • Taipei • New Delhi
Cape Town • São Paulo • Mexico City • Madrid • Amsterdam • Munich • Paris • Milan

Pearson Education Limited
Edinburgh Gate
Harlow
Essex CM20 2JE
England

and Associated Companies throughout the world

Visit us on the World Wide Web at:
www.pearson.com/uk

First published in Great Britain in 1998
Second edition published 2003
Third edition published 2013

ISBN 978-0-273-73203-7

British Library Cataloguing-in-Publication Data
A catalogue record for this book is available from the British Library

Library of Congress Cataloging-in-Publication Data
A catalog record for this book is available from the Library of Congress

ARP impression 98

Typeset in 9.5/12.5pt Charter ITC Std by 35
Printed by Ashford Colour Press Ltd., Gosport.

Brief Contents

Contents

Part One Defining services

Bart Van Looy, Paul Gemmel

Contents

Part 2 Designing services

Paul Gemmel, Bart Van Looy

Contents

Part 4 Developing services

Lecturer Resources

For password-protected online resources tailored to support the use of this textbook in teaching, please visit **www.pearsoned.co.uk/vanlooy**

ON THE WEBSITE

List of figures

Technical Notes

List of tables

Technical Notes

List of exhibits

About the authors

Werner Bruggeman is a professor in management accounting and control at the faculty of Economics of the Ghent University and at the Vlerick Leuven Ghent Management School. He is also Partner of B&M Consulting and helps companies to improve their strategy and performance management processes.

Dirk Buyens is the Academic Dean and Partner at the Vlerick Leuven Ghent Management School. As professor he is Chairman of the Competence Centre for People and Organisation. His major fields of interest are strategic HRM, organization development and strategic career management.

Koenraad Debackere is professor in technology and innovation management at the Catholic University of Leuven and Managing Director of K. U. Leuven R&D. His major research interests include innovation strategy and the management of innovation in industry and the development of government policies to support innovation in industry.

Marion Debruyne is Associate Professor and Partner at the Vlerick Leuven Gent Management school. She holds a Civil Engineering and a Masters degree and is Doctor in Applied Economics (Ghent University). After obtaining a CIM fellowship she held positions as Visiting Doctoral Fellow at the Wharton School (University of Pennsylvania), Visiting Scholar at the Kellogg Graduate School of Management (Northwestern University) and Assistant Professor at the Goizueta Business School (Emory University).

Her interests lie at the intersection of marketing strategy, innovation and competition. Her work has been published in *Marketing Science* and *The Journal of Product Innovation Management*, among others.

At Vlerick she holds the SWIFT Chair in "Market-driven Innovation" and is Programme Director of the Master in Marketing Management as well as academic director of the executive open enrolment programme "Product Management". She also teaches the Marketing Management course in the full-time and part-time executive MBA programmes. She was involved in training and coaching assignments for Abbott, Aliaxis, Dexia, Electrabel, Etex, Inbev, J&J, Manpower, Merck, Siemens and Umicore.

Patrick De Pelsmacker holds a Ph.D. in Economics from Ghent University. He is professor of marketing at the University of Antwerp and at Ghent University. His research interest include advertising effectiveness, integrated marketing communications, new advertising formats and media, ethical consumer behaviour and social marketing.

Steven Desmet studied applied economic sciences at the Ghent University, where he has been working as research assistant in (service) operations management, service productivity and quality. At the same time he worked at the Service Management Center at the Vlerick Leuven Ghent Management School. After a career as consultant for 8 years with PWC Consulting and Accenture, he is currently working for the IT department at **http://www.goudengids.be**.

Koen Dewettinck obtained his Ph.D. from the Economics and Management Department of Ghent University. He also holds a Master's degree in Work- and Organizational Psychology, from the same university. He has been a research fellow at the Weatherhead School of Management, Case Western Reserve University, Cleveland, Ohio.

Currently, Koen is partner of Vlerick Leuven Ghent Management School and Associate Professor in Human Resource Management. His research, teaching and counselling activities focus on employee motivation, employee performance management and strategic HRM. As Director of CEPP, the Vlerick Centre for Excellence on People Performance, he is working together with organizations in generating and sharing new insights, practices and tools to create high performing organizations. Koen is also Director of the Executive MBA programmes organized at Vlerick's Ghent and Leuven campuses.

Kristof De Wulf studied Applied Economic Sciences at, and holds an MBA from, University of Antwerp. He obtained his Ph.D. from Ghent University in the domain of relationship marketing and has been an associate professor of marketing for more than ten years at the Vlerick Leuven Ghent Management School. He is co-founder and CEO of InSites Consulting, a global market research firm with offices in Ghent, Rotterdam, London, Timisoara, and New York. His research focus is on customer relationship management, online and social marketing, and brand management.

Dries Faerns is Full Professor of Innovation and Organization at the Faculty of Economics and Business (University of Groningen) and Affiliated Researcher at the Research Centre of Organisation Studies (Katholieke Universiteit Leuven). He has published papers in journals such as *Academy of Management Journal, Organization Studies, Journal of Product Innovation Management, Journal of Management Studies, Technovation and Small Business Economics*. His current research focuses on the management of ambidextrous innovation strategies, performance implications of alliance portfolios and the governance of external venturing trajectories.

Dries Faems is associate editor of the *Journal of Management Studies*. He also is a member of the editorial review board of the *Academy of Management Journal* and the *Journal of Trust Research*.

Annelies Geerts holds a Master's degree in Educational Sciences and an Advanced Master's degree in Management of Public Organizations. She worked as a researcher at the Operations and Technology Management Center of the Vlerick Leuven Ghent Management School. She is currently a Ph.D. researcher at the University of Twente, Department of Management and Governance, and Affiliated Researcher at the Catholic University of Leuven, Department of Applied Economics. Her research focuses on effective innovation strategies of incumbent firms in high-velocity environments.

Paul Gemmel is professor of service management and hospital management at the Faculty of Economics and Business Administration of Ghent University. He is co-founder of the Centre of Service Intelligence (CSI), a research centre for service management at the same university. He is founder of, and scientific advisor for, a research centre for hospital management at the Vlerick Leuven Ghent Management School. In preparing his doctoral degree, he spent one year at the College of Business of the Arizona State University, Tempe, US (1992–1993). His research focus is on operations management in different service sectors such as health care and banks.

Wim Grielens is a senior consultant with IBM Global Services. He has several years of experience in applying telecommunications, collaboration and portal technology for improved operational effectiveness. He specializes in the analysis of collaboration processes. He holds a Master's degree in Applied Economics.

Wilfried Grommen is Chief Technology Officer at Hewlett Packard EMEA. His career always focused on the strategic impact IT has on business development, policy development and societal evolution. Previously he was CTO and General Manager at Microsoft EMEA. He was a leading technologist at Capco, IBM consulting and Cimad Consultants. Wilfried holds a B.S. in Civil

Engineering and Electro-Mechanical Engineering with a specialization in microelectronics from the University of Leuven.

Aimé Heene is a professor in the field of strategic management for private and public organizations at Ghent University, Antwerp University, and the College of Europe in Bruges. He specializes in competence based strategic management, management for social profit and public organizations, and the effects of European integration on business and corporate strategies. He has more than 25 years of experience in research, teaching, and consulting.

Krist'l Krols is director of the Healthcare Supply Chain Research Network at the Vlerick Leuven Ghent Management School. In close collaboration with manufacturing companies and service organizations, she undertakes research on state of the art topics in the healthcare supply chain. These topics focus on a combined improvement of efficiency, service and sustainability.

Bart Larivière is Assistant Professor of Service Management at Ghent University, where he is the founder and Executive Director of the Center for Service Intelligence. His research focuses on the link between customer loyalty and various aspects of the service encounter including service recovery, servitization, servicescape, consumer-wellbeing, and multichannel management. He intensively collaborates with Belgian companies bridging the gap between practice and academia and is co-founder of the Belgian Association for Quantitative Marketing Research (**http://www.BAQMaR.eu**), a community of marketing academicians and practitioners. His research has been published in the *Journal of Service Research*, *Journal of Service Management*, the *European Journal of Operational Research*, and *Expert Systems with Applications*. He was a finalist for best paper in the *Journal of Service Research*, and his research twice won the Best Practitioner Presentation Award at the Frontiers in Service Conference (2009; 2012), rewarding the best academic research applied to real-world situations and problems.

Pedro Matthynssens is a Partner and Managing Director of The Boston Consulting Group in Brussels. Prior to BCG he was a manager in the securities and capital markets team of IBM Global Services. He holds an MA degree in Classics from University of Leuven and a post-graduate degree in Computational Linguistics from University of Antwerp.

Niels Schillewaert is co-founder and managing partner of InSites Consulting, managing the US office. He was a marketing professor at the Vlerick Leuven Ghent Management School, obtained his Ph.D. at Ghent University and studied at Pennsylvania State University (USA) as an ISBM Fellow. Niels has received several awards for his research, is a frequent speaker at international conferences and a council member of Eşomar (**http://www.esomar.org**). His work was published in leading scientific journals such as *Journal of Marketing*, *The International Journal of Research in Marketing*, *Journal of Services Research*, *Journal of the Academy of Marketing Science*, *Industrial Marketing Management*, *The Journal of Business Research*, *Survey Research Methods and Information and Management*.

Walter Stevens has over 12 years of consulting experience with a strong focus on management development, competence management, organizational development and HR policy setting. He is one of the founders of The Competence Network (TCN) a network of experienced professionals who – starting from shared values like respect, authenticity, and integrity – deliver value to customers in the field of organizing and HRM.

Stefan Stremersch studied applied economics at Ghent University and obtained his Ph.D. at Tilburg University. He is currently assistant professor of marketing and research fellow at Erasmus University Rotterdam. He specialises in new product growth and marketing of high-tech products.

Joeri Van Den Bergh studied applied economics at VLEKHO Brussels and has a Master's in marketing (SLM) from the Vlerick Leuven Ghent Management School. He is co-author of the textbook *Marketing Communications* (Pearson) and *How Cool Brands Stay Hot: Branding to Generation Y* (Kogan Page). He is co-founder of InSites Consulting, a global marketing research and consulting agency with offices in New York, London, Timisoara, Rotterdam and Ghent.

Tine Vandenbossche received her Master's degree in psychology from Ghent University. She is scientific coordinator of the Competence Management Research Centre at the Vlerick Leuven Ghent Management School and is preparing a Master's Programme on European human resource management.

Roland Van Dierdonck is a civil and industrial engineer (Ghent University) and Doctor in Business Administration Harvard University (US). He was an assistant professor at IMD, Lausanne, visiting research scholar at the University of North Carolina, Chapel Hill (USA) and visiting professor at INSEAD (France), Rotterdam School of Management (The Netherlands) and various other schools and universities. He was Partner and professor of Vlerick Leuven Ghent Management School and at Ghent University. He was Dean of Vlerick Leuven Ghent Management School between 1997 and 2007. He became professor emeritus in January 2012. His main research interests are supply chain management, manufacturing strategy and service operations management.

Bart Van Looy was responsible for the Service Management Centre at the Vlerick Leuven Ghent Management School from the beginning of 1996 until the end of 1997. Previously, he worked as a consultant in the field of HRM and organizational behaviour. He obtained his Ph.D. from K. U. Leuven where he is currently professor at the department of Managerial Economics, Strategy and Innovation (MSI), Faculty of Business and Economics. In addition, he has a (part-time) research affiliation at the University of Twente (Institute of Governance Studies, OOHR) and teaches at the MBA programme of Flanders Business School (Antwerp). Bart Van Looy is co-promotor of ECOOM (responsible for the service and research activities pertaining to Technometrics/Patent Analysis) and responsible for the research activities of INCENTIM (Research division K. U. Leuven R&D).

Gino Van Ossel is one of Europe's leading experts in shopper marketing. He feeds his expertise into Vlerick's Retail & Trade Marketing Research Centre. He is often consulted by the media to comment on retail and consumer marketing trends. He has taught in over 25 countries spread over 4 continents. Gino Van Ossel is non-executive director of Fred & Ginger (Euronext Brussels), Formen and the Dutch Trade Marketing Association. He is also chairman of the Expert Group Retail of the Belgian Marketing Foundation.

Katrien Verleye studied socio-educational sciences at Ghent University and works as a researcher in the service management domain at Ghent University and Vlerick Leuven Gent Management School. In 2009, she was granted an I.C.M. doctoral fellowship. Her doctoral research focuses on customer participation and customer engagement behaviors in service processes. During her doctoral trajectory, Katrien was visiting research scholar at University of North Carolina at Chapel Hill (US), where she did research on service co-creation.

Kurt Verweire is an Associate Professor in Strategic Management and Partner at Vlerick Leuven Ghent Management School. He obtained his Ph.D. in 1999 at Erasmus University in Rotterdam. His major research interests are business strategy formulation and implementation.

Preface

You are looking at the first pages of the third edition of *Service Management: An Integrated Approach*. This book initially originated out of continuous discussions and research efforts that took place at the Service Management Centre of the Vlerick Leuven Ghent Management School. All too often one is tempted to take well-established insights and know-how coming from manufacturing environments and apply them to services. However, services do have some characteristics that pose specific challenges and/or require special attention, for example: intangibility poses specific challenges to communication and marketing efforts; simultaneity – i.e. the presence of the customer during the service delivery process – implies a direct link between employees' feelings and behavior and customers' perceptions of service quality; the perishable nature of service has considerable implications for managing the service delivery system and the available capacity. In addition, services are processes. They require an integrated and concerted approach; the operational service delivery system, employees and customers all need to be attuned to deliver value in a seamless way.

This awareness of the specific nature of services and, hence, service management inspired several companies, together with the Vlerick Leuven Ghent Management School, to establish a forum that allowed for exploration and in-depth discussion of the specific nature of service management. The centre followed a multidisciplinary approach from the start; people with an engineering, marketing or organizational behaviour background have been involved, and both academics and practitioners have collaborated in the discussions. Workshops have been organized covering themes such as customer satisfaction, information technology, empowerment, the service profit chain, innovation, performance management, capacity management and waiting lines, to name just a few. In-depth case studies and survey research have also been part of these exploration efforts.

During these years of working together it became clear that services need to be approached in an integrated way: the operational service delivery system, employees' competencies, behavior and feelings, and customer needs and preferences all need to be balanced, resulting in a configuration that eventually will lead to value creation and benefits for all stakeholders involved. Arriving at such a configuration implies a process which starts with defining and designing service activities that deliver value in a dynamic way.

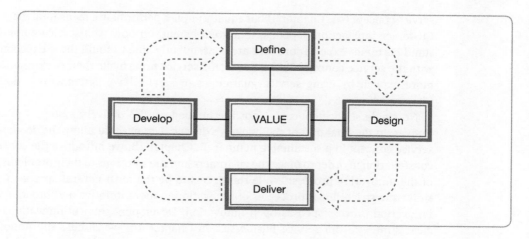

In the first part, we stress the importance of being explicit – i.e. defining – about the value envisaged by service activities. In Chapter 1, we first outline the broader evolution of services in the world economy. Next, we examine the different characteristics that distinguish services from goods and introduce relevant service classifications as not all are alike. Acknowledging the specific nature of service as well as differences among types of service is crucial for managing services effectively, as will become clear in Chapter 2. We proceed with a discussion of the critical role that the service concept fulfills (Chapter 3). The *definition* of the service concept is the starting point for the design of any service delivery system.

In Part 2 we systematically discuss the *design* of service delivery systems by adopting a process perspective (Chapter 4). As value creation processes in services involve both service employees and customers, we need to pay attention to both the behaviour of the employees and the customers in these processes. As such, a process logic should be complemented by delineating relevant HR practices in which the notion of competencies figure prominently (Chapter 5). In Chapter 6, we discuss the role of technology, in particular, information technology. Also on the level of facilities design choices need to be made as facilities are an inherent part of the service experience and play an important role in the perception of service quality (Chapter 7). Finally, one faces the challenge of 'making the intangible tangible'; branding, communication and pricing are crucial in this respect (Chapters 8 and 9).

In Part 3, we focus on how to *deliver* value for the customer. One of the key success factors in service delivery is capacity management (Chapter 10). Not only is capacity management extremely important for the financial performance of the service firm; it also directly affects the customer experiences. The same applies to the behaviour of employees: their motivation, competencies, satisfaction and commitment will impact customers' perceptions of service quality and, hence, satisfaction. As a result, human resources (HR) practices play a decisive role in the management of service operations. These are discussed extensively in Chapter 11, where we introduce three crucial notions: empowerment, competencies and collaboration. These 'internal' practices need to be complemented by a focus on the needs and considerations of customers (Chapter 12). Building and maintaining customer relationships in service situations are directly related to the principle that customer satisfaction, customer loyalty and profitability are closely intertwined with each other. Ensuring the delivery of value in any service system not only requires the presence of a service concept (see Chapter 3) but equally implies performance measurement (Chapter 13). Customer satisfaction depends, to a great extent, on how well service employees understand customer expectations and are consequently able to fulfill these expectations in line with the service concept. This is why some service firms make their performance standards more explicit by using service guarantees or service-level agreements – the subjects of Chapter 14.

No single service concept – nor the implied service delivery system – is made to last forever. In the final part of the book, we discuss avenues that allow the *development* of the service concept in a sustainable manner. In Chapter 15, we introduce the concept of value constellation in order to place the customers and the solutions to their problems at the heart of the innovation process. While this seems to be the most natural approach, it implies a shift from strict, linear processes of innovation to more iterative and broader views of the innovation process such as open innovation. Developing service innovations demands a clear strategy from service businesses. In Chapter 16, we discuss the notion of service strategy as a coalescing framework, linking processes, technology, human resources, and customers to the service concept. The ability and willingness to work internationally is becoming an additional prerequisite for service firms' growth and long-term survival. In Chapter 17, we describe in more detail the impetus towards internationalization as well as the things service firms need to bear in mind when developing an international strategy. While reading the book, it will become clear that boundaries between manufacturing companies and service providers are increasingly blurred. In Chapter 18, we look in depth at the notion of 'servitization' – that is, manufacturing companies that engage in offering services. Servitization can be considered a business model innovation for manufacturing companies, and it proves that service management is not an exclusive prerogative of the service industry but rather affects manufacturing industries to an ever larger extent.

Of course, we cannot cover all issues related to the different themes listed in the table of contents. Rather, we have tried to highlight those elements that relate directly to the nature of services or bear a crucial importance for service management. By placing service aspects in the spotlight, this book can be seen as complementary to other managerial texts focusing on a specific functional area or domain.

Paul Gemmel
Bart Van Looy
Roland Van Dierdonck
Ghent, Leuven, June 2012

Acknowledgements

The work of the Service Management Centre resulted in *Service Management: An Integrated Approach*. Without the Service Management Centre, no such book would have been written, so we are grateful for the support, both financially and intellectually, of the partners involved in the Service Management Centre: *ABB Service*, part of the Asea Brown Boveri Group; *Electrabel*, the leading Belgian electricity, gas and cable TV company; *Generale Bank*, created in 1822, now part of BNP/Paribas; *Schindler*, the worldwide market-leader in escalators and moving walkways; and, finally, *Digital Multivendor Customer Services (MCS)*, now part of the Compaq/Hewlett Packard organization.

Just looking at the table of contents and the number of authors involved demonstrates that putting this book together extended beyond the efforts of the editors. We thank all contributors for the time and knowledge they put into this book, for the patience they have displayed when confronted with our comments and suggestions, and for their openness to explore the topics at hand with us. Some people contributed to this book in ways that went beyond writing the various chapter(s). When writing the first edition, Steven Desmet was there all the time as the silent, but vitally important, man behind the scenes, always prepared to pick up the loose ends when they created problems. Ann Coopman (first edition), Isabelle De Ganck (second edition) and Ann De Smaele (third edition) coped with an endless stream of drafts and re-drafts and kept their good humour all the way through. Gino Van Ossel played a crucial role in the first years of the Service Management Centre and acted as the perfect convenor for the marketing department of The Vlerick Leuven Ghent Management School. Stratton Bull (first edition), Anne Hodgkinson (first and second edition) and Alan Anderson (third edition) were there during the whole process as 'ghost-writers', looking over our shoulders to watch the quality of the language in an extremely flexible and customer-oriented way. Rebekah Taylor, Rachel Owen, Rufus Curnow, Kathy Auger, Gemma Papageorgiou, Sarah Reeve and all other colleagues involved at Pearson Education were there as well to provide us with useful comments, suggestions and the necessary support to bring this book to its final stages. Thanks to all of you for these valuable contributions and your co-operation when putting together this book. Finally we are grateful for the continuous support and patience of Veerle, Nicole and Lucrece (first, second and third editions); this book is also indebted to the opportunities they provided for us to accomplish this work.

Paul Gemmel
Bart Van Looy
Roland Van Dierdonck

Publisher's acknowledgements

We are grateful to the following for permission to reproduce copyright material:

Figures

Figure 1.1 from Maslow, Abraham H.; Frager, Robert D.; Fadiman, James, *Motivation and Personality*, 3rd © 1987. Printed and Electronically reproduced by permission of Pearson Education, Inc., Upper Saddle River, NJ; Figure 1.4 Copyright David Maister. From D. Maister, *True Professionalism*, Free Press, New York, 1997; Figures 2.2, 2.3 from Breaking the cycle of failure in services, *Sloan Management Review*, No 32, Spring (Schlesinger, L. A. and Heskett, J. 1991), © 1991 from MIT Sloan Management Review/Massachusetts Institute of Technology. All rights reserved. Distributed by Tribune Media Services; Figure 3.4 from *Sodexho Alliance: Eating into a new market* (van der Veen, C., Duursema, H. and van der Kooij, A. 2007) Wageningen University, European Food and Agribusiness Seminar, 22 June, with permission from European Food and Agribusiness Seminar (EFAS); Figures 4.2, 4.3 from Towards a classification of service processes, *International Journal of Service Industry Management*, Vol 3, No 3, pp. 62–75 (Silvestro, R., Fitzgerald, L., Johnston, R. and Voss, C. 1992), © Emerald Group Publishing Limited all rights reserved; Figure 4.5 from Service quality deployment: quality service by design in *Perspectives in Operations management: Essays in Honor of Elwood S. Buffa*, edited by Rakesh V. Sarin, Kluwer Academic Publishers (Bahara, R. S. and Chase, R. B. 1993), with kind permission from Springer Science+Business Media B. V.; Figure 4.8 from The service blueprint, developed by Bart de Craene, Global Services Manager EMEA, Waters Corporation for his project paper Smart customer interactions enabling novel customer experiences, submitted for a project defence in the Executive Master Class in Business Process Management at the Vlerick Leuven Gent Management School, Belgium, 9 September 2011, with permission from Bart de Craene; Figure 7.1 from Structuring front office and back-office work in service delivery systems, *International Journal of Operations and Production Management*, Vol 27, No 1, p. 119 (Zomderdijk L. G. and de Vries, J. 2007), © Emerald Group Publishing Limited all rights reserved; Figure 7.3 republished with permission of American Marketing Association from Servicescapes: The impact of physical surroundings on customers and employees, *Journal of Marketing*, Vol 56, April, pp. 57–71, p. 60 (Bitner, M. J. 1992), permission conveyed through Copyright Clearance Center, Inc; Figure 8.1 from Case Study: Womble Carlyle **http://www.greenfieldbelser.com/case-studies/womble-carlyle**, with permission from Greenfield Belser and Womble Carlyle; Figure 8.2 from Cultivating Service Brand Equity, *Journal of the Academy of Marketing Science*, Vol 28, No 1, p. 130 (Leonard, L. L. 2000), Copyright © 2000, Springer Netherlands. With kind permission from Springer Science and Business Media; Figure 9.3 from *Services Marketing*, McGraw-Hill (Zeithaml, V. A. and Bitner, M. J. 1996), © 1996. Reproduced with permission of The McGraw-Hill Companies, Inc; Figure 10.7 from How long should a customer wait?, *Decision Sciences*, Vol 22, pp. 421–34 (Davis, M. 1991), Copyright © 2007, John Wiley and Sons. With permission from John Wiley and Sons; Figure 10.11 from An integrated system framework and analysis methodology for manpower planning, *International Journal of Manpower*, Vol 17, No 2, Emerald MCB University Press, pp. 26–46 (Khoong, C. M. 1996), reprinted by kind permission of MCB University Press Ltd; Figure 10.13 from *De Psychologische Beleving van Wachtrijen*, Erasmus Universiteit, Management Report Sciences, 126 (Pruyn, A. and Smidts, A. 1992), with permission from Ale Smidts; Figure 11.3 from Leadership for self-managing work teams: A typology and integrative model, *Human Relations*, Vol 48, No 7, pp. 747–70 (Stewart, G. and Manz, C. 1995), Copyright © 1995, The Tavistock Institute. Reprinted by permission of Sage; Figure 11.4 from Kolb, David A., *Experiential Learning: Experience as a source of learning and development*, 1st, © 1984. Printed and Electronically reproduced by permission of Pearson Education, Inc., Upper Saddle River, New Jersey; Figure 11.5 republished with permission of Sage Publications Inc Books from Developing and maintaining trust in work relationships in *Trust in Organisations: Frontiers of theory and research*, edited by R. Kramer and T. Tyler (Lewicki, R. J. and Bunker, B. 1996), permission conveyed through Copyright Clearance Center, Inc; Figure 11.6 from Facilitating group development: interventions for a relational and contextual construction in *Handbook of Work Group Psychology* edited by M. West (Bouwen, R. and Fry, R. 1996). Reproduced with permission from John Wiley & Sons Ltd; Figure 12.1 from Customer Loyalty: Toward an Integrated Conceptual Framework *Journal of the Academy of Marketing Science*, 22(2), pp. 99–113 (Dick, A. S. and Basu, K. 1994), Copyright © 1994, Academy of Marketing Science. With kind permission from Springer Science and Business Media; Figure 12.2 from **http:// www.netpromoter.com/np/calculate.jsp**. Net Promoter, Net Promoter Score, and NPS are trademarks of Sametrix Systems, Inc., Bain & Company, Inc., and Fred Reichheld; Figure 12.3 from Linking perceptual and behavioural customer metrics to multiperiod customer profitability: A comprehensive service-profit chain application, *Journal of Service Research*, Vol 11, No 1, pp. 3–21 (Larivière, B. 2008), Copyright © 2008, Sage Publications. Reprinted by permission of Sage; Figure 12.4 from *Valuing Your Customers: From Quality Information to Quality Relationships Through Database Marketing*, McGraw-Hill Book Co. Ltd (Jenkinson, A. 1995), Copyright Angus Jenkinson; Figure 12.5 reprinted by permission of *Harvard Business Review*. From Putting the service-profit chain to work by Heskett, J. L., Jones, T. O., Loveman, G. W., Sasser, W. E. and Schlesinger, L., March–April 1994. Copyright © 1994 by the Harvard Business School Publishing Corporation; all rights reserved; Figure 12.6 republished with permission of American Marketing Association from The impact of customer relationship characteristics on profitable lifetime duration, *Journal of Marketing*, Vol 67(1), pp. 77–99 (Reinartz, W. J. and Kumar, V. 2003), permission conveyed through Copyright Clearance Center, Inc; Figure 13.1 reprinted by permission of *Harvard Business Review*. From The balanced scorecard – measures that drive performance by Kaplan, R. S. and Norton, D. P., January–February 1992. Copyright © 1992 by the Harvard Business School Publishing Corporation; all rights reserved; Figure 13.2 from EFQM Excellence Model, EFQM, Brussels Belgium, **http://www.efqm.org/**; Figure 13.4 adapted from The market share impact of service failures, *Production and Operations Management, An International Journal of the Production and Operations Management Society*, Vol 8, No 3, pp. 208–220 (Hays, J. M. and Hill, A. V. 1999), Copyright © 2009, John Wiley & Sons. Reproduced by permission of John Wiley & Sons, Inc; Figure 13.5 from *Operations Management*, 4th ed., Pearson Education Ltd. (Slack, N., Chambers, A., Johnston, R. 2004); Figure 15.1 adapted with the permission of Free Press, a Division of Simon & Schuster, Inc., from *Revolutionizing Product Development: Quantum Leaps in Speed, Efficiency, and Quality* by Steven C. Wheelwright and Kim B. Clark. Copyright © 1992 by Steven C. Wheelwright and Kim B. Clark. All rights reserved; Figure 15.2 reprinted by permission of Harvard Business School Press. From *Open Innovation: The New Imperative for Creating and Profiting from Technology* by H. W. Chesbrough, Boston, MA 2003. Copyright © 2003 by the Harvard Business School Publishing Corporation; all rights reserved; Figure 15.3 from *Open Services Innovation: Rethinking Your Business to Grow and Compete in a New Era*, Jossey-Bass (Chesbrough, H. 2011), Copyright © 2011, John Wiley and Sons. Reprinted with permission from John Wiley and Sons; Figure 15.4 from A process view on managing quality during the creation of technical innovations: lessons from field research, *R&D Management*, Vol 27, No 3, July, pp. 197–211 (Debackere, K., Van Looy, B. and Vliegen, J. 1997), Blackwell Publishers 1997. Article first published online: 17 DEC 2002, DOI: 10.1111/1467-9310.00057, reprinted by permission of John Wiley and Sons; Figure 15.5 republished with permission of Academy of Management from The locus of control in the R&D matrix, *Academy of Management Journal*, Vol 28, No 1, pp. 67–87 (Katz, R. and Allen, T. 1985), first pub 1963, Copyright © Academy of Management, 1963, permission conveyed through Copyright Clearance Center, Inc; Figure 16.1 reprinted from The nature of strategic planning, *Long Range Planning*, Vol 30, No 6, p. 934 (Heene, A. 1997), Copyright 1997, with permission from Elsevier; Figure 17.2 from *Organisational Culture and Leadership*, 1st ed., Jossey-Bass Publishers (Schein, E. H. 1985), Copyright © 1985 Edgar H. Schein. With permission from John Wiley and Sons; Figure 17.5 from *Managing Across Borders: the transnational solution* by Sumantra Ghoshal and Christopher Bartlett, published by Random House Business Books. Reprinted by permission of The Random House Group Limited. Reprinted by permission of Harvard Business School Press. From *Managing Across Borders: the transnational solution* by Bartlett, C. A. and Ghoshal, S., Boston, MA 1989. Copyright © 1989 by the Harvard Business School Publishing Corporation; all rights reserved.

Tables
Table 4.1 reprinted by permission of Harvard Business School Press. From *Designing Care: Aligning the Nature and Management of Healthcare* by R. Bohmer. Boston, MA 2009, pp. 128–129. Copyright © 2009 by the Harvard Business School Publishing Corporation; all rights reserved; Table 5.1 adapted from Competencies management: Beheersen of begeleiden? in *Tijdschrift voor HRM*, Vol 3, 2002, No 2, pp. 31–60 (Faems, D. 2002), Business Unit HRM, Kluwer B. V.; Table 7.2 adapted from Service firm location decisions: Some midwestern evidence, *International Journal of Service Industry Management,* Vol 5, No 3, pp. 49 and 52 (Schmenner, R. W. 1994), © Emerald Group Publishing Limited all rights reserved; Table 10.1 from *Psychologische Beleving van Wachtrijen*, Erasmus Universiteit, Management Report Sciences, 126 (Pruyn, A. and Smidts, A. 1992), with permission from Ale Smidts; Table 10.2 from Using quality function deployment to improve customer service, *Quality Progress*, November, pp. 39–63 (Graessel, B. and Zeider, P. 1993). Reprinted with permission from *Quality Progress* ©1993 American Society for Quality. No further distribution allowed without permission; Table 11.1 from Job satisfaction, service capability and customer satisfaction: An examination of linkages and management implications by Schlesinger, L. A. and Zornitsky, J. (1991). Reprinted with permission from *HRPS*, Volume 14, No 2. Published by HR People & Strategy, all rights reserved. **www.hrps.org**; Table 11.2 from The empowerment of service workers: What, why, how and when, *Sloan Management Review*, Spring (Bowen, D. and Lawler, E. 1992), © 1992 from MIT Sloan Management Review/Massachusetts Institute of Technology. All rights reserved. Distributed by Tribune Media Services; Table 13.1 with kind permission from Springer Science+Business Media, *European Journal of Nuclear*

Medicine and Molecular Imaging, Patients' and personnel's perception of service quality and patient satisfaction in nuclear medicine, Vol 29, 2002, De Man, S., Gemmel, P., Vlerick, P., Van Rijk, P. and Dierckx, R., Copyright © 2002, Springer Berlin/Heidelberg; Table 14.2 from Evaluation of hospital service level agreements, *International Journal of Health Care Quality Assurance*, Vol 22, No 5, pp. 483–497 (Berbée, R. G., Gemmel, P., Droesbeke, B. Casteleyn, H., Vandaele, D. 2009), © Emerald Group Publishing Limited all rights reserved; Table 15.1 from Entering new businesses: selecting strategies for success, *Sloan Management Review*, Vol 23, No 3 (Roberts, E. B. and Berry, C. A. 1985), © 1985 from MIT Sloan Management Review/Massachusetts Institute of Technology. All rights reserved. Distributed by Tribune Media Services; Table 17.2 from *Managing Across Borders: The Transnational Solution* by Sumantra Ghoshal and Christopher Bartlett Published by Random House Business Books. Reprinted by permission of The Random House Group Limited. Reprinted by permission of Harvard Business School Press. From *Managing Across Borders: the transnational solution* by Bartlett, C. A. and Ghoshal, S., Boston, MA 1989. Copyright © 1989 by the Harvard Business School Publishing Corporation; all rights reserved.

Text

Extract on pages 105–106 from Digital finally overtakes physical in US music market by Tim Bradshaw, FT.com, 6 January 2012, **http://blogs.ft.com/tech-blog/2012/01/digital-overtakes-physical-in-us-music/#axzz23o9Piqw0**, © The Financial Times Limited 2012. All Rights Reserved.; Epigraph on page 135 from Hansard, House of Commons Rebuilding, HC Deb 28 October 1943 vol 393 cc403–73, contains Parliamentary information licensed under Open Parliament Licence v1.0; Extract on page 158 from Case Study: Womble Carlyle **http://www.greenfieldbelser.com/case-studies/womble-carlyle**, with permission from Greenfield Belser and Womble Carlyle; Exhibit 8.1 from Digital Marketing, **http://lexicon.ft.com/Term?term=digital-marketing**, © The Financial Times Limited. All Rights Reserved; Extract on page 241 translated from *Het Nieuwsblad*, 18 September 2010, © Het Nieuwsblad; Extract on page 242 translated from article Colruyt gives up the revolutionary snake queue, *Gazet van Antwerpen*, 30 March 2011; Extract on pages 246–247 reprinted from Julian E. Orr: *Talking about Machines: An Ethnography of a Modern Job*. Copyright © 1996 by Cornell University. Used by permission of the publisher, Cornell University Press; Exhibit 11.2 republished with permission of Sage Publications Inc Books from Structural constraints in learning in *Learning to Work*, edited by B. Geer (Marshall, H. 1972), permission conveyed through Copyright Clearance Center, Inc; Exhibit 13.1 from Servqual: review, critique, research agenda, *European Journal of Marketing*, Vol 30, No 1, pp. 8–32, Appendix (Buttle, F. 1996), © Emerald Group Publishing Limited all rights reserved; Exhibit 14.1 from Designing service guarantees – is full satisfaction the best you can guarantee?, *Journal of Services Marketing*, Vol 15, No 4, pp. 282–299 (Wirtz, J. and Kum, D. 2001), © Emerald Group Publishing Limited all rights reserved; Exhibit 16.1 from *Even a Giant can Learn to Run* by Steve Lohr. From The New York Times, 31 December 2011 © 2011 The New York Times. All rights reserved. Used by permission and protected by the Copyright Laws of the United States. The printing, copying, redistribution, or transmission of this Content without express written permission is prohibited; Exhibit 17.1 from Walmart comes shopping in Europe, *Financial Times*, 21 December 1997, p. 23 (Tomkins, R.), © The Financial Times Limited 1997. All Rights Reserved; Exhibit 17.2 from Why Walmart decided to pack, *Financial Times*, 29 July 2006 (Gerrit, W.), © The Financial Times Limited 2006. All Rights Reserved.

Publisher's acknowledgements

The publisher would like to thank the following for their kind permission to reproduce their photographs:

48 John Foxx Collection: Imagestate. 242 Photopress.be.
All other images © Pearson Education

In some instances we have been unable to trace the owners of copyright material, and we would appreciate any information that would enable us to do so.

PART ONE

Defining services

Bart Van Looy • Paul Gemmel

Any book on services should start with an account of the nature of services. What makes services so special that a complete book should be devoted to managing services? In Chapter 1, we first outline the broader evolution of services in the world economy: services account for an ever-increasing part of wealth creation in economies all over the world. Next, we examine the different characteristics that distinguish services from goods. This leads on to the idea of service classification; not all services are alike. Acknowledging the specific nature of services as well as differences among different types of service is crucial for managing services effectively, as will become clear in Chapter 2. Equipped with these insights, we proceed with a discussion of the critical role that the service concept fulfills (Chapter 3). Service firms face the challenge of developing a coherent and internally consistent concept that is targeted to a specific segment of a market. The definition of the service concept, together with the target market, is the starting point for the design and the management of any service delivery system.

While these first chapters might suggest a sharp distinction between services and goods, it is becoming clear that boundaries between manufacturing companies and service providers are increasingly blurred. In the final part of the book, we will return to this phenomenon to take an in-depth look at the notion of 'servitization' (Chapter 18) – that is, manufacturing companies that include services in their offering as well. Thus, managing services likewise becomes a challenge for manufacturing companies.

Chapter 1

The nature of services

Steven Desmet • Bart Van Looy • Paul Gemmel • Roland Van Dierdonck

Objectives

By the end of this chapter, you should be able to discuss:

- the importance and contribution of services to our world economy
- the driving forces behind the growth of services
- the characteristics that distinguish services from goods
- how these characteristics can be used to arrive at service classifications

Introduction

John Lewis was feeling hungry after a long day's work. He particularly wanted to have a pizza. He was already picking up his phone to order one and have it delivered to his home, when he realized that he had other options that could satisfy his pizza needs:

1 He could go to the supermarket and buy the necessary ingredients such as flour, mushrooms, and pepperoni, to make the pizza himself. This would be the cheapest alternative for him, costing roughly €3.

2 Rather than buying the ingredients, he could buy a frozen pizza in the same supermarket for €4.

3 He could indeed order the pizza and have it delivered to his home. However, the price tag attached to this alternative jumped to €6.

4 He could go and eat the same pizza in the restaurant operated by the same company that was delivering the pizza at home. The price would be about €7.50.

5 The option of going to the restaurant made him also consider going to Luigi's restaurant, a new Italian restaurant where customers are seated and served at the table, where tables are covered with tablecloths, and Italian music is played by a live band. However, this option was pretty expensive. He imagined that he would easily pay €15 for the pizza and a glass of wine.

John was overwhelmed by the choices he had and did not know how to compare them. How did the various alternatives differ? What was the extra value he received for the higher prices he had to pay? He was particularly puzzled by the fact that somewhere along the spectrum from buying ingredients to visiting the Italian restaurant he had crossed the line from buying a good (i.e. a tangible product) to buying a service since, according to what he remembered from his course in economics, products such as flour and mushrooms were classified as 'goods', while restaurants were classified as 'service' companies.

A lecture or a class is undeniably a service, but what if the same lecture is recorded on tape and sold? Does this fall into the category of goods or services? What is the difference between a pizza you buy in a store (a good) or the same pizza you eat in an Italian restaurant (a service)? What makes buying a truck different from leasing one? Is IBM a manufacturing firm or a service organization?

This is a book about service management and it is, therefore, important to understand what makes a service a service. What distinguishes services from goods? Are all services similar? If not, how can we understand these differences? These are all questions that will be addressed in this chapter. However, we will start by illuminating the growing importance of services for our economies and the driving forces behind this growth.

Next, we shall explore the defining characteristics of services and shall attempt a definition. We shall use the characteristics, intangibility and simultaneity, to distinguish different types of services and to develop some relevant classification schemes.

The growing importance of services

Economists like to divide our industries into three or sometimes even four broad sectors:

- The *primary* sector – farming, forestry and fishing.
- The *secondary* sector – the industrial sector, including gas, mining and manufacturing, electricity, water and construction.
- The *tertiary* sector – a synonym for the service sector.

Some economists have mentioned an evolution to a *quaternary* sector, but there is some disagreement over which services are tertiary and which are quaternary. Some say the quaternary sector consists of the more intellectual services, while others say it comprises social services or non-commercial services. When speaking of the service sector, we actually mean the whole service sector including the quaternary sector. 'Services' therefore becomes a label covering a wide variety of business. As a result, further refinements can be useful.

Broadly speaking, a distinction can be made between the following categories of services:

- *Distributive services* include transportation, communication and trade.
- *Producer services* involve services such as investment banking, insurance, engineering, accounting, bookkeeping and legal services.
- *Social services* include health care, education, non-profit organizations and government agencies.
- *Personal services* include tourism, dry cleaning, recreational services and domestic services.[1]

The contribution of services to the creation of wealth

The service sector's contribution to our economy has long concerned economists and philosophers. Some economists feared that the transition from an industrial economy to a service economy would lead to a halt in economic growth. The view that service is less – or not at all – productive is not confined to the second half of the twentieth century, as can be seen from the following quotations:

> 'Productive is all labour which fixes and realises itself in a particular subject or vendible commodity . . . unproductive is all labour which generally perish in the very instant of their performance.'
> (Adam Smith, 1776)[2]

> 'Services and other goods, which pass out of existence in the same instant that they come into it, are of course not part of the stock of wealth.'
> (A. Marshall, 1920)[3]

Adam Smith, one of the founding fathers of economics as a science, stated in his book, *The Wealth of Nations,* that labour was only productive if it increased the value of the item for which the labour was employed. Therefore, the services of priests, lawyers and doctors, as well as labour in trade, were not productive. Marx and Lenin held similar views on the non-productivity of trade. This explains why, in the formerly Socialist countries, little attention was given to services and the service industry.

The majority of economists agree today that services make an important contribution to economic development. Producer services, for instance, have influenced positively the manufacturing sector's effectiveness. Moreover, value creation is not confined to producing and consuming goods; enhancing quality of life by means of services can be equally important. Indeed, this can be seen as one of the driving forces behind the growing importance of services as will be explained in the next section.

Service industries are now the largest contributors to employment and gross domestic product in most countries. This has not always been the case. Food production (agriculture and livestock breeding) was the world's main economic activity for many centuries and still is in many developing countries, especially in sub-Saharan Africa. Over the decades, however, there has been a clear shift towards the tertiary sector. After the Industrial Revolution in the second half of the eighteenth century, the secondary sector's share of economic activity started to increase, first in Europe and then spreading to the rest of the world. By the beginning of the twentieth century, it had become the largest sector. The service sector grew steadily and became the major contributor to GDP in the 1950s.

The service sector has thus experienced a steady increase in importance in the world economy. Although the significance of the service sector can vary significantly when comparing developed and developing countries, the rise of the service sector can be considered a general trend.

Let us take a closer look at the figures, starting with the developed market economies (*see* Table 1.1). Services presently amount to an average of 74% of GDP in these economies.

The situation is slightly different in the formerly Communist countries of Eastern Europe (*see* Table 1.2). In general, the service sector is following the same pattern as in the developed market economies – that is, the relative importance of services is increasing. However, the actual share of the service sector in GDP is still below the level of the developed market economies. In most of these countries, there was agricultural over-population until the 1960s[4] and in some countries, such as Bulgaria and Romania, the agricultural sector is still

Table 1.1 Contribution of service sector* to GDP in some developed countries, 1970–2009 (%)

	Belgium	France	Japan	Netherlands	United Kingdom	United States	Average of developed countries
1975	56	60	52	60.3	58.1	64.1	58.4
1985	66	66	58.8	62.5	60	67.7	63.4
1995	70	72	64.9	69	67	72.6	68.4
2000	71.5	74.3	67.17	72.4	71.7	75.3	71.3
2005	75	77	69.3	73.7	75.8	76.9	73
2009	77.6	79.4	70.4	74.3	78.1	77.1	74.2

*Service sector defined by the International Standard Industrial Classification: wholesale and retail trade and restaurants and hotels (division 6); transport, storage and communication (division 7); financing, insurance, real estate and business services (division 8); community, social and personal services (division 9).

Source: UNCTAD (2010) *Handbook of Statistics*; United Nations Conference on trade and development, New York and Geneva: United Nations.

Table 1.2 Contribution of service sector* to GDP in some Eastern European countries, 1980–2009 (%)

	Czech Republic	Hungary	Poland	Romania
1985	–	42.1	34	27.3
1995	56.7	62.6	56.8	38.6
2009	67.7	67	64	55.7

*Definition of service sector as in Table 1.1.

Source: UNCTAD (2010) *Handbook of Statistics on CD-ROM*; United Nations Conference on trade and development. New York and Geneva: United Nations.

very large. The main explanation, however, is that during the Communist era greater priority was given to the manufacturing sector. Some services were viewed as non-productive, in line with the thinking of Marx and Lenin, or labelled as bourgeois. Only a limited number of service activities were stimulated, notably those that were closely associated with the Socialist view of society – for example, social security, education, science and sports. This approach hampered the development of producer services as well as personal services, which are an important source of growth for the service sector in market economies. This explains why several services, such as financing and insurance, were and still are underrepresented, compared with the developed market economies. The almost total lack of producer services under the former Communist leadership has been cited as one of the main causes of economic stagnation in these countries.[5] With the breakdown of the Communist regimes and the transition towards market economies, we observe a fast increasing contribution by the service sector to these economies.

A similar trend can be detected in countries like China, Russia and India (*see* Table 1.3). The service sector's increasing share of the economy can thus be seen as a universal trend. We have shifted from an industrial society of machine operators to a post-industrial society of service workers. The dominance of the secondary sector has been eclipsed by the rise of the service sector. In the following section, we shall take a brief look at factors that explain this phenomenon.

Table 1.3 Contribution of service sector* to GDP in some developing countries, 1970–2009 (%)

	China	India	Russia	Total Developing Economies
1975	22	38	–	40.8
1985	31.5	41.6	–	45.6
1995	33.7	45.2	52.9	52.9
2000	38.8	50.3	53.5	53.44
2005	40.5	53	56.4	55.6
2009	41	54.6	62.4	60.28

*See Table 1.1.

Source: UNCTAD (2010) Handbook of Statistics; United Nations Conference on trade and development. New York and Geneva: United Nations.

Driving forces behind the growth of services

The growth of the service industries cannot be confined to one single explanation; rather, a combination of different factors have all played a part in the sector's increasing importance. In general, two groups of factors can be discerned:

- Increasing consumer incomes and sociological changes have led to a greater demand for services.

- Increasing professionalism in companies and technological changes have brought about the creation of new services, notably of producer services.

The impact of income changes on buying behaviour

In the nineteenth century, the statistician Ernst Engel observed a phenomenon that is now called *Engel's Law*. When people are poor, they have to allocate all or a large part of their income to the necessities of life – namely, food and shelter. When incomes rise, people spend more on food, but not all of the increase in income is spent on food, since this need can be saturated. As a result, the proportion of total spending on food diminishes as income increases. Instead of spending their extra income on food, people spend it on clothing, recreation, personal care, travel and luxury items. People with higher incomes tend to spend relatively more on services and less on goods.

Disposable incomes have risen in most countries in the last few decades. As a result, the demand for both social and personal services – such as leisure, private health care, hotels and restaurants – has increased. New consumer services, such as fitness services, have been developed in order to satisfy people's needs for services. Such a development can be explained by referring to the well-known Maslow pyramid of needs, where a distinction is made between basic and complementary needs (*see* Figure 1.1). People first seek food and shelter before they can satisfy other needs, such as leisure. If millions of people are unable to fulfill even their most basic needs, services directed at their secondary needs will be hard to sell.

Sociological and demographic changes

Many services once provided by consumers themselves or performed on a voluntary basis are now being outsourced to service providers – for example, food services, laundry services and beauticians.

7

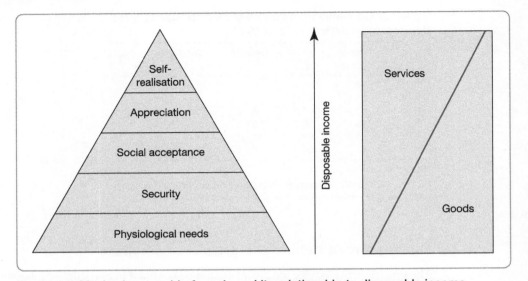

Figure 1.1 Maslow's pyramid of needs and its relationship to disposable income

Source: Maslow, Abraham H.; Frager, Robert D.; Fadiman, James, *Motivation and Personality* (3rd edn). © 1987. Printed and Electronically reproduced by permission of Pearson Education Inc., Upper Saddle River, NJ.

The traditional family of a working husband, a housewife and two children is being replaced by the dual-income family. Since such a family has less free time, it has to outsource many activities to service providers. Instead of eating at home or washing the car, the members of the family go to a restaurant or use a carwash. Furthermore, a higher percentage of women in the labour force lead to a greater demand for day-care nurseries and maid services. This phenomenon is sometimes referred to as 'doing each other's laundry'. Instead of you doing your own laundry, you pay someone else to do it and hence contribute to the increasing output of the service sector; basically, the only thing that has changed is a switch in service provider. However, many new services have been created to fulfill the changing needs of the different subgroups in our population. Since these dual-income families have a higher total income, they spend more money on services in line with the reasoning of Engel's Law.

Another trend is the increase in life expectancy, which is leading to a greying population. This has increased the demand for nursing homes, health care services and specialized travel agencies. These services are no longer organized from a voluntary perspective; they have become professional service industries.

Finally, legal advisers and income tax consultants have become necessary due to the increasing complexity of life.

The growing importance of producer services

Growing disposable incomes, as well as changes in behaviour, certainly contribute to the growth of services, but nowadays it is clear that the role played by households is declining in importance.[6]

During the 1960s, social services were the biggest contributor to rising employment in the service sector. These services, mainly provided by the government under the label of state welfare provision, included health care, education and military services. During the

1970s and 1980s, the growth in these services slowed down and producer services became the fastest growing segment.[7] Producer services are the services used in the production process of both goods and services, as opposed to consumer services, which are directed at the final consumers. There has been an increasing demand for these producer services, in both manufacturing and service companies, leading to the creation of many service companies offering these services. Companies hire law firms for their legal counselling, consulting firms for their management problems, and advertising companies for their advertising campaigns. Other examples of producer services are maintenance, data processing, transport, R&D and surveillance. This growth in producer services indicates that services do not replace manufacturing, but rather contribute to the production of value added in manufacturing firms. These services not only facilitate, but also make possible, the goods-producing activities of the manufacturing sector.

However, it should be noted that at least part of the growing contribution of the service sector to our economies can be attributed to a reclassification of jobs. While many manufacturing firms previously executed these jobs themselves, they have now outsourced them to service companies. Therefore, while these jobs were previously considered a contribution to manufacturing output, these same tasks now provided by service firms are counted as a contribution to service output.

Technological developments

Technological progress has also been an important factor, especially in microelectronics and telecommunications. Although advances in information technology are not directly correlated to the rising importance of services, they have certainly made a contribution to the diversification of the services available and towards the creation of new services.[8] Technological development has made possible the creation of whole new service sectors like telecommunications, software development and engineering, to name just a few. This technological evolution is also continuously affecting the way services are delivered – for instance, in banking, shopping and transportation. New technologies have created economies of scale and scope, which have allowed completely new service products to move through established networks or systems with little added cost.[9] The impact of information technology and the use of the Internet are discussed in further detail in Chapter 6.

Services: what makes them special?

Producing a definition of services is not an easy task. Several scholars have tried to define the notion. For example, you can define services by saying what they are not, as attempted by Quinn and Gagnon:

'Services are actually all those economic activities in which the primary output is neither a product nor a construction.'[10]

A more positive and more substantive definition of services has been advanced by Kotler:

'Any activity or benefit that one party can offer to another that is essentially intangible and does not result in the ownership of anything.'[11]

This definition suggests that services centre on intangibility. There is more to it, however, as the more extensive definition by Grönroos suggests:

'A service is an activity or series of activities of a more or less intangible nature that normally, but not necessarily, take place in interactions between the customer and service employees and/or physical resources or goods and/or systems of the service provider, which are provided as solutions to customer problems.'[12]

A careful reading of this definition reveals that services are activities or processes characterized by two central notions: *intangibility* and *simultaneity*:

- *Intangibility* simply means that the result of a service transaction is not a transfer of ownership, as in the case of physical goods. A service is a process or an act.
- *Simultaneity* means that the realization of a service implies the presence of provider as well as customer; both play an active role in the realization of services. Production and consumption are intertwined and services come into being in the simultaneous interaction between consumer and provider.

Services can thus be defined as:

'all those economic activities that are intangible and imply an interaction to be realised between service provider and consumer.'

Both intangibility and simultaneity imply further characteristics:

- Intangibility implies *perishability*. Services cannot be kept in stock like goods. It is not possible to produce services at one moment in time, store them, and take them from the shelf to sell when appropriate, as it is with goods.
- Simultaneity implies *heterogeneity*. The fact that both provider and customer need to interact at a certain point within the service delivery process opens up possibilities for variation. Customers, service providers, the surroundings, and even the moment of interaction are all sources of variation; consequently, service delivery processes will tend to be characterized by increased heterogeneity.

Table 1.4 illustrates some of the differences between services and goods.

Table 1.4 Differences between services and goods

Services	Goods
• An activity or process	• A physical object
• Intangible	• Tangible
• Simultaneous production and consumption: customers participate in production	• Separation of production and consumption
• Heterogeneous	• Homogeneous
• Perishable: cannot be kept in stock	• Can be kept in stock

A closer look at services

Intangibility

In the literature on the differences between goods and services, the intangibility of services is the characteristic most frequently cited. While goods are produced, services are performed. A service is an act or a deed that we cannot take home with us. What we can take home is the effect of the service. When you go to a cinema, you cannot take home the service you receive, but you should be relaxed or impressed by the experience. As a result, there is no transfer of ownership involved in the delivery of services as opposed to goods:

> 'Services by their very nature are physically intangible; they cannot be touched, tasted, smelt or seen. This contrasts with the physical substance or tangibility of goods. In addition to their physical intangibility, services can also be difficult for the mind to grasp and thus can be mentally intangible.'[13]

Of course, not all services show the same degree of intangibility; few services are 100% intangible, just as few goods are 100% tangible. Instead, many offerings[14] – both goods and services – have both tangible and intangible elements. They can be placed on a continuum ranging from low to high intangibility. In a fast-food restaurant, for instance, the tangible component of the offering – the food – plays an important role. In a three-star restaurant, on the other hand, the more intangible factors such as the behaviour of employees, the atmosphere and the image might become more important. Services can also imply 'facilitating goods', i.e. tangible elements that embody the service offered, as in the case of car rental. Leasing companies offer financial services; however, these are linked inherently to physical goods, namely cars. The same is true for textbooks that support educational services.

What are the implications of this intangibility?

The intangibility of services makes products difficult, and sometimes impossible, to evaluate before and sometimes even after purchase. How can a customer try out an offering before it is purchased if it cannot be seen, heard, felt, smelt or tasted? Zeithaml[15] has developed a framework to clarify this issue. She distinguishes between three categories of qualities related to offerings:

1 *Search qualities* – attributes that a consumer can determine prior to purchase. Thus, search qualities include attributes such as colour, price, feel and smell. You can smell perfume or you can evaluate the colour or style of clothes and the decision as to which perfume or what clothes to buy is based on these qualities.

2 *Experience qualities* – attributes such as taste and wearability that can only be discerned after purchase or during consumption. Hairdressing services clearly fall into this category. You cannot evaluate the quality of a haircut before the hair has been cut. However, once your hair has been cut, you can decide whether you like it or not.

3 *Credence qualities* – attributes that the consumer may find impossible to evaluate even after purchase and consumption. When you pick up your car at the garage, do you have the skills to evaluate whether your brakes are properly aligned? The difference between credence and experience qualities is subjective. If you know a lot about cars, you will have no difficulties in evaluating the brake alignment of your car. It then becomes an experience quality. However, most people do not have the skills to evaluate that service, and thus it becomes a credence quality.

The intangibility of services means that experience and credence qualities will tend to dominate, whereas search qualities dominate in the choice of tangible products (*see* Figure 1.2). Clothes and cars can be evaluated and even tried out before being purchased. However, in many services, especially those provided by professionals and specialists, credence qualities dominate. Most customers do not possess the required skills to evaluate whether a doctor's medical diagnosis is correct or not.

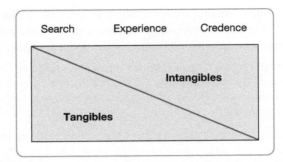

Figure 1.2 The different kinds of qualities and their importance for tangible and intangible products

The domination of credence qualities has serious implications, especially in terms of the marketing of services. Since customers cannot evaluate a service before consuming it, it is important to provide clues as to what can be expected during the service delivery process so that customers can make some kind of pre-purchase evaluation of the service. As a marketing strategist, you have to give credible proof of the competitiveness of your product; you face the challenges of *'making tangible the intangible'* to facilitate the evaluation process for the customer.[16] Consider, for instance, 'dress codes' used within consulting firms, which tend to induce an impression of seriousness, professionalism and technical expertise – that is, characteristics that are inherently linked to the nature of the service they are offering.

It should be noted that 'making the intangible tangible' is often quite the opposite strategy to that of a manufacturer of a good. Here, the intangible aspect of the offering tends to be stressed in the communication with the customer. As Rushton and Carson observe:

'Because at the centre of a tangible product there is something solid, something 'real', it seems that both customers and marketers are able to move to the realms of intangibility when it comes to identifying and assessing what the product can deliver.'[17]

Many car manufacturers do this in their advertising campaigns, as shown by slogans such as BMW's 'Sheer driving pleasure' or Smart's 'Open your mind'.

Striking a balance between tangibility and intangibility is not simply a question of communication, however; it is also an issue of strategic importance. This will become clear when we discuss the notion of *servitization* – that is, the practice whereby manufacturing firms extend their offerings by including services (*see* Chapter 18). Service companies may go in the opposite direction. By including tangible components in their offering, they try to overcome the limitations of 'selling capacity'. This idea is explored further in the discussion on service strategy (*see* Chapter 16).

Simultaneity

A second common characteristic of services is the simultaneity of production and consumption. Whereas goods are produced first and then consumed, services are produced and consumed at the same time. The customer takes part in the production process and consumes the service as it is being produced. For example, when attending a lecture, the student listens and learns (i.e. consumes the service at the same time as the lecturer gives the lecture). The pilot flies a plane at the same time as the passenger is transported. While the movie is being shown, the audience is watching it. It should be stressed, however, that the degree of overlap can vary significantly from service to service, ranging from a small degree of overlap in a bank or a car repair shop to a high degree of overlap in a hospital or a smart restaurant. The at least partial overlap between production and consumption means that there is personal contact during the service delivery process: service employee and customer interact during the service delivery process. This is not necessarily the case with goods, since goods can be produced and consumed separately. This makes the human factor in services crucial.

Therefore, careful attention must be paid to the employees dealing with the customer. They represent the company providing the service and the customer will identify their actions and behaviour with the company. For certain services (for instance, entertainment and professional services), customers not only expect a high quality service but are also interested in the person providing the service. Customers want to be serviced by a certain top accountant, chef or top professor; they do not want 'just anyone' to perform these services.

At the same time, in some cases, the customer must be just as 'educated' as the employee. How well certain services are performed depends not only on the performance of the service provider but also on the ability of the customer to specify or perform his or her own part of the service. If a tax consultant does not receive the right information from the client, or if a customer is unable to specify clearly which haircut he or she desires, there could be disappointment with the outcome.

Where production and consumption occur simultaneously, clearly the customer has to be present at the place where the service is provided. This means that the service provider has to make the service accessible to the customer. Services are therefore *'place dependent'*, and not all services can simply be 'traded'. As Bateson states:

'There is little point in McDonald's deciding to follow the lead of Ford or Procter & Gamble and build a huge, capital-intensive factory. The ability to produce one billion hamburgers a year in Michigan does not help consumers elsewhere in the world who are waiting for their food. Instead, place of consumption is important.'[18]

Service companies will thus require their own type of internationalization strategies. This is an issue we shall explore in Chapter 17.

Heterogeneity

Heterogeneity is related to the potential of variability in the performance of services. As already explained, services are processes implying simultaneity and, therefore, they bear a larger risk of being different depending on circumstances such as the employee involved, the particular customer, the physical setting or even the hour of the day.

Where does this heterogeneity come from? In general, there are three possible sources:

1 *The service provider*. Most services involve an (inter-)active role on the part of service employees. Humans are not robots, able to repeat consistently the same action day in and day out without error. Therefore, a first source of heterogeneity is the service employee involved in the service delivery process. Humans, consciously or unconsciously, vary their actions and sometimes make mistakes. People can be moody, which may lead them to treat the customer in a less friendly way. As a result, the outcome of the service delivery process is more susceptible to variation than in the case of goods, as evidenced in the following remark by an airline manager:

'Two cabin crews can go through the same motions, do the same tasks, and yet the service given can be worlds apart. So much depends on how they do the things they do – what mood they're in – and that we just can't control, we can only try to influence.'[19]

2 *The customer.* The state of mind or the personal situation of the customer strongly influences his or her behaviour, as well as his or her perception of the service. As a result, each customer will experience the service rendered differently. In addition, it should be mentioned that a particular customer will be influenced by the presence and behaviour of other customers.

3 *The surroundings.* Several external factors may influence the customer's perception of the service – for example, whether you visit Disneyland on a rainy day or on a sunny day; whether there is a long or a short queue in the bank; or whether or not there is a lot of turbulence on a flight. These are all factors that will make a big difference to the customer. However, the problem is that many of these factors are difficult, if not impossible, for the service provider to control.

This heterogeneity of services creates one of the major problems in service management – that is, 'how to maintain an evenly perceived quality of the services produced and rendered to the customer'.[20] Even with a highly standardized service product, such as a McDonald's cheeseburger, variability will occur. The complexity of the service does not allow for control of all the process parameters, to ensure a consistent, high quality output. Even if the same ingredients and the same process parameters, such as time and temperature, are used all over the world, the McDonald's service in Paris might be experienced as different from that in London, Tokyo or New York, simply because the context is different in terms of type of customers, neighbourhood, social acceptance, etc. The fact that the outcome of the service delivery process is variable creates uncertainty and higher risk for the customer who wants to purchase a service. How, therefore, can a company make sure that it delivers consistently high quality services to its customers?

One option is to increase the quality control, just as manufacturing companies do, in order to detect 'bad service' and prevent it from reaching the customer. This can be done by performing a quality check when the service is produced but before it is delivered to the customer. Obviously, this is not as easy for services as it is for goods. First, service output is essentially intangible so what should be checked? Second, production and consumption of the service occur simultaneously, making it difficult to check the quality of the produced service before it is consumed. Bad quality therefore cannot, in most cases, be detected and prevented before the customer 'consumes' the service.

Better planning of the service encounter – that is, the moment of interaction between service provider and customer – could reduce the degree of variability. Training employees to interact with the customer, to behave consistently and to deal with new situations can improve the homogeneity of their actions. Adopting uniform production procedures is also common practice in this regard. This means incorporating the principles and techniques of manufacturing firms into service organizations. The success of McDonald's, for example, can be attributed in large measure to this approach.[21]

The downside of this industrial approach, however, is the lack of personalization of the service offering. Customers receive a standardized package, which is not always exactly what they would like to have. An alternative to reducing heterogeneity can lie in developing strategies that build on this inherent heterogeneity and making it into a strength. At most pizza chains, every customer is able to choose his or her own toppings. By providing their services in such a way, the heterogeneity of customer preferences is taken as a starting point, and the service delivery system is designed to cope with this variety of preferences.

Heterogeneity, then, has wide-ranging implications for the operational side of the service delivery system. Things become even more complicated when one realizes that services are also perishable.

Perishability

Unlike goods, services cannot be stored. This is not only due to their intangibility but also to the limitations of simultaneous production and consumption. Once a service has been produced, it has to be consumed, otherwise it is of no use. If a plane leaves the ground with empty seats, the sales are lost forever. They cannot be inventoried and sold the next day. Empty seats are of no value. The same applies to restaurants with empty tables, service maintenance engineers with no machines to maintain, or hairdressers with no clients. As Lovelock states:

> '. . . unused capacity in a service organisation is rather like a running tap in a sink with no plug: the flow is wasted unless customers (or possessions requiring servicing) are present to receive it.'[22]

If the demand for these services were constant, there would be no problem. If the number of passengers an airline had to fly from New York to Paris were 150 a day, every day, airlines would build planes with exactly 150 seats and there would be no empty seats. Of course, we do not live in a world where demand is constant. On the contrary, demand for most services is rather volatile and cannot always be predicted. In restaurants, peaks of demand occur at noon and in the evening; for public transportation services, peaks are just before and after office hours; the first frost is a peak for plumbers. The fact that services cannot be stored makes the volatility of demand a bigger problem for service producers than for goods producers. When demand is lower than production, goods can be stored. If demand is higher than production, the accumulated stock of goods can be sold to accommodate the surplus in demand. Thus, stock can be used as a buffer to demand variability. This is not the case for services.

Managing supply and demand in services is therefore dependent on capacity management, as we shall see in Chapter 10.

The role of service classifications

Services are different from goods: intangibility and simultaneity imply heterogeneity and perishability. These elements pose specific challenges for the management of the service delivery process. Commercial policies, service employees and operational issues are all affected by these characteristics. However, not all services are alike. The management of a hairdressing salon will be different from the management of a consulting firm, just as the management of a fast-food restaurant will be different from that of a bank. Therefore, before developing a guiding framework to look at the managerial consequences of the different service characteristics (Chapter 2), we need to refine our insights into services.

Service classifications are very helpful in this regard. There is a plethora of classification schemes depending on the particular combination of different dimensions. However, the relevance of certain dimensions will vary depending on the question asked. If, for example, the nature of skills required for customer-contact personnel is being considered, it will be more relevant to take into account dimensions that address the nature of the interaction between customer and front-line employees than to focus only on the degree of intangibility. When examining the impact of information technology on the service delivery process, it is necessary to look more at the character of the different exchange moments and less, for instance, at the fluctuations of demand over time.

In Exhibit 1.1, we have listed a number of dimensions that can be used to generate useful insights.

Exhibit 1.1 Methods of classifying services

Degree of intangibility

This dimension has already been discussed extensively. All services can be placed on a continuum ranging from low to high intangibility. The higher the intangibility, the more difficulties customers experience when evaluating the offering. Intangibility also poses problems for the operating system since intangible things cannot be stored. Intangible things are also difficult to standardize, making their quality much more dependent on the employee providing that particular service.

Degree of customer contact required

One of the characteristics of high-contact service organizations is the fact that demand for the service is often instantaneous and cannot be stored, and that a flaw in the service operating system will have an immediate, direct effect on the customer.[23] The interaction between the employee and the customer means that the service employees have to be both competent and communicative. Therefore, it becomes even more important to select and train employees that fit these criteria in order to perform their jobs well as front-office employees.

Degree of simultaneity

This is not necessarily the same as the previous dimension. Production and consumption can occur simultaneously without the customer being present. Home-banking or phone-banking, for instance, allows the customer to consume the service without face-to-face contact with the service provider. Consequences of this dimension were discussed earlier in this chapter.

Degree of heterogeneity

Both the employee and the customer are a source of heterogeneity. As a result, there will be more heterogeneity in high customer contact organizations. Standardizing the operating system might be a way to reduce this heterogeneity.

Degree of perishability

This dimension is of course closely related to the degree of intangibility and the degree of simultaneity. The lower the goods component in the offering and the more consumption and production overlap, the higher the degree of perishability. As a consequence, these offerings cannot be stored. Managing the operation system by means of capacity management thus becomes more complex. Capacity management itself will influence both the employees and the customers. For example, capacity management approaches might be aimed at shortening waiting times for customers but, at the same time, cause employees to adopt a more flexible approach.

Degree of demand fluctuation over time[24]

This dimension is related to the previous point. The more demand fluctuates, the more capacity management becomes important. In restaurants and hotels, for instance, this problem is more acute than it is in banks and insurance companies.

Degree of service customization[25]

Unlike goods, which are mostly purchased 'off the shelf', services can be much more customized. This is especially true when there is a high degree of overlap between production and consumption. The service provider can tailor the service to the needs of the customer. Professional services, hospitals and upmarket restaurants are examples of services where there is a high degree of customization. This certainly demands different employee competencies as opposed to more standardized services.

Degree of labour intensity[26]

Service businesses differ in their labour intensity. Communications companies, amusement and recreation companies, hospitals and transport companies are all examples of low or moderate labour-intensive companies. For instance, despite the fact that hospitals have many employees, there is a great deal of very expensive equipment present, thus increasing the capital intensity. Professional services and personal services represent the opposite end of the spectrum, having a high labour intensity. According to the labour intensity of a business, different challenges will arise. Managers in low labour-intensive service businesses have to think of capital decisions, technological advances and capacity management. Human resource management, including training, hiring, and rewarding, is a top priority in the management of high labour-intensive businesses.

Service direction: towards people or equipment[27]

Personal services, hotels, restaurants and schools are services where the recipients of the service are people, while freight transportation, accounting, and laundry services are aimed at tangible objects or intangible items. The management consequences of this include, for instance, the fact that people-oriented services require the presence of the customer and as a result employees need to have different skills.

Classification schemes should be relevant in practice; there is no point in making them just for the sake of segmenting the service sector into neat categories. Rather, classification schemes should generate insights that inspire managerial action. We will now take a closer look at some specific classification schemes.

Intangibility and simultaneity

A first and obvious classification is based on the dimensions of intangibility and simultaneity since these figure dominantly in our definition of a service (*see* Figure 1.4).

In the upper right-hand corner of the matrix are the pure services – that is, those customized services with a high degree of intangibility and a high degree of simultaneity. Typical labour-intensive services such as professional services fall into this category. In the bottom left-hand corner, we find the more tangible services. The boundaries between the latter category and goods become blurred sometimes, as in the case of CDs and books.

Figure 1.3 Service classifications based on intangibility and simultaneity

What does this classification teach us? As intangibility increases, marketing strategy might change – from stressing the intangible components to stressing the tangible components, for example. When simultaneity increases, there is greater interaction between consumer and service provider, leading to different skill requirements. Employees have to be competent and their attitude towards the customer also becomes important. They must possess good communication skills. This classification scheme can also be used to distinguish between different internationalization strategies for service firms,[28] as we will see when looking at internationalization strategies in Chapter 17.

Maister's framework: combining the degree of contact with the degree of customization

Although Maister has developed this framework specifically for professional service firms, it has a wider validity among different sorts of services firms. Here, the degree of contact with the customer and customization of the process are used as dimensions. The result is the traditional two-by-two matrix with four situations: the pharmacist, the nurse, the brain surgeon and the psychotherapist (*see* Figure 1.4).[29]

In the case of the '*pharmacist*', customers want the service to be delivered according to strict technical standards at a minimal cost. Conformance to specifications is important, resulting in standardized processes with a limited degree of customer contact. Think of the retail activities of your bank: you want to be informed about the state of your account as well as having easy access to money, when necessary, without paying too much – if anything at all. Going to the pharmacist for an aspirin represents a similar situation: the client wants to buy well-established products and procedures, not innovation and creativity. It is

	Standardized process (*Execution*)	Customized process (*Diagnosis*)
High degree of client contact. Value is rendered in the 'front room', i.e. during interaction with the client	**NURSE** **Key skill:** making client experience comfortable and user-friendy in going through pre-set process	**PSYCHOTHERAPIST** **Key skill:** real time diagnosis of complex, ill-specified problems
Low degree of client contact. Value is rendered in the professional's 'back room'. Client focus is on results only	**PHARMACIST** **Key skill:** supervision of low-cost delivery team	**BRAIN SURGEON** **Key skill:** creative, innovative solutions to one-of-a-kind problems

Figure 1.4 Maister's framework of service classification
Source: Maister, D. (1997) *True Professionalism*, Free Press, New York. Copyright David Maister.

clear that, for these types of services, the industrial approach – whereby one relies on procedures, systems and technology – might be eminently suitable.

'*Nurses*' share with pharmacists the high degree of standardization that this category implies in terms of well-established and familiar services. However, the degree of customer contact here needs to be considerable to obtain customer satisfaction. As Maister explains:

'. . . the nurse delivers relatively familiar (or "mature") services that do not require high levels of innovation. However, it differs from the pharmacist practice in that the emphasis is not only on the ability to make the pill (which still may be required), but also on the ability to counsel and guide. The client wants to be nurtured and nursed: "Help me understand what is going on; explain to me what you're doing and why; involve me in the decision making; help me understand my options. Be with me and interact with me throughout the process, until this is all over. I need a front-room advisor, not a back-room technician."'

It is crucial to pay enough attention to the moment of interaction for these services. Nurses are the example *par excellence* here, although some hospitals tend to forget this in attempts to cut down on personnel costs. As a patient, however, minimal industrial treatment is often not appreciated, although it might be viable from a purely medical point of view.

The '*brain surgeon*' situation is characterized, on the one hand, by a high degree of customization, creativity and even innovation but, on the other hand, involves rather low levels of customer interaction. Professional services such as tax specialists, lawyers or doctors might fall into this category; as a service provider you offer the skills to solve the customer's complex problem. The customer, unaware of the technicalities of the service delivery process, does not engage in the technical processes to obtain the solution; he or she just wants you to deliver it. Professional technical skills, creativity and being at the frontiers of development are crucial here.

Finally, the *'psychotherapist'* combines these professional skills with a high degree of customer interaction; in this case, one is faced with problems whereby the customer wants to be – and even must be – involved in the process to arrive at solutions. There is no use in paying a psychotherapist without also engaging in the process. The same applies to some consulting services – for example, when it is necessary to work with a management team to ascertain what can be done to get the company back on track.

So this framework starts to give us an idea about what might be important for managing services depending on what kind of service provider you want to be.[30] The nature of the interaction with the customers plays a crucial role, a point we will further elaborate in Chapter 2.

Conclusion

Services are undeniably different from manufactured products or 'goods', as we like to call them. The distinguishing factors are the intangibility and the simultaneity of production and consumption. When managing service firms, these characteristics should be kept in mind.

We have seen how these characteristics have an impact on such marketing issues as promotion, product positioning and customer interaction. Similarly, these characteristics have clear operational and technological implications, more specifically in areas such as capacity management, process development, and facilities management. Likewise, the relevancy of HR practices will be dependent on the characteristics of the service delivery system. In this chapter, we also touched upon some strategy implications such as growth, internationalization and focus. These issues will be developed in more depth in the following chapters.

It should also be remembered that not all services are alike. There are various dimensions that distinguish different kinds of services and on which classification schemes can be based. Such schemes are only useful insofar as they give additional insights into how to manage these various types of firms. This point will be further elaborated on and refined in the next chapter.

Review and discussion questions

- Discuss the following extract on the relative importance of manufacturing and services to economies:

  'The relative importance of manufacturing and services to economies, and the inter-relationship between the two have been the subject of much discussion through the years. Some have urged that the decline in manufacturing and the corresponding shift to services is unsupportable in the long run, since services depend critically on manufacturing for their existence. In the absence of manufacturing, service sectors are seen as collapsing. On the other hand, a forceful case was made at the Forum that services have become a major driving force in economic growth. Rather than services following and supporting manufacturing, manufacturing is seen as flowing to those countries and areas where the services infrastructure is efficient and well developed.'   (OECD, 2000)

- Discuss the different characteristics of services. How might they affect the nature of services management?

Suggested further reading

Edgett, S. and Parkinson, S. (1993) 'Marketing for service industries – A review', *The Service Industries Journal*, Vol 13, No 2, pp. 19–39. This article gives a detailed review of the literature on the characteristics of services. It focuses on the four main characteristics – intangibility, simultaneity, heterogeneity and perishability. Each characteristic is explained in depth and implications for service management are discussed

Kingman-Brundage, J., George, W. R. and Bowen, D. E. (1995) 'Service Logic: achieving service system integration', *International Journal of Service Industry Management*, Vol 6, No 4, pp. 20–39. This article advances the multi-dimensional nature of service management. The service logic model provides a common language for a cross-functional discussion of service issues, by using the three management functions active in the creation and delivery of services: marketing, operations and human resources. Decisions taken in one domain cannot be considered in isolation from the other domains

Levitt, T. (1972) 'Production-line approach to service', *Harvard Business Review*, Sept–Oct, pp. 41–52. Service companies can learn a lot from manufacturing companies. If companies could stop thinking of service as servitude and personal administration, they would be able to improve its quality and efficiency drastically

Lovelock, C. (1988) *Managing Services: Marketing, operations and human resources*. Englewood Cliffs, NJ: Prentice-Hall. This excellent book on service management devotes a chapter to service classifications. Besides explaining a number of classifications in detail, it also contains a literature review on service classifications

Maister, D. (1997) *True Professionalism*. New York, NY: The Free Press. An excellent discussion of the service concept and its managerial consequences for different types of service

Notes and references

1 An overview of this classification can be found in Browning, Harley L. and Singlemann, Joachim (1978) 'The transformation of the US Labor force: The interaction of industry and occupation', *Politics and Society*, Vol 8, pp. 481–509
2 Smith, A. (1776) *The Wealth of Nations*. Reprinted 1991. Loughton: Prometheus Books
3 Marshall, A. (1920) *Principles of Economics*. Reprinted 1997. Loughton: Prometheus Books
4 Caselli, G. P. and Pastrello, G. (1992) 'The service sector in planned economies of Eastern Europe: Past experiences and future perspectives', *The Service Industries Journal*, Vol 12, No 2, April
5 Illeris, S. and Philippe, J. (1993) 'The role of services in regional economic growth', *The Service Industries Journal*, Vol 13, No 2, April, pp. 3–10
6 Caselli, G. P. and Pastrello, G. (1992), op. cit.
7 Elfring, T. (1989) 'The main features and underlying causes of the shift to services', *The Service Industries Journal*, Vol 9, No 3, July, pp. 337–356
8 Daniels, P. W. (1993) *Service Industries in the World Economy*. Oxford: Blackwell Publishers.
9 Quinn, J. B. and Cagnon, C. E. (1986) 'Will services follow manufacturing into decline?', *Harvard Business Review*, Nov–Dec, pp. 95–103
10 Ibid.
11 Kotler, P. (1997) *Marketing Management: Analysis, planning, implementation and control*. Englewood Cliffs, NJ: Prentice-Hall
12 Grönroos, C. (1990) *Service Management and Marketing: Managing the moments of truth in service competition*. Lexington, MA: Lexington Books, p. 27

13 Bateson, J. E. G. (1977) 'Do we need service marketing?', in Eiglier, P., Langeard, E., Lovelock, C. and Bateson, J. (eds) *Marketing Services: New insights*. Cambridge: Marketing Science Institute

14 The word 'offering' is used here instead of 'product' to stress the difference between this and goods. In the remainder of the book we shall use the word 'product' to refer to services and goods

15 Zeithaml, V. A. (1981) 'How consumer evaluation processes differ between goods and services', in Donnelly, J. H. and George, W. R. (eds) *Marketing of Services*. Chicago, IL: American Marketing Association, pp. 186–190

16 Levitt, T. (1981) 'Marketing intangible products and product intangibles', *Harvard Business Review*, May–June

17 Rushton, A. M. and Carson, D. J. (1985) 'The marketing of services: Managing the intangibles', *European Journal of Marketing*, Vol 19, No 3, pp. 19–40

18 Bateson, J. E. G. (1989) *Managing Services Marketing*. Orlando, FL: The Dryden Press

19 Rushton, A. M. and Carson, D. J. (1985), op. cit., p. 37

20 Grönroos, C. (1990), op. cit., p. 30

21 Interested readers are referred here to the work of Levitt who pioneered this approach in the 1970s and is still worth reading. *See* Levitt, T. (1972) 'Production-line approach to service', *Harvard Business Review*, Sept–Oct, pp. 41–52 and Levitt, T. (1976) 'The industrialisation of service', *Harvard Business Review*, Sept–Oct, pp. 63–74

22 Lovelock, C. (1981) 'Why marketing management needs to be different for services', in Donnelly, J. H. and George, W. R. (eds) *Marketing of Services*. Chicago, IL: American Marketing Association, p. 5

23 Chase, R. B. (1981) 'The customer contact approach to services: theoretical bases and practical extensions' *Operations Research*, Vol 29, No 4, pp. 698–706

24 Lovelock, C. (1988) *Managing Services: Marketing, operations and human resources*. Englewood Cliffs, NJ: Prentice-Hall

25 Haywood-Farmer, J. (1988) 'A conceptual model of service quality', *International Journal of Production and Operations Management*, Vol 8, No 6, pp. 19–29

26 Schmenner, R. W. (1986) 'How can service businesses survive and prosper?', in Lovelock, C. (ed.) *Managing Services: Marketing, operations and human resources*. Englewood Cliffs, NJ: Prentice-Hall, pp. 25–36

27 Thomas, D. R. E. (1978) 'Strategy is different in service businesses', *Harvard Business Review*, July–Aug, pp. 158–165

28 Vandermerwe, S. and Chadwick, M. (1989) 'The internationalisation of services', *The Service Industries Journal*, Vol 9, No 1, pp. 79–93

29 Maister, D. H. (1996) *What Kind of Provider Are You?* Boston, MA: Maister Associates, Inc.

30 It should be clear that Maister's typology does not define specific services but rather different market segments

Chapter 2

The nature of service management

Paul Gemmel • Bart Van Looy

Objectives

By the end of this chapter, you should be able to discuss:

- the nature of service management
- the meaning of 'value' in service
- the framework of maintenance-interactive, task-interactive and personal-interactive services
- how the nature of the interaction has an impact on service management
- why it is important that employees and customers are integrated in the service chain
- how employee and customer satisfaction can be linked with profitability
- the working of the cycle of failure and the cycle of success in service firms

Introduction

With more than 13 million passengers passing through Terminal 1 of London Heathrow each year, keeping it clean is a huge task. Cleaning firms compete robustly for such contracts, mostly by undercutting prices. Since cleaners' wages are by far the biggest cost, this competition leads to continuous pressure on the wage bill. But on the fringes of Heathrow, one man stands up to change all that: Waldemar Schmidt, the head of the European operations of ISS, one of the biggest cleaning contractors in the world. He says that cleaning contractors should compete less on squeezing wages, and more on quality and services. In partnership with the British Airport Authority (BAA), ISS designed a new kind of cleaning contract, putting the emphasis on productivity and performance rather than costs. Wages were raised from £3.50 to £5 per hour and new recruits were trained before starting on the job. ISS management offers the following arguments for this new way of working: 'What we try to do, is to make our people part of the airport services because then they can come into the positive circle where happy or satisfied employees are generating happy or satisfied customers, and satisfied customers will generate satisfied shareholders'. As a condition of the new contract, ISS cleaners have to be able to guide passengers around the airport. Cleaners are also more easily identified by name cards and photographs, positioned outside the toilets. The terminal management used to evaluate contractors based on the number of cleaners they had on site. Instead, they try now to find out what the passengers themselves think by asking them questions on a five-point scale concerning the cleanliness of toilets and the availability of soap and towels. The new contract also includes some more objective cleaning standards that allow them to come up with quality scores. The general manager of Terminal 1 helped to design the new contract and is very enthusiastic about this new approach to cleaning: 'When tendering for cleaning contracts, all that was happening was that the cleaning companies were paying their staff less and less and we were getting poorer and poorer quality'. Despite the expensive training and the higher wages, the new contract seems to make business sense. 'It is costing us no more than the original cleaning contracts. We are getting appropriate cleaning and our passengers are happy as well because they are getting the information'. As BAA management looks at the surveys they have done, it is evident that their passengers give the issue of cleaning much higher emphasis now. They also get many more compliments about the cleaning than they had before. So, they do not wish to go back to the old way of working based on low wages.[1]

The nature of service management

To understand the nature of service management, one has to understand how value in a service business is created for the customer. Value can be defined as the 'customer's eye view' of the benefits and costs related to the exchange of goods and services.[2] In the case of cleaning, the benefit for the customer is the cleanliness of the facilities and the costs is the price of the contract. The story of BAA and ISS illustrates that it is not that simple to define service value in terms of 'benefit and costs'.

A first point is that the value of cleaning is subjective. The perception of value or the perceived service value is far more important in many service settings than what can be measured by 'objective' service standards. This is the reason why, in their new way of working, BAA places emphasis on measuring the perception of passengers about the cleanliness of the facilities.

Second, ISS wanted to enhance the value proposition by adding other types of service such as guiding passengers around the airport. To do this in a successful way, they increased the wage level to attract higher skilled people and invested heavily in training. Do the perceived benefits of being able to guide passengers around the airport outweigh the additional costs of transforming cleaners to airport service operators? This type of question is fundamental to doing business in services. ISS knows that due to the higher labour costs, this contract is not the cheapest in the market. Nevertheless, ISS hopes that BAA will choose them again when the contract comes up for renewal.

Third, the BAA-ISS case shows that one needs to understand how value is created in the customer process. Do ISS cleaners who are able to give information to customers create more or better value than cleaners who are not able to do this? Understanding the value-creation process from the customer's point of view is one of the foundations of the Service-Dominant Logic:[3] It is not by selling a cleaning contract that ISS is creating value, but by understanding how cleaning contributes to the performance of the airport terminal services.

In the Service-Dominant Logic (SDL), value creation is linked to a relationship-oriented perspective rather than a transaction-oriented perspective.[4] In the transaction-oriented perspective, management is focused on the distribution of product or service that has been pre-produced for customers. The customer is viewed as a recipient of goods or services. In the relationship-oriented perspective, goods and services are co-created to acquire the benefits of specialized competences (knowledge and skills).[5] In this logic, the needs of the customer are the starting point of doing business, and the customer is actively involved in the creation of the right service offer. The customer can participate in the creation, the design and the delivery of the service.[6] The active involvement of the manager of BAA in the design of the contract with ISS results in a clear and common understanding of its value.

By making cleaners part of the airport services, ISS and BAA understand that the creation of value in services starts with the motivation of the service employees. The value in service is created through the interaction between service employees and customers. The primary focus of service management should be on how to manage this interaction between employees and customers. This interaction can be different depending on the kind of service. By asking cleaners to give information to the passengers, they bring these employees in contact with the customers. This has important implications for the nature of service management.

In the sections of this chapter that follow, we introduce a framework to characterize the nature of interaction between employees and customers and show how this has an impact on the nature of service management. We further show how value in service is created through the interaction between employees and customers.

The nature of the interaction

Interaction between the customer and the service delivery system is frequently identified as a dimension that allows us to characterize and classify services (*see* Chapter 1). The nature and the intensity of interactions can be very different in service settings. If you go to a bank to withdraw money, the interaction is quite different from the interaction with your architect, which in turn is different from the interaction with your psychotherapist. These differences have led Mills and Margulies[7] to develop a classification scheme around three basic types of interaction: maintenance-interactive, task-interactive and personal-interactive services. Let us take a closer look at how Mills and Margulies define these different types of interaction.

Maintenance-interactive services

When you withdraw money from your account at the bank, the direct interaction between the employee and yourself as a customer is short and rather standardized. The interaction is basically a cosmetic one because it often goes no further than polite social niceties and gestures. Convenience or comfort is the main concern in this type of interaction. The amount of information transmitted between service employee and customer is often limited. The importance of the information input by the customer into the production function – as it pertains to the completion of the employee's task – is considerable, because the customer knows just what is desired. The employee in a maintenance-type organization tends to make few judgements, and those that are made are generally of a simple nature. This is why the employee decision unit is capable of providing services for a relatively large number of customers. The direct interface between the employee and the customer allows widespread interchangeability of activities – that is to say, it is not necessary to have one employee serve the same customer repeatedly.

Task-interactive services

In task-interactive services – for instance, interaction with an architect – there is uncertainty in the transaction. By uncertainty, we mean that customers are generally less precise, not about *what* they need, but *how* to obtain or accomplish it. To a very significant extent, the interaction revolves around the task to be performed. The client has no – or limited – knowledge of the techniques required to provide adequate answers to the questions posed. Such techniques are almost exclusively in the domain of the service provider.

Generally, the information provided by the customer is not critical, a fact that reflects the client's relatively low level of awareness of the problem at hand. The duration of the relationship is generally relatively long, because the flow of information is extensive. The interaction is usually intensive, yet there is an expected termination of the relationship – for example, an engineering firm will give an estimate of the time required for a task. The decisions made by the employee are complex and sometimes require novel solutions to unusual, and even unique, problems.

In the task-interactive service firm, the client is perceived as being in a dependent position. This power disparity exists because the service employee controls more information relative to the client. The relationship is intense, and there is usually little substitutability of service employees in the interaction, since the extensive technical process implies switching costs.

Personal-interactive services

In personal-interactive services – for example, in the case of the psychotherapist – there is not only uncertainty but also ambiguity. Ambiguity means that one is not only looking for answers but that even the relevant questions seem unclear. The employees in these situations provide a personal service to clients/customers, who are typically unaware or imprecise about both what will best serve their interest and how to go about remedying a situation. A client with an emotional problem may seek help from an organization providing counselling, but may be unaware of the extent of the problem. Customer and service provider engage in a process that involves tackling the ambiguity. In this process, the skills of the service provider are crucial; however, besides the technical expertise required, as in the case of task-interactive services, personal and social skills and competencies are equally crucial in personal-interactive services.

Given the complex nature of this type of interaction, the professional service provider tends to dominate during the interaction. This is evident in teacher-student and counsellor-patient relationships. The client/customer is in a subordinate role, and the interaction is usually a personal one. The information provided by the client is often of a confidential nature, and it is unusual in these organizations for employee substitution to take place after a relationship between the employee and client has been established.

The personal-interactive service firm is the most dynamic of the service organizations – dynamic in the sense that each task – and even each episode – requires novel solutions, with the decisions of employees tending to be complete and judgmental. The employee operates with considerable autonomy. Standards and guidelines are difficult to establish in this setting.

Going back to the example of BAA and ISS, it is clear that asking cleaners to guide passengers in the airport is more than just adding a task to their job profile. Giving information is part of a task-interactive service job while cleaning has more the characteristics of a maintenance-interactive service. In this transition from a maintenance-interactive service to more task- or personal-interactive jobs, ISS needs employees with additional skills and competences, which is reflected in their hiring and training practices.

Furthermore, within the same type of service, different approaches are possible: as a consultant, you can position yourself as a technical expert (task-interactive) or as an integrated problem solution provider (personal-interactive). Such a choice will affect the way you have to design and manage the components of your service organization, as will become clear in the next chapter and the remainder of this book.

The nature of the interaction and service management

Different types of service might imply different forms of management. In order to understand this relationship, we introduce the service triangle.

The triangle concept was first suggested by a Canadian scholar, John Haywood-Farmer, as a tool to aid understanding of quality management issues in various service situations.[8] We have adopted and adapted the model and, in so doing, have come to the conclusion that its value extends beyond quality management issues. The (adapted) model is schematically represented in Figure 2.1. A service organization is conceptualized as consisting of three components. At the top of the triangle we find the organizational component. By this, we mean everything that 'belongs' to the organization itself and is clearly identified with it: processes, procedures, systems, structures, infrastructure, physical components, reputation, etc. Some people refer to this as 'structural capital'.

At the bottom, we find the 'human capital'. People come to work bringing with them technical skills, a behavioural repertoire, as well as personal characteristics. By *technical skills*, we mean all the characteristics related to doing a good job as a professional doctor, lawyer, hairdresser, cook, or whatever. This includes skills closely associated with the profession, which the individual possesses after having received the necessary education (technical knowledge, diagnostic and advisory skills, and so on). By *personal characteristics*, we refer to those characteristics not associated with any particular profession but with a particular person: traits, motives, and self-identity, but also fundamental values and norms that shape basic attitudes to, for instance, work or customers. Finally, the *behavioural repertoire* refers not so much to educated skills but rather to well-trained competencies. This includes the qualities of such daily routines as communication skills, politeness and

Figure 2.1 (a) The Service Triangle; (b) The Service Triangle and types of interactive services

attentiveness. Rather than putting the last element at the base line of the triangle, we prefer to locate it at the top of the triangle since this behavioural repertoire is influenced, if not dictated, by organizational actions such as corporate training or even standard operating procedures – for example, the duration of eye contact between the cashier and the customer at McDonald's, or having to say 'Thank you and have a nice day' at certain supermarkets. As a result, we end up with a triangle with two human components at the bottom (*see* Figure 2.1(a)).

A look at any particular service organization reveals that its centre of gravity – which is determined by the relative weight given to each component – will be closer to one of the sides of the triangle (*see* Figure 2.1(b)). Everyone would agree that McDonald's is positioned much closer to the top of the triangle. The success of McDonald's depends very much on the company's system, structure, policy, infrastructure and technology, as well as the systematic training of the 'behaviour' of its service employees. Consider, for instance, the existence of the 'hamburger university' and a large set of standard operating procedures that describe and control the behaviour of the employees. The technical skills required are rather limited. One does not have to be a good cook to perform well at McDonald's, and given that the contact is very brief and superficial, personal characteristics as defined earlier are of little importance. Maintenance-interactive types of service are located here.

A traditional university hospital or a law firm is, in most cases, situated towards the right corner of the triangle. Such an organization is largely dependent on the quality – that is, the 'technical skills' – of the professionals who work for or, perhaps more precisely, who make up this organization. The brain surgeon is probably the example that best illustrates this position. The same is true for most task-interactive services.

A student café might be an example of an organization that is situated at the left corner of the triangle. Its success is very much dependent on the personal behaviour and attitudinal characteristics of the operator or owner, and/or of the other guests. A student's favourite café may not have the best beer, or the cleanest, most modern or best equipped facilities. The owner may not be particularly skilful at serving beer. The owner may simply be someone students can relate to – a 'cool' person. It is clear that the more personal interactive services are, the more the service system should be positioned towards this point of the triangle.

By mapping the different types of interaction on the service triangle, we better understand how the nature of the interaction can have an impact on different aspects of service management:

- The competences of the service employees can be very different in the three types of service interaction. Whereas bank tellers need to be polite and have to possess the necessary skills for handling customer transactions, they are usually not involved in the service transaction on a deeper, more personal level. Under normal circumstances, neither bank tellers nor fast-food restaurant employees are expected to explore ways of looking at the world or to engage in discussions relating to their own opinions or self-image with customers in order to deliver an adequate level of service to them. Therapists, career counsellors or process consultants, on the other hand, do address these issues when they are doing job counselling and giving legal advice or therapy. These professionals not only need technical expertise but they are also involved with their customers on a more personal level during the interaction process. Here, personal characteristics do play an important or even decisive role.

- The nature of interaction between service provider and customer will correlate with the degree to which the information technology developments affect the way services are delivered and consumed. Services that imply short, standardized information transactions will be more easily delivered by new technologies than services that require a more complex type of interaction. It is far easier to substitute 'physical' maintenance interactions with their 'technological' counterpart.

- The different types of interaction lead to different types of service process. Maintenance-interactive services that are more oriented towards the top of the triangle have a focus on equipment, low contact time and low degree of customization. This makes it possible to process customers en masse, as in, for example, a bus transport company. Personal- and task-interactive services place more emphasis on the people, and have longer contact time and greater customization, as in professional service companies.[9]

- In task- and personal interactive services, a relationship-oriented perspective on the interaction is more important than in maintenance-interactive services. According to the relationship perspective, the focus of marketing is to facilitate and support task-interactive and personal-interactive customers in the consumption and use of the service throughout the relationship.[10] The focus of marketing in maintenance-interactive services is based more on the principles of mass-marketing, which means applying the 4P model of the marketing mix.

- The role of the customer is very different in maintenance-interactive services as compared with task-interactive and personal-interactive services. In maintenance-interactive services, the customer can more easily take on part of the job that eventually leads to self-service. In task- and personal-interactive services, the extent of customer participation is a crucial factor in the creation of the service. In other words, maintenance-interactive services are more open to co-production and task-interactive and personal-interactive services to co-creation.[11,12]

The interaction between employees and customers in the service chain

In practice, it is difficult in a service operation to distinguish clearly between the service, the process of providing the service, and the system and procedures that deliver it. One of the unique attributes of service is the customer's participation in its production, which we called simultaneity in Chapter 1. The service itself always concerns an act involving the customer; as a result, quality will also be perceived by the customer in terms of this interaction.

Simultaneity as an inherent characteristic of service means that service organizations have a permeable boundary between themselves and their customers. There is both psychological and physical closeness between service providers and consumers. Service employees and consumers frequently work together, observe each other and interact. As a consequence, what employees experience in their work is communicated to consumers. Dissatisfied, unmotivated or frustrated employees bring their feelings with them when interacting with the customer, and these feelings are transmitted during interactions. We can all tell stories about how the behaviour of service employees in a restaurant affects our global impression of the overall service quality. Whereas in some, the customer is given the impression that he or she is lucky to be served at all, in others the customer emerges after the meal feeling well looked after.

The permeable boundary between employees and customers

Schneider and Bowen have documented this relationship extensively.[13] In a series of studies on the relationship between the experiences of employees at work and customer perceptions of service quality, the findings point to the same conclusions over and over again. The way employees feel and act has an impact on the quality of the service delivered: satisfied people deliver good-quality service and thus value. This is also what Waldemar Schmidt of ISS was aiming at when he introduced a new way of working in the BAA-ISS partnership:

'What we try to do, is to make our people part of the airport services because then they can come into the positive circle where happy or satisfied employees are generating happy or satisfied customers . . .'.

Let us take a closer look at one of studies of Schneider and Bowen. To examine the relationship between employees' perception of, and satisfaction with, HR practices and customers' evaluation of service quality, data was gathered from 28 branches of a service company. Employees could express their satisfaction with features such as work facilities, supervisory characteristics and development opportunities. At the same time and independently, data was collected on customers' perceptions of service quality. Both elements of the study were strongly correlated. We would like to stress that the data stemmed from the same company. The type of service and the overall routines in these 28 branches were the same. It was the difference in employee satisfaction, therefore, that became the single crucial element that accompanied – or put more strongly, caused the differences in – customer perception of service quality.

Heskett, Schlesinger and Sasser also stress the connection between employee and customer satisfaction in the service profit chain model, developed at the Harvard Business School.[14] Here, the relationship between employee and customer satisfaction is called the 'satisfaction mirror'. Empirical evidence supporting this effect is abundant: data collected at Rank Xerox or MCI Communications, to name but two, reveals positive relationships between the two elements. Employees feeling enthusiastic about their job not only communicate this feeling both verbally or non-verbally but are also eager to work hard towards satisfying their customers. Customers treated in this way start to act reciprocally, increasing employee satisfaction even further. Moreover, employee loyalty is crucial; employees who stay on the job long enough not only develop their skills to a high level but also start to know customers and their specific interests and needs. This will allow them to provide an even better, personalized and customized service. Thus more value is created and, in consequence, customer satisfaction is increased. This is exactly the same argument that Waldemar Schmidt of ISS used in designing a new way of working with BAA.

We can conclude from these authors, therefore, that much of what happens inside a service organization cannot be hidden from the customer with whom the organization's employees interact. Achieving high levels of service quality and customer satisfaction imply that consideration is being given to employee satisfaction as well.

Employee and customer satisfaction leading to profitability

It can be argued that, despite the link between employee and customer satisfaction, neither is an ultimate goal for service companies. A link is needed with the notion of profitability. Otherwise, the notion of happy employees relating to happy customers will only be thought of as a pleasant side effect – a 'plus' but not an 'essential' to doing business.

Here, the work of Heskett, Sasser and Schlesinger provides us once again with crucial insights. They connected employee satisfaction, customer satisfaction, and profitability in the well-known service profit chain. It all starts from the notion of service: service capability influences employee satisfaction. Employee satisfaction in turn will lead to employee loyalty and will affect the service employees' efforts to achieve productivity and quality goals. This, in turn, will affect the value created for, and perceived by, the customer. Value creation will lead to satisfied customers and eventually loyal customers, and this loyalty will in turn contribute to profitability.

Schlesinger and Heskett[15,16] demonstrate very clearly this dynamic interplay between the 'inside' and the 'outside' of the service firm – that is, the interplay between employees' satisfaction and behaviour and customers' perceptions of service quality, and hence satisfaction – when describing different 'cycles' that may occur in managing services.

As a first example, the 'cycle of failure' is summarized here (see Figure 2.2). This cycle very often begins when an organization is looking for cost reductions in the short run.

In an attempt to reduce costs in the short run, companies start to look for people willing to work for wages marginally above statutory minimum levels. Jobs are reduced to a series of simple and boring tasks that require almost no training, since training costs money. Involving people in the company itself – in decisions, or simply more in their own jobs – costs time and effort as well, so it is easy simply not to bother. Technology is used to install some degree of quality control.

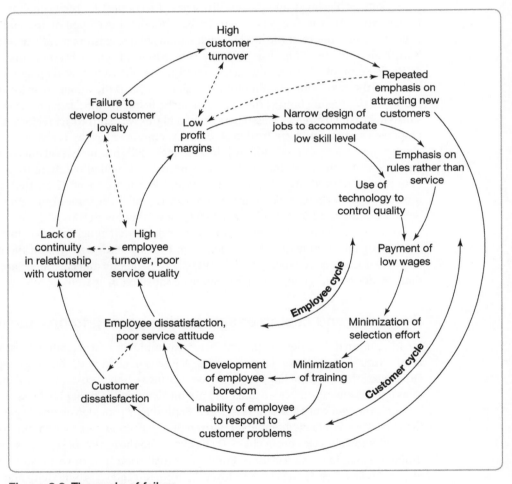

Figure 2.2 The cycle of failure

Source: Reprinted from Schlesinger, L. A. and Heskett, J. (1991) 'Breaking the cycle of failure in services', *Sloan Management Review*, No 32, Spring, pp. 17–28. © 1991 from MIT Sloan Management Review/Massachusetts Institute of Technology. All rights reserved. Distributed by Tribune Media Services.

The rationale goes something like this:

'Of course, people are not really motivated when working in such a system and yes, they do leave the company frequently and after a short period of employment, but who cares? The pool of unemployed people out there is large, and we can easily find new employees.'

While, in the short run, employee costs might be minimized, it is clear that, in the long run, the effects are disastrous. The dynamics installed at the employee level lead to indifferent attitudes towards customers. These in turn translate into poor perceptions of service quality by the same customers, which result in further increases in employee dissatisfaction, and lead to lower sales and profit margins. This will eventually inspire the next 'squeezing round' and everything will start all over again.

Several factors explain how companies can get 'seduced' into this cycle. Technology is assumed to be the saviour that will allow a company to reduce the unpredictability of human behaviour, so investing in technology is seen as more important than investing in people. While the use of technology for some service industries will increase in the future, it is clear, however, that it will be difficult for many services to replace the human factor completely. We will discuss this issue in greater detail in Chapter 6 when we examine the relevance of IT developments to service encounters.

It is also argued that factors such as the inadequate level of talent in the labour pool, the failure of educational systems and the loss of past values, such as the work ethic, force companies to take such an approach. What we tend to forget here is that companies do play a role in society and that the concepts and views with which they approach the labour force tend to be self-reinforcing.

Perhaps most important in creating the cycle of failure are the pressures for short-term performance, and linked to this, the lack of accurate information. Too many companies still fail to compute, or are unable to compute, the impact of employee turnover on customer retention, or how customer acquisition costs relate to customer retention costs. The costs of wages and training, on the other hand, can be calculated exactly. The short-term savings become clear from a look at the accounts. While improving recruitment, training and development, and rewards and recognition are all acknowledged to be important, the budget has to be managed. Long-term trends occur more slowly and less dramatically and, hence, are usually at the bottom of managers' lists of priorities. Since it is hard to quantify the impact of long-term events on intermediate earnings, efforts put into improving the quality of the workforce tend to be minimal. Moreover, since 'only what gets measured gets managed', the impact of the inner part of the cycle of failure is often not known or calculated.

These dynamic relationships can also take on a positive face. Schlesinger and Heskett juxtapose the cycle of failure described above with its counterpart, *the cycle of success* (*see* Figure 2.3). Here the dynamics going on inside the company positively affect what goes on outside, and vice versa.

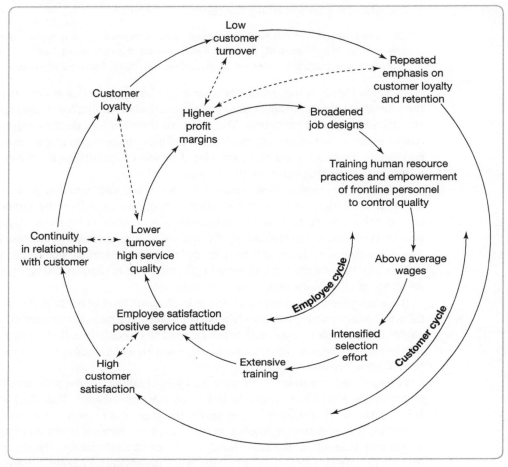

Figure 2.3 The cycle of success

Source: Reprinted from Schlesinger, L. A. and Heskett, J. (1991) 'Breaking the cycle of failure in services', *Sloan Management Review*, No 32, Spring, pp. 17–28. © 1991 from MIT Sloan Management Review/Massachusetts Institute of Technology. All rights reserved. Distributed by Tribune Media Services.

Conclusion

Months passed, and the pioneering ISS contract came up for renewal. After all, Waldemar Schmidt of ISS hoped that the new way of working with BAA would lead to a long-term relationship and that they would be able to keep the contract. That is the only way to be sure that the positive satisfaction mirror between the cleaners and the customers finally reflect on the happy shareholders of ISS. ISS knows that competitors will come in and emulate their pioneering cleaning contract. Although BAA management is very enthusiastic about this cleaning contract – they helped design it – how confident can Waldemar Schmidt be that the contract will be renewed?

Understanding the value as perceived and determined by the customer and/or consumer is at the heart of service. Adding other types of service to the value proposition, as in the case BAA and ISS, is only worthwhile if the customer perceives this as useful. Otherwise, it only adds costs without any benefit accruing in the eyes of the customer. The concept of 'value' is at the centre of the service profit chain, showing that a large part of this value is created in the interaction between the service provider and the customer. At the same time, we need to appreciate that the nature and intensity of these interactions can vary considerably between service settings. Personal-interactive services such as strategic consulting have to be managed differently from maintenance-interactive services such as pizza for home delivery. Most firms are confronted with a mix of the different types of interaction. When studying the value proposition of bank branches, one will find examples of all types of interactive service. As a service manager, one should be aware that the nature of the interaction has an impact on many building blocks of services, such as the design of processes and the environment (Chapters 4 and 7), the role of people (Chapter 5), the role of technology (Chapter 6), and the role of customers (Chapter 12). To be sure that all components fit together, service firms need a clear service concept, which will be discussed in the next chapter.

Review and discussion questions

- Select a service firm and look for examples of maintenance-, task-, and personal-interactive services in this service setting. Does this firm take into account the different natures of these types of interactive service? Use the service triangle to describe how they approach each type of interactive service.

- Look for an example of a service firm where a clear cycle of failure is working. Describe how the cycle of failure is working. Try to figure out what kind of issues caused the start of the cycle.

- List different examples of service experiences where the negative or positive employee behaviour had an impact on customer satisfaction (or dissatisfaction). What can we learn from these examples in terms of service management?

- Based on what you have learned in this chapter, discuss the following question: 'How confident can Waldemar Schmidt be that ISS will keep their contract with BAA?'

Suggested further reading

Heskett, J. L., Jones, Thomas O., Loveman, Gary W., Sasser Jr., W. Earl and Schlesinger Leonard A. (2008) 'Putting the Service-Profit Chain to work', *Harvard Business Review*, July–August 2008

Mills, P. K. and Margulies, N. (1980) 'Towards a core typology of service organisations', *Academy of Management Review*, Vol 5, No 2, pp. 255–265

Vargo, Stephen L. and Lush, Robert F. (2006) 'Service-Dominant Logic: What it is, what it is not, what it might be', in Lush, R. F. and Vargo, S. L. (eds) *The Service-Dominant Logic of Marketing: Dialog, Debate, and Directions*. Armonk, NY: M.E. Sharpe, pp. 43–56

Notes and references

1 This is based on a TV programme 'Contract Cleaning in the B.A.A.', BBC2 in the Learning Zone, 08/01/1996, 0640

2 Heskett, J. L., Sasser, W. E. and Schlessinger, L. A. (1997) *The Service Profit Chain*. New York, NY: The Free Press, p. 12

3 Vargo, Stephen L. and Lush, Robert F. (2006) 'Service-Dominant Logic: What it is, what it is not, what it might be', in Lush, R. F. and Vargo, S. L. (eds). *The Service-Dominant Logic of Marketing: Dialog, Debate, and Directions*. Armonk, NY: M.E. Sharpe, pp. 43–56

4 Grönroos, C. (2007) *Service management and marketing: Customer management in service competition* (3rd edn), Chichester and Hoboken, NJ: J. Wiley & Sons, p. 26

5 The 'relationship' approach in service marketing will be further discussed in Chapter 12

6 The role of the customer in service management will be further elaborated in Chapter 12

7 Mills, P. K. and Margulies, N. (1980) 'Towards a core typology of service organisations', *Academy of Management Review*, Vol 5, No 2, pp. 255–265

8 Haywood-Farmer, J. (1988) 'A conceptual model of service quality', *International Journal of Production and Operations Management*, Vol 8, No 6, pp. 19–29

9 Different types of service processes are further discussed in Chapter 4

10 Grönroos, C. (2007) op. cit., p. 27

11 Co-production means that customers are involved in service production and delivery processes through self-service (such as customers using ATMs or pumping their own petrol) and co-operation with front-line employees (such as customers giving guidelines about their haircut to the hairdresser). Co-creation was recently conceptualized as collaboration between service providers and their partners (such as customers and other organizations within their supply chain or value network) in the creation of value through shared inventiveness, design, and other discretionary behaviours (see Chapter 12 on the role of customers)

12 Further discussed in Chapter 12

13 See Schneider, B. and Bowen, D. (1985) 'New service design, development and implementation and the employee', in W. George, and C. Marshall (eds) *New Services*. Chicago, IL: The American Marketing Association; Schneider, B. and Bowen, D. (1993) 'Human resource management is critical', *Organizational Dynamics*, pp. 39–52; and Schneider, B. and D. Bowen (1995) *Winning the Service Game*. Boston, MA: Harvard Business Press

14 For an excellent overview, see Heskett, J., Sasser, W. and Schlesinger, L. (1997) *The Service Profit Chain*. New York, NY: Free Press

15 Schlesinger, L. A. and Heskett, J. (1991) 'Breaking the cycle of failure in services', *Sloan Management Review*, No 32, Spring, pp. 17–28

16 See also Heskett, J. L., Jones, Thomas O., Loveman, Gary W., Sasser Jr., W. Earl and Schlesinger, Leonard A. (2008) 'Putting the Service-Profit Chain to work', *Harvard Business Review*, July–August

Chapter 3

The service concept

Paul Gemmel • Bart Van Looy

'Service should be like a gentle wind. You feel the breeze – it's there – but you don't see the breeze, it is not in your face'[1]

Objectives

By the end of this chapter, you should be able to discuss:

- why service firms need a service concept and how the service gap model can guide us to implement this service concept effectively
- how service firms define a service concept
- how service firms implement a service concept and the five steps that make up the implementation process

Introduction

Unlike other airline companies, Singapore Airlines (SIA) has been profitable for the last 30 years, in good times and bad. What makes SIA's management different from its competitors? The company's success formula is explained in a recent book, *Flying High in a Competitive Industry: Secrets of the World's Leading Airline*, by Loizos Heracleous, Jochen Wirtz and Nitin Pangarkar.[2]

SIA has a very clear service concept. The mental picture that people have of Singapore Airlines is one of service excellence. This is consistent over time, and over many different countries and cultures around the world. Not only is this mental picture perceived by the company's customers, but its employees believe in it as well. They are proud to work for SIA and eager to deliver excellent service.

The service concept of SIA is reflected in Figure 3.1. It adopts human resource management practices company-wide that attract, motivate and retain employees who contribute to the objectives of high utilization of resources and to the highest quality of

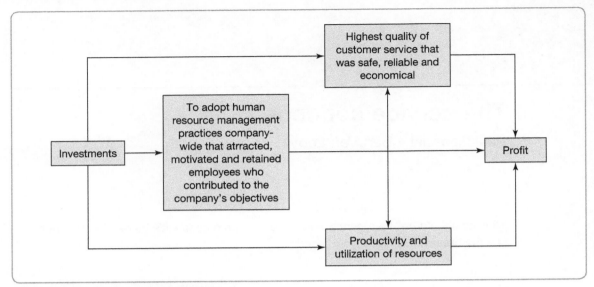

Figure 3.1 The service concept of SIA

Based on: Heracleous, L., Wirtz, J. and Pangarkar, N. (2005) 'Singapore Airlines: Aligning strategy and organization', Case 5 in Wirtz, J. and Lovelock, C. (eds) *Services Marketing in Asia – A Case Book*. Prentice Hall.

customer service that is safe, reliable and economical. This results in earnings that provide sufficient resources for investment and satisfactory returns for shareholders.

Developing a clear service concept to support a clear mental picture held by many different stakeholders starts with understanding the expectations and needs of these customers, employees and other stakeholders. SIA uses many different feedback mechanisms to understand its customers: in-flight surveys, crew feedback, customer complaints, focus groups, and even flights with competitive airlines, the so-called spyflights. The crucial point is that these feedback mechanisms are constantly used to come up with new ways of fulfilling the needs of the airline's demanding customers.

It is quite clear that not all airline passengers have the same needs. The industry has created different classes (economy, business, first) to serve the diverse needs of its various customers. SIA suites, i.e. fully separated compartments with a high level of luxury, are offered on the Airbus 380 planes to accommodate the high expectations of long-distance passengers. The challenge is to offer the right level of service at the right price to the right customer.

Although SIA strives for service excellence, it does so cost-effectively. The new Airbus 380, for example, which can carry more people in non-stop flights from Singapore to the US, appeals to passengers because they do not like stop-overs. But non-stop flights also have the advantage of costing less, since the most expensive part of a flight is taking off and landing. As well, SIA has a very young fleet: the average age of its planes is 5 years while the standard in the industry is 10 years. The interior and equipment of these planes are up-to-date and well suited to the current needs of passengers. At the same time, newer planes have lower maintenance and repair costs, and more efficient fuel use.

The key driver of cost-effective service excellence is innovation. Their trick is to innovate in such a way that the innovations lead to cost savings as well as better service.

Understanding that innovations do not happen by themselves, SIA has set up a structure for innovation. The service innovation department consists of a small group of people whose key task is to conceive innovative ideas and then take the best of those ideas through the development cycle to commercial introduction. As well, this group stimulates all other departments to contribute to continuous improvement. For instance, the ground services department redesigned the online check-in service, which built on the usage of telephone and SMS check-in services.

Maintaining a consistent service concept is not possible without substantial investment in employee training. 'Training is a necessity, not an option,' Dr Cheong Choong Kong, SIA's former CEO, once said. 'It is not to be dispensed with when times are bad. Training is for everybody.' Cost-effective service excellence through innovation and training has proven to be a recipe for success for SIA. Can it do the same for your service firm?

What can service managers learn from SIA? Service organizations should start to develop a very clear service concept. This is not only important in setting the right expectations with regard to customers, but it is also instrumental in guiding employees to offer the right level of services at all places in the organization and at all times. The biggest challenge in achieving this goal is to create a consistent mental picture of what kind of service provider the service firm aims to be, to align the strategic capabilities (such as service excellence and cost-effectiveness) to this service concept, and finally to design a service delivery system (training, service design, innovation, . . .) where all components contribute to the realization of the strategic capabilities and thus the service concept. In this chapter, we will focus on why it is so important for firms working in a service world to communicate a consistent and clear mental image of what type of service provider they are, how they can achieve this and what the specific challenges are for services in making this happen.

Why do we need a service concept?

Somebody once defined a service as a 'product in the making'. This refers in particular to a service as an experience or a process. In service delivery, there is no marked point at which a transaction of ownership of the product takes place. There is no clear end product on which all attention is focused. As with all products, services address a range of different customer needs.

With tangible products, these needs are translated into specific (technical) characteristics and product specifications. Once defined, product development, production and even marketing all focus on these characteristics and specifications. With services, such a natural focal point does not exist. Nevertheless, customers, employees and shareholders do have a mental picture of the service provided by the organization. This 'service in the mind' has been defined as the service concept.[3] It is important to understand that the 'service in the mind' is sometimes radically different from either what is intended or what is experienced.

Service firms have a strong service concept when the 'service in the mind' of all relevant stakeholders is the same.

The service concept of SIA is not one of a transportation company but of a unique travel experience provider: 'shiny new planes on the outside and warm, great service on the inside'.[4] The service concept is made tangible through the Singapore Girl: 'The Singapore Girl was conceived, a personification of oriental charm and friendliness, which the airline made real through careful recruitment and painstaking training. Effective and original advertising, together with word of mouth praises from satisfied passengers, create an aura of superior service and style. The aura, once established, had to be sustained through constant training, clever advertising and ingenuity in the cabin'.[5]

The service in the mind of stakeholders (such as customers, management and employees) can divert from the service as delivered and experienced by the customers. This leads to the so-called 'customer gap', i.e. the gap between customer expectations and perceptions.[6] Customer perceptions are the subjective assessments of what the customer actually experiences. Customer expectations consist of what a customer believes should or will happen. These beliefs are the 'service in the mind' for the customer. They are formed by customer needs, the word-of-mouth communication, previous experiences, and the external communication by the service firm. Without a strong service concept, there are many reasons (the so-called provider gaps) why the service provider is not able to fulfill these customer expectations. The 'Service Gap' model (*see* Figure 3.2) helps to identify these reasons using four 'provider gaps': the knowledge gap, the standards gap, the delivery gap, and the positioning gap:[7]

Figure 3.2 The Service Gap model

Source: Adapted from Zeithaml, V. A., Bitner, M. J. and Grembler, D. D. (2006) *Services Marketing: Integrating customer focus across the firms*. New York, NY: McGraw-Hill International edition.

- **The knowledge gap.** Management of the firm might have the wrong perception of customer expectations. Management of SIA know that they have very demanding customers. Passengers expect more from SIA than from any other airline company. As already explained, acquiring profound knowledge of – and understanding – customer needs is crucial in any business. Although this seems to be evident, service firms do not always delve into the minds of their customers to come up with the right service. Marketing research, listening to the front-line employees, and developing a relationship with the customer can all help to minimize this gap. SIA gives considerable attention to customer feedback and employs a variety of mechanisms such as crew feedback, customer complaints, focus groups, and passenger opinion surveys.[8]

- **The standards gap.** The service standards and the service designs should accurately reflect the perceptions of management. Due to the intangible nature of services, it is not easy for management to clearly communicate to their own employees what they want to achieve. 'Achieving service excellence in a cost-effective way' is not an easy message to communicate to the thousands of SIA employees. It all starts with a very clear statement by management that SIA has no desire to be the largest airline company, just the most profitable one.[9] Service firms have to set up performance management systems that communicate the right customer-driven standards throughout the company (*see* Chapter 13). They have to make sure that these customer-driven standards are translated into the service delivery system. SIA uses several incentives to make clear to its employees what is really important at SIA. For instance, bonus schemes are based on team performance and not on individual performance. SIA wants its people to work as teams and not just as individuals. The employees have profit sharing plans; in other words, they are very well aware that they have to do whatever is necessary to deliver services in a cost-effective way.

- **The delivery gap.** The service employees are not necessarily performing up to the standards set. SIA very well understands that the most important 'asset' in achieving excellent customer service is its employees. 'The crews are great at carrying out service procedures, but [SIA management] want them to really connect with customers, who are sophisticated travellers. . . . Customers desire individual pampering'.[10] Acquiring the right balance between standardization and personalization is one of the main objectives of the extensive training of SIA employees. 'Training is next to godliness at SIA'.[11] If we want employees to perform well in service provision, we need to support them with the right HRM strategy (*see* Chapter 11). Not only do the employees need to perform well but also the customers, because customers, as stated earlier, are involved in the production and creation of the service (*see* Chapter 12). This means that management has to manage their performance as well.

- **The positioning gap.** Customer expectations are influenced by promotion and other types of external communication. By positioning itself as an excellent service provider, the expectations of SIA customers are raised. 'Some customers actually will tell us that if we weren't SIA, they wouldn't have complained'.[12] Promising more than the firm can deliver will have a negative impact on the customer. 'Not being able to meet promises' compromises the reliability of the service.

The gap model teaches us that we need to be more explicit about the service concept in service settings because services – due to their intangibility and simultaneity – are in greater danger of concept dilution. As we shall see later, it is important in services to grant a level of autonomy to personnel and, in particular, to front-office personnel (*see* Chapter 5). However, variations in employee behaviour, competence, attitude, etc., can result in the service becoming diluted as it becomes exposed to random interpretation by field personnel. The customers themselves are, of course, a second source of dilution. Passengers of SIA can have many different requirements, but it should be clear to SIA staff what requirements can be fulfilled and what can not, depending on the kinds of passenger they are confronted with. Even in focused organizations, such as Club Méditerranée, employees are confronted with this phenomenon: 'What can you do with tourists who do not like the holiday philosophy of Club Med?' To satisfy these customers, service workers may need to deviate from the defined service concept. This can mean that the service organization begins to lose its focus.

A service company has, therefore, to be very clear what its service concept is, both towards its customers, and also towards its own employees.

Defining the service concept

According to J. Heskett, a service management expert at Harvard Business School, any definition of the service concept must answer the following three questions:[13]

- What are the important elements of the services to be provided, stated in terms of results, produced for the customer, for the employee and the company?
- How are these elements supposed to be perceived by the target market segment? By the market in general? By the employee? By others?
- What efforts does this suggest in terms of designing, delivering and marketing the service?

While the first two questions are more related to the knowledge gap, the last question concerns the standards, the delivery, and the positioning gap.

While it is clear that a service concept needs to address customer needs, it is also important that a service concept addresses employee needs. Ultimately, service workers are carrying out the service concept, and this is especially true for those who interact with the customer. In this respect, the service concept must involve a common set of values to which core groups of employees can subscribe. It is therefore important to note that Heskett also talks about the results for, and the perception by, employees. As an example, let us go back to the case BAA-ISS introduced in the previous chapter: employees working in maintenance and housekeeping functions commonly have a lack of self-respect – and often a lack of satisfaction with their work. When firms such as ISS want their employees to have respect for the customer, they need to encourage employees to develop a sense of self-respect and personal satisfaction. Therefore, the new way of working in the BAA-ISS case (which can be labelled as a new service concept) must include 'improved self-respect, self-development, personal satisfaction and upward mobility'.

When defining the service concept, the requirements for other elements of the service system and the perception of these elements by customers and employees must be considered. For instance, the setting should be adjusted to the needs of the customer. Restaurants targeting different age groups find it challenging to select music – not to mention volume levels – that is acceptable to all.

When defining a service concept, a service firm must try to preserve consistency between the front- and back-office elements of the service system. This involves alignment, which is more than a simple extrapolation of policies that are appropriate in the 'front office' without questioning the necessity or even the desirability of these policies for the back office, and vice versa. One such problem occurs in day clinics in hospitals. Nurses and administrative personnel in such clinics are used to working from 9.00 a.m. to 5.00 p.m., while physicians do not always respect these time limitations. This leads to overtime work, which can be the source of dissatisfaction when the overtime becomes structural. Working hours, shifts, quality control systems, the social skills of the workers and the physical environment are examples of elements that may require alignment from the front office to the back office.[14]

The service concept, once defined, becomes a blueprint that communicates to employees what service they should provide and to customers what service they should expect to receive. The past success of Club Méditerranée partially depended on the very clear definition and communication of its service concept, both to (potential) customers and to employees. If you visit the website of Club Med, you are first asked to indicate which profile best fits you as a customer (family, single or couple). Furthermore, Club Med uses the site to explain its holiday philosophy very clearly. This holiday philosophy can only be realized when the employees of Club Med, the so-called GOs,[15] and the customers, the so-called GMs,[16] completely believe in it.

Once the service concept has been defined, it will have a major impact on the components of any service delivery system since it will be noticed as soon as implementation begins.

Implementing the service concept

Given the heterogeneity of the needs of customers and employees and the variability introduced through the interaction between customers and employees, implementing the service concept is a difficult balancing act. To do this successfully, five tasks are particularly crucial: (1) segment the market, (2) target the various customer segments and design a portfolio of 'service products', (3) select a coherent model of service provision, (4) make the organization ready to support the service provision model, and (5) continuously monitor the extent to which the service concept is implemented.

Segment markets

Since different customers have differing needs and expectations, it is essential to analyse the market and to define the different segments that exist. Each segment contains customers who have more or less the same needs and therefore can be treated as one single submarket. At the same time, each segment should be as differentiated as possible from all the other segments, so that it can be served differently (as it should be). In the airline sector, for instance, segmentation could be based on the purpose of travel, business or recreation, and on the distance of the flight, short- or long-distance.

In segmenting a market, two broad groups of variables are generally used:

● the benefits sought; and
● the customer characteristics.

Figure 3.3 Market Segmentation for the after-sales service market of an industrial resin manufacturing company

Source: Forsyth, John E., Gupta, Alok, Haldar, Sudeep and Marn, Michael V. (2000) 'Shedding the commodity mindset', *The McKinsey Quarterly*, November, Fig. on p. 81.

The benefits sought are, in principle, the most important segmentation criterion. After all, underlying the segmentation effort is the fact that different groups of customers have different needs. They should therefore be treated differently – requiring, as a consequence, a different service concept. Segments should be as internally homogeneous as possible, so that customers belonging to the same segment are looking for the same benefits.

One study[17] that focused on the after-sales service business found that, when customers are segmented according to what they need, they tend to fall into one of at least three common categories (*see* Figure 3.3):[18]

- The basic-need customers want a standard level of services with basic inspections and periodic maintenance;
- The risk avoiders are looking for avoiding big bills but care less about other elements, such as response times;
- And the hand-holders need high levels of service, often with quick and reliable response times, and are willing to pay for the privilege.

But what are the benefits sought by the customers, certainly when talking about standard and high levels of after-sales service? Basic need customers look for on-time delivery and a reasonable price of the product. Risk avoiders want a consistent product performance over time and a large selection of products. Hand-holders ask for a high level of technical support and frequent interaction with sales people or a dedicated account manager. If one moves from basic-need customers to hand-holders, the more personal interactive service ingredients become relevant (*see* Chapter 2).

In principle, benefit segmentation should be the primary consideration of any marketer. However, from a managerial point of view, it is important to be able to set an indicator that permits the allocation of individual customers to specific segments. Marketers, therefore, try to match the benefit segments to specific customer characteristics, such as their geographic and socio-demographic status. By considering a consumer's age and gender, or the size and industry of an organizational buyer, marketers will try to assess the customer's needs and, consequently, the benefit segment the customer belongs to. Other important customer characteristics in consumer markets are psychographic in nature, while business-to-business marketers will also consider operating characteristics and purchasing approaches. For instance, one study of the customer needs of a large equipment manufacturing company discovered that some customers were willing to pay for immediate service to fix mission-critical products; while others were willing to wait longer (depending on the situation).[19] The level of mission-criticality of the equipment seems to be an important operating characteristic for a business customer in the after-sales services market. In addition, some psychographic characteristics such as risk tolerance can also have an important impact.

However, it is becoming increasingly difficult to match the benefit segment to customer characteristics. For example, situational segmentation criteria indicate that the same customer will have different needs depending on his or her buying situation. The same business customer can have mission-critical equipment as well as non-mission critical equipment – acting as a hand-holder in the former case and as a basic-need customer in the latter.

Exhibit 3.1 describes a case of how the benefits sought by customers can change over time. In the facility service industry (as well as in some other service industries), business customers increasingly look for the benefit of 'one-stop service solutions'. This means that one service provider should be able to offer multiple types of (facility) services and should focus on the operations as well as the management of these services. Service companies should decide whether or not to offer different types of service, even if historically they have been specializing in only one of these service businesses. This goes back to the fundamental strategic question of 'what business are we in?'.

Exhibit 3.1 'One-stop service provision' in the facility services industry

The facility services industry includes a range of business support services such as security, cleaning, property services, catering and office support. Many companies working in this industry were used to offering just one type of facility service (for instance, Sodexo focused on food services). The needs of customers changed over time and business customers increasingly asked for a 'one-stop service' situation where a single-service provider integrated many different services into its offering.[20] Today, Sodexo offers other soft facility services (such as cleaning) and hard facility services (such as maintenance of equipment). In some cases, business customers even look for one service provider that is able to take over the whole management and delivery of facility services. This is called integrated facility management (IFM). In the next step, the management and delivery of facility services and real-estate services are bundled in one package, i.e. facility estate management. Some service providers, such as Jones Lang Lasalle, are able to offer facility estate management services to some of their customers worldwide. Nevertheless, it is important to note that Jones Lang Lasalle works with subcontractors to supply some soft and hard facility services. Figure 3.4 summarizes this evolution in the facility service industry market.[21] A key strategic question for the different facility and real estate service firms is whether it is a legitimate strategy to expand the range of service products they offer in response to the changing

Figure 3.4 The changing Facility Service and Real Estate Service (Management) Market

Source: van der Veen, Casper, Duursema, Hester and van der Kooij, Alex (2007) 'Sodexho Alliance: Eating into a new Market', Wageningen University, European Food and Agribusiness Seminar, 22 June.

needs of their business customers. In other words, do you as a service provider offer one type of service or multiple services, and do you focus on operations, management and/or integration? Cohen *et al*. argue, in their *Harvard Business Review* article, that 'few companies have made money by becoming a "one-stop service provider"',[22] an observation we will further explore when discussing growth strategies for service firms (*see* Chapter 16).

Targeting market segments and designing a portfolio of service products

As each segment has significantly different needs, the service offered should be customized for each segment. Competitors who try to be everything to everybody, by offering a standardized service concept to all segments, will quickly find themselves relegated to the second best solution for each segment, whenever a more appropriate product is available. Exhibit 3.2 shows how banks ought to take into account the reality that there are very different market segments in their business, and that it is impossible to serve all these customers with the same standard service. Designing a portfolio of service products and targeting the right selection of market segments is, therefore, an important strategic decision for every service firm.

In evaluating different markets, the firm must look at two factors: the overall attractiveness of the segment and its compatibility with the organization itself. The attractiveness of a segment depends on its size and on how well it is already being served. The latter reflects the willingness to pay premium prices as well as an opportunity for the firm to outperform competitors. There should also be a match between the segment and the organization, its core capabilities, its objectives and its resources.

Exhibit 3.2 Targeting market segments in the banking sector

In the banking sector, highly focused players seem to be achieving major successes at the expense of banks trying to offer everything to everybody. In this sector, the following customer segmentation can be made:

- Urgent purchases. Banks' market share in consumer credit is decreasing in favour of the sellers of durable consumer goods. Loans for buying a car, a TV set or a piece of furniture can often be obtained directly from the seller. As customers are eager to buy, they tend to choose the convenience of one-stop shopping and do not even invite the bank to make a quotation.

- Regular purchases. Direct (home) banking offers the consumer the convenience of managing regular bank transactions from home, and at competitive prices. This is because the direct bankers have no need for a network of branch offices and can therefore achieve lower cost levels. Traditional banks have successfully responded to this threat by offering direct bank services, which complement their existing distribution channels.

- Large quantities. For mortgages and standardized medium-sized investments – for instance, bonds and savings deposits of over €10,000 – competitive prices prevail over service. As a result, specialist financial institutions, such as the Hypotheker in the Netherlands, concentrate on these specific products. Like the direct bankers, they have developed a lower-cost distribution system than the traditional banks.

- Difficult job and advice. Specialist banks and investment consultants, such as the bank J. Van Breda & Co. in Belgium, target self-employed customers and entrepreneurs looking for advice. Again, they have developed a distribution network with fewer branches than the traditional banks, but they assign key account managers to their customers and adopt a very personal 'relationship' approach. Traditional banks have responded by creating a different segment for this type of client and by serving them in a similar way.

Another aspect of targeting is communication. The communication strategy of service companies should develop a particular concern for creating the right expectations and making sure that the 'right' customers are channelled to the right delivery system (*see also* Chapter 12). Club Med must ensure that customers who dislike 'being organized' do not spend their holidays with them.

In some cases, targeting can be implemented by explicit – or sometimes implicit – selection mechanisms. The Shouldice Hospital applies a very explicit selection mechanism: patients have to fill in a questionnaire and, on that basis, surgeons determine the suitability of patients for the 'Shouldice treatment'.[23]

When a service company decides to offer different service products to different market segments, it is important to make clear what the consequences are for the service concept. A nice example here is the distinction between first, business and economy class in airline travel. It is clear that first and business class customers expect another level of service than economy class customers. In an ideal world, a service company can completely separate these market segments and offer them a distinct service concept. This is what happens in the hotel sector. But the airline companies do not have a choice: they have to put these different types of passenger on the same plane. This increases the probability of dilution of the service concept for passengers – but also for employees. Employees need to be aware that they cannot give the same amount of attention to economy class passengers as to business class passengers but, at the same time, they must avoid creating the perception that economy class customers are less valuable. The more economy and business class customers are separated from each other in terms of service provision, the easier the airline company can meet the 'service in the mind' of these different groups of passenger.

Selecting a coherent model of service provision

The example of the different passenger segments in the airline industry demonstrates that the nature of services commonly introduces wide variation in terms of customer needs or employee needs. Therefore, a clear service concept needs a coherent model of service provision that is focused on a particular market segment. The Shouldice Hospital near Toronto in Canada was one of the first clinics to understand that, by focusing on only one surgical procedure (simple abdominal hernia), they were able to offer a 'Club Med-like' services experience to their patients in a very cost-effective way. The Shouldice staff members are able to concentrate their talents and energies on one clear goal: performing abdominal hernia operations. All facilities and infrastructure are designed to cater for this one group of patients with very homogeneous needs. The Shouldice example of 'focused factory' has opened the eyes of many managers of general purpose hospitals, providing procedures ranging from appendectomies to ultrasound tests. These general purpose hospitals cannot duplicate the performance of Shouldice because their staff's focus is diffused over a wider range of services.[24] Today, the idea of focused factories has led to a revolution in the healthcare market. All over the world, focused clinics and hospitals are emerging (*see* Exhibit 3.3).

Exhibit 3.3 The University Hospital Ghent becomes a Club Med[25]

'What a view. I would like to stay for hours and look at how beautiful the city of Ghent is', exclaimed Beatrice, a patient who, full of admiration, was looking at the historical three towers of the city of Ghent from an enormous window on the sixth floor of the University Hospital building. The atmosphere in the reception area of the Day Surgery Clinic creates a relaxed feeling. A fellow patient is reading a book. A boy is playing a game in the children's corner. The mother is watching television. Beatrice is walking in her bathrobe to the surgery room. 'I will have a small operation on the eye. I am not anxious. The ambiance is so relaxed here that you feel no stress. It looks like a hotel'. The Ghent University Hospital has given its Day Surgery Unit a complete make-over. The purpose is that patients are no longer aware that they are in a hospital. 'We treat patients as our guests', explains the nursing head of the Day Surgery Unit, 'We do not intend to become a wellness centre, but we want to create a relaxed ambiance. The patients (or

Source: John Foxx Collection. Imagestate.

guests) coming to this Day Surgery Unit are not really sick. They come for a minor operation and only stay for a couple of hours. Because patients are less stressed, their rehabilitation will go faster. We want to avoid these "guests" being mixed up with real sick patients'.

When there is no focus, it is very difficult to develop a service delivery system that fits heterogeneous needs. Other examples of 'focused factories' in the service industry are McDonald's fast-food restaurants, Benetton and Club Méditerranée. These service firms all focus on a well-defined market segment and have designed their services in accordance with the characteristics of customer needs or expectations in this market segment.

It should be emphasized that focusing does not necessarily mean narrowing the product range. In some instances, it might be the opposite. One successful example of focusing is a cinema complex in Ghent, Belgium. Despite the fact that, in that city, one cinema after another was closing its doors, an entrepreneur opened a complex of 12 cinemas in the early 1980s. Everybody predicted a short life for this organization. However, quite the opposite happened: it was and still is a tremendous success. The entire service delivery system was focused on the service concept of 'choice'. People do not go to the cinema with a specific film in mind but make their decision after they have entered the system. Since then, the entrepreneur has repeated his success in various other Belgian and European cities and has evolved as Kinepolis Group into one of the bigger players in the European Cinema Industry.

Making the organization ready to support the service provision model

The main challenge in focusing the service delivery system is maintaining coherence among the various elements of the service delivery system and consistency over time. Important issues include:

- *Communication to, and selection and training of, employees.* When the integrity of the service concept is to be maintained in a situation where it is either impossible or undesirable to control the 'input' of customers, we have to make sure that employees are well informed about the service concept and their role in that concept. Service organizations should devote as much effort to internal communication as they do to external communication. In the case of Club Med, it is important that the GOs are totally customer-oriented, and that they are creative and innovative in dealing with customer needs. Club Med can attain this objective by carefully selecting their employees. It is also possible to induct employees into the Club Med culture.

- *Separating front-office and back-office activities.* The presence of the customer in the service delivery system (front office) limits the degree of freedom in the design of the service delivery system. The skills of front-office workers are clearly different from those who always work in the back office. However, differences between the back and front offices increase the chance of the firm losing its focus. It is important that there is consistency between the front-office and back-office elements when policies are formulated in the context of a service concept.[26]

- *Incorporating the focus into the service delivery system.*[27] Exhibit 3.3 clearly shows that the service delivery system and the 'servicescape'[28] in the new day surgery unit is completely different from a general purpose hospital. The patients – or should we call them guests – are welcomed in a homely atmosphere with a nice view over the city of Ghent; patients are allowed to walk to the operating room, and they are given personal guidance. This improves the customer experience. The focused factory in this hospital leads to higher labour and capital productivity since the care process can be organized as an assembly line.

- *Setting up the information systems.* In defining and implementing the service concept, service firms need to collect feedback information on how different stakeholders experience 'service in the mind'. This topic is elaborated further in Chapter 13.

Monitoring the implementation of the service concept in a continuous way

Service firms should continuously monitor their ability to create the right 'service mindset' across different stakeholders. Being able to meet (or even exceed) customer expectations is one indicator of success. Therefore, the Service Gap model introduced at the beginning of this chapter can be used as a tool to monitor the implementation of the service concept. A good service concept is essential in order to address potential gaps (knowledge, standards, delivery and positioning).

Conclusion

The nature of services requires service firms to be specific about the market segments they are going to serve and the needs they will address. A clear service concept identifies the 'what' and the 'how' of the focus. However, a service concept has to go further than simply identifying market segments; it must address any aspect of the service organization's marketing, human resource management and operations management. The content and process of these functional areas of management are discussed in the following parts of this book, respectively. In doing so, we will illustrate why we need to take into account the nature of the interaction in the service process (*see* Chapter 2). This, together with the competitive strategy deployed by the organization, will ultimately define the appropriate service delivery system. The success of SIA relies not only on the presence of a clear service concept; it is able to make its service concept a reality, every day, over and over again. This is only possible through the selection of the right strategy (*see* Chapter 16) in line with the service concept, the alignment of operational capabilities to their strategy and service concept, the nurturing of and investing in capabilities and core competences that support the strategy, and the need to understand and foster strategic innovations (*see* Chapter 15).

Review and discussion questions

- Look for a service that is not delivered up to your expectations. Describe the service and the firm delivering the service. Using the gap model, which gaps are responsible for not being able to meet your expectations?
- Life is easier for service firms that are able to focus on well-defined market segments. This means that a 'we do everything for everyone' strategy is not the best strategy in service markets. Look for firms in different service sectors with a 'everything for everyone' strategy. Do they have competitors that are much more focused? How do these generic service providers react to this competition? Who is performing best in terms of profit and growth?

● It is a fact that many utility companies providing gas, electricity, water and waste processing are taking a second look at this multi-utility concept, with many of them going back to a reduced utility scope. What is your opinion of this development? Are there other examples of service industries where customers are asking for 'one-stop service provision'?

Suggested further reading

Heracleous, L., Wirtz, J. and Pangarkar, N. (2009) *Flying High in a Competitive Industry: Secrets of the World's Leading Airline*. McGraw Hill Education (Asia), 246 pp

Notes and references

1 Deshpande, Rohit and Hogan, Hal (2003) 'Singapore Airlines: Customer Service Innovation', *Harvard Business School case*, No 9-504-025, p. 11

2 Heracleous L., Wirtz, J. and Pangarkar, N. (2009) *Flying High in a Competitive Industry: Secrets of the World's Leading Airline*. McGraw Hill Education (Asia)

3 Johnston R. and Clark, Graham (2001) *Service Operations Management*. Pearson Education, p. 29

4 Deshpande, Rohit and Hogan, Hal (2003) 'Singapore Airlines: Customer service innovation', *Harvard Business School case*, No 9-504-025, p. 5

5 Dr. Cheong Choong Kong, 'SIA's former chairman and CEO' in Heracleous, L., Wirtz, J. and Pangarkar, N. (2009) *Flying High in a Competitive Industry: Secrets of the world's leading airline*. McGraw Hill Education (Asia), p. 65

6 Zeithaml, V. A., Bitner, M. J. and Grembler, D. D. (2006) *Services Marketing: Integrating customer focus across the firms*. New York, NY: McGraw-Hill International edition, pp. 33–34

7 Adapted from ibid.

8 Heracleous, L. *et al.* (2009), op. cit.

9 Heracleous, L., Wirtz, J. and Pangarkar, N. (2005) 'Singapore Airlines: Aligning strategy and organization', Case 5, p. 61 in Wirtz, Jochen and Lovelock, Christopher. *Services Marketing in Asia – A Case Book* (eds) Prentice Hall

10 Deshpande, Rohit and Hogan, Hal (2003), op. cit., p. 11

11 Ibid., p. 10

12 Ibid., p. 9

13 Heskett, J. L. (1986) *Managing in the Service Economy*. Boston, MA: Harvard Business School Press, and Heskett, J. L. (1987) 'Lessons in the service sector', *Harvard Business Review*, Vol 65, No 2, Mar/Apr, pp. 118–26

14 In Chapter 7 we will further discuss how to structure the front-office and back-office

15 GO stands for 'Gentil Organisateur' or gentle organizer

16 GM stands for 'Gentil Membre' or gentle member

17 Bundschuh, R. G. and Dezvane, T. M. (2003) 'How to make after-sales services pay-off', *The McKinsey Quarterly*, No 4, pp. 2–13

18 Forsyth, John E., Gupta, Alok, Haldar, Sudeep and Marn, Michael V. (2000) 'Shedding the commodity mind-set', *The McKinsey Quarterly*, November

19 Bundschuh, R. G. and Dezvane, T. M. (2003), op. cit., p. 6

20 Ventovuori, Tomi (2007) *Research Reports 9, Doctoral Dissertation*. Espoo: Helsinki University of Technology Construction Economics and Management

21 Van der Veen, Casper, Duursema, Hester and Van der Kooij, Alex (2007) 'Sodexho Alliance: Eating into a new market', Wageningen University, European Food and Agribusiness Seminar, 22 June

22 Cohen, M. A., Agrawal, N. and Agrawal, V. (2006) 'Winning in the aftermarket', *Harvard Business Review*, May, pp. 129–138

23 Heskett, James and Roger Hallowell (2004) 'Shouldice Hospital Limited (Abridged)', *Harvard Business School case*, No 9-804-002

24 Herzlinger, Regina (1997) *Market-Driven Health Care: Who Wins, Who Loses in the Transformation of America's Largest Service Industry*. New York, NY: Perseus Books

25 Adapted and translated from press article in *De Standaard*, 17 March 2011

26 In Chapter 7 we will argue that designing the front office and back office structure is much more complex

27 A more elaborate discussion on service (process) design will take place in Chapter 4

28 The servicescape model is explained in Chapter 7. The servicecape includes the design of the physical environment (with or without customer input) housing the service encounter

PART TWO

Designing services

Paul Gemmel • Bart Van Looy

Designing service offerings pertains to all features offered by the service, the nature of the facilities where the service is provided as well as the technologies that support the front and the back office

Part 2 begins with a chapter on process design (Chapter 4). Services are processes characterized by simultaneity (see Chapter 1). It is therefore important to design service processes in such a way that they are reliable and that address customer needs and preferences effectively and efficiently. The presence of the customer in the process creates specific challenges for service process design. One of them is how to deal with customer-induced process variability. How do you deal with customers who do not want to collaborate in the service process? Although services are inherently variable to some extent, a more systematic approach to monitoring and evaluating processes can reduce or accommodate the process variability. These and other issues related to process design are discussed in Chapter 4.

As the processes in services involve both service employees and customers, we need to pay attention to both the behaviour of the employees and the customers in these processes. After exploring the notion of HRM and its relevance for services in Chapter 5, we introduce the idea that, for the design of service activities, a process logic (*see* Chapter 4) should be complemented by delineating relevant competencies. We end Chapter 5 by looking specifically at the notion of 'role stress', and how it can be avoided by designing relevant practices upfront.

In Chapter 6, we deal with technology, in particular, information technology. IT is important because most services are rich in terms of information exchange. We, therefore, discuss the impact IT might have on services and service processes, including how IT has transformed the physical marketplace with the introduction of its 'virtual' counterpart – the market space. The impact these IT developments have on service transactions will vary according to a number of factors: the behaviour of customers and service providers, as well as the nature of the service transaction itself.

Facilities are part of the service experience and often play an important role in the perception of service quality. Chapter 7 deals with design decisions related to facilities. It starts with a comparison of back-office and front-office activities. We then focus on the front office, addressing questions such as where to locate the service unit, and how to design the servicescape where customers interact with the firm. Finally, we will argue that all design components should reflect the service concept (Chapter 3) in order to convey the envisaged value proposition in a convincing and powerful manner

Conveying a service story in the right way is one of the building blocks of service branding, which is discussed in Chapter 8. By 'making the intangible tangible', service branding is an important element in developing trust between the service company and its customers. This is the remit of those involved in service marketing and can be achieved by clearly promoting the service offering and by setting a price level that fits the competitive positioning of the service firm. These two marketing tasks are discussed in Chapters 8 and 9 respectively.

The single most important activity in promotion is communication. A service concept must be developed and then communicated in a clear and consistent way so that, when buying in a service situation, the risk to the customer is reduced. A coherent communication strategy implies decisions on communication channels and tools as well as having a communication plan. The simultaneity of production and consumption in services means that the delivery system itself (and especially the employees) becomes an inherent part of any communication strategy.

Pricing is another very 'tangible' aspect of service marketing. In Chapter 9, we develop a framework for setting the price of a service offering in service firms. Four steps are discussed: pricing objectives, pricing strategy, pricing structure, and pricing levels/ tactics. The choice of pricing strategy has an impact on many other aspects of service management. Not only is the competitive position of the service firm influenced by pricing but price levels can also be used to manage service demand in accordance with the capacity of the firm.

Chapter 4

Service process design

Paul Gemmel

Objectives

By the end of this chapter, you should be able to discuss:

- the different types of service process and how the choice of a certain process impacts the management of service processes
- to what extent manufacturing-based methods such QFD, ISO9000, Six Sigma and Lean can be used in a service context
- how the customer experience can be integrated into the service design using methods such as Service Blueprinting
- the different sources of customer-induced variability and how to manage this
- the meaning of lean consumption

Introduction

Grupo Fernando Simao (GFS) is a Portuguese automobile dealer group.[1] At some point in time, it was concerned with the inefficiencies in its processes at one of its dealerships.

First, GFS looked at the steps a typical customer took to get a car fixed – from contacting the dealership to arriving home with the vehicle repaired (the so-called customer activity chain). The customers spent an average of 95 minutes in this process. When the customer returned to pick up the car, 60% of the time the car was not ready. Thus, a large part of the time that the customer spent in this process was wasted.

Next, GFS studied the different steps that were required to maintain or repair the car in the garage. The group discovered that this internal process took, on average, 202 minutes of paid time, only 27% of which created any value for the customer. A closer look revealed that technicians, the sole creators of customer value, were creating value during only 45% of their paid work time (see Figure 4.1). One of the major problems was that the technicians discovered additional problems when working on the car. Because they needed the permission of the customer to repair these additional problems, they could not proceed with the repairs. This interruption led to a lot of wasted time for the technicians.

Figure 4.1 The average time (in minutes) spent by customers and provider in a car repair process: distinction between value-creating time and non-value creating time

Source: This figure is based on information from the article: Womack, J. P. and Jones, D. T. (2005) 'Lean consumption', *Harvard Business Review*, March, pp. 58–68 and the paper of Venkat, K. and Wakeland, W. W. (2006) 'Using simulation to understand and optimize a lean service process', *Proceedings of the 2006 Spring Simulation Multi-Conference*.

Sergio, the manager, was looking at the graph (*see* Figure 4.1), which showed the average time customers and the car dealership needed to spend in the service delivery process. He asked himself the question: 'Why do we need 202 minutes of paid time, only 27% of which creates any value for the customer?', 'Why is almost half of the customer time wasted?' and 'Why are we not able to meet the completion time?' Sergio really wanted to improve the performance of this process. Therefore, some process changes were necessary.

To be able to deliver services in a cost-effective way, service firms need to manage their processes. As in any firm, this means that service firms have to study the ordering of their work activities and how these activities take an input, add value to it, and provide an output to an internal or external customer. This is the provision process. The story of GFS demonstrates that the customer not only 'takes' the output but 'co-produces' the output. In other words, the customer also goes through a sequence of actions (such as making a booking, driving the car to the dealership, discussing the repair . . .) that make up the customer activity chain. There are, of course, many interaction points between the provision process and the customer activity chain in services. Being able to manage these interaction points, the underlying provision process and the customer activity chain, is the main task of process management in services.

An adequate process management starts with defining the processes. This includes the choice of process type. This choice must reflect the service concept, which in itself is related to the target market segment (*see* Chapter 3). Next, the process must be designed as a sequence of several tasks. In this process design or redesign, the customer activity chain as well as the provision process should be taken into account.

Defining the service process

A three-star French restaurant looks quite different from a fast-food restaurant such as McDonald's for a variety of reasons. Both of these restaurants, in turn, are quite different from a Benihana restaurant,[2] a Japanese-style restaurant where the meal is prepared in front of the customers on a hibachi cooking table. One of the major differences is the process type. The French restaurant has many characteristics of a so-called '*job shop process*' and has a functional layout; the fast-food restaurant has many characteristics of a *line process* and has a line layout; the Benihana restaurant, with its insistence on grouping customers in 'batches' of eight in the bar before preparing and serving the meal, seems more like a *batch process*. These differences demonstrate that the traditional distinction in manufacturing between different processes applies equally to service companies. As with manufacturing firms, the main determinant of the type of process is the transaction volume. The higher the volume, the more a line process will be appropriate; the lower the volume, the more a job shop process will be used. In extreme cases such as management consultancy, a project approach might be desired. This relationship between process type and volume is illustrated in Figure 4.2.

The matrix in Figure 4.2, as it applies to manufacturing sectors, has the process type as a multi-dimensional construct. Several different manufacturing dimensions are combined. Correlated with process type are such variables as:

● product range (from narrow to broad);

● size of the (customer) order (from large to small);

● degree of product change accommodated (from standardized products to completely customized products);

● degree of innovativeness (from low to high);

Figure 4.2 The relationship between process type and transaction volume

Source: Silvestro, R., Fitzgerald, L., Johnston, R. and Voss, C. (1992) 'Towards a classification of service processes', *International Journal of Service Industry Management*, Vol 3, No 3, pp. 62–75.

- degree of automation (from highly automatic to purely manual work); and
- capital intensity *versus* labour intensity.

Something similar has been proposed by Silvestro et al.,[3] whose conclusions are illustrated in Figure 4.3. These researchers propose using the number of customers (or customer files) processed by a typical unit per day as a volume measure. On the *y* axis, they have a composite variable composed of the following sub-variables:

1 *Equipment/people focus.* Equipment-focused services are those where the provision of certain equipment is the core element in the service delivery. People-focused services are those where the provision of contact staff is the core element in service delivery.

2 *Customer contact time per transaction.* High customer contact time per transaction is where the customer spends hours, days or weeks in the service system, per transaction. Low customer contact is where the contact with the service system is a few minutes.

3 *Degree of customization.* A high degree of customization is where the service process can be adapted to suit the needs of individual customers. A low degree of customization is where there is a non-varying standardized process; the customer may be offered several routes but the availability of routes is predetermined.

4 *Degree of discretion.* A high degree of discretion is where front-office personnel can exercise judgement in altering the service package or process without referring to superiors. A low degree of discretion is where changes to service provisions can be made only with authorization from superiors.

Figure 4.3 Relationship between process type and transaction volume, according to Silvestro *et al*.

Source: Silvestro, R., Fitzgerald, L., Johnston, R. and Voss, C. (1992) 'Towards a classification of service processes', *International Journal of Service Industry Management*, Vol 3, No 3, pp. 62–75.

5 *Value-added back office/front office*. A back-office oriented service is where the proportion of front-office (customer contact) staff to total staff is low. A front-office oriented service is where the proportion of front-office staff to total staff is high.

6 *Product/process focus*. A product-oriented service is where the emphasis is on what the customer buys. A process-oriented service is where the emphasis is on how the service is delivered to the customer.

Integrating these variables leads to a construct that, combined with volumes, results in three types of service process: professional services, service shops and mass services (*see* Figure 4.3). Some scholars propose a fourth type of service process, 'the service factory'.[4] The service factory is situated close to the mass services but is differentiated from it in its rather high degree of capital intensity.

At the core of the process classifications in Figures 4.2 and Figures 4.3 is the so-called product-process matrix. There is a tight connection between the nature of the product and the type of process used to produce it. Much the same is true for services: the nature of the process by which a service is delivered depends on the nature of the service.[5] Exhibit 4.1 shows how this product-process matrix has been translated into a healthcare environment and how the process choice has an impact on the further design of the operational system.

The different types of service process lead to different challenges for the management of operations, HRM and marketing.

For instance, on the operations side with mass services, service specifications are determined prior to the service delivery to the customer. In professional services, the service specifications are developed together with the customer during the service delivery.[6] While the challenge of the mass service provider is to identify customer needs and to build them into the service process, the challenge of the professional service provider is to be able to adapt to changing customer needs during the service process. The development of clinical guidelines in the medical world is useful to make best practice more explicit, but they need to be adapted to the health needs of the specific patient facing the physician (*see also* Exhibit 4.1).

Different service processes require different styles of HRM where the styles can be differentiated by the amount of employee involvement and participation in shaping the service encounter. Social and interpersonal skills are less important in a fast-food restaurant than in a three-star restaurant. Given their highly educated personnel, it is a challenge in professional services to manage the career development of employees, whereas service factories and service shops are more concerned with workforce scheduling.[7]

From a marketing point of view, one should put more emphasis on the employees and their competences in professional services (the bottom of the service triangle, *see* Figure 2.1(a) in Chapter 2), and on the physical components and the procedures in mass services (the top of the service triangle, *see* Figure 2.1(a) in Chapter 2). In professional services, one should be aware that every service employee contributes to the image and thus the service concept of the firm. In mass services, the marketing will focus more on the technology, allowing the delivery of services to a large number of customers.

Finally, a service firm must be sure that the type of process is well-fitted to the needs of well-defined customer segments. Customers in a fast-food restaurant do not expect to be treated as they would in a three-star restaurant. These fast-food customers want fast service in a standardized way and are not willing to pay for a customized approach. An in-depth study of customer requirements is, therefore, the starting point in the successful management of service processes.

Exhibit 4.1 The Product-Process Matrix in health care[8]

In his book *Designing Care: Aligning the Nature and Management of Health Care*, Richard Bohmer recognizes that, in healthcare, the nature of the process by which a service is delivered depends on the nature of the service, but it would be dangerous to apply unmodified tools from production and assembly industries such as the product-process matrix.[9] Figure 4.4 shows a modified 'product-process' matrix in healthcare. The nature of the service in healthcare is generally determined by the extent to which the underlying health problem is structured. Health problems are more structured when they are 'well-defined and easily recognized, so that their causes can be rapidly identified by one or two diagnostic tests and, once a cause has been found, the solution is immediately apparent'.[10] Diabetes is, today, an example of a structured health problem as opposed to complex cancers, which are not all structured. The nature of the service (structured versus non-structured health problems) determines the nature of the care process. The process used for non-structured health problems is called 'iterative', being composed of multiple cycles of hypothesis proposition and testing, and where each cycle builds on the former.[11] This is in contrast to the process for structured health problems, which tends to be more linear: the process is rather an orderly sequence of steps.

The design of the operating system (including components such as services offered, human assets, process choice, policies, technology choices, and physical surroundings) is completely different in iterative care as compared to sequential care. This is summarized in Table 4.1.[12] For instance, the process type used in sequential care resembles an 'assembly line' while the process type in iterative care is more like a job shop. In terms of the framework of Silvestro *et al*. (*see* Figure 4.3) sequential care corresponds more with mass services and iterative care more with professional services. Table 4.1 also teaches us that many other design and management components are influenced by the type of care delivered: the organizational mission, the beliefs and approach (or values and strategy), the scope of services, the management policies, the human resources, the technology used, and the degree of

Figure 4.4 The product-process matrix in health care

Source: Based on Bohmer, R. (2009) *Designing Care: Aligning the Nature and Management of Healthcare*. Harvard Business Press, pp. 69–85.

collocation. The differences between these two types of care are so fundamental that Bohmer[13] advises running multiple separate operations systems, each specifically configured to the needs of either iterative care patients or sequential care patients. In practice, this means that sequential surgery procedures such as hip replacements should not be performed together with complex cancer treatments in the same organizations. This is a call for more 'focused' organizations such as free-standing surgery centres taking on the more sequential care patients. In fact, this call is not new and goes back to the idea of 'focused factory' as introduced by Skinner in the 1970s. Skinner noted that 'simplicity, repetition, experience, and homogeneity of tasks breed competence'.[14] Operational focus makes employees more effective and experienced in the tasks required for success. Operational focus can be achieved 'by focusing the entire organization on a limited set of services (for example disease- or body system-specific specialist surgical hospitals) or by focusing one unit within an organization on a limited range of activities (the hospital within the hospital)'.[15] One of the best well-known classical examples of a clinic focusing the entire organization on one set of services is Canada's famous Shouldice Hernia Center.

Table 4.1 Operating systems for sequential and iterative care

Components	Sub-components	Operating system for sequential and iterative care	
		Sequential care	Iterative care
Organizational mission	Value proposition	Efficient delivery of a problem solution	Evaluation and management of complex, difficult, and multiple problems
Beliefs and approach	Basic philosophy	Ideal exists	Ideal unknown
	Approach to uncertainty	Reduced before care commences	Reduced during care
	Strategy	Manage toward ideal	Discover ideal
Scope of services	Scope of services	Narrow	Diversified
	Capacity utilization	Higher	Lower
Process type	Type of process	Sequential	Iterative
	Degree of standardization	Higher	Lower
	Production model	'Assembly line'	'Job shop'
Management policies	Organizational design	Centralized	Decentralized
	Span of management control	Wide	Narrow
	Physician performance measurement and incentives	Process based	Outcome based
	Approach to improvement	Drive out variation	Exploit variation for learning
Human Resources	Idealized employee motivation	Conformer, rule follower	Problem solver, experimenter
	Motivation	Doing a repeated task well	Trying new things to see what will happen
Technology	Type of technology	Specialized	General purpose
Physical site	Degree of collocation	Decentralized	Centralized

Source: Reprinted by permission of Harvard Business School Press. From *Designing Care: Aligning the Nature and Management of Healthcare* by R. Bohmer. Boston, MA 2009, pp. 128–129. Copyright © 2009 by the Harvard Business School Publishing Corporation; all rights reserved.

Designing the service process

A process (as a sequence of activities) must deliver the expected outcomes in a reliable way and at a satisfactory level of quality. In manufacturing, systematic analytical methodologies are used to design processes that are reliable and satisfactory. The same is true for services although the methodologies need to take into account that the customer activity chain and the provision process should be looked at in an integrated way. In the next paragraphs, we will show how a blend of manufacturing-based methodologies and service-specific techniques can help to design the service process. Service process designers should consider how to bring customer needs into the process, how to map the customer activity chain and the provision process, and how to deal with some specific challenges in process management such as variability and waste.

Designing customer requirements into the service process

Increasingly, service management scholars are proposing the use of more systematic approaches to designing customer needs into the service processes. One of these approaches, borrowed from the manufacturing industry, is quality function deployment (QFD). QFD translates customer needs and preferences into operational goals for the firm. In a manufacturing context, QFD is very popular as it creates a bridge between the engineer and the customer. Applications of this technique have considerably reduced the cost of design and development of new products. The service applications of QFD are rather limited but are nevertheless promising.[16]

Figure 4.5 shows an example of the best known QFD matrix, the House of Quality,[17] applied in the environment of a car dealership.[18] In this House of Quality, the customer quality criteria[19] are linked to some service company facets such as the skills and training of the employees and the availability of resources (equipment). For instance, it is impossible to diagnose a problem correctly without the right equipment and knowledgeable people. The value in each cell is the multiplication of the following elements:

- the relative importance, indicating how important this quality criterion is compared with the other criteria;[20]
- the strength of the relationship (this refers to the second part of the Figure 4.5 where a strong relationship is equal to 9, a medium relationship is equal to 6 and a weak relationship is equal to 3);
- the critical incidents, indicating the number of fail points in a certain period of time;
- the competitive benchmarking, indicating how important these service quality criteria are for competitors;
- the scores on the customer quality criteria.

One study argues that QFD is particularly promising in service transactions delivered by airlines, resort hotels, leisure activities, education, and healthcare services.[21] Other scholars are much more careful in their evaluation of the use of QFD in services, questioning whether subjective customer needs in a service context can be defined objectively. There is no magic formula for translating customer needs into characteristics of service processes. Moreover,

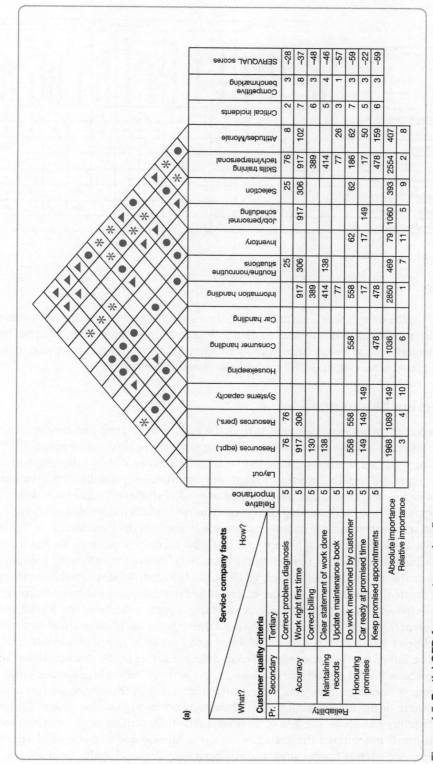

Figure 4.5 Partial QFD for an auto-service firm

Source: Bahara, Ravi S. and Chase, R. B. (1993) 'Service quality deployment: quality service by design', in Sarin, Rakesh V. (ed.) *Perspectives in Operations Management: Essays in Honor of Elwood S. Buffa.* Norwell, MA: Kluwer Academic Publisher.

(b)

Pr.	Secondary	Tertiary	Relative Importance	Planning				Procedures							Personnel		
				Layout	Resources (eqpt.)	Resources (pers.)	Systems capacity	Housekeeping	Consumer handling	Car handling	Information handling	Routine/nonroutine situations	Inventory	Job/personnel scheduling	Selection	Skills training tech/interpersonal	Attitudes/Morale
Reliability	Accuracy	Correct problem diagnosis			*	*						●			●	*	▲
		Work right first time			*	●					*	●		*	●	*	▲
		Correct billing			●						*					*	
	Maintaining records	Clear statement of work done			●						*	●				*	
		Update maintenance book									*					*	●
	Honouring promises	Do work mentioned by customer			*	*			*		*			▲	▲	●	▲
		Car ready at promised time			*	*	*				▲		▲	*	▲	●	
		Keep promised appointments							*		*					*	●

Strength of relationship

✳ Strong   ● Medium   ▲ Weak

Figure 4.5 (cont'd)

there is the danger that designers may make a subjective interpretation of customer needs, which then starts to live a life of its own.[22] Whatever the outcome of this discussion, service managers need to design customer requirements into the processes to be able to deliver the right level of service, and QFD can be helpful in this perspective.

Service blueprinting

Much of the work in service process design was done by G. Lynn Shostack, who introduced an analytical tool for process design and mapping, called service blueprinting.[23,24] In more recent work, service blueprinting has been recognized as a highly effective and adaptable technique for service (process) design and improvement, quality improvement, service innovation and strategic change focused around customers.[25] Figure 4.6 shows a service blueprint for the car dealership GFS, which wanted to study the problem of on-time perform-ance and waste of time in its process (see the example in the introduction to this chapter).

A service blueprint is a picture or a map that accurately portrays the service system so that the different people (including the customer) involved in delivering it can understand and deal with it objectively. A service blueprint in Figure 4.6 displays the service process of the car dealership by showing the customer activity chain, the points of customer contact, the activities of the contact employees and the support processes. The service blueprint is different from other process mapping tools through the use of three 'lines' on the blueprint: the line of interaction, the line of visibility and the line of internal interaction.[26] The lines can be linked to swimlanes connected to different actors in the process. Under the line of interaction but above the line of visibility, the actions[27] of onstage contact employees are shown. A customer discussing the maintenance task with the service advisor at the reception desk of the car dealership is an example of an onstage visible action. Under the line of visibility but above the line of internal interaction, contact employees are working for a customer but without the customer involved. An example of this type of action is when the service advisor further prepares and prints out the work order for a specific job after

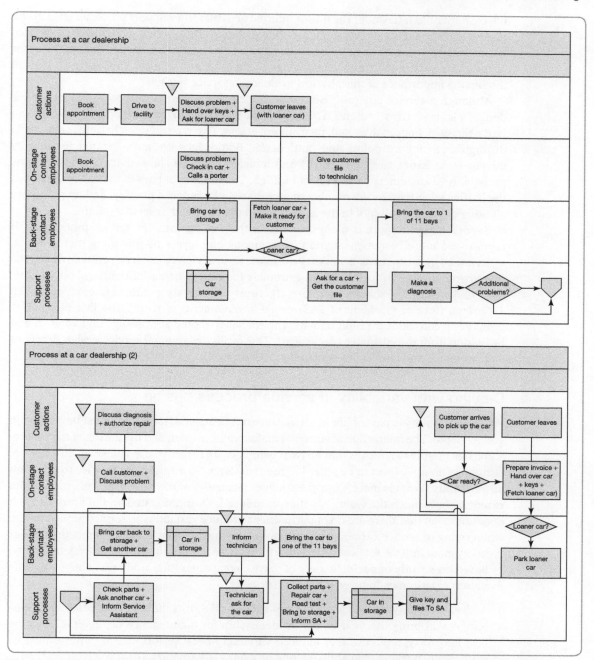

Figure 4.6 **The service encounter: a blueprint for a service delivery process in a car dealership**

Source: These figures are based on information from the article: Womack, J. P. and Jones, D. T. (2005) 'Lean consumption', *Harvard Business Review*, March, pp. 58–68 and the paper of Venkat, K. and Wakeland, W. W. 'Using simulation to understand and optimize a lean service process'. *Proceedings of the 2006 Spring Simulation Multi-Conference*.

the customer has left. Under the line of internal activities, the support processes such as the reservation and registration systems are shown. Finally, the physical evidence of the service is integrated into the blueprint. This is the physical evidence of the service such as the décor of the garage, written documents, employee's clothing, and so forth. In Chapter 7, we will discuss the importance of this physical evidence in service settings.

Although a service blueprint can be used for many different purposes such as service design, it is also extremely useful in identifying the weak links in the chain of actions, which can be the target of, first, analysis and, then, improvement. Two types of weak link are traditionally distinguished: failure points and bottlenecks. Bottlenecks are more related to capacity management issues (*see* Chapter 10) and indicate points in the activity chain where the probability of customers having to wait is high. The number of bays in the car dealership is the bottleneck if it limits the number of cars that can be serviced per day. Failure points are all other types of weak spot in the activity chain that can lead to service failure.

Service blueprinting has many benefits in the management of service processes.[28] It reinforces a more customer-oriented focus among employees by providing them with an overview so they can relate 'what they do' to the service viewed as an integrated whole. The interaction in service processes is an extremely important aspect influencing both productivity and quality. We should, therefore, rigorously identify the points of interaction, which J. Carlzon (former president of SAS) called 'the moments of truth'. The line of visibility promotes a conscious decision on what the customer should see onstage and what should be hidden from the customer (backstage). This facilitates rational service design decisions on front-office and back-office activities (*see* Chapter 7).

Dealing with variability in service process design

Process variability is part of life in service environments and, therefore, must be studied in greater depth. The interaction of customer and service provider, and the impact of the servicescape (*see* Chapter 7), means that no two customers are served in the same way. In addition, customers do not expect to be served in the same way. So it would not be wise to drive out all variability. What is more, customers judge the quality of the service process to a certain extent by how much the variability they introduce is accommodated and not reduced.[29] It does not mean that there are no opportunities to reduce variability in service processes but, when trying to reduce variability, one should take into account that customers themselves are a key input into the service process and, thus, are an important cause of process variability.

Based on a study of a wide variety of service companies, one study was able to identify five types of customer-induced variability:[30]

1 *Arrival variability*. For a car dealership such as GFS, it is difficult to predict when customers will bring their car to the car dealership for maintenance or repair. This is the best known type of customer-induced variability because this arrival pattern must be studied when trying to analyse waiting problems (*see* Chapter 10).

2 *Request variability*. Customers bringing their car to the garage can ask for a rental car or not – and sometimes they even specify the type of rental car. The fact that the desires of the customer can vary poses real challenges for virtually every kind of service business.

3 *Capability variability*. Customers differ in their capabilities to perform tasks in the service process. Customers calling in to make an appointment for their car may or may not be able to explain what the technical problems are.

4 *Effort variability.* When customers must perform a role in the service process, it is up to them to decide how much effort they apply to the task. When customers in GFS are not willing to drive their car to the right bay in the garage, the service advisors will not be able to force the customer to do so.

5 *Subjective preference variability.* Customers vary in their opinion about what it means to be served well. Some customers appreciate it when they have contact with the technicians while others do not want to be bothered with this kind of contact.

Generally, service managers have two basic strategies to deal with these different types of variability: reducing the amount of variability or accommodating the variability.[31] A classic way to reduce variability is to limit the number of request options. In the garage example, this means that only one type of rental car is available for customers. To compensate for the capability variability, service advisors can be trained to do a quick diagnosis of the car so that they take over the work of the customer. Most of the time, accommodation can be achieved through highly skilled and trained front-office employees who adapt the service offering to the needs of the customer. Of course, this increases the cost of the service delivery, while variability reduction might lead to lower quality of the service experience. The real challenge is to find a way of working that leads to the same service level without increasing the costs. One example of dealing with different types of customer variability in the car dealership is that they take the initiative to schedule for preventive maintenance on a certain day and pick up the car at the customer's home while delivering the rental car. The customer is perhaps even prepared to pay a premium price for this additional service and the car dealership is able to schedule its work much better.

The previous discussion on variability makes clear that service processes are inherently variable. This makes service operations different from manufacturing operations where there is virtually complete control over the cost and quality of production inputs. This also means that it is not straightforward to implement variability-reduction strategies such as ISO 9000 and Six Sigma in services.[32]

An ISO 9000 quality management system requires that customer expectations be documented as specifications, methods of measurement be defined, and the service process be monitored to ensure that the services conform to these specifications. A growing number of service firms apply ISO 9001 as part of their quality management initiatives. Familiezorg Oost-Vlaanderen, a home health care organisation in Belgium, received ISO 9001:2000 certification in 2004. Its quality management handbook documents all core, supporting and decision processes. Familiezorg Oost-Vlaanderen recognized the advantage of uniformly structured documents in making the organization more transparent not only for its own employees but also for its customers. The implementation of ISO 9001:2000 can be seen as one way to make the service concept more tangible. Other examples of the application of ISO 9000 can be found in many service companies delivering maintenance-interactive services such as maintenance, catering and security.

In services, ISO 9000 is used more for the maintenance-interactive type of service (*see* Chapter 2) or in the back-office of other types of service. The importance of applying ISO 9000 principles in the front office may not be evident at first sight. Customers and employees usually do not have a common understanding of the specifications of the service. Consequently, it is difficult to measure conformance to specifications. This does not mean that a service firm with predominantly front-office operations cannot benefit from an ISO 9000 certification. One study found that ISO 9000 certification creates a better balance

67

between the quality management perspectives in the back and front offices.[33] Quality certification leads a high-contact service (with a large front office) to shift its unilateral emphasis on external quality dimensions to a more balanced emphasis on both external and technical quality. This better balance also supports the consistency of quality management policies and, more generally, of the service concept in the back and front offices (*see* Chapter 7).

Generally, the same remarks pop up when using Six Sigma in service processes. A major goal of Six Sigma is to reduce process variability. Jack Welch, former CEO of GE and one of the most important adepts of Six Sigma, makes this very clear:

> 'We have tended to use all our energy to "move the mean to" . . . reduce order-to-delivery time to . . . 12 days. . . . The problem is, as has been said, "the mean never happens", and the customer . . . is still seeing variances in when the deliveries actually occur – a heroic 4-day delivery on one order, with an awful 20-day delay on another, and no real consistency . . . Variation is evil.'[34]

For sales and service organisations, unmanaged variability in the quality of the customer experience represents a significant threat to the enterprise's sustainability because customers experience variation, not averages.[35] The customer experience in a garage can be very different depending on how the customer is being served. If, on one day, a customer is confronted with a service advisor who is unfriendly and unwilling to help, this one experience will not be negated by the many other positive experiences.

A large part of the inherent variability in the service processes is driven by people (employees and customers) in the service encounter where interactions take place. While designing service processes, service managers must focus on managing the variability in these local people processes (the 'who' and 'how' of service delivery) (*see also* the next chapter on the role of employees in service design).

Dealing with waste in service process design

After developing and studying the service blueprint in combination with some more subjective insights into the customer experience, management of the car dealership GFS were able to identify improvement suggestions for the redesign of its processes. For instance, GFS could pre-diagnose the problem by phone whenever possible and confirm the diagnosis as soon as the car arrived.[36] By asking the right questions from the very start when the customer was calling in for an appointment, the service advisor no longer needed to call the customer to authorize the repair work. By implementing these and other improvements, GFS was able to come up with the results as shown in Figure 4.7. It reduced the average time customers spent in the process by 30% and the average time service employees spent in the process by 50%. These gains created a win-win situation. Customers' time was no longer wasted, and GFS could handle a greater volume of business. But what was even more important was that GFS's technicians were now creating value during 78% of their work time.[37] One could say that GFS had driven different types of 'waste' out of its service process and its customer process. In other words, the service experience at GFS car dealership became 'lean'.

Although lean management has its roots in the (car) manufacturing industry,[38] it has generally been accepted as a useful approach in service settings, such as car dealerships, to improve their processes. Exhibit 4.2 illustrates how the quality and productivity of a food service operator improves after redesigning its processes using lean management principles. Lean management has successfully been applied to push the performance of service firms to new heights. The Rotterdam Eye Hospital, an independently operating eye hospital in Rotterdam (the Netherlands) applied lean management in combination with care pathways

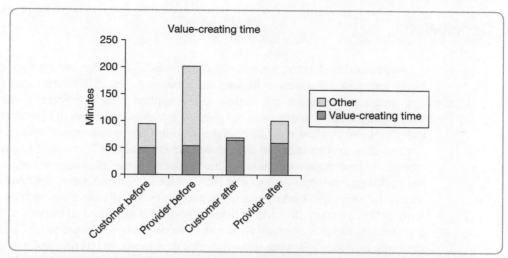

Figure 4.7 The average time (in minutes) spent by customers and provider in a care repair process before and after the process redesign

Source: This figure is based on information from the article: Womack, J. P. and Jones, D. T. (2005) 'Lean consumption', *Harvard Business Review*, March, pp. 58–68 and the paper of Venkat, K. and Wakeland, W. W. 'Using simulation to understand and optimize a lean service process'. *Proceedings of the 2006 Spring Simulation Multi-Conference*.

to level the workload of professionals and to synchronise capacity with demand.[39] Other examples can be found in the banking and insurance industry[40] and in local government.[41] Some studies recommend combining 'Lean' and 'Six Sigma' to produce 'Lean Six Sigma', especially for services[42] given the fact that many 'Lean' and 'Six Sigma' studies share a common focus on 'time' but deal with different aspects of time management. Furthermore, Six Sigma is able to give more structure to Lean initiatives that are growing from the bottom up. The usefulness of Lean (and Six Sigma) in services can be summarized in the following statement by Womack and Jones:

'Lean production transformed manufacturing. Now it's time to apply lean thinking to the processes of consumption. By minimizing customer's time and effort and delivering exactly what they want when and where they want it, companies can reap huge benefits.'[43]

Exhibit 4.2 Lean Cuisine[44]

'Beset by waste and operational variability, food service operators are taking a page from industrial manufacturers and applying lean-production approaches to their own operations. Lean techniques seek to improve product and service quality while simultaneously reducing waste and labour costs. For food service operators, the additional trick is to link such improvements to customer loyalty. For one operator, this effort meant tackling unpredictable demand and excessive error rates and wait times (ten minutes for simple sandwiches) on orders. The operator mapped daily changes in demand to highlight fluctuations, introduced a self-service counter, and redesigned kitchen and food preparation procedures to standardize sandwich making and eliminate waste, which consequently fell by 40 per cent. Meanwhile, labour costs dropped by 15 per cent and service times improved by one-third. Best of all, sales increased by 5% and margins on affected products more than doubled, since employees could spend more time influencing customers and less time apologizing to them.'

Conclusion

To conclude this chapter, we will illustrate in Exhibit 4.3 the implementation of Service Blueprinting in a Business-to-Business environment. The exhibit illustrates that the tools and methods discussed in this chapter can be applied in many different service processes – not only in a B-to-C environment but also in a B-to-B environment. It also demonstrates that every tool and method must be configured to fit the specific service context in which it is applied. The project team, in the example from Exhibit 4.3, decided to expand the service blueprint format with three additional components: the customer support processes, the backstage customer actions and the onstage customer actions. Splitting the customer actions into onstage, backstage and support processes allowed them to map the customer journey from the very start where the service need is identified all the way to the successful problem resolution. Designing processes in services where one has to take into account the customer experience is much more complex than in manufacturing and asks not only for a thorough knowledge of the different tools and methods (such as QFD, service blueprinting, Six Sigma, Lean management etc.) but also for creativity to fit these tools and methods to the characteristics of different types of service process.

Exhibit 4.3 Service Blueprinting at Waters Global Services Department[45]

Waters Corporation is a world-leading supplier of products and services to laboratories. The service blueprint was developed as part of a project that specifically focuses on the Global Services Department of Waters Corporation,[46] located within the Northern European region. Within this region, the various countries (UK, Ireland, Sweden, Norway, Finland and Denmark) had different operating modes for handling various types of customer service request in their business communication. This way of working had a negative impact on productivity and led to poor customer satisfaction. The need to reduce the variability in the interaction with the laboratories was identified. The decision to redesign their business communications management system was taken as an opportunity to optimize the service delivery process in order to attempt to improve productivity and customer satisfaction.

Service blueprints were created in order to map out the customer activity chain and the interaction of the customer with their own processes. The aim was to identify possible obstacles to delivering world-class customer experience, allowing for process redesign tailored to the customer's expectations. Figure 4.8 shows an example of one blueprint resulting from this exercise, more specifically, the blueprint for prepaid repair services.

The starting point of the exercise was a series of in-depth customer interviews in which the project team attempted to obtain a clear understanding of the various process steps the customer would take from service request to resolution. However, it became clear from the very first interview that the basic format of service blueprinting as described earlier in this chapter was insufficient for their purposes. All customers interviewed, indicated that they had to undertake quite a few steps before requesting service from any service provider. In fact, they all had their own more or less comprehensive internal process to follow before they contacted the Global Services Department of Waters. In some cases, the internal customer process handled the request and terminated the request without contacting the Global

Figure 4.8 Part of a Service Blueprint for the Prepaid Repair Services at the Global Services Department of Waters Corporation

Source: This Service Blueprint was developed by Bart de Craene, Global Services Manager EMEIA, Waters Corporation for his project paper 'Smart customer interactions enabling novel customer experiences', submitted for a project defence in the Executive Master Class in Business Process Management at the Vlerick Leuven Gent Management School, Belgium, 9 September 2011.

Services Department of Waters, leading to an incomplete service record history on the part of Waters Company and often causing dissatisfaction with the end user on the customer side. For this reason, the project team decided to expand the service blueprint format with three additional components: the customer support processes, the backstage customer actions and the onstage customer actions. Splitting the customer actions into onstage, backstage and support processes allowed the project team to map the customer journey from the very start where the service need was identified all the way to the successful problem resolution. The additional granularity above the line of interaction introduced an increased level of detail on the customer side in the service blueprinting (*see* Figure 4.8). The ability to map out the end to end service process from the customer's point of view, including the customer's own internal process, allowed the project team to interlink the processes from both the service provider and customer sides. The understanding of the customer's internal process led to the identification of possible interaction points between the customer activity chain and the provision process, enabling the customer to put the service request earlier into the supplier's organisation and, therefore, achieving a shorter time to service.

Adding internal key performance indicators to the bottom of the service blueprint secured transparent communication with their business customers, indicating the importance of minimizing the time between service need identification and contacting the service organization, without having to bypass the customer's own internal process.

Review and discussion questions

- Take an example of a service company (or take the service company you are working for) and determine the dominant process type. What are the consequences of this type of process for the design and the management of the processes?
- Discuss the advantages and the disadvantages of using QFD, ISO 9000, Six Sigma and Lean in service companies. Is there any relationship between the process type (mass service, service factory, etc.) and the possibilities for using these kinds of tool?
- How do you incorporate the customer experience into service process design?
- Think about a specific service process and give examples of the customer-induced variability in these processes.
- Take the same service process and try to understand the meaning of customer actions, onstage contact employee actions, backstage contact employee actions, support processes and physical evidence.

Suggested further reading

Bitner, M. J., Ostrom, A. L. and Morgen, F. N. (2008) 'Service Blueprinting: A practical technique for service innovation', *California Management Review*, Vol 50, No 3, pp. 66–93

Frei, Frances X. (2006) 'Breaking the trade-off between efficiency and service', *Harvard Business Review*, November, pp. 93–101

Womack, J. P. and Jones, D. T. (2005) 'Lean consumption', *Harvard Business Review*, March, pp. 58–68

Notes and references

1 This case is based on information from the article of Womack, J. P. and Jones, D. T. (2005) 'Lean consumption', *Harvard Business Review*, March, pp. 58–68. It is also based on the paper of Venkat, K. and Wakeland, W. W. 'Using simulation to understand and optimize a lean service process'. *Proceedings of the 2006 Spring Simulation Multi-Conference*

2 Benihana case (1972) *Harvard Business School case study*, 9-673-057
3 Silvestro, R., Fitzgerald, R., Johnston, R. and Voss, C. (1992) 'Towards a classification of service processes', *International Journal of Service Industry Management*, Vol 3, No 3, pp. 62–75
4 Schmenner, R. W. (1995) *Service Operations Management*. Englewood Cliffs, NJ: Prentice Hall, pp. 10–11
5 Bohmer, R. (2009) *Designing Care: Aligning the Nature and Management of Healthcare*. Harvard Business Press, p. 166
6 Silvestro, R. (1999) 'Positioning services along the volume-variety diagonal. The contingencies of service design, control and improvement', *International Journal of Operations and Production Management*, Vol 19, No 4, pp. 399–420
7 Rohit, Verma (2000) 'An empirical analysis of management challenges in service factories, service shops, mass services and professional services', *International Journal of Service Industry Management*, Vol 11, Issue 1, pp. 8–25
8 This exhibit is based on the book of Bohmer, R. (2009), op. cit.
9 Ibid., p. 166
10 Ibid., p. 79 and 80
11 Ibid., pp. 87–88
12 Ibid., pp. 128–129
13 Bohmer, R. M. J. (2005) 'Medicine's Service Challenge: Blending custom and standard care', *Health Care Management Review*, Vol 10, No 4, pp. 322–333
14 Skinner, Wickham (1974) 'The Focused Factory', *Harvard Business Review*, Vol 52, No 3, pp. 113–121
15 Bohmer, R. (2009), op. cit., p. 135
16 Dubé, L., Johnson, M. D. and Renaghan, L. M. (1999) 'Adapting the QFD approach to extended service transactions', *Production and Operations Management*, Vol 8, No 3, pp. 301–317
17 Hauser, J. R. and Clausing, D. P. (1988) 'The House of Quality', *Harvard Business Review*, Vol 66, No 3, May–June, pp. 63–73
18 Bahara, R. S. and Chase, R. B. (1993) 'Service quality deployment: quality service by design', in Sarin, R. V. (ed.) *Perspectives in Operations Management: Essays in honor of Elwood S. Buffa*. Norwell, MA: Kluwer
19 The customer quality criteria are in this example described in terms of the Servqual dimensions (*see* Chapter 13): reliability, responsiveness, assurance, tangibles and empathy
20 Here only the reliability Servqual dimension is shown
21 Hauser, J. R. and Clausing, D. P. (1988), op. cit.
22 These scholarly opinions are based on an informal e-mail discussion about QFD with the following people: Mr Frede Jensen, Prof. Glenn Mazur, Dr Lary Menor, Prof. J. A. Fitzsimmons, Prof. A. Johne
23 Shostack, G. L. (1985) 'Planning the service encounter', in Czepiel, J. A., Solomon, M. A. and Surprenant, C. F. (eds) *The Service Encounter: Managing employee–customer interactions in service businesses*. New York, NY: Lexington Books
24 Many process mapping techniques exist, and process mapping has many other purposes. This goes beyond the scope of this book. The reader interested in learning more about process mapping can refer to, for instance, the structured analysis and design technique and the service logic map. For references, *see* Congram, C. and Epelman, M. (1995) 'How to describe your service: An invitation to the structured analysis and design technique', *International Journal of Service Industry Management*, Vol 6, No 2, pp. 6–23; and Kingman-Brundage, J., George, W. and Bowen, D. (1995) 'Service logic: Achieving service system integration', *International Journal of Service Industry Management*, Vol 6, No 4, pp. 20–39
25 Bitner, M. J., Ostrom, A. L. and Morgen, F. N. (2008) 'Service Blueprinting: a Practical Technique for Service Innovation', *California Management Review*, Vol 50, No 3, pp. 66–93
26 Ibid.
27 An action is a set of operations performed by an actor; this is different from an activity, which is a collection of actions undertaken with a given purpose (*see* Patricio, L., Fisk, R. P. and Cunha, J. F. (2008) 'Designing multi-interface service experiences: The service experience blueprint', *Journal of Service Research*, Vol 10, No 4, p. 17)
28 Bitner, M. J. *et al.* (2008), op. cit.
29 Frei, Frances X. (2006) 'Breaking the trade-off between efficiency and service', *Harvard Business Review*, November, pp. 93–101
30 Ibid.
31 Ibid.

32 For more information on Six Sigma, we refer to the following book: Van Snee, R. D. and Hoerl, R. W. (2005) *Six Sigma Beyond the Factory Floor*. Pearson Education, USA, 312 pp

33 Dick, G., Gallimore, K. and Brown, J. C. (2001) 'ISO 9000 and quality emphasis: An empirical study of front-room versus back-room dominant service industries', *International Journal of Service Industry Management*, Vol 12, No 2, pp. 114–136

34 George, L. M. (2002) *Lean Six Sigma: Combining six sigma quality with lean speed*. New York, NY: McGraw-Hill

35 Fleming, J. H., Coffman, C. and Harter, J. K (2005) 'Manage your human sigma', *Harvard Business Review*, July–August

36 Womack, J. P. and Jones, D. T. (2005), op. cit., p. 65

37 Ibid.

38 Lean management is an operations management strategy that was originally developed in Japan as the Toyota Production System (TPS) by the Toyota Motor Corporation in the 1940s to survive in the automobile industry. Toyota gradually developed multiple operational and socio-technical tools to reduce costs and lead times, while improving quality. Womack, J. P., Jones, T. D. (and Roos, D.) have made an important contribution to the diffusion of the ideas of Lean Management with their book *The Machine that Changed the World* and with different articles in the *Harvard Business Review* such as (1994) 'From Lean Production to the Lean Enterprise, *Harvard Business Review*, Vol 72, pp. 93–103, and (1996) 'Beyond Toyota: how to root out waste and pursue perfection', *Harvard Business Review*, Vol 74, No 5, pp. 140–151

39 Vliet van, E. J., Bredenhoff, E., Sermeus, W., Kop, L. M., Sol, J. C. A. and van Harten, W. H. (2011) 'Exploring the relation between process design and efficiency in high-volume cataract pathways from a lean thinking perspective', *International Journal for Quality in Health Care*, Vol 23, No 1, pp. 83–93

40 Swank, Cynthia K. (2003) 'The Lean Service Machine', *Harvard Business Review*, pp. 123–129

41 Furterer, Sandra and Elshennawy, Ahmad K. (2005) 'Implementation of TQM and Lean Six Sigma Tools in Local Government: a Framework and a Case Study', *Total Quality Management*, Vol 16, No 10, pp. 1179–1191

42 George, L. M. (2003) *Lean Six Sigma for services*. New York, NY: McGraw-Hill

43 Ibid., p. 59

44 McPherson, J. R. and Mitchell, A. V. (2005) 'Lean Cuisine', *The McKinsey Quarterly*, No 1

45 This exhibit is completely based on a project performed by Bart de Craene, Global Services Manager EMEA, Waters Corporation. The project was described in a paper, submitted for a project defence in the Executive Master Class in Business Process Management at the Vlerick Leuven Gent Management School, Belgium, 9 September 2011

46 Waters Corporation, founded in 1958 by James L. Waters and headquartered in Milford, Massachusetts, US, is the world leading supplier of ultra-performance liquid chromatography, high performance liquid chromatography, mass spectrometry, thermal analysis, and rheology instrumentation and consumables. Around the world, Waters products are used by pharmaceutical, biotechnology, industrial, university, and government research and development, quality assurance, and environmental testing laboratories. For these customers, Waters provides technology that gives scientists fundamental data on the composition of natural products and synthetic chemical mixtures, and the physical properties of materials

Chapter 5

Designing human resources practices that matter for service organizations

Bart Van Looy • Koen Dewettinck • Dirk Buyens •
Walter Stevens • Dries Faerns

Objectives

By the end of this chapter, you should be able to discuss:

● how the nature of services – in particular, its simultaneity – explains the crucial role of HR practices for services

● relevant HRM models that can be used as the basis for designing relevant HR practices

● the general outline of competency-based HR practices

● how one can start to operationalize the notion of competencies, and what relevant tools might look like for proceeding on the level of identifying relevant and existing competencies

● different types of competencies and how their importance relates to different types of service

● the relevance of the notion of role stress for service organizations

● what role stress means for the individual employee and which forms it takes

● how the design of work practices can influence front-line employees' experience of role stress and how role stress can be minimized for front-line employees

Introduction

Imagine you are shopping in a large department store in one of Europe's many famous shopping streets.

You arrive at the counter with several items you would like to buy and you think you are lucky: there are no customers waiting at the desk and there are three members of staff just waiting to serve you. At least, that is how it looks to you at first. As you approach, you notice that they are talking to each other. Is this a staff meeting perhaps?

You put all the items on the desk in front of the lady you like the most (at first sight) and you smile. Important issues are obviously being discussed; your presence is hardly noticed. After a minute, you remove the smile and clear your throat to gain attention. Too modest. The discussion continues and, worse, another staff member joins the debate.

'Do I pay here?' you ask finally, choosing English as the best hope of achieving a lingua franca. One of the three employees makes a half-turn, picks up the pile of goods, takes out scissors, and continues the discussion with her colleagues. You sigh with relief; things are at least progressing. Price tags are removed by means of the scissors and put in a pile. Suddenly there are two piles – goods and price tags. Job done, scissors put away, discussion continues.

The two who have dominated the discussion leave; end of discussion, you hope. Silence falls – for a moment. Number two takes the goods and starts to organize them so they fit nicely into a bag. You have your credit card ready when you notice that the price tags are still there in their nice pile. The conversation starts up again. No, it is not about new ways of organizing floor space, recent changes in working conditions, or the latest initiatives aimed at improving customer satisfaction. No, it is about one of their colleagues having an affair with someone working in the warehouse.

You tap your credit card on the desk. An employee looks up. 'Can I pay with this card?' 'Yes', she replies. 'And when?' you enquire. A name is shouted out. Customers begin to look in your direction. You start to sweat a little and feign a weak smile. The employee who left a couple of minutes earlier starts to move in your direction again – only slowly, as the story of the affair has to be related to a colleague filling the racks. You produce the 'I don't want to be annoying, but I have a plane to catch' routine. Another shout.

At this point, you begin to consider the possibility of walking out. You hesitate a moment too long; someone picks up the pile of price tags. Between tags three and four, a short break seems appropriate; the colleague filling the racks is obviously in need of some more details.

Finally, you get to pay. You lurch out of the store. Out on the street, you open up the bag to see the clothes you have bought. They look great; it was all worth it. Then, your eye falls on the pair of socks you just bought – to be precise, the place where the price tag was removed – to find a gaping hole. The scissors.

For a moment you consider the possibility of going back into the shop. Then you look upwards and see that it is a beautiful day, too nice a day to spend in a department store.

Services are processes involving both service employees and customers. The simultaneity of services leads to an inherent link between employees' behaviour, their motivation, competencies, satisfaction and commitment, and customers' perceptions of service quality and, hence, satisfaction as became apparent in Chapter 2. As a result, human resources (HR) practices play a crucial role in the management of service operations. In this chapter, we highlight distinctive HR practices that are especially relevant for services. After exploring the notion of human resources management (HRM) and its relevance for services, we introduce the idea that, for the design of service activities, a process logic (*see* Chapter 4) should be complemented with delineating relevant competencies. We end this chapter by looking specifically at the notion of 'role stress', and how it can be avoided by designing relevant practices upfront.

The nature of services

In practice, it is difficult in a service operation to distinguish clearly between the service, the process of providing the service, and the system and procedures that deliver it. One of the unique attributes of services is the customer's participation in its production, which we called simultaneity in Chapter 1. The service itself always concerns an act involving the customer; as a result, quality will also be perceived by the customer in terms of this interaction.

Simultaneity as an inherent characteristic of services means that service organizations have a permeable boundary between themselves and their customers. There is both psychological and physical closeness between service providers and consumers. Service employees and consumers frequently work together, observe each other and interact. As a consequence, what employees experience in their work is communicated to consumers. Dissatisfied, unmotivated or frustrated employees bring their feelings with them when interacting with the customer, and these feelings are transmitted during interactions. We can all tell stories about how the behaviour of service employees in a restaurant affects our global impression of the overall service quality. Whereas in some, the customer is given the impression that he or she is lucky to be served at all, in others, the customer emerges after the meal feeling totally spoiled and well looked after.

Schneider and Bowen have documented this relationship extensively.[1] In a series of studies on the relationship between the experiences of employees at work and customer perceptions of service quality, the findings point to the same conclusions over and over again. The way employees feel and act has an impact on the quality of the service delivered: satisfied people deliver good-quality service!

Let's take a closer look at one of their studies. To examine the relationship between employees' perception of and satisfaction with HR practices, and customers' evaluation of service quality, data was gathered from 28 branches of a service company. Employees could express their satisfaction with features such as work facilities, supervisory characteristics and development opportunities. At the same time and independently, data was collected on customers' perceptions of service quality. Both elements of the study were strongly correlated. We would like to stress that the data stemmed from the same company. The type of service and the overall routines in these 28 branches were the same. It was the difference in employee satisfaction, therefore, that became the single crucial element that accompanied – or, put more strongly, caused the differences in – customer perception of service quality. As explained in Chapter 2, the service profit chain model – developed by Heskett, Schlesinger and Sasser[2] – takes this observation as one of the cornerstones of the model. Here the relationship between employee and customer satisfaction is called the 'satisfaction mirror'. Empirical evidence supporting this effect is abundant: data collected at Rank Xerox or MCI Communications, to name but two, reveals positive relationships between the two elements. Employees feeling enthusiastic about their job not only communicate this feeling both verbally or non-verbally but are also eager to work hard towards satisfying their customers. Customers treated in this way start to act reciprocally, increasing employee satisfaction even further. Moreover, employee loyalty is crucial; employees who stay on the job long enough not only develop their skills to a high level but also begin to know customers and their specific interests and needs. This allows them to provide an even better, personalized and customized service. It creates more value, which, in turn, increases customer satisfaction and, as demonstrated in Chapter 2, benefits profitability.

We can conclude from these authors, therefore, that much of what happens inside a service organization cannot be hidden from the customer with whom the organization's employees interact. Achieving high levels of service quality and customer satisfaction implies that consideration is being given to employee satisfaction as well.

Since managing human resources is of vital importance, let us take a look at what is most important in terms of human resources management for service firms.

Exhibit 5.1 Rising sales at Au Bon Pain[3]

Au Bon Pain is a chain of French bakery-cafés on the East coast of the US. Initially, store managers were being paid salaries marginally above local market averages and were allowed very little discretion regarding how they managed their stores. A 'carousel' pattern of high manager and employee turnover was normal for the firm.

To turn things around, new contracts were developed, which involved the company and store managers splitting any profits above a certain target. At the same time, managers were given freedom to modify procedures, staff policy, and even the layout of the store.[4] Headquarters started to redefine their own role. Instead of putting emphasis on control, field coaching and consulting became the priority. In a number of cases, this led to a doubling of sales volume.

One local manager, taking things even further, started to look for people willing to work 50–60 hours per week. The increased productivity and the longer work hours allowed him to reduce the head count by about 70%. Absenteeism dropped to almost zero (as a missed day meant lost overtime pay). Turnover for the low-skilled, entry-level jobs went down to 10%, whereas 200% is quite normal in this industry. Sales soared as customers noticed the changed atmosphere and started to develop relationships with the people they saw every day behind the counter. His front-line employees earned approximately double the industry norm.

Human resource management for services

HRM: What is it?

The concept of HRM was already being adopted on a larger scale in the 1970s.[5] Formerly, employees were regarded for the most part as a cost but, with the evolution of human capital theory, it was argued that people should be seen as an asset as well. Later on in the 1980s, it was felt that human resources management could and should be tied into a company's business strategy, since committed personnel were shown to make a substantial difference in an era of increasingly stiff global competition. This position has now been widely accepted and is the main difference between HRM and 'classical' personnel management. The traditional tasks of personnel management have been enlarged from a basic managing of the workforce to larger, more global issues – such as the organization's culture, new types of training, and contributing to or even forming organizational direction.[6]

Different models can be found within the domain of human resources management. We will discuss two of these models, each of which we believe makes a valuable contribution to our understanding of HRM. Considered together, they provide us with an integrated comprehensive view of what HRM entails:

- The *Michigan model* stresses the idea of strategic matching and the basic building blocks of HRM.

- The *Harvard model* directs our attention to the diversity of stakeholders involved and introduces the four Cs of HRM.

The Michigan model: linking HR practices and business requirements

In this model, the resource side is emphasized. People in organizations are resources and should be managed in a way that is consistent with organizational requirements. Congruence with organizational strategy and effectiveness is crucial; we should look for the 'fit' between human resources and business strategies. Human resources management should be in line with, and help to achieve, business goals. Being supportive in this way means developing appropriate HRM systems – such as selection, performance appraisal, rewards and development.[7]

This way of thinking stresses the importance of developing strategic contingencies, whereby human resource practices are designed according to the type of strategy being adopted. For instance, if a company is striving for differentiation by means of innovation, creative and innovative people should be selected, and the company should invest in a broad range of competencies, foster cross-functional co-operation, and design dual-ladder careers.

While this approach may be attractive at first sight, it has its shortcomings. HRM is cast rather reactively; once the strategy is defined, the human resources are 'adapted' to it. Such a HRM approach reduces the importance of the human factor to a large extent – not necessarily the most appropriate course of action in a service environment.[8] The quality of service delivery will depend on the commitment of the service employees to the defined service concept. Casting your employees in a mere 'compliance' role does not seem the best way to create this commitment. That is why it is important to address HR values and practices when defining the service concept (*see* Chapter 3) – a process in which employees could also be involved.

It is also worth noting that, in this model, strategy is approached as a rational process with generic typologies of strategy as valid starting points.[9] However, generic strategies such as cost leadership or differentiation are not as mutually exclusive as was once thought. Moreover, strategy has as much to do with process as with content. Strategy formation and change often shape an incremental process that has its own, often not so rational, logic. HR practices can also play a role in this process of change. In this context, defining HRM as selection, performance appraisal, rewards and development is too narrow a definition.

We need, therefore, to complement this view with other models that do more justice to the complexity faced.[10]

The Harvard model: stakeholders working on the four Cs

A less prescriptive model was developed at the Harvard Business School.[11] Here, the human aspect of HRM is stressed. HRM is defined here as:

'all management decisions and actions that affect the nature of the relationship between the organization and the employee.'

This implies a broader range of areas than in HRM as defined by the Michigan school. Beer and his colleagues define four HRM policy areas: human resource flows, reward systems, employee influence and work systems:

1 *Human resources flows* are comprised of activities related to managing the flow of people in, through, and out of the organization: recruitment and selection, placement, development, performance appraisal, promotion and termination.

2 *Reward systems* imply everything that is related to attracting and retaining employees: pay systems, motivation, and benefits.

3 *Employee influence* refers to the levels of (employee) authority and power and the way in which they are designed within the organization.

4 Finally, *work systems* refers to the way that work is designed and the arrangements of tasks and technology that achieve optimum results.

The Harvard model recognizes different stakeholders, each with their own interests: shareholders, management, employees and unions, government and the community. Outcomes that need to be achieved in these different policy domains and among the different stakeholders involved are called the four Cs:[12]

- *Commitment* of employees to their work and organization.
- *Congruence* between the objectives of the different stakeholders – employees and their families, the organization and its objectives, shareholders, community and society at large.
- *Competence* now and in the future – to what extent can one attract, keep and develop the skills and knowledge of the people involved.
- *Cost effectiveness* – what are the consequences of certain policies in terms of wages, benefits, turnover, motivation, employment and so on? Costs can be considered at the individual, organizational or even societal level.

This model integrates all stakeholders as well as the content and process of HRM and strategy. It can be noted that this integration is conceived mainly in terms of implementation rather than in terms of formation. It goes without saying, however, that more bottom-up approaches – whereby employees actively contribute to the definition, and design relevant practices including roles and objectives – can be reconciled within this framework, as will become apparent in Chapter 11 (people practices that enable service delivery).

A competency-based HR framework

HR practices establish a balance between – and connect – employees and the organization. They act as an interface between organizational goals and characteristics (e.g. structures) and the individual, working in the firm. In the past, the organizational characteristics tended to dominate the discussion; most of the efforts in designing an operational HR system went to job design, task profiles, recruitment procedures, and so on. Introducing the notion of competencies provides opportunities to create greater balance between organizational requirements and the functioning of employees.[13] More specifically, competency systems can be developed to link the strategic core competencies of the organization with the individual competencies of the employees. Following Prahalad and Hamel (1990), core competencies have to be defined as 'specific combinations of internal resources that can constitute a competitive advantage for the organization'. Thus, these core competencies should be in line with the envisaged service concept (*see* Chapter 3). Individual competencies, on the other hand, are defined here as human characteristics related to effective performance. These characteristics can be seen as indicating ways of acting, behaving or thinking. These individual competencies are considered more or less generalizable over the range of situations and enduring over a period of time.[14]

Figure 5.1[15] outlines such an approach. Both organizational goals and structure, as well as the individual competencies and performance, find a place here. Developing a match between them is the continuous challenge for HR practices.

The organizational mission and vision, and their translation into the firm's core processes structure (*see* Chapter 4) bring us eventually to different roles and jobs. Roles and jobs are not the same: roles are situated more directly in concrete activities (e.g. selling projects) whereas jobs are (often) a combination of roles. It is crucial here to explain not only what needs to be done, the areas of performance, but to indicate *how* one can achieve this and what kind of competencies are needed with regard to the areas of performance.

Take the example of a sales engineer selling sophisticated technical systems to professional users. In terms of areas of performance, one can stipulate that the sales engineer should promote the systems in question, sell them, and take care of the customer relationships established. These areas can be complemented by specific performance objectives, such as realizing a certain turnover in new sales and achieving an adequate level of customer retention and loyalty (e.g. at least one out of two existing customers should place an order again within the next year).

However, these elements – areas of performance and objectives – do not say anything about how to 'go for it'; that is, which competencies are needed to succeed as an individual in the job. So, defining necessary or required competencies explicitly adds value to HR practices. The notion of roles integrates both elements: areas of performance and competencies necessary to achieve results.

Figure 5.1 Quintessence Performance and Competency Management Model
Source: © Quintessence Consulting Belgium.

When competencies are made explicit, they offer a guiding framework for both recruitment practices and development actions when complemented with a gap analysis. Let us return to our sales engineer. Required competencies include, among others, customer orientation, interpersonal understanding, empathy, initiative, technical expertise, and persuasion. Comparing the level of the required competencies with the information gathered during the recruitment or promotion/mutation process allows one to make relevant decisions both in terms of hiring and in terms of instruction and/or development programmes.

Working on the tension between desired and actual competencies is not only relevant for recruitment or promotion/mutation. Given the ever-increasing rate of change companies face today, it should become a 'daily' routine. This can be achieved by complementing the 'classical' performance management process, which focuses on the realization of objectives, with a competency management process addressing competency levels and their evolution over time as depicted in the upper right half of Figure 5.1.

We just have illustrated why gap analysis can be seen as a useful approach for comparing the desired and actual competency levels of employees. However, this approach can entail the risk of 'organizational rigidity', a risk that is not implied in the 'system' itself but rather in the process characteristics of the deployment trajectory. Recall that everything starts with the mission and vision of the organization, which we called the service concept (*see* Chapter 3). As one starts to organize competencies accordingly, i.e. in line with the required service strategy, one bears the risk of reducing what is needed to what is needed *today*. Stated otherwise, one might arrive at a situation in which too much 'homogeneity' has been created, which limits the potential of the organization to adapt to changing circumstances.

In today's changing environments, organizations have to reconsider the desired competencies on a regular basis, in order to be able to respond to changes that challenge the competitive position of the organization. So, one should not push the use of the aforementioned approach (Figure 5.1) to the extreme where only competencies are to be found in the organization that reflect the '*hic et nunc*' strategic position of the company. Keeping open possible avenues to the future will imply – besides allocating some resources to 'playground' activities (*see* Chapter 15 on innovation) – adopting a more process-oriented approach towards competencies. Such an approach[16] goes beyond the 'control' logic that can easily become infused in HR systems. Within the framework of competencies, a more process-oriented orientation implies several points of attention. First of all, 'meta-competencies' enter the stage. Such meta-competencies relate to capabilities to change and redefine existing competencies. On the organizational level, this introduces notions like 'double loop learning' or even the idea of the learning organization.[17] More recently, the notion of dynamic capabilities is being advanced in this respect.[18] On the individual level, one can easily see the relevance of competencies that relate to learning and innovation. Conceived like this, it is possible to achieve an appropriate balance between stability or continuity (identity), on the one hand, and novelty or change (flexibility), on the other hand. Secondly, a more process-oriented approach will benefit from adopting principles rather than strict rules,[19] a direct consequence of the co-evolving nature of strategy processes and their deployment. Finally, and in line with the previous remarks, it will come as no surprise that a process-oriented approach will advocate designing definition and implementation projects with respect to competencies as a joint effort between line management and HR staff. Such a stance will ensure the relevance, transparency and, hence, the acceptance of any system. Table 5.1 summarizes some of the key characteristics to be found in control-oriented versus process-oriented approaches regarding competencies.

Table 5.1 Characteristics of Competence Management deployment processes

	Control-oriented model	Process-oriented model
Strategy		
Strategic vision	Strategy as a planning process aimed at 'adapting' to the (industrial) environment, resulting in a rather static view of competitive advantages	Strategy as a learning process in which 'co-evolving' processes figure prominently. Competitive advantage looked upon as inherently dynamic
How is strategy created?	Autonomous decision of management	Continuous interaction between different stakeholders
HRM		
HRM objectives	Create an 'external' fit between HRM and strategy by designing HR tools and designs that reflect the current strategy	Support and facilitate the definition and deployment of the strategic process, enabling organizational change
Function of HRM	Controlling (steering, governing and controlling)	Facilitating (supporting, facilitating and mobilizing)
Competencies		
On an organizational level	Core competencies as the translation of the strategy defined at the top	Core competencies as a context specific translation of the core activities of the organization. In addition, meta competencies are introduced as operational principles that allow us to combine stability and flexibility
On an individual level	Generic defined individual competencies that reflect the current core competencies and, hence, bear the risk of neglecting the role of change and transformation	Context specific individual competencies that reflect as well development related competencies (reflection, innovation, learning and transformational capabilities, . . .)
Competency system	Top-down linkage between strategy and individual competencies via core competencies	Interaction between meta competencies, core competencies and individual competencies that stimulate evolutionary development of strategy
Used by HRM as	Controlling instrument	Facilitating instrument

Source: Adapted from Faerns, D. (2002) 'Competencies management: Beheersen of begeleiden?', *Tijdschrift Voor HRM*, Vol 3, No 2, pp. 31–60.

By now we hear you thinking, 'OK, this might be a nice overall framework, which includes some relevant accompanying guidelines with respect to deployment processes, but how can it work in practice? How can you make this notion of competency concrete so that it can become a practical aid for linking organizational goals with employees' functions and be an integral part of HR practices? And what do approaches that can identify and assess competencies look like?'

Identifying and assessing competencies

Making competencies workable as a concept in HR practices requires a vocabulary that defines competencies and their gradations, as well as adequate techniques for collecting relevant information on the presence of these competencies.

As stated above, competencies can be viewed as human characteristics that relate to effective performance. These characteristics can be seen as indicating ways of acting, behaving, or thinking.

Relevant techniques include assessment centres as well as behaviourally-oriented interviews. Both approaches start from concrete behaviour in order to assess the presence of a competency. As such, they tend to differ rather significantly from more classical 'paper and pencil' instruments used in assessment contexts, such as personality questionnaires or IQ tests. Not that these become obsolete; in practice, combining more classical tools with competency-based approaches will yield the most complete insights.

But before digging into these concrete competency instruments, we first have to say something about developing a relevant vocabulary or a competency dictionary.[20]

Identifying relevant competencies

We face two challenges here: defining specifically what is meant by a particular competency and its constituting elements, and then identifying varying degrees within a certain competency. Take, for instance, customer service orientation. Here, focusing on the client's needs and a willingness to act on them are crucial. In this competency, one can distinguish different levels, as illustrated in Table 5.2.

How does one arrive at the delineation of these competencies and their levels? Starting from scratch implies a rather intensive exercise. By looking at 'model' behaviour in a certain situation by means of observation or behavioural event interviews (*see* below), one starts to identify and describe as precisely as possible relevant behaviours reflecting the meaning of the competency. Working with contrasting exemplars is useful: Who is a role model for our idea of customer orientation and who demonstrates just the opposite? Once a list of relevant behaviours is developed, degrees need to be identified. This can be done by ranking different descriptions referring to the same competency in terms of intensity, completeness or scope. Such varying degrees of the competency in question allow one to define more precisely what is meant, for instance, by customer orientation (*see* Table 5.2).

It should be clear that this description, brief as it is, covers a great deal of work: gathering data (descriptions) on relevant competencies, analysing them in terms of content and gradation, or working on issues such as reliability and validity by means of statistical analysis. In practice, it will not always be possible to develop these kinds of definition completely on one's own. Hence, it is advisable to turn to specialized agencies or sources that offer workable models and instruments, and eventually modify and adapt these to particular needs.

Once relevant competencies, including sub-dimensions and gradations, have been defined, one is well equipped to develop competency profiles. Working with a team of experts on certain activities and roles (supervisor, organization specialists from the HR or Quality department, employees themselves) allows one to determine the relative importance of different competencies for a particular job as well as the required levels for each competency. The different activities and roles one has to perform form the starting point here.

Table 5.2 Customer orientation as a competency

Level	Description
Level 1	Shows consideration for customers, behaves in a friendly manner
Level 2	Investigates the needs and desires of customers; takes time to gain an insight into customers' problems
Level 3	Takes concrete actions to meet customers' preferences or to solve customers' problems
Level 4	When undertaking actions, the specific needs or requests of customers are taken into account explicitly: the action undertaken reflects the problem at hand and the specific concerns of the customer
Level 5	Provides the customer with systematic feedback on the steps undertaken and the progress of the process
Level 6	Looks for ways to improve customer service, based on concrete experiences with customers, their requests and the problems experienced.

Source: © Quintessence Consulting Belgium.

One can also turn to examining – by observing – the best practices and translating these into a competency profile. The following figure gives a concrete example of the result of such an exercise carried out in a distribution company. Starting from a dictionary containing 36 different competencies, an iterative process was undertaken whereby different experts in the distribution company become involved in judging the relevance of the different competencies for the activities and roles of front-line employees, as well as the desired level for each competency, resulting in the profile that can be found in Figure 5.2. Determining the appropriate competencies is achieved by confronting the experts with different descriptions of specific behaviour.

Progress monitoring, customer orientation and oral presentation are a few crucial competencies for the front-line employees in this company. The ability to develop a broader vision or analysing complex problems are less important competencies here.

This profile can then serve as a guiding framework for the processes of recruitment and promotion/mutation, as well as for development. Here, the profile must be compared with the actual presence and degree of the competencies at hand. This also requires data on existing competencies and an approach to gathering relevant information.

Before explaining how information on existing competencies can be gathered, we want to stress that, in order for competency profiles to become an effective part of daily practice,

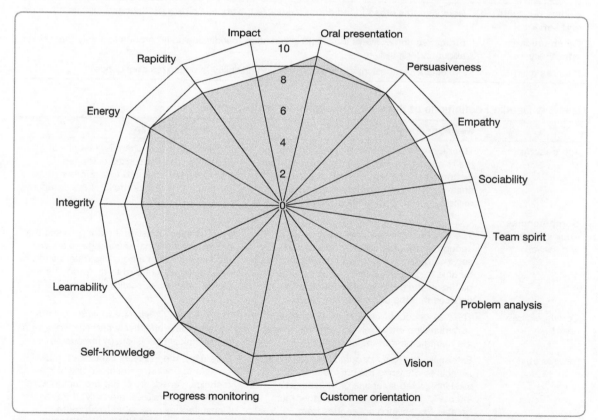

Figure 5.2 Most important competencies for front-office personnel in a distribution company

Source: © Quintessence Consulting Belgium.

they have to be as context-specific as possible. As an example, Table 5.3 shows the definitions of three competencies, used in the competency profile of sales people.

Although these definitions seem to be quite good at first sight, a more detailed analysis of the different functions that are present in the sales department makes it clear that these competencies are too abstract and, therefore, rather unpractical. After all, a large number of functions are present in the sales department. The job descriptions of two of these functions, 'key account manager' and 'presales consultant', are mentioned in Table 5.4. Based on interviews with employees that performed these jobs, one can obtain a more detailed description of the competencies mentioned above for each function. These alternative competency descriptions are also illustrated in Table 5.4.

By comparison with the original definitions, these competency descriptions are much more job-specific. Moreover, these alternative competency descriptions clearly illustrate that the content of the two functions is different, although both functions are part of the same sales department. Therefore, such context-specific competency descriptions are much more useful when the organization wants to implement a competency-based HRM to improve the effectiveness and efficiency of the core activities that employees have to perform.

Table 5.3 Definitions of three competencies for 'salespeople'

Competency	Definition
Knows products and services	Demonstrates breadth and depth of knowledge about ChipX's product and service offerings
Communicates effectively	Structures and conveys ideas and information to individuals and groups in a way that brings about understanding
Inspires trust	Projects a personal image of credibility and reliability that inspires confidence

Table 5.4 Detailed definitions of three competencies for 'salespeople'

	Key Account Manager	Presales Consultant
Job description	The Key Account Manager is responsible for the relationships with a number of important customers. He/she has to contact these customers on a regular basis and try to discover sales opportunities	The Presales Consultant is a technical specialist who possesses extended knowledge with regard to a number of products from the portfolio of the company
Competencies		
Knows products and services	The Key Account Manager must possess enough knowledge about products and services of the company. By this he/she must be able to offer the customer an accurate picture of the portfolio of products and services that the company can deliver	The Presales Consultant must possess the necessary technical knowledge to answer technical questions from customers and/or colleagues with regard to the products in which he/she is specialized
Communicates effectively	The Key Account Manager must be able to communicate effectively and efficiently with the management of the customer	The Presales Consultant must be able to communicate effectively and efficiently with the technical specialists of the customer
Inspires trust	Externally, the Key Account Manager must be able to convince the customer to buy total integrated solutions of the company Internally, the Key Account Manager must be able to convince colleagues from different teams to invest time and effort in projects for which he/she is responsible	Externally, the Presales Consultant must be able to convince the customer of the technical superiority of the product in which he/she is specialized Internally, the Presales Consultant must be able to promote products in which he/she is specialized

Gathering relevant information on existing competencies

Many techniques are available for assessing competencies or capabilities. We shall concentrate here on some new techniques – or at least relatively new – focusing on people's behaviour more than on their 'talk'. Since competencies underlie people's characteristics, indicating ways of behaving or thinking, they must somehow be observable in practice. By taking actual practice, i.e. behaviour, as a starting point, one can avoid the pitfalls of more traditional approaches (for instance, focusing on overall personality traits that might be of minor relevance to the concrete tasks at hand, or mistaking what is said for what is actually done).

The most straightforward way to make inferences about competencies is simply to observe behaviour. One needs to observe in a systematic way, however. Techniques used in 'assessment centres' have been flourishing in recent years. One can also try to derive the presence of competencies by means of interviews. Here again, specific approaches are developed. Let us look at these two techniques.

Assessment centres

In an assessment centre, simulations are set up that correspond to the actual role to be performed. Contextual elements can be brought in as well. For instance, in the case of the front-line employee in the distribution company, one can create a desk situation whereby customers and potential customers enter at random, telephones start to ring at the worst possible moment, and so on. Observing the actual behaviour of people in these types of situation allows one to assess the actual competency levels. The defined competencies and their gradations are the guiding framework here. By linking actual behaviour to those definitions, one starts to sketch a profile of existing competencies. When, for instance, during such a simulation exercise, people start to connect different elements with which they are faced, a certain level of the 'problem analysis' competency is indicated: they are now able to relate different aspects of a certain problem.

Although this might sound rather straightforward, in practice one should not underestimate the efforts it requires. First of all, one needs to design a relevant situation that allows the people involved to demonstrate relevant behaviour and, hence, competencies. Designing 'real' situations is the challenge. Secondly, making the link from behavioural observations to a specific level of a particular competency asks for certain skills as well: the behaviour must be registered as correctly as possible, then the observed behaviour must be linked with its most adjacent competency and, finally, the level of the competency inferred must be judged. Multiple observations are often required to accomplish this. These different steps require some skill; assessors most definitely need to be trained! On the other hand, the benefits of this approach are great: it yields information that is highly relevant to the activities in question while, at the same time, the outcomes are not obscured by more general psychometric data, often not easily accessible or relevant and, sometimes, even contradictory. This approach is highly recommendable, especially for front-line employees, as the behaviour here is directly experienced by customers.

Behaviourally oriented interviews

Assessment centres are of course not cheap; they require a serious investment in time and resources if one wants valuable information. Interviewing is, in this respect, more 'efficient'. Different approaches have been developed recently in an attempt to combine the best of both, gathering data on concrete behaviour and obtaining this information by conducting interviews. We will discuss two approaches here: behavioural event interviews[21] and interviewing by life themes.[22]

In behavioural event interviews, one does not ask questions such as 'How many people did you manage?', 'How did you feel?' or 'Why did you do this or what would you do in the future?' Although these types of question might reveal much about facts, emotional states, and after-the-fact rationalizations, they often teach us little about actual skills or competencies. The core of behavioural event interviewing consists of focusing on concrete events that have taken place within the professional activities of the interviewee. These might be successes as well as failures (to get a balanced view, both types should be included). Next, one asks for a detailed description of the event: 'What happened?', 'Who was involved?', 'What did you think, feel, or want to do during the course of the event?', 'What did you actually do?' and 'What was the outcome?' By gathering this kind of concrete situated data, it becomes possible to assess actual competency levels. The procedure here is roughly the same as described in the case of assessment centres.

Just as it can be advisable to record the observation by means of videotapes in concrete simulations like assessment centres, here, taping the interview can be worthwhile, allowing one to recheck certain conclusions and even to bring in different assessors – not present at the interview – to eliminate interviewer biases. Also, recorded material can be very useful for the person involved as well: it can be introduced into the development process in order to involve him or her to recognize, understand, accept and assess development needs.

A variation on this approach has been developed whereby the focus is on 'life themes': by identifying star performers, distinctive characteristics connected to life themes are established; the emphasis is on attitudes and values (e.g. customer orientation, flexibility) more than on technical skills and specific knowledge. The development of specific questions around these life themes provides a basis for holding interviews, which can then be recorded. After being transcribed, the interviews are analysed by experts to derive a life-theme profile. Several companies have even started to use telephone interviews to obtain this type of data. Although this sounds like a very efficient way to collect data, it has some drawbacks. When using telephone interviews, the starting tools need to be very well developed (structure of interview, type of situation, what-if rules to decide when to ask additional questions), implying a great deal of effort in terms of development. This makes the technique more relevant when one needs to hire on a large scale for the same job (e.g. 500 crew members for fast-food restaurants) as compared to looking for only one particular employee. Moreover, it tends to limit the amount of information passed through. While this might reduce the impact of some biases, it can also mean not noticing relevant aspects in (non-verbal) behaviour. So, while it is true that this approach is used more and more in service industries, especially in the US,[23] its relevance will depend on the specific situation. Relying solely on this type of information will be hazardous, which is in fact the case with every technique.

Besides assessment centres and behaviourally oriented interviews, many organizations use surveys to measure the competency level(s) of their employees. In this kind of survey, employees have to rate themselves on a number of questions, which should result in an image of the extent to which the respective employee masters the different competencies that are mentioned in the profile. Although this method has considerable cost advantages, we do want to express some cautions regarding the systematic use of this approach. After all, it will be impossible to circumvent all the possible biases that come along with this kind of self-assessment. Moreover, the use of surveys implies that, more often than not, an abstraction has to be made of the working environment. Hence, such surveys make it very difficult to execute a detailed and context-specific analysis of the competencies that are stressed in the profile. Hence, this method bears the risk of resulting in an approach whereby one throws the baby out with the bathwater.

So far, we have discussed how the notion of competencies can be integrated in an overall HR approach. We have also been looking at how to identify and assess relevant competencies. Equipped with this background, we are ready to address the next issues: what types of competency are important for services and how can one develop them.

Competencies for service organizations

Distinguishing between different types of competency

Broadly speaking, three types of competency can be distinguished: a person's behavioural repertoire, technical competencies including skills and knowledge, and finally, personal characteristics such as motivations, traits and self-identity:

- *Behavioural routines* are those competencies situated more 'on the surface', including traits such as politeness and friendliness. They refer to the behaviours displayed in brief encounters – for example, looking at customers when addressed, or a cheerful manner when speaking on the telephone.[24]

- *Technical competencies* refer to the sometimes broad range of knowledge and skills required to perform a certain task or job. Knowledge relates to the information a person holds in specific content areas, whereas skills are the actual ability to perform a certain physical or mental task. A surgeon's knowledge of nerves and muscles in the human body, a service technician's grasp of the lift's electrical circuits, a dentist's skill in filling a tooth without damaging nerves, and a computer programmer's ability to organize thousands of lines into a smooth-running computer program are all examples of technical competency.

- *Personal characteristics* are a mixture of motivations, traits and a person's self-concept. As such, they form the core of an individual. *Motivations* are forces that move people to act in certain ways; they drive, direct and select action. Achievement orientation is an example of a motive; achievement-motivated people set more challenging goals for themselves and take personal responsibility for accomplishing them. They believe that their personal actions make a difference and want to realize certain objectives as well. *Traits* refer to more or less consistent responses to situations or information; they range from mere physical attributes, such as good eyesight or adequate psycho-muscular abilities, to more complex psychological traits such as emotional self-control or the ability to cope with stress. Finally, the notion of *self-concept* refers to a person's values and self-image; how the person perceives him- or herself and others. Service employees who see people and, hence, customers as seeking short-term profit at others' expense will approach customers with a basic attitude of mistrust, unlike those people who see the interaction between providers and customers as a potential win-win situation.

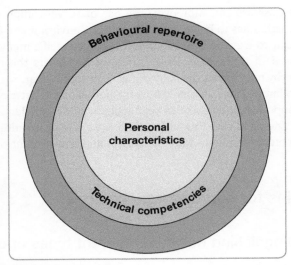

Figure 5.3 The three layers of competency

These different layers of competency are depicted in Figure 5.3. These three types of competency vary in terms of profoundness. While the behavioural repertoire can be seen as situated more on the surface, personal characteristics really form the core of the person.

Of course, these three types of competency are also interrelated and influence each other reciprocally. Personal characteristics can affect the development of technical competencies, as in the case where achievement orientation results in making the sacrifices necessary to become an engineer. Adopting new behaviour can lead to a modification of one's self-concept – for example, when someone discovers that she has a gift for public speaking after simply having done it. Acquiring behavioural skills therefore influences a person's sense of identity.

Linking competencies to services

The relative importance of each of the three different types of competency is not the same for all forms of service encounter. Whereas bank tellers need to be polite and have to possess the necessary skills for handling customer transactions, they are usually not involved in the service transaction on a deeper, more personal level. Under normal circumstances, neither bank tellers nor fast-food restaurant employees are expected to explore ways of looking at the world or engage in discussions relating to their own opinions or self-image with customers in order to deliver an adequate level of service to them. Therapists, career counsellors or process consultants, on the other hand, do address these issues. These professionals not only need technical expertise but they are also involved with their customers at a more personal level during the interaction process. Here, personal characteristics do play an important or even decisive role.

The service classification framework developed by Mills and Margulies[25] (explained in Chapter 2) can be useful in understanding the relative importance of the different competencies in relation to the nature of services.

As you may recall, Mills and Margulies made a distinction between three sorts of service transaction: maintenance-interactive, task-interactive and personal-interactive:

- *Maintenance-interactive services* imply rather short interactions and the complexity of the task is rather limited – for example, the work done by bank tellers, hotel receptionists and service employees in fast-food restaurants or shoe stores.

- *Task-interactive services* centre around the technicality of the task, where the customer has a definite question but does not have the knowledge or skills necessary to provide the answers. This type of service provider needs to handle uncertainty. Examples of these services are tax consultancy or computer programming.

- In *personal-interactive services* the provider engages in a much deeper process with customers to clarify, circumscribe and fulfil the needs at hand, which are often situated at a more personal level. Job counselling, legal advice and therapy are examples of these services.

Obviously all three sorts of competency – behavioural routines, technical competencies and personal characteristics – are present and to a certain extent important for all three types of services. When serving a hamburger one needs to be polite, as well as have the necessary technical skills to handle the food served. Moreover, having a positive attitude when interacting with people facilitates being friendly and helpful. Computer programmers need to be technical experts, but friendliness and being able to take a customer's viewpoint into account are also assets in this job. Therapists will benefit from having a mature and healthy personality, but being polite and friendly as well as having a profound knowledge of human nature are also essential here. It cannot be said, therefore, that a certain type of competency is irrelevant for some types of service. However, their relative importance certainly differs for each of the three types of service (*see* Figure 5.4).

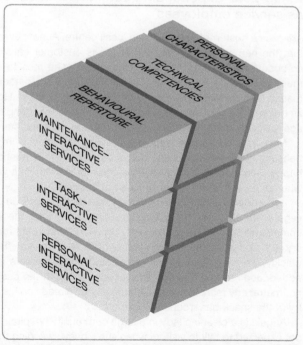

Figure 5.4 The relative importance of the three types of competency in different types of service

In maintenance-interactive services, the behavioural repertoire plays a dominant role. Technical knowledge and skills are necessary but are less important. Personal characteristics merely have a facilitating role. In task-interactive services, technical competency plays a major part. In personal-interactive service encounters, the personal characteristics of the service employee become equally important.

This framework should not be used, however, to design uniform competency development strategies for the service organization as a whole. A bank, for instance, has employees performing tasks that fall into the category of maintenance-interactive services as well as highly specialized people performing task-interactive services. Branch managers might even take on the role of counsellors for certain customers. This framework should be used to look at the relevance of different sorts of competency to the diversity of roles often present within the whole service organization. When designing roles, based on the service concept (Chapter 3) and the implied processes (Chapter 4), one should be particularly cautious as ill-designed roles might result in role stress, which is highly dysfunctional for the motivation of service employees as will become apparent in the next section. First, we highlight the nature of role stress and its consequences. Next, we discuss design practices that might avoid and remedy this phenomenon.

Role stress among front-line employees

Exhibit 5.2 Experiencing conflicts with various expectations of roles as service employees

Ariane is a customer service rep in a call centre. Almost every day, her manager emphasizes that the number one priority in her job is customer satisfaction. Being committed to the company, her department and her manager, she tries to create customer satisfaction as much as possible. For example, when she feels a customer needs some more detailed information on a certain topic, she's very happy to provide it. However, Ariane is not recognized as being a top performer because, according to the company's appraisal system, her average 'calls handled' count is not up to the departmental standard . . .

Mark is a consultant who regularly has dinner with important customers. He does so because he knows that these dinners strengthen the relationship and make the customers happy. Sometimes, when Mark has come home very late yet again, his wife Carol wonders whether he is married to her or to his customers . . .

Joe works in a fast-food restaurant. Yesterday, a customer asked for a burger without any vegetables. Because the full-option burgers roll from the kitchen to his desk, Joe did not immediately know how to respond. Once, the restaurant manager told him that quick delivery is the company's interpretation of qualitative service. 'But to have the burgers delivered quickly, we can't take specific requests from customers into consideration,' the manager added. Joe realized that this answer was not what the customer was waiting for, but it did not matter any more, since the customer was already on his way out, shouting that he 'would try at the snack bar around the corner' . . .

Angela is a cleaning lady in a large community hospital. Her boss has told her that she is not expected to talk to visitors when she's busy sweeping the floor. Every time when a visitor asks for directions to a particular department, she feels very unsure about how to respond . . .

What do Ariane, Mark, Joe and Angela have in common in the above situations (Exhibit 5.2)? They all are experiencing conflicts with various expectations of their roles as service employees. Although these single incidents may not have such a deleterious effect on their well-being or performance, the continual feeling of being torn apart by conflicting and unclear expectations from different constituencies they come into contact with (management, customers, family, colleagues . . .) clearly does. Those feelings have been called 'role stress' and are the central point of interest in the rest of this chapter.

Relevance of role stress for the service encounter

Front-line employees are employees involved in customer work. The term refers to special types of organizational service positions that involve interaction with both the organization and its customers.

As we stressed in the introductory chapter on the nature of services, simultaneity is an inherent characteristic of service work. This means that quite often the customer takes part in the production process and consumes the service as it is being produced. The (at least) partial overlap between production and consumption implies that there is personal contact during the service delivery process; customers and front-line employees are simultaneously involved in the service delivery process. Front-line work thus involves job expectations that arise from both the organization and the customers, whether in the context of closing a transaction or offering post-transaction problem-solving and/or technical support.[26] So, one of the key characteristics of services, i.e. simultaneity, might imply the presence of multiple and sometimes even conflicting expectations. Bateson[27] even went so far as to suggest that a service encounter can be viewed as a 'three-cornered fight', with the customers, the server and the service firm all vying for control. He argues that front-line employees seek to control the service encounter as a means of safeguarding their mental and physical health. Yet, customers also seek to control the encounter since they not only consume the service but also help to produce the service. Meanwhile, the organization itself seeks to control the encounter through its systems of policies, procedures and supervision. It is in this context of the service encounter, which can be considered a compromise between partially conflicting parties, that role stress takes shape. As argued by Singh,[28] the apparent conflict between satisfying management and customers and of meeting productivity and quality goals emerges as a consistent underlying theme in the study and management of front-line employees.

Role stress defined

Role theory in organizations

The central theoretical framework for understanding role stress in organizations was developed by Kahn *et al.* (1964).[29] Although their work dates from the 1960s, it is still extremely relevant today, especially for those studying front-line service jobs.

The origins of role theory emphasize its focus on interactivity within social exchange patterns. Role theory would argue that the social exchange that occurs between two or more people demonstrates certain patterns that are determined to a large extent by the role expectations and actual roles which each person adopts. The life of the individual can thus be seen as an array of roles played in the particular set of organizations and groups to which he or she belongs. These groups and organizations, or rather the subparts of each, which affect the person directly, together make up his or her environment. Characteristics of these organizations and groups (company, union, church, family and others) affect the person's physical and emotional state and are major determinants of his or her behaviour.

Different kinds of role stress

According to role theory, role demands and performance expectations from one or more people or groups to a focal person can take the form of different role stressors. The three major role stressors that were identified are *role conflict, role ambiguity* and *role overload*.

Role conflict

Role conflict occurs for an actor when the actor perceives that sets of demands from two or more constituencies to which an actor is held accountable (a) are incompatible or inconsistent with one another in such a way that both sets cannot be met and (b) are simultaneously pressed on the actor.

Kahn and his colleagues made a distinction between different types of role conflict:

- *Intra-sender role conflict* refers to different prescriptions and proscriptions from a single constituent that may be incompatible. For example, a supervisor may request a subordinate to acquire material that is unavailable through normal channels and, at the same time, prohibit violating normal channels.

- *Inter-sender conflict* refers to the situation when pressures from one role sender oppose pressures from one or more other senders. The pressures on a foreman for close supervision from his superiors and for looser supervision from his subordinates provide an example of inter-sender conflict.

- *Inter-role conflict* refers to the situation when role pressures associated with membership in one organization are in conflict with pressures stemming from membership in other groups. Demands from role senders on the job for overtime or take-home work may conflict with pressures from one's spouse to give undivided attention to family affairs during evening hours. The conflict arises between the focal person's roles as worker and partner/parent.

- *Person-role conflict*. An example of this is the conflict that may exist between the needs and values of a person and the demands of his or her environment. It can occur when role requirements violate a person's moral values or needs and aspirations.

All these types of role conflict have one major characteristic in common: members of a role set exert role pressures to change the behaviour of a focal person. Since the focal person is already 'in role', already behaving, and already maintaining some kind of equilibrium among the disparate forces and motives that he or she experiences, the generated pressures represent new and additional forces with which he or she must cope. In this sense, these pressures threaten an existing equilibrium. Moreover, the stronger the pressures from role senders toward changes in the behaviour of the focal person, the greater the conflict created for him or her.

Role ambiguity

Role ambiguity,[30] on the other hand, can be defined as the degree to which information is lacking regarding:

- the scope and limits of one's responsibilities;
- expectations associated with a role and the methods and behaviours for fulfilling one's job responsibilities;
- which expectations take priority or, stated otherwise, which elements of the role are most important;
- the standards by which one's performance is appraised.

Each member of an organization must have certain kinds of information at their disposal if he or she is to conform to the role expectations held by members of the work environment. A person may be uncertain about many facets of their social or physical environment. Organizations have several frequently encountered areas of ambiguity which people often find stressful. Singh and Rhoads[31] found that front-line employees may experience uncertainties about the expectations of the organization, their manager and managers of other departments, their colleagues, customers and families and, finally, expectations concerning ethical behaviour. These authors thus found seven facets of ambiguity in front-line employees' jobs (*see* Figure 5.5[32]). For example, front-line employees may experience uncertainties towards customers about how to behave when customers complain, but they may also be uncertain about which positive attributes of their products to highlight when presenting them to customers. Finally, front-line employees may also be uncertain about how to interact with their customers.

Role overload

Role overload, finally, occurs when an employer demands more of an employee than he or she can reasonably accomplish in a given time, or when the employee simply perceives the demands of work as excessive.[33]

Figure 5.5 Ambiguities faced by front-line employees

Source: Based on Singh, J. and Rhoads, G. K. (1991) 'Boundary role ambiguity in marketing-oriented positions: a multidimensional, multifaceted operationalization', *Journal of Marketing Research*, Vol 28, August, pp. 328–338.

To understand role overload, it is useful to distinguish between quantitative and qualitative overload. When quantitative overload is experienced, the employee is fully capable of meeting role demands. The problem is that there are too many role demands (e.g. too many customers within a given period of time) for the employee to handle. Given more time, and perhaps resources, the employee who is quantitatively overloaded could meet these role demands. On the other hand, when an employee is qualitatively overloaded, the demands of the role exceed his or her skills and abilities. In this case, even with more time and resources, the employee will not be able to meet the role demands. In the case of qualitative overload, individuals' skills and abilities do not allow them to meet their role demands adequately.

Handling role stress for front-line employees

Role stress's subversive effects

Numerous studies have focused on the relationship between the occurrence of role stress and the feelings and behaviours of those experiencing it.[34] One conclusion that can be drawn from these studies is that role stress clearly has a negative impact on employee satisfaction and employee commitment. Furthermore, it has been shown that role stress also negatively influences employees' willingness to stay in the organization.[35] Given the ideas behind the service profit chain discussed in Chapter 2, one could even state that too much stress will affect customer satisfaction and, hence, loyalty and even profitability.

Looking at the behavioural consequences, there is evidence that role stress not only has a negative impact on employees' productivity but also on the quality of the services delivered by those employees. The relationship between role stress and performance has been predicted by both cognitive and motivational explanations.[36] From a cognitive perspective, role stressors hinder performance because the individual faces either a lack of knowledge about the most effective behaviours to engage in or an almost impossible situation in which to achieve everything expected. Therefore, regardless of the amount of effort expended, behaviours are most likely to be inefficient, misdirected or insufficient. A motivational perspective would predict that performance is negatively correlated with role stressors because they are negatively associated with effort-to-performance and performance-to-reward expectations.

Given the subversive impact of role stress on service employees' feelings and behaviours, it is worthwhile for managers in a service context to try to minimize role stress as much as possible. It has been shown that a mixture of different elements within the work context influences the level of role stress experienced by service employees. These relate to leadership, empowerment and formalization. We will review those different elements first; next, we will point out some directions for choosing an approach that fits your service organization.

Leadership and role stress

Since the supervisor plays an integral part in a service employee's role performance, for instance, by providing key resources and by motivating personnel, it is important to take leadership into account when considering the work context in which role stress occurs.

Leadership behaviour has been extensively studied for several decades.[37] The focus was primarily on identifying and categorizing what the leader does – i.e. his or her behaviour. Different researchers have found a differing number of factors underlying leadership behaviour, varying from one to five. Nevertheless, although sometimes called different names, the same two major dimensions of leadership consistently emerged: leader initiating structure and leader consideration.[38]

Leader initiating structure relates to the way in which a supervisor guides employees, provides a psychological framework that clarifies roles, monitors subordinates' activities and stimulates them to display better performance. Leader initiating structure thus refers to the leader's task-oriented activities.

Leader consideration, on the other hand, is the degree to which a supervisor creates an atmosphere of affective support and socio-emotional concern for the well-being of subordinates. Leader consideration thus refers to the leader's people-oriented activities.

Both these dimensions of leadership behaviour have shown to affect role stress.[39] Task-oriented leadership behaviour provides employees with information about what is expected in their role. Consequently, these behaviours allow the leader to reduce role stress among front-line employees. As may be expected, task-oriented leadership behaviour is especially effective in reducing front-line employees' role ambiguity. Apparently, leader initiating structure helps clarify roles but does little to reduce conflict. Providing expectations unilaterally may preclude the subordinate from resolving conflicts that become clear in response to initiating structure.

People-oriented leadership behaviour, rather than exclusively serving a social or emotional role, appears to also serve an instrumental or task role. As employees gain knowledge about what behaviours are rewarded, indecision as to which role expectations to fulfil and which to ignore may diminish, thus reducing conflicts that may have arisen due to unclear role priorities. In contrast with task-oriented leadership behaviours, leader consideration may include some level of participation (e.g. the supervisor asks about and shows concern for subordinates) that affords subordinates the opportunity to discuss and resolve conflicts.

In summary, it seems that both task-oriented and people-oriented leadership behaviours have a reducing impact on role stress. When considering the role of service managers and others who take up a leadership role in the service organization, it is therefore important that these people not only be trained to be able to clarify what they expect from their subordinates, but they should also know that showing consideration and affective support clearly has a diminishing impact on front-line employees' role stress level.

Minimizing role stress by empowering employees . . .

As we will discuss extensively in Chapter 11, empowerment assumes that to a large extent employees are capable of co-ordination, planning and control of service quality. Empowerment is also referred to as the 'involvement model'[40] and can be achieved by implementing practices that distribute power, information, knowledge and rewards throughout the organization. Employees experience greater autonomy and freedom to take initiatives. The empowerment approach thus strives for competent, motivated employees who experience autonomy and, consequently, can take the necessary actions to satisfy customers' needs during the 'moment of truth'. Thus, empowerment might contribute to front-line employees' confidence to handle the heterogeneity encountered during service encounters; if employees feel competent and find themselves in an organization that provides the necessary information and support, as discussed in the previous chapter. If these conditions are not satisfied, one bears the risk of ending up with merely an increase in job stress because of the lack of clear guidelines or prescriptions on how to behave in all kinds of situations.

... or by formalizing?

The idea of formalization reflects the production-line approach, a still popular view of managing service employees.[41] The production-line approach for services suggests that a technocratically conceived service process is the best way to serve the customer. This approach emphasizes:

1 task simplification;

2 clear task division;

3 replacement of human labour with equipment (hard technology), systems (soft technology) or a combination of the two (hybrid technology); and

4 little decision-making power for employees.

Although the idea of the production-line approach to services stems from the 1970s, it is still a very relevant viewpoint that is highly visible in contemporary service organizations. The 'McDonald's' approach is the most eloquent example. Another context where the production-line approach can be clearly recognized is the call centre industry. Call centre operators' response to customers is quite standardized. Employees usually have a clear idea of what to do, and service levels are enhanced using high-tech solutions.

Central to these service contexts is the idea of formalization. Formalization is the extent to which work activities are governed formally by administrative rules, policies and procedures. The degree of formalization of the work context will influence service employees' role stress. Written rules and procedures governing the work activities theoretically make it clear to service employees what is expected of them. In this sense, formalization ought to reduce role stress, since it serves to specify legitimate role senders and ways of behaving. This reducing impact, however, will manifest itself only to the extent customers comply with these 'prescriptions'. This is more often than not the case for front-line employees involved in service work such as serving fast-food. For other workers involved in less standardized services and who have to respond immediately to customers' requests and sometimes improvise, the existence of written rules and procedures may have a counterproductive effect on their levels of role stress. This may especially be the case when those rules and procedures do not fit the situation at hand, but it can also apply when these rules are in conflict with the solution the service employee has come up with.

Choosing the right way to handle role stress

Empowerment and formalization reflect two major perspectives on service employee management. As described above, both empowerment and formalization can reduce or increase feelings of role stress among service employees. But, when to choose one over the other? Already glimpsing around the corner is the idea that choosing either one approach will depend on the nature of the service encounter that can be characterized by the degree of service interactivity. As you may remember from the first chapter, Mills and Margulies[42] identified service interactivity as an important dimension characterizing services. They identified three basic types of interaction between the customer and the service provider: maintenance-interactive, task-interactive and personal-interactive services. These three types of service interaction mainly differ according to:

- the degree to which the initial problem and possible solutions are clear to the customer and/or the service provider;
- the amount of input required from the customer into the service delivery process;
- the amount and type of judgments to be made by the service employee.

If we integrate this classification scheme into our empowerment versus formalization debate, a clear picture starts to emerge on how to address role stress within different service encounters. Let us take a closer look at a typical maintenance-interactive service job, that of a waiter/waitress in a restaurant. Both the restaurant customer and the server have a fairly clear view of the service delivery process. They both know what the initial problem is (the customer is hungry or thirsty) and possible solutions (the server can offer the customer a range of dishes and drinks). Furthermore, the customer only has to make a choice and communicate it to the server (information input from the side of the customer is rather limited). Finally, the server knows what to do once the customer has made a choice: he or she must inform the kitchen of the new order, and should be as friendly as possible when serving the customer. The server is thus not required to make many decisions.

The service delivery process in the restaurant situation described above is rather standardized. Some kind of fixed scenario applies to all service deliveries. In such a context, it is important that the service employee has a clear view of this scenario and how he or she should behave. This can be done by providing the server with some rules and procedures. In this particular situation, formalization seems to be the key to diminishing ambiguity and conflict about the server's role, and thus is the key to minimizing role stress for these kinds of service encounters.

For contrast, let's take a closer look at the job of a business consultant. The service encounter between the business consultant and the customer is very often characterized by a great deal of uncertainty and ambiguity. In such personal-interactive encounters, both the consultant and the customer may lack a clear view of what the concrete problem is and how this problem should be solved. In such situations, the customer and service provider engage in a process that involves tackling these kinds of ambiguities. The interaction between the service provider and the customer shapes the solution to the problem and thus the service delivery process. In these situations, the input of the client is of crucial importance in

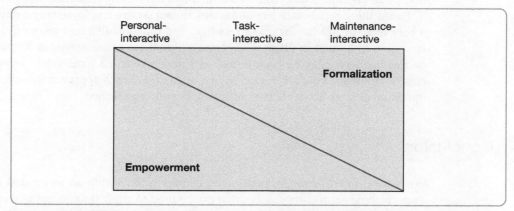

Figure 5.6 Minimizing service employees' role stress through formalization or empowerment

reaching a satisfactory solution, and the consultant is required to judge how the customer can best be helped through a complex series of decisions.

In these kinds of service encounter, one may expect that providing the service employee with only an exhaustive set of specific rules and procedures will not be sufficient. Instead, trusting in the consultant's professional standards, i.e. empowerment, will be a better option. The – competent and motivated – employee is then given the freedom to behave using his or her personal knowledge to judge how the customer may best be served. In these situations, empowerment will be a better option for dealing with service employees' role stress.

Returning to our initial question, we may conclude that service interactivity is an important aspect of the service task to be taken into consideration when deciding how to deal with and minimize role stress among service employees. The rationale we developed is that formalization may be most appropriate to address role conflict when service encounters are of a maintenance-interactive nature. The more the encounter evolves towards personal-interactive services, however, the more the empowerment approach may become the better option for minimizing role stress. Figure 13.2 illustrates this idea.

Impact of co-worker support on role stress

As mentioned in this book's first chapter, one core characteristic of service work is its heterogeneity or variability. Since services are processes where customers and employees interact with each other, the encounters carry a greater risk of difference depending on circumstances such as the particular employee or customer involved, the physical setting, or even the time of day. As a result of this variability, front-line employees are frequently confronted with unforeseen situations. In cases where service employees need to deal with the situation at hand, as argued in the chapter on collaboration, having support from colleagues is often an advantage.

It has, indeed, been proven that having the opportunity to share experiences with others in generically similar positions and to profit from similar experiences clearly diminishes role stress as experienced by service employees.[43] Kahn and his colleagues[44] argued that these kinds of professional and quasi-professional identifications may provide the person with referent group support in the conflicts and ambiguities he or she faces. They can provide either techniques for resolving such stressors, or simply reassurance that the person's difficulties are not so much the result of personal shortcomings as the common fate of those who occupy an organizational position that involves interacting with customers.

Establishing collaborative relationships among service employee teams thus seems to be a core issue in striving for role stress-free, and thus satisfied and productive, employees. However, as argued in Chapter 11, establishing those relationships in a team, with more parties involved, may be complicated and may take some time. When trying to achieve collaboration and co-worker support in a team, one should approach this effort as a developmental process in which trust must be gradually established.

Conclusion

We started this chapter by positioning competencies within an integrated HRM model. Some techniques and approaches that can be used to apply the concept of competencies to organizational practice were described, including the process of defining competencies and the role of assessment centres and behavioural event interviews.

Equipped with this more general background we developed a more detailed view of competencies and their relevance for services. Three types of competencies were distinguished: behavioural repertoire, technical competencies and, finally, personal characteristics. Although these three types of competencies are intertwined and will present themselves together in almost any situation, the importance of these different types of competencies varies, depending on the type of service activities under consideration. The behavioural repertoire is most important for maintenance-interactive services, while technical competencies are dominant when discussing task-interactive services. Finally, personal characteristics are crucial for personal-interactive services.

We then looked at the notion of role stress. Role stress refers to the feeling of being torn apart by conflicting and/or unclear expectations from different constituencies with whom service employees come into contact (management, customers, family, colleagues, etc.). We showed that role stress clearly has a negative impact on employee satisfaction, commitment and willingness to stay in the organization. Furthermore, we discussed the negative impact that role stress has on service performance (i.e. both service quality and service productivity).

Given the subversive effects of role stress, we argued that minimizing role stress should be a core aspect of any strategy for improving service performance. We dealt with four main characteristics of service employees' work environment that are relevant in this respect: leadership behaviour, degree of formalization, degree of empowerment, and co-worker support. Regarding leadership behaviour, we made it clear that both task-oriented and people-oriented leadership behaviours are crucial in attempting to minimize service employees' role stress levels. We further presented formalization and empowerment as two important ideas to consider when reflecting on the work context in which role stress occurs. We saw that both empowerment and formalization, although they reflect two different and almost contradictory viewpoints on how service employees should be managed, can decrease or increase role stress. The degree of interactivity between the service provider and the customer was shown to be an important work characteristic that can inform the decision about which of these two approaches to take in order to minimize role stress. Finally, we emphasized that co-worker support, which can be established through a developmental team-oriented process, can contribute significantly to reducing role stress levels.

Review and discussion questions

- Despite the crucial role of human resources, and hence human resources management, in relation to value creation, many companies still do not adopt HR practices accordingly. Why is this the case? What is needed to arrive at a more widespread implementation of HR investment principles?

- Would you agree with the statement that certain competencies are irrelevant for certain service jobs (e.g. personal characteristics for service employees working in cleaning companies)? If yes, can you give examples?

- It is often said that people are the most valuable assets of an organization. What are the consequences of this statement for competency management within service organizations? Would this imply as well forms of 'competence accounting' and 'competence valuation'?

- Is role stress a variable that should be 'reduced to zero'? Why (not)?
- For some managers, stress is just an individual 'problem'; do you agree? What arguments do you see in favour of this view? And which corroborate the opposite? What are the implications of these viewpoints for HRM practices?

Suggested further reading

Kahn, R. L., Wolfe, D. M., Quinn, R. P., Snoek, J. D. and Rosenthal, R. A. (1964) *Organizational stress: Studies in role conflict and ambiguity*. New York, NY: John Wiley & Sons

Schlesinger, L.A. and Heskett, J. (1991) 'Breaking the cycle of failure in services', *Sloan Management Review*, Spring. This article provides a clear account of the dynamic interplay between employees and customers in services

Schneider, B. and Bowen, D. (1995) *Winning the Service Game*. Boston, MA: Harvard Business Press. An overview of how the human factor is interwoven into the process of delivering services and how HR practices should reflect this

Troyer, I., Mueller, C. W. and Osinsky, P. I. (2000) 'Who's the boss? A role theoretic analysis of customer work', *Work and Occupations*, Vol 27, No 3, pp. 406–469

Notes and references

1 *See* Schneider, B. and Bowen, D. (1985) 'New service design, development and implementation and the employee', in George, W. and Marshall, C. (eds) *New Services*. Chicago, IL: The American Marketing Association; Schneider, B. and Bowen, D. (1993) 'Human resource management is critical', *Organizational Dynamics*, pp. 39–52; and Schneider, B. and Bowen, D. (1995) *Winning the Service Game*. Boston, MA: Harvard Business Press

2 For an excellent overview, *see* Heskett, J., Sasser, W. and Schlesinger, L. (1997) *The Service Profit Chain*. New York, NY: Free Press

3 For more details on this example, *see* Schlesinger, L. A. and Heskett, J. (1991), 'Breaking the cycle of failure in services', *Sloan Management Review*, No 32, Spring; Heskett, J., Sasser, W. and Schlesinger, L. (1997), op. cit.

4 Of course, one should stay within certain standard parameters

5 Notable predecessors include H. Munsterberg, M. P. Follet and C. Barnard who pioneered some of these ideas already in the first half of the twentieth century

6 For a more extensive and excellent discussion on these developments, *see* Sparrow, P. and Hiltrop, J. M. (1996) *European Human Resources Management in Transition*. Prentice Hall

7 *See* Tichy, N., Fombrun, C. and Devanna, M. (1982) 'Strategic human resources management', *Sloan Management Review*, Vol 23, No 2, pp. 47–61; and Fombrun, C., Tichy, N. and Devanna, M. (1984) *Strategic Human Resources Management*. New York, NY: Wiley

8 In fact, we do not believe in this approach for manufacturing firms either

9 Sparrow, P. and Hiltrop, J. M. (1996), op. cit.

10 Besides the models we discuss here, we refer the interested reader to the ideas developed by Creed and Miles on HR investment principles, as well as the work of Ulrich on adding value to HR practices: Miles, R. and Creed, W. (1995) 'Organizational forms and managerial philosophies – a descriptive and analytical review', *Research in Organisational Behaviour: An annual series of analytical essays and critical review*, Vol 17, pp. 333–372; Ulrich, D. (1997a) *Human Resource Champions, The Next Agenda for Adding Value to HR-practices*, Boston, MA: Harvard Business Press; Ulrich, D. (1997b) 'Measuring human resources: an overview of practice and prescription for results', *Human Resource Management*, Vol 36, pp. 302–320.

Ulrich, D., Brockbank, W., Yeung, A. and Lake, D. G. (1995) 'Human resource competencies: an empirical assessment', *Human Resource Management*, Vol 34, No 4, pp. 473–495; and Yeung, A., Brockbank, W. and Ulrich, D. (1995) 'Lower cost, higher value: Human resource function in transformation', *Human Resource Planning*, Vol 17, No 3, pp. 1–16

11 Beer, M., Spector, B., Lawrence, P., Mills, D. and Walton, R. (1984) *Managing Human Assets*. New York, NY: Free Press; and Beer, M., Lawrence, P., Mills, D. and Walton, R. (1985) *Human Resources Management*. New York, NY: Free Press

12 Beer, M. *et al.* (1985), op. cit.

13 Opportunities are no guarantees; one can also design competency profiles from a one-way perspective (from the organization towards the individual who has to comply). Acknowledging competencies, however, brings back employees (instead of jobs) into the picture

14 Definition adapted from Spencer, L. and Spencer, S. (1994) *Competence at Work*. New York, NY: Wiley & Sons

15 Figures 5.1, 5.2 and Table 5.2 courtesy of Quintessence Consulting Belgium

16 *See*, for instance, Whittington, R. (1993) *What is Strategy and Does it Matter?* London: Routledge; or Hendry, C. and Pettigrew, A. (1986) 'The practice of strategic human resource management', *Personnel Review*, Vol 15

17 On single and double loop learning, see Argyris, C. (1994) *On Organisational Learning*. Oxford: Blackwell Publishers; on learning organizations, see Senge, P. (1990) *The Fifth Discipline*. New York, NY: DoubleDay

18 For a comprehensive overview of this notion, *see* Teece, D. (2007) 'Explicating dynamic capabilities: the nature and microfoundations of sustainable enterprise performance', *Strategic Management Journal*, Vol 28, pp. 1319–1350

19 A point stressed by Janssens, M. and Steyaert, C. (1996) 'Culture and HRM practices: operational and ethical principles', *Tijdschrift voor Economie en Management*, Vol 41, No 3, pp. 327–354

20 *See* Spencer, L. and Spencer, S. (1994), op. cit.; Van Beirendonck, L. (1998) *Beoordelen en ontwikkelen van competenties* (Assessing and developing competencies). Leuven: Acco

21 *See*, for a fuller description, Spencer, L. and Spencer, S. (1994), op. cit.

22 *See also* Heskett, J., Sasser, W. and Schlesinger, L. (1997) *The Service Profit Chain*. New York, NY: Free Press

23 *See* Heskett, J. *et al.* (1997), op. cit.

24 Smiling when speaking on the telephone makes your voice more cheerful

25 Mills, P. K. and Margulies, N. (1980) 'Towards a core typology of service organisations', *Academy of Management Review*, Vol 5, No 2, pp. 255–265

26 Troyer, I., Mueller, C. W. and Osinsky, P. I. (2000) 'Who's the boss? A role theoretic analysis of customer work', *Work and Occupations*, Vol 27, No 3, pp. 406–469

27 Bateson, J. E. G. (1985) 'Perceived control and the service encounter', in Czepiel, J. A., Solomon, M. R. and Surprenant, C. F. (eds) *The Service Encounter: Managing employee/customer interaction in the service business*. Lexington, MA and Toronto: Lexington Books, pp. 67–82

28 Singh, J. (2000) 'Performance productivity and quality of front-line employees in service organizations', *Journal of Marketing*, Vol 64, No 2, pp. 15–35

29 Kahn, R. L., Wolfe, D. M., Quinn, R. P., Snoek, J. D. and Rosenthal, R. A. (1964) *Organizational Stress: Studies in role conflict and ambiguity*. New York, NY: John Wiley & Sons

30 The reader may recall from the first chapter that one of the main characteristics of personal-interactive services, according to Mills and Margulies' definition of different service types, is ambiguity. Mills and Margulies approach the idea of ambiguity from the perspective of the customer. In personal-interactive services, the customer is typically unaware or imprecise about both what will best serve his or her interest and how to go about remedying a situation. Within the context of role stress, (role) ambiguity refers specifically to an unclear situation about how to perform a role within the organization, from the perspective of the employee

31 Singh, J. and Rhoads, G. K. (1991) 'Boundary role ambiguity in marketing-oriented positions: a multidimensional, multifaceted operationalization', *Journal of Marketing Research*, Vol 28, August, pp. 328–338

32 Ibid.

33 Jones, B., Flynn, D. M. and Kelloway, E. K. (1995) 'Perceptions of support from the organization in relation to work stress, satisfaction, and commitment', in Sauter, S. L. and Murphy, L. R. (eds) *Organizational Risk Factors for Job Stress*. Washington, DC: American Psychological Association, pp. 41–52

34 For an overview of evidence on the impact of role ambiguity on employees attitudes and behaviours, *see* two meta-analytic studies: Jackson, S. E. and Schuler, R. S. (1985) 'A meta-analysis and conceptual critique of research on role ambiguity and role conflict in work settings', *Organizational Behavior and*

Human Performance, Vol 36, pp. 16–78; and Tubre, T. C. and Collins, J. M. (2000) 'Jackson and Schuler (1985) revisited: A meta-analysis of the relationships between role ambiguity, role conflict and job performance', *Journal of Management*, Vol 26, No 1, pp. 155–170

35 Brown, S. P. and Peterson, R. A. (1993) 'Antecedents and consequences of salesperson job satisfaction: A meta-analysis and assessment of causal effects', *Journal of Marketing*, Vol 30, pp. 63–77; Fisher, C. D. and Gitelson, R. (1983) 'A meta-analysis of the correlates of role conflict and ambiguity', *Journal of Applied Psychology*, Vol 68, No 2, pp. 320–333

36 Jackson, S. E. and Schuler, R. S. (1985), op. cit.

37 House, R. L. (1971) 'A path-goal theory of leader effectiveness', *Administrative Science Quarterly*, Vol 16, Sept, pp. 321–329

38 Wetzels, M. G., De Ruyter, K. and Lemmink, J. (1999) 'Role stress in after-sales Service Management', *Journal of Service Research*, Vol 2, No 1, pp. 50–67

39 Jackson, S. E. and Schuler, R. S. (1985), op. cit.

40 Bowen, D. E. and Lawler, E. E. (1995a) 'Empowering service employees', *Sloan Management Review*, Vol 37, Summer, pp. 73–84; Bowen, D. E. and Lawler, E. E. (1995b) 'Organizing for Service: Empowerment or Production Line?' in Glynn, W. J. and Barnes, J. G. (eds) *Understanding Services Management*, Chichester: John Wiley & Sons, pp. 269–294

41 Levitt, T. (1972) 'Production-line approach to service', *Harvard Business Review*, Vol 50, Sept–Oct, pp. 41–52; Levitt, T. (1976) 'Industrialization of service', *Harvard Business Review*, Vol 54, Sept–Oct, pp. 63–74

42 Mills, P. K. and Margulies, N. (1980) 'Towards a core typology of service organizations', *Academy of Management Review*, Vol 5, No 2, pp. 255–265

43 *See*, for example, Wetzels, M. G. (1998) *Service Quality in Customer-Employee Relationships: An empirical study in the after-sales services context*, Doctoral Dissertation, University of Maastricht; Newton, T. J. and Keenan, A. (1987) 'Role stress reexamined: an investigation of role stress predictors', *Organizational Behavior and Human Decision Processes*, Vol 40, pp. 346–368; Schaubroeck, J., Cotton, J. L. and Jennings, K. R. (1989) 'Antecedents and consequences of role stress: a covariance structure analysis', *Journal of Organizational Behavior*, Vol 10, pp. 35–58

44 Kahn, R. L. *et al.* (1964), op. cit.

Chapter 6

(Information) Technology and services

Bart Van Looy • Wilfried Grommen • Wim Grielens •
Niels Schillewaert • Pedro Matthÿnssens

Objectives

By the end of this chapter, you should be able to discuss:

- why information technology is important for services
- what is meant by 'virtual value creation' and what the implications are of working in the market space
- the factors that will influence the degree and extent to which combining market place and market space might be relevant
- relevant action strategies that might be deployed when shifting into the direction of virtual service transactions

Introduction

Digital finally overtakes physical in US music market

'It's a moment that many tech industry observers have predicted for the best part of a decade: the US music market is now more digital than physical, by volume at least.

According to figures from Nielsen SoundScan and Billboard Magazine, digital music unit sales accounted for 50.3 per cent of all music purchases in 2011, the first time that threshold has been crossed in the world's largest music market. The US is more advanced in digital than most of Europe. In the UK, figures this week showed that digital albums still account for less than a quarter of the market, although downloads of individual tracks far outstrip CD singles. One in three albums is digital in the US, while Americans bought 100m more digital tracks overall in 2011 than the prior year, up 8.4 per cent. Rap, electronic, latin and even country albums saw the biggest increases in US digital album sales, outpacing the overall average growth of 20 per cent.

But in spite of the digital growth, there are signs that the decline of CDs is slowing. Total album sales were up for the first time since 2004 and physical album sales fell 5 per cent in 2011, significantly less than the 19.5 per cent decline reported in 2010 over the prior year.

Says music analyst Mark Mulligan of the flip from physical to digital dominance: "This is obviously an important milestone, but it is as much of a reflection of how much the total market has declined as it is of how strongly digital is performing. In this context, the big slowdown in CD sales decline is important, though . . . we are looking at volumes so heavy discounting will affect revenues more markedly."

Mr Mulligan says that around 25 per cent of music fans are now buying digital, "way ahead of many European territories". "So these figures show the US consolidating its role as the most powerful digital music market but also raise questions about why other markets aren't performing as strongly digitally." But while it's the biggest, the US is not the first global market to make the shift. For the real leaders in digital music, look to Asia, where digital sales in China, Indonesia, South Korea and Thailand overtook physical back in 2009, according to the IFPI.'

(FT, 6 January 2012 11:41 am by Tim Bradshaw)

Services are processes characterized by both simultaneity and intangibility; they are also rich in terms of information exchange. As such, they are strongly affected by developments related to information technology. In this chapter, we explore in greater detail the role that information technology can have in managing service transactions.

We begin with a general introduction to the different stages in the development of information technology, and we will discuss the economic implications of the network era as it manifests itself today. Next, we examine the impact IT developments can have on service transactions: replacing and/or complementing the traditional, physical 'marketplace' by its virtual counterpart, the 'market space'. We will argue that the impact these IT developments will have on service transactions depends on a number of factors: the behaviour of customers and service providers as well as the nature of the service transaction itself. Maintenance-interactive services are most easily 'digitalized'; this will be more difficult for task-interactive services, and the process will be least viable for personal-interactive services. This is explained by the notion of 'media richness' – that is, new technologies are often less rich in terms of interaction possibilities than face-to-face meetings. Hence, complex service transactions will continue to involve a great deal of direct contact between service provider and customer.

At the same time, it is important to keep in mind the complex social adaptation processes surrounding every technological evolution. We will examine past technological developments (during the nineteenth century the hottest thing around was the bicycle) and learn by relating these to the actual IT developments.

Finally, ingredients for relevant action strategies that allow combining market place and market space activities into coherent service delivery systems will be discussed.

The network era – where do we stand?

As became clear in Chapter 1, the service sector is the largest and most rapidly growing segment of the economy for most of the industrialized world. In terms of technology, information technology is dominant: IT accounts for more than 80% of the technology purchased by service sector firms and is the predominant focus of service sector R&D staffs. This does not imply that other technology is not relevant; just think about the technologies deployed by medical staff for diagnosis or intervention.[1] It does however justify this book's focus on information technology and the way in which it may affect service delivery processes. And here we have been witnessing some turbulence during recent decades, directly related to the explosive growth and diffusion of Internet technologies. Let us briefly look at what the network era[2] implies and how it is being used today; this sets the stage for a more in-depth examination of the impact of information technology on service delivery processes.

The network era

After the batch era, the time sharing era, and the still ongoing client/server era, a new episode in the development of IT is in full swing. *Network computing* – that is, the increasing range of possibilities for doing transactions by means of electronic media – has become an integral part of our lives and organizations. Workstations such as servers, mainframes or PCs have been linked by means of networks of wires, satellite or infrared connections permitting transactions on an ever-larger scale (*see* Figure 6.1).

Batch work involved processing only one, often very complex, 'batch' of transactions at the same time. *Time sharing* introduced possibilities for switching between jobs. Still, the three different logics that can be discerned in any computer application – presentation, application and data logic – were still heavily concentrated in each operating unit.[3] *Client/ server systems* started to 'disconnect' these different logics. It became possible to have data, applications and presentation devices on different workstations. The scale on which exchange took place was still rather limited, however. Network computing reduces these limitations.

Basically, network computing extends the range of transactions (communication, publicity, solution definition, ordering, solution delivery or fulfilment, payment, satisfaction analysis and follow-up business) that can be executed or enabled electronically, reducing the time required to initiate, execute and conclude them. In addition, network computing extends the reach of the players, permitting them to establish these interactions with

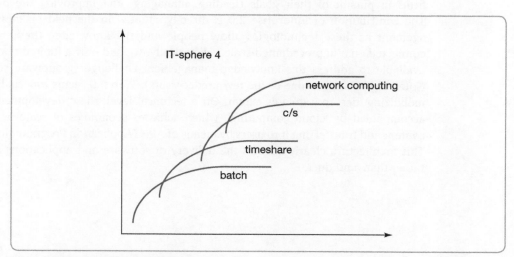

Figure 6.1 **Network computing**

partners independent of distance and time constraints. In short, it expands the market for providers and buyers from local to global, at a fraction of the cost of traditional market development.[4] This evolution results from an alignment of the interface issues underlying this network computing breakthrough. Over the years, many initiatives have been developed towards standardizing communication between information devices to create *platform independence*. The adoption of the TCP/IP protocol suite has accelerated these developments. This 'suite' bundles agreements (made between the main players within the industry as well as governments) related to information device interface standards. HTML[5] is perhaps one of the best-known protocols. This protocol, together with many others, has fuelled the spectacular growth of the Internet over the last few years. HTML conventions define the 'electronic' standards for presenting texts and figures including 'links' with other texts.[6]

The *Internet*, in its incarnation as the World Wide Web (WWW), can be considered a specific form of network computing. One of the distinguishing characteristics of the WWW has been its universal standard browser interface to a world of online textual and pictorial resources. This is currently being extended to sound (see introductory case on digital music) and moving images (video-like data streams). In addition to the increase in media types, the Internet offers an increasing number of possibilities of real online transactions, where dynamic and customized responses to individual requests become possible. Whereas Web 1.0 can be depicted as an 'information retrieval' platform, Web 2.0 is creating a participation platform. It combines rich applications (enabled by Ajax and Flash) with a service-oriented architecture (e.g. feeds, RSS, mashups) and builds on network protocols to include the end user in content creation (e.g. Facebook, YouTube, Wikipedia, Twitter, Flickr). In particular, the increased possibilities for interaction are affecting the organizational practices of enterprises. Web 2.0 technology is 'deeply social', offering people and communities ample opportunities to meet, share and create content. As procedures and rules of engagement are often 'light' (e.g. contributing to content creation for Wikipedia), content creation is becoming a 'democratic' process leading to vibrant, virtual communities.

Enterprise 2.0 can be seen as the use of these emergent social software platforms by firms in pursuit of their goals (leading, managing, and improving the organization). The contribution of Enterprise 2.0 is directly situated in the field of knowledge management as these technologies allow people and the knowledge they embody to be connected on a unprecedented scale.[7] Historically, we had only a limited number of tools available to address this knowledge management challenge (groupware such as Lotus Notes can be seen as one of the few predecessors). Web 2.0 seems especially relevant in mobilizing 'ties' to a greater extent. On a technical level, these developments are being accompanied by 'cloud computing', which achieves economies of scale by centralizing content and transferring it to users by means of APIs (Application Programming Interface). This architecture clearly enables the delivery of software and applications as a 'service' rather than a product.

The Internet: fact and fiction

'It is impossible for old prejudices and hostilities to exist any longer, now that such an instrument has been created for the exchange of thought between all the nations of the earth.'
(Victorian enthusiasts acclaiming the arrival of the first transatlantic cable in 1858)

As observed by *The Economist* a while ago, the Internet does certain things extremely well, while not doing other things at all, or at best very partially.[8] Social media are not only affecting societal developments – see, for instance, the role these media have played during the 'Arab Spring', which started in Tunisia in 2010 – but are also having a considerable impact on business activities. Recent figures (2009/2010) indicate that, in developed economies, internet adoption rates exceed 75% while broadband adoption exceeds 25%.[9] A recent Harvard study reveals that the internet is most commonly used to find information (81%); to look up the news (76%); for online banking (74%); to check the weather (65%); research a product or service before buying (63%); visit a brand or product Website (61%); pay bills (56%); watch a video clip (51%); use a price comparison site (50%); listen to an audio clip (44%). It can be said that, for a lot of individuals in the industrialized world, e-mail is the most important new form of personal communication since the advent of the telephone. Moreover, the introduction of Web 2.0 enabled a number of new social media that flourish on a global scale (Facebook, Linked In . . .). Also, a majority of firms have linked their systems directly with those of their suppliers and partners, allowing them to do business around the clock. At the same time, several firms heavily use Internet technology to reach and to conduct transactions with end consumers.

As for e-commerce, at the beginning of the new millennium (2001),[10] online sales accounted for about 1% of US retail sales. Ten years later (2010), this figure amounts to 5%, with current growth in double digits. The economic value in the business-to-business realm is estimated at several times the volume being realized in business-to-consumer environments.[11] Note that there are considerable differences between industries: for travel and lodging, the Internet has become indispensable for a majority of customers. As explained later in this chapter, it comes as no surprise that online transactions are manifesting themselves most prominently in 'maintenance-interactive' services.

It is clear, however, that e-commerce has not lived up to the expectations voiced during the mid-1990s. One of the major reasons for this discrepancy stems from confusing the use of the Internet for commercial purposes with actual purchasing by means of the Internet. An example clarifies this point: while only 5% of retail sales take place over the Internet, as many as 63% of customers use the Internet at some point to obtain information and compare prices. This growing popularity of the Internet for purchasing purposes is also reflected in advertising behaviour. In 2012, the amount spent on online advertising is expected to exceed the amount spent on advertising in newspapers and magazines.[12] Online advertising continues to grow in most countries at double digit rates with search-engine advertising claiming the lion' share. The growing popularity of this type of advertising certainly coincides with the observation that people are spending more time online than watching television. But it is also clear that the medium itself allows for much more targeted communication and is superior in terms of efficiency since pay-per-view and pay-per-click (or even pay-per-transaction) practices are standard.

While using the Internet for shopping has some interesting advantages (such as a considerable expansion of the range offered, combined with increasing opportunities for time-price comparisons[13]), one should be aware that Internet transactions do not succeed in replicating the social function of shopping. Neither does online purchasing generate the serendipity and impulse purchases that come from visits to a shopping centre.[14] In addition, the Internet does not offer the instant gratification sought by many consumers buying 'physical' goods, as the separate delivery process entails delay. Also, a majority of people prefer physical contact for what have been called 'high touch' products: goods such as shoes and clothes, as well as vegetables and meat, that one likes to see, feel, fit or even taste before buying. This is far less the case for products such as books, computers or CDs. It could even be argued that the more 'digital' that products or services are, the more relevant the Internet will be for their delivery. We will develop this logic in the next pages.

At the same time, it is evident that all is not well on this front. Music, for instance is easily delivered over the Internet, at a reasonable quality, and as the astounding growth of a number of file sharing sites has demonstrated in the past, there is plenty of demand. But the record companies have not found a way of getting people to pay for music distributed in this way at levels comparable with the turnover realized by selling CDs. At the same time, it is Apple (with iTunes) that accounts for the majority of online music sales. More recently, Spotify has been successfully experimenting with a subscription-based business model (streaming). Note, however, that it took more than a decade before the first signs of sustainable business models emerged in this industry (music retailing), an issue we explore further in discussing the socio-technical nature of technological developments.

Getting people to pay for content is a problem for other business too.[15] The online editions of several newspapers started off charging subscriptions, but most of them have abandoned that model. They found that too many rival services are available free. On the other hand, it is clear that offering free services or goods is not exactly a sustainable business proposition. So, in one way or another, agreements will be worked out between consumers, content providers, and network and other service providers to arrive precisely at more sustainable value propositions. Such arrangements will achieve greater feasibility to the extent that enabling technologies (related to security, payments, and identification, including geo-location) become available. Note that, while several of these technologies are already available, their present form is often not perceived as fair or convenient for – and by the majority of – consumers.[16]

What do these observations teach us?

First of all, as the last examples clarify, information technology in general, and Internet technology in particular, are technologies that are constantly 'under development'. Not only does this mean that technology is sometimes unstable or even just clumsy,[17] it also implies that, in a number of cases, clear business models and rules are lacking. The current situation with respect to intellectual property rights illustrates our point. Although everyone agrees that the current situation is not feasible in the long run, no clear scenarios – or business models – have yet emerged. So, being active in Internet technology requires an ability to address the ambiguity or 'interpretative flexibility' (a notion that we will explain in detail in the following pages), which characterizes the actual deployment of the Internet.

Secondly, the emerging picture seems to suggest that we should use Internet technology for what it does well. In certain instances, this might imply a full transactional cycle, in which information technology is used at all stages of the service delivery process,[18] ranging from orientation to closing (buying) and evaluation. In many cases, however, information technology will only be useful for certain parts of the service delivery process. This observation inspires us to plead for combining both the market space and the market place. In deciding upon an appropriate mix of both, we would also stress the importance of taking into account the nature of the service delivery process as well as the specific context of use.

The impact of IT developments on service encounters

Market space: value creation in the virtual world

The introduction of new information technologies can shape the service transaction process and, hence, influence the ways in which business is carried out. Nowadays, the global deployment of the Internet has led many to believe that their business may run into trouble without a presence on that medium. We will look in more detail at what doing business in the 'virtual' world, or the market space, implies.

Virtual value creation: three stages

Value creation in the 'virtual world' involves working with information; it is information that flows through new media. Globally, working with information can be depicted in three ways; often they present themselves in consecutive stages:[19]

1 In the first or the *visibility* stage, companies acquire an ability to 'see' physical operations more effectively through information. At this stage, large-scale information technology systems are put in place to monitor and co-ordinate activities in the physical value chains. Here, information is treated as a supporting element of the value-adding process, not as a source of value itself. In other words, managers use information to monitor or control their processes, but they rarely use information to create new value for their customer.

2 In the second stage, called *mirroring*, companies replace physical activities with virtual ones. They start to create a parallel value chain in the market space. These activities, however, mirror the ones that were taking place in the physical world. An example is the offering of opportunities to listen to new CDs, which previously was only possible at the local music shop but now can also be done via the Internet. Here, disintermediation, involving intermediaries being removed from the value chain, will often be the case; mirroring will imply, in most cases, a cost advantage for 'virtual' distribution systems (*see* below).

3 In the third stage, information is used to establish new services as well as new customer interactions and relationships. Managers draw on the flow of information in their virtual value chain to deliver value to their customers in new ways by looking for *virtual value creation* – virtual in the sense that it is performed through and with information. Creating value in a virtual value chain involves a sequence of five activities: gathering, organizing, selecting, synthesizing and distributing information.[20]

A nice example of rethinking and combining information so as to create new services is Pacific Pride, a company that sells diesel fuels for trucks.[21] It has created a distribution system that includes ATMs at local gas stations, allowing truckers fast and efficient access to fuel. At the same time, the information gathered in this way is used to provide the transport companies with detailed information on fuel purchase, and with accounting reports as specified by the customer. This creates added value for the customer in terms of higher quality information that helps them control their transport activities and enable them to improve the efficiency of their activities. Pacific Pride even offers a credit line for some customers. These new service offerings allow it to charge prices that correspond to margins twice as high as the industry standards.

In fact, working in this way with information allows us to rethink the way we offer services, and possibly the services themselves. A service offering can be seen as a mixture of content, context and infrastructure.[22] What the new information technology offers us are new ways of configuring our service offerings: content, context and infrastructure can be mixed differently. These new possibilities allow us to reconfigure service offerings and design new services. Federal Express understood that its customers wanted immediate and accurate feedback on the packages they delivered and, therefore, built an easy-to-use and very effective service on the Web. FedEx customers can now track their packages at every stage of the delivery and check the signature of the recipient, if necessary. FedEx saves a considerable amount of toll-free phone charges, but its biggest benefit seems to be customer loyalty. Customers will not run to the competition with such impeccable service at their fingertips.[23]

Doing business in the market space or by means of the virtual value chain thus implies new ways of combining and distributing information. It also requires a thorough knowledge of the actual marketplace, as well as seamless information flows.

Value creation in the virtual world assumes a thorough knowledge of the 'real' world; it is the actual behaviour and preferences of your customers that allow a successful design of new service offerings. The monitoring service offered by the trucking company (described in Point 3 above) would never have been offered if the company had not been aware that such a service would add value. However, this knowledge should not be seen as a starting point for only mirroring the physical activities of the classical marketplace. Instead, this knowledge can be used as a starting point for designing new complementary activities.

A good understanding of the company's value chain and customers' situation is not enough; there must also be a seamless flow of information. The recent advent of middleware messaging products and data-warehousing and data-mining software allows a company to integrate islands of information and to structure this information into more than a by-product. The next step would then be to look for new opportunities to create value.

Dis-intermediation or re-intermediation?

The introduction of the market space will have implications for the way in which business will be done. One of the most debated issues centres on the notion of *dis-intermediation*. Cynthia Moore describes dis-intermediation as:[24]

> '. . . the removal of intermediaries from the industry value chain. In other words, it is cutting the middleman out of the loop.'

This implies an imminent threat to certain job categories. Commodities such as books, CDs, certain off-the-shelf financial products and airline travel will no longer require the services of a middleman or broker. Unless the customer perceives the activity of the intermediary as an added value, this position will be under scrutiny. Recent IT developments will urge many intermediaries to look for more added value in their offerings, otherwise their profession could be forced into obsolescence.

However, the intermediary could follow a more drastic approach and seize the opportunity of new IT developments to create additional or new value for customers. This is called *re-intermediation* – the creation of new value between producers and consumers by exploiting the new information technologies, such as the Internet. An example of this is portal sites such as those developed by Yahoo.

Marketplace or market space? The driving forces

No one can deny that market spaces are increasingly present every day and that, on a number of occasions, they replace existing marketplaces.

The extent of, and speed at which, this replacement takes place will not be the same for all types of service, however. In this section, we will provide a framework that can help us to assess the impact of the recent information technology developments. We will examine the different forces that are at play:

- the customer's preferences and actual behaviour;
- the service provider; and
- the nature of the service process.

Customers' preferences and behaviour

New technologies will be adapted by customers to the extent that they better fit their needs. However, new technologies also entail new ways of acting and behaving. As such, they imply a learning and development phase characterized by uncertainty. Predicting the outcomes of such an adaptation and learning process is always a hazardous enterprise. One has only to recall the predictions of the paperless office made some decades ago. Rather than formulating absolute predictions, we shall discuss some major trends that are already visible. These trends will exert their influence on the ongoing adaptation and development process.

The changing preferences of the consumer: in search of convenience

In a rapidly changing world, consumers are changing their lifestyles: the notion of free time is more differentiated in character,[25] more of that time is spent on doing things they really want to do (instead of queueing in a supermarket), communicating with the rest of the world and the environment. Furthermore, customers have a wide variety of choices in brands, stores, shopping methods and communication channels. Companies are now offering the customer more convenience because the customer is asking for it. The customer's new attitudes are most prevalent in the following four domains:

- *Instant satisfaction.* When a customer buys a new product today, he or she wants it delivered 'yesterday'. The success of distributors like IKEA is a shining example. You buy a new dining-room table on Saturday morning and invite your friends to dine from it the same evening. Car manufacturers that can deliver a car in less than 3 weeks have a huge competitive advantage. The pre-selection of products or services will, in the near future, become more and more virtual. The pre-selection of goods will take place in a market space. The final selection and delivery, however, will continue to occur in a market place. This phenomenon may put 'hybrid' configurations combining both market place and market space in an advantageous position. This phenomenon may also lead to situations where the market place 'triumphs' over the market space. For instance, 'fun shopping' on a Saturday afternoon is only fun if you come home with new items. Only in as far as the underlying products can be digitalized, will Internet technology be able to meet this requirement.

- *Consumer control.* Customers want to decide when the interaction with others (and other companies) should take place. Pay-TV channels without advertising are increasingly successful. Customers are demanding privacy (and the law is on their side). Customers decide whether they want to be in a database or not. The locus of control for interactions is shifting in favour of the customer.

- *A more personal interaction, back to nature.* The knowledge of individual customers' needs that companies can gather through technology harks back to the days when the butcher and the baker knew their clientele personally. In that setting, customer service relationships were built in face-to-face transactions.[26] Bringing back the individual transaction with the help of technology not only gives a competitive advantage because of the personal approach, it is also a channel through which market information can be gathered.

The changing needs of customers, as discussed above, provide indications about the things companies will have to focus on in the near future. Those companies that do not take into account customer needs will undoubtedly lose market share. As we look at the changing needs of the customer, we notice that IT can provide solutions to these needs. Increasingly, accurate information can be delivered from the company to the customer and vice versa. What is important, however, is that this information at a certain point in time becomes value, for which people are willing to pay. This will become clear further on in this chapter.

Developing new behaviour: dealing with uncertainty about the offer and the medium

As we mentioned earlier, in a buying process, customers show a certain amount of uncertainty related to the product or service itself. Buying a product or service in many cases means taking a risk. The lower the perceived risk of buying a product or service is, the greater the chance the customer will actually buy the product. During the decision phase, all kinds of questions appear in the mind of the customer. Does this product fit my specific needs? Is the service quality guaranteed? Is the product damaged in any way?

When providing services or products in the market space as opposed to the marketplace, uncertainty about the product is an even bigger problem because of the lack of risk-reducing factors. In the market space, the customer cannot touch, feel, smell or even see a product sufficiently. We could say that when buying products or services in a market space there is a higher risk perception than in a marketplace.

Of course, the nature of the offer is of extreme importance. Buying CDs, for instance, is a relatively low-risk process. The quality of the product is very much the same world-wide; there are no compatibility problems because the disc plays just as well on a Chinese player as it does on an American one and, except for the imperfections of live recordings, the quality of the music on the disc is guaranteed. Buying a CD in the market space is far less risky than, for example, buying a CD player in the market space. There is more quality uncertainty with the latter. You can buy a Philips or a Sony player but, even then, you do not know if the player will arrive at your home in one piece.

When using new media such as the Internet or other online computer media for communication or distribution purposes, therefore, we have to deal with the acceptance and use of the new media by the customer. Indeed, the average customer is not aware of the possibilities and richness of a computer-mediated environment. Moreover, even if the customer is aware of the characteristics and capabilities of a medium, it does not guarantee an awareness of its convenience and timeliness. One has to be aware of the features before knowing the benefits of the service.

The uncertainty about the delivered product or service, then, is higher in the market space. The challenge here is to provide risk-reducing elements to eliminate the customer's risk perception – for example, by delivering information, branding, or providing service guarantees.[27]

Service providers looking for cost effectiveness

Many services can be delivered through multiple media. It is impossible to separate distribution media from service. In most cases, the distribution channel is a part of the service, both from the viewpoint of the medium's share of the total service cost and from the customer's viewpoint.

All distribution channels have an initial fixed cost (investment) and an operational cost. Innovations in service delivery over the past two decades have dramatically lowered the cost of setting up and running a distribution channel. Starting and running a virtual service company that uses the Internet as a medium is tremendously cheap in comparison with a company that distributes its services in offices with marble halls and well-paid employees. As a result, the economics of services distribution has changed radically over the last two decades and is likely to change in the coming decade. Many service suppliers that have been around for a while have built diverse and extensive distribution systems with different cost structures.

Often a small percentage of customers subsidizes the cost of the more expensive distribution medium for the majority of the consumers – that is, most consumers are not really worth the expensive distribution medium from a profitability perspective but only enjoy the channel because a small minority of the consumers make the channels profitable overall.

Such a distribution pattern is untenable, especially as competitive wars swirl through an industry. Competitors start undercutting each other's media costs. New entrants only use low-cost media to offer services. High-cost media are thrown on the defensive. Profitable customers will not tolerate the large channel cost that is factored into their service cost, and they will seek out more economical alternatives rather than subsidizing the channel for non-profitable consumers. The inattentive service provider will be left with a distribution medium that loses money.

In addition, many service industry players do not know what return they are receiving on service delivery investments. This is where modern cost/benefit ratio diagnostics come into play. Even when good statistical information is available, however, the complexity of the supplier-medium-consumer relationship described here does not allow for simple remedies. Although cost structure is important in the choice of the service medium, it cannot be the only basis for action but has to be regarded as part of a holistic view of service consumers and their unique behaviour, needs and profitability dynamics.

A look at banking today reveals the complexity banks face in realigning their retail distribution systems. Customers can do business with their banks through multiple channels: branches, kiosks, call centres, telephones, personal computers, automated teller machines (ATMs), digital televisions, electronic purses, smart cards and so on. The number of media is steadily increasing. Electronic transactions are much cheaper than people- or paper-based ones. This is no simple basis for action, however. Banks realize that what drives their costs is how customers behave and not the cost of a service transaction. The first step in making the most of service delivery media is to understand the evolving behaviour of customers – how the customer changes and what those changes mean for retail banks. Furthermore, adding a new, cheaper electronic distribution channel does not cut total distribution costs *per se*; customers will start using the cheaper distribution channel but will not necessarily make less use of the more expensive one. As banks make more media available, they experience an increase in overall activity. Clients are tending to make vigorous use of the entire range of delivery channels at their disposal. Additionally, a service transaction in one service medium might translate into multiple service transactions in another medium. For example, instead of making a single large withdrawal when the customer visits the branch, ATM customers make many more visits to the machine, withdrawing much smaller amounts, and checking their balance more frequently. The increase in activity, in general, conceals the substitution of activities across channels. Often banks invest in every delivery channel in order not to risk losing the customer rather than having a cost-based justification for their investments.

Although adding cheaper service delivery channels is therefore likely to cause a reduction in the use of a bank's more expensive delivery channels in the long run, it is difficult for many reasons to predict the pace and volume of the reduction. Accordingly, banks prefer to focus on optimizing the use of their service media by the consumer rather than deciding not to invest in or close down a channel.

Banks should focus on customer segments that use multiple distribution channels and cost more than the revenue they represent for the bank. The banks should then define these customers' service needs and the ways to meet them in a manner that is less detrimental to the bottom line. The bank can then begin creating a service delivery system consisting of the right media mix that works for the customer and the shareholder.[28] The type of service – that is, the nature of the service delivered – will have to be taken into account as well, as we will demonstrate in the next section.

Nature of the service process

Of course, not all services will be affected to the same extent by the fact that the market space is taking over some of the traditional marketplace activities. If you are looking for advice on a way to carry out a re-organization, if you need some personal counselling and advice on how to develop your career, or if you are looking for support to improve the relationship with your spouse, you will probably want to have a face-to-face meeting with a counsellor. On the other hand, you will not be looking for a profound personal discussion when you want to rent a DVD or when checking your bank account.

Services vary, then, in terms of the extent to which they require close and in-depth interaction between the customer and service provider. It is clear that this dimension – the degree and nature of interaction between service provider and customer – will correlate with the degree to which the information technology developments affect the way services are delivered and consumed. Services that imply short, standardized information transactions will be more easily delivered by new media than services that require a more complex type of interaction. As a matter of fact, in the more complex cases, the medium is part of the service. Delivering the service by another medium is changing the product itself.

To see this differential effect, it is useful to re-examine the typology of services that was developed by Mills and Margulies and has been discussed in Chapter 2.[29] Here, a distinction was made between three basic types of services and service organizations: maintenance-interactive services, task-interactive services and personal-interactive services:

- *Maintenance-interactive* service operations can be found in financial institutions such as banks and insurance companies. The direct interaction between provider and customer is usually rather predictable and standardized (e.g. the interaction between a bank teller and a customer). The service is based on the provider seeing to the maintenance of some goods or assets for the customer.

- Examples of *task-interactive* types of service can be found in engineering and advertising. Here, the interaction between customer and provider is based on technical problem solving, related to finding ways to obtain or accomplish something. Customers ask for assistance and interact with service providers in order to have specialized knowledge and skills at their disposal. Complex financial engineering can also be an example of task-interactive services: companies will often offer a variety of services. The bank not only performs a number of maintenance-interactive services but also delivers task-interactive services.

- The third type of service operations can be described as *personal-interactive*. Here, service providers work with customers who are not only unsure exactly how to solve their problems or satisfy their needs but also want to know how best to serve their own interests. An example here is, of course, a psychotherapist, but this type might also include a whole range of professional services, such as lawyers or consultants.

The type of interaction between service providers and customers will vary between these three types of service transaction (*see* Figure 6.2). The complexity of interaction will be greater in task- or personal-interactive types of service than in maintenance types of service. This will, in turn, affect the sensitivity to recent information technology developments; it is far easier to substitute 'physical' maintenance interactions for their 'virtual' counterpart.

The basic idea behind this model is the so-called '*information richness theory*'. However, this framework does not explain everything. We need to go one step further and position the characteristics of new media within their context of use; this will bring us to the notion of *virtual communities*. We will examine both ideas in greater depth in the next section.

Linking service transactions and media channels

Information richness theory was developed in the 1980s[30] to help companies prescribe the appropriate channels, given certain information-processing requirements. Information-processing requirements should be understood as the degree of uncertainty or equivocality reduction that an individual is looking for in the interaction. Communication channels can differ in terms of richness; face-to-face communication is richer than, for example, EDI (electronic data input) transactions. For instance, if you only need to know the status of

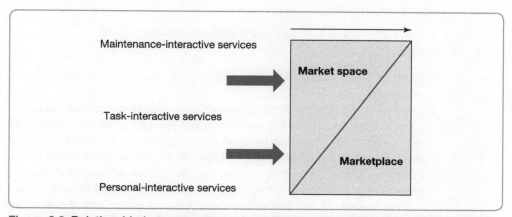

Figure 6.2 Relationship between nature of service and relevance of the market space

your bank account, you do not need a face-to-face meeting with the local bank manager; an ATM or an electronic bank link will provide you with all the necessary information. On the other hand, if you want to discuss possible ways of investing your money, taking into account the fiscal situation and so on, a face-to-face meeting can be the most effective way to proceed.

So let us examine more closely both factors: types of interaction and media richness.

Defining and linking types of interaction and media richness

As already argued, interaction may imply uncertainty or ambiguity. Uncertainty can be seen as the 'difference between the information required and the amount of information already possessed'.[31] However, this definition implies an ability to assess the degree and content of the information required. This is not the case for equivocal or ambiguous situations – that is, situations characterized by the existence of multiple and possibly even conflicting interpretations. Given a certain situation, it is impossible to decide what input is necessary. Uncertainty, then, is seen as a measure of the ignorance of a value of a variable, whereas equivocality is a measure of the ignorance of whether a variable exists. Whereas uncertainty relates to answering well-defined questions, equivocality or ambiguity implies that the right questions are still being sought.

If you want to know the status of your bank account, you find yourself in a situation of uncertainty: you know the variable, the question, and you are looking for a precise answer to that question. However, if you are looking for advice on how best to manage your deposits, you do not know all the different elements that are involved – for instance, the range of possible products and their rates of return, or the effects of tax legislation. Not only are you looking for answers, you are not even sure what questions should be asked. This situation involves equivocality or ambiguity.

Media differ in their ability to transfer rich information. If you meet someone in a face-to-face setting you will obtain more information, not only from their voice but also from gestures or facial expressions. Thus, more information can be transferred in a face-to-face meeting than with e-mail or a fax. Consequently, a face-to-face meeting is seen as a richer medium. The richness of an information handling medium can be expressed by the following characteristics:

1 the opportunity for timely feedback;

2 the ability to convey multiple cues;

3 the tailoring of messages to personal circumstances; and

4 language variety.[32]

Based on these criteria, different media can be classified on a scale of low to high richness (*see* Figure 6.3).

Information richness theory teaches us that effective communication or interaction will occur when there is a fit or a match between the media characteristics (richness level) and the information-processing requirements (uncertainty or equivocality). Thus, when we need to pass on simple information required for uncertainty reduction, we can use a lean medium. Complex, vague or ambiguous information demands rich media such as a telephone call or a face-to-face meeting – the media most suited for equivocality reduction.

This framework can be linked to the previous one, where the nature of services was linked to the relevance of the market space. Figure 6.4 depicts the relationship between the

Figure 6.3 Degree of richness of task-interactive services

Figure 6.4 The relationship between the nature of a service, information richness demands and the relevance of the market space

nature of a service, the demands in terms of information richness and, thus, the relevance of the market space.

Does this framework allow us to predict which services will become virtual and which will not? Of course, it provides us with good insights. However, it should be noted that one-to-one relationships, such as those depicted in this simplifying framework are seldom as straightforward in practice; life is more complicated. Information richness theory starts from the assumption that rational knowledge of the characteristics and the applicability of the various media will eventually drive their use. However, people's actions or interactions are not necessarily based on 'rational' considerations alone. Situational constraints, as well as symbolic considerations, will also influence the selection and use of certain media. People will use certain media because these are the only ones available, to show that they have mastered them, because they attach a certain symbolic meaning or emotion to them, or because they are allowed to use them, and not just because they are the most effective. Just think about the e-mails you receive every day. How many of the messages you receive are relevant or accurate? Some might just be better put on a database, so you could look for the information when you need it, instead of muddling through a list of relevant messages every day. Others are so delicate in content that they only raise questions and are probably better suited to a meeting or discussion.

Most importantly, it is becoming increasingly clear that everyday practice is rooted in social behaviour and, hence, the use of media will also be strongly influenced by the social practices surrounding these media. Effectiveness will in one way or another always connote effectiveness within a certain social community.

It is of no use to have telephones and e-mail connections everywhere in order to speed things up if people are slow to adopt them or do not use them at all. This observation stems directly from the fact that interaction is a two-way street. A caller or sender cannot successfully complete a communication via certain media unless the intended recipient uses them as well.[33] When deciding on a certain media channel, it is important to take into account not only the appropriateness of a certain medium to a communication task but also whether the intended recipients are likely to use, react and respond to messages in that medium within the desired time frame. This brings us to the notion of *communities of practice*. The development of new technologies can be seen as a process that is situated in a context of use, with actors shaping and also being shaped by the possibilities of technological characteristics. This is clearly illustrated in the work of Bijker *et al*. An examination of their findings and concepts can add to this discussion.

Technology's social dimension: the example of the bicycle

It is very difficult to assess today what current IT developments imply for the future. Making predictions and, hence, establishing actions and strategies based exclusively on technological characteristics can be a hazardous way to progress. This does not mean, however, that we should sit around waiting to see what happens. Much can be learned from recognizing the nature of technology development. This process can be understood not only as a 'technology' story but also as an inherent social negotiation and construction process.

It would be a mistake to look at IT developments and their impact only from a technical or rational point of view. Technological developments can follow strange patterns. Our PC keyboards still follow an Azerty or Querty logic designed specifically to *avoid* fast typing, which jammed the keys and levers in the earliest typewriters. Designs for improving both speed and accuracy have been developed during the intervening years but none has succeeded in replacing the 'good old-fashioned' keyboard.[34] Closer to home, we only need to look at the case of Apple and Microsoft. In the 1980s, Apple was already offering the devices that made user-friendliness a reality and allowed intuitive manipulation of the PC functions. These features were only offered by Microsoft with the release of Windows 95, but it was Microsoft that emerged as the most profitable in that time period (second half of the nineties).

Introducing the social dimension will bring us to a view of technology development that is richer because it takes into account the concept of social practice and user groups. Including this social dimension will create a greater generative potential in terms of action strategies regarding individual roles and positioning in the evolving stream of events. However, it will not always lead to clear-cut answers, as technology is not the only consideration. This will be illustrated later on, when we develop the notion of virtual communities. However, before we start looking at possible action strategies, let us first examine what we mean when we describe technological development as a social negotiation and construction process. We will do this by going back to the end of the nineteenth century, when bicycles were the 'hottest' thing around.[35]

Bijker[36] reconstructs the development of the bicycle by tracing it back to the earliest known drawings of a bicycle, made by a pupil of Leonardo da Vinci. (Exhibit 6.1 covers the historical analysis in greater detail.) In this account of the development process, it becomes clear that technological characteristics are not the only drivers of the use and evolution of the bicycle. First came the low-wheeled ancestors, then the appearance of high-front-wheeled vehicles, and the final stabilization of, once again, low-wheeled bicycles. How can we explain this evolution process?

A first element to be taken into account is the notion of relevant social groups. Relevant groups can be initial users, producers, non-users, or 'would-be' users. In the history of the bicycle, the initial users were young, healthy, upper-class sportsmen. The first vehicles had no cranks or pedals but were propelled by the feet pushing the ground, which, given the average road conditions, had some severe safety drawbacks and posed some serious problems for one's shoes. The initial users were interested in the first bicycles as an elegant pastime which could be exploited to impress the ladies with their athletic prowess. This group was especially interested in speed, so producers made the bicycle faster by increasing the size of the front wheel. The high front wheel also situated the driver above his fellow citizens, which was another part of the thrill for this social group. Safety was not a primary concern, since mastering such a high-risk piece of machinery was a challenge in the first place. However, other people started to notice the new technology and were affected by it, not least because the first cyclists were using the pavement and not the road. Exhibit 6.1. contains some references to colourful discussions around issues such as safety, women's dress and price.

What is striking here is that the same piece of machinery was perceived differently by different social groups. Different groups held different views on what the bicycle meant, its use, and its problems and possible solutions. As a result, there was no single unambiguous view on what the bicycle was. Aspects of speed, safety, dress and the like were seen and experienced differently by sport cyclists, touring cyclists, elderly men and women.

As Bijker states, this condition can be referred to as '*interpretative flexibility around the technical artefact*', i.e. the bicycle. Problems and solutions were seen and experienced differently depending on the viewpoint, situation and context of use. This interpretative flexibility around the same technical device is central to the social construction and negotiation process. In consecutive steps, opinions are articulated, actions undertaken and adaptations to the technical design are worked out and examined by the different groups. Producers try to create a 'dominant' design by announcing and promoting the one best vehicle they have produced. The design of the bicycle ultimately stabilized, as did its use among various social groups.

Finally, the *closure* and *stabilization* stage occurred. The introduction of the air tyre created closure and stabilization for the bicycle. The air tyre was conceived as a solution for the vibration problem and, thus, was only relevant to the users of the low-wheeled bicycle. For the group of sporting cyclists using high-wheelers, vibration was an inherent part of the game and not seen as a problem. However, when the new tyre's implications for speed became apparent, the perceptions of sporting cyclists started to change. The whole issue of air tyres was redefined in such a way that it solved the problems of several social groups. Sportsmen were pleased with the high speed, and the broader public was pleased with the anti-vibration solution. This eliminated the safe low-wheeled bicycle's most serious drawback.

It is clear that, during this social process, consensus was achieved at a certain point. This closure led to a decrease in interpretative flexibility. In addition, consensus among the different relevant social groups about the dominant meaning and uses of the technology emerged. Closure mechanisms can be *rhetorical* (by claiming that one has the perfect solution or by massive promotion and advertising, although, in the case of the bicycle, this was not quite successful), or can take the form of a *redefinition* of the problem (as was the case here). Different groups could thus take advantage of the same technological solution. Power will also have an impact upon this social negotiation process. Once there is closure, it can be difficult to understand or even see the diversity that was present in the early stages.

What this tale teaches us is that we must not only take into account technological features but we should also look at the different social groups involved, their use of the technology and the range of preferences, problems and solutions. This diversity of actors, preferences and problems will result in periods of 'interpretative flexibility' moving towards closure and stabilization through a complex social construction and negotiation process. It is risky to look only at the technology without taking into account the different players, their problems, preferences and their context of use. Just think of all the predictions made a decade ago about how, with the introduction of computers and communication media, the 'paperless office' would put an end to the paper industry.

Perhaps within 10 years people will wonder how it was possible during the 1980s (and even now) that people were producing text by means of a word processor (digital medium), then transmitting it by means of a fax (analogue medium) while, at the other end of the fax machine, the information coming through was often stored (read typed in again) using a computer. Another example that clarifies our argument can be found in today's banking industry. At the beginning of the 1980s, banks in Europe were exploring new distribution channels that had become available through the different IT developments. At the same time, the ATMs were developed, as were opportunities for home banking, tele-banking and self-banking:

- *Home banking* requires some hardware at home, usually a terminal and a modem.
- With *tele-banking*, the customers only need a telephone, albeit a digital one: they can interact by using the number keys to indicate commands, numbers of bank accounts, and amounts of money.
- In *self-banking*, the customers access a (small) branch of the bank that has no personnel at all. However, it can be accessed at almost any hour of the day, and the customers can perform all the operations they wish by means of the available terminals.

What has happened with these different types of new information technology? Up to now, self-banking has proved to be the most successful in Belgium. However, only one of the major banks adopted this kind of distribution channel right from the start. Other banks misjudged their customers' preferences and the context of use. In the case of home banking, only a limited number of customers have a personal computer at home. Several banks mis-calculated the speed with which users would pick up the new technologies and integrate them into their daily routines. In the case of tele-banking, customers often feel insecure about typing in all the different numbers (which involve their own money) without getting any visible feedback on their accuracy. This immediate feedback can be received, even on paper, in the case of self-banking. Thus, although self-banking can be described as less convenient for customers (one has to go to the 'self-bank') and more expensive for the banks, it seems to best suit the concerns and habits of a majority of customers within a certain time window.

Exhibit 6.1 The development of the bicycle: a socio-technological tale[37]

'The bicycle: the awakening of a new era . . . Cyclisation: the era of the bicycle, that is, the new time with richer, broader and more mobile civilization . . .'[38]

The bicycle started off as 'prince of the parks'. Aristocratic young men drove high-wheeled bicycles in Hyde Park to show off to their lady friends in the 1870s and 1880s. The 'safety' bicycle, a low-wheeled vehicle with a diamond frame and a chain drive on the rear wheel (similar to the one we know today), did not emerge until the following decade. As Bijker illustrates, the bicycle's evolution shows an increase and subsequent decrease of the front-wheel diameter, beginning and ending at about 22 inches and reaching a peak of 50 inches.

All the technical elements needed to modify the very first bicycle – the so-called 'running machine' – into the bicycle we know today were available right from the start. Why did it take so long, and why did inventors and builders make this 'strange detour from the sure path of technological progress'? Bijker explains this evolution by demonstrating that it was not only a 'technical' story: it involved people – users as well as non-users – playing different roles and affecting the chain of events related to the bicycle's development. In short, the evolution of the bicycle should be understood as a social construction process of technology. Here is what happened.

A pupil of Leonardo Da Vinci made a drawing of a bicycle as early as 1493, but the idea remained dormant until 1791, when eccentrics were observed riding in Parisian parks on something resembling an ancestor of the modern bicycle. This 'célirifère' was shaped like a wooden horse, had two wheels arranged in a line, and was pushed by the feet. The first steering mechanism was added in 1817 by Karl von Drais. The 'Draisienne', as his vehicle was called, was fast but was very demanding on shoes, and it remained difficult to steer. In 1839 Macmillan added cranks, driven by a back-and-forth motion, to the rear wheel, so that the feet could be raised off the ground. During the 1860s in France, Michaux added several improvements to the Draisienne and started to mass-produce this improved vehicle. His 'vélocipède' became a commercial success, although Michaux himself was not the first to either produce the vélocipède or invent its best features. His success was related to frequent minor improvements and an active promotion policy. The Franco-German war of 1870–71 halted the vélocipède's development in France and Germany, and the English took the lead. Rowley Turner, an agent in Paris for his uncle's company, Coventry Sewing Machine Company, brought a vélocipède back to Coventry and convinced his uncle to start manufacturing them.

It should be noted that the original vélocipède's wheels differed only slightly in size. When Starley and Hillman in England (working at that time for the Coventry Sewing Machine Company) patented the 'ariel' model in 1870, it reflected the trend of enlarging the front wheel. As the vélocipède had front-wheel cranks, this increased its speed. To promote their bicycle, Starley and Hillman made a memorable trip from London to Coventry, travelling 96 miles in a single day. This remarkable ride boosted the bicycle's image as a sport machine. Records were set and contested all over England, and track racing started on the continent as well. Cycling had always been seen as an athletic pursuit, since driving a Draisienne or vélocipède demanded both energy and acrobatic skills. As it was not easy to mount a high-wheeled bicycle, enlarging the front wheel only added to the challenge.

Once seated, however, riding was experienced as pleasant and comfortable. The rider sat upright, high above the ground. Cycling had an element of showing off but was also associated with progress and modern times.

The only social group actually riding bicycles at that time were young men, but this does not mean that other people had no opinion of the bicycle or influence upon its evolution. Anti-cycling sentiment escalated. One of the reasons was the satisfaction with which bicyclists elevated themselves above their fellow citizens. Their presence was also seen as a threat to pedestrians. Confrontations between bicyclists and pedestrians or coach drivers, frequently ending in insults, were commonplace.

Two problems remained. First, many people could not afford to buy a bicycle and, second, the safety problem was a barrier, especially for older people. The bicycle's design at that time implied a serious risk, as the centre of gravity was situated above the front wheel. Riders were prone to going head over heels after encountering a small obstacle like a stone or a hole in the road.

Women faced additional problems, typified by the following passage written in the *Münchner Zeitung* in 1900, reporting on a man and woman riding a two-seater bicycle:

'The numerous public walking in the Maximilian Strasse yesterday at noon witnessed an irritating spectacle that gave rise to much indignation . . . Unashamed, proud as an amazon, the graceful lady displayed herself to men's eyes. We ask: is this the newest form of bicycle sport? Is it possible that common decency is being hit in the face without punishment in this manner? Finally: is this the newest form of advertising for certain female persons? Where are the police?'

While this article reports on an unassuming low-wheeled two-seater in 1900, you can imagine the atmosphere in Victorian England two decades earlier. Some bicycle producers tried to solve the 'dress problem' by installing both pedals on one side of the bicycle and modifying the handlebars (making one longer than the other) so it could be 'side-ridden'. Other, less 'technical' solutions were tried and had greater success: changing the design of women's clothing led to new standards of fashion.

The safety problem was solved in several ways. One consisted of the invention of the tricycle, which had two front wheels. This also helped to solve the problem of women's dress, especially after Queen Victoria described the performance of a female tricyclist as 'really very graceful and one which by no stretch of the imagination could be termed unladylike'. The introduction of tricycles allowed women and older men to engage in cycling, and many proceeded to do so. This made bicycle producers acutely aware of other potential markets and they began to produce new and different bicycles in addition to the tricycles. Although it was easier to keep one's balance on a tricycle, it retained or even introduced several safety problems. Having three tracks made a tricycle more exposed to the perils of the road. The lack of effective brakes (the rider had to 'reverse the action of the machine') also caused serious problems. Attempts to solve the safety problems consisted of efforts to improve the bicycle's basic design. This was mainly done by moving the saddle backward and modifying the size of the wheels. Other attempts included the replacement of the pedals with a lever mechanism, the introduction of gears, the addition of a chain drive linked only to the front wheel, and even the reversing of the front and rear wheels, with the latter becoming the larger one.

In 1879, H. Lawson patented a bicycle more similar to the one we know with the drive, which included a chain, moved to the rear wheel. This machine, called the 'bicyclette', was promoted heavily but never became a commercial success, although many bicycle historians describe the bicyclette as 'ahead of its time'. As it still had a larger front wheel, it was perceived as 'grotesque' and compared with a crocodile because of its elongated frame. Starley, a nephew of the pioneer of the same name, was more successful in 1884. Together with his partner, Sutton, he launched the 'Rover', which had 36-inch front and rear wheels and a chain drive to the rear wheel. Sales started to boom when the Rover started beating records and winning races.

In 1888, it was written that:

'no radical changes have been made in the construction of cycles during the past year, and the tendency is to settle down to three types of machines: the ordinary bicycle [which at that time had a larger front wheel], the rear driven safety bicycle [like the "Rover"] and the direct front-steering tricycle.'[39]

However, before the end of that year, Dunlop had patented[40] his air tyre and applied it immediately to the design of his own bicycle. Although the text of the patent stressed its anti-vibration effects, in practice the air tyre also considerably increased a bicycle's speed. Pneumatic tyres won races and, thus, commercial production of air tyres for bicycles began. The first tyres were very expensive (a quarter of the cost of an entire bicycle or tricycle), easily punctured, and made cyclists vulnerable to side-slipping. However, the air tyre's success on race tracks was enormous and, within a year, no serious racing man bothered to compete on anything else.

Thus, the 'safety' bicycle was born. It combined safety with speed, while the dominant design up to that time was fast, due to its large front wheel, but not at all safe. Improvements in the following years included solving the problems of the chain drive by constructing effective chain casings, an agreement on the best kind of foot motion (up-and-down *versus* rotary), and the emergence of the diamond frame. A period of closure and stabilization around the new dominant design started and the large front-wheel bicycle faded very quickly into obscurity.

Action strategies for the new media

So far, we have explored recent IT developments and have seen that value creation is more and more a question of working with information – gathering, organizing, selecting, synthesizing and distributing information. This creation process assumes a thorough knowledge of the 'real' world. Opportunities for new service offerings can be found here. A second argument is related to the suitability of the recent IT developments for managing the service delivery process. We suggested that the relevance of virtual value creation will vary depending on the type of service. However, it is important to note that what eventually will happen depends on the actions of customers, producers, and authorities. Even the implementation of 'hard' technology is embedded in a social negotiation and construction process.

We can now start thinking about action strategies. These can be divided into those that mirror action strategies already existing in the 'physical' world, and those that are specific to the new technology available. In the latter case, virtual value creation will be essential; the new technology and media will be used to develop new forms of interaction with the customer resulting in 'new' services as new forms of co-ordination and co-production come into place. For example, in the case of the use of network computing for providing 'distant shopping' services (whereby the customer can choose what he or she wants to buy from home instead of going to the supermarket), supermarkets are experimenting with screens where the customer can 'virtually' walk through the store. However, this leads to time lost in front of the screen. An alternative approach involves the customer asking directly what he or she is looking for. Helping the customer to make choices and providing different kinds of advice, recipes and so on mean that a whole new form of shopping becomes possible for supermarkets.

We shall discuss action strategies that explore new 'virtual' ways of creating value. These involve new forms of distribution, often based on the idea of bundling or unbundling services into their components, and the development of learning relationships. We will argue that all these 'new' concepts and approaches will only work as long as they are able to create value which is also perceived as such. And while this might sound like stating the obvious, the impression remains that, especially as far as Internet initiatives are concerned, the value equation has been out of balance, i.e. much more has been spent than can be justified by the resulting value creation afterwards. Hence, we will devote specific attention to approaches that restore the balance in this respect. And here, the 'old' knowledge we already have about developing a relevant market approach will turn out to be extremely important. In fact, the ideas of segmenting and targeting, pointed out in the discussion of the service concept in Chapter 3, and service branding (Chapter 8) remain as relevant as ever. So we will start with a brief discussion of these strategies.

Segmenting and targeting

Segmenting has many advantages, and targeting even more. By targeting a specific segment, a company can upgrade the level of service offered to the customer. The smaller the segment, the more customized the market approach to the customers in that specific segment can – and to an extent must – be. Very small and well-defined market segments, known as *hyper-segments*, offer the advantage of treating the customer on a very personal basis. However, targeting a very small segment, by definition, means offering a product or service to a small number of customers, implying that there is little money to be made. IT can help solve this problem. Very small local (hyper)segments are becoming large global segments. For example, one major financial corporation in the US has set up a banking service targeted at women in the process of divorce, offering a number of services directed to their specific needs. Offering this banking service in one local area would never be affordable but, if it can offer this service on the Internet, it can deliver it throughout the entire country. Note that segmenting and targeting will result in a marketing mix that includes online media (advertising as well as presence on social media). Currently (2011), search engine advertising is still dominant (with advertising turnover achieved by Google still tenfold the advertising turnover realized by Facebook), but a presence in social media has become a necessity in order to reach audiences and customer segments effectively.

Branding

A brand can be defined as:

> 'a name, term, sign, symbol or design, or a combination of them, which is intended to identify the goods or services of one seller or group of sellers and to differentiate them from those of competitors.'[41]

Branding will become more important as the amount of information around us increases. Customers drowning in information will develop a tendency to choose speed, convenience and/or easy accessibility, which for many will mean choosing the provider they know or have already heard of. Established brands will thus have a certain advantage with regard to the new media. Furthermore, branding will take away some of the customer's inherent uncertainty about an offer or service provider. As we look for news or current affairs on the Internet, we shall likely end up at the CNN site, since it is known for providing information and news services. However, this advantage should not be seen as absolute. In the end, the services provided by means of the new media will make the difference. Also, branding is an essential cornerstone when it comes to developing trust between service providers and customers. Finally, an important point relates to extending the idea of branding to the new media. For example, creating an attractive Internet site will entice certain groups of 'surfers' to regularly check out the site. People will log on not only because of the product or service offerings but also to experience the site in and of itself.

Developing learning relationships[42]

A company aspiring to give its customers exactly what they want must look at the world through new eyes. It must use technology to assume two roles: a mass customizer that efficiently provides customized goods and services, and a one-to-one marketer that elicits information from each customer about his or her specific needs and preferences. These two concepts bring producer and customer together in what we call *a learning relationship*. This is a relationship that becomes more responsive over time as the two parties interact with each other, collaborating to meet the consumer's needs.

In learning relationships, individual customers teach the company more and more about their preferences and needs, giving the company an enormous competitive advantage. The more customers teach the company, the better it becomes at providing exactly what they want in the way they want it, and the more difficult it will be for a competitor to entice them away. Even if a competitor were to have precisely the same capabilities, a customer already involved in a learning relationship with the first company would have to spend an inordinate amount of time and energy teaching the competitor what the company already knows. A company that can cultivate learning relationships with its customers should be able to retain their business virtually forever.

Learning relationships is not the same as database marketing. Mass marketers use information technology to define the most likely buyers of the products they sell. For the most part, the information comes from simple transactional records and public information compiled by specialist firms. The mass marketer generates a list, based upon this data, of the most likely prospects and solicits them with offers or messages. Companies only guessing at the tastes of potential customers often flood them with information. By contrast, the one-to-one marketer conducts a dialogue with each customer, one at a time, and uses the increasingly detailed feedback to find the best products or services for that customer. Bank of America offers the 'Build Your Own Bank' feature to its customers on the Internet. Customers can develop their own bank site tailored to their specific needs. They do not need to go through all the data and features on the BofA website; they receive only what they are interested in.

Although many companies are moving toward this model, few have fully implemented it or combined it with mass customization.

Bundling or unbundling products and services

'Product bundling is used in almost every industry, but frequently it is not part of a specific and intentional strategy. Unfortunately, failing to consider bundling as a strategic marketing variable may unnecessarily reduce the performance of the firm.'[43]

The electronic travel desk is a service delivered via the Internet where businessmen can make reservations for business trips. Not only does the travel desk reserve the airplane tickets, but through the travel desk menus you can reserve your hotel room, rental car and concert tickets, and indicate that you are a vegetarian so that you are given appropriate meals. Bundling products and services in the travel industry can go even further. If you are interested in going on an adventurous holiday, this 'extended' service can mean that the travel agency decides where you should go, makes reservations for the different hotels, flights, water-ski and/or rafting facilities, and even buys appropriate holiday clothes for you.

By bundling products and services, you upgrade the level of delivered service, but you downgrade the level of possibilities for the customer to choose from. Interactive media are ideal not just for offering the customer a broad array of possibilities but also for knowing ahead of time which possibilities the customer might want; thus, *tailor-made bundling* (and hence *un-bundling*) becomes a possibility for many services, as the Bank of America example above clearly illustrates.

New forms of distribution

With the rapid growth of interactive media, consumers are being offered a broad range of possibilities for buying products or services. As we have already seen, an increasing number of distribution channels are offering a wide range of products to the customer.

Distributors, traditionally, fulfil different functions for their customers:

- bridging the distance between producer and consumer;
- setting the time of delivery;
- adjusting the form of the product;
- setting quantity;
- offering assortment;
- providing information;
- post-sales activities;
- the sale itself.

Many of the functions cited above can be provided in a market space rather than a marketplace. The question is whether the retailer or the producer will carry them out. Consider, for instance, home delivery, which bridges the distance gap as well as the time gap. Three principal parties can deliver this service: the retailer ready to change his processes, the producer who eliminates links in the value chain, or a third party who specializes in distribution. Hence, what can be expected in the near future is the emergence of new value configurations, whereby providing relevant information to customers will be an important competitive issue.

Providing information by means of the market space is, in one way, the easiest and, in another way, the most difficult function to achieve. Providing advice via electronic media is probably better and more efficient in the eyes of the consumer, who wants the locus of control. However, electronic media can only deliver to two of our senses, eliminating smell, feel and taste from the selection process. For certain customers, this might lead to a dual use of both place and space: a pre-selection of possible deliverers of services or products is made via electronic media, and the selection of the final supplier can take place in the 'real' world.

Avoiding the commodity magnet: Value, value, value

As became clear above, there is a danger that companies will not meet the expectations put forward when drawing up their Internet deployment action plans. And, although the number of customers ready to engage in certain web enabled service transactions has been overestimated in several cases, it seems that the most common mistake lies in a phenomenon called 'commoditizing'. Figure 6.5 depicts products or services on two axes: price, i.e. a reflection of the value of a certain service given prevailing market circumstances, and 'cost to serve', which relates to the amount and costs of the actual resources an organization needs to deliver the service at hand.

The commodity magnet, a concept advanced by Rangan and Bowman,[44] reflects the idea that forces are pulling 'high value, high cost' services away towards areas in which the cost to service actually exceeds the market prices asked. Such forces include competition, the presence of demanding customers who are unwilling to pay for additional services and options and the presence of low/no cost alternatives provided by competitors. The Internet has been particularly guilty in flirting with so-called 'new economic laws' that, in the end, turned out to be a form of wishful thinking.[45] On a company level, at certain junctures this 'new economics' implied an almost complete lack of attention to metrics that actually assessed the value creation of companies, such as profit. Instead growth, especially in terms of the customer base, was emphasized. Recall the famous quote by Jeff Bezos, CEO of Amazon, who only a few years ago claimed that if 'Amazon were profitable anywhere in the near future, it would be purely accidental'. This one-sided emphasis on growth metrics, as opposed to value-creating indicators, surely contributed to fuelling the growth of the 'magnet'. And, while selling at prices below the 'cost to serve' threshold makes sense for a certain phase of growth,[46] it is clear that, in the longer run, someone needs to pay for the service delivered. Indeed, it is exactly this longer perspective, which includes considering the resources required to accomplish this 'skimming strategy' successfully, that seems to be absent. Companies made huge investments in back-office infrastructure, personalization software and the like without addressing the value equation: Who is willing to pay what for

Figure 6.5 The commodity magnet and how to handle it

what kind of service? Instead, services were offered free, based on the premise that one should grab customers first and once this is accomplished, thinking about revenues and margins could then begin; 'the "lock in customers first, ask questions later" premise'. Thus – and this will come as no surprise at this stage – value creation should be a central idea not only when defining and designing the service concept (*see* Chapter 3) but also when considering the use of Internet technology in your service delivery system. And there is some good news in this respect: value creation through the deployment of Internet technology is indeed feasible. Recently, Amit and Zott pointed out four ways to create 'e-value'.[47] They arrived at these four models by analysing actual practices that are profitable today. These four ways relate to enhanced levels of efficiency; bundling resulting in superior value, increasing customer retention and, finally, the production of novelty. Efficiency, the first strategy, is straightforward; to the extent that Internet technology results in efficiency enhancements relative to offline business (or other online initiatives), it will flourish. Efficiency can be obtained by customers because they experience improved search and bargaining processes; but service providers can also achieve considerable savings. Low-cost airlines such as Virgin Express and Ryanair rely heavily on the Internet to sell tickets for exactly these reasons. The case of Cisco is well known in the business-to-business environment; by installing an extranet that connects 32 suppliers, Cisco was able to redeploy 50 agents who had been busy in the past collecting information on components. Moreover, Cisco is now able to make in-hours supply chain decisions that took almost a week in the past.[48]

We have already discussed the idea of bundling; let us add here the idea that bundling does not limit itself to online offerings alone. One can easily define packages that combine elements of the market space with marketplace ingredients, such as ordering online while picking up goods at a physical shop. Likewise, newspapers and magazines are starting to offer bundles of subscriptions for printed copies with online access and services. Increasing customer retention implies finding ways to motivate customers to engage in repeat trans-actions and/or to improve their associations. The most obvious way to enhance customer retention takes on the form of introducing special bonuses for repeat purchases. Familiarity with the interface of a website may also contribute to retention. Using a certain interface implies learning and, once this has begun, it creates incentives to continue the interaction, especially if the savings in doing so are considerable. For instance, once all of your delivery and payment details have been entered into a certain shopping site, you will tend to check there first. Needless to say, this type of lock-in behaviour is only interesting in so far as opportunities for customizing and personalizing are actually being exploited in a mutually beneficial way. Finally, novelty can be traced back to the third stage discussed earlier in this chapter – that of virtual value creation. Here, one tries to create value by offering completely new services, which would not be feasible without Internet technology; examples include the 'reverse markets' introduced by Priceline.com; or the customer-to-customer auction formula introduced by eBay that allowed customers to auction low-value items successfully.

Conclusion

In this chapter, we began with a brief overview of technological developments related to the emergence of network computing. We then looked at what can be described as the transition from marketplace to market space, as more and more services are delivered by means of electronic media. As a first step, we discussed the particularities of this virtual value chain; handling and combining information in new ways is crucial. That this transition is not as general as one is sometimes led to believe became clear when we discussed the driving forces that influence the extent and speed with which this transition has been taking place. Customer preferences and behaviour, cost considerations on the part of service provider, and finally the nature of the service process all play their part here. To clarify the role that the nature of the service process plays in this respect, we introduced some insights on information richness. Here, it was clear that maintenance-interactive services will be affected to a greater extent than task- and personal-interactive services. We also argued that the social side of technology development and diffusion processes should also be acknowledged. Finally, we sketched some relevant action strategies that could be deployed when companies are starting to move in the direction of virtual transactions.

Review and discussion questions

- It is clear that certain business models do actually work on the Internet and that there are even companies who make a profit using them. Notable examples include eBay (auctioning), Google, Facebook and Amazon.com (e-tailing). Can you come up with other profitable companies that rely heavily on Internet technology? What makes them distinctive? How do they avoid the 'commodity magnet'? To what extent do these companies combine the market space with the market place?

- Sceptics may argue that e-commerce will never be more than a phenomenon like mail order sales, appealing to certain segments of the market but, all in all, remaining a modest phenomenon. Would you agree? Why and/or in which cases?

- Some futurologists indicate that what is happening now on the Internet is just the beginning of the 'digital age'; in a couple of decades, we will be surrounded by 'ambient intelligence', and ubiquitous computing will make the way we work and live today very much 'outdated'? Would you agree with such viewpoints? What kind of technologies would be needed? And how would it alter human behaviour specifically? Why?

Suggested further reading

Amit, R. and Zott, C. (2001) 'Value creation in E-business', *Strategic Management Journal*, Vol 22, pp. 493–520. This article provides an in-depth discussion of a variety of strategies one can deploy to use Internet technology in a sustainable way

Rayport, J. F. and Sviokla, J. V. (1994) 'Managing in the market space', *Harvard Business Review*, Vol 72, No 6, pp. 141–150

Rayport, J. F. and Sviokla, J. V. (1995) 'Exploiting the virtual value chain', *Harvard Business Review*, Vol 73, No 6, Nov–Dec

These articles provide an excellent overview of what the market space implies.

Daft, R. H. and Lengel, R. H. (1986) 'Organisational information requirements, media richness and structural design', *Management Science*, Vol 32, No 5, pp. 554–571

Markus, M. L. (1994) 'Electronic mail as the medium of managerial change', *Organisation Science*, Vol 5, No 4, pp. 502–527

McAfee, A. P. (2009) *Enterprise 2.0*: New collaborative tools for your organization's toughest challenges. Harvard Business Press

People interested in information richness theory and its (social) extensions are advised to read these two works

Bijker, W. E. (1995) *Of Bicycles, Bakelites and Bulbs*. Cambridge, MA: MIT Press

We highly recommend this work on the, often neglected, social side of technology development

Pinch, T. and Bijker, W. (1987) 'The social construction of facts and artefacts: or how the sociology of science and the sociology of technology might benefit each other', in Bijker, W. E., Hughes, T. and Pinch, T. *The Social Construction of Technological Systems*. Cambridge, MA: MIT Press

Notes and references

1 We should mention recent developments on the level of 'fabrication' technologies. Neil Gershenfeld (2004) advances the idea that as computing has become 'personal', so fabrication technologies in the future will become 'personal' as well. This implies local production of unique pieces, enabled by the introduction of new production technologies (e.g. 3D printing). While this development will affect primarily manufacturing industries, implications in terms of service activities (e.g. spare parts, distribution) might unfold. See Gershenfeld, N. (2007) *Fab: The Coming Revolution on Your Desktop – from Personal Computers to Personal Fabrication*. Basic Books; as well as the special report published by *The Economist* (2012): 'The third industrial revolution', Vol 403, p. 8781)

2 Nowadays also referred to as the era of ubiquitous computing, clout computing or even 'ambient intelligence'

3 In every computer application or program, one can always make a distinction between three different 'logics': presentation, application and data. Presentation logic involves all 'dialogue' features and codes that allow for interaction between machine and user: the user interface. Think about all the screens you have seen passing when entering data into a certain program; you were interfacing with the presentation 'logic'. Application logic refers to the build-in intelligence of a program; all 'algorithms' that make computations or transactions in a particular program possible. Finally, data logic refers to all codes applied to handle and manage the data used in the program

4 The network era has become possible because certain discrete developments started to combine. There is increasing compatibility among the main players in the field, especially with regard to interfacing issues. Bandwidth is expanding and more and more actors are becoming linked by integrating the development of networks with new and complementary developments in the fields of processors, security technologies and the like

5 Hyper Text Mark-up Language

6 Likewise, XML, Extensible Markup Language, is an open standard that facilitates extension of the use of 'tags' so that content and form can be transmitted in a much more refined way

7 For a detailed account on Web 2.0, see McAfee, A. P. (2009) *Entreprise 2.0: New collaborative tools for your organization's toughest challenges*. Harvard Business Press

8 *The Economist*, 19 August 2000

9 http://www.oecd.org/statisticsdata/

10 Note, however, that this figure varies greatly from industry to industry; the online share in 1999 for toys amounted to less than 0.5% (US and Europe), and for travel varied between 0.5% (Europe) and 1.5% (US), but the online share for services such as financial brokerage amounted to over 14% (US) and 5% (Europe). Likewise, online shares for computer hardware and software went to nearly 10% (US). *Source*: 'First America, then the world. E-Trends', *The Economist*, 2001

11 Data from the US Census Bureau indicate that business-to-business on-line transactions exceed retail activities tenfold in monetary terms (2009/2010). In terms of share of total value shipped, the ratios are 30% versus 5%. For updates, see: http://www.census.gov/econ/estats/

12 http://www.emarketer.com/PressRelease.aspx?R=1008788

13 Armstrong, A. and Hagel, J. (1996) 'The real value of on-line communities', *Harvard Business Review*, Vol 74, No 3, p. 134

14 Of course, using electronic catalogues has advantages as well. One can bring different products to the attention of customers in a customized manner while, at the same time, other items of interest can be pointed out. This can be done through preferences expressed by customers themselves, or derived from analysing the purchasing behaviour of other customers

15 This is most notably the case for pure 'information'. As argued by a number of economists, the marginal cost of reproducing information equals zero so the price of these 'information' products tends to converge to zero as well (unless intellectual property rights are present and accepted by all parties involved in the transactions). For more on the 'economics of information', we refer you to Foray, D. (2004) *The Economics of Knowledge*. MIT Press

16 Look at, for example, 'Digital Rights Management' systems. Several of them imply some kind of 'box' that contains both the content (e.g. a software package or music) and the rights you have acquired to this content (e.g. installing it once, or playing it endlessly). In order to actually enjoy the use of the content, consumers need specific software that facilitates decoding. Few customers are willing to install such systems, especially when the same content can be acquired relatively easily by taking a different route

17 Just imagine introducing cars into the market that contain as many 'bugs' as software packages include upon launch

18 *See* Figure 8.3 on service delivery and promotional channels as discussed in Chapter 8

19 Rayport, J. F. and Sviokla, J. V. (1994) 'Managing in the market space', *Harvard Business Review*, pp. 141–150

20 Rayport, J. F. and Sviokla, J. V. (1995) 'Exploiting the virtual value chain', *Harvard Business Review*, Nov–Dec

21 *See* Rayport, J. F. and Sviokla, J. V. (1994), op. cit.

22 The newspaper provides us with an example: here, the information (content) can be consumed by reading it at home, or at the office (context), and is delivered via a complex infrastructure, involving typesetting, printing, distribution, and so forth

23 Rayport, J. F. and Sviokla, J. V. (1995), op. cit.

24 Moore, C. (1996) 'Disintermediation: Communications technologies are having some impact', *Dataquest*, June

25 For some people, less free time tends to be the case; for others, free time becomes the rule (e.g. the elderly)

26 McKenna, R. (1995) 'Real-Time Marketing', *Harvard Business Review*, Vol 73, No 4, pp. 87–95

27 Still, one has to realize that adaptation will not happen overnight. In this respect, the well-known distinction between innovators (about 2.5% of the market), early adopters (13.5%), early majority (34%), late majority (34%) and laggards (16%) as developed by Rogers in the 1960s can be kept in mind: it takes time to get the majority of customers to make the shift

28 Here, cost considerations should be matched with the customers' perceptions of value; *see also* Chapter 9 on pricing. However, as a service provider, every sound policy starts with a clear insight on the cost structure of the activities contained in each service transaction

29 For a full discussion of this service classification, *see* Mills, P. and Margulies, N. (1980) 'Towards a core typology of service organisations', *Academy of Management Review*, Vol 5, No 2, pp. 255–265

30 Leading authors here were Daft, R. H. and Lengel, R. H. (1986) 'Organisational information requirements, media richness and structural design', *Management Science*, Vol 32, No 5, pp. 554–571

31 Galbraith, J. (1977) *Organizational Design*. London: Addison-Wesley

32 *See* Huber, G. P. and Daft, R. H. (1987) 'The information environments of organisations', in Jablin, F., Putnam, L., Roberts, H. and Porter, L. (eds) *Handbook of Organisational Communication: An interdisciplinary perspective*. Newbury Park: Sage Publications, pp. 135–148

33 *See* for a more extended discussion Lee, A. (1995) 'Electronic mail as a medium for rich communication; an empirical investigation using hermeneutic interpretation', *MIS Quarterly*, June, pp. 143–157; and Markus, M. L. (1994) 'Electronic mail as the medium of managerial change', *Organisation Science*, Vol 5, No 4, pp. 502–527

34 For an account of the historical developments, *see* David, P. (1985) 'Clio and the economics of Qwerty', *Economic History*, Vol 75, pp. 227–232. The original Qwerty and Azerty formats were developed so that typing would not go too fast as this might lead the mechanical devices to run into trouble. Despite the change from mechanical to electronic technology, more efficient formats have not been able to replace the Qwerty and Azerty formats

35 The following illustration is based on the work of Pinch, T. and Bijker, W. For a complete overview of this view on technology development, *see* Pinch, T. and Bijker, W. (1987) 'The social construction of facts and artefacts: or how the sociology of science and the sociology of technology might benefit each other', in Bijker, W., Hughes, T. and Pinch, T. (eds) *The Social Construction of Technological Systems*. MIT Press; and Bijker, W. E. (1995) *Of Bicycles, Bakelites and Bulbs*. Cambridge, MA: MIT Press

36 *See* Bijker, W. E. (1995) and Pinch, T. and Bijker, W. (1987), op. cit.

37 This tale is based on the extensive descriptions given by Bijker. Interested readers can find the 'full' story as well as an extensive discussion of the development process of bakelite and bulbs in Bijker, W. (1995), op. cit.

38 Ibid. p. 40

39 *Engineer* (1888) in Bijker, W. (1995), op. cit.

40 In 1845, William Thomson had already patented a form of air tyre. They were used on carriages at that time but never became a success, as they were expensive and other anti-vibration alternatives were available. However, it meant that Dunlop's patent was invalid, as he was informed in 1890. Using complementary patents, Dunlop and his company prospered after all

41 Kotler, P. (1983) *Principles of Marketing* (2nd edn). Englewood Cliffs, NJ: Prentice-Hall

42 Pine II, B. J., Peppers, D. and Rogers, M. (1995) 'Do you want to keep your customers forever?', *Harvard Business Review*, Mar/Apr, pp. 103–114

43 Paun, D. (1993) 'When to bundle or unbundle products', *Industrial Marketing Management*, Vol 22, pp. 29–34

44 Ranga, V. K. and Bowman, G. (1992) 'Beating the commodity market', *Industrial Marketing Management*, Vol 21, No 3, pp. 215–224

45 Whether or not 'new' economic laws prevail in the information or knowledge society remains a highly debated issue. The authors of this chapter are doubtful. For a recent overview of the debate, see for instance 'New Economy? What's left?' Special Report, *The Economist*, May 2001

46 *See* Chapter 9 on pricing strategies for new products/services

47 Amit, R. and Zott, C. (2001) 'Value creation in e-business', *Strategic Management Journal*, Vol 22, pp. 493–520

48 *See* (2001) 'Trying to connect You: A supply side revolution'. *The Economist*, E-trends

Chapter 7

The role of facilities management in designing the service experience

Paul Gemmel • Roland Van Dierdonck • Steven Desmet

'We shape our buildings and afterwards our buildings shape us'

(Winston Churchill commenting on the bombed
House of Commons in 1943 – as recorded in Hansard)

Objectives

By the end of this chapter, you should be able to discuss:

- the nature of facilities management in services and, in particular, how facilities management decisions influence the customer
- how facilities management is not a purely technical or even operational decision but should involve marketing and HRM aspects as well
- the design parameters that can help to structure back-office and front-office configurations
- the various considerations in locating a service unit and some basic location concepts
- the notion of servicescape and which factors to take into consideration when designing the servicescape
- the notion of service experience design and how all different aspects discussed in Chapters 4 to 6 can contribute to it

Introduction

A University of Leicester study found that in-store music had a significant effect on purchasing and, in particular, on product choice. The results were published in *Nature*,[1] a respected scientific journal.

Royalty payments for non-broadcast commercial uses of music in 1995 amounted to £53.8 million in the UK alone.[2] However, research on music and consumer behaviour[3] has almost completely ignored the potential effect of in-store music on purchasing and particularly on product choice. By investigating the purchasing of German and French wines, the researchers found that musical 'fit' has a profound influence on product choice.

To test this, four French and four German wines were displayed in a supermarket drinks section. The wines were matched between the countries for their price and dryness or sweetness. Each of the four shelves contained one French and one German wine and appropriate national flags. The position of the wines on the shelves was changed halfway through the 2-week testing period. French accordion and German Bierkeller pieces were played on alternate days from a tape deck situated on the top shelf. Shoppers buying wines from the display were asked to complete a questionnaire by two experimenters, with 44 shoppers consenting.

When French music was played, 40 bottles of French wine were sold and 8 bottles of German wine. When German music was played 12 bottles of French wine were sold and 22 bottles of German wine. French wine outsold German wine when French music was played, whereas German wine outsold French wine when German music was played ($P < 0.001$) despite an overall bias in favour of French over German wine sales. Questionnaire responses indicated that the French music made them think of France ($P < 0.001$). Respondents did not differ in their general preference for wines from these two countries ($P > 0.05$), and only six respondents answered 'yes' to the question, 'Did the type of music playing influence your choice of wine?' Customers did not seem aware of the effect that music had on their selections.

The anthropologist E. Hall, in his book, *The Silent Language*,[4] stated, 'Space speaks' – highlighting, namely, that the physical environment in which the service takes place is observed by the customer and 'speaks' to him or her about what to expect and how to behave. The physical environment (or the '*servicescape*' as Mary Jo Bitner[5] calls it) in which the service process takes place is not only part of the service delivery system but is actually part of the product, which is the service itself.

In this chapter, we deal with those elements of the service experience that have an impact on how the service is offered and, more particularly, the context of use and the emotional components of interaction. The customer experience in a hotel is, for example, not only related to the basic processes such as making bookings, cleaning rooms and delivering room service (as discussed in Chapter 4) but also to subtle clues such as the thread count of the sheets, the mood and décor of the room and the attitude of the receptionist.[6] Clues generally fall into three main categories: functional clues, humanic clues and mechanic clues.[7] Functional clues concern the 'what' of the service experience; humanic clues are based on the behaviour and appearance of service employees; the mechanic clues come from actual objects or environments and include sights, smells, sounds, tastes and textures.[8] In this chapter, we will focus on mechanic clues. The management of these mechanic clues is traditionally studied in the field of Facilities Management, including location decisions and back-office/front-office design decisions. The importance of these mechanic clues in the service experience has led to service-specific models such as the servicescape framework, which will also be discussed in this chapter. Finally, we will argue that all design components (functional, humanic and mechanic clues) should be linked with the service concept (Chapter 3) and the service process (Chapter 4) to deliver a service experience that will be able to tell a service story in the most powerful way.

The nature of facilities management in services

Facilities management is concerned with all the physical aspects of the service delivery system, ranging from such major strategic decisions as where Disney should build its next theme park down to very detailed decisions such as posting the signs to the ladies' toilet in a restaurant. In a manufacturing environment, facilities management belongs in the domain of production or operations management and includes decisions such as plant location, process choice, and design, automation, layout and task design. In a service organization, however, it is more difficult to assign the responsibility to one of the traditional functional departments as the activities of facilities management cross the boundaries between organizational structuring, marketing, organizational behaviour, product development and operations management. Decisions in these domains affect human resources goals (e.g. the motivation of workers), operational goals (e.g. the quality and efficiency of the service processes) and marketing goals (consumer attraction and customer retention).

Issues relating to facilities management decisions were among the first to be studied in the so-called scientific management movement. At the beginning of the twentieth century, Frederic Taylor and Frank Gilbreth concerned themselves with task and process design, including time and motion studies. Somewhat later, Roethlisgberger studied the impact of environmental factors on human aspects such as motivation and productivity. Plant and warehouse location models were among the first applications of operations research models developed during the Second World War, and layout studies have traditionally attracted the attention of many researchers and practitioners, especially in the industrial engineering field. Ergonomics is another related field, where the impact of the work environment on workers' psychological and physiological needs is studied.

This type of research has produced insights, concepts and models that can be usefully applied to solve facilities management problems in service sectors. However, in these traditional approaches little or no concern is given to the customer. Purchasers of goods usually do not visit the factory where the goods are made. Purchasers of services are present in the 'service factory' and participate (sometimes in a very active way) in the service delivery process. When making decisions related to location, physical setting and process design, a service company has to take the customer and his or her explicit and implicit needs and expectations into consideration and has to realize that the outcome of these decisions is actually part of the product. Almost all researchers in the field of service management refer to the importance of 'tangibles' in the total service package (*see* Chapter 1). In addition to this direct effect, the facilities also have indirect effects on other elements of the service package such as convenience (in particular, accessibility) or functionality.

Product, promotion and place constitute three of the four Ps (the fourth being 'price') in the traditional marketing mix. Obviously facilities management will have a direct impact on the 'place' element. Facilities also have an impact on both the product and, as can be inferred from the quote 'space speaks', on the communication or promotion elements of the mix. It is no wonder that marketers have not only discovered the importance of facilities management but recently have added some interesting dimensions that help to take the customer experience into account.

The intangibility of services also makes facilities management in this context different to that experienced in an industrial context. Many services are high in experience and credence attributes. They have fewer intrinsic features upon which to base an evaluation of quality. Therefore, the building, decor, employees' attire, background music, physical surroundings and locations are all used by the customer to infer quality.

The conclusion is very clear. In services, the customer and his experience must be integrated into the management of facilities. Of course, this generally makes those decisions more complicated. Too much attention to operational priorities frequently runs counter to achieving customer satisfaction (and vice versa). As Lovelock[9] noted, the goals of operations in facilities management include:

- controlling costs;
- improving efficiency by ensuring proximity of operationally related tasks in layout decisions;
- achieving economies of scale or logistics efficiency in location decisions; and
- enhancing safety, security and standardization in work design decisions.

However, quite often this results in a customer:

- becoming confused;
- being shunted around unnecessarily;
- finding the facilities unattractive and inconvenient; and
- finding employees unresponsive to individual customer needs.

This was exactly the situation Jan Carlzon discovered on his appointment as president of SAS. In his book, *Moments of Truth*,[10] he describes many facilities management decisions, such as the layout of the Copenhagen air terminal and choice of aeroplane type, which were the result of an internally and operationally oriented culture at SAS. The cultural change that he had to effect was best expressed by his well-known slogan, 'We fly people, not airplanes'.

Back office versus front office

Not all service activities should be performed in the presence of the customer. Given that the customer brings an additional element of complexity to the facilities management decisions, it is useful to make a distinction between the 'back office' and the 'front office':

- The *back office* consists of the activities that can be physically and/or temporally separated from the customer.

● The *front office* consists of the activities that have to be, or which an organization wants to be, performed while the customer is present.

Facilities management decisions regarding back-office operations can differ greatly from those for front-office operations, as illustrated in Table 7.1. We can conclude from this table that designing the back office is 'easier', at least from an operations management point of view. One of the major reasons for this is that customer objectives do not have to be directly taken into account in making facilities management decisions regarding back-office activities:

● Location can be decided based on the availability of skilled or cheap (human) resources.

● Economies of scale can be achieved by centralizing activities; this makes computerization viable since the transaction volume necessary for making such an investment can be more easily reached.

● The labour force does not have to possess the social and communication skills necessary to interact with the customer.

● The company does not have to deal with demand fluctuations to the same extent – that is, production can be more level.

● The often considerable additional investments needed to make the 'factory' appealing to the customer are unnecessary.

Generally speaking, the operations manager has more freedom when the customer does not have to be taken into account and, thus, does not have to sacrifice customer satisfaction in the name of operational efficiency and employee satisfaction (or vice versa).

Furthermore, in the back office a major source of uncertainty – the customer contact – is eliminated from most of the activities. In other words, the 'technical core' can be isolated from environmental fluctuations. Therefore, traditional efficiency can be aimed for in the back office, which supports a *strategy of cost leadership*.

The benefit of the front office, however, is that it quite often supports one form or another of a *differentiation strategy*. It is in the front office that the service can be adapted to particular customer needs. The front-office personnel interact with customers and, by doing so, can make a difference to customer satisfaction. It is also in the front office that the physical setting can be used to influence customer expectations, as we will see later in this chapter. The customer's behaviour can also be influenced more effectively from here. A final point is that the customer's perception of quality can be affected not only before but, more importantly, during and after the actual process.

Table 7.1 Major design considerations for back office and front office

	Back office	Front office
Location	Operations may be placed near the supply of skilled or cheap resources and facilities	Operations must be near the customer
Process design	Focus on efficiency through economies of scale Support of a smooth service delivery process	Focus on the needs and wants of the customer Use the customer as co-producer
Design of the physical setting	Make the factory appealing to the employees	Make the factory appealing to the customer and the employees
Operations strategy	Low-cost strategy	Differentiation strategy

The design decision to structure the front-office and back-office work between back office and front office is, according to the previous findings, mainly based on how much customer contact is required in a particular service delivery process and on which activities are carried out with customer contact and which without.[11] In this view, designing the back-office and front-office structure requires decoupling high-contact activities from low-contact activities, placing them under separate supervision and assigning the low-contact activities to one group of employees and the high-contact activities to another.[12] In more recent studies, it is argued that there are more complex ways to design front office and back office than the decoupling recommended in the customer contact approach. Based on a study of five different banks from a co-operative banking group in the Netherlands,[13] it has been concluded that identifying three separate design decisions provides a better insight into their back-office/front-office structuring:[14]

- The decision on where customer contact occurs in the service delivery process;
- The decision on which activities are decoupled from each other;
- The decision on how employees are grouped together.

Figure 7.1 shows how the five different banks designed their back-office and front-office work using these three design decisions in providing business loans.[15] This figure demonstrates that the customer contact decisions in the process of providing business loans did not differ among the five banks. However, there was some considerable variation in the decoupling decisions of the five banks. Banks A, B and E designed a decoupled process to free sales capacity, matching worker skills and tasks, benefiting from specialization effects and establishing separation of duties. Banks C and D chose a coupled process. The former,

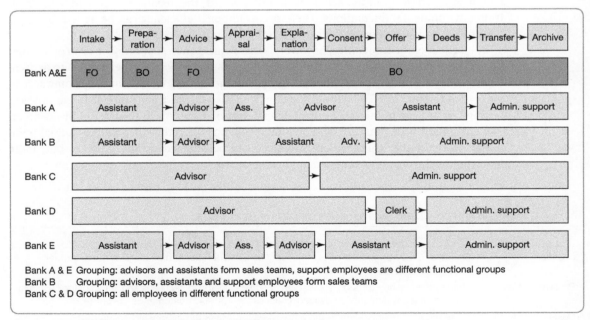

Bank A & E Grouping: advisors and assistants form sales teams, support employees are different functional groups
Bank B Grouping: advisors, assistants and support employees form sales teams
Bank C & D Grouping: all employees in different functional groups

Figure 7.1 The design decisions for providing business loans

Source: Zomderdijk, L. G. and Vries, J. de (2007) 'Structuring front office and back-office work in service delivery systems', *International Journal of Operations and Production Management*, Vol 27, No 1, p. 119.

to avoid handovers of work between consecutive employees and to increase efficiency; the latter, to contribute to the quality of the services delivered since, in a coupled process, the bank advisors possess all relevant customer knowledge and deal with all customer-related matters. With regard to the grouping decisions, Banks A, B and E chose a market grouping through the establishment of sales teams to improve co-ordination, while Banks C and D chose functional grouping of employees to facilitate cross-fertilization among business advisors, continuity of service delivery, and scale economies in the utilization of support employees.

This example illustrates that the same service delivery process (in this case, the provision of business loans) can be configured in different ways, depending on the strategic priorities and the service concept these banks put forward. This case example demonstrates that designing front-office and back-office work is a much more complex decision; this is certainly true in complex service systems that are faced with different types of customer through different channels using different technologies.

Location

Exhibit 7.1 Determining the site of EuroDisney[16]

In the 1980s, the Walt Disney Corporation's top management was confronted with the decision whether or not to open a new theme park in Europe. Besides its world-famous theme park in California, it had already opened theme parks in Florida and Japan, both of which had proved to be successful. Although an estimated 2 million Europeans visited the US sites each year, Disney felt that the European market had much more potential. The population of Europe exceeded that of the US by 150 million people, in roughly half of the land mass. However, the distance between the two continents was seen as the major obstacle. If Disney wanted to access this huge market, then Disney would have to come to Europe.

Once the decision was made to pursue the European market, a second and equally important decision had to be made. Like the US, Europe is a huge territory, with many possible sites to be considered. Where would EuroDisney be built?

What kind of parameters would Disney's management take into account in this decision? Some factors would have remained the same even if this decision was concerned with where to locate a manufacturing plant: for example, the quality of the transport infrastructure, the degree of government support or the available space for such a large compound. However, since this decision involved a service, one very important new parameter came into play: the customer. Since the customer would be travelling to EuroDisney, a central location would be advantageous. Locating EuroDisney in a far corner of Europe, such as the south of Greece or the north of Finland, would mean a far greater travel distance for most of its customers. Undoubtedly, analyses were made and models used to roughly estimate the optimal location, taking into account the geographical distribution of the potential visitors.

The weather was clearly another important factor in determining the location. Since walking around Disneyland would be much more pleasant in a warm and sunny climate, many countries were dropped from the list of possibilities, such as those located in Scandinavia or Central Europe. Ultimately, the choice came down to two sites – one in Spain and one in France. Although Spain had the advantage of better weather, the French site was eventually chosen due to its proximity to a mass market of customers, better transport infrastructure and government inducements.

'There are three important things in retailing: location, location, and location', stated Lord Seif, the chief executive of the UK-based retail company, Marks & Spencer. This quotation highlights the importance of one major element of facilities management for service organizations.

Exhibit 7.1 illustrates how locating a service facility differs from locating a manufacturing firm: the customer has to be taken explicitly into account. In services, the customer and service provider have to be brought together in a service environment. A large goods-producing facility can be set up in one country and the goods exported to another country, but this is not possible for services. Services are intangible and can neither be stored nor transported. As a result, either the consumer has to go to the service provider (for example, in going to a restaurant) or the service provider has to go to the customer (as in home pizza delivery).

A different location for the same service may lead to a totally different service experience, such as the difference between a Disneyland theme park in a warm climate *versus* a theme park in a cold and rainy one. This highlights the fact that the surroundings and the atmosphere in which the service takes place are an integral part of the service itself, as will be discussed further in this chapter.

We will now explore the question of how a service company decides where to locate its service facility.

Factors influencing the location decision

The location problem can be dealt with on several levels. A location for a service facility might have to be found on another continent, country, state, city, block or street. Depending on the size of the area under consideration, the importance attached to factors that determine the final choice of location will change. Remember the factors that Disney's management considered in deciding where to locate a new theme park in Europe. How different will they be for McDonald's when it considers where in Paris it should open a new drive-through restaurant? Disney's management was considering such factors as the availability of an adequate labour force and transport infrastructure, the climate and the degree of government support, but McDonald's local management will be thinking of quite different things. Factors such as traffic density, location of the competition, legal considerations including zoning and building regulations, available space and easy access will be of greater importance.

The next step is the domain of *micro-scale location*, dealing with the precise position within the chosen city centre, regional shopping centre, inner city arterial, secondary shopping district or retail warehouse park.[17] At this level of detail, factors such as the presence of magnet or attractor stores, the effect of exit and entry points on consumer circulation patterns, and the maximal walking distance between stores play a role. This micro-level leads us beyond the scope of this book, so we will limit our discussion to the higher levels.

A large-scale survey in 1994 among 926 service firms in five mid-western US states, representing almost 100,000 employees, investigated which factors could influence the location decision, first when choosing a general area and then, more specifically, when choosing the particular site (*see* Table 7.2).[18]

The most important factors influencing the location decision at a more general level were the availability of good infrastructure (for example, available roads and communication), ability to attract labour and proximity to customers. However, several differences emerge in

Table 7.2 Factors influencing the location decision

General area			Particular site		
Factors (in order of importance)	*Services for which higher than average influence*	*Services for which lower than average influence*	*Factors (in order of importance)*	*Services for which higher than average influence*	*Services for which lower than average influence*
Good infrastructure	Transportation – warehousing, Wholesaling	Education – social	Adequate parking	Restaurant – retailing	Construction Wholesaling
Proximity to consumers and buyers	Auto sales-service Banking Hospitals Retailing Wholesaling	Education – social Professional service Utilities	Attractive building	Banking Insurance – real estate	Construction Utilities
Ability to attract good labour	Hospitals Personal-business services	Retailing Utilities	Attractive rent cost	Retailing	Banking Construction Hospitals Hotels Utilities
Attractive place to live	Personal-business services		Specialized space needs met here	Transportation – warehousing	Retailing
Low rents, building costs		Banking Hospitals Utilities	Easy commute for employees	Professional service	Auto sales-service Education – social Hotels
Favourable taxes	Auto sales-service	Banking Education – social Hospitals Personal-business services	High customer traffic in area	Auto sales-service Banking Hotels Restaurants Retailing	Construction Professional service Utilities Wholesaling
Favourable governmental policies	Transportation – warehousing	Personal-business services	Easy commute for managers and owners	Professional service	Auto sales-service Education – social Hospitals
Proximity to suppliers and services	Transportation – warehousing	Retailing	Favourable governmental policies (zoning, traffic, etc.)	Restaurants – wholesaling	Professional service
Labour costs	Transportation – warehousing, wholesaling	Amusement Personal-business services Utilities	Favourable taxes at site	Auto sales-service wholesaling	Hospitals Professional service Utilities
Labour 'climate'	Personal-business services Restaurants Wholesaling	Amusement Utilities	Proximity to suppliers and services		
Proximity to competitors	Auto sales-service Banking	Amusement Education – social Personal-business services Utilities	Proximity to competitors	Auto sales-service Banking	Amusement Education – social Personal-business services Utilities
Being near other company facilities		Hospitals Personal-business services	Being in fully developed site	Wholesaling	Construction Insurance – real estate Restaurant Utilities

Source: Adapted from Schmenner, R. W. (1994) 'Service firm location decisions: Some midwestern evidence', *International Journal of Service Industry Management*, Vol 5, No 3, pp. 49 and 52.

the importance of these factors depending on the type of industry. Sectors such as hospitals, education and social and personal services attach in general relatively less importance to the location factors than sectors such as transportation, warehousing and wholesaling, indicating that they are relatively immune to many of the general area factors. For instance, since customers are generally less willing to travel greater distances for more common services, it is clear that services such as food retailers or banks attach more importance to being located close to their customers than professional or educational services.

At the level of choosing a particular site, more specific and practical factors come into play. Adequate parking emerged as the most important factor, followed by three factors related to the building and its costs. Again, the more retail-oriented services such as stores, banks and restaurants attach more importance to these location factors, while hospitals and utilities assigned less weight to them.

Clearly the nature of the service has a key influence on the relative importance of factors determining the location choice. A service company, providing a maintenance-interactive type of service that relies on customers passing by, cannot afford to pay too much attention to labour factors or the degree of government support in its location decision. Since convenience and comfort are keywords, such a company often has no choice but to locate itself where the customers are. However, services such as most professional services do not need to be located right beside the customer and have more freedom in their choice of location.

A company has to ask the question 'What is the value of the service to the customer?' and, more importantly, 'What is the extra value of that service compared to the competition?' It would be unreasonable to expect a customer to drive an hour to reach a certain fast-food restaurant when another chain is just 5 minutes away, no matter how good the cheese-burger tastes. However, that same customer might be willing to drive for an hour to a distinctive three-star restaurant. Thus, the freedom of locating a facility will be influenced by the perceived value of the service.

As already mentioned, however, advances in IT also play a role. IT can sometimes create a substitution for transportation, which means that the customer and service provider need not always have physical contact. These advances do not have the same impact on all service sectors. The impact will be greater for the more maintenance-interactive type of services, such as banks with their ATMs and internet banking, or the retail sector and its home shopping network, than for the task- or personal-interactive services, such as architects and physiotherapists. When looking at the bank sector, for example, Table 7.3 shows that customers are willing to travel a longer distance (in time) for specialized transactions than for standard transactions. As internet banking has become the standard channel for the delivery of standard transactions, it is quite clear that internet banking has a big impact on

Table 7.3 The distribution of customers based on their willingness to travel to a bank branch for standard and specialized transactions[20]

Travel time (minutes)	Standard transactions	Specialized transactions
0–5	100%*	100%
5–10	72.4%	90.4%
10–15	25.4%	66.0%
15–20	5.6%	33.9%
20–25	2.8%	17.2%
>25	0.9%	6.2%

* = % of customers still willing to come to the bank branch.

the location decision of bank branches. It is no longer required to have 'a bank branch on every street corner' because customers are willing to travel longer distances for the more specialized transactions (with a higher added value). This is one of the reasons why many small local bank branches have disappeared during the previous years.[19]

Location models

A number of models, with a varying degree of complexity, have been developed to aid companies in decisions regarding the optimal location. It is outside the scope of this book to discuss these models in detail. We introduce the general ideas behind these models and then give one example in Exhibit 7.2.[21]

Location models can basically help companies in answering two simple questions: 'How many sites should I build?' and 'Where should I build them?'

How many sites?

Since a service facility can cover only a certain geographical area, a service provider wants to reach the maximum number of customers with a minimal number of service facilities. Just what this number should be is difficult to determine. It depends on such things as the type of service offered to the customer, the infrastructure required to deliver that service and the strategy of the service firm.

In order to find the optimal number of sites, a balance must be struck between the number and cost of facilities, on the one hand, and the transportation costs of bringing service provider and consumer together, on the other (*see* Figure 7.2). Transportation costs decline when the number of sites increases, since the distance between the provider and consumer of the service decreases. Furthermore, revenues will probably rise since a company can expect customers to visit the facility more frequently when the distance is shorter. On the other hand, the cost of building and operating facilities increases with the number of facilities.

We have already seen that there is a correlation between the value of a service to the customer and the efforts that customer is willing to make to purchase that service. Hence, a

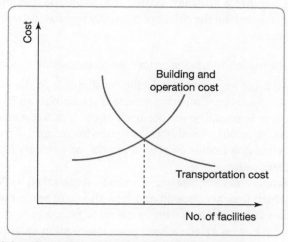

Figure 7.2 Determining the optimal number of service facilities

company cannot expect to serve a whole metropolitan area with just one fast-food outlet, while one Rolls-Royce garage might suffice.

A single-site service facility location problem can easily be solved mathematically in most cases. The problem becomes much more complicated when models for locating multiple sites are involved. The process of data collection itself is also more difficult, since the visiting patterns become more complex.

Where?

Proximity to customers was obviously one of the prime determinants of location in the survey in Table 7.2. Many models are based on this principle. They define the best location of a service facility as one that minimizes the distances between the customers and the facility. Other models – the so-called 'gravity models' – are more profit-oriented; they examine the sites with the highest potential for attracting customers. Before we can use any of these models, however, we will first look at two questions that arise:[22]

- How should we optimize our model? Should we use a minimization of distance, a maximization of profits or some other criterion?
- How should the geographical demand for the service be estimated (or where can an estimate be obtained)?

1 *Optimization criteria*

Two criteria immediately come to mind. One is *minimal transport distance or time* – for instance, in the case of a courier-service company building a new distribution centre for package handling. The other is *maximal profit* – for instance, in the case of a retail outlet trying to find an area with the highest market potential.

More social considerations can also be used, especially in the public sector. For example, a public hospital might aim to have all patients able to arrive at the hospital within 30 minutes, or a fire department might wish to locate fire alarm boxes in such a way that the distance any person must travel to the closest fire alarm box is minimized.

The choice of criteria is an important decision, since different criteria may point to different optimal locations. For instance, using only the minimum total travel distance criterion might point to a centrally located site, while the maximum reach of customers approach might recommend the choice of a densely populated area, not necessarily closest to all of its customers.

2 *Determination of geographical demand for the service*

As stated before, locating a facility so that it is in the vicinity of the target population is important in almost all service sectors. The ability to estimate the potential of customers in an area is crucial to the accuracy of the location analysis, and also to the service firm's success. It would probably be very unwise to open a trendy new discotheque in a rural area populated mainly by retired people, or to locate a motel alongside a road with little overnight traffic.

Thorough market research should be undertaken to determine who the customers are, and where they are located and how they will reach the facility. Locating the customers involves several options. One of the most extensive sources of customer information is, of course, the census data, which gives information on variables such as age, marital status and number of children for a whole country. Other possible sources include magazines and journals that release annual surveys on the buying power of the population or computerized databases available from private firms.[23]

A central location close to the customer was an important parameter in Disney's location decision. Disney had estimated that 17 million people lived within 2 hours of the Paris site by car; 109 million lived within 6 hours of the site by car; and 310 million could reach the site by plane in less than 2 hours. On top of that, the opening of the Eurotunnel in 1994 made EuroDisney accessible from the UK in 4 hours by car.[24] The fact that it was accessible to such an enormous market was one of the primary reasons why Disney decided to locate its theme park near Paris.

Several facility location techniques and models exist. The appropriate one to use will depend on the nature of the facility location problem. Exhibit 7.2 gives one example of a location model. While this model has the advantage that the location decision takes multiple factors into account, it is clear that it is rather general and simplistic and that other models are required to make a more complex location decision.[25]

Exhibit 7.2 A simple qualitative model to locate a restaurant[26]

Consider the example of a restaurant manager having to choose between four possible sites for a new restaurant (see Table 7.4). The manager has drawn up a list of factors that are important to his decision, such as the view from the terrace, the available parking space and the proximity to the customer. He attaches weights to these factors to depict relative differences in importance. Each site under consideration is then scored on these factors (see Table 7.4) and, finally, a weighted average score for each site is calculated. For instance, Site A gets a score of:

$$\frac{(5 \times 7) + (10 \times 7) + (15 \times 9) + (20 \times 9) + (30 \times 8) + (20 \times 7)}{(5 + 10 + 15 + 20 + 30 + 20)} = 8$$

In this case, Site A is clearly the best potential site of the four.

Table 7.4 Choosing a restaurant site

Factor	Weight	Site A	Site B	Site C	Site D
Visibility from the street	5	7	8	8	6
Available parking space	10	7	9	8	4
Closeness to suppliers	15	9	6	7	8
Accessibility by car	20	9	5	6	8
View from the terrace	30	8	7	5	8
Closeness to customer	20	7	6	7	8
Average score		8	6.5	6.35	7.5

Designing the servicescape

The 'service factory' environment has a strong impact on the customer's perception of the service experience. Before even entering the service facility, consumers commonly look for clues about the firm's capabilities and quality. Observe your own behaviour on your next trip to an unfamiliar city when you are looking for a place to eat. Since services are so intangible, the physical environment outside and inside is very influential in communicating an image and in shaping your expectations. As we mentioned earlier, the physical environment contains many mechanic clues from which customers can form an idea about the quality of the service.

Moreover, the 'environment' in which the service is delivered becomes part of the service (i.e. the product). While the customer is in the servicescape, the service provider is addressing not only his or her 'substantive' need but also the entire person with all his or her needs and senses. A certain meal, for instance, will be perceived entirely differently when served on the sunny, quiet terrace of a family-owned and -operated restaurant in Provence, from when the same meal is served in the restaurant of a busy international hotel in Paris. The passenger flying from London to New York in business class receives exactly the same 'core service' element as the tourist class passenger – that is, transportation from London to New York in a certain amount of time – but the business class passenger is willing to pay two or three times more, mainly due to the difference in 'servicescape'.

For these reasons it is clear that the physical setting influences the customer's 'ultimate satisfaction' with the service. When designing this environment, therefore, a company should explicitly take the customer into consideration. The environment should support the needs and preferences of the customer. Bitner[27] was one of the first marketing specialists to discover the importance of the physical setting and its interaction with the customer. She developed a model that enables us to see how the environment is perceived by the customer and how it affects his or her behaviour, degree of satisfaction, and in turn loyalty – that is, return behaviour. Figure 7.3 illustrates this conceptual model.

Figure 7.3 A framework for understanding environment-user relationships in service organizations

Source: Bitner, M. J. (1992) 'Servicescapes: The impact of physical surroundings on customers and employees', *Journal of Marketing*, Vol 56, April, pp. 57–71.

In this model, recognition is not only given to the customer but also to the employee. The response of the employee is important because, as indicated earlier, employee satisfaction is important for the success of a service. In addition, the physical setting will directly affect the nature and quality of the interaction between the customer and the service provider, which, as was mentioned, is an important element of the service 'bundle'. As the sociologists Bennett and Bennett[28] stated:

'all social interaction is affected by the physical container in which it occurs.'

Ideally, the physical environment should support the needs and preferences of not only the customers but also the needs and preferences of the employees. We will focus here, however, on the customer side.

Elements of the servicescape

Bitner defines the servicescape as:

'all objective physical factors that can be controlled by the firm to enhance (or constrain) employees' and customers' activities'.

Based on a comprehensive review of the servicescape research, Ezeh and Harris operationalize this definition as: 'the design of the physical environment (with or without customer input) housing the service encounter, which elicits internal reactions from customers leading to the display of approach or avoidance behaviours'.[29]

The customer perceives the servicescape holistically. While distinct stimuli are perceived, it is the total configuration of stimuli that determines responses. When enjoying the dinner in the restaurant in Provence, we will probably notice the various individual elements such as the sunset, the lavender fragrance, the quiet landscape and the temperature, but we will also have an overall perception. The wine experiment described in our introductory case study is an excellent illustration of this point. However, when designing the servicescape we have to take a more analytical point of view. The model in Figure 7.3 suggests three (composite) dimensions: (1) the ambient conditions, (2) what we call spatial layout and process and (3) signs, symbols and artefacts:

- *Ambient conditions* refer to largely background characteristics such as noise, temperature, scent, lighting, aesthetics and colour – in short, all the elements of our environment that affect our five senses. The background music in shopping malls or the clatter of dishes if we are sitting too close to the kitchen in a restaurant, the aroma of freshly baked croissants in a French bakery or the polluted river we smell from the café terrace in an old city on a hot day, the coolness of the air in the hotel lobby of an international hotel in Barcelona in the summer, or the cold when we are walking around in Disneyland Paris in the winter are all examples of positive or negative ambient conditions.

- *Spatial layout and process* includes the elements of the environment that are closely related to the core element of the service. It includes items such as machinery, equipment and furniture that are necessary to deliver the service. This dimension refers to the way they are arranged and the physical and psychological (indirect) effects they have on the customer. A lift that is out of order, tables placed too close together in a Parisian bistro, the uncomfortable chairs in a waiting room, and obviously disorganized and inefficient routines are all examples of processes that can have a negative impact on the customer.

This is the traditional domain of operations management, but it is important to note that these elements not only affect the efficiency of the process and the quality of the output, but also have a direct impact on the customer.

- *Signs, symbols and artefacts* are the many items in the physical environment that serve as explicit or implicit communications to its users about the place. Signs such as labels on doors or instructions on how to proceed are used for directional purposes (e.g. to show the way to the toilets), or to communicate rules of behaviour (e.g. to reserve parking spaces for disabled persons). Signs, of course, also communicate indirectly to customers such things as the firm's degree of professionalism or its respect for the customer.

  Other elements in the environment – such as the look and feel of the furniture in the reception area of the hotel, the decoration in the bank manager's office, the floor covering in the consultant's office, the tablecloths in the restaurant, the plastic utensils in the fast-food restaurant, and diplomas on the wall of the lawyer's office – communicate less directly but are no less effective in communicating the value of the service, norms and expectations for behaviour or the trustworthiness of the service provider.

The servicescape model as described by Bitner does not include the people component as an element in the servicescape framework. According to this vision, the servicescape influences the human behaviour. Some authors believe that the people in an environment determine the kind of environment they are in.[30] The number, appearance and behaviour of service personnel can have an important impact on the perceived servicescape.[31] Physicians in the Mayo Clinic, for instance, wear business attire at work. 'The wearing of business attire rather than white coats is recognized by our patients as a unique dress code that projects an aura of expertise and respect for the patient accompanied by warmth and friendliness.'[32] Just as airline passengers have no desire to see their pilot in a golf shirt, neither do ill patients want to see their doctor similarly dressed.

The number, appearance and behaviour of other customers in the environment can also be considered part of the servicescape. How other customers are dressed and behave can reflect their social status, which is then reflected on to the service context where these customers are present.

How does a customer respond?

As indicated in Figure 7.3 the customers' (and similarly the employees') response to the environmental stimuli can be found to consist of a *cognitive* response, an *emotional* response and a *physiological* response.

A cognitive response

This refers to the effect the environment has on the customers' understanding, beliefs and convictions. Stimuli have to be seen as a form of non-verbal communication. The floor coverings, the dress of the receptionist or clerk and the language used on the telephone 'tell' the customer something about the firm and the expected outcome. These stimuli influence the customer's perception of, for instance, how successful or cosmopolitan the company is. For example, Bitner found that a travel agent's office decor affected customer perception of the travel agent's behaviour. The fact that stimuli from the servicescape help customers to mentally categorize the service firm is also indicative of a cognitive response. People always try to label objects or other people. Elements of the servicescape help customers to classify and 'recognize' the firm and the expected quality. For most people in Belgium, the aroma of freshly baked pastry or bread is an unmistakable sign of what is called a 'warm baker' – that is, a baker who bakes the bread himself. A bit of dirt on the vegetables helps people to perceive them as fresh. A waiter in fancy dress helps us to classify the restaurant as 'chic' and elegant.

An emotional response

This is perhaps less rational but no less effective in influencing a customer's behaviour. It appears that as far as emotional responses are concerned, environments can be character-ized by two qualities.[33] The first is the extent to which the environment is perceived as being *'pleasant or unpleasant'*. Obviously, people want to spend more time in pleasant environ-ments and want to leave unpleasant ones as soon as possible, or avoid them entirely. The second quality is *the degree of arousal* – that is, the amount of excitement the environment generates. Research indicates that arousing environments are viewed positively unless the excitement is combined with unpleasantness. This means that unpleasant environments that are also high in arousal are particularly avoided. The key here seems to be the extent to which customers perceive themselves as having personal control. People like crowded marketplaces as long as they do not feel they 'have to go' there. Particular to understanding customers' emotional responses to an environment is that environment's complexity and coherence. According to Bitner, *complexity* (visual richness, ornamentation, information rate) has been found consistently to increase emotional arousal, whereas *coherence* (order, clarity, unity) has been found to enhance positive evaluation.

A physiological response

The servicescape also affects customers in concrete physiological ways. People will stay in a restaurant longer if the seats are comfortable. Noise might cause physical discomfort in a hotel. The temperature and humidity in a classroom will have an impact on the students and their behaviour. Putting pure comfort or discomfort aside, physiological responses also influence unrelated beliefs and feelings. When the temperature is too hot or humid, for example, customers are more aware of feeling crowded. Feelings of discomfort will be transferred to the rest of the service system. For instance, it is difficult to enjoy a meal or show when there is an unpleasant odour.

As indicated in Figure 7.3, these responses are not automatically or deterministically related to the stimuli. The mood of the individual customer when he or she enters the service-scape, the perceived degree of control, and the plan or purpose for being in the environment are all situational factors that may affect the response. Personality characteristics, such as arousal-seeking versus arousal-avoiding behaviour, and certain cultural factors will influence, for instance, how people respond to noise, odours,[34] temperature and other stimuli.

Social interactions

The responses that have been described so far are individual responses of customers. However, the servicescape might also have an impact on the social interaction among the customers and between the customers and the employees. This is obvious in the case of space and layout. When social interaction between customers is an important aspect of the service concept, the physical setting should encourage interactions and discourage people's natural tendency to isolate themselves from 'strangers'. A U-shaped setting in the classroom stimulates interaction between participants and also makes it clear from the very beginning that people should be active and interactive. A high window in a bank protected with bullet-proof glass makes it very clear that long conversations are not wanted.

However, the other elements of the environment, such as the ambient conditions or signs, may have a similar effect. A yellow line in the front section of a bus makes it very clear that interaction between the driver and the passenger should be strictly limited to functional conversation. The noise and lighting in discos does not invite people to have long conversations. Establishing office hours as a university professor might improve the professor's efficiency but will certainly also give the message to students that conversation should be short and kept strictly to business.

Servicescape and business results

As we have already noted, the servicescape will affect not only the customer's initial purchase behaviour but also the perception of the final quality of the experience, and thus the degree of customer satisfaction (*see* Exhibit 7.3). Given the relationship between customer satisfaction (and employee satisfaction) and profit established in the service profit chain, the link between servicescape and business results seems obvious. However, more direct evidence is available about the relationship between the servicescape and business results. Individuals generally react to physical settings with one of two opposing behaviours: approach or avoidance. *Approach behaviours*, according to Mehrabian and Russell,[35] 'include all positive behaviours that might be directed at a particular place, such as desire to stay, explore, work and affiliate'. *Avoidance behaviours* reflect the opposite – in other words, a desire not to stay, explore, work or affiliate.

Such behaviours and their impact have been studied in detail in retail stores where a clear relationship was found between the perception of the environment and approach/ avoidance behaviour as evidenced by shopping enjoyment, returning, spending money, time spent browsing, and exploration of the store – all factors that have a positive effect on business results. Approach/avoidance behaviours have two subcomponents: attracting or deterring entry by the customer, on the one hand, and influencing the degree of success of the customer in experiencing plans once inside.

The servicescape will not only affect the customer's behaviour and satisfaction but also those of the employee. One study shows that the convenience, safety, and pleasantness of the servicescape significantly affected the job stress and satisfaction of nurses in a hospital.[36] Safety, for instance, had nearly identical effects on job satisfaction as teamwork. HRM in service firms should take the servicescape into account in addition to the more common variables such as teamwork and supervisor support. Hence, the design of service facilities cannot simply be delegated to architects, designers, and facility planners. It is a central marketing and human resources issue.[37]

In more recent years, the impact of the servicescape on employees and customers has been studied in different environments. Exhibit 7.3 shows the application of the service-scape in a leisure service setting, more specifically casinos.

Other studies look at the 'online servicescape' or 'e-servicescape'. A cross-sectional survey of online shoppers suggests that the 'e-servicescape' is composed of three dimensions: aesthetic appeal (e.g. Is the website visually appealing?), the layout and functionality (e.g. Is it easy to use and is the information relevant?) and financial security (e.g. Are there efficient payment procedures?).[38] It is interesting to observe that, in this online environment, these servicescape dimensions have a real impact on the purchase intentions of online shoppers.[39]

Exhibit 7.3 The impact of casino servicescape on gaming customers[40]

Following the trend in Las Vegas, mega casino resorts with exotic themes have been built in Macau and Singapore. Wynn Macau, MGM Grand Paradise Macau and the Venetian Macau are all examples of casinos built in Macau with a capital expenditure of more than $1 billion. As with the casinos in Las Vegas, the designers gave considerable attention to the physical appearance, outside as well as inside the building. But do these investments pay-off? In other words, are gaming customers more satisfied, do they stay longer, and have they a stronger inclination to return?

As in other services sectors, the servicescape in casinos is made up of different dimensions. A positive ambience can make gamblers feel better in a service area. Many environmental conditions contribute to this ambience such as the temperature, the air quality – but so do the visual and auditory features of slot machines. Gaming customers often feel excited when it is crowded. Crowding affects how gamblers navigate through the servicescape to find their favourite games. This is why a somewhat crowded environment may create a sense of excitement among gamblers. It also gives them a sense of perceived control in the casino. Gamblers seem to believe that greater control will lead to an improved chance of winning. Another dimension of the servicescape is seating comfort. Seating comfort is particularly important for gaming customers who need to sit for long hours in order to enjoy the entertainment. Finally high-quality decor and clean surroundings may reduce the poor social image of casinos, which give gamblers a more pleasurable feeling inside the casino complex.

Based on a survey of 513 customers at one of the Macau casinos,[41] it was found that the five servicescape dimensions (ambient conditions, navigation, seating comfort, interior decor and cleanliness) did have an impact on customer satisfaction and on the intention to revisit, but this did not necessarily translate into a desire to stay longer in the casino. In other words, the huge investment in a casino's physical environment did appear to benefit the casino operator.

From facilities management to service experience design

In the previous paragraphs, we introduced many different aspects (such as back office/front office, location, servicescape) that, traditionally, are studied in the field of facilities management. The importance of facilities management is underestimated in most service organizations. It is frequently dealt with on a too superficial level or in a too technical manner that ignores the customer. In some sectors, such as retailing, the location decision is given some top management attention but, in others, even this decision is not handled properly, let alone other facilities management decisions.

The real challenge in designing services is not to identify the servicescape dimensions or to develop a service blueprint but to bring everything together in one holistic approach, as is clear from the story of the Mayo Clinic in Exhibit 7.4. *'Clearly identify a simple, consistent message, and then manage the evidence – the buildings, the approach to care, even the shoelaces*

– to support that message, day in and day out.[42] No single department or function can make this work. Service experience design requires an interdisciplinary approach. Therefore, marketing, operations and HRM specialists, architects, organizational behaviour experts and others should be included.

Exhibit 7.4 Clueing in customers at the Mayo Clinic[43]

During a 6-month stay as observers, two service marketing professors set out to understand why the Mayo Clinic has been an excellent care and service organization since its establishment more than 100 years ago. They found the clinic continuously sent out clues about the kind of service provider it aimed to be: functional clues, mechanic clues and humanic clues.

Functional clues are about the 'what' of the service experience, revealing the reliability and the competence of the service. In the US News America's Best Hospitals lists, the Mayo Clinic Rochester is mentioned every year as one of the few hospitals big in multiple specialities. Sixteen per cent of 1000 respondents in a survey sent to US households indicated that they would choose (for themselves or a family member) to attend the Mayo Clinic for treatment of a serious medical problem, such as cancer, heart surgery, or neurosurgery, if their insurance cover or financial resources permitted them. This is almost two-and-a-half-times greater than the second-ranked academic institution.[44]

Mechanic clues come from actual objects or environments and include sights, smells, sounds, tastes and textures. From public spaces to exam rooms to laboratories, Mayo facilities have been designed explicitly to relieve stress, offer a place of refuge, create positive distractions, convey caring and respect, symbolize competence, minimize the impression of crowding, facilitate way finding, and accommodate families.[45]

Humanic clues emerge from the behaviour and appearance of service providers (choice of words, tone of voice, body language, appropriate dress . . .). Mayo explicitly and systematically employs people who genuinely embrace the organization's values. Employed people are trained in the 'patient first' mentality. Once employed, doctors and nurses go through an orientation process designed to reinforce a patient-first mentality. Patients are served by teams of different professionals, co-ordinating resources to provide the best possible care.

Functional, mechanic and humanic clues cannot be incorporated into the service system if the Mayo Clinic is unclear about the story it wishes to communicate to customers or potential customers. 'The question for managers is whether the clues tell the intended story' – i.e. the story of the service concept. The next challenge is to make the story happen every day, every hour, every minute so that the experience of the patient tells him that he comes first. From the way it hires and trains employees, to the way it designs its facilities, to the way it approaches care, Mayo offers patients and their families concrete and convincing evidence of its strengths and values. This is the only way for the Mayo Clinic to clue in its customers and really turn the clinic into a living, breathing advertisement for itself.

Conclusion

The importance of facilities management is underestimated in most service organizations. It is frequently dealt with at a too superficial level or in a too technical manner which ignores the customer. Facilities management decisions such as back-office and front-office design, and the servicescape can be considered as mechanical clues which create the more tangible elements of the service experience.

Hopefully, this chapter has made two messages clear. The various facilities management decisions are strategic decisions, since they have an impact on the business – that is, the type of service offered to the customers and the type of customers it attracts. As illustrated in the example of the Mayo Clinic (Exhibit 7.4) a company should have a clear understanding of the desired service concept and the target market it wants to serve. These decisions also have an impact on such competitive strategic variables as the perceived quality and cost-effectiveness of the service.

The second message we hope to have conveyed is that no single department or function should make these decisions alone. Facilities management requires an interdisciplinary approach. Therefore, marketing and operations specialists, architects, organizational behaviour experts and others should be included in these decisions.

Review and discussion questions

- Select a specific service process in a firm and describe the extent of customer contact, the amount of coupling of activities and how the employees are grouped in performing these activities.

- What are the most common elements used in determining a specific location of a service firm? What are the decision variables in the location models for service firms?

- Select a service setting (such as casinos in Exhibit 7.3) and describe the different dimensions of the servicescape in this setting.

- Look for companies (other than the Mayo Clinic) that are successful in linking the service concept, and the design of the service system and service encounter. How do they clue in their customers?

Suggested further reading

Berry L. L. and K. D. Seltman (2008) *Management lessons from Mayo Clinic: Inside one of the world's most admired service organizations*. New York, NY: McGraw Hill 265 pp

Bitner M. J. (1992) 'Servicescapes: The impact of physical surroundings on customers and employees', *Journal of Marketing*, Vol 56, April, pp. 57–71

Patricio L., Raymond P. Fisk, João F. e Cunha and L. Constantine (2011) 'Multilevel Service Design: From customer value constellation to Service Experience Blueprinting', *Journal of Service Research*, Vol 14, No 2, pp. 180–200

Notes and references

1 North, A., Hargreaves, D. and McKendrick, J. (1997) 'In-store music affects product choice', *Nature*, 13 November, p. 132
2 (1996) *The Value of Music*. London: National Music Council

3 North, A. C. and Hargreaves, D. J. (1997) in Hargreaves, D. J. and North, A. C. (eds) *The Social Psychology of Music*. Oxford University Press, pp. 268–289; and Areni, C. S. and Kim, D. (1993) *Advanced Consumer Research*, Vol 20, pp. 336–340

4 Hall, E. (1959) *The Silent Language*. New York, NY: Doubleday and Co, p. 158

5 Bitner, M. J. (1990) 'Evaluating service encounters: The effects of physical surroundings and employee responses', *Journal of Marketing*, Vol 54, April, pp. 69–82; and Bitner, M. J. (1992) 'Servicescapes: The impact of physical surroundings on customers and employees', *Journal of Marketing*, Vol 56, April, pp. 57–71

6 Berry, L. L., Wall, Eileen A. and Carbone, Lewis P. (2006) 'Service clues and customer assessment of the service experience: Lessons from marketing', *Academy of Management Perspectives*, May, pp. 43–57

7 Haeckel, S. H., Carbone, L. P. and Berry, L. L. (2003) 'How to lead the customer experience', *Marketing Management*, Vol 12, No 1, pp. 18–23

8 Berry, L. L. *et al.* (2006), op. cit., pp. 43–44

9 Lovelock, C. (1988) *Managing Services: Marketing, operations and human resources*. London: Prentice Hall

10 Carlzon, J. (1989) *Moments of Truth*. London: Harper Collins

11 Zomerdijk, L. G. and de Vries, J. (2007) 'Structuring front office and back-office work in service delivery systems', *International Journal of Operations and Production Management*, Vol 27, No 1, p. 111

12 Ibid., p. 111

13 Ibid., pp. 108–131

14 Ibid., p. 127

15 The information in this figure and the explanation that follows is based on Zomerdijk, L. G. and de Vries, J. (2007), pp. 117–122

16 Based on 'Euro Disney: The first 100 days', *Harvard Business School case study*, 9–693–013

17 Brown, S. W. (1994) 'Retail location at the micro scale: Inventory and prospect', *The Service Industries Journal*, Vol 14, No 4, October, pp. 542–576

18 Schmenner, R. W. (1994) 'Service firm location decisions: Some midwestern evidence', *International Journal of Service Industry Management*, Vol 5, No 3, pp. 35–56

19 Of course this is only one of the reasons. The call for more operational efficiency and the bank crisis have led to a rethinking of the design of the bank branch network

20 This is based on a survey of 246 rural customers of one Belgian Bank in a region with seven small towns. This survey was performed by Mieke Van Oostende in a student project under the supervision of Roland Van Dierdonck on location in services, at the Faculty of Economics and Business Administration, University of Ghent, 1997–1998. If the travel time is 0–5 minutes, 100% of the customers will continue to come, and 72.4% are willing to come to the bank branch if the travel time is between 5 and 10 minutes. This means that 27.6% of the customers do not accept a travel time of more than 5 minutes

21 For the reader interested in a comprehensive overview of location models, we refer to Brandeau, M. L. and Chiu, S. S. (1984) 'An overview of represented problems in location research', *Management Science*, Vol 35, No 6, June, pp. 645–674

22 This paragraph is in part based on Fitzsimmons, J. A. and Fitzsimmons, M. J. (1994) *Service Management for Competitive Advantage*. New York, NY: McGraw-Hill Inc., 462 pp

23 The magazine *Sale and Marketing Management* annually releases a survey of buying power which measures the overall retail demand in an area as a percentage of total demand in the US. CONSU-DATA is an example of a computerized database. It contains information data from more than 4 million Belgian households such as social class, type of car or house, composition of the household and so on

24 'Euro Disney: The first 100 days', op. cit., p. 8

25 Much more complex location models have been developed in the last 50 years. Examples are the use of trading areas (utilizing the Huff formula) in the location of bank branches, gravity models in retail management and multi-site location-allocation models. One more recent example is found in the article by Lixun, Zhang and Rushton, Gerard (2006) 'Optimizing the size and locations of facilities in competitive multi-site service system', *Computers and Operations Research*, Vol 35, pp. 327–338. These authors recognize that 'the development in recent years of rich spatial data that contain demographic data at fine geographic detail and transportation infrastructure data that permit prediction of spatial choice for specified alternative facilities has, perhaps curiously, led to a decline in practice in the use of formal models' (p. 327). In other words, decision makers are using software for business applications based on access to geographic information. This does not mean that these decision makers have no need of

decision support systems to model the expected results of their decision making with respect to the attainment of objectives as well as realism with respect to the available geographic information. The more complex location models take into account many more criteria that are important for the customer. For instance, Zhang and Rhuston want to maximize consumer utility and, thus, the service quality of an organization, subject to constraints such as queuing time and the cost of setting up and/or closing branches. A good example of how Geographical Information Systems can be used for site selection can be found in the following article: Junjie, Wu, Chen, Jian and Ren, Yili (2011) 'GIS enabled service site selection: Environmental analysis and beyond', *Information Systems Frontier*, Vol 13, No 3, pp. 337–348

26 Waters, D. (1996) *Operations Management: Producing goods and services*. Harlow: Addison-Wesley Longman, Chapter 19

27 Bitner, M. J. (1992) 'Servicescapes: The impact of physical surroundings on customers and employees', *Journal of Marketing*, Vol 56, April, pp. 57–71

28 Bennett, David J. and Bennett, Judith D. (1970) 'Making the scene', in Stone, G. and Farberman, H. (eds) *Social Psychology Through Symbolic Interactionism*. Waltham, MA: Ginn Blaisdell, pp. 190–196

29 Ezeh, Chris and Harris, Lloyd C. (2007) 'Servicescape research: A review and a research agenda', *The Marketing Review*, Vol 7, No 1, pp. 59–78

30 Schneider, B. (1987) 'The people make the place', *Personnel Psychology*, Vol 40, No 3, pp. 437–453

31 Ezeh *et al.* (2007) based on Baker, J. (1987) 'The role of the environment in marketing services: The consumer perspective', in Czepiel, J., Congram, C. A. and Shanahan, J. (eds) *The Services Challenge: Integrating for Competitive Advantage*. Chicago, IL: American Marketing Association, pp. 79–84

32 Berry, Leonard L. and Seltman, Kent D. (2008) *Management lessons from the Mayo Clinic*. New York, NY: McGraw-Hill, pp. 174–175

33 This is largely based on the work of Mehrabian, A. and Russell, J. A. (1974) *An Approach to Environmental Psychology*. Cambridge, MA: MIT. They state that the emotional context of servicescapes can be captured by three dimensions: pleasure, arousal and dominance. However, dominance is not as commonly used by servicescape scholars as pleasure and arousal in empirical studies

34 Victor (1992) makes a distinction between olfactory cultures and non-olfactory cultures. In non-olfactory cultures, as in most western cultures, 'smell' is not considered a major source of messages. Odours are masked as much as possible. In olfactory cultures – for instance, most Arabic societies – smells communicate emotions such as fear and tension, and relaxed friendliness. *See* Victor, D. A. (1992) *International Business Communication*. New York, NY: Harper Collins

35 Mehrabian, A. and Russell, J. A. (1974) *An Approach to Environmental Psychology*. Cambridge, MA: MIT

36 Parish, J. T., Berry, Leonard, L. and Shun, Yin L. (2008) 'The effect of the Servicescape on Service workers', *Journal of Service Research*, Vol 10, No 3, pp. 220–238

37 Ibid., p. 234

38 Harris, Lloyd C. and Goode, Mark M. H. (2010) 'On-line servicescapes, trust, and purchase intentions', *Journal of Services Marketing*, Vol 24, No 3, pp. 230–243

39 Ibid.

40 Based on Lam, L. W., Chan, Ka, Davis, W. Fong and Freda, Lo (2011) 'Does the look matter? The impact of casino servicescape on gaming customer satisfaction, intention to revisit, and desire to stay', *International Journal of Hospitality Management*, Vol 30, pp. 558–567

41 Ibid.

42 Berry, Leonard L. and Bendapudi, Neeli (2003) 'Clueing in customers', *Harvard Business Review*, February

43 This exhibit is based on Berry, L. L. and Bendapudi, N., ibid., pp. 100–106; Berry, L. L., Wall, E. A. Carbone, L. P. (2006) 'Service clues and customer assessment of the service experience: Lessons from marketing', *The Academy of Management Perspectives*, Vol 20, No 2, pp. 43–57; Berry, Leonard L. and Seltman, Kent D. (2008), op. cit.

44 Based on research from the Professional Research Corporation as mentioned in Berry *et al.* (2008), op. cit., p. 188

45 Berry *et al.* (2003), op. cit.

Chapter 8

Service branding and promotion

Paul Gemmel • Patrick De Pelsmacker • Joeri Van Den Bergh

'Service branding is a lot like advertising, except that it turns a company into a living, breathing advertisement for itself'[1]

Objectives

By the end of this chapter, you should understand:

- The role of service branding for service firms
- How to build a service brand
- The special characteristics of the promotion of services
- The different communication tools at our disposal for promotion at different stages in the service process
- How the mix of communication tools is linked to the type of service
- A guiding framework to develop the outline of a promotion plan

Introduction

While Womble Carlyle was not the first law firm to recognize the value of advertising, it was among the first to understand each communication must sustain the look and feel of every other.[2]

Womble's most innovative contribution to law firm advertising arose not by design but by coincidence: people fell in love with the bulldog. The bulldog entered the firm's life in good fun, featured in the firm's annual Client Service Award. Shortly after, the dog showed up on the firm's holiday card. Within 2 years, the bulldog became an icon for the firm.

The second and third ad series focused entirely on the bulldog. The bulldog playing Twister announced the opening of the firm's Washington, D.C. office (see Figure 8.1) and showed up as a backlit diorama in Washington's Ronald Reagan National Airport.

Ironically the bulldog, which is named Winston (Winston-Salem, Winston Churchill), has come to humanize the firm, giving to its lawyers the same qualities we associate with man's best friend – loyalty, friendliness and intelligence.

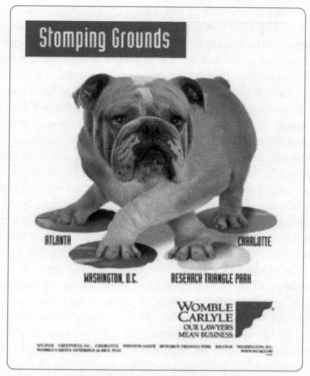

Figure 8.1 A bulldog as a mascot of the law firm Womble Carlyle

Source: A case study of Greenfield/Belser (**http://www.greenfieldbelser.com/case-studies/womble-carlyle**) Greenfield/Belser is a US-based national leader in brand strategy and design, focused exclusively on professional services marketing, and a firm that led the revolution in legal industry branding.

Bulldog Winston has become the personification of what the law firm, Womble Carlyle, a professional service firm, stands for in terms of service: loyalty, friendliness and intelligence. Womble Carlyle 'humanize' their service concept, which makes it very clear for their customers but also for their employees. This means that everyone is focused on the same 'story', the story that the firm wants to tell. It is pretty clear that advertisement and other promotion tools are important in building this image. At the same time, it introduces the challenge for the lawyers of Womble Carlyle to make what is promised in the advertisements happen every day.

In Chapter 3, we introduced the 'Service Gap' model to explain why there might a gap between the expectations of customers and their perception of the service delivery. This model demonstrates that customer expectations are not always set in the right way. This might be the consequence of (1) ineffective management of customer expectations, (2) over promising and (3) inadequate horizontal communication, i.e. communication among the internal stakeholders.[3]

Customer expectations are influenced by their personal needs, past experiences, word-of-mouth (*see* Chapter 12) and communication by the firm. Within service environments the importance of alignment between internal and external communication needs to be stressed. A service is a performance that involves the co-operation and co-ordination of several parties. The quality of the service rendered is inseparable from the quality of the service provider. A rude or slow waiter, for example, can ruin what otherwise might have been perceived as a fine meal. This means that the communication effort will not only have to encourage the customer to buy but, through internal communication, will also have to encourage the employee to perform. However, it is important that this internal flow of information and communication is in line with the external communication. We will argue in this chapter that building a strong service brand is a necessary step in linking the internal and external communication to the service concept. Otherwise, the disparity between the inside and the outside of the service organization will lead rather quickly to friction.

Promising only what is possible is a good general principle of communication. Service company employees pay attention to their own company's ads and are influenced by them, albeit not always positively. When promotional communication promises more than what is possible, the seeds of problems are sown. Expectations raised by promotional messages are brought to the service encounter by customers who find themselves faced with desperate or cynical front-line employees, who then set about creating their next 'dissatisfied' customer. Raising expectations too high may easily lead to dissatisfied consumers, since a reinforcing effect is expected. Service employees may feel betrayed by their organization's service concept as they are not backed up by adequate support.

One of the major issues in setting customer expectations right is the alignment of the service mind-set in all different functions within the company. Sales, marketing, operations, HRM, design and development, organizational behaviour experts all have different views as internal stakeholders on what the meaning of good service is. Having a strong service concept, as introduced in Chapter 3, is the first step in aligning the mind-set of all internal stakeholders but, in order to design and implement the service experience in a successful way, we need an interdisciplinary approach, based on sufficient horizontal communication.

In this chapter, we will focus on different tools that can be used by service managers to set customer expectations in the right way. We first offer an overall framework of service branding as a means of making the service concept more explicit for internal and external stakeholders. We will then elaborate on the promotion of services and on how external communication plays a role.

Service branding

'A strong brand is a safe place for customers'.[4] This is even more true in a service context where customers are confronted with intangible products. Service customers are continuously looking for clues that confirm they are making, or have made, the right choice. If the many different types of clue (functional, mechanic and humanic, *see* Chapter 7) all fit together into one consistent and simple message and, if this message is in line with what the organization has promised and with what other customers tell, the service has a strong brand. In studies of the Mayo Clinic[5] and SIA,[6] brand cultivation was found to be a principal driver of success: the brand preference of the Mayo Clinic is nearly 2.5 times greater than the second leading health care institution in the US; the value of the SIA brand was placed at $354.7 million, the eighth highest among Singapore companies. The theme park 'De Efteling' has, for years, been listed in the top 10 of the best known brands in the Netherlands. These examples show that service branding is as important as product branding.

A service brand is defined as '*a blend of what the company says the brand is, what others say, and how the company performs the service – all from the customer's point of view*'.[7] To 'create

Figure 8.2 A service branding model

Source: Berry, Leonard L. (2000) 'Cultivating Service Brand Equity', *Journal of the Academy of Marketing Science*, Vol 28, No 1, p. 130.

a distinct mental picture [or service concept] for customers' and to prevent the value proposition becoming a commodity are the ultimate goals of service branding.[8] Figure 8.2 shows the relationships among the principal components of a service brand: the presented brand, brand awareness, external brand communication, brand meaning, customer experience and brand equity.

The organization's presented brand is the organization's controlled communication of its identity and desired brand image through means such as the brand name, logo, and advertising.[9] SIA has been running the highly successful Singapore Girl campaign for years. The Singapore Girl is the personification of the presented brand. This Singapore Girl is so strongly linked with the organizational brand that many of the commercial ads use the following sentence: 'Singapore Girl, you are a great way to fly'. SIA's success with its presented brand was acknowledged by Madame Tussaud's wax museum when, in June 1993, the Singapore Girl became the only commercial figure in the world-famous museum.[10] The museum described the Singapore Girl as 'one of the world's most instantly recognizable faces'.[11] The recall level of the advertisements with the Singapore Girls is 5 times higher than the recall levels of comparable campaigns of other airline industries. The customer's ability to recognize and recall a brand can be described as *'brand awareness'*.

Not all communication about the firm's identity and purpose can be controlled by the company. When Singapore Airlines was mentioned as the best Airline Worldwide 2010 in the *Flug Revue Award* (Germany's monthly aviation magazine), this strengthened the SIA brand. This type of publicity is an example of *external brand communication*. Another type of 'uncontrollable' external brand communication is word-of-mouth communication. External brand communication is not always positive. Despite her success, some sources in the media complain that the Singapore Girl concept is sexist, outmoded and largely intended to serve male passengers' fantasies of desirable Oriental women.[12] Today, social media increase the importance and the impact of non-controllable external brand communication.

The presented brand, the external brand communication, and the service experience all contribute to the *brand meaning*. Brand meaning is what immediately comes to consumers' minds when Efteling or Disneyland Paris are mentioned. The fundamental difference between brand awareness and brand meaning is illustrated when SIA is compared with Ryanair. Both airlines companies are very well known in their respective market segments, but the dominant perception of the customer is very different. The Ryanair brand stands for basic services, i.e. transporting passengers in an efficient way. The SIA brand stands for superior service and style. In the minds of the customers, Asian Hospitality springs to mind when SIA is mentioned. Even if another Asian airline starts to offer better levels of hospitality and service or an even younger fleet (e.g. Jet Airways in India has a fleet with an average age of 3 years – it is a new entrant, however), the customer perception may be rather slow to change. This shows that the the implication of durability and sustainability is embedded in the SIA brand, giving SIA a degree of marketing advantage over competitors. This marketing advantage can be considered as positive *brand equity*, which is based on brand meaning and brand awareness. Brand equity can also be negative. The brand equity of the Belgian national public railway company is negative, mainly based on the customers' perception that trains are rarely on time. In the case of the railway company, the inability to perform their core services well creates a negative perception of being an unreliable service provider.

Building a strong service brand must be the result of conscious decisions and strategies implemented over a long period of time. One of the most remarkable findings in the study of service companies with a successful brand such as SIA, the Mayo Clinic and Efteling is that their message is simple, consistent over time, and that they make it happen every day, every hour, every minute in the experience of their customers. This is clearly illustrated in the following quotation from Dr Cheong Choong Kong, SIA's former chairman and CEO:[13]

'The Singapore Girl was conceived as a personification of oriental charm and friendliness, which the airline made real through careful recruitment and painstaking training. Effective and original advertising, together with word of mouth praises from satisfied passengers, creates an aura of superior service and style. The aura, once established, had to be sustained through constant training, clever advertising and ingenuity in the cabin.'

From the quote of Dr Cheong Choong Kong one can learn that the brand must be explained and sold to service employees. The attitude, belief, value and behavioural style of employees reflect the brand. The employees carry the brand identity into the eyes of consumers. Using a sample of international customers and employees of five-star hotels in Bangkok, a study found that strong hotel brands are characterized by a strong employee commitment to support the brand.[14] This means that, in service companies such as hotels, internal service branding is as important as external branding. Internal service branding must first guarantee that employees understand the brand, and must generate commitment to the brand. Together with other design options such as processes, technology, facilities and prices, service employees are the most important asset in creating a distinct service brand.

The quotation from Dr Cheong Choong Kong also refers to the importance of clever advertising. That is why we will give some attention to how to promote services through different communication tools.

Promoting services

The success of service branding depends on how services are promoted. To develop a promotion campaign, we need to find out what drives groups of people to consume a particular service. This brings us back to the need for focus and the notions of segmenting, positioning and targeting (*see* Chapter 3). This knowledge then becomes a starting point for defining

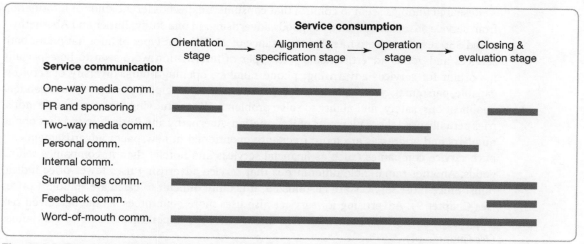

Figure 8.3 The service delivery process and the relevance of promotional channels

Source: Based on Pieters, R., Roest, H. and Koelemeijer, K. (1995) 'Ze zei mener tegen me. Servicecommuniatie in Serviceconsumptie', *Tijdschrift voor Marketing*, Oct, pp. 30–45.

the content of the promotional campaign; the needs to be addressed by the developed service concept should be the basis of the promotional efforts. Just look at some restaurants in your neighbourhood: the appeal of some is their speedy delivery; some offer a family experience; some use fashionable and exotic characteristics to attract customers; and others stress the exceptional quality of the food itself.

Since services are processes, we should first develop a model linking the different stages of the service process with the different communication tools at our disposal at these stages. The service consumption process looked at from a promotional point of view can be depicted as consisting of several phases or stages (*see* Figure 8.3).[15] During the *orientation* or *awareness* stage, (potential) customers gather information, evaluate possible service providers and choose one to interact with. They then open the interaction. During the *alignment and specification* stage, the problem is defined, possible solutions are explored and an agreement reached on one or more of the solutions. During the *operation* stage, the actual service is being delivered. The *closing and evaluation* stage consists of ending the interaction between the service provider and the served customer and evaluating the balance between expectations and experiences. The result of this exercise is an adaptation of the customer's expectations.

As shown in Figure 8.3, different promotional media may be used, depending upon the stage in the service consumption process.

One-way communication

This includes the traditional marketing communication elements: advertising, sales promotions, sponsoring and direct marketing. They are one-way because the customer cannot interact with the service provider. One-way media are often used to influence the customer's orientation stage to attract customers to the next stages. They can also be used in the specification stage – for example, a printed catalogue of a mail order company.

Research findings seem to confirm that consumers expect different kinds of information from service advertising than from goods advertising. In one study, Butler and Abernethy[16] asked 550 respondents to rate the importance of 25 different types of information for both services and goods advertisements. Ten types of information were seen to be especially important for services advertising: phone number, opening hours, diversity of services, capable personnel, years of experience, concerned and helpful personnel, independent qualifications, safety, and ability to solve problems. When studying whether service industries actually used those elements of information, Abernethy and Butler[17] found that phone numbers and addresses are more frequently mentioned in newspaper advertisements for pure service companies (such as financial services and hotels) than in companies selling goods. Another remarkable difference is that service advertising uses fewer price indications. Since most services are customized, it is quite difficult to calculate standard prices (*see* Chapter 9). Advertising for services also uses more guarantees, as the perceived risk is higher than in goods industries. This underwrites the importance of service guarantees (*see* Chapter 14).

Research by FHV/BBDO,[18] a Dutch advertising agency, confirmed Butler and Abernethy's findings and added that advertising for services puts more emphasis on the company image. A strong corporate image, built through the service brand, augments the tangibility and clarity of services and diminishes the perceived risk. The same BBDO research also found differences in the execution of the advertisements:

- Services advertising uses more text and fewer images. Intangibility makes services harder to comprehend and thus requires more explanation, which also reduces perceived risk.

- Services advertising uses fewer colours. This might simply be a result of lower communication budgets in service industries; it could also be the result of the inclination to make more serious ads.

- Advertising for services has longer headlines – again, the need for more explanation.

On the other hand, when advertising for services, creativity can overcome the need for long texts and explanation. Remember that one picture can say more than 1000 words. If an image can be found that reflects the service concept, this can make words obsolete – as can be seen from the Womble Carlyl advertisement in Figure 8.1.

Two-way and interactive media communication

New technologies, such as the Internet, are tools that allow customers to have direct contact with the service organization without human (personal) interference. This two-way media communication is particularly useful at the operations stage – for example, buying airline vouchers on the Internet, but it is clear that these media can be used as well for other stages in the process (e.g. creating awareness of new offerings by means of e-mail and measuring the effect of an advertising campaign).

Internet applications are well fitted to customize the communications messages according to the web behaviour of the recipient and to the purchasing behaviour of website users.[19] Internet booksellers such as Amazon.com are able to track the purchasing behaviour of a customer and, based on that behaviour, they customize a part of the website to the customer's preferences, or they send an e-mail with new books of interest to that customer.

Internet and other digital media such as mobile phones (both SMS and MMS), social media marketing, display advertising, search engine marketing are shifting media communication to the new era of digital marketing. Digital marketing requires a new approach to marketing and a new understanding of customer behaviour. For example, it requires companies to analyse and quantify the value of downloads of apps on mobile devices, tweets on Twitter, likes on Facebook and so on. Exhibit 8.1 shows how Pizza Hut has launched a successful digital media campaign by increasing customer involvement and engagement (*see also* Chapter 12). Potential customers are now paying attention to the products and services of Pizza Hut in a voluntary way. This is in sharp contrast to a 30-second television spot interrupting a viewer's favourite programme. This is the basis of a new communication strategy, called 'permission marketing'. Digital media have allowed marketers to establish strong relationships with individual customers whereby the customers themselves make the choice to engage with a firm.[20]

Exhibit 8.1 A digital media campaign at Pizza Hut

'One successful digital media campaign was by Pizza Hut, which created an app that allowed customers to create their own pizza by dragging their chosen toppings onto a graphical pizza base. The iPhone would then determine which of the chain's thousands of locations the customer was nearest. The company advertised the new app online, in print, and on television – even winning a placement in Apple's own iPhone commercial.

Within two weeks, the Pizza Hut app was downloaded 100,000 times and, within three months, iPhone users ordered $1m worth of pizza. The app now has millions of users across the iPhone, iPad, and Android platforms.'[21]

FT *Source*: Financial Times Lexicon (**http://lexicon.ft.com/Term?term=digital-marketing**)
© The Financial Times Limited. All Rights Reserved.

 ## Public Relations and sponsoring

Palmer defines public relations as 'the deliberate, planned and sustained effort to establish and maintain mutual understanding'.[22] It is a collection of techniques used to optimize the relationship between a company and the public. These techniques include press events, press releases, press conferences, participation in exhibition and sponsoring. PR is important for services for the following reasons:

1 It has to communicate and guard a good corporate image.

2 Services are evaluated in a subjective way (personal experiences) and this evaluation is rapidly diffused through word-of-mouth information exchange processes. PR makes sure that the service organization is playing an active role in this process and can prevent negative rumours circulating about the company or its products/services.

3 In some countries, service firms in the social profit sector are not allowed to advertise. In these cases, PR is the most important tool in presenting the service brand to the public.

The ultimate outcome of the different PR techniques is publicity, defined by Kotler and Armstrong[23] as 'securing editorial space (i.e. not paid space) in all media read, viewed or heard by a company's customers or prospects, for the specific purpose of assisting in the meeting of the goals'. Publicity is stimulated by press events, press releases and press conferences. It is cheap, has high coverage and comes from a reliable and independent source. On the other hand, publicity is almost uncontrollable and thus can turn out to be negative. Therefore, good relations with the press and experienced PR people are necessary.

Service companies often participate in exhibitions with the objective of generating awareness, rather than selling. A service exhibitor's stand should make the intangible tangible; the exhibitor should lower the risk and give clearly understandable explanations of the rendered services. A service company can also organize events to obtain press attention (free publicity) and to increase awareness.

Consumers today pay more attention to culture, environmental issues and general welfare. Service industries have understood this and are sponsoring related organizations and events. Sponsoring culture is popular among service marketers because it has positive associations – quality, seriousness and importance. Sponsoring sports is also attractive as it can lead to increased exposure, can support corporate images or alter negative attitudes towards a company. Sponsoring offers some segmentation possibilities. By choosing the right events, certain target groups can be reached very effectively (e.g. youth and music events).

It should be noted that in a service company – due to simultaneity – everyone is responsible for public relations. The crucial role of personnel (especially front-office personnel) was discussed in Chapter 5.

Personal and internal communication

Personal communication aimed at selling the service offered is defined as 'the oral presentations and/or demonstrations to one or more (potential) buyers for the final purpose of making sales'. Personal selling can fulfil two functions that facilitate the more effective selling of services: *servicing and monitoring*. By servicing, we mean front-office personnel informing and advising customers and, by doing so, addressing specific points of concern. By *monitoring*, we mean front-office personnel trying to detect customer needs and problems and reacting appropriately. Personal selling has advantages over other communication tools in that it offers opportunities for establishing relationships. Frequent, and sometimes confidential, contacts between personnel and clients can lead to close relationships that will in return lead to loyalty. Another advantage is that it offers cross-selling opportunities. With closer personal interaction, employees can detect additional customer needs and can provide information on other services. A prerequisite here is a good knowledge of the complete range of services as well as a sound appreciation of customers' needs. Of course, the personal contact between service provider and customers does not end at the moment of sale. Customers see the contact personnel as a personification and an integral part of the services they pay for. Personnel is a tangible element for them and, thus, much easier to evaluate.

To achieve consistency in the personal messages communicated, it is important to pay particular attention to all communication between personnel, i.e. *internal communication*. In services, it is particular important that there is good internal communication between the front office and the back office. For example, an employee at the counter may speak the customer's language and understand his or her needs but, when the back office produces incomprehensible documents or invoices, anything gained by such efforts will be lost. This highlights the need for good employee motivation, education and an integrated process view. Every service must first be sold to a company's own employees before it can be sold to consumers.

Surrounding communication

This deals with all kinds of communication related to the physical environment in which services are consumed. Bateson comments on the importance of the point of sale, store, office or outlet.[24] The architecture, lighting, temperature, furnishings, layout, colour and artefacts present in the firm's facilities all communicate non-verbally to the customer how the firm sees itself and how it wishes the customer to behave when entering the premises. This brings us back to the statement that 'space speaks', as discussed in Chapter 7 when talking about the servicescape.

Feedback communication

After service consumption, the customer compares experiences with expectations, and may express incomplete satisfaction to the front-office personnel, to management or, worse, to other customers or third parties such as consumer organizations. It is advisable to structure feedback communications and to actively play a role in this evaluation process – for example, by using suggestion boxes, evaluation cards or service departments. In Chapter 13, we will discuss in greater depth how to manage this customer feedback.

Word-of-mouth communication

As stated earlier, the intangible nature of services makes it more difficult to assess qualities and effects before consuming them. As such, customers will talk about experiences and will actively solicit opinions of people who went through the 'service experience'. Note that this word-of-mouth communication can appear throughout the entire service delivery process. To create positive word of mouth, it is important to have the consumer feel that he or she is understood and that the service company is working out solutions, offering an honest and realistic view of what to expect. Service organizations can adopt a proactive approach towards worth-of-mouth communication by encouraging customers and potential customers to exchange experiences and insights. Discussion meetings, customer meetings, workshops and conferences can be organized on topics of interest. Some companies have even set up special organizations to handle this area of their activities.[25] Word-of-mouth is recognized as one of the most important behaviours associated with loyalty (*see* Chapter 12).

Establishing the right mix

The service marketer must strive for an optimal integration of all these tools in order to fulfil the marketing communications goals. Finding the right combination of elements, what is called the *communication mix*, has a great influence on the success of the communication campaign. Each element has its specific advantages and disadvantages and each has a different price.

After the previous explanation, it should come as no surprise that the effectiveness of the individual elements of the communications mix is different for services. A survey[26] that looked at the importance of different communication elements in inducing buying behaviours found important differences between goods and services (*see* Figure 8.4).

Front-office management and personnel are typical communication tools for a service environment. The absence of impulse purchase decisions for services means that sales promotions are used more often for advertising goods rather than services. The effect some sales promotions have on impulse purchases explains the upward curve of the goods line in Figure 8.4. Sales promotions are used in services to stimulate repeat purchases and to

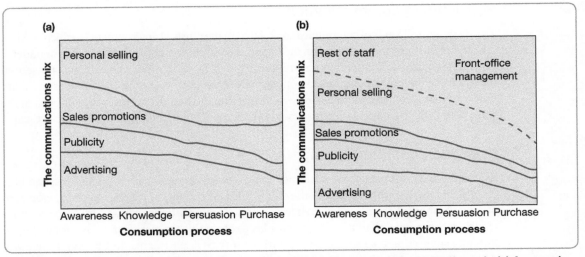

Figure 8.4 The relative importance of the individual elements of the communication mix (a) for goods and (b) for services

Source: Tettero, J. H. and Viehoff, J. H. (1994) 'Marketing voor dienstverlenende organisaties', in *Beleid en Uitvoering*. Deventer: Kluwer.

balance out demand and supply. However, publicity and PR are more commonly used in services. A strong corporate image as evidenced in the service brand is needed to compensate for the lack of tangible product characteristics. This observation can be extended to the importance of the physical settings and surroundings as well as word-of-mouth communication, elements not included in this survey. Given the intangible nature of services, both the location and design of the service facility (*see also* Chapter 7), as well as the physical appearance of the staff, will be more important when deciding to purchase services rather than products. One can extend this reasoning even further in order to delineate differences between different types of service. It will come as no surprise that we refer again to the three different types of service delineated by Mills and Margulies: maintenance-interactive, task-interactive, and finally personal-interactive services (*see* Chapter 2). Since maintenance-interactive services are more like products, given the lower levels of uncertainty involved, the appropriate communication mix can be seen as one that is more suited to goods (*see* Figure 8.4); for task and personal-interactive services, the relative importance of personal communication and word-of-mouth will be higher.

Finally, it should be stressed that all the elements of the communications mix interlink with each other and must all contribute to the goals of promoting services. Several goals of service promotion can be identified such as creating a brand identity, positioning the brand, and creating demand.[27] In other words, building a strong service brand seems to be at the heart of an effective service promotion campaign. Only then can a message strategy, which includes all different (intangible and tangible) characteristics of the service, be developed in a coherent way. It is easier for a salesperson to sell a certain service if the company has a good reputation thanks to advertising and PR. Advertising will have a greater effect if it is supported by in-store communications. Sales promotions have to be communicated to generate action. Customers will only rely on the services of an advertised company if they have confidence in the capabilities of front-office employees and vice versa. Hence, promotion directs our attention again to the need for an integrated and holistic approach to designing and operating the service delivery system.

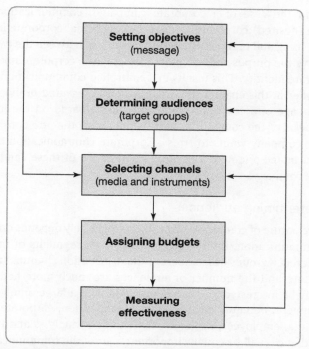

Figure 8.5 The stages in drawing up a communication plan

Drawing up a promotion plan

The different stages in building up a communication plan are presented in Figure 8.5.

Setting objectives

The objectives of a communication plan, or the messages that are to be conveyed, depend upon a number of factors. First of all, in a marketing communication campaign, the objective of the campaign will target one particular level in the hierarchy of effects:

- creating the need for the product category;
- building brand awareness;
- spreading information;
- developing a favourable attitude, purchase intention, behaviour facilitation and trial purchase;
- inducing loyalty; or
- enhancing customer satisfaction.

Furthermore, the actual service characteristic or benefit to be stressed will depend upon the strengths and weaknesses of the service promoted, the target group at which the service is aimed, and the positioning decision that has been made. In other words, the definition of the service concept – 'a desired unique place in the mind of the consumer' – comes first, and the communication strategy should then be based on it.

In the case of a corporate campaign, communication objectives will be based on the (desired) corporate identity and the actual corporate image (as reflected in the brand meaning and brand awareness) and the gap between the two. Corporate campaigns always serve the purpose of bringing or keeping the corporate image in line with the desired corporate identity. This results in a controlled communication of its identity, which we called earlier in this chapter the organization's presented brand (*see also* Figure 8.2). Thus, the message of a corporate campaign will be based on the image attribute(s) – that is, the aspects of the company's identity and image that are considered to be important and that the company wants to stress. Corporate communication objectives are mostly long-term and image-oriented. The ultimate objective of these campaigns is to create goodwill for the company.

Determining audiences

The nature of communication objectives largely depends on the target groups. In marketing communication, the target groups may be segments of final customers, opinion leaders, reference groups or members of the distribution channel. In corporate communication, the nature and the number of audiences are much more heterogeneous. Indeed, companies may be interested in creating goodwill with a large number of audiences such as the government, potential employees, the competition, corporate buyers, local communities, the media, employees, suppliers, shareholders, analysts and the general public. Since not all audiences will be equally important, part of the communication plan will consist of a selection or ranking of the most important audiences. Two audiences are important in almost every corporate campaign – the media and the company's employees – because they both serve as intermediate groups for the other audiences. Therefore, internal communication and communication with the media are extremely important, especially in a service environment in which personal contacts and reputation are important determinants of perceived quality.

Selecting channels

Next, communication channels and instruments have to be selected. Communication media and instruments were discussed earlier in this chapter. It is important to stress once again that 'the medium is the message' – that is, that the instruments and media used have to be consistent with the message conveyed and its target groups; the two have to support each other. Furthermore, a strict timetable has to be adopted that is in line with the objectives of the communication campaign.

Assigning budgets

Various methods may be used to determine a communication budget. Unfortunately, many companies still use 'percentage-of-sales', 'availability-of-funds' or 'imitate-the-competition' methods of determining a budget. All these methods have the disadvantage that there is no relationship between the budget and the communication problem at hand. The best way of setting a communication budget is the 'objective-and-task' method in which communication objectives are defined as precisely as possible, the necessary media and instruments are decided upon, and a budget is calculated based on the efforts necessary to reach the objectives. To apply this method, a clear idea of the communication objectives and the necessary input is required.

Measuring effectiveness

The effectiveness of a communication campaign can be measured in two ways, directly and indirectly. Direct measurement of effectiveness implies measuring the impact of the campaign itself: Do members of the target groups recall having seen the communication? Did they pick up the important elements of the message? Did they understand it? Did they consider it credible or personally relevant? Although direct measurement provides interesting data for campaign evaluation and further campaign development, indirect brand-level or company-level measurement is perhaps more relevant.[28] In indirect effectiveness measurement, the effect of the campaign on the service or company is assessed. A communication campaign has been effective if it has realized its objectives. As a result, measuring effectiveness boils down to comparing the situation of a service or a company before and after the campaign with respect to the objectives of the campaign in terms such as (brand) awareness, (brand) meaning, attitude towards the brand, company image and purchase intention. The results of the effectiveness measurement will be input into the next communication campaign, together with the necessary market and customer research, leading to new or adjusted objectives.

Conclusion

From the Service Gap model, we learn that the service delivery should be in line with customer expectations. This is not always easy, but the good news is that these expectations can be influenced or even manipulated. In this chapter, we have discussed several tools that can be used in branding and promoting the service. Although the promotion tools used for services are generally the same as for tangible goods, the mix of these tools and the content and execution of these tools have to be designed to fulfil the specific characteristics of services such as intangibility and simultaneity. For a service company, it is crucial to make the 'intangible' service concept more tangible. This starts at the strategic level of the company. A strong service brand is an important element in the competitive strategy of the organisation. All internal and external communication efforts such as advertising and PR must then be configured in such a way that they are in line with the service brand but also support the building of the brand in a consistent way over time. This is the only way to create a strong brand 'as a safe place for customers'.

Review and discussion questions

- Look up examples of service companies with a very strong service brand. Using the different components of the service branding model (*see* Figure 8.2), discuss how these companies are able to build a strong service brand. Discuss the mix of promotion tools these companies are using to communicate the service brand to the external and the internal stakeholders.

- Look up examples of advertisements for 'pure' goods and 'pure' services. Compare the content of these advertisements.

Suggested further reading

Berry, Leonard L. (2000) 'Cultivating service brand equity', *Journal of the Academy of Marketing Science*, Vol 28, No 1, pp. 128–137

Berry, Leonard L. and Seltman, Kent D. (2008) *Management lessons from the Mayo Clinic*. New York: McGraw-Hill Inc., p. 276

Notes and references

1 Berry, L. L. and Bendapudi, N. (2003) 'Cleuing in Customers', *Harvard Business Review*, February, pp. 100–106

2 A case study of Greenfield/Belser (**http://www.greenfieldbelser.com/case-studies/womble-carlyle**) Greenfield/Belser is a US-based national leader in brand strategy and design, focused exclusively on professional services marketing, and a firm that led the revolution in legal industry branding

3 Zeithaml, V. A., Bitner, M. J. and Grembler, D. D. (2006) *Services Marketing: Integrating customer focus across the firms*. New York, NY: McGraw-Hill International edition

4 Stan Richards, founder of Dallas-based advertising agency The Richards Group, as mentioned in Berry, Leonard L. and Seltman, Kent D. (2008) *Management Lessons from the Mayo Clinic*. New York, NY: McGraw-Hill Inc., p. 190

5 Ibid., p. 276

6 Heracleous, L., Wirtz, J. and Pangarkar, N. (2009) *Flying high in a competitive industry: Secrets of the world's leading airline*. McGraw Hill Education (Asia), p. 246

7 Berry, Leonard L. (2000) 'Cultivating service brand equity', *Journal of the Academy of Marketing Science*, Vol 28, No 1, p. 129

8 Ibid., p. 131

9 Ibid., p. 129

10 Heracleous *et al.* (2009), op. cit., p. 66

11 Ibid., p. 66

12 Business Travel on **http://www.MSNBC.com**. 'Singapore Girl, *Asia's Barbie, to get new look?* Critics claim long-running campaign is sexist, outmoded', 23 January 2007

13 Heracleous *et al.* (2009), op. cit., p. 65

14 Kimpakorn, N. and Tocquer, Gerard (2010) 'Service brand equity and employee brand commitment', *Journal of Services Marketing*, Vol 24, No 5, pp. 378–388

15 Based on Pieters, R., Roest, H. and Koelemeijer, K. (1995) 'Ze zei meneer tegen me. Servicecommuniatie in serviceconsumptie', *Tijdschrift voor Marketing*, Oct, pp. 30–45

16 Butler, D. D. and Abernethy, A. (1994) 'Information consumers seek from advertisements: Are there differences between advertisements for goods and services?', *Journal of Professional Services Marketing*, Vol 10, No 2, pp. 75–91

17 Abernethy, A. M. and Butler, D. (1992) 'Advertising information: Services versus products', *Journal of Retailing*, Vol 68, No 4, pp. 398–419

18 FHV/BBDO (1983) FHV/BBDO is a full service communication agency based in The Netherlands. Since 2000, it has been known by the name FHV Group

19 Bruhn, Manfred and Georgi, D. (2006) *Services marketing: Managing the service value chain*. FT Prentice Hall, p. 288

20 Lovelock, C., Wirtz, J., Hean, T. J. and Xiongwen, L. (2005) *Services Marketing in Asia: People, Technology, Strategy*. Pearson/Prentice-Hall, p. 171

21 *Source*: Anindya Ghose, NYU Stern

22 Palmer, A. (1994) *Principles of Services Marketing*. London: McGraw-Hill

23 Kotler, P. and Armstrong, G. (1991) *Principles of Marketing*. Englewood Cliffs, NJ: Prentice-Hall

24 Bateson, J. (1992) *Managing Services Marketing: Text and readings*. Chicago, IL: Dryden Press

25 For example, DECUS, a customer organization set up by Digital. DECUS publishes a magazine and regular conferences and workshops are held related to all sorts of IT issues of interest to customers. Through DECUS, Digital is keeping in touch with customer needs and considerations, and it is playing an active role in the word-of-mouth communication process

26 Tettero, J. H. and Viehoff, J. H. (1994) 'Marketing voor dienstverlenende organisaties', in *Beleid en Uitvoering*. Deventer: Kluwer

27 Banwari, Mittal (1999) 'The advertising of services: Meeting the challenge of intangibility', *Journal of Service Research*, Vol 2, No 1, pp. 98–116

28 *Source*: Ibid., p. 118. Jacoby, J. and Chestnut, R. W. (1978) *Brand Loyalty. Measurement and Management*. New York, NY: Ronald Press/John Wiley

Chapter 9

Pricing services

Marion Debruyne

Objectives

By the end of this chapter, you should be able to discuss:

- the setting of pricing objectives as the starting point for any price-setting decision for services
- the three basic strategies for setting prices in accordance with a certain objective – cost, customers (value) and competition (the three Cs)
- the choice of strategy – skimming or penetration – to reflect the fact that the customer value of a service is not stable over time, and such changes in value must be reflected in price setting
- decisions regarding how a pricing structure is made up, which price level will actually be charged, and why and when short-term promotional price initiatives are used

Introduction

George Downey, business unit manager of a large multinational company offering telecommunication services, is working on next year's business plan. The launch of a new project, planned for next year, is his main preoccupation, as it will determine the company's future competitive position. The company is planning to enter a new and potentially rewarding market as an Internet access provider.

After numerous discussions and meetings with his colleagues and co-workers, they finally agree on most of the points. There is only one item to be settled: the issue of price. The opinion of the financial manager is clear: he wants a high unit contribution. To achieve this, the company should set the price high. The sales manager, on the other hand, argues that this is unrealistic. Since many competitors are entering the market, the only way to gain a significant market share is by pricing low, perhaps with the new service bundled into a package along with regular services. Others claim that the price should be adjusted for different customer segments, allowing separate price structures for corporate and individual customers.

All these arguments leave the business unit manager with nothing but a new set of questions. Should he price high or low? How will competitors react? Could the sales revenue be guaranteed at high prices? How will this affect the other services the company offers? Should he allow for price reductions and, if so, in which cases? Should he charge a fixed monthly subscription rate or should he charge by the hour?

This chapter aims to provide answers to all these questions by offering a general step-by-step framework to guide pricing decisions.

Developing a framework for pricing decisions

The questions raised in the introductory case study perplex many service marketers. Of the classical four Ps of the marketing mix (product, place, promotion, and price), it is price that usually receives the least attention, even though the pricing decision probably has the greatest impact on a company's profits.

We can use the price structure in Figure 9.1 to illustrate the leverage effect price has on profits. If prices drop by five percentage points, profits are cut by half, from 10% to 5%. To keep the same profit, the volume sold should increase by 20%, which is very unlikely considering the concept of price elasticity.[1,2] Generating a 20% increase in volume, when prices drop by 5%, requires the price elasticity to exceed 4. By comparison, the price elasticity of cola in Belgium is 0.44, indicating that a price decrease of 1% causes a volume increase of 0.44%.

In addition to this leverage effect on profits, pricing behaviour affects customer satisfaction and customer loyalty, thus impacting on the long-term profit potential. Research[3] indicates that 'pricing' – for example, prices, rates, fees, charges, penalties, coupons, price promotions and price deals – ranks third on the list of reasons for switching service provider (after core service failures and failed service encounters). When asked 'Why did you switch

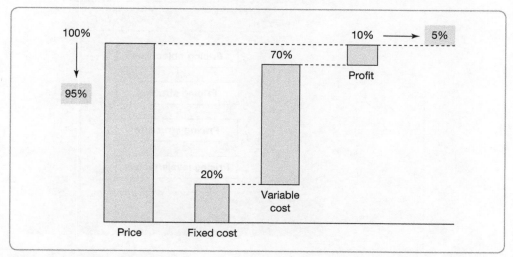

Figure 9.1 A price structure

service providers?' more than 30% of all respondents who had switched service providers responded that this was due to a price issue, such as high prices, price increases, and unfair or deceptive pricing practices.

In spite of its obvious importance, not many service marketers deal with the pricing issue in a structured or creative way. One major cause of this neglect is that many separate issues are involved in pricing decisions. It is not surprising that George Downey in our case study cannot find a solution to his problem, since the questions he is asking himself are all concerned with different issues. These questions all relate to price, but they cannot all be handled in the same way.

To develop an effective approach to pricing decisions, the service provider has to consider the different stages in the decision-making process. Figure 9.2 illustrates the various steps necessary in setting the price of a product or service.[4]

The first question a service marketer ought to ask is what he or she wants to achieve with the pricing strategy. This seems obvious, but it is often completely overlooked in practice. Determining the *objective* you want to obtain by setting a price is the first step in the pricing process, and it can help to resolve other questions at an early stage. George Downey could relieve much of his worry by just thinking about what he wants to accomplish. Every pricing decision can then be seen in the light of that objective. He should consider, for example, whether he wants to achieve a considerable market share immediately after the launch or if he wants to build it up step by step.

The second step in the pricing process is about determining which *pricing strategy* the company will follow. A pricing strategy provides general guidelines that relate to all the

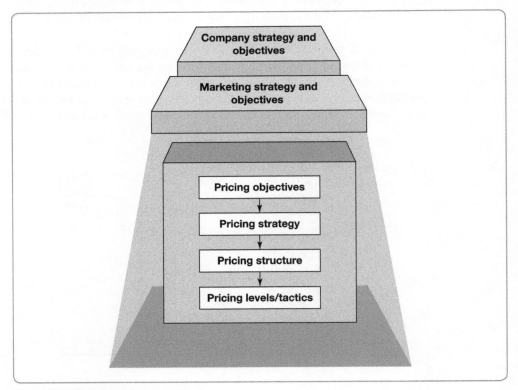

Figure 9.2 The pricing process

pricing decisions about a single product line or company. The company can, of course, alter the pricing strategy to adapt to changing circumstances. There are three main determinants on which the pricing strategy can be based – referred to as the three Cs – cost, customer and competitor. Each of these will be discussed later in this chapter.

Once the pricing objective and strategy are clear, decisions have to be made on the *pricing structure*. This means the service provider has to decide:

- which aspect of the service will be priced;
- what will be included for that price;
- on which unit the price will be based;
- if there will be a differentiation among customers; and
- what the payment conditions will be.

Imagine, for example, that you are the manager of a restaurant. Would you charge for food and drinks separately? Are you going to provide a fixed-price meal, with wine included, as a bundle? Would you charge extra for the service, or would it be included? Can the customers eat as much as they want or will they pay by the portion? Would you allow student discounts? Do the customers have to pay cash?

All these questions concern the price structure. Once this structure has been established, the service marketer has a clear overall framework into which decisions concerning pricing level and tactics have to fit. The *price level* is the actual price that is asked for a service. *Price tactics* refer to periodic price promotions or other short-term actions.

A service marketer therefore has to go through several steps to develop a pricing policy – from determining a pricing objective and strategy to the price structure, level and tactics. Obviously, the price element of the marketing mix cannot be isolated from the other three Ps. The pricing of a service has to be embedded in the marketing strategy and must be consistent with the other marketing activities relating to this service. The pricing process, as illustrated in Figure 9.2, is overshadowed by the overall marketing strategy and is in continuous interaction with other marketing measures. We shall now discuss each of the stages of the pricing process in greater detail and the specific issues involved in pricing services.

Pricing objectives

Let us return to the case study described in the introduction to the chapter and, in particular, the argument unfolding between the sales manager and the finance manager. The focus of their argument is the decision on whether to set prices high or low. It is clear that they have different objectives, making consensus around the pricing topic virtually impossible. It is, therefore, necessary for them to first discuss pricing *objectives*, before beginning to discuss different pricing *strategies*.

Reaching maximum profit is not always the key objective. Many others are possible, such as:

- acquiring a desired market share;
- maximizing long-term profit;
- maximizing short-term profit;

- avoiding cannibalizing other service offers;
- achieving the speedy exit of marginal competitors;
- being the price leader;
- avoiding price wars;
- generating traffic;
- communicating a particular image;
- making a fast recovery of investments;
- crowding out new market entries;
- regulating demand;
- securing key accounts;
- using spare capacity.

These pricing objectives can be divided into two categories: *short-term tactical moves* and *long-term strategic moves*. The decision to lower prices temporarily to make better use of existing capacity is a decision that can be taken further down the line than decisions that will shape the future of the company, such as setting the price at such a level as to reach the desired market share and signal the envisaged service concept.

In addition, choices with respect to pricing objectives are usually influenced by the dominant form of regulation in the market. A service company can be:

1 subject to *government regulation* (for example, railways, post offices and universities);
2 subject to a certain amount of *self-regulation* (for example, lawyers and doctors); or
3 services where the *market mechanism* decides (for example, cleaning services, hotels and catering).

Companies in the first category – those subject to government regulation – will have to consider the specific task in society for which they are sustained by government. Social and political goals will influence the pricing objective. For example, the Belgian government decided to take measures against ozone pollution. To discourage car use, it stimulated railway travel by offering special train fares during the summer period, when ozone levels are at their highest. Clearly, the pricing objective for these tickets was not to maximize profits but to realize an environmental goal (reducing ozone pollution) as well as a political one (creating goodwill with the public).

The second category of services – those subject to a certain amount of self-regulation – will try to establish a stable market situation and fair prices. Their pricing policy is devoted to continuity and stability. Doctors, for example, agree on general tariffs, in consultation with the doctors' association, social security agencies and the government.

The last category of services deals with a total free-market situation. The number of possible pricing objectives in this situation is almost endless. The choice of pricing objective in this case is primarily influenced by the company's strategy and objectives. Suppose the company pursues a niche strategy. The pricing objective has to be in line with that strategy. Maximizing market share would be a useless pricing objective in this case. On the other hand, if the company follows a strategy of cost leadership, it would be an appropriate goal.

Finally, the current market situation will also affect pricing objectives. Pricing objectives have to be realistic and feasible, and they will often involve intimate knowledge of the market and the competitors presently in the marketplace.

Pricing strategies

A pricing strategy establishes a general framework for pricing decisions and determines the way in which the price will be set. There are three main determinants on which the pricing strategy can be based – cost, competitor and customer. Although we discuss cost-based, customer-based and competition-based pricing strategies separately, a combination of the different perspectives seems to be necessary to compensate for the weaknesses each pricing perspective entails. In addition, price limits set by government through regulation must also be taken into account when setting prices.

Cost-based strategies

Marketers most often set their prices in accordance with the cost of the product or service. This means they focus entirely on the cost of providing a service to determine the price that is asked for it. A study by Morris and Fuller reveals that in industrial services, the process of estimating and covering costs is perceived by managers as far more important in setting prices than competitor- or customer-based considerations.[5] Mark-up pricing and target return pricing are the most common cost-based pricing strategies.

Mark-up pricing is probably the easiest way to set a price based on costs. A fixed margin is added to the service's cost to determine the price. The price is then calculated as follows:

$$\text{Mark-up price} = \frac{\text{Unit cost}}{1 - \text{Desired mark-up\%}}$$

Take, for example, a unit cost of £1600. A desired mark-up of 20% sets the price at:

$$\frac{1600}{0.8} = £2000$$

Target return pricing is based on the desired return on investment (ROI):

$$\text{Target return price} = \text{Unit cost} + \frac{\text{ROI} \times \text{Investment}}{\text{Expected number of units sold}}$$

An investment of €1,000,000, a desired ROI of 15%, and an expected volume of 1000 would construct a price of:

$$1600 + \frac{1,000,000 \times 0.15}{1000} = €1750$$

Cost-based strategies are fast and easy, and they can reveal the minimum price level necessary for the company to remain profitable. As such, cost-based price strategies do have their uses. However, cost-based strategies also show some major disadvantages from a marketing point of view:

● If the price is based on cost alone, then the pricing objective can only be to reach a certain profit level, because that is an integral part of the price formula (mark-up percentage or ROI). As has been explained above, many other pricing objectives exist for which, consequently, cost-based pricing is not effective.

● Cost-based strategies require an estimation of the number of units likely to be sold. It is clear, however, that this number will be greatly influenced by the price itself, taking into account the price elasticity of demand. In the case of high elasticity, using the sales volume to determine the price is pointless.

- Service managers should also take into account the *price cross-elasticity of demand*. This is the relative change in demand of one service caused by the change in price of another service. This price cross-elasticity could be important for additional services linked to a primary service or product. For example, the demand for computer training will be greatly influenced by the demand for computers and thus by the price of new computers.

- Cost-based strategies assume that the cost of providing a service or product has something to do with the value of the product or service. However, different organizations can have different costs for producing the same service, depending on their efficiency. The cost of a service, therefore, reflects the efficiency or inefficiency of the service provider to a greater extent than the value of the service delivered. Consequently, different companies, although providing the same service and thus creating the same value for the customer, will set different prices if they rely on their internal cost structure.

- Cost-based strategies have an entirely internal focus and do not in any way take market considerations into account. Obviously, in reality, customers are not in the least interested in what it costs the company to deliver a service; they are only interested in the benefits and values it offers them. Prices obtained by looking only at cost ignore market demand and can be much lower or higher than the customer is prepared to pay.

The cost of a service delivery is difficult to measure, due to the intangible nature of services. It is therefore crucial to monitor all the processes involved to keep track of the costs incurred for every service offered (*see* Chapter 13 on performance measurement). The cost of a service is not a static concept. Economies of scale and learning effects influence the cost and can change it over time.

It is clear from the above list of disadvantages that the cost of producing a service cannot be used as the sole determinant of price. However, it is still very important to have a detailed insight into costs, not only to determine the bottom price level, but also to be able to monitor and analyse every service offered. Service marketers can consider the cost of providing a service when setting the price, but it should also be correlated to the actual value the service delivers to the customer. In other words, their pricing strategy should also be based on customer value.

Customer-based strategies

Customer-based pricing focuses entirely on the market. The basic concept is that the price should be commensurate with the value the service actually delivers to the customer. In the end, it is the customer who will judge whether the price is fair or not and use it as a primary decision and evaluation criterion. Consequently, customers must feel they are receiving value for money.

Some service marketers measure the value construct as an equation incorporating the features and benefits of the service, with each additional benefit involving a price increment. However, this does not always correspond with the value as it is perceived by the customer. Consumers define value in four different ways:[6]

- '*Value is low price.*' Some consumers equate value with low price, indicating that what they give up in terms of money is most salient in their perceptions of value.

- *'Value is whatever I want in a service.'* Some consumers emphasize the benefits they receive from a service as the most important component of value.

- *'Value is the quality I receive for the price I pay.'* Some consumers see value as a trade-off; the money they pay is exchanged for the quality they receive.

- *'Value is what I receive for what I give.'* In this definition, the customer not only weighs up the quality and benefits of the service but also takes into account sacrifice components other than the price (for example, time and effort).

In one overall definition, perceived value is:

'the consumer's overall assessment of the utility of a service, based on perceptions of what is received and what is given.'

In any case, the key is to determine the perceived value of the service to the customer, and set the price according to this value. The concept of 'perceived value' has been explored by Zeithaml, using the model shown in Figure 9.3. As can be seen, the concept of perceived value is related to a number of other concepts:

1 *Intrinsic and extrinsic attributes.* The specific features of the service will influence the perceived value. Take the example of a sports centre. This centre's attributes would be its name, the opening hours, which sports can be practised there, the location, the availability of parking, the infrastructure, the professional qualifications of the instructors, and so on.

There is a distinction between intrinsic and extrinsic attributes. *Intrinsic* attributes cannot be changed without altering the nature of the service itself. They are part of the delivered service. In the case of the sports centre, the infrastructure and the skills of the instructors are examples of intrinsic attributes. *Extrinsic* attributes are not really part of

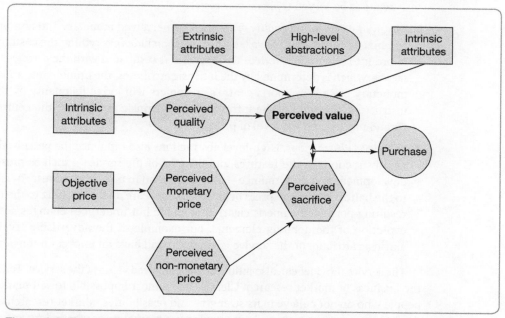

Figure 9.3 The model of 'perceived value'

Source: Zeithaml, V. A. and Bitner, M. J. (1996) *Services Marketing*. Reproduced with permission of The McGraw-Hill Companies, Inc.

the service the customer consumes. As such, they are not really an essential part of the service but are secondary variables that determine the total framework in which the service is offered. Objective price and brand name are the most important extrinsic attributes. The advertising of the sports centre is another example of an extrinsic attribute.

2 *Objective and perceived prices.* The *objective price* of a service is the actual price asked. This objective price often differs from the *perceived monetary price* because customers forget or misunderstand prices, or simply do not pay attention to them. For example, you could presume a bus ticket cost €0.87, even though in reality it now costs €1.12.

Service marketers should also understand that service buyers pay a *non-monetary price*, in addition to the monetary price. The monetary price should already take into account, and compensate for, this non-monetary price. These non-monetary customer costs result primarily from the fact that consumption and production of services coincide and that customer participation is thus required. The customer has to invest time and effort to be able to receive the service, which implies *opportunity costs* (the customer is prevented from doing something else in the meantime) and *convenience costs*. The customer also has to invest time and effort, or *search costs*, to select the right service. *Psychological costs* are also incurred resulting from the uncertainty felt while selecting, consuming, and evaluating a service. Search costs and psychological costs can be quite high because of the intangibility of services.

The various types of non-monetary costs can be illustrated with the example of visiting a restaurant. The customer:

– looks for an appropriate restaurant (*search costs*);
– worries whether the price/quality will be all right (*psychological costs*);
– goes to the restaurant (*convenience costs*);
– waits to be served (*opportunity costs*).

3 *Perceived sacrifice and quality of service.* The perceived monetary and non-monetary price combine to form the *perceived sacrifice*. This includes everything the customer has to lose in order to obtain the service. This sacrifice is compared with the *perceived quality of the service*, which is determined by the intrinsic attributes, the brand name and the perceived monetary price. The sports centre's customers will judge its quality by the skills of its instructors, the state of the infrastructure (intrinsic attributes), the centre's reputation (brand name), and the level of prices.

4 *High-level abstractions.* High-level abstractions also influence the perceived value. These are abstractions of the features and benefits of the service – such as prestige, personal development and performance – and correspond to universal values. For example, going to the hairdresser can express beauty, personal care and well-being to the customer. The resulting perceived value is clearly not stable but undergoes changes according to the evolution of the defining elements. For example, if the advertising level, which is an extrinsic attribute of the service, changes, it will have an impact on the perceived value.

The service provider can also influence the perceived value of the service. Take, for example, the business of market research. Clearly, it is almost impossible to sell market research to people who do not believe in its strengths and possibilities. Market research companies are dependent on marketers who know how to use market research, understand and believe in its value, and recognize the role of market research in marketing strategy. This is why service marketers should distinguish between a service's actual value and its potential value. The actual value is the value customers perceive at this moment. The potential value is the value the service provider could attain with continuous marketing efforts. For example, the customer could need more 'education' to fully understand the benefits a service offers. The intangible nature of services can make it more difficult to explain their uses and benefits.

Value-based pricing is based on the fact that the 'perceived value' is a fundamental consideration in setting a price, and this price as such already communicates a certain value to the customer. As can be seen from the model in Figure 9.3, the actual price influences the perceived value. This is a concept explored by Berry and Yadav.[7] They identify three different strategies that aim to capture and communicate the value of a service, according to what value means to the buyer:

- satisfaction-based pricing;
- relationship pricing; and
- efficiency pricing.

Satisfaction-based pricing

Satisfaction-based pricing eliminates the uncertainty that accompanies the purchase of a service. These kinds of strategy primarily aim to reassure the customer that he or she cannot go wrong when buying this service. Service providers can do this in several ways:

- *Benefit-driven pricing.* Service companies can explicitly price the aspect of the service that directly benefits customers. The underlying principle is that customers feel less uncertain and more satisfied if the unit in which the price is measured seems logical to them and the price is related to the benefits the service provider delivers. Benefit-driven pricing could certainly be beneficial for professional services such as legal services, which cause a great deal of uncertainty for the client, especially when lawyers charge by the hour. The cost-benefit analysis of a legal procedure cannot be estimated in advance, since the costs are not related to the benefits. Uncertainty when shopping for legal assistance is greatly reduced when prices are set according to the benefits delivered – for instance, by charging a percentage of the awarded claim (benefit) – especially when the outcome of the lawsuit is unpredictable.

- *Flat-rate pricing.* Of course, there are cases in which customers are more or less certain about the benefits they will receive, yet uncertain about the costs. To relieve this uncertainty, prices are agreed in advance. Flat-rate pricing only makes sense if the flat-rate price is attractive to the customer, compared to what he or she would expect to pay normally, and the company has to dispose of a cushion for unanticipated costs, through a highly efficient and streamlined cost structure. Lawyers, for instance, could also opt for flat-rate pricing instead of benefit-driven pricing. This could prove especially useful in lawsuits where the outcome is largely foreseeable.

- *Service guarantees.* These also belong to the category of satisfaction-based pricing. They are certainly the most extreme form of value-based pricing. Statements like 'If you're not completely satisfied, we don't expect you to pay' (Hampton Inns) guarantee service delivery of high perceived value (*see also* Chapter 14).

Relationship pricing

Relationship pricing encourages long-term relationships with the company that the customer views as beneficial. This pricing technique should not be confused with flat-rate pricing. Flat-rate pricing concerns the price of one project, while relationship pricing should encourage the customer to expand his or her purchases, both in time and in volume. The two most important pricing issues in relationship marketing are long-term contracts and price bundling:

- *Long-term contracts*, which offer customers price and non-price incentives to enter into relationships lasting several years, can change the buyer-seller relationship into a partner alliance based on mutual trust and collaboration ('win-win' philosophy).
- *Price bundling* aims at an extension of the relationship in terms of volume instead of time, by selling two or more products/services bundled together. Think of current offerings from telecom operators, which include a bundle of telephone services, internet access and (digital) TV. We shall discuss price bundling in greater detail later in this chapter, when we address the price structure decision.

Efficiency pricing

Efficiency pricing is based on understanding and managing costs, in order to accomplish cost reductions, which are then passed on to the customer. The 'efficiency pricer' must find a continuous challenge in eliminating non-value adding activities and, hence, streamlining the service processes by constantly questioning the way in which things are done. By working on the cost side in this way, the service provider can then offer the lowest price. A typical example of efficiency pricing is McDonald's. Costs can be minimized through a production-line approach to the service delivery. As we have already stated (*see* cost-based strategies), understanding costs is particularly difficult for service companies. Moreover, attempts at improving efficiency might have a negative impact on the quality of service delivery.

Exhibit 9.1 Pricing service innovations throughout the life cycle

The customer value of a service is not stable; it changes over time and differs between separate customer segments. Service marketers should keep this in mind when setting the price of a *new* service. They have to consider the price's evolution over time, together with the service life cycle.

For example, George Downey in our introductory case study is wondering about the price of an Internet connection. Should he begin with low prices, in order to gain a large market share right from the start, or should he aim for a select public and start out at a high price? Such concerns centre on a choice of strategies: penetration pricing and skimming pricing.

Skimming strategy

A skimming strategy is characterized by a maximum price setting at every stage of the life cycle. The basic premise is that there is always a group of customers willing to pay more for a service than others. The perceived value of the service is higher for these customers. The service price is then set at this level to maximize unit contribution. Over the life cycle, the price is decreased, to gradually win the customers with a lower perceived value who want to pay less. As the life cycle progresses further, the market is developed, step by step.

A skimming strategy has several advantages:

- The total profit is maximized over the life cycle of a service. At every point, the service provider asks for the maximum price, fully exploiting the perceived value of each segment.
- Price skimming supports the long-term development of the market, gaining the market step by step.
- The introductory price communicates a quality image, reassuring the customer and taking away any doubt about the performance to be expected. Since the price itself is already

an indication of value and influences the perceived value, it can sustain the image of a high quality service. This is particularly important since the intangible nature of services makes them harder to judge before purchase.

- Investments are quickly regained, aided by the high unit contribution.
- Starting with a high price allows for reductions later.
- Since the market is not fully attacked from the beginning and only a fraction of the potential customers are prepared to pay the introductory price, the necessary capacity can be limited at first and then be built up gradually. The service provider does not need full capacity from the start.

A skimming strategy does have some disadvantages, however:

- A skimming strategy involves a higher risk, since there is a possibility that the service will not be accepted at all due to its high price.
- New market entries are stimulated by the creation of an attractive market with high margins and growth potential.

With a skimming strategy, severe competition can be expected right after the introduction of the new service, when a number of competitors, attracted by the profits to be gained, also enter the market. This will cause pressure on prices. Setting a low price from the beginning could discourage new market entries and avert price wars. A good illustration of this is the Belgian cellular telephone market. Belgacom launched its product and services lines under the umbrella of their expiring monopoly. After the entry of a second provider, Mobistar, prices dropped dramatically, indicating clearly the skimming practices adopted initially by Belgacom.

Penetration strategy

Introducing a new service at a low price in order to obtain rapid market penetration is called penetration pricing. This pricing strategy is used to gain a large market share in a short time. If the service can be quickly imitated, penetration pricing can be beneficial. Furthermore, if the hesitation of customers to try out the new service needs to be overcome, offering the new services at the lowest price possible or even free is advisable. The introduction of automatic teller machines (ATMs) is a good example of this. At first, this service was offered free by most banks; once customer familiarity with the service became widespread – which is necessary for the ATM network to become sustainable in the long run – pricing was introduced in many countries.

A number of conditions need to be fulfilled and so it is essential that the implementation of a penetration strategy is handled carefully:

- The market has to adopt the service quickly, without a long test period.
- The elasticity of demand should be high, providing a high demand at low prices. If the demand does not vary with the price, there will be no point in offering low prices, since this will only damage the profitability of the service provider.
- The service provider should be aware of the possibility that the low price will communicate low quality and value to potential customers. This, combined with the fact that many services are difficult to evaluate before purchase (or even after it) could create uncertainty and doubt. Contrary to the service provider's intentions, this could actually inhibit fast, large-scale adoption. Take the example of market research studies. No one would want a study that only costs $100, since the price would indicate that this study could not possibly have been executed thoroughly and professionally.
- The necessary capacity to sustain a rapid market development should be present from the outset.

Competition-based strategies

This category of pricing strategies is entirely based on the firm's actual and desired competitive position. The prime motivation for this kind of pricing strategy is to reach a desired position within the competitive field. Such a position can be reached through the following pricing strategies: *experience-curve pricing, going-rate pricing, price signalling* and *price leadership*.

Experience-curve pricing

Let us consider a competitive market with experience effects – for instance, the market for Internet access providers – as shown in Figure 9.4.

When company A sets prices at or even below current costs, the price-sensitive customers of companies B and C will switch to company A. This will make it possible for A to gain experience more rapidly, thus outpacing the competition and eventually driving competitors out of the market. In addition, company A's low price can encourage more customers to enter the market, once again giving company A the opportunity to exploit economies of scale.

Experience-curve pricing – that is, pricing aggressively at or even below current costs – can be used when:

● experience effects are strong;
● the firm has more experience than its competitors;
● customers are price-sensitive.

Going-rate pricing

This pricing strategy involves charging the most prevalent price in the market. In some service markets, demand is so price-sensitive that a firm would risk losing most of its business if its prices became higher than those of competitors. On the other hand, charging lower prices would result in immediate retaliation from competitors. Within going-rate pricing, a distinction can be made between 'naive' and 'sophisticated' going-rate pricing.[8]

In *naive going-rate pricing*, a firm automatically sets its prices at the same level as its competitors, without analysing demand or costs. An example of this situation can be found

Figure 9.4 Chart showing relative positions of companies in a competitive market

in a busy tourist zone where a number of restaurants 'cluster' together. To attract price-sensitive tourists, restaurants will set the 'Daily Special' at the going rate, while more specialized dishes, for which competition is more 'fuzzy', are priced at a premium.

In *sophisticated going-rate pricing*, a 'follower' follows the pricing decisions of the 'leader'. This can be observed in the banking sector, where the leader determines the rate changes in a specific segment (mortgage loans, deposit accounts, etc.) and is then followed by smaller banks within that segment.

The use of going-rate pricing has two main advantages for service businesses:

1 *Simplicity*. It is much easier to make price decisions on the basis of the going rate than to set prices according to customer value or cost, given the difficulties in measurement in a service environment.

2 *Price peace*. Going-rate pricing prevents price wars.

Price signalling

Service offers often differ in quality and average total cost. Suppose there are only two different quality levels, high and low, and associated with these quality levels are average total costs of €100 and €120 respectively. Service firms can choose from three different strategies:

1 charging €100 for low quality;

2 charging €120 for high quality service; and

3 charging €120 for low quality.

The third option is called price signalling.

There are three underlying conditions necessary for price signalling to be an equilibrium strategy:[9]

- Consumers must be able to obtain information about price more easily than information about quality. In many service businesses this will be the case, since the inherent intangibility of services makes it more difficult for customers to gain information about the quality of the service.

- Customers must want the service enough to risk buying the higher-priced service even with no guarantee of high quality.

- There must be a sufficiently large number of informed consumers who can understand quality and will pay the high price only for the high quality service. This ensures a sufficiently positive correlation between price and quality, so that uninformed consumers who infer quality from price will find it, on average, worthwhile to do so.

The restaurant business is a typical service business where these three conditions are fulfilled. Consumers can gain access to price information by looking at the menu, which is often placed outside at the entrance to the restaurant, but information about the quality of the food served inside is more difficult to obtain. However, there will be a sufficiently large number of customers who can understand quality, thus ensuring a positive correlation between price and quality. Finally, many customers want the high quality enough to take some risks.

Although this pricing strategy will maximize short-term profits, it will be disastrous for most businesses in the long run, because it is based on cheating the customer. Duped customers will go away dissatisfied, spreading their bad experience by word of mouth, which makes acquisition of new customers ever more difficult. And since customers are constantly being fooled, development of a loyal customer base is impossible. However, there are certain service providers for whom a price signalling strategy can be beneficial, even in the long term. What visitor to the Piazza della Signoria in Florence or the banks of the Canal Grande in Venice has not felt cheated by the local restauranteurs? Restaurants in tourist hot spots such as these do not need loyalty to be profitable. They just need one shot at every tourist visiting these cities. There is thus no need for loyalty or positive word of mouth.

Price leadership

A price leader exerts a dominant influence on market prices for a service delivery, giving direction to market price levels and patterns by initiating price increases or decreases. The price leader is commonly a market leader, the biggest selling service firm in that specific service segment. For example, in mortgage loans, the price leader will determine interest levels for mortgage loans. The price leader will often behave very aggressively towards competitors when they are, in its opinion, misbehaving. Further characteristics of the price leader include:

- it is often a low-cost producer;
- it has strong distribution channels;
- it is often recognized as being in the technical forefront of service development;
- it has superior financial resources.

Handling fierce price competition in a service environment

Since the fixed/variable cost ratio is high in a considerable number of service businesses, the marginal profit contribution is almost equal to the revenue obtained. In the presence of competition, the result can be an intense price war, since price cuts are immediately matched by competitors. Considering the enormous impact of prices on the company's profits, the result can be devastating. The huge price war raging in the English Channel crossing market is a case in point. Since the construction of the railway tunnel ('the Chunnel'), the price of crossing the Channel has collapsed. The three main players (ferries, airlines and the tunnel) are competing by using ever cheaper offers to tempt potential customers, up to the limit where crossing the Channel by ferry can cost next to nothing. Clearly, this price war has brought few benefits to the competitors. No single price advantage is maintained for any length of time, since it is always being matched by a competitor's offer. The impact on the value perceived by customers is also detrimental. Customers' perceptions of the 'normal price' to cross the Channel are completely distorted by the continuous price cuts. The suppliers' emphasis on price in their messages to the customer only enhances this price sensitivity.[10]

In waging a price war, two key issues must be watched closely: *security* and *flexibility*. A sufficient degree of security against enemy attack is essential if an offensive strategy is to be pursued. Key customers must be looked after, with attention concentrated where the bulk of the business is done. In military terms, defend your vital targets at all costs. In Pareto terminology, fight to retain the 20% of your customer base that delivers 80% of your sales. In this case, price discrimination can offer interesting perspectives. Besides security, flexibility is a key issue in waging a price war, since prearranged plans may have to be altered to meet changing situations.

In most cases, none of the parties engaged in a price war is a winner in the end. Thus, preventing a price war seems at least as important as fighting it. This can be achieved in the following two ways:

1 *Threats*. Competitors are left in no doubt that price attacks will be retaliated against immediately.

2 *Price agreements*. Explicit or implicit agreements excluding price competition between competitors in oligopolistic markets enhance profits for all parties.

An example of the second option can be found in the Belgian telecommunications industry. Proximus (Belgacom, AirTouch) was the only cellular phone operator in Belgium until 1996, when a second operator, Mobistar (France Télécom), entered the market with very low prices. Proximus responded by dropping its prices to some 4% above Mobistar's. The combination of the price drop with press releases from Proximus, stating that the GSM market was big enough for both competitors to be profitable, averted a price war. Consequently, Mobistar also stated its intention to prevent a price war under any circumstances. Take note that price agreements are subject to regulation since it implies a loss of 'consumer' welfare, as we will discuss in the following pages.

Finding a balance between the different pricing strategies

The three determinants of price (cost, competitor and customer value) are clearly all important and ignoring any of them could be a major mistake.

The cost of providing a service determines the bottom price level. The perceived value of the service by the customer determines the top level. The competitors' price is the moderating variable that forces service providers to strike a balance between cost and customer value. However, determining how each of the three determinants will affect price must be examined in the light of the pricing objective.

To clarify this, let us return to the situation described at the beginning of the chapter. George Downey, who is responsible for a telecommunications company's expansion into providing Internet access, has to determine the price for this service. With profit optimization as his objective, he will aim at the segment that has the highest perceived value and is prepared to pay the most for an Internet connection. This way, he can skim the market incrementally, continuously looking for those high-value customers. This would be the ideal way to work in a monopoly situation but, as more and more competitors enter the market, each fighting for its share of the cake, there will doubtless be more and more pressure on prices. Furthermore, as Internet access becomes more common, the perceived value will be eroded. Lowering prices will further this erosion.

Another scenario would be to depart from a market objective – to develop the market as quickly as possible. The cost then will determine the bottom price level. George Downey should aim at the mass market and lower the threshold as far as possible. He should achieve this by not only setting low prices but also by taking away any customer doubts – by allowing a free test period, for example.

No matter what pricing objective George Downey chooses, there is one factor he should never lose sight of: his pricing strategy has to be embedded in the total marketing strategy. The process of segmenting, targeting and positioning determines who the customers are, as well as who the direct competitors of the company are (aiming at the same segment). Consequently, George Downey should regard service value only through the eyes of his target group and study the actions of those competing for the same segment. This also means that the pricing strategy must be in line with the service strategy and the implied service concept.

In line with the arguments developed in the first chapters of this book, it can be also noted that the nature of the service delivery process itself plays a role here. Recall the typology stemming from Mills and Margulies outlined in Chapter 2. A distinction has been made between maintenance-interactive, task-interactive and personal-interactive services. These services vary in terms of the amount of uncertainty and complexity entailed in the service transaction itself. The standardized nature of maintenance-interactive services implies that cost-based and competition-based considerations might dominate the final outcomes in terms of pricing strategy. As these types of service are much easier to compare, cost and competitive considerations will prevail. Also these types of service are often more capital- and hence technology-intensive. This phenomenon might lead one to emphasize experience-curve pricing as outlined above. Such phenomena are less in evidence in the case of task- and especially personal-interactive type of service. Characterized by high levels of uncertainty or even ambiguity, pricing these types of service will be much more closely related to the dynamics outlined by Zeithaml (see Figure 9.3) whereby intrinsic and extrinsic attributes are of a less tangible nature than in the case of maintenance-interactive services.[11] Note also, that for these types of service, one often does not pay for a certain transaction or outcome. Rather, fees depend directly on the time spent by the service provider; think of counselling but also of professional consulting services. And while this phenomenon, which can be linked directly to the uncertain nature of these service delivery processes, might create transparency in terms of budget (one can compare hourly/daily fees), the heterogeneity of both inputs and process ingredients will, in the end, lead again to idiosyncratic value perceptions. So, finding a balance in terms of pricing strategy necessitates taking into account both the competitive strategy and the nature of the service delivery process.[12]

Government policies restraining pricing policy

We stated above that pricing decisions can be studied from three perspectives: a cost perspective, a customer perspective and a competitor perspective. In most Western economies, however, government policies aimed mainly at protecting the consumer will also play a large part in pricing strategies. In economics, it is a widespread belief that competition is the most effective way to achieve low consumer prices. In practice, however, services are more likely than goods to be supplied in non-competitive environments. This has forced many Western governments to intervene directly in pricing decisions. These interventions take the following forms:[13]

- *Price agreements.* Since many service industries are oligopolistic in nature, companies can enhance profitability through price agreements. These in fact eliminate competition, which results in higher prices for the consumer. Such activities have been declared illegal by many European countries, both individually and in combination through European legislation. (Initially, Articles 85 and 86 of the Treaty of Rome; nowadays, the Treaty of Lisbon prohibits anti-competitive agreements in Article 101(1), including price fixing.) In the UK, an agreement between the four largest betting shop operators not to compete on price was declared illegal in 1986. In Belgium, the government determines maximum price levels for petrol.

- *Monopoly pricing.* In order to protect customers from exclusion, governments might want to avoid competition for some services. Nonetheless, to keep prices within certain bounds, governments can use regulatory bodies that determine the level and structure of charges made by these service companies (e.g. Ofcom which regulates the British telecom industry).

- *Price communication*. Governments can specify the manner in which prices should be communicated. For instance, the Belgian government, through the Consumer Protection Act 1991, requires that all prices should be communicated with VAT included. For financial services, there are specific requirements about the communication of debit and credit rates, exchange rates, and so forth.

- *Tie-in sales*. Most governments, recognizing that some forms of bundling (*see* later in this chapter), in particular some forms of tie-in sales, inflict substantial harm on the general public, have forced companies to limit the use of these techniques (in the US by the Clayton Act, in the European Union by directives of the European Commission). These cases are mostly related to limiting the use of bundling due to anti-competitive pressures.

Pricing structure

The pricing structure takes into account a set of product, customer and purchase characteristics that will have an effect on price levels.

Price discrimination

Price discrimination can be defined as the charging of different prices to different market segments. Price discrimination should not be confused with price differentiation, which involves the service provider charging lower prices due to economic factors, such as extra-large orders. Nor should price discrimination be confused with the efforts of managing demand, since price discrimination is not meant to shift demand to off-peak periods. It is meant, rather, to augment profits from price-insensitive segments, and to generate more business from price-sensitive segments.

Service providers can discriminate between segments with different price sensitivities, charging high prices to customers almost insensitive to price changes, and charging low prices to price-sensitive customers. Price discrimination is only possible when:

- different segments have different price sensitivity;
- the different segments are identifiable, and a mechanism exists to charge them different prices;
- the different segments are fully separated – that is, individuals in the low-price segment cannot pass their right to use the service on to another segment;
- the segments are large enough to make the discrimination worthwhile;
- the cost of the price discrimination strategy does not exceed the incremental revenues obtained;
- the use of different prices does not confuse customers;
- competition is limited (preferably a monopoly).[14]

The time-dependent nature of services makes price discrimination possible. Different prices at different times of the day are often feasible because demand is also time dependent. Rail companies, for instance, can charge higher prices during peak hours (since commuters cannot shift to off-peak hours), thus increasing profits obtained from these segments.

It should be noted that price discrimination is not always meant as a profit-enhancing mechanism. In many public utilities, for instance, it is common to give discounts to certain customer segments – senior citizens, minors, large families – for social reasons.

Price-line decisions

When making price-line decisions, two important factors should be studied: price consistency and price lining.

Since services are by their nature intangible, the service offerings of different providers cannot easily be compared. Thus, the price of the service offering itself will often communicate the service level of the provider. When pricing different services or products, the service provider has to keep the overall targeted position in mind. This is called *price consistency*. For instance, imagine the confusion of a guest in a five-star hotel if he or she were to see that breakfast cost only $1.95.

Price lining, on the other hand, involves dividing the product assortment into different price ranges. Through this pricing method, a service provider can maximize sales by offering different value (price-quality) propositions. The Marriott Hotel group, for instance, offers a full range of hotel chains including Ritz-Carlton and Bulgari (premium price/quality), Mariott (high price-good quality), Courtyard (average price-standard quality) and Fairfield Inn (moderate price-quality). Marriott is thus able to enlarge its customer base by offering a hotel for every segment. Moreover, Marriott eliminates loss of a customer's lifetime value, if they want to move up or down to a different price category.

Pricing complementary services

Companies that offer complementary products or services sometimes take a small profit margin on the main purchase, such as a car, but take a high margin on complementary products or services (accessories or maintenance). This pricing approach can be very profitable, unless there are more focused competitors, selling those complementary services at a lower margin. In industrial markets, for instance, installations sometimes are sold at low margins, which is compensated for through high margins on maintenance services. This technique is called *installed base management*. The low margins on installations boost sales (penetration), thus enlarging a company's installed base and expanding the potential market for the service department. Since the high margins on services will attract entrants to this market, one has to be able to build and sustain a competitive lead to secure these high margins.

Price bundling

Price bundling is the practice of marketing two or more products and/or services in a single package for a special price and is sometimes called *'package' pricing*.[15] It is a potentially powerful method for exploiting profit potentials and maximizing profits in any company that offers multiple products and/or services.

Bundled accounts that roll together credit cards, cheque accounts, certificates of deposit and consumer loans have become big sellers for many banks. One of the biggest selling points is their convenience. The marketing angle aside, these accounts are intended to reduce the overhead and support costs of taking in new deposits and making loans.[16]

There are two possible approaches to price bundling: pure or mixed price bundling:

1 In *pure price bundling* (or 'tie-in sales'), the services and/or products are available only in bundled form and cannot be purchased separately. Pure price bundling is only applicable in the rare cases in which a firm holds monopoly power over one of the components of the bundle.

2 In *mixed price bundling*, the customer is offered the opportunity to either buy the bundle or to buy its different components separately. Typically, there is some price incentive for purchasing the bundle, although bundling can simply take the form of add-on services. There are two forms of mixed price bundling: mixed-leader price bundling and mixed-joint price bundling:[17]

   – In *mixed-leader price bundling*, the price of one (or several) of the services/products is discounted while the other is purchased at the regular price. For example, some theatres and opera houses offer discounts for parking, with the theatre ticket serving as proof. This type of price bundling is not very frequent in service industries, compared to the mixed-joint form.

   – In the *mixed-joint* form, a single price is set when the different services are purchased jointly. In 1994, De Generale Bank introduced the G-Global Club in Belgium. A large number of banking transactions are free of charge for members of the club, as are debit and credit cards (including Eurocheques), in exchange for a monthly fee of €5.58. Examination of the charges to non-members shows that a club membership costs about €24.79 more per year than the fees charged by the bank to non-members. This difference is more than compensated for through large discounts offered to the members of the club by hotels, restaurants and even a travel agency. This price bundling effort has been profitable for De Generale Bank (the club had 150,000 members in 1996), it does not necessarily mean that it will be profitable for all banks.

A price bundling approach (mixed or pure) is only profitable when the following conditions are met:

1 *Government regulation permits price bundling.* Tie-in sales, for instance, are illegal in many European countries.

2 *The value offered by the bundle to the customer exceeds the value of the different components of the bundle,* where value is defined as 'what a customer gets for what he sacrifices'. Here are a few cases where this condition is fulfilled:

   – customers believe that substantial time and effort will be saved in one-stop shopping (*convenience*);

   – customers who have little knowledge about the bundled product(s) or service(s) believe that buying the bundled offer is less risky (*risk reduction*);

   – the bundle is offered at a *price discount*.

3 *Customer needs are similar,* and thus can be satisfied with one bundled offer. When customer needs are diverse, the bundled offer might not fully satisfy customers and consequently may create opportunities for more focused companies.

Pure price bundling is very common in the computer and software industry, for instance. PCs are delivered with a software package already installed. If most customers want to use another supplier's software, however, this bundled offer does not increase value for the customer and, eventually, results in higher prices for the customer and/or lower margins for the supplier. In consequence, this customer can be tempted to switch to more focused ('unbundling') suppliers.

Although it is not strictly speaking a condition, proprietary control over one of the components of the bundle greatly reduces the risk of duplication in the case of pure price bundling.

A successful price bundling effort can enhance profits and support the competitive position of a firm in several ways. First, it may enable the firm to gain a *cost advantage*, especially when bundled offers are standardized, since standardized bundled offers cost less to produce than several customized individual products or services. Second, when using a mixed-price bundling strategy, price bundling can be used as a *discrimination* device, charging different prices to different customer segments, based on their buying behaviour. Finally, price bundling may enable the firm to offer a *differentiated product or service*, by providing an overall solution to the customer's needs.

Managing demand

The nature of services, with characteristics such as intangibility, simultaneity and, above all, perishability, coupled with capacity constraints, suggests that demand should be managed in an effective way to maximize profits. Most service industries are characterized by varying demand curves over time, which follow a daily, weekly, annual, seasonal, cyclical or random pattern. These fluctuations in demand foster the need to manage capacity (*see* Chapter 10). In the case of rail services, for example, workers and students must generally arrive at work or school at a specified time, which creates peaks around certain time periods. Resort hotel demand will be higher during prime holiday months than it is in the off-season, while capacity is more or less fixed. Furthermore, resort hotel demand curves show that the market is much less price-sensitive during prime holiday months than it is in the off-season.

Profits can be maximized through setting prices according to price sensitivity. In high season, the price for a room per night can be double the off-season price. Thus, tourists taking their holidays outside prime holiday months due to price discounts level out demand, with higher profits for the hotel as a consequence of better capacity utilization.[18]

In addition, when different customer segments have different demand patterns over time, targeting these segments and thus expanding business through other segments can also significantly enhance profitability. Exploiting these other segments will often require a different price positioning effort. Capacity utilization of fast-food restaurants, for instance, is very low during the afternoon, yet this is the preferred time for children to have birthday parties. Arranging children's birthday parties can thus enhance capacity utilization and, in this manner, augment profitability for fast-food chains such as McDonald's. Of course, pricing decisions will also be of great importance in attracting this additional business. Demand management can also be addressed in the broader context of yield management, which will be discussed extensively in Chapter 10 on capacity management.[19]

Pricing levels and tactics

Price levels refer to the actual price that is charged for a service, including any specific promotions being offered. Price tactics involve short-term promotional price initiatives. The aim of such actions can differ from case to case and promotional pricing can be tailored to suit a particular objective. Examples of promotional goals and their complementary actions are:

- *Quantity discounts*. The service provider offers a discount to customers dealing in greater volume – for example, transportation companies offering discounts for every additional truck engaged.

- *Temporary discounts* (time shift). Prices are lower at certain times or on certain days – for example, off-peak hours in a squash centre, or hotel discounts at weekends.

- *Promotional discounts* (generate trial). The service can be set at a lower price for a limited period of time to attract new customers.

Promotional pricing is difficult for services, however, when customers lack precise reference prices. If such price transparency does not exist, promotional discounts become quite useless. This transparency of price information is determined by three factors:

1 *The availability of price information* – can I get information about the price of a particular service?

2 The effort it costs to get that information – what do I have to do to receive it?

3 The clarity of the price information – is it understandable?

Another important criterion – *the comparability of competing service offers* – can be defined using the same three variables as above:

1 *The availability of information on the result of a service offer* – can I get information about the performance of a particular service offer?

2 *The effort it costs to compare service offers* – what do I have to do to be able to compare service offers?

3 *The clarity of the comparison* – is it in any way possible to compare, even if I have the necessary information?

The combination of these two criteria – transparency of price information and comparability of the results – creates a framework in which every kind of service can be represented (*see* Figure 9.5).

Services that are easily comparable and that possess a high transparency of price information are most appropriate for discount pricing actions. The customers of these services are more likely to know reference prices and can judge the promotional price compared to it. The effect of price discounts on services with low transparency of price information is questionable. The price discount can create greater clarity (which is not always beneficial to the service provider) but it can also confuse the customer who cannot distinguish the discount price from the normal price. For services with a low degree of comparability, it is more important for the customer to receive assurance of quality, since the result of the service is difficult to judge beforehand.

The framework in Figure 9.5 does more than determining when discount prices can be useful. Given that the basic aim of discounting prices is to obtain more income by lowering

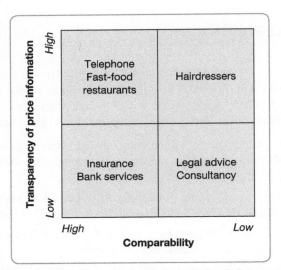

Figure 9.5 Matrix representing criteria for implementation of discount pricing

the price, discounting assumes that decreasing the price will have a positive effect on sales. In reality, the usefulness of price discounts will be determined by the price competition that exists in the market and the vulnerability of the service provider when it comes to pricing.

Clearly, markets with a high transparency of price information and a high degree of comparability experience greater price competition, and are forced either to use price discounts (in order to keep or attract customers) or to expand their sales volume. The matrix in Figure 9.5 provides a means of escaping this trap, making price discounts obsolete:

1 *Reducing the transparency of price information*. Creating complicated price structures is a possible way to lower the transparency of the price information. However, this is a dangerous path to walk alone since it can increase the insecurity of the customer, who prefers to know what to expect. De Generale Bank takes this approach with its G-Global Club that, in one way, enhances transparency by attaching a clear, fixed price to a bundled set of services. On the other hand, the individual services can no longer be distinguished, making it impossible to know what they cost.

2 *Reducing the comparability of the offer*. The service provider can implement this by differentiating its offer from that of its competitor's. Customization of the service is one possible way to do this. Clearly, when the offer is completely adapted to a customer's needs, it becomes difficult for him or her to compare several offers.

According to the framework described, there are two ways to escape from severe price pressure: by making it more difficult to see through the pricing or by making it more difficult to see through the offer.

Conclusion

In this chapter we have provided you with an overview of the major elements playing a role in pricing services.

It is important to take time to think at the beginning of the pricing process. Determining in advance what you want to achieve with your pricing strategy is a necessary, but often neglected, first step in developing a sound pricing approach.

Within the pricing process, it helps to make a distinction between pricing objectives, strategy, structure, level and tactics. They all refer to a single pricing process but consider separate questions.

In terms of pricing strategy, the costs, competition and the value as experienced by customers should all be taken into account. Also, the nature of the service delivery process itself might affect the relevancy of these different elements. It is important to know exactly what drives costs and to make sure that the pricing strategy is in line with the overall marketing strategy. Pricing is a valuable instrument when targeting a particular segment and positioning the company in relation to competitors. Perhaps the most difficult task is determining what value means to the customer and adapting the pricing strategy to reflect this. What value means for customers is dynamic as well; this became clear when discussing pricing strategies for innovations.

Anticipating competitors' moves and avoiding price wars by differentiating your product from that of the competition are important tactical considerations. Regulations governing the market dynamics are another issue to be taken into account.

Finally, being clear about your prices is more important than developing all kinds of promotions.

Review and discussion questions

- Being first in the market allows deploying different pricing strategies; which one would you prefer under which conditions?

- The idea of price bundling is not only very fashionable but also very controversial (e.g. Microsoft). Under what conditions would price bundling be relevant and acceptable?

- With respect to e-business, pricing seems to be extremely difficult. What do you consider as relevant approaches to price the (different?) services the Internet entails? And which part should be paid by whom? Would bundling be a relevant concept in this respect?

Suggested further reading

Berry, L. L. and Yadav, M. S. (1996) 'Capture and communicate value in the pricing of services', *Sloan Management Review*, Summer, pp. 41–51

Dolan, R. J. and Simon, H. (1997) *Power Pricing*. New York, NY: The Free Press. This is the most comprehensive book on pricing. Highly recommended

Leszinski, R. and Marn, M. (1997) 'Setting value, not price', *The McKinsey Quarterly*, Issue 1

Shoemaker S. (2003) 'The future of pricing in services', *Journal of Revenue and Pricing Management*, Vol 2, No 3, pp. 271–279

Taher, A. and El Basha, H. (2006) 'Heterogeneity of customer demand: Opportunities for pricing of services', *Journal of Product and Brand Management*, Vol 5, No 5, pp. 331–340

Notes and references

1 Considering that the fixed costs can be spread over a larger volume, an increase of 20% in volume will be sufficient to cover the price decrease

2 Price elasticity is defined as the ratio of the relative change in volume to the relative change in price: Elasticity $= ((\delta V/V)/(\delta P/P))$. Depending on the price elasticity of the service, the total demand will vary more or less according to the price. If the price elasticity is high, the demand will increase relatively more than the price decreases, and vice versa

3 Keaveney, S. M. (1995) 'Customer switching behaviour in service industries: An exploratory study', *Journal of Marketing*, Vol 59, April, pp. 71–82

4 Morris, M. and Cantalone, R. (1990) 'Four components of effective pricing', *Industrial Marketing Management*, Vol 19, pp. 321–329

5 Morris, M. H. and Fuller, D. A. (1989) 'Pricing an industrial service', *Industrial Marketing Management*, Vol 18, pp. 139–146

6 Zeithaml, V. and Bitner, M. J. (1996) *Services Marketing*. New York, NY: McGraw-Hill, pp. 496–498

7 Berry, L. and Yadav, M. (1996) 'Capture and communicate value in the pricing of services', *Sloan Management Review*, Summer, pp. 41–51

8 Giletta, M. (1992) 'Prix: de la maîtrise des prix à la maîtrise des coûts', *Vuibert Gestion*, p. 22

9 Tellis, G. J. (1986) 'Beyond the many faces of price: An integration of pricing strategies', *Journal of Marketing*, Vol 50, October, pp. 146–160

10 Garda, R. and Marn, M. (1993) 'Price wars', *McKinsey Quarterly*, Issue 3

11 A point we will further explore in Chapter 17

12 For a further elaboration of the relationship between service characteristics and pricing decisions, *see* Taher, A. and El Basha, H. (2006) 'Heterogeneity of customer demand: opportunities for pricing of services', *Journal of Product and Brand Management*, Vol 5, No 5, pp. 331–340

13 Palmer, A. (1994) *Principles of Services Marketing*. New York, NY: McGraw-Hill, pp. 257–258

14 Bateson, J. E. G. (1989) *Managing Services Marketing*. The Dryden Press, p. 363

15 Guiltinan, J. P. (1987) 'The price bundling of services: A normative framework', *Journal of Marketing*, Vol 51, April, pp. 74–85

16 Radigan, J. (1992) 'Bundling for dollars', *United States Banker*, Vol 102, No 9, September, pp. 42–44

17 Guiltinan, J. P. (1987), op. cit.

18 Note that such practices might negatively affect customer loyalty as convincingly demonstrated by Shoemaker (2003). Thus, service firms should consider simultaneously short-term benefits and potential (medium term) negative effects before engaging in such practices. *See*: Shoemaker, S. (2003) 'The future of pricing in services', *Journal of Revenue and Pricing Management*, Vol 2, No 3, pp. 271–279

19 Yield management is the process of allocating the right type of capacity to the right kind of customer at the right price so as to maximize revenue or yield – Kimes, S. E. (1989) 'Yield management: A tool for capacity-constrained service firms', *Journal of Operations Management*, Vol 8, No 4, October, pp. 348–363

PART THREE

Delivering services

Paul Gemmel • Bart Van Looy

Service delivery focuses on how to interactively create value for the customer. Service employees, as well as customers, play an active role in the realization of services. Each service encounter involves employees and customers with their own expectations and experiences and, therefore, delivery will depend on the behaviour of employees and customers.

One of the key success factors in service delivery is capacity management (Chapter 10). Not only is capacity management extremely important for the financial performance of the service firm but, in addition, its outcome has a direct impact on the customer. It affects waiting times for the customers but, more importantly, capacity is part of the service offering. Capacity management is not only important but also complex, given the simultaneity and intangibility of the service. Capacity management involves managing not only supply but also demand. With the particular problems of managing supply and demand in services, handling customer waiting times are often inevitable. As a result, Chapter 10 includes a section on the psychology of waiting.

The simultaneity of services leads to an intimate relationship between employees' behaviour, their motivation, competencies, satisfaction and commitment, and customers' perceptions of service quality and, hence, satisfaction. As a result, human resources (HR) practices play a crucial role in the management of service operations. These are discussed extensively in Chapter 11, where we introduce three crucial notions that service-oriented HR practices should address: empowerment, competencies and collaboration.

Two levels of empowerment can be discerned – empowerment at the individual level and at the organizational level. Empowerment at the individual level is closely related to the notion of motivation. We will examine the meaning of empowerment as a motivational construct and its implications for leadership. With empowerment at the organizational level, redistributing power, rewards, information and knowledge are seen as crucial. It will become clear that organizations functioning in this way tend to achieve higher levels of employee and customer satisfaction and, even, profitability.

While, in Chapter 5, the contours of competence based HR practices have been highlighted, we complement this perspective by discussing competence development strategies in Chapter 11. In talking about competence development, it is tempting to approach this process solely from an individual perspective. However, competence development has a highly relational side. We highlight the importance of collaborative relationships in Chapter 11, thereby completing our overview of competencies and their development.

When managing services, it is crucial to have detailed knowledge about the needs and considerations of customers, as discussed in Chapter 12. Customers are asked to consider a purchase that is very difficult to evaluate beforehand. Furthermore, since customers are participating in the production and even the creation of services, it is a much more intimate activity than simply buying a product. A service company must find out the needs and the motivation of its customers, and interact in such a manner that customers become engaged emotionally.

It should come as no surprise that the most important focus in service marketing is on building and maintaining relationships. Chapter 12 therefore discusses *relationship marketing*. Building and maintaining relationships in service situations are directly related to the principle that customer satisfaction, customer loyalty and profitability are closely intertwined with each other.

Dynamic changes in the environment and heterogeneity due to the interaction of employees and customers in the service delivery process continuously harbour the risk of losing focus. Therefore, it is important to define a clear service concept as described in Chapter 3. However, defining a service concept is only one part of the story. Making sure that the employees in the organization underwrite and sustain the service concept is the other (more difficult) part. In Chapter 13, we introduce a fundamental requirement in this respect, i.e. the design and implementation of a performance measurement system. Whilst a performance measurement system can guide the organization in the right direction, it can just as easily misdirect it if the performance measures chosen are not aligned with the service concept.

Customer satisfaction depends, to a great extent, on how well service employees understand customer expectations and are consequently able to fulfill these expectations in line with the service concept. This is why some service firms make their performance standards more explicit by using service guarantees or service-level agreements – the subjects of Chapter 14. In these types of arrangement, the service provider makes explicit the level or quality the customer may expect and, sometimes, backs up these promises with a pay-out. This kind of arrangement gives the service provider the opportunity to track service failures and to continuously improve the service offering, crucial to developing and maintaining a long-term relationship with customers.

Chapter 10

Capacity management

Roland Van Dierdonck • Paul Gemmel

Objectives

By the end of this chapter, you should be able to discuss:

- the specific nature of capacity management in services and why capacity management is important
- ways of determining how much capacity to make available, given a certain demand pattern
- how to schedule the available capacity facing a variable demand pattern
- how capacity management involves the management of demand, and how the demand pattern can be influenced
- the concept of yield management
- how waiting in a service organization is inevitable and how the perception of the waiting experience can be managed

Introduction

The change in value of EuroDisney stocks more than anything else illustrates the difficult introductory period of Disneyland Paris. The initial euphoria disappeared very quickly after the opening of the park in April 1992. Financial restructuring and management changes have now put the company (it is hoped) on the path to profitability, but no one can deny that the company has, thus far, not been the success envisaged at the start. What went wrong?[1]

As usual, it was probably a mixture of various factors: financial, cultural, marketing and many others. Poor capacity management certainly played a part. The park was designed to have a maximum capacity of 50,000 visitors per day. Admission gates were to be closed after this figure was reached, with additional visitors being admitted as visitors left the park for the remainder of the afternoon and evening. For instance, on one occasion in the opening 3 months, the gates of the park were closed from 11.00 a.m. to 3.00 p.m.

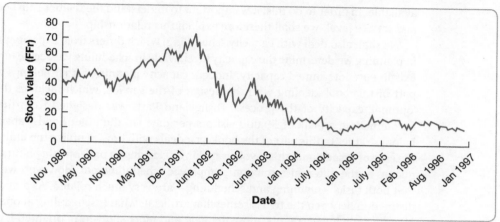

Figure 10.1 The value of EuroDisney stock, Nov 1989 to Jan 1997

because the park had reached capacity; a large number of additional guests were admitted only after 3.00 p.m. The result was long queues at certain times and a great deal of customer dissatisfaction.

While it may be true that Europeans in general, and the French in particular, are less tolerant of queues and are less disciplined while queueing, compared with Americans, it is undoubtedly true that there was a capacity problem. Take, for example, the 50,000 person peak-capacity design. With 29 rides and attractions in its first phase, this meant that at peak times there were 1724 (50,000/29) customers per ride per day. Compare this with the peak capacity of 90,000 at Disney World in Florida, where there are 72 attractions, leading to an average of 1250 customers per ride per day. No wonder the queues at Disneyland Paris were longer than visitors were used to in Florida. For an organization for which repeat business and word-of-mouth advertising are very important, this causes a serious problem.

Another capacity issue was that to break even there needed to be 11 million visitors a year. This meant an average of about 30,000 per day. Given the high seasonality of the business and a peak capacity of 50,000, an average of 30,000 seemed unrealistic. How many visitors could reasonably be expected in the winter season in Paris? Not only did winter visitors have to put up with the sometimes inclement weather but, adding insult to injury, they came to the conclusion that, in order to reduce costs, Disneyland Paris had closed many attractions for the season. It is highly probable that visitors felt cheated because the 'service concept' had been ruined.

Disneyland Paris made serious mistakes in its capacity management. However, the case is certainly not unique. Capacity management is crucial to almost all service businesses. The purpose of this chapter is to explore some of the issues related to capacity management. We shall identify typical problems and describe solutions – or at least approaches to tackling such problems.

We begin by defining 'capacity,' and identifying the essence of capacity management. We go on to deal with the issue of capacity planning – that is, determining the size of the capacity or providing an answer to the question of how much capacity should be made available. In order to do this, it is important to understand the relationship between capacity and service level; we shall therefore explain this relationship.

We shall also deal with capacity scheduling, which differs from capacity planning in that in planning we determine the capacity level, while in scheduling we decide how to utilize the existing predetermined capacity. Indeed, capacity planning rather belongs to the previous part of this book dealing with the design of the service, which includes determining the 'optimal' capacity of the process. Disneyland Paris was designed from the beginning to accommodate a peak of 50,000 visitors per day. On the other hand, capacity scheduling belongs rather to this part of the book as it deals with how to utilize the built-in capacity. In the case of Disneyland, this involves making decisions on park opening hours, managing the queues at the different attractions, employee scheduling, etc. However, we have to admit that both tasks – planning and scheduling – are very much related. As a matter of fact, the distinction between the two is somewhat artificial: what is scheduling at one level becomes planning at a lower, that is, more detailed and more short-term oriented level. As a result, we concentrate on integrated systems for managing capacity, which we call service requirements planning. This includes the application of Just-In-Time principles. We will pay particular attention to the issue of staffing in a service environment.

An alternative to managing capacity is to try to influence demand so that it matches capacity as far as possible – a process known as demand management. Various ways to manage the demand are presented. Particular attention will be given to the concept of yield management.

When managing capacity, the consequences of capacity shortage or excess must be considered. One of the consequences of a shortage is that customers will have to wait. As we shall see, however, waiting is not a purely rational issue: we shall look at the psychological factors involved in waiting experiences and their management consequences.

We begin with an example of an organization involved in inspecting car emissions that is facing capacity related problems described in Exhibit 10.1. Throughout the chapter, we shall refer back to Exhibit 10.1 to illustrate the application of concepts or techniques that can help us to analyse the problems and provide solutions.

Exhibit 10.1 The Belmont Case[2]

Karel Verschaeve was coming to the conclusion that something had to be done about the capacity of his car-emission inspection stations. Over the preceding few months, the number of complaints by customers as well as by employees had drastically increased. In particular, professional drivers had become visibly more irritated by the long waiting times at the inspection stations. The Ministry of Transport had even forwarded him a couple of letters of complaint.

Inspection of car emissions

Since 1 July 2008, the emission norms had become much more severe in an attempt to protect the environment and in particular to reduce the ozone concentration in summer. All cars, regardless of their age, had to be inspected for composition and level of emission of various pollutants. In the past, such inspection had been part of the general technical inspection. For private cars, this meant that they were only inspected 3 years after having been purchased.

The existing vehicle inspection stations could not handle the increased volume of business and, furthermore, the existing equipment was not suited to the more severe norms. The new

---

equipment required a high level of investment and special expertise was required to operate the equipment, and so the authorities had decided to build specialized emission-control centres. In order to limit the total investment, the number of centres had been limited to one for every large metropolitan area.

Karel Verschaeve was the general director of all inspection centres. He was happy about this appointment, especially because the Minister of Transport had promised him a large degree of autonomy. Both the Minister and Verschaeve wanted to make a 'showcase' of the inspection centres. In particular, they wanted to demonstrate that an operation did not have to be privatized to be run efficiently and effectively. He recalled very vividly the political resistance which arose when the Minister decoupled the emission inspection centres from the general technical inspection centres. The latter were operated by private institutions.

The situation in Belmont

Belmont was the largest city and the capital of the country. There was one inspection centre for the entire metropolitan area. The complaints referred to earlier were mostly related to this inspection centre. In this centre, there was a total of 11 inspection lines to test the emission gases of the car. The test itself was rather short: between 2 and 5 minutes. However, it was clear that the test itself was the bottleneck. The steps that preceded and followed the test were of an administrative nature and went very smoothly thanks to automation. The two steps in the process lasted 4 and 2 minutes respectively. For these administrative processes there were in total 24 stations (see Figure 10.2).

It was estimated that in the Belmont metropolitan area there were about 260,000 cars registered, which all had to come to the inspection centre at least once a year. Roughly 20% of the visits were repeat visits. When a car was refused, it had to be presented for re-inspection within 2 weeks of the first visit. The opening hours of the inspection centre were between 8.00 a.m. and 4.00 p.m. on weekdays, over 50 weeks per year, excepting statutory holidays.

The demand was not evenly spread over the year. From February to May the average demand was about 10% higher than the annual average. There were also clear fluctuations during the day. The peak occurred early in the morning shortly after opening. The variable cost of an inspection was about €3, the bulk of this amount (around 80%) being direct labour costs. The customers paid €8 per inspection.

Karel Verschaeve assumed that it would be very difficult to increase the number of inspection lines. The investment required to install an additional line was estimated to be at least €250,000. The funds needed for such additional equipment had not been budgeted for. Although he did not want to exclude any particular option, he was convinced that he had to look for other, more creative solutions to solve the capacity problem.

Figure 10.2 Flowchart showing the inspection process at Belmont

Source: Based on Belmont case in Hill, A. (1991) *Minnesota Pollution Control Agency*. University of Minnesota.

Capacity and capacity management

Capacity is a complex concept

The concept of capacity is used in our everyday language quite frequently. The capacity of my fuel tank at home is 5000 litres; the capacity of the boot of my car is 466 litres, while the car can transport five people; the university hospital has 1100 beds; the aeroplane on the daily flight between Brussels and New York contains 320 seats; the Belmont inspection centre has 11 inspection lines. This notion of capacity is very close to the dictionary definition of capacity:

'the ability to hold, receive, store or accommodate a certain volume.'

This definition of capacity is inappropriate in most organizations for a variety of reasons:

1 It refers to capacity of input resources: the trunk of the car, the size of the tank, the number of beds or seats, or the number of parallel lines. It does not necessarily tell us anything about the output. The output is of course a function of the 'capacity' of the input resources, but usually of a particular combination of input resources. For example, in a hospital, resources include not only beds, but also nurses, surgery rooms and various materials.

2 Service times are frequently inherently variable so that, although a certain resource might usually be the cause of the bottleneck, on some occasions the problem might lie elsewhere. In the Belmont case, for example, although the inspection lines are the bottleneck, the registration process could also slow things down, as sometimes for a particular reason and sometimes for no reason at all, many customers may need a good deal of help in doing the paperwork.

3 The traditional input resources definition of capacity lacks the time dimension. It is a static concept and it is a dynamic concept that is needed. We do not know the capacity of a restaurant unless we know the average time customers stay there. It is clear that the capacity of a restaurant with 120 seats is much higher in the case of a fast-food restaurant with a throughput time per customer of 20 minutes or less, than in the case of a traditional French restaurant with a throughput time per customer of 120 minutes. To calculate capacity, we must incorporate a time dimension appropriate to the use of the assets. Capacity is therefore most appropriately expressed in so many 'output' units per hour, per day, per week, per month or per year.

Returning to the Belmont case in Exhibit 10.1, we can say that the capacity should be expressed in 'cars per day'. Assuming an 8-hour day and assuming that the inspection lines are in fact the bottlenecks, we can say that the capacity is 188.57 cars per hour or 1508 cars per day (*see* Figure 10.2).

Since time is an integral part of the capacity concept, capacity can be increased or decreased by influencing the processing time. In the Belmont case, if the time required to test the car increases by 20% (from an average of 3 minutes 30 seconds to 4 minutes 12 seconds) the capacity of the inspection centre will decrease by 20% to 1257 cars.

This reduction in capacity resulting from an increase in processing time has recently become particularly clear in the Belgian prison system. As in almost every other country, Belgian prisons are overcrowded (because of a lack of capacity). In order to solve the problem, the Belgian Justice Department adopted the policy of granting earlier parole. This seemed to be a much 'cheaper' solution to the capacity problem than building more prisons.

Fixed versus variable capacity

When we refer to capacity, we usually mean the fixed or installed capacity of the operating system. In the Belmont case, capacity is a function of the number of inspection lines. However, to achieve a capacity of 1508 cars per day an adequate number of inspectors is also required. If for one reason or another, only 10 inspectors are available, the effective capacity will only be 1370. Nevertheless, most people will express capacity as a function of the number of inspection lines, because the inspection line resource is of a more fixed nature than the inspector resource. The inspector resource is presumed to be more variable. What is fixed or what is variable depends very much on the time horizon. Changing the number of inspection lines requires a long-term perspective as such a decision would require a long-term forecast of capacity needs. Likewise, the number of rooms in a hotel would not be changed without an examination of capacity needs over the following year or more, since this type of decision requires large financial commitments which are also more or less irreversible. If a capacity need is only going to last a week or so, it will probably not be necessary to change the number of lines in an inspection centre or the number of beds in a hotel.

In the long run, all capacity is variable, of course. The shorter the time horizon, the more constrained an organization is by the fixed and limited capacity of the resources. Considered in the long term, capacity management in a supermarket chain will mainly be concerned with the number of stores and their location; in the shorter term, capacity management will be concerned with the size of the store in the form of incremental additions or partial closures. As the time horizon decreases further, concern will be focused in turn on the number of check-outs, the opening hours and, finally, the staffing schedules.

Specificity of capacity management in services

The nature of capacity management is illustrated in Figure 10.3.[3] In essence, it involves two decisions:

1 How much capacity to make available (= capacity planning).
2 How to utilize the existing capacity (= capacity scheduling).

These two questions are hierarchically related – that is, the answer to the first question is the starting point for the second. This issue can also be considered within the framework of differentiating time horizons. The first question poses a capacity problem in terms of a long-term horizon. This restricts the shorter time-horizon capacity problem with which the second question is concerned. A supermarket, for instance, wants to decide how many check-out counters to install. Once installed, it starts to think about utilizing this resource effectively, by deciding on the staffing level and opening hours, but also by trying to influence the demand pattern. In the Belmont case, the number of inspection lines will probably be arrived at based on long-term patterns of demand; only afterwards will such issues as opening hours, staffing, and influence-demand patterns be addressed.

However, the decisions are not strictly sequential; there is usually a high level of interaction between these two levels. When there is a difficulty in changing opening hours or influencing the demand patterns in a certain period, a company might go back to the first

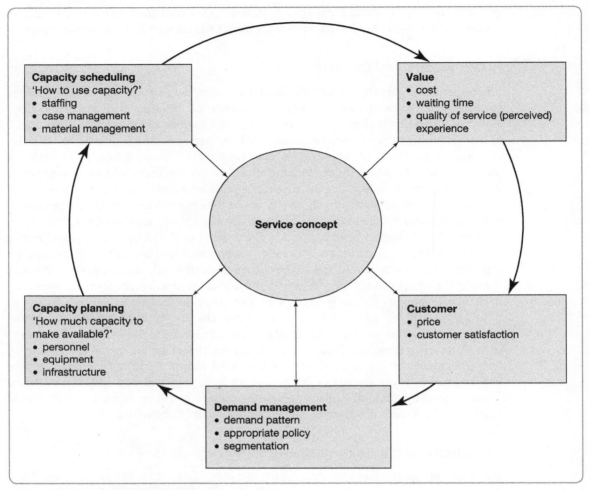

Figure 10.3 The nature of capacity management

decision and adapt the number of lines. Alternatively, a company might come to the conclusion that changing opening hours or influencing the demand patterns is the easier choice, and accordingly it would then go back and change the number of inspection lines.

There are, of course, many similarities between the capacity management problems in the service industry and in manufacturing industries. We can learn a great deal from the systems that have been developed in these fields and the experience that has been gained. However, there are a number of particularities, resulting from the fact that services are intangible and consumption and production occur simultaneously, that must be kept in mind when managing capacity in services:

● *Intangibility,* for instance, means that services cannot be stored. Excess capacity cannot be utilized when there is no demand. Excess capacity is lost when the demand is not there. Output cannot be put into stock to be sold later. An airline that has scheduled a Boeing 747 between Amsterdam and New York with only 240 passengers loses forever the unoccupied excess of some 120 seats or, at least, the profit potential of these excess seats.

- *Simultaneity* also means that inventories cannot be used to balance supply and demand or – even better – to absorb demand fluctuations. This is the case both for seasonal and random fluctuations in demand. Statistical variation in demand patterns cannot be 'absorbed' by safety or other buffer stocks: the uncertainty in demand patterns penetrates (part of) the operating system. Expressed in technical terms, the arrival pattern in many services is *stochastic*: capacity management must inherently deal with uncertainty. This uncertainty is increased because not only is the arrival pattern stochastic but also the service process. In particular, the time it takes to process a customer or a request varies statistically. The time of a haircut or an intervention by a helpdesk is stochastic. This is mainly a result of the *heterogeneity* of services.

Uncertainty is, thus, inherent in the capacity management problem in services.

Capacity as part of the service concept

The way a service organization answers the two basic questions, however, will determine the value of the product we offer to the customer. It is clear that the capacity management solutions will have an impact on the cost of the service and, therefore, on the price the customer has to pay.

But is goes further. As a result of the simultaneity, imbalances in capacity and demand are visible to customers and will affect them. When the capacity is limited, the customer has to wait. The customer will perhaps be turned off by long waits, especially when the queues are not managed correctly. At the other end of the scale, excess in capacity might also have a negative effect on the atmosphere and, therefore, the quality experienced by the customer.

We could go as far as saying that, in many instances, capacity is part of the product. The atmosphere in a football stadium is very much influenced by the number of people in the stadium relative to its capacity. Watching football in a stadium with a capacity of 100,000 with only 10,000 spectators is a totally different experience – and therefore a totally different product – from watching the same game with the same number of spectators in a stadium with a capacity of 10,000. The experience and, therefore, the 'product' in a restaurant that is only one-third full is a different experience from that in a restaurant that is close to its effective capacity. An empty restaurant will also probably be seen by the customer as a sign of poor quality, while a restaurant that is fully occupied will be perceived as a good restaurant.

The opposite is true in an aeroplane environment. An aeroplane that is fully occupied offers a hustled, nervous type of experience, while an aeroplane that is only half full not only gives you greater physical comfort, but also projects an atmosphere of calm and relaxation.

The absolute size of capacity also has an impact on the customer or on the customer's perception of the service encounter. Coming back to our restaurant example, it is clear that the restaurant with 50 places is much more intimate, exclusive and relaxing than a restaurant with a capacity of 200 places. The latter creates the impression of being a mass-production kitchen; it looks impersonal and standardized.

Demand management

Given the direct interaction between capacity and customer, it is clear that capacity management should not only deal with the supply side but also with the demand side. This means that it is important in capacity management to understand demand patterns and to try to influence them, because it might be easier – or, at least, more cost effective – to adjust the demand to the given capacity in the short term.

All these factors demonstrate that capacity management in service industries is not a numbers issue or a purely technical problem. It is a question beset with many intangible, difficult to quantify issues, which require a good understanding of the psychology of the customer. When designing a service, it is important to keep in mind the way in which a customer will 'feel' the capacity.

Capacity as a strategic weapon

Services are intangible, which makes it very difficult to take out a patent on a product to protect against imitation. A process can sometimes be patented, but very frequently another means is needed to protect against imitation when that process is successful. Economists speak of 'barriers to entry'. By this, they mean obstacles that make it difficult or unattractive for potential competitors to enter the market. A patent could be such a barrier. However, capacity and the way in which capacity is or is not built up can be another factor that will influence the entry behaviour of potential competitors. If a new service is successful it will certainly draw attention to itself and, if the market is large enough, will quickly lead to imitation. In order to protect against such imitation, the service organization sometimes has very little choice but to build up capacity very quickly, thereby closely following the evolution of the demand. By so doing, the innovating company turns its time advantage (being the first one) into another, such as location or reputation; above all, this makes it risky for a potential competitor to enter the market. If the innovating company lacks the financial needs or management talent to build up capacity quickly, it will often resort to franchising, which provides not only capital but also the management capacity to manage dispersed operations.

It is clear that a capacity strategy to deter competition is not without risk. The new service concept might enjoy temporary, short-lived success. Many theme restaurants have experienced this fate.

Planning capacity

Capacity, service level and waiting

In the Belmont case, customers were complaining about long waiting times, a situation not unique to this organization. We have all been in situations where we have had to wait against our will and were frustrated by the length of the waiting time and/or by the circumstances under which we had to wait. Table 10.1 is based on a Dutch study[4] and gives an overview of the frequency of various waiting situations and average waiting times. Various studies have indicated that, in many services, the final level of customer satisfaction will depend to a great extent on the length of waiting times and on how waiting has been perceived by customers. The utility company, Florida Light and Power, came to the conclusion that there was a strong correlation between waiting time on the telephone and the level of satisfaction[5] (*see* Table 10.2).

Table 10.1 Various categories of waiting situations: frequencies and average waiting times

	Frequency	Average waiting time
1. Check-out counters in supermarket, small stores, etc.	22.1%	7.6 min
2. Appointments with friends, business associates, etc.	13.6%	22.0 min
3. Public transport	12.4%	11.0 min
4. Bars, restaurants, etc.	10.6%	13.0 min
5. In traffic	9.5%	10.4 min
6. Services with a counter (banks, post office, etc.)	8.5%	7.7 min
7. Services with reservations	5.0%	26.0 min
8. Cultural/sports events	2.7%	12.1 min
9. Other	15.6%	19.9 min

Source: Pruyn, A. and Smidts, A. (1992) *De Psychologische Beleving van Wachtrijen*. Erasmus Universiteit. Management Report Sciences, 126. Based on the diaries of 243 persons with 3566 waiting situations.

Table 10.2 Mean satisfaction rating by length of time on hold

Mean rating*	Time on hold
1.32	Less than 30 seconds
1.57	30 seconds to 1 minute
1.67	1 to 2 minutes
2.14*	2 to 3 minutes

*On a scale from 1 to 5, where 1 = very satisfied; 5 = very dissatisfied.

Reprinted with permission from *Quality Progress* © 1993 American Society for Quality. No further distribution allowed without permission.

As stated earlier, services and service processes are inherently stochastic, therefore waiting is almost inevitable in service organizations. However, there is a strong relationship between capacity utilization and the length of the waiting time (*see* Figure 10.4). The relationship is usually exponential.

For instance, in the Belmont case, applying the queueing theory (*see* Technical note 1), we can prove that with an average capacity utilization of 90%, the average waiting time will be 2 minutes 5 seconds and the average number of customers waiting will equal 5.9. On the

Figure 10.4 Capacity utilization and waiting time

Figure 10.5 Capacity utilization and waiting times in a bank

days or moments of the day, however, when the arrival rate is 10% higher – that is, the utilization is 99% – we can expect an average waiting time of 29 minutes 6 seconds and an average number of customers waiting of 90.6.

In a study in a Belgian bank, we were able to establish a clear relationship between waiting time and capacity utilization. We produced simulation models for a number of branches in order to determine the optimal number of employees staffing the counters, taking into account the customer arrival patterns and the bank's service levels in terms of acceptable customer waiting times. Figure 10.5 depicts the relationship between capacity utilization and average waiting time for one particular branch. With three employees, the average waiting time for the customer is only 12 seconds. This is quite obvious given the low capacity utilization of only 37%. With two employees and a capacity utilization of 57%, the average waiting time increases slightly to 1.4 minutes. It can be clearly seen that employing only one person is totally unacceptable in terms of customer waiting times. The high capacity utilization of 95% leads to average waiting times of 38 minutes. The acceptable level of capacity utilization seems to be in this case between 60% and 70% since, beyond this point, an exponential growth will occur in customer waiting times.

If customers have to wait, they experience the general service level as low and become dissatisfied. In other circumstances, waiting is simply not feasible. When there are too few rooms in a hotel or too few seats on an aeroplane, customers have to be turned away. Not only is the gross profit potential lost as the customers are turned away, but there is also a loss of future earnings as the customers might never return.

When customers are able or willing to wait, service level can be defined as:

$$P = 100\% - \text{probability of an excessive wait}$$

When the customer is not willing to wait, service level can be defined as:

$$P = 100\% - \text{probability of having to turn away a customer}$$

What constitutes an excessive wait in the first case depends on the situation. Thirty seconds waiting for someone to pick up the telephone is usually considered excessive, while most of us are willing to wait for 30 minutes in a hospital to see a particular specialist. Each organization has to determine what an excessive wait is.

Let us assume that, in the Belmont case, 20 minutes is considered excessive. With a capacity utilization of 90%, the probability of a certain customer having to wait 20 minutes is rather small. At peak times with a capacity utilization of 99%, however, the probability of an excessive wait is equal to 54%,[6] leading to a service level of 46%.

Determining the capacity level

Cost of waiting is known

The first question in capacity management is how much capacity should be made available given a certain 'expected' demand pattern. This decision is basically a trade-off between the cost of additional capacity, on the one hand, and the value of a higher service level or the cost of a lack of service level, on the other (*see* Figure 10.6). The optimal capacity level depends very much on the evolution of both cost curves. Economists will tell us that it makes sense to increase capacity as long as the marginal cost of adding a capacity unit is lower than the marginal benefit of increasing the service level.

In the Belmont case, an additional inspection line requires an investment of €250,000. Assuming the usable lifetime of this equipment to be 5 years, the annual equipment costs are €50,000. An operator must be hired to run the line and paid €15 per hour. Standard queueing theory (*see* Technical note 1) teaches us that, by adding a twelfth line, the average waiting time per customer will drop in peak months from 5 minutes to 1.2 minutes. However, assuming a morning peak during which the demand is 5% higher than average, the average waiting time will drop from 1 hour to 2.2 minutes or a gain of 57.8 minutes. Let us then assume that we add an inspection line that is operated part-time from 8.00 a.m. to 10.00 a.m. for the period February to May, costing in total €21,000 (€15/hour × 14 weeks × 5 days × 2 hours). The depreciation charge for the installation is €50,000, so the total yearly cost of increasing the capacity is €71,000. The benefit is a reduction in waiting time of 57.8 minutes per customer during that period. This drop will affect 26,278 customers (= 187.7 customers at peak/h × 14 weeks × 5 days × 2 hours).

If we assume that the 'value of waiting for the customer' is €12.5/hour, the increased value for customers is therefore:

Figure 10.6 Determining the capacity level

213

$$26{,}278 \times \frac{57.8}{60} \times 12.5 = \text{€}316{.}430$$

Given that this value is higher than the marginal cost of expanding the capacity, it is worthwhile expanding the capacity to 12 lines. Expanding the capacity from 12 to 13 lines has the same marginal cost, but the marginal benefit in terms of reduced waiting times is a drop in average waiting time of only 1.4 minutes. The value of this reduced waiting time is:

$$26{,}278 \times \frac{1.4}{60} \times 12.5 = \text{€}7{.}664$$

Therefore, it does not seem to be worthwhile expanding to 13 lines.

Often the benefit to the customer or, conversely, the cost of waiting to an external customer, is difficult to determine. However, if we are speaking of internal customers – that is, the organization's own employees – the cost is easier to determine. For instance, in the case of a large hospital that is considering investing in an additional lift to reduce personnel waiting time, the cost of waiting is simply the salary cost associated with the waiting time.

An interesting study in which the cost of waiting was traded off against the cost of increasing capacity was carried out by Mark Davis.[7] He first established a relationship between waiting time and customer satisfaction in a fast-food restaurant. In a second step, he established a relationship between customer satisfaction and the return behaviour of the customer, with which he could associate an increase or reduction in revenue and margin. Combining the two relationships, he was able to define a cost function related to waiting time:

$$w(t) = 5.47 + 16.54t$$

where the cost of waiting $w(t)$ is expressed in dollars and the waiting time (t) in minutes.

He concluded that each minute the customer had to wait cost about \$16.54. This had to be traded off with the cost of installing capacity $C(t)$. In this case, adding capacity was mainly a matter of adding more personnel paid at \$7.50 per hour. Applying standard queueing theory, one can establish a relationship between the number of workers and the average waiting time. Including the labour cost in the equation leads to a relationship between $C(t)$ and the waiting time:

$$C(t) = 52.98 \times t^{-0.09}$$

The total cost is therefore:

$$T(t) = 5.47 + 16.54t + 52.98 \times t^{-0.09}$$

As can be derived from Figure 10.7, the minimum total cost is reached for $t = 0.32$ minutes. In order to achieve this, eight servers were required.

Cost of waiting is not known

When dealing with external customers and when it is impossible to determine the cost of waiting, the problem can sometimes be approached from the other direction. Usually, it is easy to determine the cost of expanding capacity. Theoretically, as stated earlier, capacity should be increased as long as the marginal cost is lower than the marginal benefit of an increased service level. If service level is expressed as an average waiting time, the question then becomes whether or not the marginal cost of increasing capacity is lower than the

Figure 10.7 Optimal waiting time in a fast-food restaurant

Source: Davis, M. (1991) How long should a customer wait?, *Decision Sciences*, Vol 22, pp. 421–34. With permission from John Wiley and Sons.

reduction in total average customer waiting time multiplied by the cost of waiting per time unit. As a formula this becomes:

$$a < b \times \Delta_w \times N$$

where:

a = marginal cost of capacity expansion
b = cost of waiting per time unit and per customer
Δ_w = the marginal reduction of average waiting time per customer
N = total number of customers whose average waiting time will be reduced over the time horizon considered

As long as $b > \dfrac{a}{\Delta_w \times N}$, expansion is worthwhile.

If $b < \dfrac{a}{\Delta_w \times N}$, expansion should not take place.

While it is difficult to estimate the exact value of b in many cases, it is possible to evaluate whether this value is higher or lower than $\dfrac{a}{\Delta_w \times N}$.

For instance, in the Belmont case, we concluded that a = €71,000, Δ_w = 57.8 minutes and N = 26,278, therefore:

$$\frac{a}{\Delta_w \times N} = \frac{71,000}{57.8 \times 26,278} = €0.047$$

As long as b is estimated to be higher than €0.047/minute, expansion can go ahead. If b is estimated to be lower than €0.047, expansion should not be considered.

Customer is turned away

Until now we have assumed that lack of capacity leads to waiting time – that is, that the service level could be related to waiting time. In many situations, customers cannot or do not want to wait when there is insufficient capacity. Customers go to the restaurant next door when they see that there is a long queue. Similarly, when a hotel or airplane is fully booked, the customer has to look for an alternative. In these cases, the cost of capacity shortage is the lost margin. In these instances, an approach referred to as marginal analysis can be applied. According to this approach, the optimal capacity level C^* is that level for which the probability that demand (D) will exceed capacity is equal to:

$$P(D > C^*) = \frac{C_o}{C_s + C_o}$$

where C_o is the cost of having one capacity unit in excess and C_s is the cost of having one capacity unit too few.

Here is an example to illustrate this concept. A hotel has to decide how many rooms to provide in a new hotel at a certain location. Management knows that the demand at that location is normally distributed with an average of 250 rooms per night and a standard deviation of 20. If on a particular day the hotel has to turn away a customer because it is fully booked, it loses the gross margin on the room of €50 (C_s is therefore €50). It also knows that if the hotel has one room unoccupied on a particular day, it has a cost which is equal to the depreciation of the capital invested in the room per day and the cost of the upkeep of that room (cleaning, heating, etc.). This cost is estimated to be €12.5 (C_o in this case is therefore €12.5). In this case the optimal capacity – that is, the optimal number of rooms C^* – will be such that:

$$P(D > C^*) = \frac{12.5}{50 + 12.5} = 0.2$$

In other words, the capacity of the hotel should be such that there is a 20% probability that the demand on a given day will be higher than the available capacity. Statistical calculations teach us that in order to have a 20% chance of exceeding the level C^*, the capacity should be equal to 267.[8]

Scheduling capacity

Given a certain 'fixed' or 'structural' capacity level, it is important to work out how we should utilize capacity to maximize service to the customer on the one hand and minimize costs on the other. The assumption is that the 'fixed' capacity is given. Furthermore, in order to serve the customer, the organization has to provide other resources, such as materials and human resources. This is referred to as 'service resources planning'. The key role of human resources in services means accurate scheduling of these resources so that they match the demand patterns as closely as possible is of crucial importance. Exhibit 10.2 illustrates the experience of capacity scheduling at McDonald's.

Exhibit 10.2 Capacity scheduling at McDonald's[9]

At McDonald's, the objective is to keep a customer waiting no longer than two minutes in a queue and no longer than 60 seconds at the counter. A restaurant is 'producing' meals to stock – or, more precisely, assembling (collecting the sandwich, the fries, etc.) – and to order. A stock (or a bin) of sandwiches divides the back office from the front office. Each restaurant has its own historical overview of the distribution of sales during the week and during the day. Tables 10.3 and 10.4 give examples of these distributions.

Based on historical data of weekly volumes, these distributions make it possible for the restaurant manager to predict the work volume (expressed in $) for any moment of the day. With these data the manager determines the staffing schedule each Wednesday for the following Sunday through to Saturday, using the guidelines shown in Table 10.5.

When the volume at a certain time is estimated to be $240, for instance, eight employees are scheduled in total: two at the grill, two at the counter, two at the drive-thru windows, one at the bin, and one with a flexible task (the floater). The bin plays an important role in the actual production scheduling (i.e. deciding which and how many hamburgers to make at a particular moment). The bin acts as the interface between the back-office personnel in the

Table 10.3 Distribution of sales throughout the week at a typical branch of McDonald's

	Percentage of week's customers
Sunday	14.0
Monday	12.3
Tuesday	12.4
Wednesday	13.2
Thursday	14.8
Friday	16.3
Saturday	16.8
	100.0

Table 10.4 Distribution of sales throughout the day at a typical branch of McDonald's

For hour ending at ...	Percentage of day's sales
8.00 a.m.	3.4
9.00 a.m.	4.1
10.00 a.m.	4.0
11.00 a.m.	3.9
12.00 noon	7.5
1.00 p.m.	14.9
2.00 p.m.	9.1
3.00 p.m.	5.0
4.00 p.m.	3.5
5.00 p.m.	5.5
6.00 p.m.	9.1
7.00 p.m.	8.4
8.00 p.m.	5.6
9.00 p.m.	5.3
10.00 p.m.	4.6
11.00 p.m.	3.4
12.00 p.m.	2.5
	100.0

Table 10.5 Staffing at McDonald's

| | Total number of staff | Workstations | | | | | | $ per hour volume guidelines |
		Grill	Windows	Drive-Thru	Bin	Fry	Floaters*	
Minimum to open	4	1	1	1	–	–	1	$120
	5	1	1	1	–	–	2	150
	6	2	1	1	–	–	2	180
	7	2	2	1	–	–	2	210
	8	2	2	2	1	–	1	240
	9	2	2	2	1	–	2	275
	10	3	3	2	1	–	1	310
	11	3	3	2	1	1	1	345
	12	3	3	3	1	1	1	385
	13	4	3	3	1	1	1	425
	14	4	3	3	1	1	2	475
	15	4	4	3	1	1	2	525
	16	5	4	3	1	1	2	585
Fully staffed	17	5	5	3	1	1	2	645

*Floaters 'help the cause': patrol the car park, entrance and toilets; restock; cover on breaks.

kitchen and the front-office personnel at the counter and at the drive thru windows. If hourly sales volume exceeds $240, a person is specially assigned to 'run' the bin. This person manages the flow of products into the sandwich-holding bin, calling for production as needed, wrapping the sandwiches when they are passed up, and keeping the bin stock organized and fresh. The person 'on the bin' uses certain rules of thumb to determine how much stock is appropriate. For instance, when volume is between $600 and $700/per hour, 20–24 hamburgers, 20–24 cheeseburgers, 9 Big Macs, 3–4 Quarter Pounders, 3–4 Quarter Pounders with Cheese, and 6–7 Filet o' Fishes are kept in stock. The distribution per type of sandwich is pretty well known and relatively stable over the week and during the course of the day.

Service resources planning

In the Belmont case in Exhibit 10.1, it is clear that, in addition to the inspection lines and registration desks, there is also a need for people to staff these stations and for supplies, such as the filters and documents used at these workstations.

At first sight, scheduling the human resources in this case would appear to be very easy. One inspector is needed per line and one administrative employee per desk. However, given the seasonality of the demand pattern, it is not always necessary to staff all the lines and all the desks at 100% capacity. The availability of human resources could be adapted to the expected demand pattern, as the restaurant manager does at McDonald's (*see* Table 10.5).

Successful completion of an inspection requires supplies – that is, various documents and materials consumed during the actual inspection. In this case, the cost of the supplies will probably be small compared to the cost of the other resources. Management will therefore pay little attention to optimizing the availability of these supplies, making sure that there are always sufficient levels in stock. A high safety stock will be maintained. In other cases, such as restaurants like McDonald's, the materials are relatively important not only because their share in the total cost of the service is high but also because freshness is an important quality factor.

Independent versus dependent demand

An important concept to consider when managing the 'other resources' in service organizations is the notion of *independent, dependent, pseudo-independent* and *pseudo-dependent* demand items:

- *Independent demand items.* In a supermarket, sugar is in most cases an independent demand item – that is, the demand for sugar is not (directly) dependent on the demand for any other item in the supermarket. Therefore, the availability of the sugar can be managed independently of any other resource.

- *Dependent demand items.* In a catering company, conversely, the demand for sugar is dependent on the type and number of meals. If the planned production of meals over a certain time horizon is known, the demand for sugar can be derived from this planned production.

- *Pseudo-independent demand items.* On an aeroplane, the demand for sugar is theoretically a dependent demand item, dependent on the number of passengers and their preference when drinking coffee or tea. However, few airlines will derive the demand pattern for sugar from the planned number of passengers. They will probably always have a fixed supply of sugar on the plane, regardless of the number of passengers they have on board. The cost of managing the availability of sugar on board more precisely by deriving it from the scheduled number of passengers will probably be higher than the cost of excess stock of sugar they carry by managing it independently. Sugar is therefore a pseudo-independent demand item – that is, it is managed as if it were an independent item.

- *Pseudo-dependent demand items.* A pseudo-dependent demand item is an item that is not directly and deterministically dependent on the demand of another item, but where there is some sort of relationship which can be used to determine the demand more precisely. For instance, the demand for tennis facilities at a vacation resort can be derived from the number of villas or bungalows which are occupied.

Managing independent demand items

When the demand for a resource is independent, or when a company wants to manage it as if it were an independent item (i.e. it is a pseudo-independent demand item), and when the resource is a non-material resource, such as equipment or human resources, the approach discussed earlier can be used. When we are talking about a material resource, however, like the sugar in the supermarket, the various existing inventory management models can be used. We refer the reader to the standard textbooks on inventory management or production management for a detailed discussion of these models.

Management of dependent demand items using the MRP logic

When managing a dependent demand item, an approach called '*service resources requirements planning*', analogous to the manufacturing resources planning (or MRP) approach utilized in manufacturing organizations, can be used. Figure 10.8 depicts the framework of such an approach in a hospital.

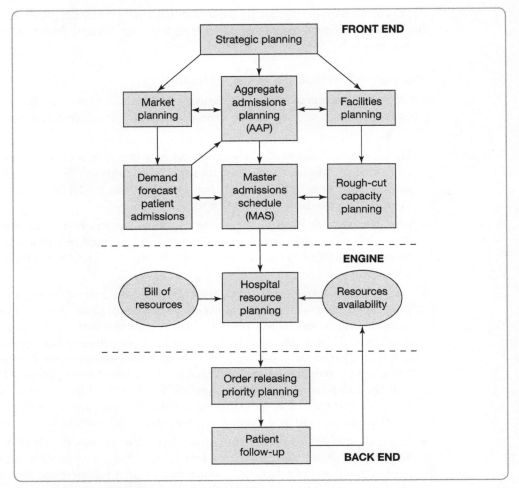

Figure 10.8 Hospital resource planning system

The key elements of this approach are the *master schedule* (in the hospital application, the master admission schedules), the *bill of resources*, and the *data file on availability of resources*:

- The *master schedule* expresses the known or forecast demand for so-called 'end products'. In the case of a hospital, for instance, this is the planned admission schedule or the planned discharge schedule of patients. For an airline catering company, this might be the actual and/or forecast number of passengers on a certain flight.

- Returning to the case of the hospital, each type of patient can be assigned a certain *bill of resources*. This is a projection of the amount and timing of resources that will be consumed by this type of patient during his or her stay in hospital. In order to do this, patients are classified into different groups – the so-called DRGs or diagnostic-related groups. For each DRG, a specific bill of resources such as time in the operating theatre, time of the surgeon, medicines and so on, is determined. In the airline catering company, there is typically a contract where the type of meals in each passenger class is specified. A further distinction has to be made between vegetarian and non-vegetarian meals, and sometimes kosher and non-kosher meals. When the actual or planned number of passengers in each of the categories on a certain flight is known, the number of each type of meals needed can be derived, as can, subsequently, the number of intermediate products, ingredients, and, over time, even human resources.

Exhibit 10.3 illustrates how this concept has been implemented in a New Orleans restaurant.

Exhibit 10.3 MRP in a New Orleans restaurant[10]

As is illustrated in Figure 10.9, the procedure starts with an aggregate daily forecast expressed in monetary terms. The forecast is estimated mathematically based on a regression analysis using trend and a series of dummy variables to account for the seasonal patterns within the week.

This aggregate forecast is disaggregated into forecasts for the various meals on the menu based on a distribution of the individual meals over the last 8 months. This process was carried out for each of the 46 meals on the menu, resulting in a master production schedule, called 'Recipe Formation'.

Figure 10.9 The resources planning procedure

Figure 10.10 A product structure tree for Veal Picante

For each of the meals, a 'product structure' or 'bill of resources' is constructed (a kind of recipe). Figure 10.10 depicts such a product structure for the 'Veal Picante' meal type. This structure includes not only material resources but also human resources. This structure together with the master production schedule allows the organization to calculate a time-phased resources plan, for instance, the 'cream' item #40011. This leads to the so-called requirements for the cream over the entire planning horizon.

Taking into consideration the *scheduled receipts*, i.e. the expected orders of cream that will be delivered and the cream 'on hand', one can calculate the net requirements – that is, the quantities of cream that should be ordered to avoid a stock out. Taking into consideration the delivery lead time and the order quantities, one can calculate the so-called 'planned orders', which are orders that have to be issued to the supplier of cream.

The advantage of a service resources requirements planning approach is that the availability of resources is integrated. The resources are available only when they are needed. When, for one reason or another, a particular resource is not available, the system tells us that the other resources normally required for the same end product are not needed either. Another advantage is that information regarding how much of the resource is required, and when it is required, is linked to the final product and kept up to date.[11]

Just-in-time in service environments

Just-in-time (JIT) is a production philosophy originally applied in Japanese manufacturing firms but increasingly used by Western manufacturers. According to this philosophy, the objective is to eliminate waste – that is, the activities, such as transport, storage, quality inspection, waiting and setting up machines, which do not add value to the product. All these non-value-added activities have one thing in common: they all lead to unnecessary inventories. JIT therefore targets the inventories and has the material delivered exactly when needed – 'just in time' to be utilized and in the quantities needed at that time. Applying the JIT philosophy not only leads to lower inventories and therefore reductions in costs and working capital but, by forcing companies to eliminate the non-value-added activities, it decreases costs even further, providing the opportunity to improve quality and delivery dependability and to increase delivery speed and flexibility.

One of the key elements of JIT is the application of the so-called *pull principle* to the issuing of work orders and purchase orders. Using the pull principle as a tool to initiate production or purchase orders means that the signal to start producing or delivering a certain item comes from the place or the workstation where the item is being used or consumed. The signal does not come from a central planning department but from the 'next' workstation. A typical example of the application of this principle is the relationship between the Volvo plant in Ghent and ECA, the supplier of seats located about 15 kilometres north of the plant. ECA starts producing a car seat after it has received an (electronic) message from Volvo that the car is at the final assembly stage. ECA has 8 hours to produce and deliver the seats before they are installed in Volvo's final assembly plant.

Examples of pull systems in service environments can be found in hospitals where a pull relationship is established between the central pharmacy and the operating theatres for the delivery of medicines and supplies. A cart filled with a limited amount of supplies is the communication device. As soon as one cart is emptied, it is wheeled back to the central pharmacy where it is filled up and brought back to the operating theatre. Similar pull systems have been established between outside suppliers and various units in a hospital – for instance, for the delivery of linen.

The scheduling system of McDonald's is another example of such a pull system. The back office is told to make additional sandwiches when the number of sandwiches in the 'bin' drops below a certain minimum. This minimum is dependent on the time of the day, as we have already described.

The JIT principles can equally be applied to service, even if the material and therefore the physical stocks are negligible or non-existent. Rather than taking inventories – which are nothing more than 'queues' of materials – as a central point of reference, a queue of customers or files can be considered.

Staffing and scheduling in a service environment

In many service systems, human resources are the single most important asset and have a predominant role in the service delivery process. Available staff should be deployed in such a way that good (or excellent) service delivery can be obtained. This is not easy in an environment which is known as inherently stochastic.

The planning and scheduling of personnel should ideally be integrated with the management of other resources. However, in this section we will treat human resources as a somewhat separate area and position it within the broader framework of manpower planning (*see* Figure 10.11).[12] The figure makes it clear that – as with capacity in general – it is first of all necessary to divide the task of planning and scheduling into different hierarchical levels. The highest level is the strategic level. At this level, the *manpower requirements* – i.e. the type and quantity – over a multiple-year horizon are determined. Strategic decisions on the design of the service operating system have a severe impact on this decision. Other decisions, such as the number and types of operating units and the days and hours each unit will operate, determine the required manpower levels.[13]

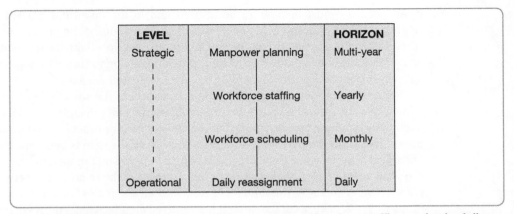

Figure 10.11 An integrated framework for manpower planning, staffing and scheduling
Source: Khoong, C. M. (1996), reprinted by kind permission of MCB University Press Ltd.

Once these overall manpower requirements have been determined, they are annually adjusted in a *staffing plan*. This plan takes into account estimates of staffing requirements as produced by individual department managers. The department manager uses overall forecasts of demand and/or subjective estimates of the current workloads in order to determine the staffing requirements of his or her department. Normally, this occurs once a year at the time of budgeting. These department level estimates are aggregated into a company figure that may be compared with the multi-year manpower requirements. Based on this information, a (re)allocation of the available personnel to the different departments or units can take place.

The staffing plan should also include policies regarding how predicted fluctuations in required human resources over a certain seasonal period will be handled. The available human resources capacity can be stretched (e.g. by means of overtime) or new interim labour resources can be acquired. These policies are generally embedded in a wider human resource management plan.

Once the human resources are allocated to a department, a *workforce schedule* specifies when (on which day and at which time) each of the allocated personnel is going to work (*see also* Exhibit 10.2). Developing workforce schedules is particularly important in those service environments where a 24-hour service delivery is guaranteed through different shifts – the police, for example. By specifying the on-duty and off-duty periods for each employee over a certain period of time, an organization tries to match capacity with demand over a short time horizon. In many service firms, the development of a workforce schedule is considered to be a very complex (and time-consuming) task due to the many constraints that must be taken into account:

1 the available (allocated) staff;
2 the wishes of the individual employees as to when they want to work;
3 the demand pattern for services over a (shorter) cycle of a week or a day.

The nature of services and characteristics, such as the simultaneity of production and consumption and the impossibility of holding an 'inventory' of services, means that it is important to develop a workforce schedule where capacity and demand are well matched. Imbalances will become clear through fluctuations in the workload of the employees. It has been proven that, in high-contact services, a work intensity that is sustained above normal levels can lead to increased fatigue, burnout and eventually increased turnover,[14] which in turn has an impact on the availability of personnel. The high turnover may be the start of 'a cycle of failure', as described in Chapter 2.

Many different mathematical models have been developed in order to find an 'optimal' workforce schedule in specific situations.[15] The complexity of a workforce schedule also makes it an interesting application for automated decision support.

The last level in the manpower planning framework is that of the *daily reassignments of personnel* due to sudden sickness leave of employees or unexpected peaks in demand. In order to cope with these daily changes, some degree of flexibility in workforce staffing and scheduling is required.

Exhibit 10.4 describes the complexity of staffing and scheduling nurses in acute care hospitals.

Exhibit 10.4 Staffing and scheduling nurses in an acute care hospital[16]

A hospital nurse staffing and scheduling survey in American hospitals (348 nurse managers) reveals that the three most important objectives of nurse managers are:

1 achieving and improving quality of care;

2 having satisfied nurses with a low turnover rate; and

3 assigning equitable workload to nursing staff by matching required staff to actual number on duty.

These objectives overrule other goals such as cost containment and productivity improvement. How do nurses typically deal with the nurse staffing and scheduling problem?

At the annual budgeting round, the nursing director is asked to project the next year's staffing needs. On average, the nursing director will develop estimates of the nursing staff needs by:

● gathering data on patient days and admissions, and sometimes on forecasts of these data;

● studying trends in the utilization of nursing services; and

● using her experience.

The nursing director must also determine how many nurses will be allocated to the different nursing departments. While the number of patients on the unit is an important indicator of staffing, the nursing director must be aware that a patient day does not have the same meaning for every nursing department. A critical care unit needs a higher level of nursing resources per patient day than a non-critical care unit. In order to take these differences into account, the average amount of nursing care per patient for each nursing department must be known. This assumes the development of time standards for a type of patient. Several methods such as work sampling and expert opinion can be used to collect time standards. Applying time standards requires the development of a patient classification system that identifies different types of patients. Besides these quantitative differences, the qualifications of a nurse working in an intensive-care unit may be different from one working in a non-critical care unit.

The staffing needs of a nursing department at a certain time are thus a function of, among others, the kind of patient cared for. This makes it extremely difficult for the nursing director to allocate a fixed number of nurses to one department for a longer period of time (for instance, one year). The changing needs demand flexibility in the allocation of nurses. One way to deal with this problem is to use a pool of floating nurses who can be reallocated as needed.

The staffing budget specifies how many nurses with a specific qualification are needed for each nursing unit. This budget is the input into the nursing scheduling decision. The head of the nursing unit determines which nurses will work at which shift and on which day. A scheduling policy will specify the rules of schedule development. The scheduling policy includes decisions on the following topics: the time period of the schedule (2, 4 or more weeks), the number of shifts per 24 hours, how nurses rotate (or do not rotate) between shifts, how nurses are assigned to shifts, how many hours a nurse works per shift (day), the pattern of days on and off.

An example of a (traditional) scheduling policy is a cyclical schedule of an 8-hour shift, 5-day working week.[17] These shifts are usually from 7.00 a.m. to 3.30 p.m., from 3.00 p.m. to 11.30 p.m. and 11.00 p.m. to 7.30 a.m. A cyclical schedule is one that repeats itself after some period of time (for example, 6 weeks). Many more complex scheduling rules have been developed – for example, a cyclical schedule of 10-hour days and 4-day working weeks. Scheduling policies vary in terms of allowable scheduling patterns and wage rates and so the cost of implementing alternative scheduling policies is also different.[18]

An attractive scheduling policy seems to be an important factor in retaining nurses; it must take into account the individual wishes of the nurses. Common requests include working a maximum of 7 consecutive days, never working on Wednesday afternoons, working only 2 weekends per month and this for the whole weekend. These wishes are further complicated with very specific requirements such as requests for a particular day off.

Scheduling nurses is a complex calculation problem with many different goals, decision parameters and constraints. In order to solve this complex computational problem, several automated scheduling procedures or systems have been developed.

On a shift-by-shift basis, non-predictable changes will occur, for instance, due to sudden sickness. Some policies must be available to deal with these daily problems. For instance, one nursing department uses a combination of overtime work, on-call staff, a pool of floating nurses from outside, and the floating of nurses between nursing units. These reassignment mechanisms assume some kind of staffing and scheduling flexibility and do not all have the same costs and benefits. Hiring nurses from outside the hospital is clearly more expensive. Floating nurses between nursing units is sometimes limited by the special skills needed.

Managing the demand side

Until now we have assumed that the demand pattern was a given – that is, that it could not be influenced by the organization. However, most service organizations, explicitly or implicitly, try to influence the demand pattern to provide a better match between demand and supply (the available capacity). It can sometimes be easier and/or less costly to work on the demand side of the service equation, rather than attempting to control supply. This is certainly the case in organizations with high capacity-related fixed costs, such as airlines, hotels and professional service organizations.

Managing the demand patterns

Influencing the demand pattern involves changing the natural demand pattern – that is, the pattern that occurs if the customers do not have any incentive to adapt the timing or quantity of the demand. Demand management therefore involves offering customers an incentive to change their behaviour or otherwise changing the drivers of demand. Effective demand management therefore involves understanding this behaviour and the demand drivers.

Understanding demand patterns

In the Belmont case in Exhibit 10.1, there are two 'seasonal' patterns. There is a *daily pattern* whereby drivers prefer to arrive early in the morning, and there is the *yearly pattern* whereby more drivers tend to bring in their car for inspection in the first 4 months of the year than in the other 8. The yearly cycle is tied to the timing of car purchases. It appears that in this case people, for a variety of reasons, prefer to buy their new cars in the first months of the year. As long as the visit to the inspection station is tied to the date of purchase of the car, these peaks at the beginning of the year will persist, whatever the incentive the inspection station gives its customers to come later in the year. To change the yearly pattern, these dates must be decoupled, which in this case requires legislative action.

This situation is fairly clear in the Belmont case, but it is not always so in other cases. The notion of dependent and pseudo-dependent demand is useful in this context. The demand for car inspection services can be considered to be dependent on the purchase of the car. The demand for train seats is influenced at peak times by the opening and closing times of schools and workplaces.

Often the demand is composed of different segments, which vary in terms of demand drivers or in their degree of sensitivity to incentives to change the demand pattern. In an ambulatory care facility, demand is made up of patients with an acute problem, on the one hand, and patients whose problems can be dealt with on an appointment basis, on the other. One such facility analysed its demand pattern and came to the conclusion that, on Monday mornings, there were significantly more patients with acute problems than on any other day of the week. To avoid excessive demand on Mondays, a policy was introduced that did not allow patients to make appointments for Monday mornings. The capacity was made available exclusively for the treatment of acute problems.

The demand pattern must be understood not only to see if the demand can be influenced but also to see the extent to which it can be influenced. For instance, price sensitivity might differ from segment to segment. Tourists are more sensitive to price reduction than businessmen and are therefore willing to stay over the weekend, if offered a cheaper plane fare. Businessmen usually prefer to return home as soon as business is over, no matter what the price is.

In the Belmont case, there are at least two segments: private individuals and professionals. A professional – such as a lorry driver, taxi driver or travelling salesperson – drives his or her car as a part of the job. Statistics tell us that early morning peaks in demand come mainly from private drivers. The daily pattern for the professional driver is much more evenly spread. This is explained by the fact that private individuals who have to bring in their car in the middle of the day have to take at least half a day off. If they can come in early in the morning, these drivers do not have to take so much time off. At most, they will be an hour late for work. The 'cost' (in terms of time off) clearly varies depending on the time of the day. For the professional driver, the cost during the day is much more even since it is not dependent on the time of the day or tied to a particular time slot.

Introducing price incentives

Price incentives (or disincentives) are the most obvious way to change the demand pattern, as was already discussed in Chapter 9. Prices for ski lift passes are obviously more expensive during the Christmas break and the winter school holidays than they are, for instance, for the

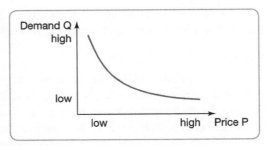

Figure 10.12 A demand curve

rest of the months of December or January. The price for electricity is lower at night than during the day. The same is true for a telephone conversation. Before applying price incentives, however, one has first to estimate the price sensitivity – not an easy task in many cases.

Price sensitivity is an expression of the relationship that exists between demand and price. In most cases when the price drops, demand will increase. The demand is said to be '*price-elastic*'. More people will be tempted to buy the product or the service when the price is lower (*see* Figure 10.12). For example, taking the Disneyland Paris case described in the introduction of this chapter, one of the actions taken by management after the rather disastrous first year was to drop prices.

Demand can be very *elastic* – producing a curve that is very steep (as it is in Figure 10.12) – it can be *inelastic*, implying an almost flat curve. For certain products such as luxury goods, the demand can even be positively related to the price.

Before experimenting with lower prices, companies should be aware that the different segments in the market may have a different price sensitiveness. Very frequently, there is a segment in the market that is very price sensitive and another that is less so. If a price incentive is offered, regardless of the segment, it goes without saying that the less price-sensitive segment will also take advantage of the price discount and, therefore, the company will lose gross margin.

The key question is, therefore, how a market should be segmented. Airlines have done it very cleverly by requiring low-fare travellers to stay over the weekend.[19] The Belgian railways offer so-called 'GO Passes' for younger people in off-peak hours and are thereby reaching a market segment that otherwise would not take the train, certainly not during off-peak hours. Hotels that otherwise depend very much on business travellers or conventions offer special rates at weekends.

Segmentation and price incentives can become very complex in certain businesses, particularly if there is a dynamic policy. This leads to the practice of yield management, as we shall explain later in this chapter.

Promoting off-peak demand

Another approach to altering the demand pattern is promoting off-peak demand. This entails seeking out different sources of demand at various periods. Seaside hotels compete vigorously during the period between October and March for conventions and business meetings. A ski resort, on the other hand, will offer a full range of summer sports like mountain biking, archery, hiking trips and white water rafting.

Offering alternative services

When the demand for a certain service becomes too high, a part of that demand can be reassigned to an alternative service. For instance, a holiday resort offered puppet shows and other entertainment for children at the times when there was peak demand for the subtropical swimming pool area.

Altering the product

When trying to alter the demand pattern, price need not be seen as the only variable. The other elements of the so-called 'marketing mix' – product, promotion and place – should also be considered. An interesting example is offered by a US resort.[20] Faced with far greater demand for tennis facilities than they could handle at peak hours, they transferred part of that demand to the early morning hours by creating what became known as the Early Bird Club. People who played tennis early in the morning were offered a free breakfast at the tennis court and started to get to know one another, teaming up for singles or doubles games. The product had become entirely different.

Advertising

Promotion might also be effective in changing the demand pattern, for example, by announcing that certain periods of the day, week or year are going to be very busy. In the US, the postal service starts early – immediately after Thanksgiving – with its campaign to stimulate people to send their Christmas cards. This is reminiscent of the summer campaign by the coal industry in the 1950s and 1960s to 'buy coal in the summer'.

In the Belmont case, a promotional campaign could be launched to let the public know that mornings are very busy.

Installing booking systems

An effective way to influence the demand pattern is to introduce a booking system. A booking system pre-sells the potential service. One can deflect additional demand to other time slots at the same facility or to other facilities of the same organization. Bookings also benefit the customer by reducing waiting and guaranteeing service availability. A problem with booking systems is that consumers may fail to honour the booking. We shall discuss this problem later in this chapter.

Another problem is, of course, dealing with the inherent uncertainties – those related to arrival, as well as those related to service times. In many service organizations, service times may vary considerably. Patients seeing a doctor or a dentist are sometimes difficult to schedule because of the (seemingly) random variations in service times. This is an even bigger problem because a customer who has made a booking does not expect to wait and will be quickly dissatisfied when he or she has to wait beyond the scheduled time.

Yield management

What is yield management?

The next time you are sitting in an aeroplane, ask your neighbour what price he or she paid for the trip. There is a good chance that a different price was paid for the same seat and surrounding service package. If the price you have paid is higher, you probably won't be very happy about it. However, don't start writing a letter of complaint to your local consumer protection agency. The airline's differentiated price practice will not be seen as unfair. You are just the victim of the yield management system of that airline. If you question your neighbour a little further you will probably find out that he or she booked much earlier than you did, is required to stay over the weekend, or is a member of a bird watching association on the way to its annual convention in Orlando, Florida.

You could have the same experience if you stay in a hotel, rent a car or even attend a hospital. These are all examples of service organizations that practise so-called 'yield management', also called 'revenue management'.

When an airline schedules a plane on a certain day for a certain route, the capacity for that day on that route is fixed. While the airline wants to sell that capacity to passengers who are willing to pay full fare, it probably knows that on that day there are insufficient passengers willing to pay the full price. Given the fixed nature of the capacity and the fixed nature of the cost of operating an airline, where variable costs are low, the airline will of course be tempted to reduce its sales price to fill up the remaining seats. However, it has to make sure that the passengers who are willing to pay full fare do not take advantage of this price reduction but, on the other hand, make sure that they do not feel cheated or unfairly treated by the airline. The problem is more complex in the case of an airline, since it normally cannot take a wait-and-see attitude (i.e. wait to see how the airline fills up and depending on the occupation rate decide to drop prices). It has to make the decision on what prices to charge to which type of customers well in advance. This means that it has to decide beforehand what maximum capacity it will set aside for the lower paying categories. Exhibit 10.5 describes a simple example of a yield management system.

Yield management has been defined as 'the process of allocating the right type of capacity to the right type of customer at the right price so as to maximize revenue or yield', where yield is defined as 'the ratio of revenue realized over revenue potential'.

Yield management techniques began to be used around 1950, when they were applied to the airline and the hotel industry. The deregulation of the airline industry in the US in the late seventies stimulated the introduction of yield management significantly. Let us illustrate yield management with the TPA example.

Exhibit 10.5 Yield management at Transpacific Airlines

Let us assume that Transpacific Airlines (TPA) has scheduled a flight between London and Sydney on a particular day. The plane has a capacity of 300 passengers. The airline knows that there are two categories of customers interested in this trip. A first category – Category A – is willing to pay £1000, while the marginal cost to serve this type of passenger is only €100. The second category – Category B – is only willing to pay €500, while the marginal cost is €80. The airline also knows that on that particular day an average of 175 passengers is willing to pay full fare. However, the actual number may fluctuate. Let us assume that the actual number is normally distributed with a standard deviation of 50 passengers. Similarly, TPA knows that on average 150 passengers are willing to pay the lower fare and that the standard deviation of the demand in this group is 25. How much capacity should TPA set aside for Category B?

It can be shown that the optimal number of seats to set aside for the lower paying category is such that the expected marginal revenue for both categories is the same. If we assign a fixed number of 120 seats to Category B, the remaining 180 are assigned to Category A. The probability that demand will exceed 180 in Category A is 46%. Therefore, the expected marginal contribution of this seat is therefore $0.46 \times 900 = €414$. The probability that the demand in Category B will exceed the assigned number of seats is equal to 88%. Therefore, the marginal contribution of the seat above 120 is 0.88 × 420 = €370. The latter category is below the marginal contribution of the former one, and so the number of seats assigned to Category B should be reduced. When we reduce the number of seats to 116.1, the expected marginal revenue for both categories is the same (= €405). The optimal (static) policy is therefore to allocate 184 seats to Category A and 116 seats to Category B.

The total capacity of the aeroplane is 300 seats and the maximum yield per seat is £900 or the maximum total yield is 900 × 300 = €270,000 or 100%. If at a certain time the aeroplane is filled with 200 passengers paying full fare (€900) and 90 passengers paying the reduced fare, the yield becomes:

$$\frac{(200 \times 900) + (90 \times 420)}{(300 \times 900)} = 80.6\%$$

In this simple problem, yield management appears to be a fairly static process. The lower-fare passengers will be accepted as long as the total number of passengers (300) (called the booking limit) and the number that has been set aside for this category beforehand have not been exceeded. For the high-fare paying passengers, the rule is simple. Passengers are accepted as long as there is an empty seat on the aeroplane (ignoring the fact for a moment that most airlines will probably overbook).

In reality, however, the problem is much more dynamic. The booking limit (number of seats set aside for the lower category) changes over time depending on the forecast of demand for the high category. If the conclusion is reached that the booking for the high category is slow – that is, that fewer higher-fare paying passengers are expected than originally planned – the booking limit will rise. On the other hand, when the demand for the high-fare tickets is much higher than expected, the booking limit will be reduced. To add to the complexity, there could be more than two categories. Another source of complexity is that customers who have made bookings could fail to show up. This shows how difficult it is to develop yield management systems. We refer the reader to the literature for further details.

When and where to apply yield management?

Yield management is an issue in service organizations in the following circumstances:

1 *When the organization is operating with a relatively fixed capacity* – that is, capacity that cannot be quickly changed.

2 *When it is possible to segment markets.* It must be possible to effectually segment the markets into different types of customers. For example, the airline industry distinguishes between time-sensitive and price-sensitive customers by requiring that discounted fares involve a Saturday night's stay.[21] A hotel distinguishes between transient guests who walk in and request a room and, for instance, corporate travellers who usually make bookings. The first group pays a higher price than the second group.

3 *When the capacity is perishable.* This is one of the basic characteristics of services. Capacity is inventory that perishes when it is not used. It is precisely this characteristic that makes yield management relevant. It is because capacity that is not utilized is lost forever, that service organizations are willing to sell it cheaply, so that at least some marginal revenue is earned.

4 *Marginal sales cost is low, but the cost of adding extra capacity is high.*

Almost by definition, one could say that yield management is practiced in the so-called 'for-profit' sectors. However, Metters and Vargas (1999) described how yield management can be useful in the not-for-profit sectors like child care services or even universities. In many of these institutions, there exists a form of discrimination when allocating capacity across different segments (for instance, the financial situation) and, therefore, scope for the application of yield management.

What about no-shows and overbooking?

Airlines allow customers to cancel unpaid bookings with no penalty. Even after having purchased a ticket, passengers are allowed to cancel their flights and receive at least partial refunds. On average, about half of all bookings made for a flight are cancelled or become no-shows. American Airlines estimates that about 15% of the seats on sold-out flights would be unused, if bookings sales were limited to aircraft capacity.[22]

As a result, airlines, like hotels, have very little choice but to set booking levels higher than their capacity. Of course, the problem is how high the overbooking level should be. If the level is too low, there will be a large number of empty seats; if the level is too high, there is the prospect of disappointed and often angry customers who have made bookings but are being turned away. The airline or hotel must compensate them for the inconvenience and accommodate them on other flights or in other hotels.

Determining the overbooking level can again be based on the marginal analysis described above. To illustrate this approach, let us consider the case in Exhibit 10.6.

Exhibit 10.6 The Gates Hotel, San Francisco

The Gates Hotel,[23] a very popular business traveller's luxury hotel in San Francisco, found that it frequently turned down the rental of a room that was being held for a no-show booking. Mr Barnes, the manager, felt that the hotel's policy of overbooking should be examined. He wondered how much extra capacity should be maintained to cover these commitments.

The average lost contribution for a room was $20 per night if a customer reserved the room and the hotel was unable to honour the booking. About 10% of the guests who showed up with bookings that could not be honoured could be placated without cost. Another 30% were satisfied with being 'walked' (or transferred) to another hotel at a cost to the Gates of $3 per booking. The remaining guests were so upset by this situation that the Gates could expect a loss of future business with an expected value in terms of contribution of approximately $50.

Mr Barnes reviewed his records and found that, when it was operating around full capacity, the Gates Hotel had the no-show experience summarized in Table 10.6.

Let us assume that the hotel accepts five more customers than it can accommodate. The cost of having one room unoccupied at the end of the day (C_o) is $20. The expected cost of having one room short (C_s) can be calculated as follows:

$$C_s = 0 \times 0.1 + 3 \times 0.3 + 50 \times 0.6 = \$30.9$$

As long as five or more customers do not show up, there will be no cost of overbooking, but the hotel will have to carry the cost of reduced occupancy. From Table 10.6 we can see that the probability of this happening is 27%. Therefore, the marginal expected cost of

---

Table 10.6 The Gates Hotel no-show experience

No-shows	% of experiences	Cumulative % of experiences
1	10	10
2	21	31
3	19	50
4	13	63
5	10	73
6	5	78
7	6	84
8	4	88
9	3	91
10	2	93
11	1	94
12	2	96
13	2	98
14	1	99
15	1	100

unoccupancy is $0.27 \times 20 = \$5.40$. On the other hand, if four or fewer customers do not show up, the hotel will have an overbooking cost. The probability of this happening is 63% (see Table 10.6), so the marginal expected cost of overbooking is $0.63 \times 30.9 = \$19.50$. Given that this latter cost is higher than the first cost, the hotel should overbook a lower number of customers. It can be proven that the optimal overbooking level (L) is such that: where D is the number of people that do not show up. $P(D > L)$ is then the probability that the number of people that do not show up is greater than L. We can see from Table 10.6 that the optimal level L is somewhere between 2 and 3. We would probably advise the hotel to keep its over-booking level to 2.

In reality, determining the overbooking level is usually more complex. First of all, it can seldom be approached in a static manner. The overbooking level changes over time. The earlier a passenger or guest has made a booking on an airline, the higher the probability that he or she will cancel. This means that the overbooking levels must be higher a month before the departure than a week before the departure. Furthermore, the cost of overbooking is usually not in proportion to the number of passengers. When overbooked, American Airlines offers vouchers to passengers willing to give up their seats. It works something like an auction: the value of the voucher increases until enough willing passengers are found. The higher the number of oversales, the higher the average value of the voucher the company has to offer.

The psychology and managerial consequences of waiting

Waiting is not waiting

As should be clear by now, time is a key dimension of service activities. The duration of these activities and of the whole process – the length of the waiting times, the predictability of these durations, the opening hours, etc. – are all factors that have a strong impact on the quality of the service experience. We refer back to Table 10.2 at the beginning of this chapter, which illustrates more than anything else that people do not like to wait, and that waiting undoubtedly affects our satisfaction level and our repurchase behaviour. Referring to the SERVQUAL model (*see* Chapter 13), we see that various elements are directly related to the time dimension.

As was made clear in the first part of this chapter, the first thing to do when confronted with customer dissatisfaction related to waiting times is to analyse the capacity of the process and, where possible, adjust it. However, increasing the capacity might not always be a possible, adequate, or most effective alternative. If waiting is a problem, then there are various other alternatives at a manager's disposal. The relationship between customer dissatisfaction and waiting time is not as direct or even as linear as the Florida Light and Power study (*see* Table 10.2) or the fast food example (*see* Figure 10.7). It is a more complex process where other factors than the objective waiting time play a role. One of these other factors is the subjective perception of the waiting time. Improving the customer's perception of the waiting experience can be as effective as reducing the actual length of the wait. In other words, we should focus on managing perception as much as managing capacity.

Before considering such actions, managers should be aware of how people perceive waiting and what the factors are that influence people's perception of waiting. David Maister refers to this as the 'psychology of waiting'.[24]

The psychology of waiting

Most of us have probably had similar experiences when travelling to an unknown destination. The first time you drive your car to visit a colleague or friend who lives in a place you have never been to, the drive towards the unknown destination always seems longer than the return drive. This impression disappears as you become more acquainted with the road. If you have experienced this, you have witnessed one of 'Maister's laws'.[25] David Maister, at that time a Harvard Business School professor, formulated a number of laws (without empirical testing, however) that express experiences many of us have had in waiting situations. We will briefly describe (an adaptation of) this list of laws.

Most people tend to overestimate the actual waiting time

Various studies indicate that customers cannot accurately estimate how long they have waited and usually think that they have waited much longer than they actually have. For instance, in the telephone study at Florida Light and Power referred to earlier,[26] 41% of the customers who had actually waited less than 30 seconds thought they had waited between 30 seconds and 1 minute, while 28% even thought they had waited more than 1 minute. More generally, the study indicated that the following relationships existed between real waiting time (expressed in seconds) and the subjective or perceived waiting time:

$$\text{Real time} = 11.9 \text{ seconds} + 0.276 \text{ Subjective time}$$

Other studies, at least for waits of 5 minutes or less, point to the same conclusion. In a supermarket study, the average percentage differences between the perceived waiting time was found to be between 21% and 40%.[27] A third study in a bank came to the conclusion that customers overestimated the waiting time by about 30% (4.7 minutes *versus* 3.6 minutes) with 78% of the customers overestimating the waiting time.[28] There is clearly an element of time distortion in all these situations. There are many factors that might explain this time distortion, ranging from the fact that people generally are very poor at estimating time, to the fact that waiting is an anticipatory stage, and therefore draws attention to itself and to the circumstances under which it takes place. Whatever the reason, however, such distortion exists, and there is little point in arguing about the subject of a customer's estimate.

Unoccupied time feels longer than occupied time

There is an anecdote reported by Sasser *et al.*[29] about a hotel where customers complained about the waiting times at the lifts. Not being able to immediately increase the capacity of the lift facilities, the management of the hotel installed mirrors next to the lift doors. The result was that the number of complaints dropped significantly, despite the fact that the actual waiting time had not changed. The conclusion is that when people are distracted, they are less aware of the waiting time or are more tolerant of waiting. In the bank study referred to earlier, for instance, the bank installed an electronic news board. This board displayed 15 minutes of up-to-date news and information, interspersed with ads for the bank. As a result, customers found waiting much more tolerable. When asked to describe their waiting experiences on a scale from 1 to 10 (from very boring to very interesting) the interest level increased significantly. In the supermarket study,[30] Jones and Peppiatt found that when customers were distracted by a television screen at the check-outs, the average difference between actual and perceived waiting time dropped from 71.8 to 48.1 seconds.

Pre-process waits feel longer than in-process waits

Maister states that 'people waiting to make their first human contact with the service organisation are much more impatient than those who have "begun".' This is closely related to the 'anxiety' level of people when waiting. Generally speaking, a person's anxiety level is much higher while waiting to be served than it is when being served. Imagine entering a crowded café or tea room, where waiters appear to be very skilled at ignoring your presence and avoiding your signals. You are probably very anxious for fear of being forgotten or being leap-frogged by customers who entered later. Your anxiety will magically disappear after the waiter has made eye contact with you and has somehow assured you that you have been noticed. Your tolerance for waiting increases as soon as you have the feeling of being 'in the system' rather than being 'in front of the system'.

The walk-in medical clinic at Harvard University noticed a significant drop in dissatisfaction levels due to waiting after they installed a triage system, despite the fact that the actual average total waiting time increased after the installation of the system. This contradiction was resolved after observing the fact that, in the new system, the average time a walk-in visitor waited before he or she saw a medically qualified person (the triage nurse) attending to his or her problem decreased. In the new system, the average time was 19.7 minutes, while in the old system, without the triage nurse, it took an average of 23 minutes before a first contact with a nurse or a physician took place. In addition, in the new system, the distribution of this time was much narrower than in the old system.

Anxiety makes waiting feel longer

That a trip to an unfamiliar destination seems longer than the return trip has a lot to do with the anxiety we feel about the unknown, the fear of being late. Anxiety about whether or not one has been forgotten is also the reason why pre-process waits feel longer than in-process waits, as noted above. Another source of anxiety might be the uncertainty of the length of the waiting and service time. The impatience of many motorists waiting in a traffic jam is surely more closely related to the uncertain length of the waiting than to the waiting time itself. There is also the fear of being unfairly treated as other customers pass you in the queue. All of us have had the experience of choosing a queue at a supermarket or a lane on a motorway, and then worrying whether or not we have made the right choice. Doesn't the other queue always move faster?

The supermarket study supports this hypothesis. It was found that the less familiar customers were with a supermarket, the more they overestimated the waiting time. Frequent visitors overestimated the waiting time by about 28 seconds, while infrequent visitors overestimated the same time by 167 seconds. Uncertain waits always feel longer than known, finite waits.

Unexplained waits are less tolerable than explained waits

In addition to not knowing how long you will have to wait, not knowing *why* you are waiting makes the waiting less tolerable and makes the perceived waiting time longer. Passengers waiting to board an aeroplane will be less angry when they are told that the plane is late because of weather conditions, than when they are told only that the plane is late. You will perhaps forgive your doctor's lateness when you are informed that he or she has been held up by an emergency.

The lower the degree of personal control, the less tolerance there is for waiting

While it is true that knowing why you have to wait is beneficial for the particular waiting experience, the impact of the information on the customer's overall and long-term satisfaction will depend very much on how customers attribute the cause of waiting. This is determined by two factors:

1 *The customer's perception of his or her role.* Customers who know the peak hours of a service delivery system (i.e. the motorway, the bank) but still decide to come during those hours have only themselves to blame for the waiting and delay, certainly if they had the opportunity to come at a different time. Generally speaking, the more the customers perceive themselves as having control (even while waiting), the more tolerant they are of waiting. This aspect was also illustrated in the walk-in clinic referred to earlier. In the new system there was not only a triage but a choice of doctor or nurse, while previously patients had been assigned to a doctor or a nurse on a first-come, first-served basis. This, together with a faster first contact, explains why patients were more satisfied with the changed system despite the fact that the objective waiting times were longer.

2 *Whether or not the reason for waiting is within the service delivery system.* Most people will be tolerant of waiting when the cause of the delay is beyond the control of the service organization. When a tour bus pulls into a restaurant, customers that follow will probably understand and accept that waiting is inevitable. On the other hand, when the same restaurant has accepted a wedding party and uses this as an excuse to other customers for long delays, such an excuse will not be accepted. A booking has been made for the wedding party well in advance and the restaurant should have made arrangements to cope with the increased demand. We are more tolerant when an aeroplane is late due to weather conditions than when it is late due to maintenance failure.

Unfair waits are longer than equitable waits

An otherwise very quiet waiting room with very civilized citizens can be transformed all of a sudden into a mob of angry people, when somebody has successfully 'skipped the queue'. Even the most patient customer becomes furious in such a situation. Some of us might even have witnessed fights between motorists in the street after one motorist has cut in front of another while not obeying the traffic rules.

In waiting situations, where there is no visible and/or enforced order, or when people can easily violate the 'first-come first-served' order, instead of being able to relax, the customer remains in a state of nervousness about whether his or her place in the queue is being preserved.

The more valuable the service, the higher the tolerance for waiting

When you go to a supermarket to buy a newspaper or a loaf of bread, you are not willing to wait 10 minutes behind other customers whose carts are fully loaded with groceries. Supermarkets have recognized this problem and have installed express checkouts. Airlines provide special counters for passengers that do not have any luggage to check in. There is not only a value-for-money expectation – that is, where you pay a high price, you expect high values – but also a value for waiting time. This principle not only applies to the value of the service itself but also to the perceived 'value' of the service provider. A customer is more tolerant of waiting in a bank when waiting to see the manager or being served by the manager than when dealing with a clerk. Maister illustrates this principle by referring to an old rule in academia that 'you wait five minutes for an assistant professor, ten for an associate professor and fifteen minutes for a full professor.'

An interesting consequence of this principle is the intolerance involved in waiting after the service is over. Post-process waits are perhaps even less tolerable than pre-process waits. When the service is over, there is no further expected added value. This explains the haste of airline passengers to disembark and find their luggage once the plane has landed or the impatience of hotel guests to check out, or restaurant visitors to pay the bill.

Solo waits feel longer than group waits

The supermarket study referred to earlier is one of the few studies that tested the proposition that waiting alone seems longer than waiting in a group. In this study, it was found that people who queued alone perceived the waiting time to be on average 75.6 seconds longer than the actual waiting time. This was significantly longer than for people who queued together with one or more other persons. In this category, the average difference between perceived and actual waiting time was 49.3 seconds. This is partially explained by the fact that in group waits, customers are 'occupied' and also perhaps less anxious. There is also the phenomenon that the customers, even if they do not know each other, turn to each other when the delay is announced and express their exasperation. There is some form of comfort in group waiting rather than waiting alone.

Sometimes, more positively, a sense of group community develops in queues, and as Maister states:

> 'the line turns into almost a service encounter in its own right: part of the fun and part of the service.'

However, sometimes groups can amplify feelings of discomfort and, therefore, be the cause of dissatisfaction.

◼ Managing perception of waiting times

Each of the propositions introduced above can help managers to actively influence a customer's perception of the waiting time, and by so doing influence the customer's satisfaction. The various propositions are interdependent, however, and acting on each of them separately could even be counterproductive. Take, for instance, the idea of installing television screens in queues. A Dutch hospital did just that but had to conclude afterwards that it had no effect at all on customers' satisfaction. Most people did not watch the TV and, those who did, did so only after some time, once they had finished browsing through magazines or had run out of small talk with other people. It is possible that those watching TV were those who had to wait the longest or those who were the most impatient – that is, with the lowest tolerance for waiting.

It is therefore necessary to develop an integrated view of the problem. Two Dutch researchers, Smidts and Pruyn,[31] have developed and tested such a model (*see* Figure 10.13). Largely based on this model and to a lesser extent based on the results of other studies, we developed an integrated conceptual model. This model attempts to explain customers' satisfaction or dissatisfaction with certain services. According to the model, *overall satisfaction or dissatisfaction* is influenced by *satisfaction or dissatisfaction with the wait*. Of course, this is influenced by the actual *objective waiting time*, but there are other factors that come into play here that makes this relationship indirect and more complex.

Acceptable waiting time

The first factor is what the customers consider to be *the acceptable waiting time* – his or her 'zone of tolerance'. It is beyond question that customers consider zero waiting times to be

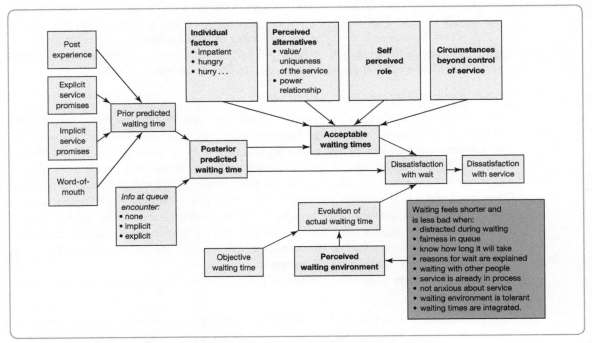

Figure 10.13 An integrated view of managing the perception of waiting times

Source: Pruyn, A. T. H. and Smidts, A. (1992) *De Psychologische Beleving van Wachtrijen*, Erasmus Universiteit, Management Report Sciences, 126.

ideal. They recognize, however, that this is not always possible because the price would be too high – hence, a tolerance for waiting. Figure 10.13 describes some of the factors that have an influence on the acceptable waiting time:

1 *Factors that are temporary and individual.* When you are in a hurry to catch a train, you will be less tolerant of people who cause traffic jams; when you are hungry, you will be more impatient towards the waiter who fails to take your order immediately. Certain persons are by nature more impatient than others. In their banking study,[32] Katz and her colleagues classified customers into three categories: the *watchers*, the *impatients* and the *neutrals*. Watchers enjoyed observing people and events at the bank, while impatients could think of nothing more boring than waiting in a queue. Neutrals fell somewhere in between. Durrande-Moreau and Usinier (1999)[33] introduced the concept of time styles. Individuals have a certain time style, which is characterized by a general attitude towards time. They use five dimensions to describe a certain time style: economicity of time, past orientation, future orientation, time submissiveness (the capacity to comply with schedules), and feeling of usefulness of time. Based on this, they identified two ideal types: quantitative individuals and qualitative individuals. 'Quantitative individuals display strong economic time and marked temporal projections, mostly towards the future, and have a sense of the usefulness and purpose of their time. On the other hand, qualitative persons display low concern with economic time, and their projections towards the past and future are less pronounced. They tend to live in the present, and have little sense and purpose of their time.'[34]

2 *Factors related to the perception of alternatives.* If the service is very valuable and unique, tolerance for waiting will be higher. Certain restaurants, certain medical doctors, and even certain management consultants work with waiting lists measured in months. In other circumstances, the same customers, who in the above situations wait patiently, become very impatient if they have to wait more than 30 seconds for someone to answer the telephone, or if they have to stand in a queue for more than five minutes at the supermarket. Uniqueness and value have of course something to do with power relationships. If you, as a customer, are clearly in a subordinated position, your tolerance for waiting will be higher. That is why, at least in Belgian universities, students have to respect the academic quarter, meaning that the professor is allowed 15 minutes of grace before students can leave a class. Would any student dare to act likewise and come 15 minutes late for an exam?

Similar conclusions could be drawn for monopolistic situations, as in many government or government-controlled systems. However, the fact that the customer has no other choice and therefore is 'forced' to be tolerant does not mean that his or her satisfaction level will not be influenced by waiting time. The extent to which the customer feels forced to use a certain service provider should be considered.

3 *Factors related to the 'self-perceived role'.* The zone of tolerance will be smaller when a customer perceives his or her control to be very small. This is one of the reasons why the multiple queueing system is preferable to a single queueing system: customers pick a queue and can at least blame themselves if their queue seems to be moving more slowly that the others.

4 *Factors that are due to circumstances beyond* the control *of the service provider.* These concern the perception that waiting is caused by circumstances beyond the control of the service provider, such as weather conditions or strikes.

Expected waiting time

As illustrated in Figure 10.13, a further important factor that influences tolerance of waiting is what Smidts and Pruyn call the *posterior predicted waiting time*.

The posterior predicted or expected waiting time is a prediction of the expected waiting time once you have entered the service system. It is a 'will' expectation, not a 'should' expectation (i.e. not a norm). It is a combination of the *prior predicted wait* and the specific *queue information* at the service encounter. For example, before setting out to the post office you might make an implicit or explicit prediction of the expected waiting time. When you arrive, you see a large number of cars and bikes parked outside the post office. You will probably adjust your expected waiting time immediately. In this example, you are receiving implicit information about the waiting time. In some circumstances, you receive explicit information about the expected queue. This happens at Disney parks where, at various points in the queueing space, boards are erected indicating the length of the queue in front of you, expressed in minutes. Some call centres do the same. They not only tell you the number of customers in front of you but will also sometimes tell you the expected waiting time.

The prior expected waiting time is the time you expect to wait before receiving specific situational information. This is, first of all, based on *past experience with similar or 'verisimilar' situations*. By 'verisimilar', we mean situations that are not exactly the same but from which we can extrapolate. Based on our experience in the bank, we can extrapolate waiting time expectations at the post office, for instance. Even if you have no experience of the immigration service at, for instance, Kennedy Airport in New York, you will have a prior expectation of a waiting time, based on your immigration experience in other countries or, even more generally, with the customs service when crossing borders by car.

A second factor is the *explicit service promise* either because the time has been explicitly advertised or promised when making reservations. Some supermarkets, for instance, promise that there will never be more than four customers waiting at the checkout. A pizza restaurant makes very explicit promises about the time it will take before you can pick up your pizza.

Even if there are no explicit promises, quite often there are *implicit promises*. As is generally the case for other quality dimensions, price is often an implicit promise with respect to waiting. If you are booked in an expensive hotel, you expect short check-in and check-out times and, more generally, short servicing times. The same is true for airlines. People who pay a more expensive fare expect shorter check-in times and expect to be able to leave the aeroplane before the other passengers.

A final factor influencing an individual's prior expected waiting time is the *word-of-mouth* information by friends, relatives, consumer reports, and so on.

Perceived waiting environment

The *perceived waiting time* is very much influenced by the *perceived waiting environment*. In this category we include all the factors that influence your perception of waiting time, while waiting, apart from the actual waiting time. They can be grouped into explicit distracters such as television, exhibits, and music or into general perceived attractiveness factors such as colour and spatial layout (*see* the servicescape in Chapter 7). It is here that the 'Maister's laws' apply. Pruyn and Smidts found that an attractive waiting environment 'directly and positively influences the satisfaction with the service. The design element of the environment may induce a positive mood, which influences *the appraisal* without necessarily influencing the perceived duration of the wait'.[35]

Appraisal of the wait

Appraisal of the wait, we should emphasize, has two components: a cognitive component that reflects the perception of the time span in terms of long or short, and an affective component that consists of emotional responses to waiting such as irritation, boredom, stress, and so on.

Conclusion

In this chapter, we have discussed various issues that need to be addressed when managing the capacity of a service delivery system in such a way as to ensure that capacity and demand match as far as possible. We emphasized that, in service industries to a greater extent than in industrial firms, management has to look at both sides of the equation: supply (i.e. capacity) and demand. Capacity management is, therefore, not only an 'operational' problem but also a marketing problem. Capacity is part of the product, as we have seen.

While there are many rational approaches to managing capacity, it is important to take into account how the results of capacity management are perceived by the customer. The customer is not always a rational human being. There are many subjective elements in the way customers perceive capacity management effects, such as waiting times. The difficult balance between rational approaches and subjective elements in capacity management is clearly illustrated in the experiment with 'snake queueing' at the discount retail company Colruyt (*see* Exhibit 10.7).

Exhibit 10.7 Snake queuing at Colruyt

In September 2010, Colruyt a major discount retail company in Belgium and France announced a 'revolution at the cash register: queueing in a snake'. This revolution was described as follows in the popular press in Belgium:[36]

> 'Finished with queueing in line, which always seems to be the slowest: Colruyt tests a simple but genial system as a result of which all customers will have to stand for up to a third less of the time in the queue at the check-out counter. Just as at the airport, we will soon be guided to the counters in one long line – the snake.'

The snake, as the system is called, is being tested in two different stores of the chain. Customers are guided into one queue and, when they reach the front of it, are invited by the first-available cashier to proceed to her/his checkout counter. To save space, the queue is organized as a snake comparable to the organization of waiting lines in airports or amusement parks. The system is not new since FNAC, the international book chain, applies this principle and many other chain stores in the world. The objective, in theory, is to reduce the average waiting time from three to two minutes. The purpose of the pilot study is to establish if it actually works in practice.

A second objective is to gain some space, again in theory. The company wants, in particular, to find out whether the snake works well at peak times, in particular, on Saturday mornings. The Commercial Director, Jean-Pierre Roelands, stated that, in addition, they want to find out how customers respond to the one-line system, and whether zigzagging along the snake with Colruyt's fairly large shopping trolleys will operate smoothly.

Gino Van Ossel, a Marketing professor at a leading Belgian Business School, believes in this concept. 'Research teaches us that queueing is very frustrating. Two out three shoppers have the impression they have chosen the wrong, i.e. the slower, line. Everybody in the same line is perceived as being fairer.' However, he shares the concerns of Mr Roelands about the versatility of the shopping carts. A second source of frustration in supermarkets, according to the professor, is the risk of being hit by other shoppers. But he believes that the problem is not as severe at Colruyt since it is not a 'fun store'. There are less couples shopping and also fewer children. That reduces the probability of collisions. He warns the company, however, to make the corridors sufficiently broad.

Precisely to improve versatility, Colruyt has decided not to introduce ribbons to guide customers along the snake, in the way that is practiced in airports. There will only be white lines on the floor. Van Ossel is aware that this requires greater discipline from shoppers. Another danger is that customers, now required to queue in one long line, may develop the negative perception that the waiting time at Colruyt is long and, therefore, might decide to shop elsewhere. The fact that the line will be continuously moving may counter this impression.

On March 30th 2011, the following article was published in one of the Belgian newspapers: 'Colruyt gives up the revolutionary snake queue'.[37] This was described as follows. 'The distribution chain Colruyt will not generalise the application of the snake concepts in its other stores. The tests in two stores have demonstrated that customers preferred the classical lines. Customers prefer to choose their check-out counter. A lot of people seem to know the cashier personally and like the opportunity to stay in contact with them. In addition, not all customers were convinced that the snake system was faster than the classical system'. Colruyt too had some doubts. 'The snake occupies more space than separate waiting lines. At peak times, the snake could be so long that the line extended right back into the shopping isles. In order to run the experiment efficiently, we need more space and this is a too big an investment.'

Figure 10.14 Snake Queueing at Colruyt

Source: Het Nieuwsblad (Belgian Newspaper), 18 September 2010. Photo courtesy of Photopress.be.

Review and discussion questions

- State the capacity of a highway with the following characteristics:
  - One lane, marked with 'kilometres' markers.
  - Speed limit 120 km/h.
  - All cars drive at the speed limit.
  - Average length of a car is 5 metres.
  - Average distance between cars: 40 metres (including the length of the car).
- How will the use of a number-taking system influence your waiting experience?
- Discuss the advantages and disadvantages of a snake-like entry system that you find at a Disney park versus the 'funnel' entry you might find at other places?
- Apply the model of Figure 10.3 to a (non-fast food) restaurant. How will capacity and capacity management influence your perception of the service offered?
- In the bank example (*see* Figure 10.5), what is the reason, despite an utilization rate lower than 95%, for customers having to wait 30 minutes? How could you reduce the working time without increasing the number of employees?
- In St Luke's hospital, there are four lifts for visitors. While the average capacity of the four lifts is sufficient to transport the visitors during the day, visitors have to wait about 3 minutes on average to get in the lift. Installing a fifth lift would reduce the waiting time to 1 minute 30 seconds. Knowing that the yearly depreciation and operational costs of a fifth lift is €30,000 and knowing that there are about 70,000 visitors a year, would you recommend that the hospital install a fifth lift?
- Is the demand for cashier resources in a supermarket dependent, independent, quasi-dependent or quasi-independent?

  What is the implication for managing these resources? Develop a resource planning system for a supermarket.
- Explain how the planning system at McDonald's described in Exhibit 10.2 can be seen as a pull system. What is the pull signal?
- Apply the demand management policies to a postal service.
- Read Exhibit 10.7 and answer the following questions:
  - How revolutionary is the snake queue concept?
  - What are the alternatives?
  - What are the advantages of both the snake queue system and of the classical multiline queueing system?
  - What do you think of the arguments used by Colruyt to bring the experiment to an end?

Technical note

Queueing systems in service environments and various forms of queueing theory are analysed in Technical note 1. The role of simulation as a tool when designing services is discussed in Technical note 2. These notes appear at the end of the book.

Suggested further reading

Kimes, S. E. (1989) 'Yield management: A tool for capacity-constrained service firms', *Journal of Operations Management*, Vol 8, No 4, October, pp. 348–363

Maister, D. H. (1988) 'The psychology of waiting lines', in Lovelock, C. H. (ed.) *Managing Services: Marketing, operations and human resources*. London: Prentice Hall, pp. 176–183

McGuire, K. A., Kimes, S. E., Lynn, M., Pullman, M. E. and Lloyd, R. C. (2010) 'A framework for evaluating the customer wait experience', *Journal of Service Management*, Vol 21, No 3, pp. 269–290

Smidts, A. and Pruyn, A. T. H. (1993) 'Customer reactions to queues: Towards a theory of waiting and delay', in Chias, J. and Sureda, J. (eds) *Marketing for the New Europe: Dealing with complexity*, Vol 2. Barcelona: ESADE, pp. 1383–1402

Notes and references

1 *See* 'Queuing for flawed services', *Financial Times*, 14 June 1992, p. 13 and *'EuroDisney Case'* (1981) Harvard Business School, 9–681–044

2 Based on 'Belmont case' in Hill, A. (1991) *Minnesota Pollution Control Agency*, University of Minnesota

3 This figure was inspired by Jaime Ribeca at IESE, Spain

4 Pruyn, A. and Smidts, A. (1998) 'Effects of waiting on the satisfaction with service: Beyond objective time measures', *International Journal of Research in Marketing*, 15, pp. 321–334

5 Graessel, B. and Zeider, P. (1993) 'Using quality function deployment to improve customer service', *Quality Progress*, November, pp. 39–63

6 Based on simulation

7 *See* Davis, M. (1991) 'How long should a customer wait?', *Decision Sciences*, Vol 22, pp. 421–434

8 In normal distribution tables we can see that the z-value corresponding with 20% is equal to 0.85. Therefore the additional number of rooms above the average should be equal to: 0.85×20, or 17

9 This description is based on the McDonald's Corporation Case, pp. 156–74 in Sasser, W. E., Clark, K. B., Garvin, D. A., Graham, M. B. W., Jaikumar, R. and Maister, D. H. (1982) *Cases in Operations Management*. Homewood, IL: Richard D. Irwin

10 Based on an article of Wacker, J. (1985), 'Effective planning and cost control for restaurants', *Production and Inventory Management*, Vol 26, pp. 55–70

11 For further information on the MRP concept the reader is referred to J. Orlicky (1975) *Materials Requirements Planning*. New York, NY: McGraw Hill

12 Khoong, C. M. (1996) 'An integrated system framework and analysis methodology for manpower planning', *International Journal of Manpower*, Vol 17, No 1, pp. 26–46

13 Siferd, S. P. (1991) 'The Ohio State University Hospital Nurse Staffing and Scheduling Survey Results', a document sent to the respondents, June

14 Pue, R. O. (1996) 'A dynamic theory of service delivery: implications for managing service quality', unpublished dissertation, Sloan School of Management, MIT, June

15 *See*, for instance, for a review of these models, Smith-Daniels, V. L., Schweikhart, S. B. and Smith-Daniels, D. E. (1988) 'Capacity management in health care services', *Decision Sciences*, Vol 19, pp. 898–919

16 Siferd, S. P. (1991), op. cit.

17 Marriner-Tomey, A. (1992) *Guide to Nursing Management*. Mosby-Year Book (St. Louis), p. 238

18 Easton, F. F., Rossinm, D. F. and Borders, W. S. (1992) 'Analysis of alternative scheduling policies for hospital nurses', *Production and Operations Management*, Vol 1, No 2, Spring, pp. 159–174

19 Smith, B., Leimkuller, J. and Danon, R. (1992) 'Yield management and American Airlines', *Interfaces*, Vol 22, No 1, Jan–Feb, pp. 8–31

20 *See* Sasser, W. E. (1970) 'Match supply and demand in service industries', *Harvard Business Review*, Nov–Dec, pp. 113–141

21 Some of the commonly used fare restrictions are: advanced purchase requirements, required Saturday night's stay over, and so on

22 Smith, B. *et al.* (1992), op. cit.

23 'The Gates Hotel', p. 101, in Sasser, W. E., Olsen, R. P. and Wyckoff, D. D. (1978) *Management of Service Operations: Text, cases and readings*. Boston, MA: Allyn and Bacon

24 Maister, D. H. (1988) 'The psychology of waiting lines', in Lovelock, C. H. (ed.) *Managing Services: Marketing, operations and human resources*. London: Prentice-Hall

25 Ibid.

26 Graessel, B. and Zeider, P. (1993), op. cit.

27 Jones, P. and Peppiatt, E. (1996) 'Managing perceptions of waiting times and service queues', *International Journal of Service Industry Management*, Vol 7, No 5, pp. 44–61

28 Katz, K., Lawson, B. and Lawson, R. (1991) 'Prescription for the waiting-in-time blues: entertain, enlighten and enjoy', *Sloan Management Review*, Winter, pp. 44–53

29 Sasser, W. E. *et al.* (1982), op. cit.

30 Jones, P. and Peppiatt, E. (1996), op. cit.

31 Pruyn, A. and Smidts, A. (1998), op. cit.

32 Katz, K. *et al.* (1991), op. cit.

33 Durrande-Moreau, A. and Usinier, J. C. (1999), 'Time Styles and the Waiting Experience: an Exploratory Study', *Journal of Service Research*, Vol 2, No 2, pp. 173–186

34 Ibid.

35 Pruyn, A. and Smidts, A. (1998), op. cit.

36 Translated from *Het Nieuwsblad* (Belgian Newspaper), 18 September 2010

37 Translated from *Gazet van Antwerpen* (Belgian Newspaper), 30 March 2011

Chapter 11

People practices that enable delivery

Bart Van Looy • Krist'l Krols • Dirk Buyens • Tine Vandenbossche •
Walter Stevens • Dries Faerns

Objectives

By the end of this chapter, you should be able to discuss:

- the relevance of the notion of empowerment for service organizations
- what empowerment means at the level of the individual employee
- the implications of empowerment for leadership
- the implications of empowerment for the organization as a whole
- the consequences of empowerment for organizations in terms of outcomes
- what the process of developing competencies looks like at the individual level
- different development strategies and what they might imply
- appropriate competence development strategies for different types of competencies
- the relationship between collaboration and learning
- why and for what type of services these dynamics are important
- the specific requirements that learning poses regarding relational characteristics in connection with the learning processes of newcomers and apprentices
- the nature of collaborative relationships and how they can develop

Introduction

Alice has a problem: her machine reports a self-test error, but she does not quite believe it. So many of the parts of the control system in this machine have failed that she suspects there is some other problem producing the failures. She is unwilling to accept that so many failures could be independent of each other. We are going to lunch at a restaurant where many of her colleagues eat to try to persuade Fred, the most experienced of them, to look at the machine with her. If this fails, she will try to get the team technical specialist to look at it. She makes copies of the information from the error log and service log to take with us. In the parking lot, she recognizes the cars of the colleagues, including that of the one she wants to recruit to help . . .

When she succeeds in getting him and the others interested, they listen to the list of problems the machine has and begin to talk about noise problems or communication problems. She repeats that she wants help, that she does not understand this series of problems, and Fred tells her she has to fix it. He looks at the logs and tells her ways of approaching the problem as a noise issue; he also tells her she cannot ignore the error code. They figure out which board the error code is actually indicating, where it is in the machine. She repeats that she wants help; he repeats that he is not going to help her, but he will tell her how to approach the problem. He shows her how to check the communication lines, and they all laugh at one of the suggested remedies for persistence of the fault – swapping all the boards in the machine, one at a time.

Fred asks her again about the error code: she tells him, adding that it is persistent, and the machine will do nothing. He says that, in that case she should be able to solve the problem right away with the procedure associated with the error code, and why is she bothering him? She reminds him again of the number of previous failures and the number of modules replaced. He asks about a specific one as she recites the list, and yes, she has replaced that one too. One of the other technicians points out that that only means that the part is new, not that it is necessarily functional, and all the others agree.

Alice repeats that she thinks there is something about that machine that is causing the failure of all these components; the other technicians all tell her just to fix the problem. Alice reminds Fred that some of the components have been replaced twice in recent months. Fred starts to tell her about running the noise test, and then says that she probably cannot do it if the machine will not run at all. Alice doubts that the machine will run long enough to do the noise test, although she has managed to read the error log; if she can't do that, she may be able to use some of the other diagnostic programs. He starts to tell her about testing communication lines . . . (J. Orr)[1]

In Chapter 5, we argued that employees make the difference in terms of creating value. Based on the insights offered by the service profit chain (*see also* Chapter 2), it became clear that customer satisfaction and profitability are driven by employee's behaviour. This not only implies that service firms need to design HR practices that foster competencies of employees, in line with the envisaged service concept (Chapter 5); practices that result in employee satisfaction are as much needed. But which practices result in employee satisfaction? Intrigued by the strong relationship between employee and customer satisfaction – described in Chapter 5 as the mirroring effect – Harvard scholars began an investigation into the sources of employee satisfaction. A study by Schlesinger and Zornitsky[2] revealed that about two-thirds of employee satisfaction levels were caused by just three factors: the latitude given to employees by their management to meet customer needs, the authority given to them to serve customers and, finally, possession of the knowledge and skills needed to serve customers.

When looking at these findings, two central notions are clear: empowerment and competence. This can be seen from an examination of the top three elements of Table 11.1. Latitude refers to the freedom employees are given to act as the situation requires. The idea of having authority to serve the customer is closely linked to latitude. These two together

Table 11.1 Sources of employee satisfaction

Determinants of employee satisfaction	Explanatory power*
Latitude is given to meet customer	36.6%
I have the authority to serve the customer	19.2%
I have the knowledge and skills to serve the customer	12.9%
Rewards are provided for serving the customer well	7.3%
Customer satisfaction is a high priority with the director/manager	4.2%
Production requirements are reasonably balanced with serving the customer	3.1%
Supervision overall is satisfactory	2.8%
Underwriting training is satisfactory	2.1%
13 other determinants	11.8%
TOTAL	100.0%

*Each figure represents the proportion of the total R2 (correlation between determinants and general feelings about capability to do the job) explained by each determinant. Explanatory power represents the amount of variance explained by the antecedents.

Source: Schlesinger, L. A. and Zornitsky, J. (1991) Reprinted with permission from *HRPS*, Vol 14, No 2. Published by HR People & Strategy, all rights reserved. http://www.hrps.org.

read like a textbook definition of empowerment while knowledge and skills clearly bring the word 'competence' to mind. In this chapter, we first discuss the notion of empowerment. While in Chapter 5, the contours of competence based HR practices have been highlighted, we complement this perspective by discussing competence development strategies, including the role collaboration (among employees) plays in this respect. Why do we want to stress the idea of collaboration? First of all, services are often provided by means of an interplay between a number of service employees; collaboration can help to deliver seamless service. Teamwork is often a prerequisite for success in services.[3] In addition, as discussed extensively in Chapter 1, services are characterized by a certain degree of heterogeneity. In other words, as a service employee, you will from time to time be confronted with the unforeseen, and often the unknown. At these moments, support from and collaboration among service employees becomes crucial. Finally, collaboration also plays a crucial role in terms of competence development; learning and improving are social processes as well, something that is often forgotten.

The role of empowerment in service organizations

During an ongoing change process, blue-collar workers in a computer firm's logistics department decided that they were as capable of taking initiatives and making decisions as their colleagues in engineering. At an after-hours meeting, they decided to ask their superiors for a mandate to handle the forthcoming move of their warehouse on their own. They formed a self-regulating project team and succeeded in transferring every piece of stock without management interference and, perhaps more importantly, without a financial loss.

After 2 years of discussion, it was agreed that the blue-collar workers in a tyre factory were to be allowed more discretion and autonomy in their jobs. As a result, several new teams started working without supervisors. During the first month, one of these semi-autonomous production teams stopped the machines for safety reasons. According to the engineers, the total cost of stopping the machines amounted to the gross yearly salary costs of three supervisors. Supervisors were re-installed after this incident.

A front-line airline employee was confronted with a queue of 30 people waiting for a transcontinental flight scheduled to leave in 15 minutes. He saw that he only had 12 places left. He also knew that the Concorde flight, due to leave 10 minutes later, still had plenty of capacity. There was no superior in the area. The last 18 passengers had the time of their lives, flying on Concorde using an economy ticket.

In a large service organization, each employee has to define the objectives and direction for his or her own job every year. After extensive preparation, all the employees gather together for two weeks to discuss and integrate their different objectives and directives. If supervisors and employees disagree on whether to include a certain objective or to pursue in a certain direction, employees are allowed to explore the proposed direction. After a 6-month experimentation period, a joint decision is made whether or not to continue. In the recent past, suggested objectives have resulted in a new product line, the formation of two new subsidiaries, and numerous quality improvements and cost reductions. Fifteen per cent of an employee's gross salary is contingent on achieving his or her own goals.

These examples make it clear that today's organizations are experimenting and sometimes struggling with new ways of collaborating. The notion of *autonomy* – the degree to which people can and do make decisions on their own within their working context – seems to be central. An increase in autonomy and taking initiative is labelled as *empowerment*. However, empowerment also goes beyond the individual employee's specific work situation. Empowerment has implications for the organization as a whole: it affects the way of working, the way of organizing, and the relationships between employees and managers. Empowerment cannot be treated as an 'add-on'; rather, it implies changes in the design of authority, responsibility, learning and benefits.

The notion of empowerment is not completely new. In the past, we have encountered concepts such as participative management, involvement of the workforce, quality of working life, the role of autonomy for job satisfaction. However, there are some significant differences. The debate on empowerment strongly emphasizes results. Today, empowerment is essentially seen as a way of improving a company's performance in terms of quality and customer satisfaction whereas, in the past, the individual employee's well-being received equal or greater attention. The market demands quick responses to specific requests, technology allows for fast communication and flat structures and people ask for more involvement and autonomy. Everything seems to point to more participation of all employees in today's organizations, on a larger scale than ever before.

Empowerment can be approached on two levels:

1 *The level of the relationship between the individual employee and supervisor*. Here, individual motivation and leadership style will be crucial.

2 *The level of the broader system, the organization*. What is important at the organizational level when speaking about empowerment? How must organizations be structured to allow for and reinforce empowerment?

The relevance of empowerment for service environments

Given the specific nature of service delivery, empowerment seems to be an issue especially important for service organizations. You will remember our discussion of the simultaneity of services in Chapter 1. Both customers and employees work simultaneously on the delivery of service. This means that employees play a crucial role in the experiences and satisfaction of the customer. Services also imply heterogeneity, part of which stems from the customer and becomes apparent only at the moment of the service delivery. This means that employees need a certain degree of autonomy during the service encounter. Standard operating procedures will not account for every customer-employee contact situation in most service organizations. As a result, the contact employees themselves play an important role in handling the customer interaction.

The significance of this autonomy will vary, however, according to the type of service activities, as well as the strategy followed.

Bowen and Lawler[4] developed a contingency model of empowerment within services. As a starting point, they observe that a number of ways of delivering services can all be very successful. These delivery methods are described by means of a continuum – with the 'production-line' approach at one end and the 'empowerment' approach at the other:

- The *production-line approach*, or the industrial way of delivering services, is characterized by simplification of tasks, clear division of labour, substitution of equipment and systems for employees, and little decision-making discretion afforded to employees.

- With the *empowered approach*, less emphasis is put on the systems surrounding the service employees, who are given more discretion and autonomy.

The empowerment approach can involve quicker online responses to customer demands during service delivery or when problems arise. Empowerment can also lead to higher levels of employee satisfaction, better quality of customer interaction, and higher levels of commitment, resulting in employee involvement, quality improvement and innovation.

However, empowerment requires greater investment in selection and training, resulting in higher labour costs. Empowerment can also possibly lead to customer impressions of not being treated correctly (because they are treated in a non-standardized way) and implies the risks of 'give-aways' and bad decisions by front-line employees.[5]

In the light of these benefits and costs, Bowen and Lawler argue that empowerment cannot be seen as the one best way to approach service industries. Bowen and Lawler define five contingencies including strategic, commercial, technological, environmental, and workforce dimensions (*see* Table 11.2). Organizations, for which the description in the production-line column seems appropriate, will gain fewer benefits from empowerment. Costs might outweigh the benefits.

Although this framework offers guidance on how important empowerment can be at an *organizational* level, we believe that empowerment can be relevant for *individual* employees in almost every situation. Consider, for example, the blue-collar workers who formed a

Table 11.2 Contingencies of empowerment

Contingency	Production-line approach	Empowerment approach
Basic business strategy	Low cost, high volume	Differentiation, customized, personalized
Tie to customer	Transaction, short time period	Relationship, long time period
Technology	Routine, simple	Non-routine, complex
Environmental	Predictable, few surprises	Unpredictable, many surprises
Types of people	Theory X manager, employees with low growth needs, low social needs and weak interpersonal skills	Theory Y manager, employees with low needs, high social needs and strong interpersonal skills

self-managing team to handle the forthcoming move of the warehouse. Within this project, they acted autonomously: they drew up a project plan, defined the individual steps, divided tasks and allocated responsibilities; they even worked out the budget and made decisions on necessary expenditures. However, about 85% of their daily activities could be described as routine; procedures and quality regulations existed and had to be followed strictly. Nevertheless, among these employees the experience of empowerment was very high.

We can look at the functioning of a fire department in the same way. When an emergency occurs, everyone has to act quickly and central co-ordination – that is, one commander – is required. When a house is burning down, who needs a group discussion on how to approach the fire? However, in preparing actions or evaluating past performance and methods, everyone's input can be valuable. At these times, giving employees the freedom and autonomy to think, speak and act can be extremely worthwhile. Stated otherwise, routinized processes and empowerment do not exclude each other as the (re-)design of these routines can be a highly participative process.

Empowerment: The employee and the supervisor

Empowerment at the level of the individual employee

Empowerment involves giving more autonomy, more freedom to employees to take decisions. Why should we do this?

The most important reason at the level of the individual employee is the belief that autonomy motivates people – that is, that people are willing to take initiatives and make decisions and that they prefer this above situations where everything regarding their jobs is dictated to them. Empowerment involves giving power and power means energy, so empowerment can be read as energizing people and increasing their motivation.

Motivation is not only a matter of autonomy, however. Intrinsic work motivation involves the elements within an individual, pertaining directly to the task, that produce energy, enthusiasm and satisfaction. Five elements seem to be crucial when talking about individual work motivation:[6]

- *Meaning* can be seen as the value of a work goal, as perceived by the individual in relation to his or her own ideals or standards. It implies that there is some sort of congruence between what an individual actually does and what he or she believes or values. The better the fit, the higher a person's motivation will be.

- *Competence* has to do with an individual's belief that he or she is able to perform the required activities adequately – that is, confidence in one's own ability to perform the tasks skilfully. Competence is also related to motivation: the more an individual feels competent, the more motivated he or she will be.

- *Self-determination* is linked with the individual's sense of having a say in initiating and regulating actions, work methods, productivity and so on. It involves the extent to which an individual can influence the way his or her activities are performed, which affects motivation.

- *Strategic autonomy* pertains to the individual's freedom to influence the content of the job. Whereas self-determination refers to the influence on the *how* of the job, strategic autonomy refers to the extent to which people can influence the *what* of the job – that is, the content and direction of activities within their jobs. The case of the blue-collar workers handling the move, described in the introduction to this chapter, involves *operational autonomy* only. Once decisions are taken regarding what can be done, the workers have the freedom to define the way the move is organized. The example of the service company that allows its employees to define their own objectives and direction involves *strategic autonomy*.

● Finally, *impact* can be viewed as the degree to which an employee can influence outcomes at work. It has to do with having a say regarding what is going on in the direct work environment, what happens in the department, and also how it happens.

All five elements contribute to intrinsic task motivation. The more they are present in the experiences of an individual in relation to his or her job, the higher the level of motivation will be. Self-determination, strategic autonomy and impact are obviously related to autonomy. However, motivation can be seen as something broader than autonomy; it also involves finding a job meaningful and having confidence in one's own competence.

It is important, therefore, when discussing empowerment at the individual employee level to keep in mind that empowerment has to do with motivation and that levels of motivation are determined by several different factors or elements. The more these elements are present in an individual's work experience, the more empowerment will be experienced and the higher motivation will be. Table 11.3 summarizes the five elements.

Now that we have identified the building blocks of empowerment at the individual level, we can start thinking about putting empowerment into practice.

When the five dimensions within the notion of empowerment are examined more closely, we observe that they are related to each other in the following way: *competence* and *meaning* seem to be necessary pre-conditions of *self-determination, impact* and *strategic autonomy*. High levels of both competence and meaning are required before high levels of autonomy can be achieved. In other words, low levels of meaning and competence are seldom seen in combination with moderate or high levels of autonomy.[7] As a result, empowerment can be pictured as a kind of pyramid, the foundations of which are formed by competence and meaning (*see* Figure 11.1).

These findings have serious managerial implications since, when implementing change processes directed towards empowerment, looking at autonomy alone can be deceptive. Sufficient degrees of meaningfulness and competence should also be present; otherwise, the seeds of autonomy will be sown on dry ground. Empowerment is a gradual process, starting with the creation of meaning and feelings of competence, and evolving towards levels of self-determination, impact and even strategic autonomy.

Empowerment has been shown to have a significant impact on employee morale and behaviour. Research[8] has indicated clearly that employees with high levels of empowerment are more satisfied, show higher levels of commitment, and higher degrees of problem-solving

Table 11.3 The five dimensions of empowerment as a driving force behind individual work motivation

Meaning	The extent to which an individual experiences a task as personally meaningful
Competence	The extent to which an individual feels confident about his/her capabilities to perform the task
Self-determination	The degree of influence that an individual has on how to perform the job
Strategic autormony	The degree of influence an individual has on the content of the job
Impact	The degree of influence an individual has on the direct work environment

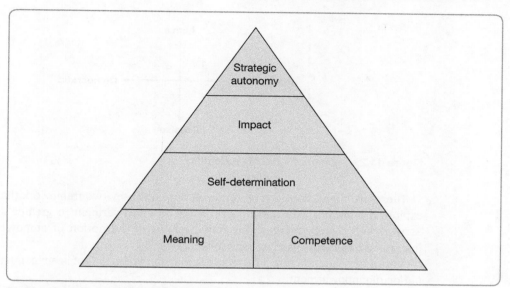

Figure 11.1 Empowerment as a pyramid

Table 11.4 Comparison of employees with high and low levels of empowerment*

	Low empowered (mean)	High empowered (mean)
Job satisfaction*	4.39	5.66
Commitment*	4.61	5.76
Innovative behaviour*	4.01	5.13

*Variables are rated on a seven-point scale and differences in means are significant at $p < 0.001$.

and innovative behaviour compared with colleagues for whom empowerment is not available (*see* Table 11.4).

Leadership and empowerment: an impossible marriage?

As we have shown, empowerment can be defined as increasing an individual's autonomy and degree of freedom. It involves giving employees more latitude in terms of decision making and actions. Does this mean that managers will become obsolete? The answer seems to be no. Setting goals and developing trust between employees and supervisors[9] will continue to be the preserve of the supervisor or manager. It is expected, however, that new forms of leadership will be developed; empowerment will have implications for the leadership style.

Before we examine and define more clearly this new style of leadership, we shall consider a general model of leadership (*see* Figure 11.2).[10] Leadership practices can be categorized on a continuum ranging from entirely autocratic to purely democratic. *Autocratic leadership* is displayed by leaders who look for sole possession of power and control; *democratic leadership* is characterized by sharing authority and power between superiors and employees.

Leadership styles can also be described according to a second dimension ranging from active to passive. A *passive* or laissez-faire leader is usually not involved in the daily activities of his or her employees and, thus, exercises little influence. An *active* leader is highly involved in employees' activities, which leads to high visibility of the leader for the employees.

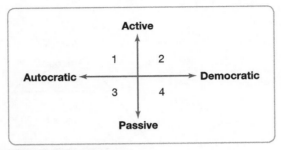

Figure 11.2 A general model of leadership

These two dimensions can be combined into a two-by-two framework that allows us to explore the notion of leadership in relation to empowerment in greater depth. In fact, Stewart and Manz[11] merged this framework with the notion of empowerment. Their integrated framework can be found in Figure 11.3.

As can be seen in Figure 11.3, some leadership styles do not seem compatible with the notion of empowerment:

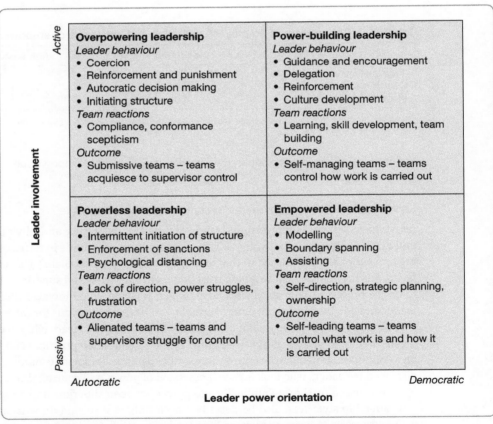

Figure 11.3 An integrated framework of leadership and empowerment

Source: Stewart, G. and Manz, C. (1995) 'Leadership for self-managing work teams: A typology and integrative model', *Human Relations*, Vol 48, No 7, pp. 747–770.

- *Overpowering leadership* – i.e. the combination of active and autocratic behaviour – tends to overwhelm the initiatives of employees, thus inhibiting empowerment.

- *Powerless leadership* combines an autocratic orientation with a passive attitude. Here, the probability that distance will occur between employees and their superior is high. This leads to leadership behaviour where little direction is given and only sanctions are taken. This will often cause stress and certainly does not seem a good foundation for building trust and support, let alone empowerment.

- *Power-building leadership* includes encouragement in terms of skill development and co-operative networks. However, in this approach leaders still retain significant control over what is going on, as employees rely on the leader to set the overall direction.

- *Empowering leadership* combines a democratic approach with a more passive way of acting. In this approach, the requirements seem to be fulfilled for empowering employees in an enduring way. Here, one can truly speak of achieving forms of 'strategic autonomy'.

Exhibit 11.1 Empowerment at Taco Bell

The changes in leadership style involved in empowerment are revealed in the following account of the change process taking place in the Taco Bell corporation, a US fast-food chain offering Mexican cuisine.[12]

In this company, a new market approach was introduced in the mid-1980s, stressing the idea of value. Value was to be understood as delivering food quickly, accurately, hygienically and at the appropriate temperature, and this in combination with the lowest costs possible. This approach involved, above all, a change in the mindset of both managers and employees: quality characteristics and low costs were to be seen as mutually reinforcing elements, not contradictory items. To arrive at this reconfiguration of the business, changes were introduced at several levels. New production techniques were developed, restaurant space was redesigned, a fully decentralized information system was introduced and even recipes were reformulated so as to allow fast delivery. These changes at the level of the supporting operational systems were complemented by training and development efforts as well as the introduction of empowerment at the level of the employees and the managers.

In the past, a strong emphasis had been placed on managerial responsibility: any problem occurring in a restaurant had to be dealt with by the manager in charge, whether it involved a major breakdown of the technical equipment or a short-changed customer. This hierarchical approach was thrown out. As a first step, the jobs of restaurant manager and district manager – supervising several restaurants – were redesigned. In the past, the district manager had played a policing role – including 'white gloves' inspections of the physical restaurants and audits of the financial books. This changed drastically: the span of control was increased from 6 to 20 restaurants. This implied an (intended) revision in the management skills and styles necessary for a market manager, as district managers were now called. Coaching and developing took the place of controlling.[13]

This could only be realized by redefining the role and competencies of the restaurant manager, whose job title was changed to restaurant general manager. As more and more decision making was delegated, managers with broader skills were required, who could take care of profit and loss, were decisive and took ownership. Training and support to help with this transition were available. The compensation and benefits package was also redesigned as to reflect this new approach: the base salary was increased and the bonus element started to reflect the idea of ownership. These changes had a significant impact: sales and profits increased (doubled or tripled) over a 5-year time period and employee and customer satisfaction evaluations did the same.

In the early 1990s, this logic was even extended by introducing 'team-managed units' (TMUs) – teams of employees sufficiently trained to manage the store without a full-time manager. Crew members were seen as the experts in delivering value to the customers. It was crucial in this respect to create a shared ownership of problems among the crew members and the skills to solve these problems. The team-managed unit concept was introduced in 1992 and was enthusiastically embraced by restaurant general managers and market managers. By the end of 1993 there were TMUs in 90% of the company stores. This transition also implied the commitment of resources to competence development; a restaurant manager had to spend about a year being trained in how to create a self-sufficient team. However, stores operating this system did perform better.

The responsibilities of the restaurant general manager also increased. Once they were freed from most of their daily activities – such as scheduling labour, ordering inventory, interviewing applicants, handling cash and making deposits, opening and closing stores – they started to take on responsibility for the new distribution channels Taco Bell had been developing, including lunch-school programmes and shopping mall restaurants. As a result of these changes, the span of control of market managers increased from 20:1 to 56:1. During these changes, customer satisfaction increased steadily, as did sales and profits.

The Taco Bell story in Exhibit 11.1 shows that empowerment might be an important element in designing future HR practices. It motivates people and hence has a positive impact on sales and profits. However, empowerment is not something to be implemented overnight. It implies a serious rethinking of leadership approach and style. Moreover, the case of Taco Bell also illustrates that changes are not limited to the employee's motivation or the managerial style of the supervisor. Superiors and employees do not work in a vacuum; they are working in a broader organization. The changes taking place in Taco Bell would not have been successful without considerable training and development efforts and without the installation of new operating systems and remuneration packages. Empowerment implies changes at the level of the organization as a whole.

Empowerment: the organization

People cannot become empowered when they are not supported by an environment that stimulates actions such as initiative taking and autonomy. We cannot expect employees to show dedication, responsibility, autonomy and initiative in their daily activities without first creating an environment in which this behaviour can be developed. What is needed is an *empowered organization*.

Empowered organizations have everything in place to facilitate the 'pushing down of information, knowledge, rewards and power'.[14] We have already discussed power in this chapter when considering the autonomy of individuals within the organization. But what is meant by information, knowledge and rewards?

Sharing information

The sharing of information is extremely important; empowerment cannot work without people being informed. To be able to take the right decisions and initiatives, employees need to be informed. Information on a range of subjects is required:

- *The service concept.* Employees need to have a clear view of the service concept they want to achieve – that is the company's objectives and values (*see* Chapter 3). A good knowledge of these values and how they relate to daily activities are prerequisites, if employees are to act according to the desired service concept. How can employees correctly evaluate the quality remarks of a displeased customer when the quality policy of the company is not clear to them?

- *The service delivery process as a whole.* Information should not be limited to an individual's own functional area; employees should have some insight into the total service delivery process and their own role within it. Otherwise, it becomes extremely difficult for people to assess the impact of their actions on the final customer experience. Withholding this broader information runs the risk of creating problems further down the service delivery process.

- *Past and current performance as well as future targets.* Employees are also entitled to be openly informed of the performance of the organization as a whole. Moreover, information is not only important in relation to how to act in the future; information on current and past activities is equally crucial. Without this kind of information employees will not know whether they are doing well – whether their actions are appropriate or not.

- *The setting of goals.* Goal setting is crucial as well. Empowerment does not involve supplying information to employees and then leaving everything open. An attitude of 'let's see what happens with these guys now they are empowered' would be disastrous. Empowerment means giving people all relevant information as well as clear objectives so that they can achieve success. Whereas employees want enough latitude to be able to deliver results, they also like to have a clear picture of their authority. Employees who know what is expected of them and who have the right information to act to achieve these goals are simply more empowered.

Heskett, Sasser and Schlesinger[15] distinguish between two different modes of setting goals:

1 With *the traditional approach*, goals define what an individual is allowed to do. Everything else is discussed with management. So as long as employees stay within the 'box', they are free to act.

2 *The non-traditional approach* simply defines what needs to be done. Additional actions to achieve better results are allowed and even encouraged as long as the 'bottom line' is respected. It is this second approach that was introduced in Taco Bell (*see* Exhibit 11.1).

The traditional approach is more hands-on. It implies a rather exhaustive definition process of what is allowed and what is not. Emphasis is refocused on conformance to rules and regulations and control. In this respect, the second is the preferred approach. However, it will demand more from employees in terms of competencies, maturity and integrity. The actual nature of the workforce will determine which of the options is chosen. To achieve real empowerment, an evolution towards the non-traditional approach will be inevitable.

Knowledge and competence development

It is clear that the successful implementation of empowerment requires competent employees with an extended range of skills. It is no longer sufficient to execute a limited number of tasks perfectly. An individual should be able to evaluate the way of working, to discover opportunities for improvement, to generate ideas and communicate them, to work in teams, to listen to colleagues and to take responsibility for the results obtained. The reverse relation also holds true; if an employer wants employees to develop these competencies, empowerment is the only option. Of course, this involves an element of change or even a transformation.

This transformation needs to be supported by a broader competence base; training programmes addressing technical skills as well as personal and behavioural characteristics will become essential. Business and management courses also need to be introduced on a larger scale. The crew members in Taco Bell had to master inventory control techniques, labour scheduling approaches or interview techniques to assess the competencies of new applicants. Increasing technical skills is not enough, however; personal characteristics, such as a customer orientation and good citizen behaviour, are also crucial as employees will have to make more frequent decisions on their own.

It is therefore crucial for today's service companies to develop continuously the competence base of their employees. Ways of developing these competencies have been explored extensively in previous sections. It is important to stress again here the relevance of the notion of *'useful slack'*. Development involves time.[16] In the stream of reorganizations, downsizing, cost-cutting programmes and rationalization, organizations sometimes reduce themselves to a minimal level that could be harmful to future development. By looking at organizations as mere mechanical constructions and by seeking only immediate results, companies might cut out their own future – the human potential. In order to face the problems and opportunities of tomorrow's markets, employees need to understand, to learn continuously, to develop a critical spirit, to look for improvements and to adapt to change. This way of working is only possible if some 'slack' is left in the organization – room for teamwork, forethought and learning. It is impossible for people to develop a mutual learning process, to discover areas for improvement or to apply all their talents when they are *continuously* fully occupied and experiencing the stress of operational activities.

Redistributing rewards

Eventually, when employees are being asked to act like 'local' managers, a rethink of recognition and rewards is inevitable. There are two reasons for this:

1 People cannot be expected to act like responsible entrepreneurs engaging themselves fully in the achievement of results in their own activity domain, if the old employer-employee logic is applied when these same results are divided among the different stakeholders. Empowerment involves the idea of variable pay; a larger part of the salary will be linked more closely to results.

2 Broadening the competence base will also affect base salary levels. Whereas increasing people's competencies and abilities is rewarding in itself, there should also be some monetary rewards – a tendency justified by the increased role employees play in the value creation process.

Is empowerment worth it?

Empowerment cannot be regarded as a quick fix.[17] It is important to consider whether all the efforts required to achieve empowerment – for example, rethinking organizational functioning, developing competencies, introducing new ways of leadership – are worth pursuing.

Empirical evidence seems to show such efforts are worthwhile. The work on the service profit chain, extensively discussed throughout this book, provides us with the necessary conceptual links between empowerment and profitability. Service capability defines employees' satisfaction, which in turn has a positive effect on service quality and productivity and, hence, customer satisfaction and profitability. Several studies have empirically demonstrated the robustness of these links. Companies involved include Taco Bell, Southwest Airlines, American Express, to name but a few.[18]

Our own research data confirms this view. Employees with a high level of empowerment are more satisfied and committed and, hence, will contribute more to productivity, quality and in the later stages customer satisfaction, loyalty and, hence, profitability.

An impressive study was undertaken recently by Lawler *et al.*[19] to investigate how involvement efforts related to business performance. About 40% of the Fortune top 1000 companies were involved in this study.

The relationship between organizational practices aimed at creating the involvement of the employees and performance was investigated systematically. With regard to involvement initiatives, a distinction was made between actions aimed at sharing information, increasing knowledge, redistributing rewards and finally delegating power and decision authority within the organization. Performance outcomes were examined at three levels: direct outcomes such as quality and productivity, profitability (also compared with competitors) and employee satisfaction. The results are clear – despite the huge amount of interfering variables not included in this analysis. A strong positive relation occurs over and over again between the degree of involvement and the level of the results.

It is clear that empowerment has many positive implications, both at the level of the individual employee and in terms of organizational outcomes. At the same time, it became clear that autonomy can only work to the extent that competencies are present. While we already discussed how to design HR practices based on the notion of competencies (*see* Chapter 5), the continuous development of competencies remains a focal point of attention. We turn our attention to competency development in the next section.

Competency development

The competence development process implies different stages. Experiential approaches to education made it clear that adults learn best if they are exposed to a process consisting of four different steps that are linked as shown in Figure 11.4.[20] Abstract conceptualization can lead to active experimentation, whereby concrete experience is gained. Reflection upon these experiences can lead to new insights.

Furthermore, development requires the presence of three different conditions:

- dissatisfaction with an existing condition (actual situation);
- clarity about a desired condition (ideal situation); and
- clarity about what to do to move from the actual to the ideal.

This means that, at the individual level, different steps or phases can be acknowledged during the development process:

1 self-assessment, involving recognition, acceptance and understanding of the need for development;
2 practice or application to acquire new competencies; and
3 follow-up.[21]

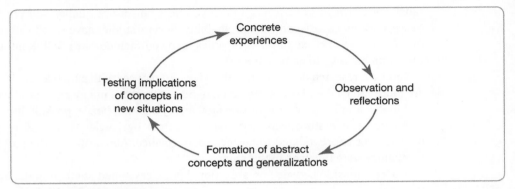

Figure 11.4 Kolb's Learning cycle

Source: Kolb, David A., *Experiential Learning: Experience as a source learning and development* (1st edn). © 1984.
Printed and Electronically reproduced by permission of Pearson Education, Inc., Upper Saddle River, New Jersey.

The *self-assessment phase* implies recognition, acceptance and understanding. *Recognition* simply means that learners need to recognize that certain types of competencies do exist and are relevant to them. *Understanding* implies the creation of a clear insight into the level of competency at hand. During the recognition and understanding stage, the person will also face issues of acceptance. *Acceptance* is not always evident, especially when speaking of personal characteristics. Early attempts to teach achievement motivation to stimulate economic development in Third World countries were criticized for being attempts at 'brainwashing'. Critics felt that psychologists had no right to 'muck about with people's minds'. These critics were assured that, in fact, a person's motivation cannot be changed unless its validity is accepted – that is, the person really sees it in his or her own self-interest to change. Brainwashing does not work: competency learners must want, and work hard, to develop a new competency.[22] Self-assessment relates therefore to obtaining an accurate view of one's own level of competency.

Practice has to do with experimenting with the competency behaviours in realistic simulations, whereas *application* refers to the application of a new competency to real job situations. Finally, *follow-up, support* and *feedback* close the circle.

It is also clear that developing competencies will require different efforts, depending on the type of competency. As they vary in terms of profoundness, different types of competency often imply a different time frame and will require different developmental approaches. Whereas competencies related to the behavioural repertoire can often be easily trained and are adopted quite quickly, the development of technical skills and knowledge can imply longer time periods. Personal characteristics are often the most difficult to develop, as they are formed and fixed during childhood and early adult years.

Moreover, competency development strategies can take on different forms. Whereas behaviour modelling is more appropriate to developing one's behavioural repertoire, technical training and education seem to be more suited to gaining technical expertise. The development of personal characteristics will often demand more intense forms of change and training, such as sensitivity training. So, once the relevant competency areas to be developed are identified, the company can choose from a number of different kinds of training or development strategies.

Choosing appropriate development strategies

Competence development can be seen as a set of activities providing the opportunity to acquire and improve competency. A variety of methods and approaches exists, and a brief overview of the main types of competency development activities is included here.

The most common methods and approaches applied are lectures and programmed instructions, behaviour modelling and role-playing, team-building efforts and personal assessment programmes, case studies and action learning, and finally simulation or vestibule training, which comes very close to on-the-job training.

Lectures and programmed instructions

Lectures, where an instructor presents material to a group of learners, are the mainstay of higher education, so they are perhaps all too familiar. The accepted shortcomings of lectures include the predominance of one-way communication; insensitivity to learner differences in learning style, ability and interest; and lack of feedback to the learner.

Although this method communicates the same message to large groups of people, it suffers from time and space constraints, as the student needs to be present at the same time as the teacher. Recent technological developments have allowed some of these constraints to be overcome. The course content is translated into programmed instructions and is subsequently made available on PCs, networks or CD-ROMs. Self-paced or programmed instruction approaches present the learner with a series of tasks, allow for evaluation of success at intervals throughout the training, and provide feedback about correct and incorrect responses as the learner advances through the training. Instruction programmes can proceed through a fixed sequence of experiences or they can skip from one point to another, depending on how well the learner is grasping different parts of the material. These programmed instructions are being made more and more available via electronic media.

Computer-based training (CBT) includes both computer-assisted instruction (CAI) and computer-managed instruction (CMI). CBT is most commonly used to deliver training about computers, but a wide range of other topics can also be addressed:

- CAI developed out of the programmed learning texts of the 1960s. In these applications, the computer simply presents a block of information and then asks the trainee questions to assess his or her mastery.

- CMI is much more complex. In this type of programme, the computer assesses the trainee's initial level of competency and then provides a customized set of learning modules and exercises. The trainee's performance is assessed frequently, and the training content is modified continuously in line with the learner's progress.

It will become clear that this approach and these methods are most suited to teaching technical knowledge and insights and are less appropriate for developing behavioural routines or personal characteristics. Moreover, programmed instruction will always be limited to what is known; it cannot anticipate new and unforeseen problems.

Behaviour modelling and role-playing

Behaviour modelling training is based on social learning theory, which states that most people learn by observing others and then copying their behaviour, when appropriate. Learning from others reduces the need for trial-and-error learning. Behaviour modelling training typically follows a fixed sequence of steps:

1 The trainer introduces a single interpersonal skill, perhaps in a short lecture that conveys some of the principles underlying the skill.

2 Trainees view a videotape of someone performing the skill correctly. Then, the trainer plays the tape again, highlighting key principles, or steps, called learning points.

3 Trainees practise the skill by role-playing with other trainees.

4 Trainees receive feedback on the effectiveness of their role-playing behaviour. Practice continues until the trainees feel confident with their new skill.

Team building and personal assessment programmes

Many organizations invest in team building and personal assessment programmes in order to develop the capacity of individuals and work groups to interact more effectively. Team building often starts with a data collection phase, utilizing questionnaires or individual interviews with team members. The trainer looks for information about how the group works together, what problems exist, and what norms are followed. This information is summarized and fed back to the group so that they can take an objective look at the way they work together and decide how they wish to change it. The facilitator helps the team understand the feedback and develops action plans for improving group processes. These plans may include training in specific skills such as active listening, problem analysis and group decision making, consensus seeking and conflict resolution. Team building without the feedback but with a heavy emphasis on group problem-solving skills is also commonly provided to new teams when self-directed work groups are set up.

Personal assessment programmes focus on the personal characteristics that people apply in their interaction with work and the social environment. Issues addressed here include coping with stress and personal organization, but some programmes dig even further into self-image or identity and how it relates to functional or dysfunctional behaviour. It is clear that these programmes are more profound on the personal level. Issues such as acceptance are crucial here.

Case studies and action learning

The *case study method*, developed at the Harvard Law School in the 1920s, presents the trainee with a written description of an actual or hypothetical problem in an organizational setting. The trainee is required to read the case, identify the problem and recommend solutions. The case study method has several intended purposes:

● It shows trainees that there is usually no easy solution to complex organizational problems.

● It helps trainees realize that different perspectives and solutions to the same case may be equally valid.

● It helps managerial trainees develop their problem-solving skills.

● Since case studies can often be worked out in groups, the development of behavioural and personal characteristics can also be addressed when cases are explored in depth over a longer time period by several people. Team building and collaboration, negotiation, and presentation skills then all become involved.

Case studies allow complex issues to be tackled in a concise format, but they remain studies; real practice is still out there in the real world. Action learning attempts to overcome this by combining formal training with practical experience. *Action learning* is an increasingly common method for middle and upper management development, which combines on- and off-the-job learning in innovative ways. The underlying idea is that formal training is good at conveying programmed knowledge (facts) but poor at teaching the student to question insights (the ability to seek out and use knowledge to solve real problems in innovative ways); yet it is precisely the latter that is most crucial to managerial success. Action-learning programmes usually feature some classroom instruction along with an applied project tackled by a team of trainees (or occasionally by individual trainees). As these projects actually take place, they are richer in terms of 'real life' context and complexity. On the other hand, as these projects are often limited in time and resources, they tend to not be as rich in terms of content as case studies.

Simulation and vestibule training

Simulation techniques create a facsimile of elements of the work setting, in which trainees try out different behaviours or strategies. The objective is to have trainees learn from their own actions, as well as from the group discussion that follows the simulation in a debriefing session. Simulations can be as simple as two-person role-playing or as complex as a sophisticated computer simulation of business processes.

Many experiential exercises are designed for more than two people. Large-scale behavioural simulations represent an increased level of complexity. These involve simulated organizations of up to 20 people in different roles, lasting from 6 hours to several days. Simulations at this level of complexity are typically used with executives rather than lower-level supervisors because sophisticated interpersonal and decision-making skills are prerequisites for learning from such an extremely complex situation.

Another simulation technique is the computerized business game. A business simulation or game may be defined as a sequential decision-making exercise structured on a model of a business operation, in which the trainee's role is to manage the simulated operation. In the game, the trainee or group of trainees is asked to make decisions about organizational matters such as investment in R&D, pricing or entering new markets. Based on these decisions, the programme provides computer-generated feedback on how the organization has performed. With this new information at hand, the trainee is asked to make another series of decisions, which are used in the next run of the simulation. The primary objectives of these business games are to teach general management skills such as decision making, setting priorities, long-range planning and effective use of time, personnel, and equipment.

Like on-the-job training, *vestibule training* requires trainees to do the whole job, using the same tools and machines that are used on the job. However, the training takes place in a vestibule, or separate workshop used just for training. Examples are flight simulators for pilots or test restaurants for hamburger chains. A trainer is present at all times, and the trainees are protected from the hustle and pressure that occur on the job itself. In Table 11.5,

Table 11.5 Different training approaches and their relevance for developing different types of competencies

	Behavioural repertoire	Technical competency	Personal characteristics
Behavioural modelling and role-playing	XXX		
Lectures and programmed instruction		XXX	
Team building and personal assessment sessions			XXX
Case studies and action learning	XXX	XX	XX
Simulation and vestibule training	XX	XX	XX

the different forms that development programmes can take are linked to the different types of competency defined above. Behaviour modelling and role-playing are most suitable when addressing the development of the behavioural repertoire. Lectures and programmed instruction are most relevant for developing technical competency, whereas team building and personal assessment sessions focus on personal characteristics. The other forms can be relevant for developing a range of competencies simultaneously. The relative importance of the different learning objectives can be used as a guideline when deciding which form to use. Finally, on-the-job and apprenticeship training can be seen as valid approaches to developing different sorts of competency.

While competency development is often perceived as a rather individual process, actually the opposite is true: learning is a highly social endeavour, as will become clear in the next section. Thus, collaborative practices deserve our attention as well.

Collaboration: integrating work and learning

In this section, we will explore the importance of collaboration and its implications for people management in service organizations. We will first look at some recent observations related to the work practice of service technicians, which highlight the benefits of collaboration. Collaboration enables people to find solutions for new and unforeseen problems as well as to create and transfer knowledge and insights – in other words, it enables people to learn. Although we start by considering the work of service technicians, we will argue that these findings are also relevant to a broader range of service situations. Learning and collaboration are not only linked in the case of well-established teams of professionals; collaboration also plays a role in the learning process of novices and apprentices. Finally, given the central role of collaboration, we will examine the development process of such collaborative relationships.

The benefits of collaboration in the workplace

The recent study by Orr,[23] from which the introductory case study was taken, can be described as an in-depth anthropological analysis of service technicians – or, as he calls it, an 'ethnography of a modern job'. It certainly provides us with some interesting findings. Over a period of several years, Orr studied the work and behaviour of service technicians working on copying machines simply by participating in their daily activities. His findings reveal the importance of collaboration for service work. The characteristics of the interaction with customers, as well as with fellow technicians, have an important influence on the effectiveness of technical repair jobs.

These findings are in sharp contrast with the predominant view of technicians, who are often portrayed as 'lonesome cowboys' working alone in the field, with technical skill and expertise their only tools besides manuals and technical documentation. Technicians' work is commonly defined as merely the diagnosis, repair and maintenance of machines. Orr concludes that the social side of work is at least of equal importance:

'. . . a large part of service work might better be described as repair and maintenance of the social setting.'

From Orr's description of Alice in the introductory case study, technical service work appears highly relational; talk is a crucial dimension of the practice of the group of service technicians to which Alice belongs. Diagnosis is aided by and in some cases takes place through a communication process involving the creation of a coherent description of the machine in question. These descriptions become the basis for technicians' discussions about their experience. During these discussions, knowledge and insights are shared and new approaches are developed. The circulation of anecdotes among technicians is the principal means by which they stay informed of the developing subtleties of machine behaviour. Let us examine this phenomenon more closely, by looking in detail at Orr's observations.

Socializing customers . . .

The starting point of diagnosis is usually a situation in which the customer has concluded that the machine has malfunctioned. The customer must then describe this situation when requesting a service call. Technicians receive a description of the problem, which is the joint product of the customer and the call operator. The technician's task when diagnosing a problem is to produce a satisfactory representation of the problem in order to allow a course of repair to be identified.

The customer who first experiences the problem is the first source of information. However, these customers may need to be trained in describing the ways of the machine. This is done by the technicians, who encourage the customers to note significant incidents relating to the machine and to talk about them in appropriate language – that is, the technicians' language. Customers are taught to create lucid representations of the situation, which the technician can use to create a coherent picture of the situation so that it can be remedied. This socialization of the customers is a substantial part of the social work of services. Technicians focus on maintaining the relations between their customers and the machines, and this is accomplished through the technician's relationship with both.

. . . and exchanging war stories with colleagues

There is a class of problems for which the machine provides no direct diagnostic information. In such cases, diagnosis is accomplished by piecing together clues gleaned from the machine and the customers. These clues do not clearly indicate a specific cause of the problem. Their significance is in what they show about patterns of machine behaviour. If interpreted correctly – and various interpretations are possible – such clues might suggest further areas of investigation that could produce a definite cause.

Some of these diagnoses actually fall into the 'known-and-recognized' class, in that the connection between the clue and the problematic behaviour is long established and well known to technicians. Creating this stock of common knowledge is achieved by technicians circulating 'war stories' among themselves. These stories are anecdotes of experience narrated with an appropriate level of context and technical detail. These stories start to circulate and through them experience becomes reproducible and reusable.

Other diagnoses are more problematic. Technicians may find themselves confronted with problems that have some familiar elements, but where the facts do not add up to a clear picture of the problem – as in the situation Alice faced in the case study. In cases like this, technicians almost invariably start looking for colleagues and a story-telling cycle ensues. Comparable stories are told or retold in the consideration of the problem.

Exchanging stories of similar experiences is a way of pushing the facts around, trying new perspectives to see if they suggest other interpretations. As a result of this process, new approaches and solutions are developed and constructed and at the same time transferred. This process can also be called *'learning'*.

Before delving into this idea of learning and its relationship to collaboration, however, we should first clarify the role of service documentation, often seen as the prime resource for learning. This will also allow us to explore and establish the broader relevance of the dynamics described by Orr.

The use of service documentation

Orr's findings clearly indicate that both interaction with customers and exchanging information and discussing problems with colleagues are crucial ingredients of the service technician's work. This finding contrasts with the prevalent practice in providing support for service technicians, which emphasizes adequate manuals or 'knowledge systems'.

Should these knowledge systems be considered obsolete in the light of these findings? Of course not; they play a supportive and hence valuable role, but this role will always be limited. Service manuals cannot replace the role discussions play when solving *new* and *unknown* problems that occur within a specific context of use. Nor do they succeed in providing a complete understanding of the machine, which is crucial in creating confidence both in the minds of customers and technicians. Let us explore both these issues.

A service manual is usually perceived as a collection of descriptive information about the machine in question. The assumption is that the technicians deduce the source of the machine's problems by obtaining information about it from the manual, which they consult whenever there is a problem with a machine. However, documentation is not simply a representation of the machine. A service manual is a device which one person (or group of people) constructs to convey information to someone else. Choices of inclusion and exclusion significantly constrain what can be done using the manual.

Often this documentation is designed not to provide information about the machine and its problems but to direct the technician to the solution through a minimal decision tree. This approach is legitimate given efficiency considerations, but it is not without consequences. The directions in this type of document are intended to prescribe the technician's behaviour from arrival at the customer site to departure. The premise is that following the instructions carefully from beginning to end will lead to the resolution of problems more quickly than could be accomplished by the technicians reasoning from their understanding of the machine alone. Such directive documentation provides only the information believed necessary for following the instructions and may omit information that would contribute to a better understanding of the problem. The effectiveness of such information depends on the success of the documentation designer in correctly anticipating and providing for the problems that actually arise in the field. Success also depends on the users' and the technicians' understanding of how the documentation should be used, and making appropriate use of it.

Even with all these elements in place, however, it is clear that it is not possible for instructions to be completely stand-alone. The knowledge relevant to the job of diagnosis cannot be set out exhaustively. The documentation mechanism is limited in its prescriptive ability. It is composed of representations and instructions that require interpretation by their users in the *context* of their application. The scope of problems and their solutions will always be limited to the already known. As a result, certain new problems will arise out of the interplay between machines and the situations in which they are used.

Accordingly, the technicians must inevitably be prepared to solve new and unanticipated problems; they must therefore develop as comprehensive an understanding of the machine as possible. When technicians use the documentation, they contrast their analysis of what the documentation is trying to convey with their own analysis of what might be wrong with the machine. They pursue those paths in the documentation that seem consonant with their hypotheses. If this is not successful, colleagues are used as a more 'flexible' source of information. Fellow technicians are probably better able to contribute to new perspectives and the iterative process of diagnosis and technical problem solving.

Moreover, the technicians use the documents in pursuit of their own goals, and these are not entirely the same as those of the documentation's designers. A technician's primary goal is to keep the customer happy and this includes, but is not limited to, fixing the machine as necessary. An important component of this goal is keeping the customer assured that the situation is under control; this involves being able to tell the customer what the machine is doing and to say when it was fixed and what was fixed. The customer must be made aware that the technician has repaired the machine in order that they will feel confident that the machine can be repaired in the future, should the need arise. Thus, a system that fixes the machine without either customer or technician knowing how or why is unlikely to be acceptable. This is why 'war stories' are becoming so important. Cause-and-effect links can be discussed, taking into account the context of use and pointing out reasonable courses of action.

These observations can also be of use in the design of relevant service manuals. Besides documenting well-known standard errors and common problems, they should also provide users with insights and understanding about the logic of the equipment at hand. Conceiving service manuals in this way makes them supportive and complementary to the collaboration process. The latter remains a crucial method of dealing with unforeseen, new and context-specific problems.

The broader relevance of collaboration to services

By now, we hear you say, what does all this mean for services in general, or for our service operations and employees in particular? Do these insights apply to all services and all situations?

As already discussed, the process of solving unforeseen, new, and context-specific problems benefits greatly from interaction or collaboration. This idea is the guiding principle for determining the broader relevance of these social dynamics for services. If you can plan everything in advance and if there are no unforeseen circumstances or uncertain situations to be faced, these dynamics are irrelevant. You just make everything explicit, translate it into procedures, prescriptions, manuals and so on, and make sure people stick to them. Collaboration has only a social, motivational or mere distraction function; it does not directly affect the job to be done.

In all other cases, these dynamics are important. As a result, these dynamics are important for many service situations. In Chapter 1, we concluded that heterogeneity or variability was one of the core characteristics of services. Unforeseen situations occur, in which service employees need to puzzle out the situation at hand. In these cases, having support from colleagues is often an advantage. Consider the airline customer who arrives at the check-in desk asking if he can change the destinations and times of his complex flight scheme. Other parties become involved when you start to make changes: waiting times will shift, luggage problems might arise. A brief exchange of viewpoints with colleagues before choosing the most appropriate action can be very useful. Alternatively, think of IT consultants who may be facing a new complex problem when working for a particular customer. As soon as they get back to the office, they may start discussing viable approaches to the problem with colleagues.[24]

Of course, the extent of heterogeneity is a very broad guideline when it comes to deciding how relevant collaboration is to a particular service. The framework of Mills and Margulies[25] provides us with more detailed insights. The different types of services – maintenance-interactive, task-interactive and personal-interactive – differ in terms of the level of uncertainty or ambiguity faced during the service encounters:

- For *maintenance-interactive services*, the level of uncertainty or ambiguity is low; hence technicians can rely more on systems, procedures or manuals.

- In the case of *task-interactive services*, uncertainty increases.

- For *personal-interactive services*, both increased uncertainty and increased ambiguity have to be taken into account.

Hence, for these last two types of services, the relational dynamics described here become more and more vital. Neglecting them can have a profound effect on performance because the essential, social ingredient of the learning process is left out.[26] This is clear not only when observing how colleagues extend their existing knowledge by exchanging, discussing and interpreting novel experiences, as described by Orr, but also when looking at the learning process of novices or apprentices.

The role of collaboration in learning

Whereas conventional explanations of learning stress internalization – whether discovered, transmitted from others or experienced – real learning implies more. Learning also means becoming a practitioner within a community.[27]

This concept of community is crucial to any understanding of the relational side of learning. A community can be seen as a set of relationships among people and activity over time, characterized by a certain common understanding about what constitutes good work practice. Communities are characterized by a degree of homogeneity in terms of interest, theory and methodology. Examples of this type of community are lawyers, physicians, engineers or butchers.

Such a community of practice is an intrinsic condition for the existence of knowledge because it provides the necessary interpretative support. Activities, tasks, functions and understandings do not exist in isolation. They only have meaning as part of broader systems of relationships. These systems arise out of and are reproduced and developed in social communities. The individual defines and is defined by these relationships.[28]

Learning thus implies not only a relationship to specific activities but also a relationship to social communities. It implies becoming a full participant, a member, a whole person – learning to function in a community, whether it is a community of physicists, engineers, classmates or scholars in philosophy or organizational behaviour.

This process of becoming a practitioner ideally takes on the form of '*legitimate peripheral participation*', as argued convincingly by Lave and Wenger.[29] The notion of legitimate peripheral participation denotes the particular mode of engagement of a learner who participates in the actual practice of an expert, but only to a limited degree and with limited responsibility for the outcomes.

Peripheral participation leads to the creation of knowledge in practice when it is approached as more than an observational lookout post; it involves participation as a way of learning. An extended period of peripheral *participation* provides learners with opportunities to take on board the culture of the practitioners. A general idea of what constitutes a community's practice is assembled piece by piece: who is involved, what is done, and what everyday life is like; how experts walk, talk and work; how people who are not part of the community of practice interact with it; what other learners are doing; and what learners need to learn to become full practitioners. It includes an increasing understanding of how, when and about what elderly people collaborate, collude and collide and what they enjoy, dislike, respect and admire. It provides paradigms, including masters, finished products and more advanced apprentices in the process of becoming full practitioners, which are grounds and motivations for learning activity. This means that legitimate peripheral participation is much more than creating initial impressions. Viewpoints from which to understand the practice evolve through changing participation in different tasks, changing relationships with ongoing community practices, and changing social relationships within the community.

This participation should be *peripheral*. Expecting the same results from newcomers as are expected from experts is asking for trouble. Conditions of participation should reflect this idea of peripherality. Space and time should be allocated to experimenting with and reflecting upon activities. Without such reflection and experimentation, no 'internalization' takes place. If a trainee has no time to live through experiences by means of reflection, discussion with other apprentices or masters, and so on, these experiences will remain superficial. Moreover, asking too much too soon can result in stress, burn-out and many quality problems.

Finally, having opportunities to participate peripherally – that is, having full access to all kinds of activities involved in practice – bring with it the idea of *legitimacy*, that the apprentice should be allowed to enter the field or the community. Introducing learning into work practice therefore implies certain characteristics of interaction. Conditions that place newcomers in adversarial relations with their managers or colleagues, or that imply exhaustive over-involvement in daily operations, partially or completely distort the prospects for learning in practice.

Exhibit 11.2, which describes the learning process of becoming a butcher in a supermarket, highlights how things can go wrong. It provides us with many examples of how access can be denied. The trade school and its shop exercises did not stimulate the essential procedures of meat cutting for supermarkets, much less make them accessible to apprentices. The on-the-job training was not much of an improvement; worse yet, the master butchers confined their apprentices to jobs that were completely removed from activities rather than peripheral to them. By doing so, newcomers are prevented from peripheral participation and thus very little learning actually takes place. Opportunities for learning are thus given structure by work practice.

Exhibit 11.2 Failing apprentices in the butcher trade[30]

A butcher's apprenticeship in the UK consists of a mix of trade school and on-the-job training. This programme was initiated by the Meatcutters' Union and culminated in the granting of a certificate. The certificate corresponded to six months of the apprenticeship and entitled the holder to receive journeyman's pay and status after two and a half years on the job . . . In preparing trainees for the certificate, the trade school class is run along traditional lines, with book work and written examinations in class and practice in shop. The work follows the same pattern, year after year, without reference to the need for apprentices to learn useful things not learned on the job. Teachers teach techniques that were in use when they worked in retail markets and that are readily adaptable to a school setting . . . Most assignments are not relevant to the supermarket. For instance, students learn to make wholesale cuts not used in the stores and to advise customers on how to cook meat. These skills are not particularly in demand and, as a result, few students bother to learn them . . . Apprentices are more interested in the shop period, where they become familiar with equipment they hope to use some day at work. However, the shop also has tasks useless in a supermarket. One of the first things learned is how to sharpen a knife – a vital task, but only in the past. Today, a company delivers sharpened knives and collects dull ones from meat departments at regular intervals . . .

On the job, learning experiences vary with certain structural dimensions of the work settings. A supermarket meat department manager tries to maximise the difference in value between the total volume of sales for the department and the wholesale meat order, plus his costs for personnel and facilities. To do this, the manager ensures that his skilled journeymen can prepare a large volume of meat efficiently by specialising in short, repetitive tasks. He employs apprentices where they can work for him most efficiently. Diverting journeymen from work to training tasks increases the short-run cost of selling meat. As a result, journeymen and apprentices are so occupied with profit-making tasks that apprentices rarely learn many tasks . . . The physical layout of a work setting is an important dimension of learning, since apprentices can gain a great deal from observing others and from being observed. Some meat departments are laid out so that apprentices working at the wrapping machines cannot watch journeymen cutting and sawing meat. An apprentice's feeling about this separation came out when a district manager in a large local supermarket told him to return poorly arranged trays of meat to the journeyman:

> 'I'm scared to go in the back room. I feel so out of place there. I haven't gone back there in a long time because I just don't know what to do when I'm there. All those guys know so much about meat cutting and I don't know anything.'

When he arrives at a store, an apprentice is trained to perform a task, usually working the automatic wrapping machine. If he handles this competently, he is kept there until another apprentice comes. If none comes, he may do this job for years almost without interruption. If a new apprentice comes, he trains him to wrap and then learns another task himself . . . Stores offer the kind of meat that customers in their area will buy . . . In poorer neighbourhoods, apprentices have more opportunity to practise cutting meat than in wealthy neighbourhoods. Where there is high volume, a division of labour among a relatively large number of workers increases efficiency . . . in this situation, not only apprentices but also journeymen will seldom learn the full range of tasks that was once integral to their trade.

Collaboration as the central theme

Now that we have an insight into the relational dynamics at play in both work practice and learning processes for apprentices, we can start thinking about the crucial points of attention. The work of Brown and Duguid is helpful here.[31] After examining the work of Orr, they identify two crucial aspects of work practice:[32]

1 *The extensive narration used*. This refers to the exchanging of stories. Stories help to diagnose the problem at hand, and they also become a means of preserving knowledge, as they function as repositories of accumulated wisdom circulating within the community of practitioners.

2 *The notion of collaboration*. The narrative process is collective, and not an individual process. Faced with difficult problems, people like to work together and to discuss problems together. This makes working an inherently social process that benefits from collaboration.

Brown and Duguid here make an analogy with the concept of 'bricolage' – that is, the ability to 'make do with whatever is at hand' – as developed by Lévi-Strauss:[33]

'. . . what one needs for bricolage are not the partial, rigid models of the sort directive documentation provides, but help to build, ad hoc and collaboratively, robust models that do justice to particular difficulties in which they find themselves.'

Exchanging, developing and adapting stories all play a crucial role in the process of augmenting knowledge, expertise and skill. However, this implies the free floating of these stories, the willingness to share, to listen and to engage in constructive dialogue. In short, this implies collaboration. Collaboration can therefore be seen as the enabling condition here.

When summarizing the different elements at play in the learning process depicted as legitimate peripheral participation, three ideas must be stressed:

1 *It is important to create a variety of learning situations*. The range of activities central to being a practitioner needs to be reflected in the learning curriculum. Job variety and rotation are crucial during this learning period.

2 *Participating in a variety of activities should take the form of peripheral participation*. Space and time should be reserved for experimenting with and reflecting upon the activities engaged in. If experiences are not reinforced by means of reflection, discussion with other apprentices or masters, and so on, the chances are high that these experiences will remain superficial. No thorough understanding is built up when short-term demands interrupt this process of 'sense-making'. When no time is left for discussion, reflection and narration – in other words, making sense of everything – people will start feeling insecure and helpless, suffer from stress, and will muddle through with their unsatisfactory understanding (because it has been experienced as incomplete), adding to what is known as the cycle of failure (*see* Chapter 2).

3 *Learning implies eventual legitimacy*. An apprentice has to be allowed to participate, to gain access, and this comes down again to establishing collaborative relationships between apprentices and masters, or between employees and their managers. If collaboration is absent, the goodwill, the patience and time, so crucial for feedback and reflection, will also be lacking.

Collaborative relationships are therefore seen as crucial prerequisites for the learning process to evolve. We should now take a closer look at what collaborative relationships mean and how they develop over time.

Establishing collaborative relationships

Collaborative relationships are crucial for learning. Working relationships characterized by openness, reciprocity, support and recognition are an essential element of the learning process. This idea has been around for quite a while and yet continues to pose serious challenges in practice.[34] A distinction can be made between different types of relationships: *dyadic relationships* involving just two persons or *team-oriented relationships* involving more people. Establishing collaborative relationships is somewhat different depending on which form of relationship is in question:

- On the level of dyadic relationships, the notion of trust can be seen as an integrating concept.

- As for teams, things are a little more complicated as more parties are involved. It is important to consider the development process taking place in this context.

Establishing trust within dyadic relationships

A distinction can be made between '*cognition-based*' and '*affect-based*' trust:[35]

1 Trust can be seen as *cognitive-based* when people act for what they take to be 'good reasons', balancing between 'total ignorance' and 'total knowledge'. Available knowledge and good reasons serve as a foundation for trusting behaviour. The extent of reliable role performance, the similarity between two parties and professional credentials are seen as factors positively influencing cognition-based trust.

2 *Affect-based* trust refers to emotional bonds between people.[36] Determinants of affect-based trust are related to insights gained in the motives of partners in the relationship; behaviour recognized as personally chosen and demonstrating care and concern (as opposed to self-interest) is seen as critical to the development of affect-based trust. Affect-based trust shows strong similarities with the concept of 'organizational citizenship behaviour' – that is, behaviour intended to provide assistance and support *outside* an individual's work role.

These two concepts are the building blocks of the process of developing trust. Four stages can be identified (*see* Figure 11.5).[37] The cognitive elements are prominent when speaking of calculus-based and knowledge-based trust. By contrast, the emotional dimensions are most critical in identification-based and diversity-based trust:

- *Calculus-based trust* can be seen as the outcome of a calculation whose value is derived by determining the outcomes resulting from creating and sustaining the relationship relative to the costs of severing it.

- *Knowledge-based trust* is closely related to the notion of predictability – that is, knowing the other sufficiently well so that the other's behaviour can be anticipated.

- *Identification-based trust* involves identification with another's desires and intentions: 'trust exists because the parties effectively understand and appreciate each other's wants; this mutual understanding is developed to the point that each can effectively act for the other'.

When a relationship develops, trust is seen as evolving from calculus-based trust towards cognition-based and (possibly) identification-based trust:

- Finally, *diversity-based trust* can be seen as the most complex form. Constructive collaboration means taking the perspectives of others into account. Tolerance of differences or

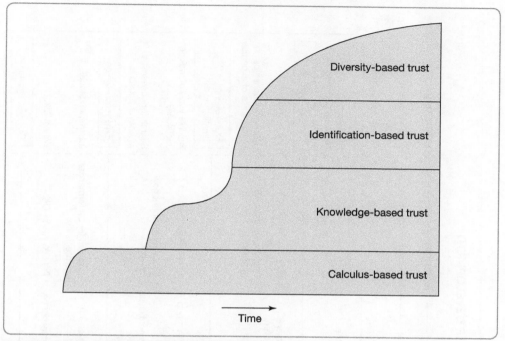

Diversity-based trust

Identification-based trust

Knowledge-based trust

Calculus-based trust

Time

Figure 11.5 The stages of trust development

Source: Adapted from Lewicki, R. J. and Bunker, B. (1996) 'Developing and maintaining trust in work relationships', in Kramer, R. and Tyler, T. (eds) *Trust in Organisations: Frontiers of theory and research*. © 1998 by Sage Publications. Reprinted by permission of Sage Publications Inc.

dealing with diversity thus becomes an inherent part of working together. In this regard, total identification with the other cannot be the final stage, since learning ultimately would be limited to the other's knowledge and competence.[38] Difference is needed in order to develop new insights and to take steps forward. In this sense, identification-based trust as a characteristic of working relationships is developed further to the next stage wherein differences are accepted and taken as a starting point for development.

Achieving collaboration within teams

Collaboration in teams is more complicated, as more parties are involved. The team or group developmental process can be depicted as involving a number of stages, with intermediate stages implying the development of collaborative relationships and trust, followed by 'productive' stages.[39]

A number of points should be kept in mind when considering how a team develops. In most cases, a team is formed around a common goal. Teamwork also implies taking up different roles and establishing working procedures. Finally, working together involves interpersonal relationships as well. In Figure 11.6,[40] these different elements are linked to the different phases that can be observed in the development process of groups:

1 In the first phase, dependency on authorities and issues concerning acceptance and inclusion are central. A well-known phenomenon, when starting a new team, is everybody looking at everybody else and asking themselves whether they will be accepted in

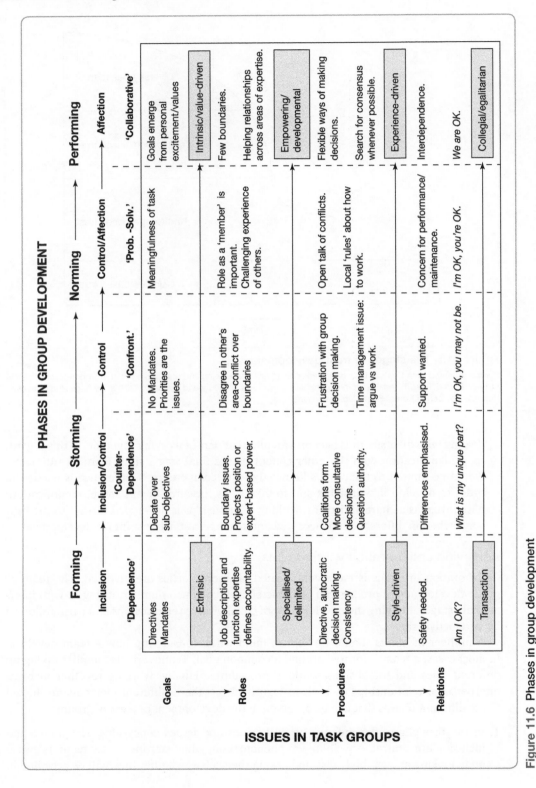

Figure 11.6 Phases in group development

Source: Bouwen, R. and Fry, R. (1996) 'Facilitating group development: Interventions for a relational and contextual construction', in West, M. (ed.) *Handbook of Work Group Psychology*. Wiley.

the team and what needs to be done. Reliance on authority is then an easy way of making the first steps. Moreover, conflicts are avoided since being accepted is preferable to being rejected, both from the point of view of the team members and from that of the supervisor.

However, this period of superficial harmony does not last long. When engaging in different activities as a team, individual members become aware that they are saying yes to a certain way of working, to a certain own role, and the team's activities. This raises doubts as to whether members really want to go along with the implicit agreements made at the start.

2 Hence, the second phase is characterized by counter-dependency and fighting; role issues, control and ways of operating are debated with less attention paid to the task in hand. While these phases seem to be less productive at first sight, they are a crucial step in arriving at the commitment and acceptance required for the final stage. The challenge here is to arrive at an open two-directional way of dealing with differences of opinion. The one-sided use of power, in which opinions are forced through, might settle the issue in question but it will also signal a return to the first mode of working, where acknowledging the technical expertise of others often plays the role of stepping stone. It is a preliminary way of expressing 'I am OK, you are OK'.

3 By the fifth and final stage, trust is established whereby respect for the other as a person – including the differences from one's own perspective and/or capabilities – is realized and a working structure has been installed, allowing the team to be productive.

Whereas this model suggests a certain linearity, it should be thought of more as a spiral; going back is often easier than moving forward. Teams struggling with the third stage often 'regress' to the first stage by allowing 'authority' to settle the ongoing disputes. Furthermore, arriving at the fifth stage does not mean that the team will remain there. Achieving this means devoting continuous efforts to the team process.

Conclusion

In this chapter, we first have been looking extensively at the notion of empowerment. At the level of the individual, empowerment can be seen as a motivational construct involving more than just autonomy: meaning and competence are crucial building blocks, while impact, self-determination and strategic autonomy complete the picture. Empowerment will have an impact on employee–manager relationships – involving a shift from active and autocratic management styles towards more democratic and even passive forms of leadership. Moreover, the impact of empowerment extends beyond the hierarchical relationship; empowerment has implications at the level of the organization as a whole. Delegating power, sharing information, developing competencies and distributing rewards in line with actual performance are the main ingredients of an empowered organization.

We then looked at competence development. Here, it became clear that different sorts of competencies require different development initiatives. The framework within which the relative importance of certain competencies was linked to the type of services provided was then expanded to accommodate different types of competence development actions.

Finally, we have discussed the relevance of collaboration for service environments. Collaboration is important because it relates directly to building and sharing knowledge;

collaboration is linked to learning. This holds true especially in situations that involve new or unforeseen events; in situations where this is not the case, (expensive) interactions can be substituted by procedures or manuals. However, services are characterized by heterogeneity; moreover, certain types of service involve by definition high levels of uncertainty or even ambiguity. Collaboration therefore deserves our attention, both in the daily work practice and in the learning process of newcomers or apprentices. We concluded this chapter by discussing the development process of such collaborative relationships.

Review and discussion questions

- Would you agree with the statement that empowerment is not relevant for low skilled employees? Why (not)?
- Does the road towards empowerment lead eventually to strategic autonomy (at the individual level)?
- In terms of implementation, what are, according to you, crucial prerequisites and/or ingredients of (change) programmes aimed at introducing – or further developing – empowerment within the organization?
- Would you agree with the statement that certain competencies are irrelevant for certain service jobs (e.g. personal characteristics for service employees working in cleaning companies)? If yes, can you give examples?
- Herbert Simon once said that 'all learning takes place within an individual's head'. Would you agree? How does this idea relate to the social dynamics outlined here?
- If these social dynamics are indeed crucial in terms of knowledge creation and diffusion, what might supportive HR practices look like?

Suggested further reading

Empowerment:

Bowen, D. and Lawler III, E. E. (1992) 'The empowerment of service workers: What, why, how and when', *Sloan Management Review*, Spring, pp. 31–39

Bowen, D. and Lawler III, E. E. (1995) 'Empowering service employees', *Sloan Management Review*, Summer, pp. 73–84

Lawler III, E. E., Mohrman, S. and Ledford, G. (1995) *Creating High Performance Organisations*. San Francisco, CA: Jossey-Bass

Stewart, G. and Manz, C. (1995) 'Leadership for self-managing work teams: A typology and integrative model', *Human Relations*, Vol 39, pp. 483–504

Collaboration and learning:

Brown, J. S. and Duguid, P. (1994) 'Organisational learning and communities-of-practice: toward a unified view of working, learning and innovation', in Tsoukas, H. (ed.) *New Thinking in Organisational Behaviour*. Oxford: Butterworth-Heinemann

Lave, J. and Wenger, E. (1991) *Situated Learning: Legitimate peripheral participation.* Cambridge: Cambridge University Press

Orr, J. (1996) *Talking About Machines: An ethnography of a modern job.* Ithaca, NY: Cornell University Press

Notes and references

1 Orr, J. (1996) *Talking About Machines: An ethnography of a modern job.* Cornell University Press, pp. 39–40

2 Schlesinger, L. A. and Zornitsky, J. (1991) 'Job satisfaction, service capability, and customer satisfaction: an examination of linkages and management implications', *Human Resource Planning,* Vol 14, No 2, pp. 141–149

3 For a very convincing plea for teamwork in professional services, *see* Maister, D. (1997) *True Professionalism.* New York, NY: Free Press

4 Bowen, D. and Lawler III, E. (1992) 'The empowerment of service workers: What, why, how and when', *Sloan Management Review,* Spring, pp. 31–39; Bowen, D. and Lawler III, E. (1995) 'Empowering service employees', *Sloan Management Review,* Summer, pp. 73–84

5 Bowen, D. and Lawler III, E. (1992), op. cit.

6 Four of these dimensions are developed by Thomas and Velthouse (1990): meaning, competence, self-determination and impact. Spreitzer (1995, 1996) later developed a scale to assess these four dimensions. Recent research on the notion of empowerment added the fifth dimension: strategic autonomy (*see* Van Looy, B., Desmet, S., Krols, K. and Van Dierdonck, R. (1998)). *See* Thomas, K. W. and Velthouse, B. A. (1990) 'Cognitive elements of empowerment: an "interpretive" model of intrinsic task motivation', *Academy of Management Review,* Vol 15, No 4, pp. 666–681; Spreitzer, G. (1995) 'Psychological empowerment in the workplace: Dimensions, measurement and validation', *Academy of Management Review,* Vol 38, No 5, pp. 1442–1465; Spreitzer, G. (1996) 'Social structural characteristics of psychological empowerment', *Academy of Management Journal,* Vol 39, No 2, pp. 483–504; and finally Van Looy, B., Desmet, S., Krols, K. and Van Dierdonck, R. (1998) 'Psychological empowerment in a service environment', in Swartz, T., Bowen, D. and Brown, S. (eds) *Advances in Services Marketing and Management,* Vol 7. Greenwich, CT: JAI Press

7 This relationship between the different empowerment sub-dimensions has been tested in a more rigorous way. Results were statistically significant. For more details, the reader is referred to Van Looy *et al.* (1998), op. cit.

8 For more details the reader is referred to Van Looy *et al.* (1998), op. cit. In this study, highly significant differences between high- and low-empowered employees, related to more satisfaction, commitment and degree of innovative behaviour have been found. The sample contained nearly 500 service employees and managers

9 Empirical evidence can be found again in Van Looy *et al.* (1998), op. cit. Here, it became clear that high-empowered employees differed from low-empowered employees in the sense that they had a more precise view of their goals. Also high-empowered employees had more trustworthy relationships with their managers

10 This framework was developed originally by Bass and Associates in the early 1990s. Given the wide empirical validation as well as acceptance, this framework is chosen as our starting point. The interested reader is referred to Bass, B. M. (1990) *Leadership and Performance Beyond Expectations.* New York, NY: Free Press

11 Stewart and Manz developed this framework in the context of team functioning. Here some adaptations are made to make the model applicable to the supervisor – employee relationship. *See* Stewart, G. and Manz, C. (1995) 'Leadership for self-managing work teams: a typology and integrative model', *Human Relations,* Vol 48, No 7, pp. 747–770

12 *See* extensive case studies developed at Harvard Business School (*Taco Bell Corp.,* 9–692–058, *Taco-Bell,* 1994, 9–694–076) as well as Heskett, J., Sasser, W. and Schlesinger, L. (1997) *The Service Profit Chain.* New York, NY: Free Press

13 This does not mean, however, that Taco Bell no longer monitored the operational performance of the restaurants. To ensure adherence to quality standards, different 'safety nets' were installed: a complaint line, mystery shoppers and regular market surveys. Information brought back to the restaurant general managers and market managers was to assist the task of improvement. Information was also used to assess the appropriate level of bonus

14 Lawler *et al.* (1995) define four characteristics of – what they call – 'high involvement' organizations: sharing information, developing knowledge, rewarding performance and, of course, redistributing power. For more details, *see* Lawler III, E. E., Mohrman, S. and Ledford, G. (1995) *Creating High Performance Organisations*. San Francisco, CA: Jossey-Bass publishers

15 Heskett, J. *et al.* (1997), op. cit.

16 We refer to the discussion of the idea of peripherality when addressing the notion of 'legitimate peripheral participation' further in this chapter

17 *See* in this respect as well the work of Blanchard, K., Carlos, J. and Randolph, A. (2001) *Empowerment Takes More Than a Minute*. San Francisco, CA: Berrett-Koehler Publishers

18 Ibid.

19 Lawler III, E. E. *et al.* (1995), op. cit.

20 Wolfe, D. and Kolb, D. (1979) 'Career development, personal growth, and experiential learning', in Kolb, D., Rubin, I. and McIntyre, J. *Organisational Psychology: Readings on human behaviour in organisations*. Englewood Cliffs, NJ: Prentice-Hall

21 Adapted from Spencer, L. and Spencer, S. (1994) *Competence at Work*. New York, NY: Wiley & Sons

22 Ibid.

23 Orr, J. (1996), op. cit.

24 As noted by Weick (1979), ambiguity, or equivocality as he calls it, drives interaction: the more ambiguity one experiences, the more one feels the need to interact with other people to make sense of the situation at hand. As 'universal' laws are rare in the social sciences, this might just be one. We highly recommend Weick's work on this topic to interested readers: Weick, K. (1979) *The Social Psychology of Organizing* (2nd edn). New York, NY: Random House; or, more recently, Weick, K. (1995) *Sensemaking in Organizations*. Beverly Hills, CA: Sage

25 Mills, P. K. and Margulies, N. (1980) 'Towards a core typology of service organisations', *Academy of Management Review*, Vol 5, No 2, pp. 255–265

26 As Maister stresses again and again when discussing professional services: teamwork is crucial. *See* Maister, D. (1997) *True Professionalism*. New York, NY: The Free Press

27 Lave, J. and Wenger, E. (1991) *Situated Learning: Legitimate peripheral participation*. Cambridge: Cambridge University Press

28 Ibid., pp. 50–56, *see also* Giddens, A. (1984) *The Constitution of Society*. Cambridge: Polity Press

29 *See* Lave, J. and Wenger, E. (1991), op. cit.

30 Adapted from Marshall, H. (1972) 'Structural constraints on learning', in Geer, B. (ed.) (1998) *Learning to Work*. Beverly Hills, CA: Sage

31 Brown, J. S. and Duguid, P. (1991) 'Organisation learning and communities of practice: toward a unified view of working, learning and innovation', *Organisation Science*, Vol 2, pp. 40–57

32 In fact, they also mention a third category; 'social construction'. This latter notion is however strongly linked with the notions of narration and collaboration. It does add the idea of (social) identity – by becoming a member, through exchanging stories and collaboration, one develops one's own identity. This identity also reflects values and visions of the community in which one is participating

33 Lévi-Strauss, C. (1966) *The Savage Mind!* Chicago, IL: University of Chicago Press, p. 174

34 *See*, for instance, Argyris, C. and Schön, D. (1974) *Organisational Learning: A theory of action perspective*. Reading, MA: Addison Wesley. The interested reader is referred to Argyris, C. (1994) *On Organisational Learning*. Oxford: Blackwell Publishers, which gives an excellent overview of more than 30 years of this scholar's work on the relationship between ways of working and collaborating and their impact on learning

35 McAllister, D. (1995) 'Affect- and cognition-based trust as foundations for interpersonal co-operation in organisations', *Academy of Management Journal*, Vol 38, No 1, pp. 24–59

36 Note the distinction made by Johnson-George and Swap (1982) between reliability and emotional trust. *See* Johnson-George, C. and Swap, W. (1982) 'Measurement of specific interpersonal trust: construction and validations of a scale to assess trust in a specific order', *Journal of Personality and Social Psychology*, Vol 43, No 6, pp. 1306–1317

37 The first three stages of this typology have been developed by Lewicki and Buncker (1996) and are based on previous work by Saphiro, Sheppard, B. H. and Cheraskin, L. (1992) 'Business on a handshake', *Negotiation Journal*, Vol 8, pp. 365–377. Based on discussions with Prof. M. Janssens (Faculty of Business and Economics, Ku Leaven), we added the fourth dimension. The three forms of trust identified by Lewicki and Bunker are: deterrence-based trust, knowledge-based trust, and identification-based trust. *See* Lewicki, R. J. and Bunker, B. (1996) 'Developing and maintaining trust in work relationships', in Kramer, R. and Tyler, T. (eds) *Trust in Organisations: Frontiers of theory and research*. Thousand Oaks, CA: Sage

38 Taking this reasoning to its limits even means that learning is not possible

39 Wheelan and Hochberger (1996) depict, for instance, four phases. We are limiting our discussion here to the work of Bouwen and Fry (1996), as they comprehensively integrate the work of their predecessors. *See* Wheelan, S. and Hochberger, J. (1996) 'Validation studies of the group development questionnaire', *Small Group Research*, Vol 27, No 1, pp. 143–170; and Bouwen, R. and Fry, R. (1996) 'Facilitating group development: Interventions for a relational and contextual construction', in West, M. (ed.) *Handbook of Work Group Psychology*. Wiley

40 Bouwen, R. and Fry, R. (1996), op. cit.

Chapter 12

Customer attitudes and behaviours towards service firms

Bart Larivière • Paul Gemmel • Kristof De Wulf • Katrien Verleye

Objectives

By the end of this chapter, you should be able to discuss:

- the attitudinal and behavioural components of customer loyalty
- different behavioural manifestations of customer engagement
- different ways in which firms can measure customer loyalty and customer engagement
- the link between customer loyalty and engagement and the firm performance
- different strategies to generate customer loyalty and engagement towards the firm
- the link between service failures, service recovery, and customer satisfaction
- relationship marketing
- customer experience management

Introduction

'You saved €7.34 using your loyalty card!' is the enthusiastic message on my receipt after packing my groceries at the checkout. Good news for me? Yes – if I am not worried that my supermarket chain is compiling a profile based on what I buy, how often I buy, and what my buying preferences are. In the end, who cares whether I buy one pizza brand over another and whether I shop every day or only once a week? Supermarkets care. By tracking as much information as possible and storing this information, supermarkets gain more insight into their customers' preferences. Moreover, based on the information concerning customers' preferences, direct marketing techniques (such as personalized mail to customers) can be used, which may contribute to generating a long-term relationship with the customer. Not surprising that we have more and more loyalty cards in our wallet . . .

As illustrated by the loyalty card example, several firms want their customers to stay loyal over a longer period of time. Over the past few years, customer loyalty has even become a top priority for many firms over the world.[1] The importance of customer loyalty implies that firms need to invest in building and sustaining strong customer-firm relationships, and thus customer relationship management. As an extension of customer relationship management, firms are also pursuing strategies to steer and encourage customers into showing engagement behaviours towards the firm. Consider, for instance, platforms to encourage customers to become involved in service innovation processes and communities where customers can connect with one another. In this chapter, we will focus on both customer loyalty and customer engagement behaviours. After describing these phenomena, we will explain why customer loyalty and customer engagement are important for the firm's performance. Additionally, we will discuss how firms can measure and manage customer loyalty and customer engagement, so that stronger customer-firm relationships are built.

Customer loyalty and customer engagement

Enhancing customer loyalty has become a popular topic for managers, consultants and academics alike.[2] The 2010 Conference Board 'CEO Challenge' Survey, comprising 444 CEOs, chairmen, and presidents, identified customer loyalty as one of the main present and future challenges for companies worldwide.[3] Numerous retailers and service providers have invested in setting up customer relationship management (CRM) systems to boost their profits via an increased level of customer loyalty. These efforts made loyalty 'big business', as it clocked in as a $10 billion industry overall, with approximately 1.3 billion people signing up to diverse loyalty programmes.[4] Do these loyalty programmes pay off? To answer this question we need to better understand what true loyalty is.

We define *customer loyalty* as:

'customer behaviour characterized by a positive buying pattern during an extended period (measured by means of repeat purchases, frequency of purchase, wallet share or other indicators) and driven by a positive attitude towards the company and its products or services.'

This definition clearly shows that customer loyalty has an attitudinal component and a behavioural component. Customer attitudes and behaviours, however, can be very different, as shown in Figure 12.1.

Based on different combinations of customer attitudes and behaviours, four types of loyalty can be identified:

- *No loyalty*. Obviously, there will always be some customers who display no loyalty to a particular company or brand.
- *Latent loyalty* applies to customers who are loyal simply because they have no other choice.
- *Spuriously loyal* customers tend to be more motivated by impulse, convenience, and habit – that is, if the conditions are right.
- *Truly loyal* customers are willing to seek out a particular service, location or brand.

Firms striving for true customer loyalty need to have a good understanding of both customer attitudes and customer behaviours. In the following paragraphs, we discuss different

Figure 12.1 The dimensions of customer loyalty[5]

Source: Dick, A. S. and Basu, K. (1994) *Journal of the Academy of Marketing Science*, Vol 22, No 2, pp. 99–113. Copyright © 1994, Academy of Marketing Sciences. With kind permission from Springer Science and Business Media.

attitudes and behaviours that are associated with customer loyalty, thereby providing greater insight into the ways in which firms can measure these attitudes and behaviours.

Attitudinal components of customer loyalty

Is it not the dream of every firm to have customers with such positive attitudes or even passion towards the firm that they start to sell these offerings to other customers? Lego has its ambassadors who give shows, and its lead users who create their own Lego businesses. Customer behaviours that extend to giving shows and building businesses stem from attitudes that include an affective commitment to the firm and a strong intention to stay with it. Commitment and loyalty intentions are two important attitudinal components of customer loyalty.

Commitment is generally described as an attachment to continue with a partner[6] or the belief that a relationship is sufficiently important to warrant strong efforts to maintain it.[7] Customers can show three types of commitment:[8]

- Calculative, continuance, or rational commitment refers to attachment based on the costs that customers associate with leaving the organization (switching costs) or customer attachment based on a lack of choice (*cf.* latent loyalty);

- Normative or moral commitment reflects attachment that derives from a customer's sense of moral obligation towards the organization;

- Affective or emotional commitment represents the customer's desire to continue their relationship with the organization because of the enjoyment of the relationship.

In essence, calculative, continuance, or rational commitment pertains to 'having' to maintain the relationship; normative or moral commitment pertains to feelings as though you 'should' maintain the relationship; and affective or emotional commitment, to 'wanting' to maintain the relationship.[9] Affective or emotional commitment can be considered the strongest and most important form of customer commitment.[10] As a result, firms should focus their attention on the customer's affective or emotional commitment towards the firm.

Loyalty intentions refer to customers' repurchase intentions, their likelihood of staying with the firm, their propensity to switch, their willingness to pay price premiums, and their likelihood to recommend the brand or firm. Firms can measure and track each of these aspects to gain greater insight into the loyalty intentions of their customers. However, the most popular measure for capturing loyalty intentions in actual practice is – without any doubt – the customer's likelihood of recommending the brand or firm. Several firms use this measure to calculate the Net Promoter Score (NPS), which is discussed in Exhibit 12.1.

Exhibit 12.1 The Net Promoter Score

The Net Promoter Score (NPS) was developed by Satmetrix, Bain & Company and Fred Reichheld, and popularized through Reichheld's book *The Ultimate Question: Driving Good Profits and True Growth*.[11]

In calculating the NPS, firms can begin by asking their customers one simple question: '*How likely is it that you would recommend [Company X] to a friend or colleague?*' A representative group of customers is required to answer this question on an 11-point scale, ranging from 0 (not at all likely) to 10 (extremely likely). Based on the respondents' scores, firms can identify three groups of respondents (*see* Figure 12.2).

As shown in Figure 12.2, these groups are:

- Detractors represent the respondents with a score from 0 to 6;
- Passives represent the respondents with a score of 7 or 8;
- Promoters represent the respondents with a score of 9 or 10.

The NPS is calculated by subtracting the proportion of detractors (the percentage of respondents who are classified as detractors in the sample) from the proportion of promoters (the percentage of respondents who are classified as promoters in the sample).

Figure 12.2 How to calculate the NPS?

Source: **http://www.netpromoter.com/np/calculate.jsp**. Net Promoter, Net Promoter Score, and NPS are trademarks of Sametrix Systems, Inc., Bain & Company, Inc., and Fred Reichheld

As shown in Exhibit 12.1, the NPS is a very simple metric to gain greater insight into loyalty intentions. By providing insight into loyalty intentions, the NPS also strengthens understanding of the firm's ability to grow. Indeed, advocates of the NPS argue that the NPS is 'the single most reliable indicator of a company's ability to grow.'[12] This statement, however, is questioned by a team of practitioners and academics who evaluated the superiority of the NPS in predicting a firm's growth in various industries, compared to other metrics for predicting a firm's growth (such as customer satisfaction, repurchase intentions, and other loyalty metrics). The most important finding of this study is that only in some cases did NPS outperform the other metrics in capturing a firm's growth.[13] As a result, it can be concluded that the NPS is a simple and useful metric for capturing loyalty intentions and for obtaining an indication of the firm's ability to grow, but firms may well benefit from looking at other metrics to gain a better understanding of their ability to grow.

Behavioural components of customer loyalty

Firms hope that a positive attitude will result in a positive buying pattern. They expect their customers to come back (customer retention) and to spend a fair amount of money (share-of-wallet).

Customer retention reflects the firm's ability to maintain existing customers. To gain insight into their ability to maintain existing customers, firms can calculate their customer retention rate over a one-year period. A customer retention rate of 90% denotes that 90% of the entire customer base remained customers during the observed year. The other 10% of the customer base – also labelled the customer defection rate (= 100% – retention rate) – includes customers who switched to another provider and/or completely defected. It goes without saying that complete defection of customers threatens a firm's profitability. On the one hand, completely defected or 'lost' customers cannot engage in repeat purchases or repatronage behaviours. On the other hand, these customers might threaten future customer acquisition by hesitating to recommend the firm or indeed spreading negative word-of-mouth about the firm.[14]

Share-of-wallet builds on the notion that not all customers are equally loyal to a firm. Firms have customers who spend most of their money in a certain category within their firm, while they have other customers who consider a competing firm as their main supplier in this specific category. Moreover, customers increasingly buy products and services from different brands and providers. As a result, multi-brand and multi-provider loyalty is the new dominant logic, as illustrated by Exhibit 12.2.

Exhibit 12.2 Polygamous loyalty at Kraft foods

Kraft Foods – the largest food and beverage company in North America – markets products that regularly find their way to 99% of all households. Kraft defines a loyal customer as a person who has bought 70% of the same brand within a category over the past 3 years. Three decades ago, approximately 40% of Kraft's customers were believed to fit this description. It is interesting to observe that today only 15% of its customers have bought 70% of the same brand within a category over the past 3 years.

As shown in Exhibit 12.2, customers increasingly spread their purchases over different brands and providers and, therefore, become more and more 'polygamously loyal'.[15] As a result, firms need to focus on the share that a customer allocates to a firm – and thus share-of-wallet (SOW). SOW is defined as *'the percentage of money a customer allocates in a category that is assigned to a specific provider'*.[16] SOW helps firms to benchmark their performance with the performance of competitors.[17] Moreover, a McKinsey report suggests that focusing on both SOW and retention can add ten-times greater value than focusing on retention alone.[18]

Customer engagement behaviours

Customers can also show their loyalty – or better their engagement – to a brand or firm through behaviours after and beyond purchase. These behaviours are labelled 'customer engagement behaviours'.[19] In this section, we discuss different customer engagement behaviours.

Customers can show their engagement towards a brand or firm via word-of-mouth (WOM) behaviours. WOM behaviours can have a positive impact on the firm if customers recommend a brand or firm to family, friends, and acquaintances or spread positive WOM via social media, forums, blogs, and so on. In an increasingly networked society, customers can even share their opinion with absolute strangers. Consider, for instance, customers who post their reviews and ratings of specific products and services online. It goes without saying that not all customer reviews and ratings reflect positive WOM. Customers can also spread negative WOM via the Internet or complain about a brand or firm to their family, friends, and acquaintances. These WOM behaviours can be very powerful, as illustrated by the example discussed in Exhibit 12.3.

Exhibit 12.3 'United Breaks Guitars'

In the YouTube video 'United Breaks Guitars', a single angry, dissatisfied customer shared his bad experience of United Airlines with the rest of the world by means of a song. More than 10 million people have seen this video clip and over 28,000 individuals have commented on it. Indeed, an entire webpage was devoted to this critical incident (**http://www.UnitedBreaksGuitars.com**). And all of this began with one single customer who was deeply dissatisfied because United Airlines broke the neck of his guitar and no one from the airline company was willing to listen to him.

In an increasingly networked society, customers have other options, in addition to WOM behaviours, to show their engagement with the firm. Customers can also show engagement by helping firms to improve the service experience for their customers. Firstly, customers can optimize their own service experience by cooperating with frontline employees. Examples include customers who provide all the information required by a lawyer to defend their case successfully and customers who, after surgery, comply with the healthful behaviours recommended. Additionally, customers can contribute to the service experience of other customers by showing empathy, giving information, or providing assistance to other customers. Consider, for instance, customers who help each other in user forums. Finally, customers can give feedback about their service experience and provide input for service improvement and innovation activities within the firm. Firms increasingly recognize that these behaviours can help them to improve the service experience of current and future customers while also controlling costs. Therefore, increasingly, firms are introducing practices to steer and encourage these customer engagement behaviours, as illustrated in Exhibit 12.4.

Exhibit 12.4 Customers helping other customers and the firm

At **http://www.ipodlounge.com**, iPod users can talk about their favourite devices. Additionally, customers can ask questions to other iPod users (e.g. 'Please help, it won't reset'). Furthermore, iPod users can show the world (and thus Apple) what they would like the next iPod to do and to look like. With more than 5 million hits a day, the website generates a lot of customer input and inspiration, which can be used for product and service improvement activities, and the development of new products and services in the future.

Although firms understand the importance of managing customer engagement behaviours, the measurement of customer engagement and customer engagement behaviours is still in its infancy. However, this is likely to change in the near future: there will be more and more opportunities to link firm databases to online information, such as posts on Twitter.[20]

Customer loyalty and engagement and the firm's profitability

In the previous section, the focus was on different behavioural manifestations of customer loyalty and customer engagement with the brand or firm. In this section, we discuss the impact of customer loyalty – and, more particularly, customer retention and SOW – on the firm's profitability. Next, we show that customers can become more profitable over time by introducing the concept of 'customer lifetime value'. We conclude this section by discussing the potential of looking at the 'total customer engagement value' to increase the firm's profitability.

Customer retention and share-of-wallet: the link with profitability

Suppose that a financial services firm serves 1 million customers, thereby having an average net contribution of €50 per customer per year and an average defection rate of 7%. In this situation – which represents the real-life situation of a Belgian financial services firm – the financial services firm has a retention rate of 93%.[21] As shown in Table 12.1, this retention rate generates a total contribution of €392.2 million after 25 years.

Suppose now that the firm was able to increase its customer retention rate by 1%, resulting in a retention rate of 94%. In this scenario, the total contribution after 25 years increases by €27.5 million (*see* Table 12.1). This example clearly illustrates that changes in customer retention rates can have a substantial impact on the firm's profitability.

Table 12.1 Real-life retention example

Retention Rate (RR)	No of customers (thousand)							Average contribution per year (in Euro)	Total contribution after 25 years (thousand Euro)	Additional contribution over 93% retention situation (thousand Euro)
	start	2nd year	3th year	4th year	5th year	...	25th year			
93%	1.000	930	865	804	748	...	175	50	392.213	0
94%	1.000	940	884	831	781	...	227	50	419.757	27.544
100%	1.000	1.000	1.000	1.000	1.000	...	1.000	50	682.518	290.305

The firm's profitability, however, does not only depend on customer retention rates. In a context characterized by polygamous loyalty, the percentage of money that customers allocate to the focal firms as opposed to competing firms – and thus the SOW – are equally important for the firm's profitability, as shown in Exhibit 12.5.

Exhibit 12.5 Share-of-wallet and profitability in a financial services firm

In a study of customers in a financial services firm,[22] customers were categorized into low, high, and full SOW groups:

- low SOW group: customers who had multiple banks and did not consider the investigated bank as their main financial institution
- high SOW group: customers who had multiple banks but considered the investigated bank as their main financial institution
- full SOW group: customers who used a single bank and considered this bank as their main financial institution.

As shown in Figure 12.3, the high SOW group had a better profitability trajectory for the company than the other SOW groups over a time window of 31 months. On the one hand, the high SOW group had a higher baseline value than the other SOW groups (*cf.* intercept). On the other hand, the high SOW groups also had a better subsequent nonlinear trajectory than the other SOW groups (*cf.* slope). It is intriguing that the high SOW group – and not the full SOW group – provides the best profitability trajectory. This finding, however, could be explained by the fact that rich customers are more likely to spread their money across different banks. In combination with the substantial difference between the low and the high SOW group in terms of profitability, this study suggests that firms should try to capture the biggest SOW.[23]

Figure 12.3 Profitability trajectories for different share-of-wallet groups: an example of a Belgian financial services provider

Source: Larivière, B. (2008) 'Linking perceptual and behavioral customer metrics to multiperiod customer profitability: A comprehensive service-profit chain application', *Journal of Service Research*, Vol 11, No 1, pp. 3–21.

Exhibit 12.5 suggests that firms need to capture the biggest SOW to increase their profitability. Moreover, firms might also benefit from expanding their relative SOW over time. To do so, firms need to be able to identify different SOW groups and optimize their relationships with different SOW groups. This is not easy, since polygamous customers receive promotions, publicity and other marketing incentives from all providers and can easily compare the providers' offerings. A customer feedback system, however, can help firms optimize their relationships with different SOW groups on condition that this system provides insight into (1) customer needs, wants, intentions, and desires and (2) the firm's performance in comparison with the performance of competitors (*see* Chapter 13). Before starting to optimize their relationships with different SOW groups, however, firms need to take the customers' potential value – and, more particularly, the customer lifetime value – into account.

Customer lifetime value: the link with profitability

Over their lifetimes, customers generate revenues for the firm. The lifetime revenue stream from a loyal pizza customer can be as much £5600. A loyal Cadillac owner may easily generate £232,000 in revenues over his or her lifetime. If you buy £70 of food products every week and you are loyal to your supermarket, you will spend £36,000 over a period of 10 years. A moderately frequent flier who travels between the US coasts once a month will generate £15,000 or more in revenues for the airline over a 5-year period. To a news vendor in Manchester, a customer who buys every daily edition of *The Times* and the *Sunday Times* is worth £10,000 in lifetime revenues. A newborn baby can soil £1000 worth of single-use nappies in its first year.

As shown by these examples, firms might benefit from taking the lifetime revenues of their customers into account. A measure that takes these lifetime revenues into account is the customer lifetime value (CLV). The CLV represents the turnover generated by the customer minus the costs of attracting, serving, and maintaining a relationship between the customer and the firm. In other words, the CLV reflects the net present value of the profits that a firm generates from a customer over a number of periods (usually 4–5 years) and, thus, the value of a particular customer. The sum of the CLVs of all of a firm's customers is labelled 'customer equity' (CE).[24] In Exhibit 12.6, we illustrate how firms can calculate the CLV for a sample of 1000 customers.

Exhibit 12.6 A calculation example of CLV

Firms can carry out their own lifetime value calculation by following the steps below:

- Select a group of customers, all of whom became regular customers at about the same time in the past (4–5 years ago).
- Calculate the retention rate by determining how many of these customers were still buying a year later. If there is enough data, determine the second-year retention rate as well. If not, estimate it for subsequent years (50% attrition is not unusual for some companies).
- Determine the average amount of money that these customers spend in a single year.
- Determine the percentage of revenue that must be allocated to direct costs.

Table 12.2 CLV calculation example

Revenue	Year 1	Year 2	Year 3	Year 4	Year 5
Customers	1000	400	180	90	50
Retention rate (%)	40%	45%	50%	55%	60%
Average yearly sale	$150	$160	$170	$180	$200
Total revenue	$150,000	$64,000	$30,600	$16,200	$10,000
Costs					
Cost (%)	50%	48%	46%	44%	42%
Total costs	$75,000	$30,720	$14,076	$7128	$4200
Profits					
Gross profit	$75,000	$33,280	$16,524	$9072	$5800
Discount rate (20%)	1	1.2	1.44	1.73	2.07
NPV profit	$75,000	$27,733	$11,475	$5244	$2802
Cumulative NPV profit	$75,000	$102,733	$114,208	$119,452	$125,056
Customer lifetime value (CLV)	**$75**	**$103**	**$114**	**$119**	**$125**

- Determine the discount rate that applies to the business (a sound rule is to double the market rate of interest).

- Put all of this data into a spreadsheet, projecting the CLV for 5 years.

- Try out some 'what-if' analyses – i.e. try to predict the effect of several marketing scenarios on CLV.

- Keep the spreadsheet active – after trying a few marketing initiatives, check their results against the spreadsheet, thereby improving your company's forecasting ability.

By following these steps, firms will end up with a spreadsheet similar to the spreadsheet in Table 12.2.

From the example in Table 12.2, the following assumptions were made:

- The retention rate increases each year because customers who showed loyalty in the past also have a greater chance of remaining loyal in the future.

- The average annual sales increase each year as a result of the fact that customers tend to spend more money if they show greater loyalty.

- Costs drop each year as a result of the fact that loyal customers require less operational handling and acquisition costs have disappeared.

- A discount rate of 20% was used.

Consultants of Bain & Co. have studied the relationship between CLV and the retention rate in a number of different industries. Their study of the US credit card industry shows that a credit card customer who leaves after the first year generates an average business loss of $21. If the credit card company can keep the customer for 4 years, the CLV amounts to $100. If the credit card company increases its retention rate from 80% to 90%, the lifespan of its customers goes up from 4 to 10 years and the CLV more than doubles – jumping from $134 to $300.[25] Moreover, keeping 5% more customers each year – i.e. a 5% increase in the retention rate each year – can boost profits by 25% to 85%, depending on the industry. In the credit card industry, for instance, a 5% increase in the retention rate each year boosts profits by 75%.

There are several ways to increase CLV. One way is to sell more and to increase customers' share-of-wallet. Companies, however, can also increase CLV if they can get customers to buy higher-margin products (up-sell), decrease marketing costs (e.g. some customers get locked into a longer contract so the company does not have to market to them so often), decrease the cost of service (e.g. airlines getting customers to use the website rather than call centre, banks migrating customers from tellers to ATMs, etc.) or decreasing the discount rate (make customers less risky). Customer relationship management is about segmenting customers based on their needs and the value they (might) represent for the company, setting the right objectives for each segment to increase CLV, creating contact points to achieve the objectives, and measuring against these goals using a customer feedback system.

From customer lifetime value to total customer engagement value

In the previous section, we focused on the importance of customer retention, share-of-wallet, and customer lifetime value for the firm's profitability. The firm's profitability, however, cannot be seen in isolation from customer engagement behaviours, such as word-of-mouth behaviours.[26] Since these behaviours can also affect the firm's profitability, a team of researchers[27] recently sought to focus on the total customer engagement value (CEV), which aggregates four components:

- Customer lifetime value: the value of customer purchasing behaviours (both repeat purchases and additional purchases through up-selling and cross-selling)
- Customer referral value: the value of customer referral behaviours (i.e. current customers who convert prospects in their social network into actual customers based on firm-initiated and firm-incentivized referral programmes)
- Customer influencer value: the value of customer influencer behaviours (i.e. current customers who influence other acquired customers and prospects through word-of-mouth behaviour, information sharing, and assistance)
- Customer knowledge value: the value of customer knowledge behaviour (i.e. customers who provide feedback to the firm on ideas for innovation and improvements)

Although it might be difficult to collect and compile all these metrics, it is argued that *'CEV provides firms with a new and more complete way of assessing their customers and allows firms to create better and more effective marketing strategies to target, acquire, and retain their best customers'.*[28]

Managing customer loyalty and customer engagement behaviours

In a customer's relationship with a particular firm, he or she can progress from being a prospect to being a customer, client, supporter and, at the top of the ladder, an advocate (*see* Figure 12.4).

Advocates are so deeply embedded in an organization that they not only show true loyalty to the firm but even show engagement behaviours to the firm by spreading positive word-of-mouth. Too often marketers stop short, being satisfied with having converted a prospect into a customer. The real value of customers, however, will only manifest itself when they can be nurtured further up the loyalty ladder. Therefore, the aim of any company should be (1) to make sure that customers do not fall from the loyalty ladder and

Figure 12.4 Customer loyalty ladder[29]

Source: From Jenkinson, A. (1995) *Valuing Your Customers: From Quality Information to Quality Relationships Through Database Marketing*. McGraw Hill Book Co. Ltd. Copyright Angus Jenkinson.

(2) boosting customers as high as possible up the ladder. In this section, several strategies to achieve this objective are discussed.

Focus on customer delight instead of customer satisfaction

Customer satisfaction is generally defined as:

> 'the customer's feeling regarding the gap between his or her expectations towards a company, product or service and the perceived performance of the company, product or service'[30]

Despite the common belief that customer satisfaction automatically translates into customer loyalty, there is often only a weak correlation between customer satisfaction and customer loyalty scores. Many satisfaction surveys reveal that 90% of the customers questioned are 'satisfied' to 'very satisfied', while only 30% to 40% of these customers repurchase the product or service. Rank Xerox discovered that the chance of repurchase among customers claiming to be 'very satisfied' was six times higher than the chance of repurchase among those who reported being 'somewhat satisfied'. There are several reasons for this weak correlation:

- Positive and negative feelings can co-exist: a customer may feel good about a company but may dislike one aspect of its service.

- Factors not directly related to the service can play an important role. It is not the restaurant's fault that your partner chooses to tell you over dinner there that he or she is leaving you, but as a consequence you may never want to eat there again.

- Customer satisfaction scores are reported by the customers themselves: self-reported scores are, to a great extent, influenced by the unstable and temporary conditions the respondent is in.

● Different types and levels of customer commitment might explain the large differences in satisfaction and loyalty levels. While customers characterized by a *calculative* commitment merely give added weight to the extra value your company can offer compared to that offered by the competition, customers who show *affective* commitment truly have a deep relationship with their service provider, and customers with high levels of *normative* commitment feel a moral obligation to maintain the relationship. While calculatively oriented customers might well be satisfied with the service offerings, they can turn out to be less loyal as a result of the fact that service offerings are easily copied by competitors. An affective or normative relationship, on the contrary, is better protected from a competitor's actions.

Despite the weak correlation between customer satisfaction and customer loyalty, customer satisfaction scores should not be rejected or replaced by customer retention or share-of-wallet measures. Firms can use customer satisfaction scores – if carefully interpreted – to get valuable information about customers' appreciation of the value proposition of their firm and compare customer satisfaction reliably over time (*see also* Chapter 13). Additionally, customer satisfaction scores can help firms to find out whether they are able to 'excite' or 'delight' their customers, since there is a close relationship between high levels of customer satisfaction (*customer delight*) and customer loyalty (*see* Figure 12.5).

As shown in Figure 12.5, the affective zone includes very satisfied customers who are very loyal to the firm and thus truly loyal customers. This zone also includes extremely satisfied customers who show extreme loyalty to the firm. These customers are labelled 'apostles'. In the indifference zone, we find customers who are not truly loyal because their satisfaction level is only moderate. Customers with low satisfaction and low loyalty are found in the attrition zone. This zone deserves particular attention because this zone can

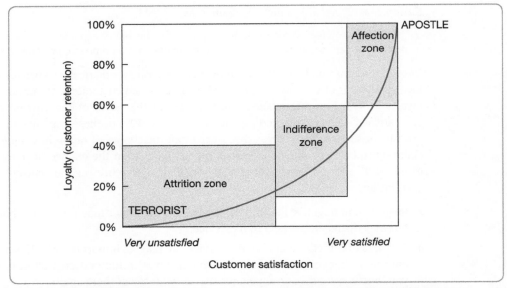

Figure 12.5 The relationship between customer satisfaction and customer loyalty[31]

Source: Reprinted by permission of *Harvard Business Review*. From Putting the service-profit chain to work by Heskelt, J. L., Jones, T. O., Loveman, G. W., Sasser, W. E. and Schlesinger, L., March–April 1994. Copyright © 1994 by the Harvard Business School Publishing Corporation; all rights reserved.

include 'terrorists'. Terrorists are extremely dangerous for companies, since they seize every opportunity to complain about their bad experiences with the company. Exhibit 12.7 shows how such terrorists can undermine the image of a company.

Exhibit 12.7 Dutch comedian declares war at customer service desks[32]

At a certain moment, customer service in the Netherlands was so bad that the Dutch comedian and columnist Youp van 't Hek decided to dedicate his column in NRC newspaper to exposing bad customer service after his own son battled a mobile phone provider for months to no avail. His own experience seems to be that these firms only respond to public humiliation by celebrities and the fear of being exposed to the public rather than actually provide 'customer service'. In late October 2010, van 't Hek tweeted about his son's broken mobile phone and went on a talk show the same day to tell his story. After appearing on TV and naming and shaming the mobile phone provider, the problem was taken care of faster than the speed of light. In other words, if you are famous and use Twitter to tell your 45,000 followers what is going on and repeat your story on TV, you will get 'service'.

Avoid service failure – or at least recover your mistakes

As suggested in Exhibit 12.7, firms not only need to satisfy, excite, or 'delight' their customers; equally important is the avoidance of service failure – or at least ensuring an effective service recovery. There is some evidence that customers are five times more likely to switch suppliers in the case of service failure and a lack of service recovery than in the case of price concerns or competitive actions in general.

Mistakes are an inevitable part of every service. Even the best service companies cannot prevent the occasional late flight, burnt steak, or missed delivery. In these situations, service firms need to take action to recover the service problem. Otherwise, service problems might lead to erosion of customer loyalty and even customer defection, as illustrated in Exhibit 12.8.

Exhibit 12.8 How service problems lead to erosion of customer loyalty

'A couple of years ago, I bought – as a customer of a telecommunication and Internet company – a new 'modem and router'. In the shop, the service advisor told me that it was easy to install the new 'plug and play' modem. At home, I immediately installed the new modem, plugged it in, but . . . it did not play. Because I had no internet connection, the only thing I could do was call the customer contact centre of this telecommunication and Internet company. I called several times on different days, but I was never able to get somebody on the phone. I didn't have the time to go back to the shop. After 3 days – without Internet connection! – I was so frustrated that I decided to switch to another internet provider, although I knew that it would take a couple of additional days to get connected. Am I the only customer having experienced this kind of bad service when trying to solve a problem?'

Certainly not. The results of a survey among more than 75,000 B2C and B2B customers show that most customers encounter problems in their interactions with customer contact centres:[33]

- 56% report having to re-explain an issue
- 57% report having to switch from the web to the phone
- 59% report expending moderate-to-high effort to resolve an issue
- 59% report being transferred
- 62% report having to repeatedly contact the company to resolve an issue

This study also showed that negative experiences with the customer contact centres lead to the erosion of loyalty, eventually resulting in customer defection. Finally, the study showed that the probability of future customer defection increases if customers have to do more work to solve their problems. As a result, firms need to remove all obstacles in their customer contact centres to avoid customer defection in the future.

To avoid erosion of customer loyalty and customer defection, firms might benefit from service recovery strategies. Service recovery is defined as '*a process that identifies service failures, effectively resolves customer problems, classifies their root cause(s), and yields data that can be integrated with other measures of performance to assess and improve the service system*'.[34] Service recovery strategies are thus much broader than complaint handling; these strategies fit within a quality management system. An effective service recovery strategy involves:

- the identification of fail points in the service process
- the elicitation of a customer reaction following an incident (this can be a complaint)
- the identification of a response to the service failure
- the identification of root causes of the failure
- the evaluation of the effectiveness of the recovery.

One of the crucial ingredients of effective service recovery is, thus, to elicit customer responses to service failures, since customers do not necessarily address their complaints to the firm. Consider, for instance, customers who do not take any action or customers who communicate their complaints only to a third party, such as a customer advocacy group.[35] If customers do not complain, firms may not be aware of the existing complaints and consequently will have no opportunity for service recovery. In Technical note 3 we discuss how to handle complaints and to develop a complaint management system in more detail.

Firms who have an opportunity for service recovery after a service failure are more able to:

- *Retain customers*. Since complaints are the expression of dissatisfaction, the way the organization deals with complaints will determine whether it will retain or lose the complaining customer. Moreover, since negative *word-of-mouth* is very likely to result from customer dissatisfaction, the business (earnings) at risk can be more than those from the complaining customer alone.
- *Continuously improve*. Customers will only go to the trouble of complaining if the service defect is important to them. Therefore, complaints provide valuable information on what is important to customers and on the frequency with which specific service failures

occur. A complaint is a 'gem', as it provides an opportunity for learning and continuous improvement.

● *Build a customer-focused organization.* The way top management treats complaints sends clear signals to all staff on how important it considers customer satisfaction and retention.

In sum, it is widely accepted that an effective service recovery will lead to positive post-complaint satisfaction and positive customer behaviour in terms of loyalty and word-of-mouth behaviour. As a result, one can even wonder whether firms, in the end, benefit from service failures? The 'service recovery paradox' holds that dissatisfied customers who are confronted with effective service recovery can become more (post-complaint) satisfied and loyal than satisfied customers who have not experienced a service failure. The existence of the service recovery paradox, however, has been questioned in some recent studies. A major study involving more than 8000 telephone interviews, for instance, showed that customer satisfaction and intention to purchase after service recovery never surpassed the satisfaction and intention to purchase of customers who did not experience a service problem in the first instance.[36]

Customer relationship marketing

In order to boost customers as high as possible up the loyalty ladder, companies can also use specific strategies for developing and enhancing customer relationships – and thus relationship marketing. Relationship marketing in itself is not a new concept. Two hundred years ago, the natural approach to the market was through relationships. Jacob Schweppes, who founded the soft drinks company bearing his name in 1790 in Geneva, had already built up close relationships with local doctors who provided poorer patients with his sparkling mineral waters. Today, however, we see an increased acceptance of the relationship concept, which can be defined as all marketing activities directed toward establishing, developing, and maintaining successful relational exchanges.[37] The renewed attention to relationship marketing refocuses the traditional transactional marketing approach by placing a greater emphasis upon the creation of customer value. In transactional marketing, marketing managers are generally concerned with the day's sales and the year's top and bottom lines. In relationship marketing, a marketer's challenge is to bring service quality, customer service and marketing into close alignment, leading to long-term and mutually beneficial customer-firm relationships.[38] In the following paragraphs, we discuss two types of relationship marketing practices: level one relationship marketing and level two relationship marketing.[39]

A first level of relationship marketing relies on pricing incentives to secure customer loyalty. This level of relationship marketing is often referred to as 'level one relationship marketing'. Level one relationship marketing implies providing customers with rewards that rely primarily on pricing incentives and money savings to secure their loyalty. Examples of tangible customer rewards are frequent flyer miles, customer loyalty bonuses, free gifts, or personalized money-off coupons. Also trying to earn points – on such things as hotel stays, cinema tickets, and car washes – are expected to help customers remain loyal, regardless of service enhancement or price promotions of competitors offering discounts, rebates or goods.

However, level one relationship marketing is considered to be the weakest level of relationship marketing. Firstly, competitors can easily imitate price. Secondly, reward programmes are frequently regarded as being cheap promotional tools, short-term fads that give something for nothing, because these programmes can affect customer behaviours (such as retention) but not customer attitudes (such as commitment). Initiatives such as Mobil's Premier Points, for instance, may help boost sales – 25% in the case of Mobil – but do little to lock in the highly promiscuous consumer. Real loyalty comes from real differentiation. The danger exists that consumers are enticed by the promotions, rather than being attracted to the products or the service. From this point of view, loyalty cannot be bought; it must be earned.[40] Finally, there is a danger in using rewards to stimulate loyalty, as illustrated by an old American joke (*see* Exhibit 12.9).

Exhibit 12.9 An American joke to illustrate the dangers of using rewards

An old man was being insulted every day by a group of 10-year-olds, who would tell him how stupid, ugly and old he was. Instead of shouting at them, he called them together and told them that any of them who shouted at him the next day would get a dollar. Excited and amazed, they all came round, hurled abuse and collected their dollars. 'Do the same tomorrow,' he said, 'and I'll give you a quarter for your trouble.' The children thought this was still pretty good, and turned out again to insult him and earn their reward. The man apologized and told them that on the following day, he could only afford to give them a penny. 'Forget it,' they said – and that was the end of his problem!

As illustrated in Exhibit 12.9, the loss of rewards is a source of dissatisfaction, which leads to a decline in desirable responses and a return to baseline performance levels. National Westminster Bank offered one point per £10 spent, then one point per £20 spent, but what could it do next? When Shell stopped distributing free savings stamps to its customers in the Netherlands, their reactions were so fierce that the company was obliged to reintroduce them. All these examples illustrate possible drawbacks of level one relationship marketing practices. Level one relationship marketing practices, however, can generate useful information for the firm on condition that firms also use this information, as illustrated by the following quote:

> 'Our lessons reflect the simple truth that excellence in marketing has always flowed from understanding how to deliver what customers need – profitably. Many retailers offer discounts, rebates or goods if customers present loyalty cards at every purchase, yet they fail to use the resulting information to tailor their offerings to individual customers' tastes, buying patterns, or value to the company'[41]

In general, 'level one relationship marketing' is more relevant in maintenance-interactive services, whereas task and personal-interactive services might benefit more from 'level two relationship marketing' (*see* Chapter 2).

Level two relationship marketing focuses on the social aspects of a relationship, exemplified by regularly communicating with customers. In general, it is recognized that buyer–seller communication enhances the prediction of behaviour of the other party and clarifies each other's roles, thereby increasing the probability of beneficial behaviours. Additionally, buyer-seller communication leads to the discovery of similarities and encourages feelings of trust, special status, and closeness. Moreover, firms can affect the strength of customer-firm relationships by customizing their communication and relationship marketing practices.

Sheth and Parvatiyar[42] confirm that *'implicit in the idea of relationship marketing is consumer focus and consumer selectivity – that is, all consumers do not need to be served in the same way'*. Consider the simple example of a person who called a local independent florist to arrange for flowers to be sent to his mother on her birthday.[43] The following year, 3 weeks before his mother's birthday, he received a postcard from the same florist, reminding him that his mother's birthday was coming up, that he had sent spider lilies and freesias the year before for a certain price, and that a phone call to the specified number would put another beautiful bouquet on his mother's doorstep. The only tools the florist needed were a PC and a large measure of common sense. The possibilities for customization are especially impressive when personal service capabilities are combined with electronic data-processing capabilities, as illustrated by these two examples:

- The Belgian supermarket chain Colruyt regularly communicates with its customers. Every fortnight, they send folders with tailor-made coupons. These folders also include recipes based on ingredients that can be bought at the store and that are often on promotion. The company stores customers' prior purchases and their prior usage of coupons in databases. The in-house data analysis team uses this information to predict customers' next purchases and subsequently selects the coupons that will be of interest to them.

- A Ritz-Carlton hotel in California stores all information from guest registration cards in a computerized system. This information is immediately displayed on terminals used by front-desk personnel when a repeat guest visits the hotel. The guest's assigned room can be pre-stocked with the brand of whisky, newspaper and hairdryer that were requested on a previous visit.

These practices allow firms to learn about specific characteristics and requirements of their customers and tailor their services to the situation at hand. The success of customer relationship marketing, however, also depends on the firm's ability to align their relationship marketing strategy to the value customers (might) represent for the firm (Exhibit 12.10).

Exhibit 12.10 The importance of customer segmentation for successful customer relationship management

As mentioned in the previous section, the value that customers (might) represent for the firm depends on their SOW and their lifetime duration. Based on the level of SOW and the level of profitable lifetime duration, four customer segments can be identified, in which each customer segment requires a different customer relationship management strategy (*see* Figure 12.6).[44]

As shown in Figure 12.6, there are four types of customer relationship management strategy. In the *high SOW-high profitable lifetime duration customer segment* (right upper quadrant), marketing strategies should aim at nurturing, defending, and retaining existing customers along with rewarding them for being such loyal customers. In contrast, *the low SOW-low profitable lifetime duration customer segment* (left lower quadrant) requires strategies to reduce marketing expenses. Moreover, firms can even consider divesting these customers or outsourcing these customers to outside agencies that can operate on a percentage basis. In the *high SOW-low profitable lifetime duration customer segment* (left upper quadrant), firms can use selective or optimal mailing/contract strategies to reduce costs or attempt to ensure up-selling and cross-selling to increase the profit potential. Finally, there

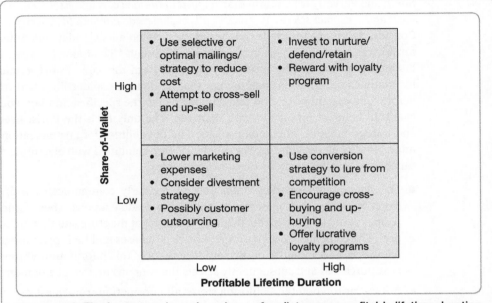

Figure 12.6 Firm's strategy based on share-of-wallet versus profitable lifetime duration

Source: Reinartz, Werner J. and Kumar, V. (2003) 'The Impact of Customer Relationship Characteristics on Profitable Lifetime Duration,' *Journal of Marketing*, Vol 67, No 1, pp. 77–99.

is the low SOW-high profitable lifetime duration customer segment (right lower quadrant). This segment requires marketing strategies that focus on luring customers' money from competitors in combination with strategies to encourage higher spending (both up-buying and cross-buying) and lucrative loyalty programmes.[45]

In sum, firms can move customers up the loyalty ladder through relationship marketing practices. Effective customer relationship marketing practices, however, require careful and intelligent use of the available resources.

Customer experience management

Joseph Pine and James Gilmore's introduction of 'the experience economy' has not gone unnoticed by service managers who consider the role of customers in services as crucial in achieving customer loyalty and long-term company success. In their seminal work on customer experience,[46] these experience gurus introduced the notion of – and the importance of creating – memorable customer experiences. As products and services become commoditized, the customer experiences that companies create will matter most. Companies are in a better position to differentiate themselves from competitors by staging experiences in their offerings; customers are even more willing to pay price premiums for these unforgettable experiences. Experiences have always been at the heart of the entertainment business – a fact that Walt Disney and the company he founded have creatively exploited. But, today, the concept of selling an entertainment experience is taking root in businesses far removed from theatres and amusement parks. Several other industries also embraced the customer experience concept:

- Nike Town London is a shop that goes beyond a place to search for shoes, sportswear and gear: shopping at Nike Town London is supposed to be real fun and entertainment.

- Volkswagen's entertainment park Autostadt in Wolfsburg (**http://www.autostadt.de/en/start/**) and BMW Welt in Munchen (**http://www.bmw-welt.com**) illustrate that successful car dealers and managers have moved from selling cars to (1) selling mobility, (2) emphasizing what customers want, and (3) providing extreme levels of fulfillment through memorable customer experiences.

- Lego is also more than toy bricks to play with: there is a Lego community where true fans can share ideas and stories that provide inspiration for creating own designs (**http://www.legoclick.com**). Lego also launched an iPhone application to convert individuals' favorite pictures into 'Lego-pixels'.

- The experience of drinking a mug of coffee at Starbucks does not need any further explanation: customers are prepared to pay additional euros/dollars just to enjoy their Starbucks and to experience the atmosphere and everything that makes this coffee different from an ordinary coffee.

The creation of enjoyable and memorable experiences can even encourage customer engagement behaviours, as illustrated by the example in Exhibit 12.11.

Exhibit 12.11 Customer experience and customer engagement behaviours

Nationwide is the world's largest building society, with around 15 million members. It is a major provider of savings and current accounts, mortgages, credit cards, personal loans and insurance products. Nationwide does a great job in leveraging customer experiences. The company slogan, since 1964, is 'Nationwide is on your side'. Matt Jauchius, Chief Marketing and Strategy Officer at Nationwide, revealed that:

'At Nationwide, we closely follow the buzz at social media. Recently, one of our customers had a claim following an accident. On his Twitter account he blogged "*I wonder whether Nationwide will be on my side?*" We took immediate action and contacted the customer even before he contacted us. That particular customer was overwhelmed by positive feelings caused by the action and service delivered by Nationwide, and so he shared his positive experience with the rest of the world through his Twitter account "*Yes, it's true; Nationwide was on my side, it's more than just a slogan!*".[47]

The example in Exhibit 12.11 demonstrates that enjoyable and memorable customer experiences can encourage customer engagement behaviours, such as WOM behaviours.

Conclusion

Over the past few years, enhancing customer loyalty has become a popular topic for managers. The Service-Profit Chain – as discussed in Chapter 2 – introduced, many years ago, the idea that customers need to be satisfied to become loyal. The insights from this chapter show that this relationship is not straightforward. A first insight is that customers must be very satisfied or delighted for them to become loyal. But even then, one must make a distinction between attitudinal components and behavioural components of customer loyalty. This chapter has shown that customer loyalty attitudes and behaviours can be very different. To stimulate both positive attitudes and behaviours – and thus true loyalty – firms can invest in (1) effective service recovery systems, (2) effective relationship marketing strategies, and (3) experience management strategies. These strategies are totally in line with the Service-Dominant Logic, which points to the fact that customers are actively involved in the service experience.

Moreover, these strategies might help firms to encourage not only customer loyalty but also customer engagement behaviours.

Review and discussion questions

- The Net Promoter Score is a simple and useful metric to capture loyalty intentions and get an indication of the firm's ability to grow, but firms might benefit from looking at other metrics as well to gain a better understanding of their ability to grow. What kind of metrics would you use to better understand the ability of a service firm to grow?

- Think about four different types of company you patronize (e.g. public transportation, bank, restaurant, hairdresser, etc.), and reflect upon the following three questions: (i) Are you satisfied/delighted with this provider and why/why not? (ii) Are you also loyal to these companies and how do you show this loyalty behaviour and (iii) Are you showing any type of customer engagement behavior (such as WOM) towards these companies?

- Consider a company where you buy regularly, and discuss your current level of experience and engagement behaviour. What would be needed to enhance your engagement behaviour?

Suggested further reading

Keiningham, Timothy L., Vavra, Terry G., Aksoy, Lerzan and Wallard, Henri (2005) *Loyalty Myths: Hyped Strategies that will put you out of business – and proven tactics that really work.* Wiley, 256 pages

Larivière, B. (2008) 'Linking perceptual and behavioral customer metrics to multiperiod customer profitability: A comprehensive service-profit chain application', *Journal of Service Research*, Vol 11, No 1, pp. 3–21

Pine, B. Joseph and Gilmore, James H. (1998) 'Welcome to the Experience Economy,' *Harvard Business Review*, July–August, pp. 97–105

van Doorn, Jenny, Lemon, Katherine N., Mittal, Vikas, Nass, Stephan, Pick, Doreén, Pirner, Peter and Verhoef, Peter C. (2010) 'Customer Engagement Behavior: Theoretical Foundations and Research Directions', *Journal of Service Research*, Vol 13, No 3, pp. 253–266

References and notes

1 Barrington, L. (2010) 'CEO Challenge 2010: Top 10 Challenges' (No. Research Report No. R–1461–10–RR). New York (February)

2 Keiningham, Timothy L., Cooil, Bruce, Andreassen, Tor Wallin and Aksoy, Lerzan (2007) 'A Longitudinal Examination of Net Promoter and Firm Revenue Growth', *Journal of Marketing*, Vol 71, No 3, pp. 9–51

3 Barrington, L. (2010), op. cit.

4 Berman, Barry (2006) 'Developing an Effective Customer Loyalty Program', *California Management Review*, Vol 49, No 1, pp. 123–148

5 Adapted from Dick, A. S. and Basu, K. (1994) 'Customer loyalty: toward an integrated conceptual framework', *Journal of the Academy of Marketing Science*, Vol 22, No 2, pp. 99–113

6 Anderson, Erin and Weitz, Barton (1992) 'The Use of Pledges to Build and Sustain Commitment in Distribution Channels', *Journal of Marketing Research*, 29 (February), pp. 18–34

7 Morgan, Robert M. and Hunt, Shelby D. (1994) 'The commitment-trust theory of relationship marketing', *Journal of Marketing*, 58 (July), pp. 20–38

8 Allen, Nathalie J. and Meyer, John P. (1990) 'The measurement and antecedents of affective, continuance, and normative commitment to the organization,' *Journal of Occupational Psychology*, Vol 63, No 1, pp. 1–18. Jones, Tim, Fox, Gavin L., Taylor, Shirley F. and Fabrigar, Leandre R. (2010) 'Service Customer Commitment and Response', *Journal of Services Marketing*, Vol 24, No 1, pp. 16–28

9 Gruen, Thomas W., Summers, John O. and Acito, Frank (2000) 'Relationship Marketing Activities, Commitment and Membership Behaviors in Professional Associations', *Journal of Marketing*, Vol 64, No 3, pp. 34–49; Kelly, Stephen James (2004) 'Measuring Attitudinal Commitment in Business-to-Business Channels', *Marketing Intelligence and Planning*, Vol 22, No 6/7, pp. 636–651

10 Fleming, John H. and Asplund, Jim (2007) *Human Sigma: Managing the employee-customer encounter*. New York, NY: Gallup Press

11 NPS website **http://www.netpromoter.com** and Reichheld, Fred (2006) *The Ultimate Question: Driving Good Profits and True Growth*. Boston, MA: Harvard Business School Publishing

12 Reichheld, Fred (2003) 'The One Number You Need to Grow', *Harvard Business Review*, Vol 81, No 12, pp. 46–57

13 Keiningham, Timothy L., *et al.* (2007), op. cit.

14 Hogan, John E., Lemon, Katherine N. and Libai, Barak (2003) 'What Is the True Value of a Lost Customer?', *Journal of Service Research*, Vol 5, No 3, pp. 196–208

15 Bennett, Rebekah and Rundle-Thiele, Sharyn (2005) 'The Brand Loyalty Life Cycle: Implications for Marketers,' *Journal of Brand Management*, Vol 12, No 4, pp. 250–263, Rust, Roland T., Lemon, Katherine N. and Zeithaml, Valarie A. (2004) 'Return on Marketing: Using Customer Equity to Focus Marketing Strategy', *Journal of Marketing*, Vol 68, No 1, pp. 109–127, Uncles, Mark, Ehrenberg, Andrew and Hammond, Kathy (1995) 'Patterns of Buyer Behavior: Regularities, Models, and Extensions,' *Marketing Science*, Vol 14, No 3, G71

16 Cooil, B., Keiningham, T. L., Aksoy, L. and Hsu, M. (2007) 'A Longitudinal Analysis of Customer Satisfaction and Share of Wallet: Investigating the Moderating Effect of Customer Characteristics', *Journal of Marketing*, Vol 71, No 1, pp. 67–83

17 Larivière, Bart, Aksoy, L., Cooil, B. and Keiningham, T. L. (2011) 'Does Satisfaction Matter More If a Multichannel Customer Is Also a Multicompany Customer?,' *Journal of Service Management*, Vol 22, No 1, pp. 39–66

18 Coyles, S. and Gokey, T. C. (2002) 'Customer Retention Is Not Enough,' *The McKinsey Quarterly*, Vol 2, pp. 81–89

19 van Doorn, Jenny, Lemon, Katherine N., Mittal, Vikas, Nass, Stephan, Pick, Doreén, Pirner, Peter and Verhoef, Peter C. (2010) 'Customer Engagement Behavior: Theoretical Foundations and Research Directions', *Journal of Service Research*, Vol 13, No 3, pp. 253–266. Bove, L. L., Pervan, S. J., Beatty, S. E. and Shiu, E. (2009) 'Service Worker Role in Encouraging Customer Organizational Citizenship Behaviors,' *Journal of Business Research*, Vol 62, No 7, pp. 698–705

20 Kumar, V., Aksoy, Lerzan, Donkers, Bas, Venkatesan, Rajkumar, Wiesel Thorsten and Tillmanns Sebastian (2010) 'Undervalued or overvalued customers: capturing total customer engagement value,' *Journal of Service Research*, Vol 13, No 3, pp. 297–310

21 The ideal situation with retention rates of 100% is utopian, because of uncontrollable reasons of defection. Natural death and moving to a foreign country (or different region) are common examples of events beyond the control of the company, which may result in customer defection

22 Larivière, B. (2008) 'Linking perceptual and behavioral customer metrics to multiperiod customer profitability: A comprehensive service-profit chain application', *Journal of Service Research*, Vol 11, No 1, pp. 3–21

23 Ibid.

24 Rust, Roland T. *et al.* (2004), op. cit.; Kumar V., Katherine N. Lemon and A. Parasuraman (2006) 'Managing customers for value: an overview and research agenda', *Journal of Service Research*, Vol 9, No 2, pp. 87–94

25 Reichheld, Frederick (1996) *The Loyalty Effect: The Hidden Force Behind Growth, Profits, and Lasting Value*. Boston, MA: Harvard Business School Press

26 Hogan, John E., Lemon, Katherine N. and Libai Barak (2003) 'What Is the True Value of a Lost Customer?' *Journal of Service Research*, Vol 5, No 3, pp. 196–208

27 Kumar, V. *et al.* (2010), op. cit.

28 Ibid.

29 Jenkinson, A. (1995) *Valuing Your Customers: From quality information to quality relationships through database marketing*. London: McGraw-Hill

30 In Chapter 13, we will return to customer satisfaction and how to measure it

31 Heskett, J. L., Jones, T. O., Loveman, G. W., Sasser, W. E. and Schlesinger, L. (1994) 'Putting the service profit chain to work', *Harvard Business Review*, Mar–Apr, pp. 164–174

32 Based on **http://www.24oranges.nl/2010/11/16/dutch-comedian-declares-war-on-customer-service-desks/**, accessed on 12 April 2011

33 Dixon, Matthew, Freeman, Karen and Toman, Nicholas *et al.* (2010) 'Stop Trying to Delight Your Customers', *Harvard Business Review*, July–August, pp. 1–7

34 Tax, S. S. and Brown, S. W. (2000) 'Service recovery: research insights and practices', in Swartz, T. A. and Iacobucci, D. (eds) *Handbook of Services Marketing and Management*. Sage Publications, Chapter 16, pp. 271–285

35 Lovelock, Christopher and Wirtz, Jochen (2007) *Services Marketing: People, technology, strategy* (6th edn), Upper Saddle River, NJ: Pearson Prentice Hall, pp. 391–392

36 Andreassen, Tor Wallin (2001) 'From disgust to delight: do customers hold a grudge?', *Journal of Service Research*, Vol 4, No 1, pp. 39–49

37 Morgan, Robert M. and Hunt Shelby, D. (1994) 'The Commitment-Trust Theory of Relationship Marketing', *Journal of Marketing*, Vol 58, No 3, July, pp. 20–38

38 Christopher, M., Payne, A. and Ballantyne, D. (1994) *Relationship Marketing: Bringing quality, customer service and marketing together* (2nd edn). Oxford: Butterworth-Heinemann

39 Based on De Wulf, Kristof, Odekerken-Schröder, Gaby and Iacobucci, Dawn (2001) 'Investments in Consumer Relationships: A cross-country and cross-industry exploration', *Journal of Marketing*, Vol 65, No 4, pp. 33–50

40 Molenaar, C. N. A. (1995) 'Loyaliteit kun je niet kopen' (you cannot buy loyalty), *Tijdschrift voor Marketing*, Nov, pp. 24–27

41 Child, P., Dennis, R. J., Gokey, T. C., McGuire, T. I., Sherman, M. and Singer, M. (1995) 'Can marketing regain the personal touch?', *The McKinsey Quarterly*, No 3, pp. 113–125

42 Sheth, Jagdish and Parvatiyar, Atul (1995) 'Relationship Marketing in Consumer Markets: Antecedents and Consequences', *Journal of the Academy of Marketing Science*, Vol 23, No 4, pp. 255–271

43 Peppers, D. and Rogers, M. (1993) *The One-to-One Future: Building business relationships one customer at a time*. London: Piatkus

44 Reinartz, Werner J. and Kumar V. (2003) 'The Impact of Customer Relationship Characteristics on Profitable Lifetime Duration,' *Journal of Marketing*, Vol 67, No 1, pp. 77–99

45 Ibid.

46 Pine, B. Joseph and Gilmore, James H. (1998) 'Welcome to the Experience Economy,' *Harvard Business Review*, July–August, pp. 97–105; Pine, B. Joseph and Gilmore, James H. (1999) *The Experience Economy: Work Is Theater and Every Business a Stage*. Harvard Business School Press, 253 pp

47 Matt Jauchius (2011) Keynote speaker, Plenary Session on: 'From Strategy to Execution: Driving Service Excellence', 20th Annual Frontiers in Service Conference, Ohio, Columbus, 1 July 2011

Chapter 13

Performance measurement systems in service firms

Paul Gemmel • Kurt Verweire • Gino Van Ossel •
Werner Bruggeman • Roland Van Dierdonck • Bart Van Looy

Objectives

By the end of this chapter, you should be able to discuss:

- the design of a performance measurement system and its alignment with the strategy, goals and the service concept

- the need for a 'balanced' performance measurement system – that is, one that includes measures on several performance areas

- the use of the balanced scorecard and the European Foundation for Quality Management Excellence model as a starting point for the design of a performance measurement system

- the importance of customers, employees and processes as the performance areas that are particularly relevant to the service firm

- the significance of service quality, service productivity, time-based performance and flexibility as the most important process measures

- the steps involved in implementing a performance measurement system

Introduction

John Brown was taking his first day off since accepting the position of CEO at G-Mart about 3 years before, but the day was not a gratifying one. He had decided to resign the week before, after much reflection, having failed to put the drifting ship of G-Mart on a new course heading for improved customer satisfaction and regained profitability.

G-Mart operates over 100 supermarkets, making it the second largest grocery retailer in the country. But, for almost a decade, G-Mart's profit margins had gradually been eroded because of a slow but steady loss of market share. The entrance of hard discounters, combined with the poor economic climate, had made all the major market players suffer, but G-Mart had turned out to be the biggest loser. Long queues at check-outs, frequent out-of-stocks, unfriendly staff, a messy store – in short, a generally unpleasant shopping atmosphere – caught G-Mart in a difficult competitive position: it was perceived both as being more expensive than the hard discounters and as offering a lower quality service than the so-called 'value retailers'.

As a result, about 3 years before, the board of G-Mart, in search of a turnaround, invited John Brown to become CEO. Brown accepted the challenge, considering it to be that once-in-a-lifetime opportunity, and gave himself 3 years to put G-Mart back on track.

The first step in this major endeavour was to redesign G-Mart's service strategy. After a period of 6 months of intense consulting with senior management, it was agreed that the first priority should be to increase customer loyalty and retention in order to stop the crumbling away of G-Mart's market share. It was also accepted that G-Mart should position itself as a value retailer rather than as a discounter. This strategy was based on the view that the hard discounters carried a less deep product range, resulting in a structural cost advantage. G-Mart would thus be a benchmark against the other value retailers. All senior managers agreed that only by offering world-class service could the company be given a competitive edge. The objective would be to increase customer loyalty through increased customer satisfaction.

As a second step, Brown launched a major internal communication campaign. Before the campaign actually started, he held a survey of all employees, which would later show whether or not his efforts were paying off. The objective was to measure both staff motivation and involvement, as well as to assess the staff's view of G-Mart's strategy and service concept. Future surveys would then show the impact of the internal communication campaigns. Not surprisingly, the first survey showed that the perception of what strategy G-Mart should adopt was highly diffuse. Some believed G-Mart should lower its prices immediately, while others wanted to take some type of 'value' path. However, the staff did express their belief in the company's future. There seemed to be a true sense of urgency and the survey's results clearly indicated that John Brown had the staff's support.

After his first year as CEO, he wanted to assess his progress. To do this he ordered a second internal survey, which showed that awareness of the new strategy was very high. Almost all employees strongly agreed that G-Mart wanted to offer its customers world-class service. Brown also organized a preliminary customer satisfaction measurement. A survey was held exclusively among G-Mart's active loyalty-card owners, as sales to card holders accounted for over 82% of all transactions and for over 90% of all sales. The results showed that the overall satisfaction index was 7.2 on a scale of 10. More alarming was that 14% of respondents could be defined as dissatisfied, having rated G-Mart a 6 or less. Furthermore, both market share and profitability were down.

With these results in mind, John Brown wanted to stabilize G-Mart's market share during his second year as CEO. Aware of the staff's motivation and its high awareness of the importance of quality service, customer satisfaction and customer retention, he was fully convinced that the customer satisfaction index would go up and that business results would start to improve. Throughout that year, he and his staff meticulously monitored the progress of sales, market share and costs, at the level of both individual stores and product categories. Store managers and store department heads alike were closely monitored on their business results.

In spite of all these efforts, however, it soon became clear that the fall in market share had not been stopped. At the end of his second year as CEO, G-Mart's profitability was at an all-time low. This was reflected in the third employee survey, which showed that employees were still supporting the world-class service strategy, but their belief in the organization's future had decreased dramatically. On the other hand, the customer satisfaction index was up from 7.2 to 7.5, while the number of dissatisfied customers had slightly decreased from 14% to 12% of the sample.

During his third and final year at G-Mart, Brown had to drink the cup of bitterness to the dregs. The disappointing financial results forced management to take drastic measures, including both a substantial wage cut and major layoffs, which resulted in strikes at several stores. The social unrest was reflected in that year's employee and customer satisfaction surveys. Customer satisfaction was down from 7.5 to 7.1 points, while the number of dissatisfied customers had increased from 12% to 16%. Moreover, employee motivation was at a record low and the staff's commitment to the world-class service strategy had decreased dramatically. Finally, the strikes had caused an additional loss of market share. Investors seemed to have lost their trust in G-Mart's future, as the price of the company's stock had decreased by over 30% during the previous 6 months.

John Brown could not help but admit that he had failed. He resigned and decided not to accept any new assignment or job offer for at least 6 months. He wanted a sabbatical leave to try to assess where he had gone wrong and what he could have done differently.

Like G-Mart, many companies claim in their mission statements that they are striving for 'customer and employee satisfaction'. Customer-focus programmes are being set up everywhere, and employee satisfaction measurement systems are being conceived. However, all is not well. While some companies have experienced early improvements, most campaigns do not get beyond the stage of mere lip service. Furthermore, the established measurement systems often produce nothing more than attractive reports. It has thus become clear that sloganeering and heightened awareness can only marginally improve actual customer and employee satisfaction, and eventually profitability. Unless a measurement system, aimed at realizing the desired service concept, is linked to the company's business practice and processes, it will not affect the way the company runs its business and, consequently, cannot have a significant impact on the actual satisfaction of its customers, employees' morale or longer term profitability.

Aligning performance measures with the service concept is extremely important in service organizations because of the danger of losing focus. Without a good insight into the service concept, the customer can build up expectations and ultimately demand a service delivery that does not fit the service concept. This may encourage service workers to disregard this concept. In the same way, when the internal service worker does not know what the goals are, divergence in behaviour – for instance, between back office and front office – is highly probable. Performance measurement and control is part of strategic performance management and is a crucial tool for helping the organization to keep focused.

To ensure that the organization moves in the direction of the proposed goals – i.e. realizing its service concept – a performance measurement and reporting system must be developed. Such a system plays an important role in motivating managers to take actions that are in line with the organization's strategy and that further its goal. The performance measurement and reporting system quantifies the degree to which managers achieve their objectives and it is the basis of the reward system. As a result, the measurement system has a significant impact on management behaviour. It is also an important communication tool about those goals and how to achieve them. It is said that 'you get what you measure'.[1]

While it is clear that performance measurement is important in services, its success depends totally on the way that the measurement system is designed and how it is implemented. In the first part of this chapter, we will argue that an integrated and balanced approach is necessary in designing a performance measurement system. Then, we will look at some service-specific aspects of performance measurement. We will go on to show how a performance measurement system as part of performance management must be implemented if the service concept is to be achieved.

Designing performance measurement systems for services

In many organizations, the performance measurement system discourages managers and employees from taking actions in the desired strategic direction. Sometimes, the measurement system points them in the wrong direction. Consider, for instance, the example of a service company where the key message of the service strategy is quality and customer satisfaction, but the performance report focuses only on costs. As a result, employees focus on improving productivity in order to reduce costs, neglecting the possible negative consequences on the quality of the service delivered. It is said that such a performance report is *not aligned with the service concept*.

The starting point in designing integrated performance measurement systems is therefore the definition of the service concept (*see* Chapter 3). The service concept is a formulation of the fundamental reason for the existence of a service firm and, thus, goals must be defined in line with this concept. The definition of the service concept does not guarantee that the service concept is being successfully implemented. Many companies do not even know if they do what they intend to do. A company striving to become the world leader should report on a regular basis the degree to which the company is actually becoming a world leader. An organization intending to delight its customers should measure and report the level of customer delight.

Far too many organizations lack performance measurements that are anchored within the service concept and goals. They rely too heavily or – even worse – exclusively on financial figures to measure how well they are doing. There are many reasons for this. Companies listed on the stock exchange are judged by their quarterly financial results. However, unlisted organizations also consider profit and/or financial stability to be their main objective and, therefore, their management control system emphasizes financial measures. Moreover, it is much easier to measure the financial situation than the more qualitative degree of employee satisfaction. However, relying on financial measures to manage an organization is like steering one's car by using only the rear mirror. Indeed, while today's financial results are the result of yesterday's performance, they are a poor indicator of tomorrow's success.[2]

The performance measurement system should be capable of giving advance warning of potential financial decline. Remember the basic idea behind the service profit chain: employee satisfaction drives customer satisfaction, which ultimately influences financial performance. Non-financial figures, such as employee satisfaction and customer satisfaction, will not only give a company additional information regarding its performance but may also present it with a warning light of possible financial decline. This way, preventative actions can be taken – something that would not be possible if only financial performance were to be considered. We, therefore, need measurement systems that give a more balanced view of performance. An important question here is which performance measures need to be included in a scorecard in order for it to be 'balanced'. Some inspiring general frameworks can be used as a starting point to design a balanced performance measurement system. In the next section, we will discuss two frequently used models that reflect an integrated and balanced view – namely, the *balanced scorecard* and the *European Foundation for Quality Management's (EFQM) Excellence model.*

These two models are designed in general terms, however: they do not always reflect the specific issues service firms are confronted with. We will, therefore, go on to develop some service-specific issues in designing a performance measurement system.

The balanced scorecard

The balanced scorecard (BSC), a framework developed by Kaplan and Norton, helps managers translate their organization's mission, goals and strategy into a comprehensive set of performance measures aimed at achieving competitive success.[3] Thus, the BSC is primarily a mechanism for strategy implementation. Figure 13.1 illustrates an example of the BSC for a large US healthcare system.[4]

The BSC is organized around four different perspectives:

- financial;
- customer;
- internal business processes; and
- innovation, learning and growth.

These four perspectives both provide an integrated balance between measures of current, short-term operating performance and future competitive performance and growth. The BSC perspectives should be considered a template and not a 'straightjacket'. Although there is no mathematical theorem proving that four perspectives are both necessary and sufficient, the four perspectives make sense for many companies, since shareholders, customers and employees are very important stakeholders in each and every company. Depending on industry circumstances and the company's strategy, one or more additional perspectives may be needed to incorporate the interests of other important stakeholders such as suppliers, the community and the environment.

The key in developing a BSC is to construct the multiple scorecard measures so that they are properly linked together and directed towards achieving a single, integrated strategy. The set of objectives and measures should be internally consistent and mutually reinforcing. The linkages should incorporate the complex cause-and-effect relationships that exist among the critical measures in the four perspectives. For example, a chain of cause-and-effect relationships can be established between improving employee skills (in the learning and growth perspective), which has a positive effect on the quality and efficiency of internal processes (in the internal business process perspective), leading to on-time delivery of orders and, as a result, a high degree of customer loyalty (in the customer perspective), which eventually influences the financial performance. The BSC thus 'tells the story of the

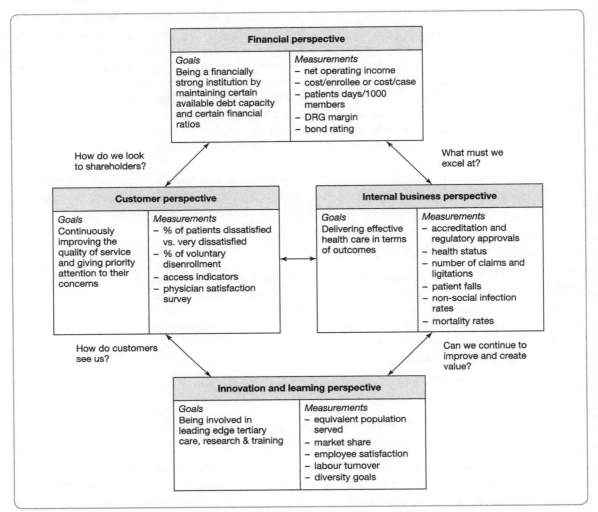

Figure 13.1 The balanced scorecard as developed by Henry Ford Health System

Source: Reprinted by permission of *Harvard Business Review*. From The balanced scorecard – measures that drive performance by Kaplan, R. S. and Norton, D. P., January–February 1992. Copyright © 1992 by the Harvard Business School Publishing Corporation; all rights reserved.

strategy', starting with the long-term financial objectives and linking them to the actions that must be taken in terms of customers, internal processes, employees, and systems to deliver the desired value.

Although the BSC was originally devised as a strategic tool at the business unit level, it can be implemented at the corporate and functional levels, and on the level of corporate support functions and shared services as well. A functional scorecard translates the functional strategy (e.g. marketing, human resources and operations) into a coherent set of performance measures. A BSC of a shared service unit (e.g. a HRM department) links the performance measures of the service unit with its goals and strategies, and aligns them with the service concept of the firm (or business unit). Because many of these shared service units are in the back office, the deployment of the BSC at unit level will guarantee a better fit between back-office and front-office activities.

The BSC framework provides a balance between:

- quantitative outcome measures and more subjective, non-financial measures of the drivers of performance;
- external measures for shareholders and customers, and internal measures of critical business processes, innovation, and learning and growth.

The full power of the BSC will only be apparent when it is embedded in an approach that implements the service organization's policy of becoming strategy-focused[5] (*see also* Chapter 16).

The EFQM Excellence Model for Total Quality Management

A second model that can be used to design an integrated performance measurement system is the *EFQM Excellence Model*, underlying the European Quality Award and proposed by the European Foundation for Quality Management (EFQM). This award is similar to Japan's Deming Award and America's Baldridge Award. As the EFQM award is the most recent, it is based on the American and Japanese experiences, and is thought to be the most comprehensive model.

The EFQM excellence model is based on nine criteria, divided into two major groups: enabler criteria and results criteria (*see* Figure 13.2).[6] The five enabler criteria are Leadership, Strategy, People, Partnerships & Resources and Processes, Products and Services. The RADAR approach is central to the use of the enablers in the EFQM excellence model. According to this four-step approach, an organization needs to:

- determine the Results it is looking for
- plan and develop sound Approaches to attain the results
- Deploy the approaches in the proper way and
- finally, Assess and Review the approaches.[7]

Figure 13.2 The EFQM Excellence Model

Source: The EFQM Excellence Model has been reproduced with the permission of EFQM, Brussels Belgium http://www.efgm.org/.

The four results criteria are Customer Results, People Results, Society Results and Key Results. In terms of the results, the questions of the EFQM model aim at defining the organization's actual performance as well as comparing the organization's performance against its own targets and, if possible, its performance compared to competitors and 'best in class' organizations.[8]

These models such as the BSC and EFQM stimulate the search for a comprehensive approach and inspire the development of concrete performance indicators that reflect the different aspects of performance a company wants to improve.

Designing a service-specific performance measurement system

While both the BSC and the EFQM Excellence Models undoubtedly have their merits, neither was developed specifically for service industries. Now that we know that a good performance measurement system must be linked to the service concept and needs to be balanced, we can start asking ourselves what the crucial ingredients are for a service-specific performance measurement system.

The service profit chain (*see* Chapter 2) should inspire us to design a performance measurement system for service firms. We have already discussed how the service profit chain implies various cause-and-effect links between the following elements: the service concept and organizational capabilities impact on employee satisfaction, which in turn affects employee retention as well as service productivity and quality, resulting in value created for customers. Creating value for customers will eventually result in customer satisfaction and lead to customer loyalty and profitability. This framework highlights which areas of attention – besides profitability – should be included in a BSC for services:

- organizational capabilities, which include skills, technology and operations;
- employees;
- customers and the value that is created for them (*see* Figure 13.3).

In Figure 13.3, we emphasize the notion of service concept, which implies a focus using certain capabilities. These elements should not be measured as such; they need, however, to be clearly defined – or designed in the case of capabilities – and will determine the relevance of specific measurements related to employees, customers and processes.

Once we understand the service concept and the focus on the target markets (*see* Chapter 3), we can start to think about the required capabilities the 'service delivery system' should possess.

The major resources enabling a firm to deliver services are technology and people (skills and knowledge). Knowledge workers are the key resource in today's service firms, and getting the most from these knowledge workers is the major challenge for the twenty-first century.[9] Although many years have been spent in getting better insight into the performance and, more specifically, productivity of physical labour, only limited attention has been paid as yet to the performance (productivity) of knowledge workers. Productivity of knowledge is much more difficult to measure because it is intangible and because quality is more important than quantity.[10] A management professor should be evaluated not by how many students are taking his course but by how many students have learned something. This is a question of quality. In Chapter 16 we will look in more depth at the issue of managing intangible resources such as knowledge.

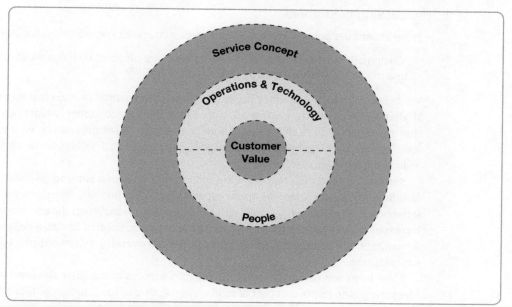

Figure 13.3 Service concept as a guiding framework

Once the capabilities have been defined, the design of the performance measurement system can begin. In designing a performance measurement system for services, special attention needs to be paid to employees, customers and processes.

Assessing employees

The importance of employees cannot be stressed enough in service operations as became clear in Chapter 11. Different elements relating to employees can be given a place in an integrated performance measurement system. *Employee satisfaction* is an absolute must. Scales are widely available on the market.[11] *Employee-retention indicators* can be easily derived from looking at seniority figures. It is advisable to document more than these two elements, however. The notions of competencies, empowerment and commitment are the next dimensions to be included. In the case of *competence development*, the efforts employed in this area as well as the progress made should be documented. While assessing performance might often take on a more descriptive and qualitative form in this context, indices can also be relevant – for instance, the number of people trained to perform certain new tasks, the speed and number of apprentices that grow out of this status and so on. *Empowerment* can be assessed on two levels: the degree to which a company is engaging in employee involvement and the level of empowerment at the level of the individual employee. These notions have been discussed extensively in Chapter 11 so, we will not repeat them here.[12]

Employee commitment to the organization, its antecedents and consequences have been investigated in great detail and critically reviewed.[13] The conclusion was that commitment is a complex and multi-dimensional concept. A well-known conceptualization describes organizational commitment of employees as being composed of affective commitment (employees' affective attachment to the organization), continuance commitment (the perceived cost associated with leaving the organization), and normative commitment (the obligation to remain in the organization).[14]

Assessing customers

From a customer point of view, a core concept is customer (perceived) value (*see* Figure 13.3):

> 'Customers will derive value according to the utility provided by the combination of attributes less the disutility represented by the final price paid.'[15]

Value seems to have a moderating role between service quality and customer satisfaction.[16] Higher levels of service quality will only result in more customer satisfaction to the extent that customers believe that value is being enhanced. Customers can be very satisfied with a lower-priced package holiday, compared to a higher-priced holiday to the same destination, as long as the value received is high.

Satisfaction and dissatisfaction are seen as two ends of a continuum, where the location is defined by a comparison between expectations and outcome. A customer will be satisfied if the outcome of the service meets his or her expectations. When the service quality exceeds the expectations, the service provider is in the happy position of having a delighted customer. A customer will be dissatisfied when the perceived overall service quality is below his or her expectations.

Most firms are using customer satisfaction surveys to measure the level of satisfaction. Measuring is an important part of management. One of the reasons for this is that what gets measured gets done. However, measurement is just a start. In their never-ending battle against kilos and calories, obese people who want to lose weight typically start by buying a bathroom scale and a book with a title like *'How to lose 10 kilos in 4 weeks without feeling hungry'*. Weighing oneself and reading about successful dieting methods, however, rarely results in weight loss. Most people on diets fail to lose weight, even though they genuinely want to, because of a lack of willpower to resist the continual temptation of tasty foods and drinks. This is the secret of the success of 'Weight Watchers'. Instead of trying to stick to a diet all alone, a 'Weight Watchers' member has the opportunity to meet fellow overweight people. During the weekly gatherings, everyone is invited to step on the scales, which creates peer pressure to sustain one's dieting efforts.

Organizations often make the same mistake. Their managers read books and attend seminars on customer focus. They make satisfaction measurement systems part of their customer focus efforts and invest heavily in buying the best possible scales – that is, a highly sophisticated customer satisfaction measurement system. All too often, however, it turns out that the books, seminars and measurement system do not trigger the desired improvement projects. These organizations are experiencing the obese person's lack of willpower. They too can benefit from the 'Weight Watchers' approach by creating peer pressure within the organization. This typically requires:

- measuring customer satisfaction for specific organizational units rather than for the organization as a whole;
- making the satisfaction data available to everyone in order to create peer pressure and healthy internal competition;
- linking a manager's appraisal to the customer satisfaction data.

Another reason for measuring customer satisfaction is being able to balance the score card. Performance measurement systems tend to be biased in favour of financial measures. In Technical note 4 we give some important suggestions for service managers when they want to develop customer satisfaction systems.

A common mistake is to deal with the customer satisfaction survey independently of all other customer feedback systems. If the aim is to prioritize improvement projects, the best results will be achieved when other sources of information are used, including more qualitative ones. Indeed, a satisfaction measure rarely reveals the underlying drivers or causes of a certain level of satisfaction. If 15% of the customers rate the meals on board a certain flight as poor, it is difficult to ascertain the reasons for this from this statistic alone. Similarly, if 15% of the customers are delighted with the meals, it is still unclear why.

Using other sources of customer feedback can be very revealing:

1 *The complaints and congratulations a company receives.* All complaints or congratulations will help to explain what the possible satisfiers and dissatisfiers are. Comparing both complaints and congratulations, on the one hand, and satisfaction scores, on the other hand, for different organizational units, can be extremely revealing.

2 *The invoked guarantees.* By inviting customers to explain why they are invoking the offered guarantee, and by linking these explanations to the satisfaction scores, a more refined insight into the underlying drivers of satisfaction scores can be obtained. The role of service guarantees will be discussed in Chapter 14.

3 *User groups and qualitative market research.* By explicitly asking customers to discuss the strengths and weaknesses, as well as their likes and dislikes, in a more qualitative manner, valuable information can be obtained.

4 *The front-line staff.* Obviously, front-line personnel can provide very useful information in assessing what the major areas for improvement or the few vital priorities are.

The service satisfaction framework (*see* Figure 13.4) summarizes the different elements of customer feedback that should be part of performance measurement systems assessing customers. It shows that only a certain percentage of customers who are dissatisfied voice their complaints, while others do not. Complaints should be considered gems for the company since they provide information helpful for continuous improvement, as well as opportunities to recover customers. A complaint management system is, therefore, an important component of a performance measurement system when focusing on customers.

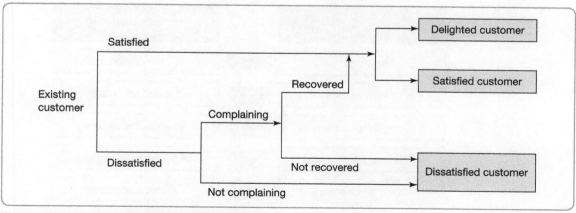

Figure 13.4 A service satisfaction framework

Source: Adapted from Hays, J. M. and Hill, A. V. (1999) 'The market share impact of service failures', *Production and Operations Management, An international Journal of the Production and Operations Management Society*, Vol 8, No 3, pp. 208–220.

A well-designed complaint management system allows for service recovery, and service recovery in itself is a big opportunity to make customers even more loyal than those consistently satisfied with the firm's service. Customer retention through effective complaint management creates more value than attracting new customers. Customers who do not complain cannot be recovered (*see also* Chapter 12). These customers tell everyone how bad the service is, and it is these customers who can deeply damage the business. In Technical note 3 we show how a complaint management system can be set up.

As already stated, the different types of customer feedback give service managers many gems to improve their system and recover from service problems. In other words, setting up a performance measurement system to capture customer feedback will only pay off when this performance information leads to actions to improve and recover the services (*see* Chapter 12).

Customers and employees interact with each other during the process of service delivery. It is quite clear that the performance of the service delivery process will strongly influence the satisfaction (and hence retention) of customers and employees. Therefore, it is important to measure and assess the process performance.

Assessing process performance

Employees perform activities that constitute the service process. It is clear that the performance of the processes is determined by the performance of the employees in this process. However, focusing on the individual employees is not enough: organizations should also consider how people interact in the process. This is also a function of the other resources: tangible resources, such as equipment or building, but also the information provided. It is also a function of the way the various activities interact, how the processes are designed, and how the processes are perceived by the customers. The design of processes has been discussed in Chapter 4. A well-accepted framework to evaluate processes and operations recognizes five performance objectives: quality, cost, speed, dependability and flexibility[17] (*see* Figure 13.5). We will discuss each of these performance objectives in a service context.

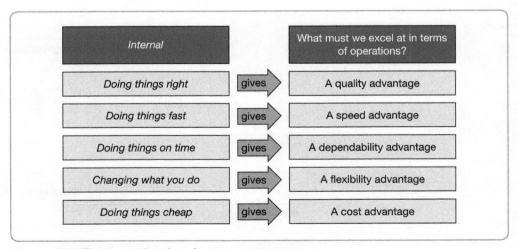

Figure 13.5 Five operational performance measures
Source: Slack N., Chambers A. and Johnston R. (2004) *Operations Management*, 4th edition, Pearson Education Ltd.

As speed and dependability are time-related performance objectives, we discuss them together under the label 'time-based performance'. As cost is related to productivity, we will focus on service productivity.

Quality: doing things right

Service quality and the measurement of service quality has been one of the most researched and discussed topics in service management.

Service quality as perceived by the customer may differ from the quality of the service actually delivered. A patient can be very dissatisfied about a visit to a doctor because he felt that the doctor did not spend enough time communicating the diagnosis of a fatal disease. The patient could not understand how the doctor could take only two minutes to give a life-changing diagnosis. Nonetheless, from a medical point of view, the diagnosis was totally correct. This leads to the distinction between technical quality, or 'what' is perceived by the customer, and 'functional' quality, or 'how' a service is provided:

> 'The latter [functional quality] is the most critical aspect and is concerned with the psychological interaction taking place during the exchange transaction. It is based on the customer's perception and is therefore extremely subjective and encompasses all the cues that the customer picks up during the transaction.'[18]

These cues not only emanate from the server but are also based on perceptions of the whole service environment (*see* Chapter 7). Passengers on the *Titanic* were delighted with the ship's accommodation. If the ship had reached its destination, many passengers would have been satisfied customers. But, as we all know, the ship sank due to the crew's lack of competence in navigating such a large ship through an ocean full of icebergs. If nothing had happened, this lack of competence (an aspect of technical quality) would never have been perceived by the customer. Therefore, it is argued that measuring service quality cannot end with measuring customer satisfaction. Technical quality, which is based on the ability of people and the service system to deliver good (professional) quality, must also be monitored. In the manufacturing industry, monitoring process capability is one of the oldest basic principles of quality management. In the service industry, process capability is considered in a very limited way due to the fact that the variability of processes is taken for granted. Nevertheless, we believe that technical quality is a major issue in many service environments, and we have therefore spent a separate chapter on designing processes (*see* Chapter 4), and have emphasized the role of employees in realizing a service quality experience.

The distinction between customer satisfaction and service quality is a very important one. Service quality is a form of attitude representing a long-run, overall evaluation, whereas satisfaction represents a more short-term, transaction-specific judgement. The level of customer satisfaction is the result of a customer's comparison of the service quality expected in a given service encounter with perceived service quality. This also means that satisfaction assessments require customer experience while quality does not.[19]

Many researchers have tried to discover which dimensions influence the quality, as perceived by the customers. Not only did they try to identify these dimensions, but they also tried to assign relative weights to these dimensions. In an ideal model, the various dimensions should be a *comprehensive set*: it should be possible to explain differences in quality perceptions as a result of differences in one or more quality dimensions. The model should also be *universal* – that is, the various dimensions should be valid, albeit with different weights, across a wide spectrum of services. The dimensions should further be *independent*, or at least measure different aspects of service quality perception. They should also be *homogeneous* and *unambiguous*. Finally, the number of dimensions should be limited.

We have to admit from the start that the ideal model meeting all these criteria does not exist yet; however, we shall describe one model that seems to be widely accepted: the servqual model.

The Servqual model was developed by Parasuraman, Zeithaml and Berry,[20] and has been presented as a service quality measurement instrument. Originally, these researchers listed ten determinants or dimensions of service quality: reliability, responsiveness, competence, access, courtesy, communication, credibility, security, understanding/knowing the customer and tangibles. Exhibit 13.1 defines each of these dimensions and gives some examples. This list was drawn up as a result of focus group studies with service providers and customers. Later, the researchers found a high degree of correlation between communication, competence, courtesy, credibility and security and, therefore, merged them into one dimension, which they called *assurance*. Similarly, they found a high correlation between access and understanding, which they merged into *empathy*.

Exhibit 13.1 Ten components of service quality

1 Reliability involves consistency of performance and dependability. It also means that the firm performs the service right the first time and keeps its promises. Some specific examples it may involve are:
- accuracy in billing;
- performing the service at the designated time.

2 Responsiveness concerns the willingness or readiness of employees to provide service. It may involve:
- mailing a transaction slip immediately;
- calling the customer back quickly;
- giving prompt service (e.g. setting up appointments quickly).

3 Competence means possession of the skills and knowledge required to perform the service. It involves:
- knowledge and skill of the contact personnel;
- knowledge and skill of operational support personnel;
- research capability of the organization.

4 Access involves approachability and ease of contact. It may mean:
- the service is easily accessible by telephone;
- waiting time to receive service is not excessive;
- convenient hours of operation and convenient location of the service facility.

5 Courtesy involves politeness, respect, consideration, and friendliness of contact personnel (including receptionists, telephone operators, etc.) It includes:
- consideration for the customer's property;
- clean and neat appearance of public contact personnel.

6 Communication means keeping customers informed in language they can understand, and listening to them. It may mean that the company has to adjust its language for different customers. It may involve:

- explaining the service itself and how much the service will cost;
- explaining the trade-offs between service and cost;
- assuring the consumer that a problem will be handled.

7 Credibility involves trustworthiness, believability and honesty. It involves having the customer's best interests at heart. Contributing to credibility are:

- company name and reputation;
- personal characteristics of the contact personnel;
- the degree of hard-sell involved in interactions with the customer.

8 Security is the freedom from danger, risk or doubt. It may involve:

- physical safety;
- financial security and confidentiality.

9 Understanding/knowing the customer involves making the effort to understand the customer's needs. It involves:

- learning the customer's specific requirements;
- providing individual attention.

10 Tangibles include the physical evidence of the service:

- physical facilities and appearance of personnel;
- tools or equipment used to provide the service;
- physical representations of the service, such as a plastic credit card.

Source: Buttle, Francis (1996) 'Servqual: review, critique, research agenda', *European Journal of Marketing*, Vol 30, No 1, pp. 8–32.

This has led to the well-known and widely used five dimensions of service quality, the so-called RATER dimensions:

- *Reliability* – consistency of performance and dependability. This means that the firm performs the service correctly the first time and that the firm honours its promises.
- *Assurance* – knowledge and courtesy of employees and their ability to inspire trust and confidence.
- *Tangibles* – the appearance of physical facilities, the personnel, the tools or equipment used to provide the service and communication material.
- *Empathy* – caring, individualized attention to customers.
- *Responsiveness* – the willingness to help the customer and to provide prompt service.

The researchers claimed that the dimensions were sufficiently generic that they could cover a wide spectrum of service sectors.

Since this pioneering work, many others have tried to duplicate these findings in a variety of service settings. Some researchers have confirmed these findings and, therefore, the model; however, most failed to do so. It was particularly difficult to find the same five generic quality dimensions – that is, the various sub-dimensions did not aggregate as in the Parasumaran *et al.* studies. Furthermore, the comprehensiveness of the five dimensions could not always be supported. In other words, it was doubted whether the service quality construct could be composed of five dimensions. One study suggests that the Servqual dimensions are likely to be industry specific.[21]

The criticism voiced of the Servqual dimensions was also related to more fundamental methodological issues and even conceptual issues, such as the presence of conceptual inconsistency in the dimensions. 'Tangibles' and 'responsiveness', for instance, are entirely different concepts. Tangibles are part of the service package but are not a quality dimension. The 'quality' of the tangibles (their appearance, availability, operating characteristics such as comfort, etc.) no doubt influences the perceived quality just as much as the 'quality' of the personnel (their appearance, competence, care, etc.). Like personnel, tangibles are not a quality dimension but an important quality-determining element influencing dimensions such as reliability, credibility and others. Another conceptual problem is related to the homogeneity of the generic dimensions. For instance, it is difficult to understand how 'factors' like courtesy and competence would always correlate and, therefore, be grouped into one category, as they are both such different concepts.[22]

Another important comment about the Servqual tool is that expectations can mean many different things to customers. Customers who have experienced the service in the past believe (predict) what actually will happen in their encounter ('predictive expectations'); other customers expect a minimum level of performance they are willing to accept ('adequate expectations'); still others expect the service to be delivered on a level equal to that of an excellent organization ('excellence expectations'). These different kinds of expectation make it difficult to analyse the Servqual results in an unambiguous way. One outcome of this discussion is the development of 'a performance-only' survey, which only measures perceptions (the so-called Serperf measures).[23] One study, comparing the Servqual and Servperf scales, draws attention to the importance of recognising the most suitable method for a service-specific research question rather than imposing a well-known measurement scale or technique that may not suit the purpose.[24]

Although researchers disagree about the manner in which service quality perceptions should be measured, they seem to agree that service quality is a multi-dimensional higher-order construct comprising several overarching service quality domains such as technical quality, functional quality and environmental quality.[25]

Notwithstanding its many criticisms, the Servqual tool has been adapted to measure service quality in a variety of service settings such as healthcare, retail chains, banks, fast-food restaurants, etc. Exhibit 13.2 shows one example of an adaptation of the Servqual tool to measure service quality in an ambulatory care (outpatient) nuclear medicine clinic.

Exhibit 13.2 Measuring service quality at an outpatient nuclear medicine clinic

A survey comprising 22 questions was taken to measure patients' perception of service quality on a 7-point scale. The survey was based on the original Servqual items. Altogether, 416 patients received the questionnaire, of which 259 were completed and returned (response rate: 62%). Using factor analysis, it became clear that the items could be grouped into five dimensions. Table 13.1[26] shows these dimensions, the different items, and the average and the standard deviation of their scores on the dimensions. Four items were not retained in the analysis due to a large number of missing values.

Table 13.1 The results of a Servqual perception measurement in a nuclear medicine clinic

Item analysis of patients' service quality perception	
Item in each dimension	**Mean and standard deviation (SD) of patients perceptions**
Tangibles-Assurance	
Has up-to-date equipment	5.99 (SD 5 1.04)
Physical facilities are visually appealing	4.88 (SD 5 1.60)
Employees are neat in appearance	6.13 (SD 5 0.91)
Physical facilities in accordance with service	5.17 (SD 5 1.49)
Shows sincere interest in solving your problems	5.99 (SD 5 1.07)
Employees can be trusted	5.95 (SD 5 0.99)
Feels safe in your interaction with employees	6.08 (SD 5 0.93)
Reliability	
When promises to do something, it does so	5.50 (SD 5 1.38)
Provides services at the time it promises	5.35 (SD 5 1.56)
Responsiveness	
Tells you when the services will be performed	4.68 (SD 5 1.88)
Gives prompt services	4.65 (SD 5 1.83)
Personnel is always willing to help	5.77 (SD 5 1.44)
Never too busy to respond to your requests	4.61 (SD 5 1.83)
Empathy	
Gives individual attention	5.01 (SD 5 1.68)
Employees give personal attention	5.35 (SD 5 1.52)
Employees understand your specific needs	5.03 (SD 5 1.57)
Convenience	
Has operating hours convenient to you	5.65 (SD 5 1.41)
Has your best interests at heart	5.90 (SD 5 1.40)
Not included in the analysis	
The personnel perform the service right the first time	
The department keeps its records accurately	
The personnel are consistently courteous	
The personnel get adequate support from the University Hospital	

Source: De Man, Stefanie, Gemmel, Paul, Vlerick, Peter, Van Rijk, Peter and Dierckx, Rudi (2002) 'Patients' and personnel's perceptions of service quality and patient satisfaction in nuclear medicine', *European Journal of Nuclear Medicine and Molecular Imaging*, Vol 29, No 9, p. 1109.

When looking at the results, a first observation is that the dimensions in this study are not the same as in the basic Servqual framework. It is generally accepted that different service environments can generate different service dimensions.

A second observation is that only the perception part of the Servqual was measured. Expectations were deliberately not measured because of considerable disagreement about the added value of measuring expectations when perceptions are already measured.

Patients give the highest score to the tangibles-assurance and convenience dimension. They have the perception that the opening hours are convenient and that employees care about their patients. The lowest scoring items are all situated within the responsiveness dimension. Patients perceive that they do not get prompt service and that they do not know when the service will be performed. One of the problems patients are confronted with in a hospital outpatient clinic is the waiting time. To better serve customers, management needs to pay more attention to the responsiveness dimension.

Productivity: doing things in a cost-effective way

Productivity of an operation measures how effectively input resources in a process are transformed into economic results for the service provider and value for its customers.[27] In a simple way, one can state that productivity is the ratio of output to input. In services, it is difficult to use such a simple productivity concept for the following reasons:[28]

- Services are at least partially intangible, which makes defining, let alone measuring, output much more difficult.

- In many service organizations, there is no one output measure that summarizes the whole activity. The output of a professor at a business school can be measured in terms of number of publications, the number of teaching hours, the quality of the teaching itself, the success of the management training programmes, etc. It is really impossible to reduce these measures to one (financial) output figure. This means that there is no information on how the service process as a whole transforms all used input resources into customer value.

- When the number of students increases in a university programme and the number of teaching staff is not adapted at the same rate, the productivity (as measured by the number of students per teacher) will increase, but this can also have an impact on the perceived quality of the output, including the technical quality (e.g. less time to prepare the courses due to a higher teaching load) and functional quality (e.g. teaching to large groups). Thus, cost-cutting initiatives can have a negative effect on the servicescape and the service process, leading to a deterioration in the perceived service quality, dissatisfied customers and eventually customer defections. In other words, productivity and perceived quality are inseparable phenomena.

- In addition, the presence of the customers in the process brings a couple of challenges in managing productivity. The customer, with his or her specific needs and behaviour, introduces a high level of variability into the service process, which will make reaching uniform productivity standards difficult. Are nurses productive when they provide care to five patients per hour? It depends on the severity of illness of these patients. Even more important, the service productivity frequently depends on how the relationship between the service provider and the customer progresses. The capability of customers to perform well in the service process is increasing the longer they stay in the relationship. This relationship is a mutual learning experience over a longer period of time. If relationships are broken and customers defect, this leads to lower service productivity.[29] This is, of course, the case for service processes where relationships are important such as task-interactive and personal-interactive services.

Based on the previous comments, it is sometimes claimed that quality and productivity cannot be improved at the same time.[30] This is not necessarily true because the quality-productivity trade-off is determined by (1) the utilization level of the available capacity and (2) the variability of demand and supply. If a service organization is working near or at full capacity, an increase in service productivity will lead to a higher work pressure, a decreased responsiveness (e.g. longer waiting times) and eventually less reliability (not being able to serve on time) or more errors; in other words, an erosion of service quality. In this situation, the quality-productivity trade-off is reinforced when there is a lot of variability in the arrival and service process (*see also* Chapter 4). One of the strategies to break this trade-off is to reduce the variability, although this is more difficult in services than in manufacturing.

The absence of one summary and absolute productivity standard in most services has lead to the development of new techniques to measure productivity. Several service organizations such as banks are working with multiple service units (branches) that are comparable in terms of productivity and efficiency. This allows these service firms to compare or benchmark the performance of one service unit with another. The requirement of working with multiple output measures (and eventually multiple input measures) in such benchmarking has created new techniques for relative efficiency benchmarking such as Data Envelopment Analysis (DEA). DEA is a linear-programming-based technique that allows us to rank service units in terms of performance by comparing several output and input measures simultaneously. In Technical note 5, we further discuss DEA and introduce an example.

In general, service firms have an advantage over manufacturing firms when performing internal efficiency benchmarking because they have a much larger network of service delivery sites. DEA is a very popular tool for internal and external efficiency benchmarking in multi-site service environments, which are confronted with multiple inputs and outputs.[31] Examples of such environments are banks, hospitals, courts and university departments.

The conclusion is that measuring productivity is more problematic and complex in a service environment than in manufacturing. Nevertheless, it is obvious that they should still be measured. Service productivity cannot be left out of an integrated performance measurement system.

Time-based performance: doing things fast and on time

Throughput time is an important performance measure, as the speed with which the service is delivered determines the competitive position of the service firm. It is *the* measure of, for example, fast-food restaurants and exhaust repair centres, but sectors like insurance companies, financial institutions, airline companies or even consulting firms can also gain competitive advantage, if they can provide a short 'delivery time'. At the airport, Ryanair is able to turn around its planes in an average of 25 minutes, which is twice as fast than more traditional airline companies. This short turn-around time increases the number of flight hours and, thus, revenue. In field services, the time to respond to a request for service when a machine breaks down determines the downtime and, thus, lost revenue for the customer.

There are some particular developments in the service sector that make short throughput time one of the basic needs of many customers:[32]

- Customers want to be served at the time and place, and in the way they prefer. Technologies such as PC banking make it possible for today's customers to be served at whatever time (and place) they prefer. Customers are becoming 'nomads in time and space'.

- At the same time, customers increasingly ask for fast responsiveness in the service delivery. Fast responsiveness does not necessarily mean that the service must be delivered immediately but that a 'time contract' is made with the customer, indicating the time by which the service must be delivered. Many examples of these 'time contracts' can be found in service level agreements (*see* Chapter 14), stating in what time frame the repair of a machine will be performed.

- Service firms are increasingly required to be permanently available for the customer. Computer firms, for instance, sell back-up room capacity to customers. If the computer system in the customer's firm fails, the customer can immediately be installed in these back-up rooms and can continue their activities.

The role of employees changes completely in these time-based service delivery environments. Managing the customer contact time becomes a major point of attention in the service delivery. Managing the customer contact time includes the following action points:[33]

- making waiting times as short as possible;
- measuring time from the customer's point of view;
- defining a service contract (guarantee or agreement) in terms of time performance (*see* Chapter 14);
- indicating what the payout will be if the firm is not able to keep the promise in the service contract;
- matching opening hours to the times customers are able to visit the service firm;
- giving some extra attention to the first and the last contact point in the service delivery;
- matching the level of service delivery to the customer requirements;
- paying attention to who accompanies the customer during the service delivery;
- anticipating defects in the service delivery process;
- guaranteeing that every moment in the service process is perceived by the customer as a quality experience.

As a result, lead time or delivery time can be included as an element of quality. However, even if the customers are not aware of or do not value short throughput times, it might be worthwhile measuring the throughput time of the processes or, more specifically, the ratio between the sum of the operating times of the steps in the process that really add value to the total time spent in the process. A ratio of less than 1% is not rare, as was the case with an insurance company where the actual time it took to process a life insurance policy was 10 days, of which only 7 minutes (= 0.16%) was actual added value time. The rest was (mainly) waiting time, transportation time, time necessary to inspect somebody's work, etc. According to the theory of time-based competition, reducing the throughput time will help companies to simultaneously:[34]

1 reduce costs;
2 improve quality dependability;
3 increase flexibility;
4 improve delivery dependability;
5 improve innovativeness by shortening the time to market for new products.

Throughput time appears, therefore, to be a universal measure encompassing a number of performance criteria. One of them is dependability, i.e. delivery at an agreed place and time, or when and where promised. Dependability is related to reliability, which is one of the most important service quality dimensions. Exhibit 13.3 shows the impact of train delays on the image (and thus branding) of a service company.

Exhibit 13.3 The punctual Belgian customer no longer trusts the train

Only one out of ten Belgian customers judge the train to be the most reliable means of transport for arriving on time at their destination. 50% prefer the car, and 30% consider the plane as the most punctual means of transport. 'Being on time' is the most important reason for 87% of respondents choosing a certain means of transport (*see* Figure 13.6).[35]

The national Belgian railway company, SNCB, received many complaints about the delays. In 2010, the company paid out €488,000 in compensation to passengers who had experienced considerable delays.[36] Some customers really become frustrated with the unpunctual performance of this railway company. On 16 September 2011, some train passengers in a local railway station became so angry over the continuous problems with the train they took to their work daily that they obstructed the rail tracks to force another train to stop and to take them to their destination. One of these passengers testified: 'I have a very good job, I like my work, but I have stress every day when I take the train'.[37] One can imagine that this kind of testimonial on national television does not contribute in a positive way to the 'service branding' and reputation of the railway company. The issue of delay and the poor time-based performance leads to the perception that the railway company is an unreliable service organization, and many customers no longer trust the railway company. The key performance indicator that customers are looking at is the 'on time arrival and departure' of the trains.

Another television programme investigated the causes of these delays.[38] The most important causes are related to the infrastructure and the capacity of the railway company. During the last couple of years, the railway company has not invested enough in the train infrastructure, leading to the breakdown of trains or problems with the railway tracks. This ageing infrastructure is faced with a more intensive usage due to increased demand. To serve this higher volume of passengers, the railway company continues to use trains that are sometimes more than 40 years old.

Figure 13.6 Customer evaluation of most dependable means of transport in Belgium

Source: Study of OIVO on Mobility (OIVO = Onderzoeks- en Informatiecentrum van de Verbruikersorganisaties; Research and Information Center of the Consumer Organisations), September 2011.

Flexibility: changing what you do

Flexibility is the ability to change the service operations in some way to adjust to the change or take into account a new situation.[39] There are different types of operational flexibility.[40] To reduce the time passengers spent at check-in, customs and security, airport authorities are considering technologies such as biometrics. These authorities are able to introduce new services as the opportunity or need arises and show some degree of *service flexibility*. Being able to offer a wide range of in-flight services (such as a choice of film and audio programmes, bar, shops) to fulfill the needs of customers from different segments is an example of *mix flexibility*. Due to unexpected higher demands, airline companies must be able to schedule extra trips and deploy additional transport capacity when the need arises. This is an example of *volume flexibility*. A last type of flexibility is *delivery flexibility*. Airline companies must be able to cope with late arrivals and other delays due to bad weather and technical problems. In some cases, the turn-around time and the boarding processes for the next trips must be speeded up.

The different types of operational flexibility can be considered as part of a larger strategy to keep up with the fast pace of change at the level of technology and customer demands. In this way, it contributes to the competitive position of service organizations as is illustrated in the following statement:

> 'Imagine an airline that uses scans of fingerprints and faces to allow travelers to breeze through check-in, customs, security and boarding in under 60 seconds and automatically get seat assignments based on their preferences. Who wouldn't choose that carrier over its competitors?'[41]

Firms that are able to combine speed and flexibility have been labelled as '*agile*'. An agile firm should design its organization, processes and services in order to quickly respond to changes within a useful time frame.[42] The railway company in Exhibit 13.3 is an example of a service firm that is not agile. In contrast, Zara, a Spanish clothing and accessories retailer based in Arteixo, Galicia has been able to gain competitive advantage in the fashion industry by adopting an agile strategy (*see* Exhibit 13.4).

Exhibit 13.4 Agility in the fashion industry[43]

The curse of the fashion industry is the time lag between the design of new clothes and their delivery to the shop floor. When a designer puts pencil to paper to create, say, a new skirt, he or she is in effect predicting what the customer will want in 6–9 months' time.

That kind of prescience is hard enough in most industries, and it is particularly painful in the fickle world of fashion. Even the most successful companies regularly get it wrong and end up with enormous amounts of unsold inventory, which they have to either mark down or send off to their outlet stores, reducing return on investment.

Zara was founded on an entirely different business process. Based in La Coruna, in Galacia, Spain, Zara owns and operates 14 highly automated factories where robots stamp, cut and dye fabrics 24 hours a day, based on the CAD-driven output of their Spanish design rooms. Its turnaround time from design to shop floor is 2 weeks.

Every store manager in each of the 2600+ Zara outlets worldwide has a handheld device that is used to tell the designers what is selling, what is not, and what customers are looking for but not finding. That information, together with other input about current popular trends, means that Zara can react at very short notice to its customers' needs.

Instead of sticking to the industry standard of seasonal deliveries, Zara outlets receive twice-weekly deliveries from La Coruna. If there is a hot new look on the fashion catwalks at the moment, chances are that Zara has an affordable version in its stores now.

Integrating the different performance measures

In the previous paragraphs, we identified many different performance measures related to employees, customers and operational capabilities. As already indicated at the start of this chapter, integrated performance measurement means that these different perform-ance measures are looked at simultaneously, and greater insight is obtained into the relationship between these different performance measures. Although the service profit chain gives a conceptual model of the relationship between performance measures such as employee satisfaction, value, and customer satisfaction, operationalization of each of the conceptual performance measures is necessary to really get an integrated view of a particular service organization. Table 13.2 shows how this operationalization is carried out for a bank.

The next challenge is to collect data on each of the performance measures in Table 13.2. Having a large sample data set encompassing all of these measures, from internal service quality to financial performance, is the main obstacle to integrated performance measure-ment allowing the relationships between these performance measures to be seen. Some empirical studies tested the link between performance measures, carried out in different service environments such as after-sales services and banking. For instance, one of these studies links survey-based customer satisfaction, service quality, and share-of-wallet meas-ures to longitudinal data on two outcome variables – customer retention and customer profitability – gathered from a financial services company's internal records.[44] Another study in the after-sales industry linked measures of role conflict, role ambiguity, job satisfac-tion, service quality (functional and technical), customer satisfaction, affective and calcula-tive customer commitment, and the intention to stay.[45]

The importance of the different performance measures depends on the kind of services delivered. The value of personal-interactive services is generally higher than for maintenance-interactive services. This means that customers are more willing to wait for the former than for the latter or, in other words, that personal-interactive services are less time-sensitive than maintenance-interactive services.

In maintenance-interactive services, productivity is a major issue. Better productivity is considered to be positively correlated with better quality. In these service environments, internal benchmarking studies using DEA are well accepted. The relationship between productivity and quality in task-interactive and personal-interactive services is much less clear. Higher nursing productivity in terms of number of patients treated per hour can lead to lower service quality because nurses no longer have enough time for each patient. In personal-interactive services, the productivity of knowledge can be considered the major challenge of the next century.

Once the service concept has been translated into very concrete performance measures, as in Table 13.2, it can be implemented through the introduction of an integrated and balanced performance measurement system.

Table 13.2 An integrated set of performance measures and their operationalization for a bank[46]

Conceptual performance measure	Subcategory	Operationalization
Profitability measures		Revenue per full-time equivalent per household
		Revenue per household
Customer loyalty measures	Checking retention	Number of customers with cheque accounts who stayed with the bank from year 1 to year 2
		Percentage change in the number of customers with cheque accounts who stayed with the bank from year 1 to year 2
	Deposit retention	Number of customers with deposits who stayed with the bank from year 1 to year 2
		Percentage change in the number of customers with deposits who stayed with the bank from year 1 to year 2
	Average investable assets	Average percentage of customer investable assets held at the bank
		Percentage change in the average percentage of customer investable assets held at the bank from year 1 to year 2
	Cross-sell	Average number of services purchase per household
Customer satisfaction measures		Percentage change in the average number of services purchased per household (year 1 to year 2)
		% ranking branch 6 or 7 (on a scale from 1 to 7)
		% ranking bank 6 or 7
		Average branch rating
		Average bank rating
Employee loyalty measures		Manager full-time average service months
		Average employee tenure (years)
		Percent of employees surveyed who are 'committed to regional's success'
		Ratio of employees surveyed who would 'leave if offered same pay elsewhere'
Employee satisfaction measures		Average of responses to 'how would you rate this organization as a place to work?'
		Average of responses to 'how would you rate your job – the type of work you do?'
Internal service quality (percent of employees rating bank a 6 or 7 in the following categories)		Communications
		Teamwork
		Training
		Reward/opportunity
		Available resources to perform job well
		Top corporate management
		Business line management
		Geographic market management
		Immediate supervisor

Source: Based on Loveman, G. W. (1998) 'Employee satisfaction, customer loyalty and financial performance: an empirical examination of the service profit chain in retail banking', *Journal of Service Research*, Vol 1, No 1, pp. 18–31.

Implementing an integrated performance measurement system

Figure 13.7 shows the steps involved in implementing an integrated and balanced performance measurement system.[47] We shall now discuss each of these steps in greater detail.

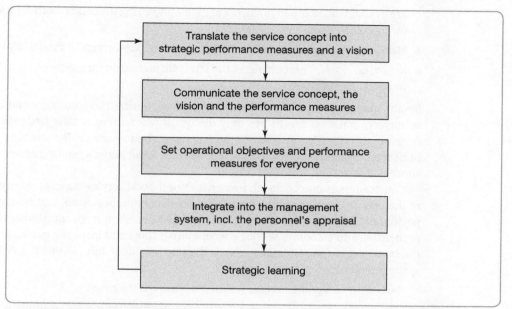

Figure 13.7 **The implementation process of a performance measurement system**

◼ Step 1 Defining the service concept in actionable terms

The first challenge is to make the service concept actionable. This is particularly relevant if the service concept is rather general in its wording. If this is the case, there is ample room for interpretation, which may result in ambiguity and differences of opinion as to what the service concept actually means. It also makes it difficult to judge to what degree the organization is delivering the service concept and thereby achieving its strategic goals.[48]

It is of key importance, therefore, that senior management selects a limited number of *strategic performance measures*. If all senior managers are committed to the same goals and measures, they are ready to deploy the service concept throughout the organization.

A fine example of this approach is the management accounting system at Rank Xerox, the first winner of the EFQM award. Rank Xerox states that customer and employee satisfaction enables the company to increase market share, which drives the financial results. The company's balanced scorecard consists of four strategic performance measures:

● *Personnel satisfaction*. Rank Xerox surveys its staff annually on their overall satisfaction. A total of 110 questions measure, among other things, the employees' relationship with their superiors and their peers, and satisfaction with their wages and salaries. The anonymous survey is mailed to the home address of the white-collar workers and achieves a response rate of about 80%. The blue-collar workers fill out the survey during working hours – for instance, in the dining hall – so that the response rate is close to 100%.

● *Customer satisfaction*. Rank Xerox mails a customer-satisfaction questionnaire to its customers and gathers the responses by telephone. This combines the completeness of a written survey with the high response rate of a telephone survey. The measurement is executed by an independent research agency on behalf of Rank Xerox. Satisfaction data are available for a broad range of customer impacting processes, both for Rank Xerox and for its competitors.

- *Market share.* This is considered to be one of the key drivers of profitability.
- *Return on assets.* This completes the strategic management control system by adding the financial perspective.

Senior management at Rank Xerox stress that, during their visits to middle and junior managers, 'business results are only discussed when there is time left'. Absolute priority is given to customer satisfaction and personnel satisfaction. By stressing the strategic performance measures, while coaching its staff, Rank Xerox's senior management turns its strategy into action.

Conciseness is one of the characteristics of a good service concept. Many formulations of the service concept are too long to be easily communicated to, and remembered by, all personnel. Therefore, many organizations have benefited from translating the more comprehensive and elaborate service concept into a short and inspiring *vision*. Probably one of the strongest vision statements ever is the late president John Kennedy's vision for the US space programme:

'Before the turn of the decade, we will put a man on the moon.'

Similar examples are abundant in service organizations. One example is DHL's service concept:

'DHL will become the acknowledged global leader in the express delivery of documents and packages.'

Although this message was not a lengthy one, DHL learned that it was not easy to convey it to all employees. Consequently, DHL crafted a simple yet very clear time-driven vision:

'To achieve 100% next-day delivery.'

Once everyone agrees on what is essentially meant by the vision, the organization is ready to kick off its internal communication effort, which is the second step in implementing customer focus.

Step 2 Communicating the service concept, the performance measures and the vision

As part of a customer-focus programme, a major airline decided to empower its cabin crew to distribute money for dry cleaning whenever food or drinks were spilled accidentally on a passenger's clothes during a flight.[49] The objective of the empowerment exercise was twofold:

1 The airline wanted to retain customers who might otherwise be dissatisfied. The compensation for the damages would minimize the customer's hassle and consequently might create some goodwill.

2 The initiative was conceived as a means of communicating to all staff that customer satisfaction and retention was a major priority. Staff had to realize that the old days of filing formal service recovery requests were over: whenever the airline made an error, it would try to make it up to its customers.

The first time one of the crew members actually paid a passenger for dry cleaning, she obviously had to hand in the passenger's receipt. The manager accepting the receipt killed the initiative by asking one simple question:

'Was there any way you could have avoided paying the compensation?'

This example illustrates the key role of middle management in any customer focus initiative. No matter how much an organization invests in internal communication efforts, eventually it is the immediate supervisors who will give a concrete meaning to whatever message is being communicated to their subordinates.

Experience has taught us time and time again that middle managers can make or break any programme. If middle managers are committed to the service concept and vision, they will set an example by communicating and supporting it through junior management to all personnel. However, if they disapprove of the concept or do not clearly understand what is actually meant by it, they will convey the wrong message to junior management, both in their deeds and in their words. In these circumstances, middle management functions as a terrorist squad fighting a guerrilla war from the inside.

Middle management's role is particularly vital in geographically decentralized organizations, with a high personnel turnover and a high percentage of low-skilled and/or part-time workers. The important role of middle management is clearly illustrated in the case of Belgium's leading fast-food chain of hamburger restaurants, Quick (*see* Exhibit 13.5).

Exhibit 13.5 'Living the vision' at Quick

The vast majority of the staff of Quick are part-timers – for instance, students trying to earn extra money. Thus, the contact personnel consider working in a Quick restaurant to be a temporary job rather than a career. This situation confronts Quick's management with the major challenge of creating a feeling of belonging among these employees. Investing heavily in training and internal communication targeted at the part-timers is not a solution because of the high personnel turnover rate: too many employees leave the organization before the investments start to pay off.

Quick recognizes the key role of its middle management and, therefore, focuses its internal communication on its restaurant managers. The underlying hypothesis is that the manager should fully understand and be committed to the Quick organization's service concept and culture. Managers will thus act according to Quick's service strategy and communicate its meaning to its staff on the job. By 'living the vision', they act as role models for all other employees and have made an important contribution to Quick's overwhelming success.

● Step 3 Set operational performance measures for everyone

With the exception of senior management, employees do not perceive themselves as having any impact on or direct responsibility for the strategic performance measures, as defined in the organization's balanced scorecard. Operational objectives that are in line with the strategic objectives should, therefore, be set for each individual and/or team. The resulting *personal scorecards*[50] complement the strategic balanced scorecards.

In developing these personal scorecards, it is recommended that the organization's key priorities are defined. Deploying these priorities from the top down, while developing the personal scorecards from the bottom up, means that all efforts are integrated into the organization's endeavour to implement its strategy.

We will first discuss the personal scorecard and then the importance of setting priorities.

The personal scorecard

A balanced scorecard, containing the organization's strategic performance measures, helps top management to monitor the degree to which it is achieving its goals and objectives. All other employees in the organization cannot be held responsible for reaching those goals, as they only have a minor impact on the organization's processes and output. Overall, the lower one is in the hierarchy, the less one's involvement is with comprehensive performance measures.

That is why leading companies invite all their staff to translate those strategic performance measures into their own operational performance measures. All employees have to specify what actions they will undertake to help the organization reach its goals. The actions have to be linked to quantifiable objectives, deadlines and performance measures.

This process is called *policy deployment* (also referred to as *management by objectives* (MBO)).[51] Again, Rank Xerox provides us with a good example. As mentioned earlier, the company uses four strategic performance measures: customer satisfaction, employee satisfaction, market share, and return on assets. These measures also function as the key indicators of senior management's performance, as they can and should be held responsible for how well the organization is doing. In the case of individual employees, however, it is difficult for them to see how their performance is linked to Rank Xerox's overall performance measures. Yet this overall performance depends entirely on the effort of all individuals. The challenge is to integrate all these efforts.

That is why each individual or team within Rank Xerox is invited to work out for themselves how they can contribute to the overall strategic objectives. They have to devise their own action plans, their own objectives and their own performance measures (*see* Figure 13.8).

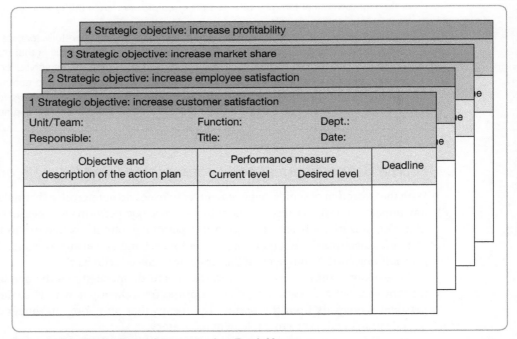

Figure 13.8 The balanced scorecard at Rank Xerox

For instance, a manager whose direct subordinates' satisfaction falls below average can set up an action plan that should result in the increased satisfaction of his own staff. The manager will be held responsible for achieving his own objective and not for the organization's overall employee satisfaction.

Setting priorities

The policy deployment process yields the highest results when the action plans are developed in line with set priorities. These priorities are determined top-down, whereby each manager sets his priorities in line with those of his direct supervisor. Top management sets the strategic priorities and then the priorities are cascaded down the organization, developing priorities for each level. Rank Xerox strongly believes that focus on the 'vital few' priorities is far more desirable than diluting the efforts by working on the 'useful many'.

Setting these priorities has a double integrating effect:

- *Horizontally*. All people working at the same level within the organization have to confer with one another when setting their own priorities. Their supervisors can function as moderators. Thus, all priorities at a single level are integrated.

- *Vertically*. Each manager is making sure that his subordinates set priorities in line with his own. Thus, the cascading process guarantees that all set priorities are in line with the vital few strategic priorities of top management.

Furthermore, the top-down approach allows for both process improvement and process re-design (*see* Chapter 4). If the approach were bottom-up, re-design would be almost impossible within the policy deployment effort. Indeed, in a bottom-up situation, every manager or team at the lowest level would come up with projects aimed at improving their own processes according to the Kaizen philosophy of continuous improvement, excluding projects that go beyond the scope of one single team or manager. With the top-down approach, however, any manager can decide whether he considers a re-engineering effort desirable for the group of processes for which he is responsible or whether he wants to leave it up to the managers below him to work independently on the sub-processes for which they are responsible.

In this stage of setting priorities for both process improvements and process re-design, the framework incorporating five performance objectives (quality, cost, speed, dependability and flexibility), which has been introduced earlier in this chapter, can be useful in evaluating the efforts and changes.

If setting the priorities is basically a top-down effort, developing concrete action plans should be more of a bottom-up process. The involvement of employees largely depends on the degree of freedom they are given to conceive their own actions, performance measures and objectives. It is extremely important in a professional service environment to ensure that a balance can be found between the personal development plans and the set priorities.

Not setting priorities can only be justified when the policy deployment technique has just been introduced. At that point in time, the first objective is to mobilize energy, so that everyone becomes involved in designing and implementing action plans. To maximize the chances of success, employees are simply invited to participate, without being steered towards set priorities. It is only after employees have mastered the philosophy and practice of policy deployment, that vital few priorities are used to focus the individual action plans on the implementation of the strategy.

Step 4 Integrate the personal scorecards into the management system

All too often organizations are reluctant to change the way they evaluate their staff. The internal communication programme, sometimes strengthened by the policy deployment effort, stresses customer satisfaction and customer focus as the number one priority. Yet, at the same time, the old criteria for appraising staff are being used; as a result ambiguous signals are being sent out.

In the last decade, several car manufacturers have developed customer-focus initiatives, resulting in kick-off meetings, training efforts and other types of internal communication efforts as well as extensive customer satisfaction surveys. The letter accompanying the survey of one manufacturer stated:

> 'In the 1990s it is no longer sufficient to build excellent cars. Customers expect outstanding service from their dealers.'

As a general rule, manufacturers trained their regional dealer supervisors to coach the dealers in analysing and using the customer satisfaction results. The objective was to encourage dealers to start service quality improvement projects in order to increase customer satisfaction.

Many car manufacturers learned the hard way that not adjusting the appraisal system undermined customer satisfaction efforts. The further use of sales volumes as the key strategic performance measure and of promotions in an attempt to boost sales volume lead to a focus on short-term sales results, at the expense of long-term customer satisfaction. One car manufacturer learned, for instance, that customers were extremely disappointed with the attention they received when their new car was delivered. Before the signing of the sales contract, the sales people gave them the royal treatment. They wanted to close a deal because their bonus depended on it. However, when the customers came to collect their new cars several weeks later, the person who had sold the car hardly paid them any attention at all whilst giving the royal treatment to a new prospect.

Time and again, it has been proven that companies have to change their personnel appraisal system so that it reflects the emphasis on customer satisfaction. Otherwise, they may become entangled in the 'what's it gonna be this year' syndrome, in which top management regularly launches a new programme, which employees perceive as the latest in a long line. They do not change their behaviour, as they think the newly launched programme will not last.

By changing the appraisal system, management can prove they means business, but it is obvious that people will only start adjusting their behaviour if their financial and non-financial rewards are linked to the strategic performance measures and to the personal scorecards. Although this is the objective, there is an important danger inherent in this approach. People will now alter their behaviour in order to obtain a positive appraisal. If the criteria are not correct, the outcome can be disastrous.

The biggest danger is that the criteria used to appraise people are wrong – either the strategic direction is wrong, or the set objectives are not in line with the strategy. In both cases, the consequences can be dramatic.

A more common problem is that the criteria are correct but not in balance. Companies can become customer obsessed instead of customer focused. Secretaries who can earn a bonus by improving their responsiveness on the telephone may end up picking up the telephone very quickly but can perform less well in all other aspects.

Step 5 Strategic learning

A final step in implementing the service concept consists of the systematic analysis of the relationship between the various performance measures. This process of strategic learning allows the organization to assess the soundness of the strategy and to optimize the chosen path. A company can try to improve its understanding of the relationship between each of these elements:

- Does improved employee satisfaction result in higher productivity, lower staff turnover and higher customer satisfaction?
- Does improved customer satisfaction result in less attrition, more retention and more referrals?
- Do improved employee satisfaction and customer satisfaction result in more revenue and lower costs, and consequently in better business results?
- How strong are these relationships?

In a study in the Netherlands on the role of after-sales services in developing relationships with customers of a large office equipment firm,[52] it was found that technical quality (the quality of the end result, i.e. repairing the machine properly) has a direct effect on affective commitment, but that the functional quality (i.e. the quality of the process, the way in which it happens) has an indirect effect on affective commitment through customer satisfaction. So the way that the field engineer interacts with the customer has an impact on satisfaction, as well as on commitment and thus on customer retention.

In the same study, the authors also tried to find the elements explaining customer perceptions of quality. High role conflict and high role ambiguity lead to lower job satisfaction for the employee and thus to lower quality. Role conflict means that the expectations of management are different from the expectations of customers. The field engineer is confronted with this clash. For example, a superior might expect a service employee to serve as many customers as possible, while each of those customers is demanding personal attention. Role ambiguity occurs when a person does not have access to sufficient information to perform his or her role as a service employee adequately.

The relationship between the personal scorecards and the balanced scorecard should be monitored. If all employees implement their action plans and meet their objectives – for instance, regarding the improvement of customer satisfaction – does overall customer satisfaction go up?

These analyses will help organizations to adjust their priorities and to fine-tune the set strategy. Calculating the results of improvement projects becomes possible.

Exhibit 13.6 Performance measurement at G-Mart (continued)

John Brown had spent a great deal of time thinking about his three years as CEO at G-Mart. He was beginning to understand what had gone wrong. The programme had started pretty well, as all employees had a strong feeling of urgency. Furthermore, the chosen strategy had been the right one. Through internal communication he had convinced all staff that delivering world-class service was the only way to regain momentum.

Where he had failed was in setting up a system to improve the service according to clearly defined priorities. In his eagerness to regain market share, he had only discussed sales figures, turnover, number of transactions conducted, and market share with his subordinates. They had repeated the same message to their people. Eventually, G-Mart became a sales-driven organization. The customer who either wanted a low price or a good service was receiving neither.

Obviously, customer satisfaction had gone up, because dissatisfied customers simply stopped doing business with G-Mart. The remaining customers seemed to be happy doing their shopping with G-Mart, but their numbers decreased.

Eventually, employees who had had their expectations raised – probably too high – saw no real improvement, so that the initial motivation and overwhelming energy turned against John Brown and G-Mart. The resulting strikes scared off the customers and finally resulted in his resignation.

He now knew what had gone wrong: his approach had been built on enthusiasm, but it had lacked an integrating system to direct the mobilized energy to the set goals.

Conclusion

The requirements of integration and balance in designing a performance measurement system for services form the basis of most of the content of this book: operations, marketing and human resources cannot be separated from each other in managing services. They are the components that make up the engine of a ship and are given orientation by a compass – that is, the service concept. To monitor the performance of the engine, it is important to have multiple indicators looking at it from different perspectives. We have also made clear that it is not enough to have a compass. It must be used to move the ship in the right direction. We therefore need a captain and a crew. If they do not understand the ship, or do not know what the ultimate destination is, the ship will not proceed in an efficient and qualitative way. The motivation of people and the alignment of their personal scorecard with the organization's balanced scorecard are crucial in implementing the service concept. The service concept must therefore be communicated in a straightforward way and attention must be paid to the system of personnel appraisal; these are the most important steps in the implementation of an integrated and balanced performance measurement system.

Review and discussion questions

- What are the similarities and the differences between integrated performance models such as the BSC and the EFQM Excellence model?
- Servqual has been used in many different sectors to measure service quality. Find in the literature a study describing the use and the results of Servqual in a certain service context. How did the study use SERVQUAL (expectations, perceptions, gaps, importance etc.)? What kind of 'service quality dimensions' were recognized? What were the (managerial) results of the study?

- DEA has been used in many different sectors to measure service efficiency. Find in the literature a study describing the use and the results of DEA in a certain service context. What kinds of input- and output variables were included in this study? What were the managerial lessons? What were the advantages and disadvantages of this DEA method?

- How can a service manager break the trade-off between service quality and service productivity?

- In Exhibit 13.3, we described the failure of the Belgian railway company to run its trains on time. This leads to dissatisfied customers. Employees are confronted with complaining and angry customers. This produces job stress and lowers motivation. How can this company get out of the cycle of failure?

- Is it possible for firms in the service business to develop organizational capabilities in such a way that they have an excellent performance in each of the operational measures (quality, productivity, time-based performance, and flexibility). Why or why not?

- What is the importance of a service concept in the implementation of an integrated performance measurement system?

Technical Note

Technical notes 3, 4 and 5 relate to this chapter. They describe in more detail the techniques of setting-up a complaint management system, customer satisfaction measurement and Data Envelopment Analysis.

Suggested further reading

Kossman, Mario (2006) *Delivering Excellent Service Quality in Aviation: A Practical Guide for Internal and External Service Providers.* Ashgate Publishing Limited, 192 pp

Schneider, Benjamin and White, Susan S. (2004) *Service Quality: Research Perspectives.* Thousand Oaks, CA: Sage, 185 pp

Sherman, H. David and Zhu, Joe (2006) *Service Productivity Management: Improving Service Performance Using Data Envelopment Analysis* (DEA). Springer, 328 pp

Notes and references

1 Bruggeman, W., Bartholomeeusen, L. and Heene, A. (1988) 'How management control systems can affect the performance of service operations', *International Journal of Operations and Production Management*, Vol 8, No 3

2 Kaplan, R. S. and Norton, D. P. (1993) 'Putting the balanced scorecard to work', *Harvard Business Review*, Sep–Oct, pp. 134–147

3 *See* the following articles and books of Kaplan, R. S. and Norton, D. P. (1992) 'The balanced scorecard – measures that drive performance', *Harvard Business Review*, Jan–Feb, pp. 71–79; (1993) 'Putting the balanced scorecard to work', *Harvard Business Review*, Sep–Oct, pp. 134–147; (1996a) 'Using the balanced

scorecard as a strategic management system', *Harvard Business Review*, Jan–Feb, pp. 75–85; (1996b) *The Balanced Scorecard: Translating strategy into action*. Boston, MA: Harvard Business School Press; (1996c) 'Linking the balanced scorecard to strategy', *California Management Review*, Vol 39, No 1, Fall, pp. 53–79

4 Based on Griffith, J. R., Sahney, V. K. and Mohr, R. A. (1995) *Re-engineering Health Care: Building on CQI*. Ann Arbor, MI: Health Administration Press

5 Kaplan, R. S. and Norton, D. P. (2001) 'Building a Strategy-Focused Organisation', *Ivey Business Journal*, Vol 65, No 5, May–June, pp. 12–19

6 EFQM Excellence Model, October 2012

7 European Foundation for Quality Management, 1999

8 Porter, L. J. and Tanner, S. J. (1996) *Assessing Business Excellence – A guide to self-assessment*. Oxford: Butterworth-Heinemann

9 Drucker, P. F. (1999) 'Knowledge Worker Productivity: The Bigger Challenge', *California Management Review*, Vol 41, No 2, pp. 79–94

10 Ibid.

11 Readers interested in job satisfaction scales that were developed rigorously and according to scientific standards are referred to Miller, D. (1991) *Handbook of Research Design and Social Measurement*. Sage; as well as Ferry, D. and Van de Ven, A. (1979) *Measuring and Assessing Organisations*. New York, NY: John Wiley

12 Relevant references for assessing levels of empowerment are Spreitzer (1996) and Van Looy *et al.* (1998b). *See* Spreitzer, G. (1996) 'Social structural characteristics of psychological empowerment', *Academy of Management Journal*, Vol 39, No 2, pp. 483–504; Van Looy, B., Desmet, S., Krols, K. and Van Dierdonck, R. (1998b) 'Psychological empowerment in a service environment', in Swartz, T., Bowen, D. and Brown, S. (eds) *Advances in Services Marketing and Management*, Vol 7. Greenwich, CT: JAI Press

13 Meyer, J. P. and Allen, N. J. (1991) 'A three-component conceptualization of organizational commitment', *Human Resource Management Review*, 1, pp. 61–89; Meyer, J. P., Allen, N. J. and Smith, C. A. (1993) 'Commitment to organizations and occupations – extension and test of a 3-component conceptualization', *Journal of Applied Psychology*, Vol 78, No 4, pp. 538–551

14 For an excellent overview of the concept 'organizational commitment', we refer to Klein, Howard J., Thomas E. Becker and John P. Meyer (2009), *Commitment in Organizations: Accumulated Wisdom and New Directions* (1st edn), New York, NY: Routledge, Taylor & Francis Group

15 Caruana, A., Money, A. H. and Berthon, P. R. (2000) 'Service quality and satisfaction – the moderating role of value', *European Journal of Marketing*, Vol 34, No 11/1, pp. 1338–1353

16 Ibid.

17 Slack, N., Chambers, A., Johnston, R. (2004) *Operations Management*. London: Pearson Education

18 Ibid.

19 Caruana, A. *et al.* (2000), op. cit.

20 Parasuraman, A., Zeithaml, V. A. and Berry, L. L. (1985) 'A conceptual model of service quality and implications for further research', *Journal of Marketing*, Vol 49, Fall, pp. 45–50; and Parasuraman, A., Zeithaml, V. A. and Berry, L. L. (1988) 'Servqual: A multiple item scale for measuring consumer perceptions of service quality', *Journal of Retailing*, Spring, pp. 22–40

21 Asubonteng, P., McCleary, K. J. and Swan, J. E. (1996) 'SERVQUAL revisited: a critical review of service quality', *The Journal of Services Marketing*, Vol 10, No 6, pp. 62–81

22 For a further critical review of Servqual, *see* Buttle, F. (1996) 'Servqual: review, critique, research agenda', *European Journal of Marketing*, Vol 30, No 1, pp. 8–32

23 Cronin, J. Joseph and Steven A. Taylor (1994) 'SERVPERF versus SERVQUAL: Reconciling Performance-based and Perceptions-minus-expectations Measurements of Service Quality', *Journal of Marketing*, 58 (January), pp. 125–131

24 Gilmore, A. and McMullan, R. (2009) 'Scales in services marketing research: a critique and way forward', *European Journal of Marketing*, Vol 43, No 5–6, pp. 640–651

25 Dagger, T. S., Sweeney, J. C. and Johnson, L. W. (2007) 'A Hierarchical Model of Health Service Quality: Scale Development and Investigation of an Integrated Model', *Journal of Service Research*, Vol 10, No 2, pp. 123–142

26 De Man, Stefanie, Gemmel, Paul, Vlerick, Peter, Van Rijk, Peter and Dierckx, Rudi (2002) 'Patients and personnel's perceptions of service quality and patient satisfaction in nuclear medicine', *European Journal of Nuclear Medicine and Molecular Imaging*, Vol 29, No 9, p. 1109

27 Grönroos, Christian and Katri, Ojasalo (2004) 'Service Productivity. Towards a conceptualization of the transformation of inputs into economic results in services', *Journal of Business Research*, 57, pp. 414–423

28 Ibid., p. 415

29 Ibid., p. 419

30 Ibid., p. 415

31 The following article gives a very good insight into the technique of DEA and also shows that DEA is frequently used in efficiency benchmarking of banks and bank branches all over the world: Avkiran, N. K. (1999) 'An application reference for data envelopment analysis in branch banking: helping the novice researcher', *International Journal of Bank Marketing*, Vol 17, No 5, pp. 206–220

32 Fessard, J. and Meert, P. (1994) *De tijd van de klant* [The customer time]. Roesebre: Roularta, p. 216

33 Ibid.

34 Stalk, G. and Hout, T. (1990) *Competing Against Time*. MA: Free Press

35 Study of OIVO on Mobility (OIVO = Onderzoeks- en Informatiecentrum van de Verbruikersorganisaties; Research and Information Center of the Consumer Organisations), September 2011

36 Newspaper *Het Nieuwsblad*, 9 September 2011

37 News broadcasting on EEN, a national television channel in Belgium, 16 September 2011

38 'Panorama', (Canvas), (Belgium), 10 December 2010

39 Kossman, Mario (2006) *Delivering Excellent Service Quality in Aviation*: *A Practical Guide for Internal and External Service Providers*. Farnham: Ashgate Publishing Limited, p. 49

40 Slack, N. *et al.* (2004), op. cit. and Kossman, Mario (2006), op. cit.

41 Wirtz, Jochen and Lovelock, Christopher (2005) *Services Marketing in Asia: a Case Book*. Singapore: Pearson/Prentice-Hall, 472 pp

42 Prater, E., Biehl, M. and Smith, M. A. (2001) 'International supply chain agility – trade-offs between flexibility and uncertainty', *International Journal of Operations and Production Management*, Vol 21, No 5/6, pp. 823–829

43 Based on a presentation of Brendan Lawlor, Process Architect, DeCare Systems Ireland, 23 November 2006

44 Larivière, Bart (2008) 'Linking perceptual and behavioral customer metrics to multiperiod customer profitability', *Journal of Service Research*, Vol 11, No 1, pp. 3–21

45 Wetzels, M., De Ruyter, K. and Lemmink, J. (1999) 'Role stress in after-sales service management', *Journal of Services Research*, Vol 2, No 1, pp. 50–67. Martin Wetzels has written a doctoral dissertation where he empirically tests the service profit chain in an after-sales service environment. In this article, the first part of the relationship (starting with internal service capability and ending with quality) is investigated. The managerial recommendations are very interesting

46 Based on Loveman, G. W. (1998) 'Employee satisfaction, customer loyalty and financial performance: an empirical examination of the service profit chain in retail banking', *Journal of Service Research*, Vol 1, No 1, pp. 18–31

47 The overall thinking in this section is inspired by Kaplan, R. S. and Norton, D. P. (1996) 'Using the Balanced Scorecard as a Strategic Management System', *Harvard Business Review*, Jan–Feb

48 Heene, A. (1995) *Bruggen Bouwen naar de Toekomst*. Tielt: Lannoo

49 Project Klachten and Luchtvaart (Complaints and Aviation Project)

50 We first came across personal scorecards at Rank Xerox, but the name itself was found in Kaplan, R. S. and Norton, D. P. (1996b), op. cit.

51 *See*, for an excellent and systematic account on MBO, Reddin, B. (1989) *The Output-oriented Manager*. Farnham: Gower Publications

52 Wetzels, Martin doctoral dissertation, Maastricht University, The Netherlands

Chapter 14

Service guarantees and service-level agreements

Paul Gemmel • Gino Van Ossel

Objectives

By the end of this chapter, you should be able to discuss:

- the components of service guarantees
- the effects of service guarantees
- how to implement service guarantees
- the core characteristics of service-level agreements
- the basic building blocks of service-level agreements and when to use them
- internal service guarantees and service-level agreements and how to implement them

Introduction

On 12 March 2008, Yves Van Vaeren was presiding over a steering committee whose aim was to launch a project to develop a monitoring tool so that the quality of service delivery between the Dog Support Unit of the Belgian federal police and the local police districts could be improved.[1] This initiative was taken after receiving several complaints from local police officers that the dog teams were not always available on time. These complaints were not in line with the service concept of excellent and community-oriented service that had been advanced by the federal police. Yves understood that supporting services such as dog support teams also contribute to this service concept.

The operational division of the Dog Support Unit (DSU) of the Belgian Federal Police sends out specialized dog teams at the request of judicial authorities and local and federal police services. Four types of specialized dog teams are distinguished: tracking dog teams, drug detection dog teams, human remains detection dogs, and attack dogs. A major group of customers are the local police districts, asking for dog support in some of their investigations. Depending on the kind of investigation, dog support may be required in the short term (urgent requests) or over the longer term (scheduled requests).

In the case of an urgent request for dog support when, for instance, a child has been signalled as missing, it is important that the local police know as soon as possible whether or not a tracking dog support team will be available at short notice. It is also important to maintain contact with the dog coaches to better explain the situation. In these situations, the local police officers are eager to call the dog coaches without first contacting the DSU. This means that the DSU does not always have a full overview of the available dog teams.

The DSU does play a central role when scheduled requests for dog support are made. When, for instance, attack dogs teams are required for a demonstration scheduled for a future date, the local police have to file this request to the DSU. In this case, the DSU collects all requests coming in over a longer period of time and informs the local police districts a couple of weeks before the event takes place whether or not a dog team is available. This confirmation is still conditional because urgent requests always have priority. This uncertainty about the availability of dog teams is the source of complaints.

Yves Van Vaeren, Director-Coordinator in the Belgian federal police, wanted to improve the service provided by the DSU. The steering committee appointed a project group including representatives of the DSU and the federal police, on one side, and the local police districts, on the other side. The project team first developed a 'dog support service catalogue' with an overview of the different types of dog team and the capabilities of these dog teams. Although this catalogue improved communication between the federal and local police, it did not contain any information about the service problems identified from the complaints: the on-time communication about the availability of dog teams and how long it would take to have dog teams on site in the case of urgent requests. Yves was aware that a tension existed between the internal capabilities of the DSU to schedule the teams in an accurate way and the expectations of the local police officers about when they hoped to get an answer to their request for support. Yves was convinced that it was important to set the expectations of the local police officers in accordance with the capabilities of the DSU. In other words, the project team should be able to develop a monitoring tool based on a agreement between the DSU and the local police districts about the minimum acceptable level of service the DSU should be able to deliver. He wondered how the project team should go forward with this project.

In pursuing customer satisfaction, every organization tries to balance its customers' expectations with the delivered service. As this service is to a great extent based on the efforts of the organization's employees, customer satisfaction largely depends on the employees' understanding of the customers' expectations.

Service guarantees and service-level agreements – related and yet different concepts – are attractive to companies because they can help to match the operational requirements of the service provider with the customer requirements and because they render the sometimes abstract service concept into a concrete and measurable performance standard.

A service guarantee promises the customer a certain service quality and backs up this promise with a payout. A service-level agreement is an agreement between the service provider and its customers quantifying the minimum acceptable service to the customer.

By communicating this performance standard to its employees, an organization can genuinely focus on what is really important to the customer. Moreover, since service guarantees and service-level agreements make services more 'tangible', they have become important communication tools that can facilitate customers' search and purchase processes by reducing the perceived risk of purchasing something. The presence of a service guarantee or service-level agreement can support the perception of service reliability, which is one of the most critical determinants of customer satisfaction.

With both concepts, service quality is made measurable. This allows all service failures to be tracked and used as input for future improvement projects.

Service guarantees

A service guarantee is an explicit promise made by the service provider to deliver a certain level of service and remunerate, in one form or the other, the customer when the promise is not kept.[2] Service guarantees are often used as a promotional tool to differentiate a firm from competitors, but they also play a role in focusing the whole organization (including processes and people) on the delivery of the service quality as promoted to the customer.

In this section, the key components of a service guarantee will be discussed, as well as the possible advantages of their use. Organizations can aim for external marketing effects as well as for internal improvements, for which the payout functions as an incentive. Special attention is also paid to the implementation of service guarantees. This is important not only to maximize the desired improvements but also to manage the business risks inherent in promising a payout in case of a service failure.

A service guarantee makes the customer a meaningful *promise* and specifies a *payout* and an *invocation procedure* in case the promise is not kept.

The promise

By introducing a service guarantee, an organization is making a meaningful and credible promise to its customers. The promise can be classified along two dimensions. In terms of content, it can either promise full satisfaction or be more specific. In terms of communication to the customer, the promise can be either explicit or implicit.

Content of the promise

A good promise is meaningful to the customer; that is, it meets the expectations and even goes beyond. A distinction can be made here between a full satisfaction guarantee, a multi-attribute specific guarantee and a combined guarantee. Exhibit 14.1 shows an example of the different types of guarantee for a photocopy service provider.

Exhibit 14.1 Three types of service guarantee[3]

A full satisfaction guarantee

We guarantee full customer satisfaction. Should you not be 100% satisfied with ANY element of our service, simply inform our staff and we will either REDO the photocopy within 24 hours or NOT CHARGE you a single cent for the entire order.

A multi-attribute specific guarantee

We guarantee to adhere strictly to your instructions such as double-sided printing, sizing and binding. Should we fail to deliver on this promise, simply inform our staff and we will either REDO the photocopy within 24 hours or NOT CHARGE you a single cent for the entire order.

A combined guarantee

We guarantee to deliver all photocopying within 24 hours, to produce high quality copies with NO smudges, spots, lines, dark areas etc., and to adhere strictly to your instructions such as double-sided printing, sizing and binding.

   Should we fail to deliver on any of the above promises or should you not be 100% satisfied with ANY element of our service, simply inform our staff and we will either REDO the photocopy within 24 hours or NOT CHARGE you a single cent for the entire order.

The most powerful type of service guarantee is the full satisfaction guarantee, as illustrated in the first example of Exhibit 14.1. The customer is guaranteed total customer satisfaction. Another example is the 'Hospitality Promise' of Holiday Inn:

> 'We promise that throughout your stay with us, we will endeavour to meet the high standards that you expect from Holiday Inn Hotels. However, should anything not be to your satisfaction, don't hesitate to tell us . . . as you are not expected to pay for unsatisfactory service.'

The most common type of service guarantee – *the specific service guarantee* – focuses on one or more service attributes such as double-sided printing, sizing and binding in the example of the photocopy services (Exhibit 14.1). There are two possible reasons for offering this type of guarantee:

1 It is possible that the core customer satisfaction criterion can be boiled down to one specific service aspect. For instance, Federal Express guarantees that all documents and packages that are sent from Europe to the US will be delivered the next day before 10.00 a.m. As reliable overnight delivery is the single most important quality criterion, the guarantee is limited to this service aspect.

2 The risk of abuse and/or the unreliability of the delivered service quality sometimes discourages organizations from offering total customer satisfaction guarantees. Therefore, they guarantee one or several service aspects that are meaningful to the customer.

Although a full satisfaction guarantee offers the widest scope, the ambiguity associated with exactly what is covered may cause its value to be discounted. Therefore, a combined service guarantee design is being proposed.[4] A combined service guarantee combines the wide scope of full satisfaction with specific elements as illustrated in the third example in Exhibit 14.1. This combination helps the customer to focus on the important service aspects and reduces the ambiguity of the full service guarantee.

In defining the promise, a company should be very careful not to send the wrong message, as the guarantee may signal that service failures are more likely to occur than would normally be expected. However, this is less harmful than launching a promise which is too limited in scope – that is, those that guarantee only less important service aspects.

Another issue in the design of service guarantees is that the guarantees are highly conditional, excluding all major causes of service failures. Lufthansa guarantees that its customers will make their connecting flights if there are no delays due to weather or air-traffic control problems. Yet these two problems cause in total 95% of all flight delays. Furthermore, the guarantee only applies if all flights, including the connecting flights, are with Lufthansa.[5]

Communication of the promise

Promises, and therefore guarantees, can be communicated explicitly to the customer. On the other hand, it is also possible to define a guarantee and not communicate it to the customer. Such implicit guarantees are less powerful than explicit ones, but they offer certain advantages.

Explicit service guarantees are the best known and most powerful type. They are communicated clearly to customers. The customer may choose the service provider over another because of the guarantee. Furthermore, the guarantee may lower the complaint threshold and can therefore be an excellent tool in a relationship marketing strategy (*see* Chapter 12).

Implicit service guarantees are the least powerful type, as the promise is not explicitly communicated to the customers. Consequently, there are fewer positive effects. The marketing effect is limited to possible service recovery benefits in case of complaining customers. Similarly, the number of payouts will be lower than with explicit service guarantees. Consequently, the smaller amount of the payout functions as a less powerful incentive for positive change.

Implicit guarantees do offer certain advantages:

1 They minimize the risk of an excessive payout in cases where the risk of a service failure is too great. The Spanish national railway company, RENFE, launched a service guarantee that promised a refund to all passengers in the case of any delay exceeding five minutes. Within 24 hours of the launch, RENFE revoked the guarantee, as technical difficulties had caused delays to 900 passengers, who were paid refunds totalling approximately €65,000.

2 Their use prevents abuse. A Belgian chain of book and CD shops applies an implicit full satisfaction guarantee. All books and CDs can be returned for a refund for any reason, even without producing any proof of purchase. However, in order to avoid being used as a library where the latest books and CDs can be borrowed at no cost, this retailer prefers to use an implicit guarantee.

3 By communicating a guarantee, the organization is actually indicating that service failures may occur. In Lufthansa's service guarantee, the company promises its customers that their luggage will arrive with them. Although this is meaningful to customers, as luggage does get lost occasionally, the perception may be created that lost luggage is more of a problem with Lufthansa than it is with other airlines. In this case, an implicit guarantee would have been more appropriate.

The effectiveness of communicating a service guarantee is also dependent on the history of the firm related to service problems. It will be difficult for a service firm with a bad service reputation to send out a credible message.

▨ The payout

When the promise is not kept, the customer will receive a *payout*. This payout will encourage the customer to communicate all service failures. This has a double effect:

- *Service recovery.* The customer who claims his payout is less likely to defect. Service recovery, i.e. taking actions to recover the damage, becomes possible for the service provider. Service recovery has been discussed in Chapter 12.

- *Service quality improvement.* Each claim not only represents valuable information about quality errors and their possible causes, but the avoidance of future payouts functions as an incentive to all staff to participate in improvement projects.

In order to achieve service recovery, the payout has to be meaningful to the customer. It should make up for all the damage and inconvenience that he or she has suffered.

For instance, if a Federal Express document or parcel sent overseas to the US has not been delivered by 10.00 a.m. the following day, there is no charge to the customer. However, this payout is not a solution for the customer whose partner on the receiving end did not receive the promised delivery. To be fair to Federal Express, we have to stress that an acceptable solution is not easy to find. On the one hand, the late delivery has occurred and cannot be rectified. On the other hand, compensating for the damage is also very difficult. The actual damage to the customer is difficult to assess, as it varies widely from one case to another and may occasionally be so high that it has an impact on Federal Express's financial results – for example, in the case of transporting human organs for transplantation.

By contrast, the payout offered by the Dutch public transportation company, Interliner, tries to solve the problem of their customers. Interliner guarantees that passengers boarding their buses will make their connecting buses and trains. Again, a refund would not adequately compensate the passenger who had just missed a connection. Therefore, every passenger who had to wait for more than 15 minutes for a connection due to a delay by Interliner can be taken to his or her destination by taxi at Interliner's expense.[6]

A payout can also be too high. Domino's Pizza offered customers its pizzas free of charge if they were not delivered within 30 minutes of ordering. Much to Domino's surprise, fewer people made use of the guarantee than expected. Market research showed that consumers felt sorry for the delivery boy. They feared that if they did not pay for the pizza he could get fired, and thereby declined the payout. Consequently, the service guarantee did not trigger the expected customer feedback on late deliveries. Domino's, therefore, reduced the payout to a discount if the pizza is delivered between 30 and 45 minutes after ordering. A refund or a fresh pizza is offered only if the pizza is more than 15 minutes late. Consequently, customers who now perceive that the 'punishment fits the crime' have started using the guarantee, providing Domino's with valuable information on the actual frequency of late deliveries.

The invocation procedure

The final component of the service guarantee is the invocation procedure. How can customers notify the organization that it has not kept its promise, and what do they have to do to collect the payout?

Invoking a guarantee should be either very easy or even proactive. Supermarkets Hoogvliet (the Netherlands) and Match (Belgium) both promise short queues at their checkouts. If all checkout counters are not manned and if you are the third (Hoogvliet) or fourth (Match) customer in a queue, you do not have to pay (Hoogvliet) or you receive a significant discount (Match).

The invocation procedure itself is the major difference. At Match, the customer has to step out of the queue and press a bell, which focuses all attention on the 'complaining' customer. Social pressure prevents customers from using the bell. The guarantee is hardly ever invoked and queues have not decreased. In contrast, Hoogvliet customers do not have to do anything at all. If they find themselves third in line, the person manning the checkout counters will proactively tell them that their groceries are free of charge.

A fine example of a full satisfaction guarantee that is easy to invoke is Superquinn's Goof Card system. Superquinn is the leading supermarket chain in the Greater Dublin area. Periodically, all customers who participate in its loyalty saving system called 'Superclub' receive a so-called Goof Card. The card explains to the customers that each time Superquinn 'goofs' – that is, produces a service failure – the customer simply has to point this out to any member of staff, and he or she will receive 30 Superclub bonus points worth about €1.

The guarantee offers unconditional satisfaction, as customers can define the goofs themselves but, in order to further help their customers, Superquinn lists 10 examples of goofs. Included are products that have passed their sell-by date, prices at the checkout that do not match the prices marked on the shelf, wobbly trolleys and labels being out of stock at the fruit and vegetable scales. In this way, it becomes a combined guarantee.

The effects of a service guarantee

Service guarantees can serve different purposes. First, such a guarantee has major internal effects on an organization's operations and staff. The payout catalyses improvement projects that focus on the guaranteed promise. As such, guarantees have proven to be a highly effective tool in steering organizations towards maximum customer satisfaction.

The internal effects should indirectly translate into marketing benefits – more precisely, increased customer loyalty and positive word of mouth. Some organizations also use guarantees to reduce the customer's perceived risk. By guaranteeing a specific outcome, the organization hopes to increase its business and to acquire new customers. It conveys the image of a reliable supplier. A side effect of this is improved customer loyalty through service recovery in case of service failure.

The internal effect on the organization's operations and staff

The benefits of service guarantees are, in many ways, similar to those of complaint management systems (*see* Technical note 3). The payout and the easy invocation procedure lower the threshold for customers to report any service failure and seize the opportunity for service recovery. Furthermore, these service failures are reported and analysed, and used to set up improvement projects aimed at eliminating their root causes.

Service guarantees seem to be more effective than complaint procedures. The payout penalizes each failure and seems to mobilize all staff to switch to prevention mode. If Holiday Inn's guests were generally dissatisfied or if Domino's delivered too many pizzas late, they would simply go out of business. The guarantee is a very effective way for management to communicate to its staff that customer satisfaction truly is a number one priority.[7]

A second advantage of a service guarantee over complaint management systems is that the promise helps to highlight what is important to the customer. This is particularly true for specific service guarantees. As the promise is related to certain aspects of the service, all staff involved will focus on these service aspects.

Service guarantees that are not clearly linked to the organization's service concept, or that put emphasis on aspects that are of secondary importance to the customer, may send the wrong signal to the staff. Similarly, aiming at zero defect operations should not be done at any price.

A fine case in point of sending out the wrong signal is Domino's. The service guarantee promises the delivery of a pizza to the customer's address within 30 minutes. While very meaningful to the customer, the guarantee may encourage the delivery staff to risk their own safety in order to meet the 30-minute target. Moreover, the delay may have been caused while cooking the pizza and not during the delivery. Domino's has come up with a very simple solution:

1 Pizzas are only delivered to customers within an 8-minute drive from the outlet.

2 Ten minutes (or a 2-minute margin) is allowed for delivery.

3 Pizzas leaving the kitchen more than 20 minutes after the order was taken are automatically stickered as 'discounted for late delivery'.

The effect is threefold:

- Back-office staff is directly confronted with service failures and the resulting payout. This increases their involvement with the service guarantee.

- The delivery staff cannot avoid the payout by speeding and thus risking their safety, in order to make up the time lost in the kitchen. The sticker already awards the penalty.

- The invocation procedure is made proactive.

The Domino's example also shows another effect of the promise; namely, that it sets clear performance standards. The snappy but non-committal 'Quick delivery' becomes '20 minutes from order-taking to start of delivery' and '10 minutes to deliver'. All staff know exactly what is expected of them.

Another internal effect of service guarantees is increased employee satisfaction and, finally, it may lead to greater staff empowerment. By advertising the guarantee, employees perceive their organization as delivering a high quality and very reliable service. Thus, they find the working environment more pleasant and their satisfaction increases. The constant customer feedback encourages a natural feeling of empowerment. With no formal 'empowering' effort, employees are allowed, expected and willing to take more initiative in trying to avoid service failures incidentally and, in setting up improvement projects, to tackle root causes structurally. Hampton Inn, a hotel chain in the US, provides us with some empirical support for this impact on its personnel. It guarantees its customers total customer satisfaction. The impact on its staff[8] was as follows:

- 69% say it makes the company a better place to work.

- 90% say it motivates them to do a better job.

- 93% say it motivates others to do a better job.

The marketing effects

Service guarantees can produce some very specific marketing effects. They are a particularly powerful way to reduce the customer's perceived risk of buying and can, therefore, attract new customers and/or new business. For example, some restaurants advertise that they can serve a three-course business lunch within an hour or it will be free. The guarantee reduces the risk for time-conscious business people that they will spend too much time in a restaurant. Similar guarantees are offered by restaurants in train stations and airports, allowing customers to judge very precisely if they have time to order a meal before their train or plane leaves.

Risk reduction is particularly useful for 'high-risk' services. Dining out at a low-priced restaurant carries a lower risk than dining at a higher-priced (i.e. high-risk) restaurant. A study looking at the impact of service guarantees on the choice of restaurants by students showed that service guarantees have marginal added value in ensuring a good dining experience for low-priced restaurants. Higher-priced restaurants seem to benefit more from service guarantees because the risk of getting the expected value is much higher.[9]

The degree of risk depends partly on the predictability of the outcome and of the possible consequences of an undesirable outcome. The outcome is less predictable with new suppliers and/or with initial purchase situations; hence, the use of guarantees to attract new customers. The consequences are typically related to the actual service: the late arrival of a package delivered by Federal Express or of a bus operated by Interliner may have major consequences.

Service guarantees make the service promise more tangible, but it is important to remember that breaking the service promise is the single most important way in which service companies fail their customers.[10]

Implementing a service guarantee

Going back to the RENFE example of the company hastily revoking its guarantee, we should stress that, in addition to the short-term financial loss, the Spanish railway company actually reinforced its image as an unreliable service provider, which was plainly the opposite of what it wanted to achieve.

This example clearly illustrates that implementing a guarantee has to be carried out with the utmost care. The consequences of an unsuccessful implementation can be very diverse. In the best case, a failure has simply been a waste of resources. This happens if the guarantee is never or rarely invoked. Payout consequently is limited, but so is feedback to the organization on service failures. There is no real incentive to set up improvement projects, and there are no opportunities for service recovery. The benefits of the guarantee are zero, while resources have been invested in its conception, advertising and implementation.

RENFE illustrates the worse case. The organization suffered significant financial losses because of the excessive failure rate and resulting payout. Hurriedly, the organization had to revoke the guarantee, sending a clear signal to both its customers and its staff that management accepts the organization cannot guarantee a reliable service.

And what about the risk of abuse?

Providing service guarantees carries the risk of abuse. If a satisfied guest at Holiday Inn abuses the guarantee to obtain a free stay, he cannot be forced to 'return' the goods as in the case of tangible products. For instance, if a customer buys a television set and is not satisfied, the invocation procedure of an unconditional satisfaction guarantee will usually require the customer to return the rejected television. This discourages abuse, as the customer wanting a TV would have to procure a new set anyway.

The importance of abuse is difficult to assess. Hampton Inn, an American hotel chain, spotted a guest who invoked its guarantee 18 times within one year. It put this customer on a blacklist.

One study finds that potential material gain has no effect on abuse of the guarantee, but the intention to repeat purchase reduces the tendency of abuse.[11] It also shows that situational and personality variables (such as satisfaction, morality and self-monitoring) reduce consumer cheating, whereas Machiavellianism increases abuse.[12]

On the other hand, if the number of abusers is limited, the vast majority of honest customers should not be punished because of a small minority of abusers.

There are different ways to manage the risk of abuse:

- *Testing the guarantee*. By using a pilot phase, it is possible to assess the actual abuse.
- *Adjusting the invocation procedure*. Holiday Inn tries to combat abuse by inviting its customers to report any dissatisfaction during the consumption of the service. At a training institute, a refund can only be obtained if the dissatisfied participant decides to leave the one-day course before noon. Abusers punish themselves: they have their money back but cannot attend the course in full.
- *Using an implicit guarantee*. The risk of abuse can be minimized by not communicating the guarantee explicitly to the customers. The example of the book and CD shop, which we described earlier, illustrates this approach.

Service-level agreements

A service-level agreement (SLA) is an agreement between the service provider and its customers quantifying the minimum acceptable service to the customer.[13] This definition reflects three core characteristics:

- It is an agreement and thus requires the approval of both parties. This is the first basic difference between a guarantee and an SLA. A guarantee is unilateral. The supplier decides on the promise, the restrictions, the payout and the invocation procedure. The supplier should, of course, take into account the customers' points of view in conceiving the guarantee, but it does not need their formal approval. By contrast, an SLA is bilateral. Both the supplier and the customer have to approve it, which can necessitate compromise. For instance, on the one hand the supplier may promise to achieve certain service levels and, on the other hand, the customer may commit to providing accurate volume forecasts and respecting specified deadlines. As a result, elements that affect the supplier's promise but that are within the customer's control become the customer's promise in an SLA. In a guarantee, they would typically take the form of 'restrictions'. An important consequence of the 'mutual' nature of an SLA is that it is by definition tailor-made. Instead of offering a standard contract with standard clauses, as does a service guarantee, customer and supplier sit down together to draft an agreement that addresses both parties' needs and interests.
- The SLA specifies the minimum acceptable service, taking into account the mutual interest of both parties. For instance, a company servicing copiers may guarantee that its repair staff can be on all their customers' premises within 60 minutes in case of a malfunction. Such a guarantee sets a clear performance standard but is not necessarily the optimal intervention time. Some customers may consider 120 minutes or 24 hours equally acceptable. Since reducing the response time typically results in higher costs, the SLA allows supplier and customer to define the minimum acceptable service level at which the total cost to both parties is minimized. An SLA should prevent unnecessary and expensive over-provision of quality.

Table 14.1 The main differences between service guarantees and service-level agreements

	Service guarantee	Service-level agreement
The needs of the customer	Identified by the manager	Communicated by the customer
The promise	Unconditional	After negotiation
The content	Standardized	Customized
The responsibility	Supplier	Supplier and customer
Number	One guarantee for all customers	One SLA for each customer
Changes	Unusual	Possible with consent of supplier and customer
The kind of customer	B-to-B and B-to-C	B-to-B
Communication of the promise	Not in the case of implicit service guarantees	Through negotiations
The payout	Proactive or when the customer asks for it	When there is a deviation from the norm
The nature of the payout	Rather a fine	A fine or a reward
Feedback on the perceived service delivery	Uni-directional	Bi-directional
The source of information for feedback	The invocation procedure	Reports and meetings

- The SLA also quantifies the service. As such, it sets clear performance standards for both supplier and customer. For instance, a supplier of information systems may promise to limit the down-time of a multi-computer service. When conceiving such an agreement, the customer's expectations have to be clearly defined. In this case, this requires defining 'availability' of the system: is it available or unavailable if one of the computers is down, or if 5% of all users cannot access it? The timing of the availability has also to be discussed. Average availability figures may hide the fact that the system is too often down when it is really needed. The same degree of clarity is, of course, required on the customer's part.

Table 14.1 summarizes the main differences between service guarantees and SLAs.

Developing SLAs creates better awareness of customer needs and enables a company to better manage its customer expectations. As with service guarantees, the internal processes should be stable enough to make the SLAs feasible. The SLAs also help to optimize allocation of scarce resources to competitive needs, for instance, by not delivering service at an unreasonably high level. Ultimately, SLAs should have a positive impact on customer retention and the development of a long-term relationship with the customer. In contrast to service guarantees, SLAs are not promotional by nature, but they play an important role as a communication tool between the (business) customer and the supplier during the negotiation and the delivery process of the service. Table 14.2 classifies the most essential objectives of SLAs into four primary and 10 secondary objectives.

Setting up service-level agreements

An SLA is a tool that can be used to help a company move towards the delivery of a service of a quality appropriate to the needs of the business. It provides an objective indication of whether the service is being delivered at a minimum acceptable level; furthermore, if such a service is not being delivered, the SLA provides what is needed to bring the service to that level.

Table 14.2 Objectives of a service-level agreement[14]

Primary objectives	Secondary objectives
1 Determining customer needs	– Controlling customer expectations – Satisfying the customer
2 Defining the necessary processes	– Efficiently allocating available resources – Controlling costs
3 Implementing a performance measurement system	– Measuring customer satisfaction – Comparing performance with competitors – Implementing employee rewarding system – Justifying the budget of a department
4 Managing the relationship between customer and service provider	– Avoiding conflicts – Increasing customer retention

Source: Berbée, R. G. et al. (2009) Evaluation of hospital service level agreements, International Journal of Health Care Quality Assurance, Vol 22, No 5, pp. 483–497.

The following mechanisms should underlie any SLA:

1 The minimum acceptable service level must be specified, as well as the commitment from the customer.

2 The degree to which the mutual promises are kept must be measured.

3 The root causes of failures should be sought and improvement projects set up.

4 Review meetings should be set up to discuss progress and to see whether the initial commitments need fine tuning.

When to use service-level agreements

As evidenced by the growing prevalence of SLAs in the ICT industry, the advantages of SLAs have been repeatedly proven by ICT providers and their customers.[15] The success of SLAs in the ICT world inspires other service sectors, such as the facility service sector (catering, security and real estate). Exhibit 14.2 illustrates how and why SLAs are used in a major security company. Service providers such as Securitas use SLAs to manage the supplier–buyer relationships in outsourcing contracts.[16] When outsourcing a service, it is essential to define the level of the service to be provided, because it would otherwise not be possible to determine whether the service provider has performed its functions adequately or not.[17]

SLAs require a considerable amount of resources. First, they have to be conceived, then measurement systems have to be installed and, finally, review meetings have to be held. Moreover, as an SLA is custom-made, the investment has to be repeated for each individual customer. SLAs also make demands on the customers' resources, as they also have to participate in the start-up negotiations and review meetings.

As a result, the benefits of SLAs can only outweigh the costs for major and long-lasting customer–supplier relationships, which yield a high dividend for the supplier and have high cost implications for the customer.

Common pitfalls when implementing service-level agreements

Many SLAs fail during implementation. The most common mistake is to assume that, once the agreement has been signed, the work is basically over. In reality, drafting and signing an agreement is only the first step. Its success depends on the way the agreement is managed afterwards. The following pitfalls are often encountered during the implementation of SLAs:

- *Poor handling of service failures.* As the objective of an SLA is to develop a communication platform on areas for improvement, service failures have to be treated as a valuable source of management information and must be dealt with constructively. One of the most common pitfalls is for customers to treat the agreement as an unconditional guarantee. Each failure is presented as a major cause of dissatisfaction. This creates a defensive attitude on the part of the supplier, who starts focusing on avoiding the reporting of failures rather than on tackling their root causes. A clear symptom of this problem is when the agreement is drafted as a legal contract. Contracts are considered binding, while an SLA is a basis for future co-operation, including future reviews of the agreement itself.

- *Inadequate definitions and poor measurements.* Inadequate definitions and poor measurements turn the focus of the review meetings from the root causes of failures to the accuracy of the service failure data. To avoid this pitfall it is important to have clear performance measures. The design of a performance measurements system (*see* Chapter 13) is a condition *sine qua non* for the successful implementation of SLAs. As many SLAs include a 'time contract', time-based performance measures such as responsiveness and on-time delivery are particularly useful.

- *Unclear definition of 'availability'.* In the example of multi-computer system, it is important to have a clear definition of 'availability'. If this definition is inaccurate, several review meetings will be required to come up with more accurate definitions and appropriate measurement systems. Moreover, supplier and customers may have different interpretations of the initial agreement, so that fine-tuning the definitions may result in an agreement that is unacceptable to one of the parties.

- *Poor measurements.* Similarly, poor measurements will result in debates on the validity of the number of reported service failures. If penalties are part of the agreement, it is particularly important that the validity and impartiality of the measurements are accepted by all concerned parties. Otherwise, the agreement, which has already consumed a fair amount of resources, will fail to yield early benefits. Eventually, this may result in an overall failure. Some have misinterpreted this point by drafting very elaborate and detailed SLAs up to 30 pages long. As the agreement is not a contract but a platform for communicating, clarity and specificity are more important than degree of detail.

- *Lack of mutual benefits.* As an SLA is demanding on both customer and supplier, both have to benefit from it. If not, the commitment of one of the partners is bound to gradually diminish.

- *Lack of commitment of both senior management and front-line staff.* SLAs are expensive. They need constant resourcing. Consequently, senior management has to be committed in order to keep the agreements alive. On the other hand, the organization will only reap the benefits if front-line staff is also involved. By having them participate at the conception stage as well as in the review meetings, one can avoid the discussion of the SLAs being confined to management meetings.

Exhibit 14.2 Service-level agreements at Securis

Security is one of our most basic needs. Many companies have been paying more attention to creating a secure environment, especially since 11 September 2001. In most cases, security services are bought from an external supplier. One of these suppliers is Securis.

Securis was founded as a Belgian aviation security company in 1985. In later years, the company diversified into permanent and mobile security. In 1999, Securis was taken over by the Swedish holding company Securitas AB, a world leader in the area of security. In 2004, Securis took on the name Securitas. Securitas has today more than 5000 employees in Belgium. Because this exhibit is based on how Securis originally implemented SLAs, we continue to use the name Securis.

SLAs were introduced in Securis several years ago following an explicit request from a customer to develop such an agreement. Securis only develops an SLA when a business customer explicitly asks for it. Each SLA has a duration of 3–5 years and is developed to meet the customer's specific needs. This requires an intensive process of negotiation between Securis and the customer about the specified quality level, the dimensions of quality to be measured, the measurement method and the consequences. The consequences may be a fine or a reward for the supplier (Securis) depending on whether or not the specified quality level is attained.

The 'A' of 'Agreement' in SLA is of great importance for Securis. In the negotiations, a situation acceptable to both supplier and customer is striven for and a balance is reached between price and quality. This aspect of mutual interest, which is so important in developing a SLA at Securis, is also recognized as one of the most difficult to realize in practice.

The SLAs at Securis do not specify the outcome of the service delivery but the resources and the efforts that are necessary to perform it. An agreement about outcomes carries too much risk, certainly when the supplier has insufficient input into the customer's business.

Compliance with the specifications in an SLA is only possible when the company has a well-functioning quality assurance system in place. Management at Securis is convinced that a good level of service quality is a condition *sine qua non* for implementing SLAs. SLAs do not lead to an improvement in quality, only to a change in the perception of quality. An SLA is very useful in making the quality perception more objective. The performance measurement system specified in the SLA permits an objective assessment of whether or not the service delivered corresponds with what has been agreed in the SLA. When this performance evaluation is positive, the operational management in charge of the execution of the SLA is rewarded at the end of the year.

The management at Securis believes that the use of SLAs can lead to a future competitive advantage if the service company proves that it is able to develop and implement a well-functioning SLA. The SLA has a positive impact on the relationship between the customer and the company. The increased transparency and objectivity in the relationship means that customers react in a less emotional way to problems. An SLA also creates some dependency in the relationship between supplier and customer, since the cost of shifting to other suppliers increases.

A properly functioning SLA creates trust in the relationship between customer and supplier and leads in the end to greater customer loyalty. But an SLA is also a double-edged sword, according to Securis management: the customer learns about the positive but also about the negative points of the company. Customers must learn to handle this kind of information.

Internal service guarantees and service-level agreements

The first SLAs were developed not between service providers and their external customers but between electronic data processing (EDP) departments and their internal customers. Information technology solutions have all too often been conceived by headquarters specialists operating from their 'ivory towers' and unaware of their users' real needs and concerns. The dissatisfaction of the end users, who, after all, are ultimately paying for all central functions, has resulted in EDP departments developing SLAs in order to become more (internal) customer-oriented.

The concept of the internal customer has proven to be very difficult to bring to life. Despite its popularity in managerial literature, organizations have learned that it is hard to establish a culture in which the internal customer is being treated with the same respect as the external one. The underlying reason for this is that the internal supplier traditionally had a monopoly, since the internal customer has no alternative source of supply. In recent years, organizations have attempted to break this monopoly, either by outsourcing some of the support functions or by allowing the internal customers to buy from external suppliers if they can get a better service.

It is not surprising, therefore, that most internal SLAs and service guarantees have been developed by so-called off-stream internal service providers – that is, those departments that require no handover of work in order to allow the internal customers to continue their work. Customer and supplier are not contributing directly to the same stream of work. For instance, finance and accounting may be responsible for invoicing but, if invoices are sent out late, the sales representatives are not directly affected in their work. Exhibit 14.3 shows an example of an off-stream internal service guarantee.

Exhibit 14.3 Filling vacancies

The Marriott's Bethesda Hotel was doing very well and required constant hiring of new staff to keep up with growth. However, all kinds of administrative work prevented the human resources department from investing enough time in finding and selecting new staff members. As a result, it was taking too long to fill vacancies.

To focus more clearly on the internal customers' needs, the human resources department launched an internal service guarantee. It promised that, within 2 weeks of a vacancy being reported to them, qualified applicants would be found. If not, the human resources department would hire temps at its own budget's expense. After introducing the guarantee, the number of vacancies decreased from 45 to 4.

Whenever the internal service provider is performing a task that must be completed before the internal customers can do their work, they are contributing directly to the same stream of work. The provider-to-customer handoff is an in-process handoff. For instance, contact personnel in a bank cannot write a quote for a loan if the credit department has not approved the loan application. Similarly, the credit department cannot approve the loan if the contact person has not properly filled out the loan application form. This in-process handoff includes the idea that 'the next process is your customer', as proposed by Ishikawa[18] in the 1950s.

Unfortunately for the in-process handoff, outsourcing is not a valid alternative, and so the service provider in effect has a true monopoly. In recent years, organizations have learned that internal service guarantees and SLAs are powerful tools in bringing the concept of the internal customer to life and to focus all functions and departments on the service experience of the final customer or consumer. In this way, internal service guarantees and SLAs become important internal communication tools. In this way, the expectations of the end-customer are translated into service levels for every department and function of the organization, across the lines of visibility and internal interaction as specified in the service blueprint (*see* Chapter 4). These were the major reasons why AZ Sint Blasius, a Belgian general hospital, developed more than 200 SLAs to describe the internal service provision of different supporting departments such as cleaning, food service, rehabilitation and pharmacy to the nursing departments.[19]

In deciding whether to use service guarantees or SLAs internally, the same arguments apply as to external ones: agreements require efforts from both the supplier and the customer. Therefore, agreements only make sense if there is a clear mutual benefit that outweighs the costs to both parties. After an evaluation of the performance of the SLAs at AZ Sint Blasius, they found that there were more problems in the implementation with the cleaning SLA than with the others.[20] According to the CEO of the hospital, this dissatisfaction is mainly caused by the unilateral nature of the negotiations that have taken place for the cleaning SLA in the past. The nursing departments were as internal customers not much involved in the negotiations on the service levels laid down in this SLA. This resulted in internal SLAs that were not able to meet the expectations of the internal customers.

The major risk in implementing internal service guarantees and SLAs is that, after the initial enthusiasm, they fade out and die a silent death. For instance, in the case of a service guarantee with a merely symbolic payout, the internal customer has only a limited incentive to invoke the guarantee. For SLAs, the required efforts are much higher. A lack of initial results may discourage service provider and internal customer from continuing the review meetings. The risk of fade-out is particularly great in the following circumstances:

- *Lack of a support structure and/or a facilitator.* Setting up SLAs and service guarantees requires a certain expertise. By establishing a steering committee, this expertise is gradually developed as more agreements and/or guarantees are launched. Moreover, the interest is kept alive by marketing these concepts internally and by formally asking for the achieved results. The facilitator should be available for daily support. Particularly in large organizations, his or her function can be compared with that of a quality manager or of a quality coach reporting to the quality manager.

- *All initiatives are isolated.* If such a support structure is lacking, guarantees and SLAs are often isolated initiatives of individual departments. Particularly for in-process handoffs, the chances of early fade-out can be reduced by launching a series of linked guarantees or agreements, gradually moving further away from the external customer. Some organizations use such an integrated but gradual approach as a preparation to launching an external guarantee.

- *Lack of integration in everyday working procedures.* Often the guarantee and the SLA add to the normal workload. For instance, they may require an additional reporting system. By integrating them into the existing working procedures and replacing existing tasks with new ones, the workload of the employees concerned is less affected. Particularly for

SLAs that require a great deal of effort from both customer and supplier, the existing reporting system should be largely replaced by the mechanisms of the agreement.

Conclusion

Service guarantees and SLAs can be valuable tools to realize customer satisfaction by creating explicit customer expectations. Moreover, they allow difficulties due to the intangibility of service to be overcome. When it comes down to making tangible the intangible, service guarantees and SLAs can play a crucial role. In this chapter, we have discussed extensively the important issues to consider when defining and implementing both service guarantees and SLAs. It has become clear that the success of implementing either one depends heavily on the joint efforts of the total organization. Although this no doubt sounds like a platitude by now, the intertwined nature of what happens inside the service organization and what customers eventually will experience cannot be stressed enough as the examples and the pitfalls described in the chapter amply illustrate. Implementing service guarantees and SLAs will require dedication and a well-balanced plan. We identified the major building blocks and guiding principles of the implementation process. Exhibit 14.4 demonstrates how these building blocks can be used to design an SLA for the services of the DSU of the federal police.

Both service guarantees and SLAs can be powerful devices to link the service delivery processes to customer satisfaction and a positive service brand (*see* Chapter 8). They can help to:

- Reduce customer buying risk and ensure outstanding service delivery.
- Ensure an adequate service recovery, which results in a more favourable image for the firm in terms of quality and value.
- Establish a company's competitive image in the customer's mind as the superior service provider.
- Enhance customer feedback, both positive and negative.

Exhibit 14.4 A service-level agreement for the services delivered by the Dog Support Unit (continued)

In trying to improve the service delivery of the DSU, the project team developed a service-level agreement between the DSU (as the service provider) and the local police districts. The design of the SLA included three stages (*see* Table 14.3).

In the first stage, customer needs were identified and confronted with the process of delivering dog support services. This led, in the second stage, to the formulation of specific service levels for different performance indicators. The discussion on which service quality dimensions should be included and how to measure these dimensions was the most crucial point in the design of the SLA. Table 14.4 shows the finally selected service quality dimensions,

---

Table 14.3 An overview of the different steps in the SLA project of the Dog Support Unit

Stage	Description	Step	Description	Tool
1	Preparation	a	Identification of the expectations of the customers (the local police districts)	Surveys (project group)
		b	Description of the service delivery process in the case of dog support	Process mapping (project group)
		c	Definition of the scope of the services	Service catalogue (project group)
		d	Investigation of the feasibility of the SLA as tool and engagement of management	Steering committee
2	Negotiation	a	Translating the expectations into measurable service performance indicators	Workshop, (project group)
		b	Formulating service levels for each service performance indicator	Workshop, (project group)
3	Management of the SLA	a	Measuring the performance of each service standard in terms of the negotiated service levels	Monitoring tool
		b	Visualising, analyzing and reporting of the current performance	Monitoring tool
		c	Taking corrective actions if necessary	Steering committee and project group
		d	Implementing the proposed changes and restarting the cycle of measuring, analyzing and improving	Steering committee

Table 14.4 The service quality dimensions, measures and service levels for the Dog Support Services

Service quality dimension	Description	Measure	Expected service level
Reliability	Availability of dog support teams at the time of request	The ratio of the number of refused requests due to non-availability of dogs	% refused requests must be lower than 5%
Speed	Time between request and intervention with dog teams in the case of urgent requests	The cut-off point for the person who makes the request. The cut-off point is the point after which it is no longer useful to send dogs. Is the intervention taking place before the cut-off point or after the cut-off point? Or is the intervention not taking place because the DSU could not deliver the dogs before the cut-off point?	% urgent requests with intervention after the cut-off point must be lower than 5% % urgent requests with no intervention because there are no dog teams available must be lower than 1%
	Response time for scheduled requests	Time between the request for dog support and the answer that the request has been honoured (or not).	% scheduled requests with more than 3 weeks between the request and the response must be lower than 5%

the way in which each quality dimension is measured and the specified level of service for each measure. This table clearly shows that a well-designed performance measurement system is at the core of the SLA. Other information included in the SLA was a description of the parties involved; the terms of the agreement; scope and exclusions; limitations; arrangements for periodic reviews; procedures for resolving disagreements; and procedures for negotiating modifications of the contract; the scope of service; the obligations of the clients; performance targets.[21]

In the third stage, the project team and the steering committee made sure that the measures and their service levels were continuously monitored and that corrective actions were taken when the service levels were not achieved. This last stage was very crucial in making the SLA a continuous monitoring tool for the delivery of dog support services. It was clear for Yves Van Vaeren that this was the monitoring tool he was looking for at the outset of the project.

Review and discussion questions

- Look up an example of a firm using a service guarantee and evaluate it (for example, does it contain all the necessary information required of a service guarantee?) What is the purpose of the service guarantee? Is it effective?

- Read Exhibit 14.2 about the implementation of SLAs at Securis. It is clear that Securis applies SLAs in its own particular way. What are the differences between the theory and the practice of developing and implementing SLAs at Securis? What are the opportunities and threats of using SLAs in a service company such as Securis?

- Evaluate the SLA between the DSU and the local police districts in Exhibit 14.4. Evaluate the approach the project team took in Table 14.3? Did the project team define the right performance measures in Table 14.4? Did they select the right service levels?

Suggested further reading

Beaumont, N. (2006) 'Service Level Agreements: An Essential Aspect of Outsourcing', *The Service Industries Journal*, Vol 26, No 4, pp. 381–395

Hart, C. W. L. (1995) 'The power of internal guarantees', *Harvard Business Review*, Vol 73, No 1, pp. 64–73

Hiles, A. (1993) *Service Level Agreements. Managing cost and quality in service relationships.* London: Chapman & Hall

Hogreve, Jens and Gremler, Dwayne D. (2009) 'Twenty years of service guarantee research', *Journal of Service Research*, Vol 11, No 4, p. 324

Marmorstein, H., Sarel, D. and Lassar, W. M. (2001) 'Increasing the persuasiveness of a service guarantee: the role of service process evidence', *Journal of Services Marketing*, Vol 15, No 2, pp. 147–159

Notes and references

1 This case is based on a project performed by one of the authors (Paul Gemmel) for the Belgian Federal Police in 2008

2 Hogreve, Jens and Gremler, Dwayne D. (2009) 'Twenty years of service guarantee research', *Journal of Service Research*, Vol 11, No 4, p. 324

3 Wirtz, Jochen and Kum, Doreen (2001) 'Designing service guarantees – is full satisfaction the best you can guarantee?', *Journal of Services Marketing*, Vol 15, No 4, pp. 282–299

4 Ibid.

5 Lufthansa Airlines, advertisement in the *Wall Street Journal*, 9 March 1987

6 Interliner was a 'fast bus' concept introduced in the Netherlands in the 1980s. The changes in bus transport organization led to the disappearance of the Interliner bus and its concept

7 Case, John (1991) 'Customer service: The last word', *Inc. Magazine*, April

8 Rust, R. T., Zahorik, A. J. and Keiningham, T. J. (1996) *Service Marketing*. New York, NY: Harper Collins College Publishers

9 Tucci, L. A. and Talaga, J. (1997) 'Service guarantees and consumers evaluation of services', *Journal of Services Marketing*, Vol 11, No 1, pp. 10–18

10 Kandampully, J. and Butler, L. (2001) 'Service guarantees: a strategic mechanism to minimize customers' perceived risk in service organizations', *Managing Service Quality*, Vol 11, No 2, pp. 112–120

11 Wirtz, Jochen and Kum, Doreen (2004) 'Consumer cheating on service guarantees', *Journal of the Academy of Marketing Science*, Vol 32, No 2, pp. 159–175

12 Ibid. Individuals with high Machiavellianism typically lack concern for conventional morality and are effective manipulators of others

13 Hiles, A. N. (1994) 'Service level agreements: Panacea or pain', *The TQM Magazine*, Vol 6, No 2, pp. 14–16

14 Berbée, R. G., Gemmel, P., Droesbeke, B., Casteleyn, H. and Vandaele, D. (2009) 'Evaluation of Hospital Service Level Agreements', *International Journal of Health Care Quality Assurance*, Vol 22, No 5, pp. 483–497

15 Hartley, K. L. (2005) 'Defining Effective Service Level Agreements for Network Operations and Maintenance', *Bell Labs Technical Journal*, Vol 9, No 4, pp. 139–143

16 Beaumont, N. (2006) 'Service Level Agreements: An Essential Aspect of Outsourcing', *The Service Industries Journal*, Vol 26, No 4, pp. 381–395

17 Davis, D. (2003) 'Service Level Agreements: What are they? Why do we need them?', *Credit Management*, May, pp. 36–37

18 Ishikawa, K. (1996) *Guide to Quality Control*. Tokyo: Asian Productivity Organization

19 Berbée, R. G. *et al.* (2009), op. cit.

20 Ibid.

21 The design of the SLA was based on the format proposed by Beaumont, N. (2006), op. cit.

PART FOUR

Developing services

Bart Van Looy • Paul Gemmel

No single service concept – nor the related service design and service delivery – is made to last forever. Thus, in the last part we discuss the process of developing services with the long-term perspective of a sustainable service business.

Innovation is currently on everyone's lips and is considered the key to rejuvenating the business. This is also true for service innovation. In Chapter 15, we introduce the concept of value constellation in order to place the customers and the solutions to their problems at the heart of the innovation process. While this seems to be the most natural approach, it implies a shift from strict, linear processes of innovation to more iterative and broader views of the innovation process such as open innovation. Open innovation advances the idea that firms can and should rely both on internal and external sources to strengthen their own innovative capabilities and market their ideas. The trend towards open innovation and its relevance for services innovation will be discussed in Chapter 15 as well.

Developing service innovations demands a clear strategy from service businesses. In Chapter 16, we discuss the notion of service strategy as a coalescing framework, linking processes, technology, human resources, and customers to the service concept. All ingredients need to be developed in an integrative and sustainable manner. While traditional perspectives on strategy provide meaningful insights for developing a service strategy, the more recent competence-based approaches seem to be especially valuable in looking at the particular strategic challenges faced by service firms today: the need for tangibility, the use of intangible resources in creating and sustaining competitive advantage, mastering the dynamics of value creation and value perception in delivering services, using technology, and managing continuity in creating competitive advantage in time and space.

The ability and willingness to work internationally is becoming an additional prerequisite for service firms' growth and long-term survival. In Chapter 17, we describe in more detail the impetus towards internationalization as well as the things service firms need to bear in mind when developing an international strategy. It will come as no surprise that core characteristics of services such as intangibility and simultaneity play a crucial role here.

While reading the book, it will become clear that boundaries between manufacturing companies and service providers are increasingly blurred. In Chapter 18, we look in depth at the notion of 'servitization' – that is, manufacturing companies that include services in their offering as well. Servitization can be considered a business model innovation for manufacturing companies, and it proves that service management is not an exclusive prerogative of the service industry but rather affects manufacturing industries to an ever larger extent.

Chapter 15

Managing innovation in a service environment

Koenraad Debackere • Annelies Geerts • Bart Van Looy

Objectives

By the end of this chapter, you should be able to discuss:

- innovations as spiral processes whereby the value constellation is taken into account
- why this idea is especially relevant for services
- how the portfolio approach is beneficial in balancing the contradictory forces present within the innovation process
- how 'make' and 'buy' are both relevant for organizing the innovation portfolio and how open services innovation can be beneficial for service firms
- how to approach the innovation process at the project level and how to anchor it within the organization
- what makes innovation in a service environment 'special'.

Introduction

'Virtual' banks and stockbrokers are emerging. They mainly consist of an electronic network and its customers. Other financial service companies supply the products. Buildings, headquarters, branches disappear.

During the mid-1990s, a large company decided to start up a subsidiary that would become a leading worldwide online hotel reservations agency. They realized that Internet technologies could enable and stimulate a new way of doing business in the travel industry. The online firm guarantees the best prices for any type of hotel. Through continuous innovation in its services, the agency aims to offer an easy-to-use, efficient and cost-effective way to book hotel accommodations. Especially for smaller hotels, the value proposition offers considerable opportunities for achieving greater global reach. Currently, the platform includes nearly 200,000 hotels worldwide and handles over 200,000 booked rooms every day. While the company builds daily on the effort of over 3000 employees, the success also has consequences for traditional travel agencies who see part of their businesses disappear.

Airline companies launch pilot projects to equip cabin crew with iPads. Using an iPad is held to have benefits for both customers and cabin crew. It enables awareness of customer preferences and a greater understanding of the travel history of each customer, allowing cabin crew to offer a more personalized service. The iPad lets cabin crew identify where each customer is seated, who they are travelling with, their frequent flyer status, special meal requests, as well as customer service updates. In addition, cabin crew will have easy access to the latest information in the air and, instead of handling a long scroll of paper after boarding, by simply refreshing their screen when the doors have closed, they will have a complete list of passengers on board through the use of wireless 3G networks.

The ever-increasing pace of change is well-known to any of today's managers. Technological, competitive and cultural pressures collide. Innovation's ability to fundamentally change the rules of competition is becoming generally recognized and appreciated. Management is caught in this vortex. Sometimes management creates the change, but all too often, management is reacting to it, or still worse, is hurt by the eternal gale of creative destruction whipped up by competitors that were not even part of the incumbents' strategic industry horizon.

We begin the chapter with a plea for a more holistic view of the innovation process. Innovation processes have been traditionally viewed as being rather linear and sequential. Shifting toward more iterative and spiral approaches fully supports the trend towards managing the value constellation of the company instead of 'merely' managing its value chain. This shift from the value chain towards value constellation deserves special attention for service firms as the notion of value constellation places customers and the solutions to their problems at the heart of the innovation process. Looking at innovations in this manner brings the dynamics of innovation into line with the notion of the service concept: everything starts from addressing a specific customer need and approaching these needs in an integrated manner. Moreover, in services, the involvement of the customer in the innovation process is not limited to explaining needs; the intangibility and simultaneity of services implies a real involvement of customers in design and development phases as well. Given the crucial importance of approaching innovation from a value-constellation perspective for services, we shall start with this idea in the first section.

Innovation is perhaps the single most destructive force in an industry.[1] When disruptive innovations unfold, existing industries are shaken up and face the risk of being destroyed and replaced by new entrants. Both research and practice have highlighted the paradoxical nature of the innovation process. On the one hand, innovation fosters endogenous firm growth through the development of competence-enhancing products, processes, and services. These competence-enhancing innovations are important since they consolidate and optimize existing commercial and technological capabilities, both at the level of the firm and at the industry level. These are the well-known incremental innovations that extend and rejuvenate existing product and service platforms. On the other hand, though, innovation can be highly disruptive, destroying a firm's commercial and technological capabilities. The advent of desk-top publishing, for instance, has signalled the destruction of many well-entrenched capabilities in the traditional pre-press industry.

The dual nature of the innovation process therefore necessitates careful managerial attention. Companies need to balance the competence-enhancing and the competence-destroying forces with their innovation endeavours. Innovation portfolios provide a powerful tool for managing this strategic paradox. The concept of the innovation portfolio and the process of portfolio management will therefore be major issues in this chapter.

The fact that innovations can both be competence-enhancing and competence-destroying of course raises another issue: how should this dual challenge be addressed, given the existing technological and market capabilities of the firm? Should internal developments ('make') be sought or should partners be found that embody the desired new capabilities ('buy')? We shall argue that a well-balanced innovation approach implies both making and buying, an idea also reflected in the notion of 'open innovation'.

Open innovation advances the idea that firms can and should rely both on internal and external sources to strengthen their own innovative capabilities and market their ideas. In addition, firms can create value from 'outsourcing' internally developed innovations. The trend towards open innovation and its relevance for services innovation will be discussed in this chapter as well.

Next, we will discuss some major insights and guidelines regarding the management of innovation projects at an operational level and consider how the innovation project can be anchored within the broader organization.

We end this chapter by questioning whether and to what extent innovation management is different in service environments compared to manufacturing environments.

Innovations as spiral processes: the value-constellation approach

Early models of innovation activities took a rather linear view of the nature of the innovation process. Innovation was viewed as a sequence of phases or activities to be carried out in a rather sequential way. The linear process started with conducting research activities, followed by development and design activities, resulting in pilot production. Once the pilot production phase was finalized, large-scale production and commercialization could begin. However, research on the management of innovation in the 1970s and 1980s concluded that the process was in essence non-linear and iterative, incorporating many feedback loops between the different activities involved. Problems detected during the design phase, for instance, can trigger a new research activity. Engineering change orders are yet another (unwanted) illustration of the non-linearity of the process. They signal design changes, even when the product has already been commercially launched.

Even allowing for this non-linearity, however, approaches to managing innovation still rely on phase-based models during which the innovation gradually becomes refined and better articulated. Between the different phases or stages, important design review moments take place, resulting in crucial stop-go decisions. Various models[2] highlight the need to distinguish between the presence of different phases, stages, or activities during the innovation process. These are still managed in a rather sequential way – for example, the idea-generation phase, the concept-definition phase, the problem-solving phase, the prototype-design-test-correct cycles, the manufacturing ramp-up and commercialization phases. However, between the different phases, stop-go decision moments and evaluations are inserted to tunnel and filter uncertainty reduction.

Recently, the emphasis has been on the *'concurrency'* of the various phases, with the objective being to maximize feedback and iteration. Interdependence and overlap between the different activities and functions involved along the innovation journey are increased. However, limits to organizational as well as human resources experimentation and information processing capabilities have been important liabilities in the attempt to achieve full-blown concurrency.

This emergence of the 'concurrency' paradigm signals the need for a still more interactive and iterative way of developing and designing new products. The innovation process has now become much more dynamic and adaptive. This is best illustrated by the rise of interactive design methodologies for software development. New software is increasingly being developed in a sequence of short-cycle iterations where analysts, testers, programmers and users provide input, evaluation and monitoring of a sequence of rapidly developed prototypes. Instead of spending a long time studying a basic software design which is then followed by a detailed design, which is in turn programmed, tested and debugged, we are now being confronted with a quite different development approach. First of all, the software is increasingly being modularized. Then, for each module, small-scale prototypes are designed, quickly built, and upgraded towards full-scale applications. Specifications and functionalities are refined in a cycle of interactions between small module design groups and users. New meta-technologies – that is, technologies that support and enable the design of new technology – such as case-tools and object orientation, further foster this evolution.

As a consequence, we can start to speak of an *innovation spiral* instead of an innovation chain. The innovation spiral points to the continuous sequence of iterations refining and articulating the firm's product, service and process platforms, with solutions to customers' needs being addressed in an integrated manner. In this way, they support the *value constellation* of the firm, rather than its *value chain*.[3] It seems to us that this interactive and iterative model for the development and design of new products is particularly relevant for services. Given the fact that services are intangible, prototyping, for example, is not possible; service providers have to move almost immediately from concept design to tests in the presence of customers. Moreover, by involving customers from the earliest stages in new and complementary development, ideas pop up, leading to an integrated solution for customers' needs instead of just a new product.

In the case of value-chain thinking, there is a tendency to focus on the activities in the value chain upstream or downstream from those conducted at present by the firm. Integrating or eliminating steps along the value chain proves an important source of innovation for many firms. For instance, an important service innovation in the airline industry is the elimination of the ticketing and seat reservation activity. These types of innovation are important, of course, although they are still the result of a rather linear analysis of the value chain along which the firm operates.

The *value constellation* takes a much more holistic view of the way in which the innovation process creates value for the final customer. The value constellation inspires innovation managers to fully understand and articulate how the products and services developed by their organization, in interaction with other (complementary) products and services, create value for the customer. This analysis can lead to the integration of activities across value chains (rather than along the value chain) into new product and service offerings. As a consequence, a service organization (e.g. an automobile association) might realize that, for their next service innovation, not only should they focus on their traditional activities along the value chain of providing automobile assistance, but they might start integrating complementary activities from related value chains with their traditional automobile assistance offerings. This might result, for example, in the (co-)development of smart cards that can be used in combination with a car radio to obtain the latest traffic and automobile assistance. Value-constellation thinking thus stimulates innovation both across and within service lines (*see* Exhibit 15.1).

Exhibit 15.1 UK's National Theatre: Expanding the customer base – encourage all stakeholders to innovate[4]

The UK's National Theatre is one of the world's leading theatres, welcoming audiences totalling more than 1.2m a year to its home on London's South Bank. But as a 'national' theatre, supported by public funding, it has a core objective of bringing theatre to all – not just people visiting or living in London.

In 2009 the National Theatre launched NT Live to stream live performances into cinemas. It had realised that improvements in digital satellite technology meant the National could reach audiences outside London, even overseas, by increasing its 'virtual' capacity.

The National Theatre had to deal with multiple challenges. The first issue was product delivery – making a broadcast capture the intensity of a live theatre performance. A similar scheme at New York's Metropolitan Opera had been successful, but pre-recorded theatrical performances by others in the past had generally been judged to feel flat. This was partly because the cameras operated around a normal paying audience – they could not move and were not in the best spots.

The NT Live answer was to offer broadcasts of one-off performances with a live audience and to work closely with actors, directors, lighting designers and camera operators to prioritize the cinema audiences and find new ways to work.

The new medium also required new rights agreements with stakeholders such as actors, directors and unions. The National negotiated with relevant trade bodies, listening to any concerns as it tailored arrangements to the one-off nature of the performances.

The National's production budgets and remit reflect those of subsidised theatre – rather than a commercial film studio – so it had to devise a business model that was financially sustainable while ensuring that the cinema tickets were inexpensive. NT Live negotiated with distributors to charge no more than £10 per ticket. This was both a financial constraint and a barrier to the scheme being undercut by others.

Finally, the initiative would ultimately be financially viable only if rolled out across the UK and overseas. The National forged a network of distributors who marketed performances to their existing audiences.

NT Live started in June 2009 with Racine's *Phèdre* – starring Helen Mirren, an actress familiar to cinema audiences worldwide – and has now broadcast 11 productions to more than 500,000 people in 400 cinemas in 22 countries.

Actors and audiences were receptive to the innovation, thanks partly to the National clearly remaining true to its core mission and values. The technology was tasked with bringing the National's high artistic quality to a wide audience, and this was possible with support from key stakeholders. The artists, the audiences, the funders and the organisation itself were all prepared to learn from the experiment.

Finally, the National was astute in recognizing that the time was right. Cinemas were now technically equipped to deliver the broadcasts with high-quality HD projectors and satellite technology to receive a live feed; consumers were both engaging with content in new ways and already enjoying live broadcasts – from rock concerts to opera.

As a pioneer in streaming live theatre, the National gained a considerable market and artistic advantage.

Taking a closer look at the concept of an innovation spiral, we find that breakthrough innovations are often the basis of a whole range of new product and service families that are marked by an increase in functional variety and application possibilities. For instance, the innovative breakthrough of using ICT technologies to provide bank services has triggered the development of a highly varied stream of service platforms, such as self-banking, phone-banking and home-banking. The result has been a range of new service-market possibilities. Not only has the reach of the service-market assortments offered been augmented but also the breadth and variety of service product-market possibilities have dramatically increased thanks to underlying process innovations.

Although anyone would agree that, once such a breakthrough has been realized, harvesting the possibilities offered should be the next step, the paradoxical nature of the innovation emerges here yet again. Indeed, without active management intervention, what was once a breakthrough innovation will ultimately result in very incremental changes. This type of incremental innovation, unfortunately, is strongly affected by imitative actions from competitors, eroding the firm's initial competitive advantage at increasing speed. Moreover, this trend often results in the incremental innovator being led by its customers and competitors, rather than it leading its customers and competitors.

As a consequence, management has to strike a continuous balance between the need for short-term incremental improvement to its existing product-market platforms and the more long-term need for fundamentally new business development.

Although the spiral model based on the analysis of value constellations allows for a more accurate modelling and understanding of the innovation process than the 'traditional' linear and value-chain oriented models, it still has one major drawback: if used inadvertently, it may once again lead to 'path-dependent' thinking. There is a risk that a company will become locked into the technical path chosen, a path that will inevitably be eroded over time.

In order to minimize the dangers of path-dependent thinking, the concept of the innovation portfolio can be used. The portfolio approach forces management to articulate its innovation efforts in several dimensions that are determinants of both the long-term and short-term survival and good health of the firm.

Innovation portfolio management

Portfolio management forces management to make the mission and nature of the organization's innovation activity explicit. The framework developed by Kim Clark and Steve Wheelwright[5] at Harvard Business School distinguishes between *research, breakthrough, platform* and *derivative projects* (*see* Figure 15.1). These different types of projects support different missions entailed in the firm's innovation efforts.

The objectives of innovation strategy[6]

Portfolios thus first of all remind us of the fact that innovation activities serve several purposes. The most obvious (and also the one involving fewer risks) is to provide support to existing business. This, of course, is a short-term objective that results in mostly incremental improvements to existing products and services: the so-called *derivative* projects.

Figure 15.1 The innovation portfolio

Besides this short-term objective, innovation efforts also aim at extending and expanding the existing product range of the organization (*platform* projects). This is achieved through the creation of new product generations for existing markets, or through the further extension, adaptation and modification of existing service families to new markets. Innovation activities also carry the seeds of creative destruction. *Breakthrough* innovations break or change the rules of the competitive game. They have the potential to fundamentally destroy and re-orient the technological capabilities as well as the market capabilities in an industry. For example, the Internet breakthrough will fundamentally re-orient the way we do business, both from an organizational perspective and from a technical and commercial perspective.

Finally, innovative companies also realize that they have to continuously rejuvenate and adjust their competence base. Hence, a final objective of an innovation strategy is the timely alignment of the firm's technical competencies (or knowledge economy) to its future product-market requirements.

The four objectives of a firm's innovation strategy can therefore be summarized as:

● support to existing operations and products;

● extension and expansion of product range;

- creation of breakthrough products and processes;
- rejuvenation and alignment of the firm's competence base.

The strategic objectives of a firm's innovation efforts have to be balanced over time. The relative weight of each objective can vary over time and place in the firm's strategy process. For instance, competitive pressures may force the firm to (temporarily) focus the bulk of its innovation investment on support to and incremental improvement of its existing product range. However, senior management should be fully aware of this distribution of focus and assess the long-term consequences of not investing (or over-investing) in particular innovation objectives and outcomes.

The first two objectives (the support to existing operations and products as well as extension and expansion of the product range) attempt to exploit powerful learning-curve effects during the firm's innovation process. The other objectives (the creation of breakthrough product and service innovations as well as rejuvenating and aligning the competence base to future needs) are more disruptive, necessitating 'un-'learning and signalling the onset of new learning curves.

The project typology, as developed by Wheelwright and Clark and shown in Figure 15.1, offers managers an instrument around which processes can be developed to ensure that the strategic objectives of the innovation process are in balance.

Types of innovation projects

As Figure 15.1 shows, the innovation project typology makes a distinction between the *service offering* and *the service delivery process*. Positioning the various types of innovation activity within the matrix highlights the fact that service offering and service process innovations are related.[7]

The creation of new service offerings to complement an existing line of service offerings is illustrated by the financial services sector. Over the last decade, the boundaries between banks and insurance companies have blurred. This has led to serious efforts by all players in the market to develop new services, resulting in new combinations of typical bank and insurance offerings. Innovations can also occur at the level of the service delivery process: banks invest in electronic banking facilities and supermarkets install optical readers linked to cash registers. Although these process innovations in some cases have not affected the basic services banks or supermarkets are offering, it has changed the delivery process and has had a significant impact on the queues at check-outs. It has also given supermarkets a better understanding of customer preferences and allowed for more efficient direct marketing, stock control and purchasing strategy.

Combining both axes – the *content* of the service offerings and the service delivery *process* – allows us to define the three types of innovation project with greater accuracy:

- *Derivative projects* imply small or incremental changes and improvements to either the services itself, the service delivery process, or both. For example, the development of a new savings account for loyal customers, or the development of express check-out counters in a supermarket.
- *Breakthrough projects* imply radical changes to existing services as well as to the delivery process. The offerings that result from a breakthrough innovation differ fundamentally from their predecessors. For example, second-hand cars are sold at several locations.

During the second half of the 1980s, Japan witnessed the emergence of Aucnet. Aucnet was founded by Masataka Fujisaki and made use of a computer and satellite communications system. Each week, sellers can call Aucnet with a list of cars they are offering. Aucnet people then travel to the seller's lots, verify the information on the cars, and collect pictures of them. All this information is then digitized and distributed to dealers who subscribe to the system. Consumers can access this system and choose from a larger variety of cars than ever before. This type of innovation has a dramatic impact both on the 'technology' used to sell second-hand cars and on the 'customer relations' through which the commercial transaction is organized.

- *Platform projects* fill the middle ground between breakthroughs and derivatives. Originating in breakthroughs, they imply significant product-market extensions and the developments of new services, both in terms of the service itself and in terms of the service delivery process, or both. For example, the breakthrough project of electronic banking led to the spin-off of a multitude of platform projects like electronic banking for larger companies, followed by electronic banking services for SMEs, and ultimately, electronic banking applications for the home. These electronic banking platforms were then further complemented with application platforms such as services to compute taxes, to prepare investment projects, etc.

From a strategic perspective, the distribution of the firm's innovation efforts into breakthrough, platform and derivative projects is crucial. Figure 15.1 shows that breakthrough projects imply fundamental changes both from a product/functional perspective and from an operations/process perspective. New core products and new core processes are created. They support the *long-term competitive position* of the company. Platform projects are positioned at the origins of the creation of new product families. They symbolize the degree of product-market differentiation and diversification the company is aiming for. As a consequence, platform projects are mostly *medium-term oriented*. Derivative projects, finally, point to incremental changes (both from a product perspective and a process perspective) that further enhance the performance (in terms of cost and/or functionality) of the firm's existing platforms. By their very nature, they are *short-term oriented*.

It is clear that the bulk of the firm's innovation efforts should go into the execution of platform projects since they represent the medium-term survival of the company. Typically, experience suggests that 50% to 60% of the firm's innovation efforts should be devoted to the creation of new platforms. Derivative projects are important since they sustain existing market relationships. However, portfolio management should be aware of the dangers involved in placing too much emphasis on derivative project activities since they quickly degenerate into imitative behaviour (as they are often driven by short-term customer requests or by the moves of competitors).

In addition to the three types of projects described above, there are more fundamental research activities which can be labelled as *research and advanced development projects*. These involve, for example, the researcher taking on new scientific or technological leads, thereby exploring fundamental know-how and know-why that may ultimately lead to the development of new competence areas for the organization. These projects are not aimed at creating specific products yet. Nevertheless, companies are recommended to frame these research and advanced development activities within a context of value-oriented thinking. In other words, the potential to contribute to value creation (even if it is still defined according to rather abstract and often subjective dimensions) should not be neglected when defining, selecting and following up those research and advanced development projects. Research and advanced development projects or activities are singled out in this portfolio model. This is because their uncertain and unpredictable nature causes extreme difficulties for predicting specific outputs and results within a pre-defined time-frame and budget constraint. It is therefore advisable to consider them as a separate, long-term investment whose progress cannot be measured against well-defined and predetermined criteria and standards. This does not mean, of course, that the quality of the effort cannot be measured and monitored. In terms of future business performance, however, outcome predictability is low.

Creating a balanced portfolio

The benefits of this framework relate to the way in which it enables the firm to manage the collection of innovation activities it is carrying out. It allows for the design of a *balanced* innovation strategy, taking into account both the shorter- and longer-term imperatives of business strategy. It is therefore interesting to map the different projects that are proposed in the innovation portfolio along a number of dimensions that make their contribution to the firm's strategy even more explicit. Typical dimensions are the following:

- *Distributions of reward expectations versus risk*. What are the potential rewards to be reaped when the new product is introduced in the marketplace (these rewards are often described in qualitative terms such as modest, acceptable and outstanding)? How do these compare with the risk that the project achieves a combined market and commercial success? The logic behind this type of criteria mapping is that more risky projects tend to be more promising in terms of rewards and benefits. This is typical of breakthrough projects. The balancing act then calls for an equilibrium between risky but potentially outstanding projects in terms of rewards and benefits on the one hand, and less risky but often also less rewarding projects on the other. Derivative projects are typical examples of projects involving little market and technology risk, while at the same time often offering limited rewards.

- *Time-to-market distributions*. We do not want the portfolio to be too long-term oriented, neglecting the need to achieve short-term, bottom-line results. However, at the same time, we should refrain from having project distributions that are too heavily oriented towards the short-term, since they signal an incapacity to develop and sustain the long-term business development process of the firm. Hence, the need to carefully monitor the time-to-market distribution in the portfolio.

- *The product and technology life cycles underlying the projects*. Product and technologies typically show S-curve life cycles. After a start-up (*embryonic*) phase, they often tend to develop rapidly, as shown by dramatic increases in sales (*product life cycles*) or technological performance (*technology life cycles*). However, there are limits to performance growth, both from a product and technology perspective. The result is that (inevitably) *maturity* sets in. Mature products and services are subject to margin erosion and sales stagnation. Mature technologies are marked by diminishing marginal returns on technological performance. Mature products and technologies are either replaced by newer ones, or rejuvenated by 'enabling' breakthrough innovations – for example, the punctuated leaps in performance increases in silicon technology as a result of breakthroughs achieved in silicon processing technologies, despite the long predicted 'maturity' of silicon-based semiconductor products. It is therefore necessary to monitor the maturity distribution of the technologies and products captured by the development projects in the portfolio. Mature portfolios are vulnerable to substitution and other competitive pressures. Portfolios that have a disproportionate presence of embryonic technologies, products or services contain a high degree of risk. Once again, there is a need to balance maturity distributions.

- *The degree of familiarity with the market and the technology.* The less the organization is familiar with the technological capabilities to be deployed in the project and/or markets to be served by the project, the higher the risk involved and the greater the need for collaboration with external partners. The market/technology familiarity distributions therefore provide yet another insight into the nature of the firm's innovation portfolio.

So far, we have discussed some of the considerations related to portfolio management in innovative environments. As was suggested during the discussion on the familiarity criterion, the portfolio also highlights weaknesses with respect to the technological and/or market capabilities of the firm. These can be solved through the management of 'make' and 'buy' decisions.

Organizing the innovation portfolio: the make-and-buy decision

The development of new business activities via the portfolio approach and methodology can be achieved through:

1 internal development activities (the 'make' decision);

2 reliance on other partners to conduct part of the development activity (the 'buy' decision); or

3 joining internal and external development capabilities (the 'co-operate' decision).

Table 15.1 reflects the spectrum along which the make-and-buy decision should be situated.

Roberts and Berry[8] point out that the relevance of the different approaches will depend on the degree of familiarity with both the technical requirements and the market requirements of the new business. Familiarity has to be interpreted from the perspective of the company analysing its portfolio. For instance, a bank may not yet be familiar with a certain new chip card technology; however, this technology may already have been around for a long time, and thus, it may not be 'new to the world' at all. Hence, familiarity points to the extent to which competencies (both market- and technology-related) are present within the firm.

By stressing both technology and market familiarity, the distinction between breakthrough, platform and derivative projects can be further enriched:

- Breakthrough projects imply increasing degrees of newness and hence will often imply less familiarity.

- Derivative projects are minor extensions of the existing competence base; the company will be familiar with both the market and the underlying technology.

- Platform projects are situated in between.

As a consequence, there is a direct link between familiarity and risk: the less the company is familiar with the market or technical aspects of the new business, the higher the risk of failure.

So Table 15.1[9] can now be linked to the familiarity concept in the following way. The more the company is familiar with the technology and/or the market, the more it can rely on internal mechanisms (such as 'making' the technology using internal development and internal ventures) or disembodied modes of technology transfer and acquisition (such as 'buying' the technology via licensing) to develop the new product or service. These modes can be deployed because the level of familiarity ensures that the organization is able to understand and to handle both the technical and the functional (or market-related) parameters involved in the project.

However, when this capacity is underdeveloped (either from a market or a technology perspective), the project will only succeed if this situation can be rectified. In other words,

Table 15.1 The make-and-buy decision spectrum

Internal developments	This implies the use and development of existing resources, meaning also that the time lag for breaking even tends to be long, especially when these new developments are related to breakthrough projects.
Internal ventures	Existing resources are grouped into a new entrepreneurial unit. Although it allows the company to hold on to talented entrepreneurs, one often observes a mixed record of success. Organizational culture is a critical element in creating and sustaining a successful internal venture process.
Licensing	Licensing allows rapid access to proven knowledge, systems, processes or technology, and reduces the financial exposure. However, the licensee remains dependent upon the licenser throughout the entire process.
Venture capital investments	By providing venture capital to small start-up firms working on relevant new developments, the firm can obtain a 'window on technology'. While this strategy allows for (initially) low levels of commitment, this type of buy decision is not without its problems. The agreement of time horizons between the capital provider and the receiver of funds is not easy, balancing financial and non-financial objectives often causes tensions, and legal problems related to property rights often surface.
Joint ventures or alliances	The competence base of the firm is linked to another company, preferably one with complementary assets. Whereas this approach allows a company to balance risks during the innovation effort, it also requires investments in developing a common infrastructure for the venture as well as establishing operational relationships at the level of the innovative staff belonging to the venture partners.
Acquisitions	In this mode, a company acquires new competencies through the acquisition of another company. In doing so, it gains access to technical capabilities and market competencies it does not possess. However, the challenges of becoming familiarized with the new competence areas and of establishing co-operative relationships between the parent and the newly acquired organization are often high. All too often, core competencies disappear during the transition period. The inability of the parent to accommodate the acquisition often results in core staff members leaving the newly acquired company. A special form of acquisition is the 'educational' acquisition. Here, the emphasis is on gaining access to the people familiar with the new business. While this allows for rapid familiarization with the technical and market aspects of the new business, the success of this approach depends to a large extent on the ability to retain the key people involved.

Source: Reprinted from Roberts, E. B. and Berry, C. A. (1985) 'Entering new business: Selecting strategies for success', *Sloan Management Review*, Vol 23, No 3. 1985 from MIT Sloan Management Review/Massachusetts Institute of Technology. All rights reserved. Distributed by Tribune Media Services.

Table 15.2 Portfolio management and the make-and-buy decision

Objective	Type of innovation	Transfer mechanism	Emphasis is on
Developing new competence	Research/advanced development	Embodied buy mode	Exploring
Creating new product and service generations	Breakthrough project	Embodied as well as disembodied buy mode	Strategic business development
Expanding actual product	Platform project	Disembodied buy mode as well as make mode	Sustaining current competitive position – Exploitation
Improving/adjusting existing product and service offerings	Derivative project	Make mode	Quick market and diffusion response

innovation projects can only succeed if, within the organization carrying out the project, there are well-developed market and technical competencies relevant to the successful completion of the project. If this is not the case, the company will have to acquire and develop these competencies. When there is a serious lack of familiarity, the organization will have to engage in an *embodied technology transfer mode*, implying not only a black box transfer of technical or market results but also a more intense and co-operative mode of transfer involving fluxes of people as the major carriers of the competencies needed. Hence, as familiarity decreases, we witness a rise in the use of such mechanisms as acquisitions and joint ventures.

In all cases, however, the familiarity discussion demonstrates that, in order to successfully 'buy' and integrate 'new' competencies, the company also has to possess or develop a base of internal competencies. This internal competence base characterizes the absorptive capacity of the company. Therefore, we cannot speak any longer of the make-or-buy decision; rather, we should refer to the *make-and-buy* decision. Indeed, competencies can only be successfully bought when they are supported and complemented by internal capabilities.

It is also obvious that the ways or sequences in which the different make-and-buy mechanisms are deployed evolve over time. When entering a new business, the emphasis will be on embodied transfer modes. The more competencies are developed internally, the more the company can engage in disembodied transfer modes and fully supported internal development approaches. Hence, the deployment of the various mechanisms discussed in Table 15.1 will change as well, involving the use of different organizational approaches as the internal competencies co-develop and co-evolve. This co-evolution, and its link to portfolio management, is further illustrated in Table 15.2.

The idea that internal development efforts should be complemented with initiatives involving external partners is at the core of the notion of 'open innovation' as advanced by Chesbrough (2003).[10] Firm competitiveness is increasingly being defined in terms of the power to innovate or the degree to which firms introduce new or significantly improved products, processes and methods. The increasing competition and globalization results in a reduction of innovation cycles: firms are forced to develop innovations in a faster way in order to survive and be successful in the long run. As knowledge and technology are crucial in the innovation process, the question can be raised whether firms are capable of acting alone in their innovation processes.

From 'closed' to 'open' innovation

Traditionally, firms developed new services by relying on internal capabilities. Being self-reliant in terms of new service development indeed offers the best guarantee that the outcomes will be unique and appropriable. Recently, our thinking about such 'closed' innovation strategies started to change, resulting in more 'open' ways of innovating. A number of reasons created this 'paradigm' shift. First, even firms characterized by considerable scale and scope start to realize that it is extremely difficult – and costly – to have in-house state-of-the-art knowledge in all – potentially – relevant fields. Second, combining one's own expertise with the expertise of competent partners might result in considerable cost savings and a reduction of risk levels – implied in all type of innovation efforts. Finally, combining knowledge and capabilities from a diversity of partners bears the potential for novelty: service offerings resulting from combining diverse capabilities may well be more novel than anything the partners involved could achieve separately. This trend towards greater collaboration in research and development activities and the increasing use of external sources for innovation is, nowadays, widely recognized under the umbrella of 'open innovation' (Chesbrough, 2003). 'Open innovation' implies two flows. First, firms should internalize external knowledge and technology to strengthen their own innovative capabilities. Second, firms should consider externalizing internally developed innovations that are not immediately relevant to their core business activities.

As illustrated in Figure 15.2, a distinction is made between the research phase and the development phase in the innovation process. The dotted line of the funnel represents the porous boundaries of the firm, the interface between what is done internally and what is

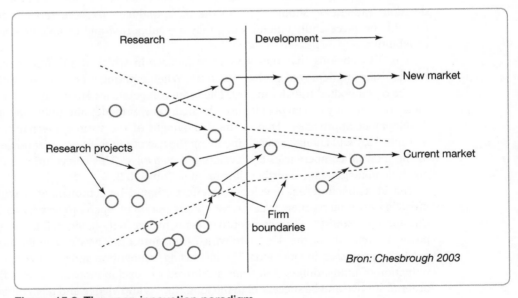

Figure 15.2 The open innovation paradigm

accessed from outside the firm. Ideas can originate from inside the firm or can be started outside the firm and then move inside. As Figure 15.2 shows, there are many potential ideas in the external environment of the firm. Open innovation assumes that firms can and should use both internal and external ideas and paths to create new services. In addition, added value can be generated when ideas, developed internally, are externalized, either by spinning out (corporate venturing), selling or licensing out relevant knowledge and technologies towards third parties.

Firms can improve their innovative capabilities by developing inter-organizational collaborations with a variety of partners.[11] Collaborations with existing suppliers and customers, potential lead users, universities and research centres, and even potential or actual competitors have been advanced as relevant in this respect.

Open services innovation

In the past, firms could easily achieve competitive advantage through product-focused innovation. Consider, for example, mobile phone manufacturers who were able to gain large profits and increase their market share due to the invention of a breakthrough product. A totally new and superior design of a mobile phone could turn the innovation into a hot item in the marketplace. Today, the way of approaching innovation has changed. Instead of focusing mainly on the product, customer experience comes into play. Mobile phone manufacturers are forced to focus their innovation efforts on the applications and services that will enrich their customers' experience in order to survive and remain competitive in their industry (*see also* Chapter 12). Opening up the innovation process, incumbent firms and new entrants are building platforms that attract other companies to design applications and services. This example clearly illustrates the shift required in approaching innovation from a more service-focused, as opposed to a mainly product-focused, standpoint. Both manufacturing and service firms should include a services perspective in their businesses. Moreover, an open services perspective is considered as an enabling framework for discovering new ways of generating profitable growth.[12]

Innovation processes that were effective in the past will not take the firm into a successful future. Knowledge and technologies are widely dispersed, making it more difficult for firms to differentiate their products and sustain that differentiation. Consequently, products can become commodities, sold on the basis of their cost and not their value. In addition, the product life cycle increases. There is only a limited time for a product to be in the marketplace before a new and improved product replaces the existing one. These economic forces should motivate firms to rethink their innovation processes and management. Applying a service perspective enables new value creation for both the firm and its customers. Innovation in services helps firms to overcome the danger of inertia related to the commoditization of products.

Open services innovation has been recently advanced as a framework for stimulating innovation and growth.[13] As Figure 15.3 illustrates, it relies upon four concepts. First, firms should think about their business as an open services business to create and sustain differentiation. Second, customers should be involved to co-create innovation in order to generate the customer experiences that they prefer. Third, open innovation practices should be applied to strengthen services innovation, making it faster, reducing the costs and risks. Fourth, business models should be transformed through open services innovation. The most important subsidiary ideas that underpin each concept are listed in Figure 15.3.

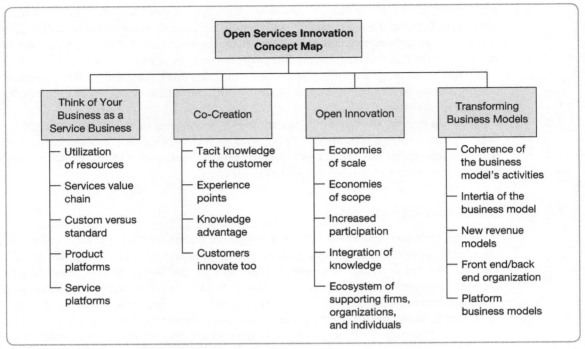

Figure 15.3 Open services innovation concept map

Source: Chesbrough, H. (2011) *Open Services Innovation: Rethinking your business to grow and compete in a new era*. San Francisco, CA: Jossey-Bass. Copyright © 2011, John Wiley and Sons. Reprinted with permission from John Wiley and Sons.

Now that we have achieved a better understanding of portfolio management as a tool for supporting the process of strategic decision making regarding product and service innovations, including the need to balance internal and external development efforts, we can start to look at the operational paradoxes in the management of innovation.

The operational management of innovation

In Figure 15.4,[14] we provide a summary overview (simplified) of the key performance variables relevant to the innovation processes at the operational level. The critical influence of information flows and communication patterns on the performance of innovation activities has been well documented and is the subject of major research attention. Not only are intense intra-organizational and cross-functional information flows and communication patterns necessary during the innovation process, but the innovative organization must also be closely linked to its broader (external) technological environment. This close relationship is symbolized by the presence of special 'network' roles during the innovation process, among which the gatekeeper figures prominently. Related studies, which have their origins in the development and the marketing of new products, have further pointed to the importance of the design and the application of appropriate work organization techniques and approaches for achieving innovative performance.[15] These include:

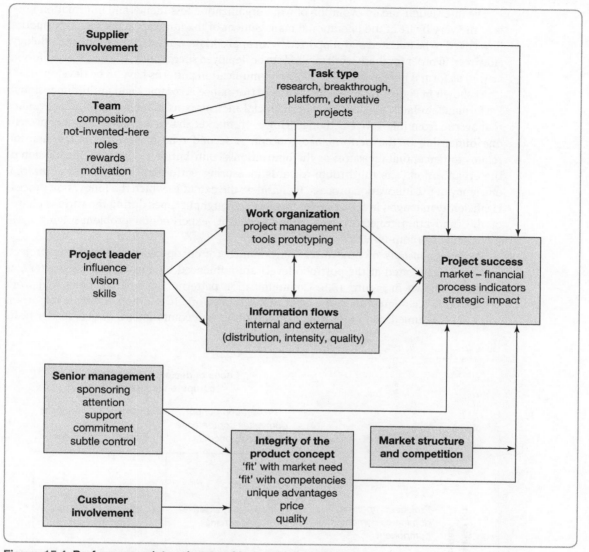

Figure 15.4 Performance determinants of innovation projects

Source: Debackere, K., Van Looy, B. and Vliegen, J. (1997) A process view on managing quality during the creation of technical innovations: Lessons from field research, Vol 27, No 3, pp. 197–211, Blackwell Publishers Ltd., reprinted by permission of John Wiley and Sons.

- the use of flowchart-based decision and monitoring models of the innovation process;
- the application of project management techniques;
- the introduction of creativity and idea-generation techniques, such as brainstorming;
- the development of selection methodologies that respond to the innovation's need for tolerating and handling uncertainty and ambiguity;
- the use and the design of grid-methodologies and techniques to define and to monitor innovation opportunities (e.g. product maturity grids, business growth matrices, quality function deployment matrices).

The interaction and co-evolution of work organization techniques and information flows is at the very heart of the operational management of the innovation process. Information flows need to be initiated and supported by an appropriate work-organization methodology. However, in order for these work methods to be deployed successfully, the necessary informal as well as formal information flows and communication patterns have to be developed.

As shown in Figure 15.4, the innovation performance is complex and multi-dimensional. Performance relates to such rational, financial indicators as market shares and revenues that accrue from innovative activities. However, market shares and revenues only present one dimension of the performance concept. A second type of performance dimension relates to perceptual measures as the innovation's contribution to the strategic mission of the organization. The third route towards measuring performance refers to the internal efficiency of the innovation process. It considers the extent to which the innovation process is efficiently managed in terms of, for instance, throughput times during the various phases of the innovation trajectory (e.g. time-to-concept, experimental problem-solving cycle times, time-to-ramp-up).

These dimensions of innovative performance (often operationalized at the project-level and aggregated at the portfolio-level) are influenced by a myriad of parameters, as is further shown in Figure 15.5. Communication patterns, information flows and work organization techniques are at the heart of this framework. In addition, there are important roles to be assumed. Senior management attitudes and commitment, project leader traits

Figure 15.5 Project performance in the innovation matrix

Source: Adapted from Katz, R. and Allen, T. (1985) 'The locus of control in the R&D matrix', *Academy of Management Journal*, Vol 28, No 1, pp. 67–87.

and behaviour, as well as team member characteristics, all exert a strong influence on the performance of innovation activities. Moreover, these have to be embedded in an appropriate motivational context, using incentive mechanisms that foster 'project ownership' rather than performance 'control'. Incentive mechanisms encouraging entrepreneurship and 'ownership' in innovative contexts therefore have to be related to the realization of project outcomes as well as to the overall success of the project in the eyes of its customer – for example, by providing substantive bonus schemes for project members if they achieve a successful project result. Of course, as suggested in Figure 15.4, the complexity of the project (research, breakthrough, platform or derivative) has an important impact on the relationships just described. More specifically, in the case of derivative or incremental projects, these performance relationships can be managed in a much more structured and formalized way than in the case of a research activity or a breakthrough project. For instance, in a breakthrough project, creating ownership may involve the development of highly visible bonus schemes that give the project members significant stakes in the project's success. For derivative projects, this should not be the case. Here, the incentive system should evaluate such 'classic' performance control criteria as responsiveness and timeliness of the project members' activities.

The involvement of external parties, more specifically suppliers and customers, is yet another well-known determinant of innovation success.[16] The relative importance of their impact varies depending on the party that obtains the highest returns from investing in the innovation. Although this is a simple criterion, it may be difficult to determine who will benefit most from a particular innovation, certainly when it pertains to emerging industries.

For example, the telecommunications industry is in a state of flux. Product and service innovations are increasingly intertwined and have a dramatic impact on our daily lives. However, it is unclear thus far who will reap the most benefits from these innovations. Many years ago, MCI was a major innovator in the industry. Today, it has been acquired by WorldCom, which is much smaller than MCI but is now one of the most admired service innovators in the industry. However, it is still unclear whether a company like WorldCom will ultimately be able to reap the benefits from those innovations, or whether it will accrue to another, as yet unknown, player in the industry. It is only when the value constellation can be articulated that we can start to analyse who should benefit most from involvement in the innovation process. In emerging industries, this value constellation is most often unclear and, hence, the relative importance of users and suppliers is difficult to establish.

As can be seen in Figure 15.4, the structure of the market or the degree of competition in the marketplace are other important parameters influencing success along the innovation journey. Turbulent market structures, marked by high degrees of monopolistic competition, strongly moderate the 'optimal' organization of the innovation process. Examples abound, such as the case of Quantum Corporation.[17] Quantum, active in the area of computer disk drives, experienced a turbulent, fast-evolving marketplace with fierce competition based on slightly differentiated product characteristics. This competitive environment necessitated an innovation function highly responsive to frequent changes in the marketplace. As a solution, Quantum based the organization of its innovation process on flexible lateral (team-based) structures, state-of-the-art functions or competencies and appropriate incentive systems. These required each team member to act as a 'cross-functional specialist' who had to strike a balance between team performance and individual performance, as well as between expertise and experience. Appropriate incentive systems were developed and implemented.

This need for 'cross-functional specialists' points to the dilemma concerning, or the tension present in, the matrix structure – a tension that is characteristic of most innovative organizations. An innovator always needs to balance the development of competencies (i.e. the development of a satisfactory absorptive capability) with the imperative to achieve the results expected from the projects and programmes in the portfolio. This dilemma is often captured by creating a matrix form of organization structure, in which competence areas and project teams are intertwined and balanced. As Figure 15.5[18] shows, successful innovation efforts require 'strong' matrix structures.

In order for competencies to be allocated to and deployed in a breakthrough or platform project, they need to be up-to-date and state-of-the-art (we intentionally leave out derivative projects, since they often require only minimal forms of project organization). Hence, successful breakthrough and platform projects will have to be embedded in well-developed competence areas. This calls for a 'strong' matrix structure, where competence areas and project management are allies in resource accumulation and deployment, rather than the one being dominated by the other. Both need to be state-of-the-art in their respective domains of expertise and experience.

Clearly, the presence of two strong components sows the seeds of a situation of conflict. However, this need not be a problem since a 'strong' matrix will certainly have some conflict between its project and competence components. What a 'strong' matrix certainly does have is an ability to solve those conflicts. In other words, these forms of organization handle the tensions that occur between their competence and project components not by being conflict-free but through their ability to manage and resolve the conflicts that inevitably occur. This is a critical capability in managing innovation matrices. Certain companies, such as Intel, have become very good at it.

This argument is further corroborated by the research results reported in Figure 15.5. Two major dimensions that relate to decision making in an innovation matrix have to be addressed:

1 Decisions about competence issues will have to be made – for example, those relating to technical issues such as the telecommunication protocol to be used in the development of a new service. Will it be the Internet protocol TCP/IP or not?

2 Decisions have to be made with respect to organizational or managerial issues – for example, those relating to the allocation of (additional) resources to a project or the evaluation of the performance of project team members.

For each of these decision areas, we have to ask what should be the most influential component. Should it be the competence component of the organization, or should it be the project component? The summary research results reported in Figure 15.5 show that the highest performance is obtained when a balance is realized between the competence and the project component. The project component then dominates organizational/managerial decision making, while the competence component dominates competence-related or technical decision making. The lowest performance occurs when the competence component dominates both organizational/managerial decision making and technical decision making on the project. In the other instances (*see* Figure 15.5), project performance is average or moderately positive.

The tension in the innovation matrix therefore calls for competencies and projects to be both well managed and state-of-the-art, instead of one dominating the other. Unfortunately, the fact that organizations have – and always will have – only limited resources available often obscures this important finding. Very often, the finite capacity problem is solved by allowing one component in the innovation matrix to control the other component on both dimensions of the decision-making process, resulting in sub-optimal performance, as demonstrated in Figure 15.5.

Even worse, all too often the finite capacity constraints are resolved by making the traditional functional (i.e. the competence-based) organization dominate decision making in both dimensions. Again, as demonstrated in Figure 15.5, this is the worst-case scenario. Typically, in such a situation, it becomes impossible for a company to grow and to retain strong project management skills and leadership. The overall result is a portfolio that underperforms and does not achieve its objectives in terms of strategic support to the growth of the company.

Managing service innovation

Now that we are acquainted with innovation and its translation into practice, the issue can be raised as to whether and to what extent innovation management is different within service environments. Innovation has long been linked to technology driven product- and process innovations in the manufacturing industry. It has, relatively recently, come more to the fore in service industries. Service firms are considered as different innovators compared to manufacturing firms.[19]

Service innovations are all around and their power in creating economic growth and well being is increasingly recognized. Frameworks concerning the strategic management of service innovation remain relatively scarce.[20] There is no consensus about the definition of service innovation. However, six dimensions are relevant in this respect: new service concept, new customer interaction, new value system or business partners, new revenue model, new organizational or technological service delivery system. A service innovation can be defined as a new service experience or service solution that consists of one or more of these dimensions.[21]

A first observation that must be made in the respect of the differences between services and manufacturing industries relates to the amount of R&D spending. R&D spending in services is increasing rapidly although, in general, this is lower for services than for manufacturing firms.[22] Recent OECD figures indicate that the total amount of all business expenditure on R&D (BERD) taking place in service industries is much less compared to manufacturing industries. Given that these same industries count for about 70% of GDP, it seems that manufacturing industries are 'outperforming' services in this area.[23] There are several reasons for this difference. The first relates to the character of innovations in services. The majority of these innovations are non-technical and involve small and incremental changes, which often require little R&D. In addition, innovation surveys have made clear that R&D expenditure is only one element of a firm's innovation expenditure. Spending linked to changes in processes, organizational arrangements, and training of staff seems to represent a larger share of expenditures for innovation in service environments.[24] Also, in services, one frequently observes 'ad hoc' innovations stemming directly from a particular request by a customer,[25] which seldom result in the formation of a 'centralized' R&D department. Hence, in service environments, R&D activities tend to be more 'hidden' and their extent less well documented. It is nevertheless clear that, during the last few decades, more R&D activity has taken place in manufacturing industries. Service industries have thus tended to play the role of 'lead user', whereby ideas and requests for new ways of delivering services resulted in the service firms' suppliers developing new technology, instead of these technologies being developed by the service firms 'in house'. A crucial role in this respect is played by the IT industry, as was made clear in Chapter 6.

While this might give a rather 'passive' view of innovation in service companies, some serious nuances can and should be made. First of all, over the last decade, R&D expenditures have steadily increased in service firms, bringing them closer to the ranges observed in manufacturing industries.[26] Secondly (and this phenomenon will be discussed in Chapter 18), the boundaries between manufacturing and service industries are tending to fade. Servitization implies that manufacturing companies will, to an ever-increasing extent, offer bundles of products and services; similarly, service firms are often very interested in complementing their offerings with products (*see* Chapter 16). As a consequence, distinctions in the way in which innovation is organized between services and manufacturing are tending to disappear in certain respects. Nevertheless, there also seem to be noticeable differences in how services and manufacturing firms approach the innovation process. These differences refer primarily to the way in which firms formalize development of innovations in the services and manufacturing sector. In addition, there is the unique way of testing new concepts with customers and the combined role of general managers and professionals in the services innovation process.[27]

Considerable differences can further be observed between industries, and even between firms within an industry, in the role and importance of innovation, and thus of R&D activities. It would appear that these differences no longer correspond to boundaries between services or manufacturing industries. Industries such as engineering and telecommunications outperform many manufacturing industries in terms of R&D intensity. In this respect, taking the nature of the service delivery process itself into account might be more relevant in explaining the R&D intensity of a service firm (or industry). We will illustrate this idea with the service classifications advanced by Mills and Margulies, as discussed in Chapter 2. Maintenance-interactive services, given their predictable and routine character, are most susceptible to standardization and are most easily translated into technology (*see* Chapter 6); it will therefore come as no surprise that the R&D intensity of such service firms is tending to resemble that of manufacturing firms.[28] As for task-interactive services, the specialized knowledge involved in their delivery means that two types of technologies play a central role. These are specialized equipment (such as medical), and more generic, knowledge-supporting technologies such as databases, expert systems and communication technologies that allow for information exchange between experts (*see also* Chapters 6 and 11). Finally, personal-interactive services seem to benefit mainly from this last type of technology; the ambiguous nature of at least part of the service transaction itself makes it extremely difficult to introduce tools or technology that complement the competencies embodied by the service provider as a person. Thus, it could be said that organizing R&D activities as outlined above might be somewhat less relevant for personal-interactive services. For task- and maintenance-interactive services, organizing innovation becomes a process very similar to the processes taking place in manufacturing environments.

Two important points need to be stressed in this respect. First of all, getting organized with respect to innovation requires an explicit R&D *investment* strategy. As demonstrated above, translating an innovation project portfolio into a range of new services will require resources, which will more often than not be human. As will be illustrated in Chapter 16, services can suffer from 'limits to earnings due to restrictions on selling capacity'. This simply means that what you can earn may be limited by the time (capacity) available within the service organization. For instance, if you are a consultant, your earnings amount to the number of hours you work, multiplied by the earnings per hour. If you decide to invest in R&D projects, this might imply that you forego short-term revenue in the hope that it will be compensated by future revenues from the new projects. The intangibility of services (since they consist mainly of know-how) poses specific problems, however; the problematic nature of intellectual property rights arrangements for services has been pointed out by several scholars. While patents offer many manufacturing industries a solid ground for safeguarding the future benefits resulting from the investments made, the intangible nature of services makes effective protection less straightforward.[29] And whereas trademarks and copyrights do exist, they are generally much easier to circumvent than patents. Hence, within services, short-term-oriented R&D projects, which entail fewer resources, tend to be favoured over projects with extended time frames and requiring considerable resources. Stated otherwise, in order to arrive at an effective realization of any innovation strategy, service firms will have to come up with a well-designed plan that addresses the way in which the results of these investments will be appropriated. We will discuss this issue in more depth in the chapter on service strategy.

Secondly, a particular phenomenon in relation to innovation and services has been advanced by Barras (1986):[30] the idea of the 'reversed product cycle'. Whereas manufacturing environments are dominated by the idea that product innovations are followed by process innovations, the opposite may hold true for services. Within manufacturing environments, the so-called Abernathy-Utterback model,[31] named after the authors who proposed it, is considered highly valuable. This model illustrates how the nature of a company's innovation activity changes as it grows and matures. During a first phase, a novel product design is subject to major changes; since product characteristics are underdetermined, product innovations are numerous. These innovations are focused on improving the functional performance of the product, rather than on reducing its (production) costs. After a while (often as a result of frequent interaction with lead users) a 'dominant' design tends to emerge, implying a stabilized product concept. The product becomes standardized and production systems become more and more efficient and reliable, precisely because the product design does not change fundamentally. Innovation during this second stage focuses on process improvements and adaptations. What Barras has been suggesting with respect to services is that the order of these stages is reversed. In certain services, such as banking, insurance and administration, Barras observed a product life cycle opposite to the traditional industrial cycle. At the beginning, there is the adoption of an item of new technology, for instance computer equipment. This first triggers the emergence of incremental process innovations resulting in efficiency improvements of the services provided. In a next step, one achieves more radical improvements in terms of service quality, to finally arrive at the emergence of new products based on these new technologies. A case in point here is the introduction of home banking, in which PCs and networks are used to connect the bank's customers to its services. Although this initially results in less expensive distribution channels, it also implies new quality achievements (availability, speed). Nowadays, the Internet banking platform is being used more and more to introduce new services (e.g. tax simulation). While it is true that this process might not hold for all service industries to the same extent,[32] it again draws our attention to the design of specific innovation trajectories – including relevant roadmaps – that fit with the specific nature of services.

Conclusion

In this chapter, we have provided an overview of the major strategic and operational imperatives that come into play during the development of new products and services. Innovation efforts should be aimed at providing solutions for customers' needs and problems. In services, it is especially crucial for companies to bear in mind the notion of value constellation; innovation efforts should, in a sense, be in line with the service concept the company is striving to achieve.

Moreover, innovation is a paradoxical process; both competence-enhancing and competence-destructive forces need to be balanced. We deliberately focused on products as well as services, since recent trends in innovation in service industries show that the two have become increasingly intertwined. Thus, the development of combined product/service offerings becomes imperative to successful innovation practice in service industries.

In order to develop these product/service platforms, firms will have to balance their portfolios. This balancing act has a cross-sectional dimension as well as a longitudinal one. From a cross-sectional perspective, portfolio management requires a balance to be struck between the longer term (breakthrough projects) and the shorter term (derivative projects). Management thus has to develop a strategic vision as to the sequence and the timing of the development of new product and service platforms.

Given the dual nature of the innovation process, both make and buy actions will be relevant for acquiring new capabilities.

Collaboration practices with external partners become increasingly important to strengthen a firm's innovative power and to gain significant competitive advantage. We have elaborated on the transition from a 'closed' towards an 'open' innovation model.

Next, we discussed the operational issues of managing innovation projects and the organizational structure in which this strategic innovation portfolio becomes embedded. As we have suggested, this structure has to be 'strong', enabling and sustaining a 'strong' project component as well as a 'strong' competence component. This balancing act is at the heart of the operational performance of the innovative service organization. Finally, we discussed differences between manufacturing and services environments in terms of defining and implementing an adequate innovation strategy.

Review and discussion questions

- How important is innovation for the long-term survival and growth of service firms? Why? Can you give examples? Would you consider this importance the same for all sorts of service industries? Why/why not?

- Suppose you are a successful R&D manager in a large manufacturing company. You are asked to develop the R&D activities of a large international bank. While the offer is very interesting, you still have your doubts; do you have all the relevant experience and do you know how to succeed? Stated otherwise, what might be different in terms of managing an R&D department in a large service firm, as opposed to managing such a department in a manufacturing firm? Would you consider these to be differences of degree?

Suggested further reading

Allen, T. J. (1977) *Managing the Flow of Technology*. Cambridge, MA: The MIT Press

Champy, J. and Nohria, N. (1996) *Fast Forward: The best ideas on managing business change*. Boston, MA: Harvard Business School Press

Chesbrough, H. W. (2003) *Open Innovation: The new imperative for creating and profiting from technology*. Boston, MA: Harvard Business School Press

Chesbrough, H. W. (2011) *Open Services Innovation: Rethinking your business to grow and compete in a new era*. San Francisco, CA: Jossey-Bass

Katz, R. and Allen, T. (1985) 'The locus of control in the R&D matrix', *Academy of Management Journal*, Vol 28, No 1, pp. 67–87

Kay, J. (1993) *Foundations of Corporate Success*. Oxford: Oxford University Press

Twiss, B. C. (1992) *Managing Technological Innovation*. London: Pitman Publishing

Van de Ven, A. H., Polley, D. E., Garud, R. and Venkataraman, S. (2008) *The Innovation Journey*. New York, NY: Oxford University Press

Wheelwright, S. C. and Clark, K. B. (1992) *Revolutionising Product Development*. New York, NY: The Free Press

Notes and references

1 *See*, for instance, Kay, J. (1993) *Foundations of Corporate Success*. Oxford: Oxford University Press

2 *See*, for instance, Saren, M. (1984) 'Models of the innovation process', *R&D Management*, Vol 14, No 1, pp. 11–24; Roberts, E. B. and Frohman, A. (1978) 'Strategies for improving research utilisation', *Technology Review*, Vol 80, No 5; Wheelwright, S. C. and Clark, K. B. (1992) *Revolutionising Product Development*. New York, NY: The Free Press; and Twiss, B. C. (1992) *Managing Technological Innovation*. London: Pitman Publishing. Errasti, N., Zabaleta, N. and Oyarbide, A. (2011) 'A review and conceptualisation of innovation models from the past three decades', *International Journal of Technology Management*, Vol 55, No 3/4, pp. 190–200

3 *See* Normann, R. and Ramirez, R. (1996) 'From value chain to value constellation: Designing interactive strategy', in Champy, J. and Nohria, N. (eds) *Fast Forward: The Best Ideas on Managing Business Change*. Boston, MA: Harvard Business School Press, pp. 39–60

4 *Source*: Schutt, B. (2011) 'Case Study: National Theatre Live' *Financial Times*, 24 August (This case study was adapted from Schutt's Judge Business School case study and teaching note 'The Work of Art in the Age of Technological Reproduction: The National Theatre Goes to the Movies', available at European Case Clearing House). Becky Schutt is a Fellow in Arts and Culture at the University of Cambridge Judge Business School

5 *See* Wheelwright, S. C. and Clark, K. B. (1992), op. cit.

6 Ibid.

7 However, both process and product innovations do not have to coincide. Just think back to the issues discussed in relation to information technology. Here we have seen that process innovations (e.g. self-banking facilities) do not necessarily imply new services; they simply mirror an existing bank office. However, in practice, new processes will often lead to new services as well; just think about the extensions of services made possible through self-banking (e.g. tax calculations)

8 Roberts, E. B. and Berry, C. A. (1985) 'Entering new businesses: Selecting strategies for success', *Sloan Management Review*, Vol 26, No 3, pp. 3–17

9 Ibid.

10 Chesbrough, H. W. (2003) *Open Innovation: The new imperative for creating and profiting from technology*. Boston, MA: Harvard Business School Press

11 Faems, D., Van Looy, B. and Debackere, K. (2005) 'Interorganizational collaboration and innovation: Toward a portfolio approach', *Journal of Product Innovation Management*, 22, pp. 238–250

12 Chesbrough, H. (2011) *Open Services Innovation: Rethinking Your Business to Grow and Compete in a New Era*. San Fransisco, CA: Jossey-Bass

13 Chesbrough, H. (2011) 'The case for open services innovation: The commodity trap', *California Management Review*, Vol 53, No 3, pp. 5–20

14 *Source*: Debackere, K., Van Looy, B. and Vliegen, J. (1997) 'Quality as a process during the creation of technical innovations: Lessons from field research', *R&D Management*, Vol 27, No 3, pp. 197–211

15 We refer to the work of Bergen, S. A. (1986) *R&D Management: Managing new projects and new products*. Oxford: Basil Blackwell; Cooper, R. G. and Kleinschmidt, E. J. (1995) 'Benchmarking the firm's critical success factors in new product development', *Journal of Product Innovation Management*, 12, pp. 374–391; Crawford, C. M. (1983) *New Products Management*. Boston, MA: Irwin; Souder, W. E. (1987) *Managing New Product Innovations*. Lexington, MA: Lexington Books; Twiss, B. C. (1974) *Managing Technological Innovation*. London: Longman; or Wheelwright, S. C. and Clark, K. B. (1992), op. cit.

16 For instance, von Hippel's research has documented well the important role played by lead users and suppliers. *See* von Hippel, E. (1988) *The Sources of Innovation*. New York, NY: Oxford University Press

17 Quantum Corporation (1992) *Business and Product Teams*. Harvard Business School Case 9-692-023

18 Adapted from Katz, R. and Allen, T. (1985) 'The locus of control in the R&D matrix', *Academy of Management Journal*, Vol 28, No 1, pp. 67–87

19 Miles, I. (2006) 'Innovation in services'. In Fagerberg, J., Mowery, D. C. and Nelson R. R. (eds) *The Oxford Handbook of Innovation*, New York, NY: Oxford University Press, pp. 433–458

20 Frei, F. X. (2008) 'The four things a service business must get right', *Harvard Business Review*, Vol 86, No 4, pp. 70–80; Möller, K., Rajala, R. and Westerlund, M. (2008) 'Service innovation Myopia? A new recipe for client-provider value creation', *California Management Review*, Vol 50, No 3, pp. 31–48

21 Ettlie, J. E. and Rosenthal, S. R. (2011) 'Service versus manufacturing innovation', *Journal of Product Innovation Management*, Vol 28, pp. 285–299

22 Although differences are considerable between industries

23 OECD (2011) *OECD Science, Technology and Industry Scoreboard 2011*. Paris: OECD Publishing, doi: 10.1787/sti_scoreboard-2011-en; OECD (2009) *Innovation in Firms: A microeconomic perspective*. Paris: OECD Publishing

24 Pilat, D. (2001) 'Innovation and Productivity in Services', in *OECD Proceedings*, Paris: OECD Publishing

25 As such, a consequence of the simultaneity and heterogeneity that characterizes services

26 For exact figures, *see* Edwards, M. and Crocker, M. (2001) *Innovation and Productivity in Services: Major trends and issues*. OECD Report

27 Ettlie, J. E. and Rosenthal, S. R. (2011) 'Service versus manufacturing innovation', *Journal of Product Innovation Management*, Vol 28, pp. 285–299

28 Whereby for services, suppliers will take care of the development of technology more often

29 For a more in-depth discussion on this topic, *see* Howells, J. (2001) 'The nature of innovation in services', in *OECD Proceedings on Innovation and Productivity in Services*, Paris: OECD Publishing; and Andersen, B. and Howells, J. (2000) 'Intellectual property rights shaping innovation in services', in Anderson, B., Howells, J., Hull, R., Miles, I. and Roerts, J. (eds) (2000) *Knowledge and Innovation in the new service economy*. Cheltenham and Brookfield, WI: Edward Elgar Publishers

30 Barras, R. (1986) 'Towards a theory of innovation in services', *Research Policy*, Vol 15, pp. 161–173

31 Abernathy, W. and Utterback, J. (1975) 'A dynamic model of product and process innovation', *Omega*, Vol 3, No 6, pp. 639–656

32 *See*, for instance, the arguments outlined above with respect to the relevancy of organizing R&D in relation to the nature of the service delivery process. *See also* Gallouj, F. and Weinstein, O. (1997) 'Innovation in services', *Research Policy*, Vol 26, pp. 537–556, on this topic

Chapter 16

Developing Sustainable Strategies

Aimé Heene • Bart Van Looy

Objectives

By the end of this chapter, you should be able to discuss:

- the basic questions or themes that have to be dealt with when defining a service strategy

- the notion of competitive advantage and how competitive forces erode this advantage

- how recent insights from resource- and competence-based views on strategy enhance our insights into the strategy process

- specific issues and challenges faced by service firms: tangibilization, the use of intangible resources, the dynamics of value creation and perception, the role of technology, and ways of managing for continuity in time and space.

Introduction

Exhibit 16.1 Even a giant can learn to run

'BECAUSE it has become so consistently successful, I.B.M. is almost boring. This is a company so predictable that its financial forecast is packaged as a "five-year road map" as if it were some sort of state planning exercise.

Yet behind I.B.M.'s relentless progress over the last decade is a game plan that has been anything but conservative. The company shed multibillion-dollar businesses. It chose higher profit margins over corporate size, and expanded aggressively overseas, seeking sales, low-cost engineering talent and quicker organizational reflexes.

All of that didn't just happen. A large portion of the credit goes to Samuel J. Palmisano, who steps down on Sunday after nearly a decade as chief executive. During his tenure, I.B.M. has been a textbook case of how to drive change in a big company – when so much of the study of business innovation focuses on start-ups and entrepreneurs.

He says his guiding framework boils down to four questions:

- "Why would someone spend their money with you – so what is unique about you?"
- "Why would somebody work for you?"
- "Why would society allow you to operate in their defined geography – their country?"
- "And why would somebody invest their money with you?"

Mr. Palmisano formulated those questions in the months after he became C.E.O. in March 2002. His predecessor, Louis V. Gerstner Jr., recruited to I.B.M. in 1993, had already pulled the company out of a financial tailspin, first reducing the size of the work force and cutting costs, and then leading a remarkable recovery.

In meetings after he took over, Mr. Palmisano told colleagues that I.B.M. was still good, but that it wasn't the standard-setting corporation that it had been when he joined in 1973 . . .

The four questions, he explains, were a way to focus thinking and prod the company beyond its comfort zone and to make I.B.M. pre-eminent again. He presented the four-question framework to the company's top 300 managers at a meeting in early 2003 in Boca Raton, Fla.

"This needs to be our mission and goal, to make I.B.M. a great company," he said, according to executives who attended the gathering.

The pursuit of excellence in those four dimensions shaped the strategy. To focus on doing unique work, with its higher profits, meant getting out of low-margin businesses that were fading. I.B.M.'s long-range technology assessment in 2002 concluded that the personal computer business would no longer present much opportunity for innovation, at least not in the corporate market.

The hub of innovation would shift to services and software, often delivered over the Internet from data centers, connecting to all kinds of devices, including PCs. Today, that is called cloud computing; when I.B.M. started promoting the concept several years ago the company called it on-demand computing.

So Mr. Palmisano led a lengthy strategic review of the PC business, deciding to sell while it was still profitable. Internal arguments against a sell-off were intense: PCs pulled in sales of other I.B.M. products in corporate accounts, the cost of electronic parts for its larger computers would jump without the purchasing power of its big PC division, and the corporate brand and its reputation would suffer without PCs, the one I.B.M. product touched by millions of people.

"I've heard every one of the arguments, every one of them," Mr. Palmisano says. "But if you decide you're going to move to a different space, where there's innovation and therefore you can do unique things and get some premium for that, the PC business wasn't going to be it."

In 2004, I.B.M. sold its PC business to Lenovo of China. Mr. Palmisano says he deflected overtures from Dell and <u>private equity</u> firms, preferring the sale to a company in China for strategic reasons: the Chinese government wants its corporations to expand globally, and by aiding that national goal, I.B.M. enhanced its stature in the lucrative Chinese market, where the government still steers business.

In total, the PC, disk drive and other hardware businesses that Mr. Palmisano sold off generated nearly $20 billion a year in sales, if not a lot of profits. The divestitures meant that I.B.M. was no longer the world's largest information technology company. Hewlett-Packard took that title and took a different strategic path as well, doubling its bet on PCs by acquiring Compaq in 2001. "You see the choice that was made, and how the economics worked out,"

Mr. Palmisano observes. Today, I.B.M.'s stock market value, at $217 billion, is more than four times that of the struggling H.P.

I.B.M. invested heavily elsewhere, buying the business consulting firm Pricewaterhouse-Coopers Consulting, for $3.5 billion in 2002, for its expertise in specific industries. For I.B.M., the emphasis was to move up from selling customers computers and software to helping them use technology to solve business challenges in marketing, procurement and manufacturing.

Corporations and governments are drowning in a flood of data from internal systems and the Web, struggling to make sense of it. To get ahead of that challenge, I.B.M. has spent more than $14 billion since 2005 buying 25 software companies that specialize in data mining and analytics, looking for useful patterns in data in fields as varied as disease treatment, traffic management and crime detection. And it has increased its research and development budget by 20 per cent under Mr. Palmisano, to about $6 billion a year.

Combining research, specialized skills and sophisticated technology is the recipe behind I.B.M.'s Smarter Planet initiative, begun in 2008. It now has more than 2,000 projects worldwide, applying computer intelligence to create more efficient systems for utility grids, traffic management, food distribution, water conservation and health care. The idea, Mr. Palmisano explains, is to "go to a space where you're uniquely positioned and use the value of I.B.M.'s integration." For him, the Smarter Planet effort is a return to I.B.M.'s roots. Shortly before he became chief executive, he dipped into corporate archives, reading speeches and memos from the founder, Thomas Watson Sr. When Mr. Palmisano was an executive assistant to John F. Akers, then the chairman, in 1989 and 1990, he had lunch with Thomas J. Watson Jr., a former chairman, once a month. The Watsons, he says, always defined I.B.M. as a company that did more than sell computers; they believed that it had an important role to play in solving societal challenges.

"It's old-fashioned, but it's motivational," he says.

And it resonates with the young people I.B.M. is recruiting these days, he says. A couple of times a year, Mr. Palmisano speaks to groups of elite students whom I.B.M. is trying to woo to its research labs. The pitch, he says, is that I.B.M. is a place where you can make a difference and do deep science. "You can change the world, and you can compete for a Nobel prize," he says, referring to I.B.M.'s five Nobel winners. (Eighty-seven percent of the candidates who were offered jobs by I.B.M. Research this year joined the company.)

Mr. Palmisano's appeal to young technologists is just one example of an answer to one of his four questions. All four, he says, must be addressed. "The hardest thing is answering those four questions," Mr. Palmisano says. "You've got to answer all four and work at answering all four to really execute with excellence."'

In this chapter, we explore the issues involved in developing a sustainable strategy for a service firm. We start off by taking a broader look at what strategy is all about. What is the nature of strategic management? What questions have to be answered when defining an organization's strategy? What are the relevant frameworks and recent insights? Equipped with this background, we shall be able to discuss some of the specific challenges involved in defining a service strategy: managing intangible resources, looking at added value carriers and the dynamics of value creation, managing for continuity, and finally the role of technology.

The nature of strategic management

The basic themes in defining a strategy

We start from the assumption that it is a fundamental objective of an organization to safeguard its longevity. In some industries, such as the dot.com industry around the turn of the millennium and the airline industry at certain moments in time, this might mean simple survival; however, generally longevity implies being successful or even gaining 'above average rents', as economists express it. As the IBM case clarifies, each firm has to develop a strategy that requires decisions regarding four basic elements: the firm's objectives, its environment, its resources and patterns of resource allocation, and finally its corporate values, norms and ethics. These elements are summarized in Figure 16.1.[1] To be effective, a well-balanced strategy needs to address all these elements in a consistent manner.

The objectives: What do we want to do?

Developing a strategy consists first of decisions regarding what it is that the company wants to do and wants to become. This means that the management has to define a desirable future for the company. This desirable future will usually be summarized in the firm's objectives, its 'business definition', its mission statement and its vision of the future. Thus, we are close to the 'service concept' notion discussed in Chapter 3: defining the service concept is an inherent part of the strategy definition exercise that service firms face.

Let us take Ikea as a first example. The desirable future as Ikea defines it reads like this:[2]

'The Ikea vision is to create a better everyday life for the many people. We make this possible by offering a wide range of well-designed, functional home furnishing products at prices so low that as many people as possible will be able to afford them . . .'

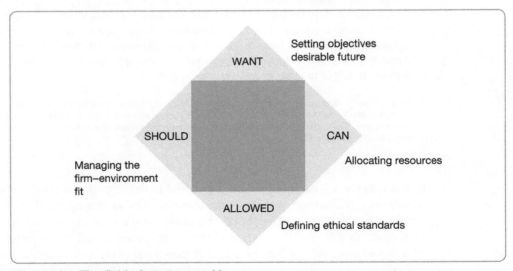

Figure 16.1 The field of strategy making

Source: Heene, A. (1997) 'The nature of strategic planning', *Long Range Planning*, Vol 30, No 6, p. 934. Reprinted with permission from Elsevier.

The environment: What should we do?

Strategy, of course, is more than a simple wish list of what management wants. A company should consider whether what it wants to do is in line with what is going on in the market, and so strategy will also imply an analysis of the firm's environment, leading to a definition of what the firm, given its environment, should achieve.

Within environmental analysis, customers and their needs and preferences will be a central focus of attention. Other elements include the existing competition, possible substitutes, the bargaining position towards suppliers, as well as regulatory elements.[3] Environmental analysis allows the firm to be connected to its environment and guarantees the alignment between the company and its environment, be it through adapting the firm to its environment or through a process of 'changing' the environment so that the needs of the environment better fit the firm's objectives and capabilities.

In the case of Ikea, this alignment exists. Large segments of the market are interested in furniture that is cheap, functional and attractive at the same time. Notice too that Ikea's offering to its customers actually shapes the market as well. The conception of furniture and how it fits into people's purchasing behaviour is altered. In the past, buying furniture was more a twice-in-a-lifetime event: a cheaper set of furniture at the beginning of adult life, followed by a more luxurious design intended to last for decades once careers work out well and the children have outgrown their 'creating-damage-all-over' phase. Now, flexibility and more frequent changes in interior have become an option within the grasp of a large group of customers.

Resources and resource allocation patterns: What can we do?

A company has to take into consideration what it can do, given limited resources. Whether a firm will be able to successfully pursue the course of actions defined depends on its resources and the deployment of these resources. Resources and their deployment determine what the firm can achieve. If we look at Ikea again, we should not forget that, behind the rather simple objective stated above, hides a complex resource allocation pattern. Ikea has contracts with about 2000 suppliers, selected to meet the manufacturing standards required. The low price is built into the production process; the flat packs used for shipping allow for a rational distribution; selling surfaces are designed in such a way that self-service and immediate take-away is made possible for the majority of products.

In terms of resources, it is important to note that – besides the classical tangible resources such as facilities, plants and so on – two types of resource are becoming more crucial everyday: the intangible resources (such as knowledge, aptitudes, attitudes, reputation, image and brand equity) and the 'firm-addressable resources'. The latter are resources that are not legally owned by the firm but are used within the processes of product design, development, service delivery, or marketing and sales. This notion of firm-addressable resources is becoming more and more important as firms start to operate in networks.[4] Strategy then does not limit itself to *one isolated* company but needs to address the network as a whole. Good examples are the so-called virtual business schools. Such schools do not have a faculty of their own but are able to 'address' a group of (visiting) faculty members employed elsewhere to teach their courses. This is, of course, the essence of supply chain management: 'controlling' the entire supply chain without owning it.

Corporate values: What are we allowed to do?

A further element defining the firm's strategy that, under the influence of corporate scandals over the last 2 years, has gained importance and, therefore, needs to be addressed up front concerns the company's values. This includes corporate norms and values and 'business ethics' through which management decides what is allowed to be achieved by the company's associates:

'Thrift, inventiveness, and hard work. Modesty and willpower. Our relationships with each other and the world around us. Co-operation and sharing, and the knowledge that we are in this together and we all need each other.'

These are the values of Ikea: it inspires the company to pay attention to ecological considerations, to work with manufacturers all over the world (in more than 60 countries), and to develop appropriate HR practices.

Such values should not be seen as something that merely scratches the surface. Situations where values are at stake are abundant, and the position a company takes influences its daily operations. Consider what happened with Barings bank, or more recently Enron and Arthur Andersen not to mention the financial crisis of 2008. Clearly, values should be a core part of the identity and, hence, mission and strategy of firms.[5]

Addressing potential conflicts

Any strategy for any company, including service firms thus needs to address four different issues: what is desirable, and what should and can be realized, in a manner that is in line with the organization's values. While these four levels sound rather simple, dealing with them in a consistent way is often complex in practice. In particular, in defining the content of strategy, many potential conflicts between the four constituting issues of strategy need to be resolved.

Conflict with the environment

One of the typical conflicts in defining the content of strategy is the tension between the objectives of the firm and the value that the environment attaches to the services offered – that is, at the price at which the firm wants to sell a service, the market might not be interested in the service concept offered. An interesting example can be found in the Belgian history of fast food. The concept, brought over from the US, started to present itself in European streets in the late 1960s. During the early 1970s, the results of the first hamburger chains were disastrous. The price at which hamburgers were offered was perceived as simply too high by customers. Just when some of the major local players in Belgium were considering abandoning this market, a form of last-chance marketing plan was launched by one of the major distribution chains. This plan consisted in essence of strong price reductions and, if sales went up, the installation of larger-scale operations. The rest is history: it is impossible to visit a single town in Belgium that does not have its own hamburger restaurant.

Conflict with available resources

Another 'classical' field of conflict arises out of the tension between what the available resources allow the firm to do and the direction in which the company wants to go. New business development may, for instance, be constrained by past history and the assets that have been built up over time. Larger organizations, in particular, tend to have difficulties in changing when the times demand it. What were once assets might become liabilities. As discussed in Chapter 6, new forms of distribution have become possible for financial services: a bank with a large network of branches should be aware that this network might be a liability as customers start to use electronic banking devices on a large scale. Competitors with a less costly distribution network might start to outperform more traditional banks. Other illustrations of the fact that changes or transformations are difficult to realize can be found everywhere: think of the difficulties the flag carriers in the airline industry have had, and still have, to survive. Organizational structure and culture, the routines and technologies developed over time, are all elements very resistant to change. For more than a decade now, national railways in Europe have been talking about changing into a customer-oriented service company, but very few have succeeded in doing so. Indeed, changing direction to realize objectives is in practice a rough job compared to defining these objectives. This type of strategic change remains one of the most difficult challenges managers face.[6]

The key to long-term survival and profitability: competitive advantage

The challenge in defining a sound and sustainable strategy is thus to come up with a consistent and integrated answer to the basic strategic questions of what management wants to do, should do, can do, and is allowed to do. This answer will result in longevity when it implies the creation of a competitive advantage.

A competitive advantage first of all refers to the 'distinctive capability' of the firm. A firm creates competitive advantage if it succeeds in becoming different from its competitors in a way that is recognized and appreciated by its (potential) clients. IKEA unquestionably has a competitive advantage: the firm succeeds in clearly distinguishing its product offering from competing product offerings, and customers assign value to IKEA's product offering as it clearly addresses their needs and preferences.

A competitive advantage also has to be sustainable. It has to create a 'time window' that lasts long enough to allow the firm to harvest the benefits of the differences, in terms of both financial profits and opportunities for building and leveraging resources to create a 'new' competitive advantage.

It is now recognized in strategy theory that a firm may pursue three types of strategy:[7]

- a cost leadership strategy;
- a differentiation strategy; or
- a focus strategy.

The cost leadership strategy aims to minimize the costs of products or services delivered to the marketplace. Discount retailers such as Aldi and Lidl apply this generic strategy, as does Easyjet or Ryanair. Policies such as limiting the product range, offering non-branded or privately branded goods or services, formalizing, standardization, automation or harvesting economies of scale, and simplification of business processes perfectly fit this strategy.

Differentiation strategies aim to create competitive advantage not by striving for the lowest possible cost structure but by maximizing value created for the customer. Companies like Esselunga (Italy) and Delhaize (Belgium) pursue a differentiation advantage in the retail sector, while Lufthansa and SIA do the same in the airline industry. The rationale behind the strategy is that the higher value that has been created will be rewarded in the marketplace by means of a price premium sufficiently large to cover the higher costs that may have been necessary to create the added value and to bring this higher value to the attention of the (potential) customer. Within this strategy, typical policies include extending the product range, offering branded goods, highly personalized 'on-the-spot' procedures and harvesting economies of scope. If value is defined as the ratio between (perceived) quality and price, it could be said that both of the above strategies result in 'similar' value propositions, but cost leaders and differentiators work for different segments.[8] The trouble starts when a company deviates from the 'value line' and becomes 'stuck in the middle'. Being 'stuck in the middle' means that, for the same price, someone else offers more quality or that the same quality can be found elsewhere at lower prices, which is not a very stable starting point for sustainable competitive advantage. Of course, a company can deviate from the value line in an opposite direction as well; this involves 'changing the rules of the game'. By introducing new ways of working – often involving new technologies – a company starts to offer the same or higher quality at lower prices than previously available. Ikea is a good example: the firm's operations managed to completely change the market of furniture distribution and sales. By combining production processes that allow for flexibility with, among other things, well-thought-out distribution practices and a specific surface layout, Ikea is able to offer what in the past seemed an impossible marriage between opposites: a broader range of furniture characterized by an appealing design at reasonable prices. In this way, Ikea started to break the industry rules, offering more value in comparison with other low-price producers. The price comparison with producers of more exclusive designed furniture is favourable, and so Ikea even attracts customers from this segment. Indeed, this example clarifies the logic behind the notion of 'blue ocean' strategies advanced recently by Kim and Mauborgne (2005).[9] They argue that firms should aim to create uncontested market space by enacting value curves that differentiate the firm from the competition. Not only is Ikea a case a point; Cirque du Soleil has also been able to create a new synthesis of circus, theatre and dance performance practices, which results in a unique value proposition. Consequently, this recent work stresses the importance of creativity and innovation on the level of the business model and, hence, the service concept.[10]

With a focus strategy, the firm applies a cost-leadership or a differentiation strategy within a particular market segment in a specialized way and, as a result of this focus, gains competitive advantage over firms applying their generic strategy on a wider market. Local retail shops often apply this kind of strategy. Specialized hospitals apply a focus strategy and can as a result gain competitiveness over general hospitals. This brings to mind the Shouldice Hospital we looked at when discussing HR practices. By concentrating on one type of medical intervention and organizing the whole hospital accordingly, Shouldice was able to become the leader in hernia treatment, with the lowest price, the highest service quality, and the shortest throughput time. In the Belgian financial industry, Bank van Breda focuses on 'entrepreneurs' and develops specific products only for this market segment.

Competition: eroding the competitive advantage to a competitive requirement

One can observe that, in almost any industry, products and services become better, more fitted to customer needs, delivered in a more reliable way, and even cheaper over time. Cars, for instance, have clearly advanced technologically over time and, at the same time, have become cheaper. Just consider how the prices of PCs are dropping at an ever-increasing pace, while performance is continuously increasing.

All this is the result of competition that makes competitive advantages erode to competitive requirements, definable as the minimal threshold that companies have to maintain in order to remain in business. The distinction between a competitive advantage and a competitive requirement is similar to the distinction that some people make between order winners and qualifiers.[11] Four mechanisms are used to erode or destroy competitive advantage: imitation, substitution, resource mobilization and resource paralysis:[12]

- *Imitation* is undoubtedly the best-known erosion mechanism and has become reinforced in the past by practices such as 'benchmarking'. Take distribution, for example: over the past decade, Aldi has introduced a low-cost approach, attracting a significant number of customers. By offering a well-balanced but, at the same time, rather restricted line of products, introducing a very sober surface lay-out and minimizing the number of staff, Aldi has been able to offer products at very low prices. At the moment, Aldi is suffering from competition rather less from the classical distribution players than from companies applying the same logic but trying to push it even further: fewer products, less 'comfort' inside the shop, and so on. Similar observations hold for Virgin, once a pioneer in low-cost flights, now being surpassed by Ryanair.

- *Substitution* often involves product innovation whereby existing products or services are replaced by new ones. The essence of substitution is that the same function with the same customer group is fulfilled by a new product or service based on a new or different technology. Examples in the manufacturing industries abound: digital *versus* mechanical watches, electronic typewriters, etc. In the service industry, one could refer to the substitution of traditional surgery methods by endoscopic methods. It is interesting to note that substitution can also be the result of 'process innovation', which can eventually lead to 'changing the rules of competition'.[13] This is the route many online stockbrokers took by completely redesigning the distribution channel.[14] It is interesting to note that, in service industries, what some see as a process innovation is actually, at the same time, a product innovation as the customer is confronted with the new process. Think, for instance, of the electronic delivery of courses (a process innovation) which, for the student, is distance learning (a product innovation).

- Some forms of *resource mobilization* such as headhunting are widespread and well known. The mechanism of resource mobilization is at work whenever resources contributing to a competitive advantage start to move or when ownership over them is changed. Resource mobilization can have different causes. It can result from an internal loss – for example, when an important employee having an important body of knowledge leaves the firm. It can also result from external causes involving a competitor's action – for instance, when an employee leaves the firm to join the competitor after having been invited by the competitor to do so.

- *Resource paralysis* is a direct attempt by competitors to reduce the value-creating potential of the firm's resources. Resource paralysis is a frontal attack that takes the form of competitors spreading rumours, provoking false complaints, using negative comparative advertising, or lobbying for the enforcement of laws that prevent their competitor from using its resources – for instance, through import barriers, standards enforcement or environmental regulations. The way Easyjet is frontally attacking Go (British Airways' low-cost carrier) in its advertisements perfectly illustrates resource paralysis. Government regulation (e.g. accreditation) in the educational field is effectively paralysing distance learning competencies of Open University courses in many fields.

The quest for sustainability

The fundamental purpose of strategy is not just to build competitive advantage but to build 'sustainable' competitive advantage. Therefore, one of the important issues in defining and implementing strategy is to define actions that eliminate the erosion mechanisms or that, at least, slow down their deployment or effects. Counter-erosion actions are aimed at extending the time window during which the competitive advantage 'exists', and they allow the firm to earn the profits that it needs to safeguard its longevity.

Over time, strategic management theory has developed several frameworks for conceptualizing and developing such counter-erosion decisions. The first approach that has been developed is based on the competitive forces model[15] discussed earlier. Based on this model, one can argue that creating and sustaining a competitive advantage implies: building barriers to entry, keeping track of possible substitutes, reducing the intensity of rivalry and building a stronger structural negotiation position towards both buyers and suppliers.

- Barriers to entry can be created by different means:

  1 *Employing economies of scale* – e.g. as in car rental.

  2 *Product differentiation* – e.g. Harvard Business School's emphasis on case research and case methodology in its programmes.

  3 *Capital requirements* – e.g. Disney who through his model parks, enormously increased the need for working capital.

  4 *Switching costs* (costs for the client when switching from one supplier to another) – e.g. the (mainly psychological) costs that a consumer is facing when switching from his traditional hairdresser to a new one.

  5 *Access to distribution channels or generally location* – e.g. with the fierce competition going on for space on the supermarket shelf, introducing a new product will require serious investment if traditional distribution channels are to be persuaded to incorporate the new product.

  6 *Property rights* – e.g. technological patents, exclusive access to certain resources or licensing agreements and even favourable locations as in the case of McDonald's.

  7 *Government regulations and policies* – e.g. in the case of energy supply in large parts of Europe.

- Possible substitutes should also be monitored. For security brokers, insurance companies or real estate agents are competitors, and the services provided are to a certain extent exchangeable: they all offer longer-term investments with a certain return. Security companies were confronted in the 1980s with the development of ever more sophisticated electronic alarm systems technology that could take over the work of guards at a much cheaper rate. Security firms had no choice but to develop service packages combining guards and electronic systems whereby the guards become highly skilled operators.

- Working on the intensity of competition itself implies complicated strategies and actions very much like a game of chess. Deciding what actions are the most relevant – working on advertising or price, or trying to increase market share by acquiring smaller competitors – depends heavily on the specific industry – that is, the number of competitors, the life cycle stage of the industry, the overall cost structure prevailing within the industry, and so on.[16]

- Sources of competitive advantage – and hence also threats to it – can also lie in the relationships with customers and/or suppliers. The relative power balance between parties – the firm, the customers, the suppliers – will influence the strength and the sustainability of competitive advantage. A limited number of customers or suppliers means vulnerability in terms of profit rates as well as long-term results; as soon as something happens within such a customer base, you feel it.

An alternative view on how to defend against processes that erode competitive advantage can be found in resource- and competence-based strategic management theories. These theories basically argue that the complexity of the system of resources used to create competitive advantage determines the sustainability of the competitive advantage created. Co-ordinated resources can, by their nature, be protected against erosion because of three characteristics: they include a certain degree of intangibility; they are time-dependent; and they are co-ordinated and, hence, complex.

Tacit knowledge, brands, reputation, networks (social capital), and organizational climate and corporate culture are all examples of resources that are difficult to imitate given their highly intangible nature. McKinsey (the consulting firm), Wal Mart or Club Med offer examples here. Characteristics such as culture, reputation and more implicit ways of working are built up over time. It is not only by bringing together a few highly intelligent people that a new McKinsey is born; equally, just throwing together a bunch of enthusiastic young people in an attractive resort by the seaside does not mean Club Med has to start worrying about its long-term future. It may take years, if not decades, for a distributor to make his employees behave as Wal Mart employees do. Moreover, often a complex process of different kinds of co-ordination of resources is involved, making it extremely difficult to imitate. This is an issue we shall discuss further when looking in greater depth at managing intangible resources.

We now have a taste of the issues involved in establishing a consistent strategy. Let us turn to some specific challenges faced by service firms.

The challenges of strategic management for services

The general issues of strategic management in service industries are not fundamentally different from those in manufacturing industries. However, there are some issues which are specific to service industries, given the specific nature of a service – in particular, intangibility and simultaneity.

The identification of the 'added value carriers'

Creating a sustainable competitive advantage means creating distinctive added value for the firm's clients in a sustainable way and 'embedding' this added value in the firm's outputs: its products. According to this line of reasoning, products can be regarded as 'carriers of added value'. As we argued earlier (*see* Chapter 1), most products are a combination of goods and services, i.e. a package of tangible and intangible elements. From this point of view, the firm has to decide:

1 What added value will be embedded in the tangible components of its offering to the marketplace.

2 What added value will be embedded in the pure service (i.e. intangible) component of its offering to the marketplace.

3 How synergy can be created between the added value in the tangible component and intangible component.

4 Whether and how the mix of tangible and intangible components itself can become an added value for its customer.

As stated, this is and should be a concern for any type of firm. However, the reason for doing so differs for service firms as opposed to manufacturing firms. Manufacturing companies may add service components to their product in reacting to the price-erosion that takes place due to competitive dynamics. Service companies may do the reverse and add tangible elements; by doing so, they may overcome the earning limitations that service companies have to face when selling 'capacity'. Moreover, by acting in this way, the service offer becomes anchored in the service company and so-called 'switching costs' for customers are built in.

Limits to earnings due to restrictions on selling capacity

Capacity management is an important concern in service companies. As has been argued before, balancing and co-ordinating the supply of capacity and market demand is one of the core problems in capacity management in service companies; it also determines, in many cases, the chance of survival of service companies.

One of the critical factors is the extent to which a service organization in general, and a professional service organization in particular, is able to 'leverage' its available capacity. Given the need for interaction between the service provider and the customer, the available time of the provider is the 'scarce' resource limiting the earning potential of the firm.

The earnings of a service firm can be expressed as follows:

Total earnings = Units of time available in service delivery × Earnings per unit of time.

If a firm wants to raise earnings it can increase the units of time available in service delivery or raise the earnings per unit of time. The first alternative means increasing the available capacity, which of course is an option at least as long as there are positive economics of scale. The other alternative, however, for increasing capacity is to increase the productivity of the service process (that is, to get more out of one unit of time) or to increase the value of one unit of time for the customer – that is, leveraging capacity.

One way of leveraging capacity is what we call the tangibilization of the product. Tangibilization, in fact, means that 'goods' substitute 'time sold' so that the embedded value is less dependent on time. This will lead the service company to take a new position on the goods-services continuum (see Figure 16.2). In fact, with the tendency towards servitization discussed in Chapter 18, one could speak of the phenomenon of 'productization' here. An excellent example of this tangibilization process can be observed in software companies, in the case of 'body-shopping activities', i.e. commercial activities whereby personnel are supplied to a customer by the service provider. Here, activities that are highly subject to the limit on earnings are substituted by selling software packages.

The added value for the customer is then the sum of the added value in the tangible components, the added value in the service component, and the added value by combining both types of components.

Figure 16.2 **Product companies and service companies moving towards each other**

The added value of software packages is less constrained by time than body shopping and thus allows the software company to raise earnings per head and to maximize the earnings of time spent. Similarly, in the maintenance services, diagnostic tools provided to the customer can replace the intervention of the technicians.

It goes without saying that extending one's offerings by adding components – whether tangible or not – should be accompanied by adequate pricing. Far too often, extensions take place – in order to differentiate – without charges to customers for the additional value creation. This approach (not charging for additional offerings) is risky in two ways:

1 Customers do not perceive the additional value or start to find it normal that it is free; they become 'spoiled' and start to ask for more.

2 Resources are required to deliver additional services: so someone has to pay the bill in the end. By not acknowledging this, the chances are high that the company is mortgaging the future developments of the organization.

Of course, adequate pricing will demand a thorough understanding of what value means to the customers; it will imply adequate information systems and policies (for instance, activity-based costing) and might imply some efforts in educating customers.

Finally, it is important to note that the tangibilization of services constitutes a move upwards in the service triangle. By doing so, the service – and also the service company – becomes somewhat more independent of its employees and their loyalty (or lack thereof) towards the organization. This leads us to the second consequence of tangibilization, the issue of anchoring the service in the firm.

Anchoring the service offer within the firm

A growing number of companies extend their service components in order to raise competitiveness and to fight against the 'standardization' or even 'banalization' of their products resulting from the competitive battle. For instance, a growing number of banks are evolving towards financial consulting. It is expected that adding this service component will contribute to the competitiveness of the firm and will help the firm overcome erosion processes caused by the competitive pressures.

Added service components have to be 'anchored'

Although this line of reasoning seems to be acceptable at first sight, the practice is highly questionable. Raising competitiveness through adding service components can indeed only be successful if one can 'anchor' the service component within the firm. This will prevent customers from using that service component to obtain better conditions from a competitor that may be inclined to supply these better conditions due to the fact that it did not have to deliver the service (the advice) offered.

If clients can 'consume' the (additional) service component offered and use this to obtain better prices or slightly better products from competitors, the strategy of extending services in order to raise competitiveness risks raising the competitor's competitiveness. Raising competitiveness through adding or extending can only be successful if the firm is able to 'anchor' the service within the firm itself, and if the firm as a result is able to 'lock in' customers.

Two forms of anchoring the service in the firm

Anchoring the service delivered within the service firm can take different forms. In all cases of anchoring, switching costs for clients are raised and, as a result, the firm succeeds in 'locking in' clients: if the client uses the service delivered to bargain for better conditions from the competitor, the client will have to overcome additional costs for doing so.

A well-known example is the pharmacist. In most European countries, a pharmacist is a highly skilled professional. The added value of the pharmacist is his or her knowledge about various types of medicines and expertise in preparing special prescriptions. The service component is without doubt very important in this 'product'. However, preparing prescriptions is becoming less important given that more and more standardized medicines are prescribed by doctors. As a result, the added value of the pharmacist (real or perceived) is decreasing, with price erosion the inevitable result. The pharmacist, however, can limit this erosion by making sure that all medicines can only be distributed by pharmacists. In other words, his or her service as a pharmacist is linked to a product which is anchored in a pharmacy. The customer is not tempted to use the service at one place and buy the drug elsewhere, as the price is the same everywhere, and the drug can in any case only be found in other pharmacies, the number of which is limited by law (in most EU countries).

Generally speaking, at least two strategic approaches to anchoring are worth considering:

- raising the uniqueness of the product component sustained by service delivery;
- creating causal ambiguity for the client.

If the firm succeeds in connecting the service offered (advice) and the unique goods, the value of the service component delivered can only be harvested in the firm itself while the added value of the service component can only be 'consumed' through consuming the product that 'materializes' the service component. This is actually what our pharmacist is doing. Whereas, at first sight, services are or can be used to 'upgrade' and 'de-banalize' goods, in fact the opposite happens here: the added value and de-banalization of services can only be sustained if these are connected to and sustained by unique goods or services. Let us take investment advice as an example. No matter how good the advice is, not being able to deliver the necessary stock transactions in a timely manner will remain a major drawback for investment consultants. Customers will try to get the advice free and spend the money (transaction costs and broker's fee) elsewhere. Harvesting the value of the additional service offered will be far easier when offering both services (transactions and advice) especially when they are blended in such a way that they create 'causal ambiguity'.

The second approach, creating causal ambiguity, implies that the service company does not reveal the component to which additional services will be connected. Clients are not given any insight into the specifics that will be used to solve the problem; the service delivered only reveals the problem-solving potential without revealing the characteristics of the components themselves. Let us look again at the situation of financial advisers: when an investment consultant talks to a potential customer about which bonds he or she should invest in, the customer can 'take' this advice and, after a few such discussions, decide for himself or herself what transactions to pursue and where. When no such clear indications on the product are offered, but instead information is given about the approach, the customer base or previous results, customers are not able to make decisions on the 'components'. As a result, uncertainty on how to achieve results is created in the client's mind. This prevents him or her from 'joy-riding'.

Of course, despite the fact that introducing tangibles in the service offering can be a visible way to create a competitive advantage and/or create higher earnings, it is important to pay careful attention to the intangibles in services, which brings us to the next topic.

Managing intangible resources

Intangibles and competitive advantage

Intangible asset stocks are central for the creation of sustainable competitive advantage in a service firm. Distinctive characteristics of tangibles and intangibles for the process of creating competitive advantage are summarized in Table 16.1.

Building competitive advantage by using intangible assets protects competitive advantage against imitation, mainly due to the intangibility of the assets and the resulting causal ambiguity. It becomes unclear to an outsider which assets are precisely used to create competitive advantage and how the creation of competitive advantage by using these assets is achieved. It is, for instance, difficult to precisely and completely understand where the competitive advantage of Disney comes from. One can argue that this competitiveness is the result of the working together of many resources of a tangible and an intangible nature: location, the attractions themselves, the atmosphere, the employees' behaviour, etc.

Whereas it is rather obvious that intangibles are highly protected against imitation, it is at the same time true that they are not necessarily equally well protected against 'resource mobilization'. Knowledge, for instance, can easily 'leave' the firm when 'key employees' are mobilized and leave the firm due to internal or external causes. Many professional service firms, such as law firms, are for this reason very vulnerable to key personnel leaving the firm accompanied often by customers who are loyal to the service provider and not to the service firm.

Table 16.1 Distinctive characteristics of tangibles and intangibles

Tangible assets	Intangible assets
Build-up time rather predictable	Build-up time less predictable
Rather easy to imitate	Difficult or impossible to imitate
Fixed reproduction costs	Economies of scale on reproduction
Depreciates through use	Grows through use
Remains if not used (leveraged)	Disappears if not used
Easy to appropriate	Difficult to appropriate
Easy to control	Difficult to control; difficult to deny access to others

The challenge for 'knowledge management' in this context is then:

- reducing the mobilization itself;
- safeguarding the firm's knowledge stock when mobilization takes place;
- preventing the deployment of mobilized knowledge stocks outside the firm that is subject to mobilization. Firms may take actions that limit the possibilities of key employees to leave the firm legally, they may articulate knowledge and embed it in large databases as consulting companies do and they may split up knowledge over groups of people as is happening in development teams.

Reducing the process of resource mobilization

How can, for instance, a business school or a law firm prevent or discourage its 'knowledge carriers', mainly personnel, from leaving the organization? Two approaches can be followed here:

- raising the dependency of the personnel;
- raising the attractiveness of the firm for the personnel.

Raising the dependency can be achieved through legal measures such as contracts that prevent knowledge carriers from leaving the firm. However, it should be noted that this approach has limited value: making people dependent by contracts (and their enforcement) often does not enhance motivation. Increasing the firm's attractiveness is, in this respect, much more advisable. It is clear that human resource policies play a key role in creating such an attractive internal environment – for instance, by offering career opportunities that cannot be obtained from the competitors or by creating a corporate culture that highly motivates employees and invites them to demonstrate loyalty to their firm. In short, HRM's crucial role in the service company's strategy must focus primarily on raising – to express it in economic terms – 'switching costs' for personnel through the creation of a highly attractive internal environment.

Safeguarding the knowledge stock

It will never be possible to completely prevent personnel from leaving the firm. It is, therefore, necessary to work out measures to safeguard the knowledge present in the firm when personnel are leaving the company. Measures to safeguard the knowledge of the firm can involve:

- the spread of the knowledge over personnel;
- articulation and codification of (mainly tacit) knowledge – for instance, in schemes, manuals, drawings, procedures and databases. This is common practice in the major consulting firms where huge databases are built to accumulate experience and knowledge that has been developed by the consultants.

Spreading knowledge over personnel, of course, guarantees that the firm can go on using the knowledge stock in its processes of product and value creation when resource mobilization has taken place. Spreading knowledge means setting up learning processes within the firm and thus managing the firm as a 'learning organisation'.[17]

Articulation and codification of knowledge are processes through which (mainly tacit) knowledge is made explicit and as a result made 'apprehensible'.[18] This is exactly what the SOP (standard operating procedures) manuals at McDonald's do. At first sight, it might seem that articulated and codified knowledge has major disadvantages compared to 'tacit' knowledge, as one could argue that the more knowledge is articulated and codified, the more it becomes 'observable' by an outsider and, thus, more easily imitated by competitors. One can, however, argue that the articulation and codification of knowledge does not necessarily imply that the value of the knowledge for creating sustainable competitive advantage is affected:[19]

- If an individual's knowledge is articulated within an organization, the ability of outsiders to apprehend the full meaning of the articulated knowledge cannot be presumed.

- Even when articulated knowledge can be fully apprehended by the outsiders, causal ambiguity about the importance of the knowledge to create competitive advantage may obscure the value of the knowledge to the outsiders.

- The value of knowledge, whether tacit or articulated, is time-dependent and erodes over time.

- Tacit knowledge is very hard to spread throughout and transfer within the organization.

- Tacit knowledge is much harder to leverage than articulated and codified knowledge.

One could thus argue that articulating and codifying knowledge has serious advantages over leaving knowledge tacit and that it should be recommended even if the imitability of articulated knowledge might seem to be higher than the imitability of tacit knowledge.

Preventing knowledge deployment and knowledge leveraging outside the firm

Knowledge should not only be spread, articulated and codified, but also 'anchored' within the company as well. Anchoring knowledge prevents the deployment or leveraging of knowledge outside the firm. This can only be achieved if the 'knowledge stock' within the firm is managed as part of the system of resource stocks and flows that make up the company.

'Anchoring' in this sense, for instance, means that knowledge of technologies is connected both to tangibles such as computer hardware and software that are put at the development engineer's disposal, and to organizational structures – for example, structures that define interfaces between the engineering and the marketing departments.

Looked at from this point of view, 'organizational knowledge management' becomes a meaningful concept differing significantly from 'individual knowledge management'. A strategic approach to knowledge management does not only incorporate managing the knowledge base of individuals but also considers 'individual knowledge management' to be part of a much larger management issue.

Mastering the dynamics of value creation and value perception in delivering services

The reader will understand by now that strategic management in any firm is about creating value for the customer. As we know, services imply that customers are actively involved in the service delivery process. This phenomenon poses some specific value related challenges:

- Service companies have to address specific problems that might result from taking over one or more of the value-creating activities of their clients. These problems relate to interdependencies stemming from 'interweaving' value systems but pertain as well to the situation that clients may be in a bad position to assess the added value delivered by the service company. In-depth knowledge of the client's value systems as well as the appropriate use of value signals will turn out to be highly relevant.

- Service companies also have to define whether and how the involvement of the client in the process of service delivery creates added value for the client. This implies that service companies will have to manage the 'actual use' of the service by the client, a process which starts when defining the service concept.

Taking over value-creating activities: dealing with interdependencies and ensuring that clients are able to assess the added value of the service

The nature of the interaction that service companies build with their clients differs significantly from that of industrial companies. Whereas industrial companies deliver inputs to the 'value system'[20] of their clients (raw materials, sub-assemblies, etc.), service companies take over one or more of the value-creating activities and thus become interwoven with their client's value system. In many cases, service companies 'take over' value-creating activities for which clients do not have sufficient resources, such as knowledge.

The fact that service companies are involved in the value system of their clients and may perform activities which are not 'mastered' by the client has serious consequences for the competitiveness of the service firm and for the perception of this competitiveness:

- Since performances of a value-creating activity in the value system are affected by the other activities in the same value system, the performance of the service company may be affected by the performance of the client in other value-creating activities.

- Clients with little or no knowledge about the value-creating activities that the service company is performing may be in a bad position to assess the added value that the service company is creating.

In order to overcome the first consequence, it can be advised that service companies aim for a very broad and deep involvement in the client's value system. A private banker offering services in wealth management has to have a complete understanding of the total assets of the customer, including his real estate position, his risk profile, family situation, life style, etc. If not, the banker might risk ending up in a situation where he advises the wrong investment. The competitive service company should be able not only to take over a limited part of the value-creating activities of its client but should be able to take over the interconnected value-creating activities as well, or should at least be able to 'manage the interfaces' between the value-creating activities taken over and the interconnected value activities that the client continues to perform itself. At the very least, service companies can undertake a very detailed and in-depth analysis of their clients' value systems so that it becomes clear to the service company and to the clients how they should both co-operate to maximize the added value.

This is, without any doubt, a major point of concern for any service company taking over activities that used to be done internally by its client, such as payroll administration, IT services, etc. For this type of service, it is undoubtedly important to establish clear arrangements on how information should be passed on.

Secondly, it may be difficult or even impossible for clients to assess the value the service company is offering and thus the competitiveness of the firm base on that value proposition, especially when the client lacks knowledge about the value-creating activities performed by the service company. As was described in Chapter 2, this is typically the case in the so-called task- and personal-interactive service sectors. In these cases, it is advisable to define in advance the performance criteria and norms as precisely and in as much detail as possible, and to agree on an 'output'-based assessment of the service the company delivered. We refer to the practice of agreeing on service level agreements discussed earlier. The emergence of 'no cure no pay' contracts fits an extreme example of this. This might require some effort but, in these cases, clients should be prevented from assessing the service company's competitiveness based on the service process alone (as they may lack the knowledge to do so). In addition, it might be relevant to compensate for the client's 'lack' of individual perception of the service company's value by introducing 'inter-subjective assessments'. 'Word of mouth' marketing is, in this respect, a tremendously valuable strategic tool for service companies, and building 'image' (as an intangible resource stock) within a relation network that sustains the perception of competitiveness of the service company is becoming a necessity for the service firm.

A consequence of the above is that service companies should also steer the client's perception of the added value created in delivering the service by the extensive use of 'value signals'. These value signals can and should be embedded in the service firm's physical elements of the service offering, its tangible resources or its outputs. For instance, good-looking and well-written reports for a consulting firm or clean trucks for a transport company are important value signals; nice, cozy branches may be important value signals for a bank; or smartly dressed technicians for a maintenance firm.

By means of value signals, the service company influences the client's perceptions of the value of the service provider. By becoming deeply involved in the client's value system, the service company can guarantee the competitiveness of its service and can guarantee that the 'actual use' of the service provided equals the 'intended use'.

Added value results from the involvement of clients in the service delivery process

It will not come as a surprise that we argue that the value the service firm offers results directly from having the client involved in the service delivery process. This is clearly the case in business schools where students have the opportunity to actively participate in the learning process. Also in the Shouldice hospital the active participation of the patients in their recovery process creates extra value for the patient. Hence, the competitiveness of any service firm will depend on how this involvement is organized. As a general rule, one could state that, in delivering services, a detailed 'knowledge and expertise analysis' should be undertaken and used to determine which activities are to be offered by the service company and which ones conducted by the client. This should be done while defining the service concept as discussed in Chapter 2. Service companies can gain competitiveness by working out a service concept in which the service company creates the most favourable conditions for the client to apply its own knowledge and expertise.

So defining the service concept should address the roles performed by both parties – customer and provider – and hence implies the following activities:

- analysing which knowledge is needed to maximize added value in the service delivery activities;
- defining which party has the knowledge;
- creating conditions for successfully applying the knowledge.

This again underscores the importance of knowledge management in a service firm. It also indicates that knowledge management includes the customer as well.

The role of technology in safeguarding the longevity of the service firm

Often service delivery is highly 'human-factor driven'. However, it can be argued that humans in service delivery not only add value to the process but can 'subtract' value as well. The major disadvantages of human-driven service delivery from a competitive point of view can be summarized as follows:

- The involvement of a human deliverer limits the availability of the service in time and space as service delivery implies the physical presence of the human service deliverer at the time and place of the service consumer. This point has been raised before when discussing the relevancy of 'tangibilization' for overcoming capacity limitations. Computer software as a substitute for 'human' teaching activities allows the student to 'consume' the teaching where and when this is most suitable to his or her needs.

- Unless highly structured and steered by strictly applied procedures, the repeatability of the service delivery process is in danger of being harmed by the human service deliverer – that is, by his or her 'on-the-spot' degree of initiative and creativity. This will be the case when this initiative results in 'sub-optimal' outcomes. In the future, one might expect artificial intelligence and expert systems intended to solve problems to become more widespread. Such systems allow problem-spotting and problem-solving independent of the specific (and limited) knowledge of a human trouble-shooter and thus will lead to the same corrective measures in all equal-problem situations. A case in point is the expert systems to be found more and more in surgery environments; these enable one to have the most advanced know-how available in all surgery rooms.

- 'On-the-spot' creativity and initiative on the part of the human service deliverer can affect the cost effectiveness of the service delivery. The introduction of technology allows the client to be involved in the service delivery process in a cost-effective way. For example, home- and phone-banking, which can be fully automated, can be cost-saving.

Substituting technology for the human factor encourages the company to clearly define in what respect and to what extent involvement of the human service provider adds value to the service delivery process, and how and where the 'personal touch' that only the human service provider can deliver adds value to the service provided. Any service firm should therefore thoroughly question when and how the personal touch that can be delivered by the human factor can add value to the service. All characteristics of the service delivery process in which this 'personal touch' does not add value should lead the service provider to investigate whether and how the substitution of the human factor by technology can contribute to the competitiveness of the service delivered. From a strategic point of view, then, technology can play a major role in safeguarding the longevity of the service firm through its impact on building and sustaining competitive advantage. Generally speaking, technology can add to the firm's competitiveness by lowering the service firm's costs or improving its competitive performance. The introduction and application of technology (such as information technology) in service delivery allows a company to:

- optimize the service delivery process;
- standardize the service delivery process and as a result guarantee the quality reliability of the services offered;
- guarantee the deliverability of the service, independent of space and time.

Through the introduction of technology, service delivery becomes an activity in which the 'human factor' is sometimes less involved and, in all cases, differently involved. This redefinition of the involvement of the human factor in service delivery adds value for customers if technology leads to reducing or even eliminating the non-value-adding characteristics of the human factor.

The foregoing reasoning does not necessarily imply that the service firm should adopt a industrialization approach. Introducing technology might allow the service firm to redefine the role and impact of the human factor to the point where it can really add value to the process of service delivery. Such a redefinition would then result not in reducing staff levels but rather in the creation of superior value by allocating resources differently.

The fundamental strategic issue raised by extending the technological base of the service firm is the identification of the contribution of both technology and the human factor to the creation of value and based on this sustainable competitive advantage. Clearly defining the role of technology and of the people delivering services in a complementary and mutually reinforcing way can enhance the competitiveness of the service firm and thus its growth, prosperity and, consequently, its potential to safeguard the employability of its people.

Managing for continuity by creating sustainable competitive advantage

As repeatedly demonstrated in the foregoing sections, managing knowledge is highly relevant to service companies, since it allows them to manage for continuity by creating a competitive advantage over time. It is crucial that competitiveness shows such continuity.

However, service companies not only have to guarantee the continuity of their competitiveness in time. For many service companies, it is at least as important to guarantee the continuity of competitiveness in space. Fast-food restaurants, cleaning companies, banks, consulting companies, transport companies and, in general, all service companies with a geographically distributed service delivery have to make sure that all their geographically spread associates deliver the service in a comparable way, and on an equal level of competitiveness, even though they may be acting and delivering the service in quite different circumstances and with totally different customers. Continuity of service delivery in space can be achieved through:

- standardization of the service delivery process;
- standardization of the service delivery output.

In the first case, the delivery of the service is made independent of the particular circumstances in which the service is delivered. Processes and procedures are standardized and do not take particular circumstances into account or only allow for minor adjustments to these particular circumstances. This approach can be highly effective for implementing a differentiation strategy in the service delivery and, at the same time, can produce economies by reducing and even eliminating uncertainty and fluctuation. Process standardization in service delivery can be applied in any case where the client is not actually involved in the service delivery – for example, cleaning companies – or where standardizing the interaction with the client adds value to the client – for instance, by guaranteeing quality reliability. Fast-food chains are perfect examples of this. Generally speaking, this approach could be regarded as suitable for all maintenance-interactive types of services (*see* Chapter 2). For this type of service growth becomes easier as licensing and franchising become more viable. In the case of standardization of output, continuity of competitiveness of the service delivery is not achieved at the level of the delivery process itself but rather at the level of the result of the delivery process. This is possible if the service company succeeds in explicitly and clearly expressing the service concept in terms of results produced for the customer. In this approach, 'service quality' is described in terms of criteria that will be used to assess the performance of the service delivered and in terms of norms to be achieved in order to judge the quality to be 'good' or 'competitive'. Take, for instance, the maintenance of lifts: the maximum duration of breakdown allowed or the intervals between lift failure and repair can be agreed. How to organize the service delivery process is a challenge for the provider and, as such, is not stipulated in contracts.

Standardizing output will often be necessary if the service delivery process involves a high degree of unpredictable involvement on the part of the client. Teaching is one of the best examples. It is difficult – if not impossible – to standardize the process of service delivery in this case due to the unpredictable and particular circumstances in which teaching has to take place. Every group of students has its own particularities. In order to guarantee continuity of competitiveness in this kind of service process, it makes sense only to standardize the output; what are students supposed to master in terms of knowledge and/or skills at the end of the course. This 'output standardization' often goes hand-in-hand with an emphasis on 'input' competencies and empowerment. Teachers need a comparatively long period of training and apprenticeship in order to develop adequate didactic insights and skills. Equipped with these skills, they are allowed considerable discretion in how to teach. Another example is physicians: here standardization with 'skills' is matched by decision latitude on how to handle a specific patient. Generally speaking, for task- and personal-interactive services, there will often be a combination of input and output standardization, while the process is far less 'determined'.

Conclusion

In this chapter, we started with an overview of relevant strategic questions and issues that needed to be addressed. Strategy is about finding answers as to what to do in order to safeguard the firm's longevity and how to do this. Crucial to long-term survival and profitability is the creation of a distinctive and sustainable competitive advantage. Recently emerging resource- and competence-based theories offer new insights here: sustainability can be realized by configuring complex constellations that create value for customers.

Services are confronted with specific strategic challenges resulting from the intangibility and simultaneity inherent in the service process. We looked at these challenges systematically: how to overcome limits to earnings due to capacity constraints, how to anchor the intangible offer within the service company, how to use the intangible nature and technology to create and sustain competitive advantage over time and space, and how to deal with the role of the customer in the value-adding process.

What becomes clear over and over again in this context is the need for an integrated approach towards service management. Customers, employees and the whole operational system have to be combined into a coherent service concept or value constellation. Strategy is as simple and as difficult as that.

Review and discussion questions

- What are the themes to be included in a service firm's strategy statement?

- Why do flag carriers in the airline industry create separate ventures in order to compete with the low cost carriers? Why don't they integrate the low cost strategy into their traditional high service strategy?

- What is the best defence against imitation by competitors? Illustrate using three concrete examples.

- What are three typical strategic issues for service firms?

- Companies like McDonald's or Disney have developed so-called universities to train their employees. How does this fit in with concerns that have been described in this chapter?

- Identify and document in your environment three retail companies that follow one of the three generic strategies (cost leadership, differentiation and focus) described in this chapter. How have they implemented their strategic choices?

- An increasing number of business schools develop web-based MBA programmes (i.e. using the distance learning concept). How would you look at this from the perspective of a traditional business school? Use the concepts developed in this chapter.

- Recall the service typology we have been using throughout the book and which makes a distinction between maintenance, task- and personal-interactive services. Would you expect differences between these types of services in terms of the strategic challenges outlined in this chapter (e.g. the issue of resource mobilization, or managing for continuity across time and space)? Which ones? And why? What strategies can firms follow to handle these issues? How would you see the – differentiated – importance of the human factor in this respect? And what about the way in which a firm interacts with its customers and how it designs its service delivery system (processes, facilities, operations management)?

Suggested further reading

For readers interested in the recent insights related to resource- and competence-based models of the firm and their particular relevance to service firms, we recommend the following works:

Hamel, G. and Prahalad, C. K. (1995) *Competing for the Future*. Boston, MA: Harvard Business School Press

Heene, A. and Sanchez, R. (eds) (1997) *Competence-Based Strategic Management*. New York, NY: Wiley

Kim, W. C. and Mauborgne, K. (2005) *Blue Ocean Strategy*: *How to create uncontested market space and make the competition irrelevant.* Boston, MA: Harvard Business Press

Porter, M. (1980) *Competitive Strategy*: *Techniques for analysing industries and competitors.* New York, NY: The Free Press. This book is very worthwhile reading, when discussing strategy in general

Notes and references

1 *Source*: Heene, A. (1997) 'The nature of strategic planning', *Long Range Planning*, Vol 30, No 6, p. 934
2 *See* **http://www.ikea.com**, March 2012
3 For a systematic framework for analyzing environments in relation to defining strategy, *see* Porter, M. E. (1980) *Competitive Strategy: Techniques for analysing industries and competitors*. New York, NY: Free Press as well as Grant, R. (2005) *Contemporary Strategy Analysis*. Blackwell Publishers
4 See in this respect also the notions of 'open innovation' and 'open business models' as advanced by Chesbrough, H. (2006) *Open Business Models*: *How to thrive in the new innovation landscape.* Boston, MA: Harvard Business Press
5 For a recent plea to fully integrate values into business practices, see Porter, M. E. and Kramer, M. (2011) 'Creating Shared Value', *Harvard Business Review*, Jan–Feb, pp. 62–77
6 For a more comprehensive discussion on strategic change, we recommend Pettigrew, A. and Whipp, R. (1992) *Managing Change for Competitive Success*. Oxford: Blackwell Business
7 Porter, M. E. (1980), op. cit.
8 D'Aveni, R. (1994) *Hyper-competition*: *Managing the dynamics of strategic manoeuvring.* New York, NY: Free Press
9 Kim, W. C. and Mauborgne, K. (2005) *Blue Ocean Strategy*: *How to create uncontested market space and make the competition irrelevant.* Boston, MA: Harvard Business School Press
10 For a recent overview of the importance of business model innovation, see *Harvard Business Review*, Jan–Feb 2011: Business Model Innovation
11 *See* T. Hill's work on manufacturing strategy
12 Rotem, Z. and Amit, R. (1997) 'Strategic defence and competence-based competition', in Heene, A. and Sanchez, R. (eds) *Competence-Based Strategic Management*. New York, NY: Wiley, pp. 169–191
13 *See*, for example, Hamel, G. and Prahalad, C. K. (1995) *Competing for the Future*. Boston, MA: Harvard Business Press
14 *See* also the work of Barras in this respect, as discussed in Chapter 15
15 Porter, M. E. (1980), op. cit.
16 For a more detailed overview of possible relevant action strategies, *see* Porter, M. E. (1980), op. cit.
17 Senge, P. (1990) *The Fifth Discipline*. New York, NY: Doubleday
18 Sanchez, R. and Heene, A. (1997) 'A competence perspective on strategic learning and knowledge management', in Sanchez, R. and Heene, A. (eds) *Strategic Learning and Knowledge Management*. New York, NY: Wiley, p. 7
19 Sanchez, R. (1997) 'Managing articulated knowledge in competence-based competition', in Sanchez, R. and Heene, A. (eds) *Strategic Learning and Knowledge Management*. New York, NY: Wiley, pp. 166–169
20 The chain of activities by which the firm builds value

Chapter 17

Managing services across national boundaries

Roland Van Dierdonck • Bart Van Looy

Objectives

By the end of this chapter, you should be able to:

- understand why and identify how services are becoming more and more international

- understand the drivers and the enablers of this internationalization trend in general and apply them to particular sectors

- understand the range of internationalization strategies and select an appropriate strategy, depending on the sector, the type of service and the local circumstances

- understand the cultural dimension of services, which necessitates an awareness on the part of service companies of ethnic and cultural differences

Introduction

The following report of Walmart's entry into the European market appeared in 1997 in the *Financial Times*.[1]

Exhibit 17.1 Walmart comes shopping in Europe

'The legendary Sam Walton and his brother, Bud, opened the first Walmart Discount City store in Rogers, Arkansas, in 1962. In the 35 years since, the mighty Walmart Stores have conquered the US with its cut-price goods, becoming by far the country's biggest retailer.

Now, it's Europe's turn. This week, Walmart took its first step into the European retail market by buying the Wertkauf hypermarket company from Germany's Mann family for an undisclosed sum. In itself, the acquisition is not large: Wertkauf has only 21 stores and its sales last year were about $1.4 billion, a flea-bite next to Walmart's $105 billion. But Walmart left no doubt that it regarded the acquisition as just the start of its European expansion.

"When we enter new markets, our first priority is to learn more about the customers, introduce Walmart concepts and philosophy, and prove ourselves," said Bob Martin, chief executive of Walmart's international division. "When we serve our customers and exceed their expectations, growth in the business will follow."

At the last count, Walmart had 1904 out-of-town discount stores in the US and another 436 Supercenters selling groceries as well as general merchandise. Its success in the US is attributable to many factors, but high on the list is corporate culture that places heavy emphasis on something that should be every retailer's top priority: customer service.

Employees in the stores are bound by the so-called 'ten-foot rule' that requires them to approach any customer who comes within 10 feet of them, look them in the eye, welcome them with a smile, and ask them what they can do to help. Shoppers are met and greeted on entering the store, and when they ask where they can find certain goods, employees are required to escort them all the way to the right place instead of pointing or telling them.

Walmart is also highly regarded for its advanced retail technology, which enables it to have the right quantities of goods in the right place at the right time while keeping costly inventories at a minimum. The company was the first retailer in the US to equip all its stores with scanners at the check-outs. Nowadays, employees carry hand-held computers enabling them to re-order merchandise, while backroom computers link each store with a sophisticated satellite system.

Since starting its international expansion in 1991, Walmart has already become the biggest retailer in Canada and Mexico. It has also dipped its toe into emerging markets, opening small numbers of stores in Argentina, Brazil, Indonesia and China. Yet retailing travels notoriously badly. Retailers that develop a successful concept in their home market usually find they need to adjust the formula to suit local conditions overseas: yet, in doing so, they risk undermining whatever it was that made them successful in the first place.

Previous US ventures into Europe have a mixed record. McDonald's and Toys 'R' Us may be growing, but Woolworth sold its UK stores, Sears Roebuck pulled out of Spain, J. C. Penney sold its Sarma stores in Belgium, and Safeway sold its UK supermarkets. If Walmart's European venture is to succeed, then it will have to overcome the obstacles that have discouraged other US retailers: much higher costs for real estate, labour and distribution than in the US, plus tastes that differ widely from one country to another.

However, European retail analysts say that Walmart has probably made the right decision by starting in Germany. Although competition is intense, the market is large and, in some ways, German retailing is not as advanced as it is in other countries. Nicholas Jones, an analyst at Goldman Sachs in London, says the depth and breadth of assortments are inferior in German hypermarkets, as are store lay-outs and visual presentation. And relatively few German retailers are equipped with the systems and logistics that are among Walmart's biggest strengths. "Walmart's key challenge is to secure critical mass so it can offer attractive prices as soon as possible," says Mr Jones. "If they can combine that with their skills in merchandising, then they will differentiate themselves very distinctly."'

Source: Tomkins, R. (1997) Walmart comes shopping in Europe, *Financial Times* 21 December.
© The Financial Times Limited 1997. All Rights Reserved.

In 2002, 5 years after the report in Exhibit 17.1 appeared, Walmart operated 95 stores in Germany with 16,500 employees. In the same year, Walmart operated more than 12,000 stores in nine countries outside the US contributing $37.4 billion to its revenues and 1.4 billion to its operating profit, an increase of 33.1% over previous years. However, in 2006 Walmart decided to give up its German operations as the *Financial Times* explained:[2]

Exhibit 17.2 'Why Walmart decided to pack'

'Walmart, the world's biggest retailer, pulled out of Germany on Friday, selling its 85 stores for an undisclosed price after eight loss-making years in which it tried to break into a market dominated by discounters.

German consumers resisted such tried-and-true US retailing strategies as providing staff to pack customers' bags at checkouts. Germans feared they would have to pay extra for the service, forcing Walmart to re-assign its bag-packers.

The sale of its 85 stores to Metro – Germany's largest retailer – marks Walmart's most significant international retreat and follows its decision this year to pull out of a smaller loss-making operation in South Korea. Michael Duke, Walmart vice-chairman, said Germany's business environment made it "difficult to obtain the scale and results we desire". It will book a second quarter pre-tax loss of $1bn as a result of the sale.

Walmart entered Germany in 1998 and bought two existing hypermarket chains, but it struggled from the outset against stiff local competition that included Metro and the discounters, Aldi and Lidl. It achieved sales of about $2.5bn in Germany last year, out of global sales of $312bn. The company also encountered difficulties in dealing with the union leadership at its German stores.

. . .

The move illustrates the power of privately owned discounters Lidl and Aldi, which have grown their share of the German grocery market to 40 per cent.

Walmart tried to respond with low prices coupled with more US-style customer service. Used to the most basic of shops, German shoppers shied away, fearing the US company would have to cover extra personnel costs by charging higher prices.'

 Source: Gerrit, W. (2006) 'Why Walmart decided to pack', *Financial Times*, 29 July.
© The Financial Times Limited 2006. All Rights Reserved.

The Walmart experience in Germany illustrates that the internationalization of a service firm is not as straightforward as it might seem: managing across national boundaries poses a serious challenge.

Service businesses are becoming more and more international with import and export figures of services on the rise.[3] This challenges the traditional belief that services by their very nature are local, not transportable and, therefore, cannot be exported. Even if this belief is accepted, it does not mean that there cannot be international trade, since customers can cross borders to 'consume' their services. An obvious example of this is, of course, tourism-related services. It comes as no surprise, therefore, that countries with a strong tourism base perform well in the international service trade. Service providers can also cross borders. ABB, for instance, has maintenance expertise in a large variety of industries but not in every country. When faced with a maintenance problem in a Dutch paper mill, they might call in an expert from Finland.

Internationalization is more than exports, however. Just as with manufacturing industries, exporting is only the initial phase of an internationalization strategy. In this chapter, we shall explore various approaches to internationalization, while taking the specificity of services into consideration.

The simultaneity of consumption and production is one of the major characteristics of a service. This has three major consequences for internationalization:

1 *Customer accessibility to the service delivery system.* This means that exports, although not excluded, can only be considered in a few instances or in a very limited way. Service firms will have to establish foreign operations much earlier in their life cycle than manufacturing industries. If Disney wants to grow in the theme park business it has little choice other than to set up theme parks in Japan and Europe. This holds especially for task-interactive and personal-interactive services since the scope for leveraging technology is more limited (*see* Chapter 5).

2 *The need for personal contact between the customer and the service provider.* This does not only have logistical consequences, as described in the previous point, but requires particular skills on the part of the provider: language, cultural fluency, sensitivity for and knowledge of the local situation.

3 *Handling differences in culture.* In most service 'encounters', there is an interaction, sometimes an intensive one, between the service delivery system and the customer. In certain service environments, for instance, customers are expected to behave in a certain way. This type of behaviour is often culture-dependent. For example, in a business school using interactive teaching methods, students are expected to participate and to defend their personal view. However, this may be in conflict with values and norms of non-Western cultures. In Western Europe, the attitude towards complaining is quite different from that in the US. Therefore, quality-control systems that work well in the US might not work well in Europe. There is not only the culture (i.e. norms and values) of the customer to take into account but also the culture of the personnel. For instance, the extent to which the behaviour of the personnel (an important part of the service) can be 'controlled' by the organization will vary from country to country. Europeans will more readily consider something as belonging to their private 'space' than, say, North Americans, and they will therefore reject too much control over something they consider to be private. This means that it will not always be possible to 'transfer' a service concept 'undamaged'. The behaviour of both customer and personnel is part of the service.

In the remainder of this chapter, we will first explore why companies would want to internationalize. We will see that, generally speaking, internationalization motives are of a strategic nature; companies internationalize because they hope to improve or defend the current competitive position. As mentioned earlier, services are very sensitive culturally. We have included a framework to assess, or at least understand, cultural differences across countries or regions. Based on the insights gained in the previous sections, we will then describe the application, in the service sector, of a model that describes various approaches to internationalization.

Why internationalize?

In service industries, the basic motives for internationalizing are not very different from those in manufacturing industries. Companies, by nature, want to grow and, instead of diversifying in their own country, they therefore expand by going abroad. In many cases, it is easier to sell the same product in another country than to make and sell another product in an existing market. The chances that the company will stay closer to the core business are greater in the former case than in the latter. In the case of Walmart, there are few opportunities for expanding in North America.

Growth is not the only reason for companies to go abroad. Quite often, by becoming bigger they are better able to exploit static and dynamic economies of scale. The effort a company like SAP or Microsoft has to make to develop software is the same, whether or not they do this for their domestic market or a worldwide one. This is not very different from the motives that drive pharmaceutical companies to enter global markets, for example. Dynamic economies of scale or learning curve advantages are as relevant to the McDonald's corporation (for instance, both in setting up and operating a new restaurant) than they are in an automotive factory.

More generally, it can be said that the usual motive for going international is leveraging a competitive asset. This asset can be a well-designed service concept and/or a well-designed and well-operated service delivery system, such as a Disney theme park or a Walmart retail concept. It can be specific knowledge or know-how, as in the case of large consulting firms such as McKinsey, or it can be an image or reputation, such as Harvard Business School or, closer to home, INSEAD.

Companies also become international to add value to their product. The more international a company such as Federal Express, Hertz, ABB Services or Ernst & Young Consulting becomes, the more attractive is its service. The same applies to the Vlerick Business School, which now runs campuses in Western Europe (Belgium), Russia and China. The School will serve its regional market much better by becoming international and accepting foreign students. The other students in the class will learn more about foreign cultures and about doing business internationally by interacting daily with foreign students, than by taking a battery of courses in international business. Likewise, a company may wish to tap into cheaper or more valuable local resources. One of the traditional reasons why manufacturing companies have set up plants in countries with low labour wages is to take advantage of cheap labour resources. This trend is found increasingly in information-intensive service organizations such as software development (in India) and insurance back-office processing (in Ireland or even the Philippines). Companies set up foreign operations not only to tap into cheaper regions but also into scarce resources. For instance, call centres and translation services are set up in Belgium because of its available pool of multilingual people. Likewise, most banks have an office in financial centres such as London and New York because of the expertise and information available there.

It goes without saying that 'going international' provides learning opportunities for firms. This trend is becoming more and more prevalent in manufacturing industries. Companies set up and manage a network of plants with opportunities for exchange and transfer of learning across plants. While it is rare, if not unknown, for a service organization to set up a foreign operation with this as the initial reason, there are quite a few organizations that extensively transfer knowledge, experience and practices across 'offices' in various parts of the world. Food Lion, the American subsidiary of Belgium's second biggest supermarket chain, Delhaize, is an interesting outpost for Delhaize to learn firsthand about innovative practices in supermarkets in the US.

Finally, it should be noted that customers are becoming international. This is especially the case for service-to-business industries, such as consulting, accounting, market research and maintenance. However, it might also be the case for consumer services such as department stores or health care, even if such companies only cater to expatriate managers and their families.

The motives and drivers described in the previous section help a service company to decide whether or not there is a strong pull or push to internationalize. However, before companies develop action strategies, they should be aware of cultural differences across various regions in the world.

Culture and cultural differences

Services, especially personal-interactive services, are experiences and, therefore, neither culture-free nor culturally neutral. The transaction is often much more than a specific exchange at a certain moment in a certain place. A service concept not only expects employees to act or behave in a certain way but also customers to act or behave in a certain way. The Club Méditerranée experience would not be a Club Med product if the employees (GOs) and the customers (GMs) did not behave in the 'Club Med' way. Not only would customers damage the quality of the experience for themselves but also the quality of the experience for the other visitors. Behaviour, people's actions, and the interaction between people are all governed by culture – that is, values, beliefs and implicit assumptions.

For example, in the US, customers are used to having their groceries packed by super-market personnel. Europeans resent this (see the Walmart account) because they interpret it as unnecessary or even as an invasion of their privacy. How can a stranger pack a customer's groceries if he or she does not know when and how the customer plans to store the various items? In France, a car-rental agent addressing a customer by his or her first name is considered rude. On the other hand, the practice in some French restaurants of men and women using common toilets is unheard of for American visitors, as is allowing dogs into restaurants. Disney's policy of requiring its employees to adhere to certain hygiene and dress standards is considered an intrusion on (French) employees' privacy and is, therefore, resisted by them. It is impossible for French customers and employees to understand how a dinner (or even lunch) experience can be complete without wine. Lovelock and Yip[4] explain that 'McDonald's' has a different meaning for Americans than for non-Americans. When an American goes to a McDonald's restaurant in a foreign country it means 'us', something to be trusted, a piece of back home. For the non-American, going to the local McDonald's means 'them', a foreign experience, something different.

An employee working in a call centre in Tiruchchir in the South of Tamil Nadu (in India) talking to an American in Texas complaining about his gas bill from his local utility company should not only have an American, if not a Texas, accent but should also know something about the outcome of yesterday's Super Bowl.[5]

Service organizations wanting to set up foreign operations should be more culturally aware for all these reasons. We shall now describe a framework to help companies understand and analyse various cultures.

The concept of culture

When we refer to culture, we do not so much mean the concept of corporate culture but rather national, or more accurately, ethnic culture. (As a matter of fact, the concept of corporate culture is derived from the notion of ethnic culture as anthropologists have defined it.) Probably the best-known of these anthropologists is Margaret Mead,[6] who defined culture as 'a shared pattern of behaviour', and later refined this to 'a system of shared meaning or understanding that drives behaviour'. This of course comes very close to what has been defined earlier as 'corporate' culture – that is, 'a pattern of beliefs and expectations shared by the members of a group'. In any group, these beliefs and expectations produce norms, which powerfully shape the individual members' behaviour.

Culture is visible and observable via *people's artefacts and behaviour*. Artefacts can be pieces of art such as music, poetry, painting or architecture ('Culture with a capital C'), but they can also be a decorated Christmas tree, a cuckoo clock, a strict gun-control law, garlic sauce, or eating French fries with ketchup. Another visible aspect is human behaviour – for instance, driving on the left-hand side of the road, eating with one hand on one's lap, or saying 'yes' while thinking 'no'. Figure 17.1 illustrates how the same hand movement is interpreted differently in three different countries.

Artefacts and behaviour are the things we notice immediately when we arrive in a foreign country. They can be a source of amusement, irritation or confusion for visitors. When questioned about this, the insiders quite often do not know why they are behaving the way they do, or do not see anything particularly strange about the artefacts. As a matter of fact, they are surprised and sometimes irritated by the series of seemingly stupid questions they may be asked about their culture.

Delving a little deeper, it can be seen that the artefacts are based on *fundamental beliefs and values or norms* that people have.[7] Beliefs are statements of facts – the way things are. Values are expressions of the preferred status about what should be, or about ideas. The Japanese say 'yes' even though they mean 'no' because they find this the proper thing to do (i.e. a value); they do not want to offend others or to make them lose face. That the French cannot imagine having dinner without wine is based on values they hold with respect to wine.

These beliefs and values can only be understood, however, when one is aware of the basic underlying assumptions, what some call the *underlying world view*. These underlying assumptions prescribe ways of perceiving, thinking and evaluating the world, oneself and others. They are often implicit. Thus, when we talk about culture, we should be aware of this complex construction (*see* Figure 17.2). If we really want to appreciate culture we should therefore try to understand the inner core. It is here that cultures are fundamentally different. It is also at this level that cultural changes are difficult to bring about. People might be persuaded to change their behaviour, or even change beliefs, but to change fundamental assumptions is much more difficult, if not impossible.

Dimensions of cultural differences

In what way do these underlying assumptions differ from group to group? Various researchers have used different, albeit related, dimensions to describe these differences. We shall describe the dimensions defined by F. Trompenaars[8] (for other authors, we refer the reader to the literature). These dimensions are summarized in Table 17.1:

1 The first dimension concerns how a society deals with its rules. Does one believe that there is a universal truth, or does it all depend on the particular instance or situation? On

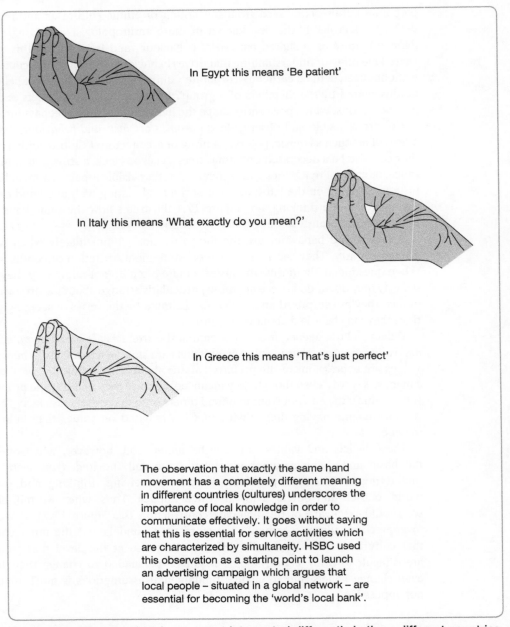

In Egypt this means 'Be patient'

In Italy this means 'What exactly do you mean?'

In Greece this means 'That's just perfect'

The observation that exactly the same hand movement has a completely different meaning in different countries (cultures) underscores the importance of local knowledge in order to communicate effectively. It goes without saying that this is essential for service activities which are characterized by simultaneity. HSBC used this observation as a starting point to launch an advertising campaign which argues that local people – situated in a global network – are essential for becoming the 'world's local bank'.

Figure 17.1 The same hand movement interpreted differently in three different countries
Source: Based on HSBC.

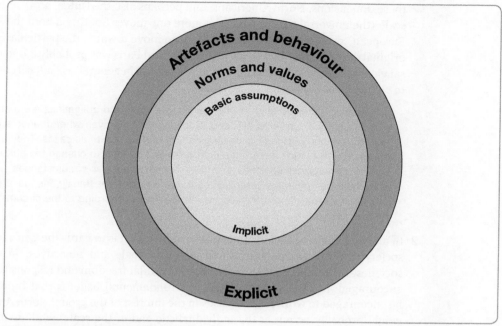

Figure 17.2 The structure of culture

Source: From Schein, Edgar H. (1985) *Organisational Culture and Leadership* (1st edn), Jossey-Bass Publishers. Copyright © 1985 Edgar H. Schein, this material is used by permission of John Wiley & Sons, Inc.

Table 17.1 Dimensions to characterize underlying assumptions

1 Universalism Apply rules and procedures universally to ensure equity and consistency	↔	**Particularism** Encourage flexibility by adapting to particular situations
2 Individualism Encourage individual freedom and responsibility	↔	**Collectivism** Encourage individuals to work for consensus in the interest of the group
3 Affective neutral We must control the expression of our emotions so that we can consider issues objectively	↔	**Affective** Be able to express whatever we think or feel openly and freely
4 Specific It is important to keep business separated from other aspects of life	↔	**Diffuse** Recognise that the integration of different aspects of the total person can stabilize and deepen relationships
5 Achievement We need to appreciate and reward the things our people do and achieve based on skills and knowledge	↔	**Ascription** Respect 'who' our people are, based on their own experience and past record
6 Future We can get the present of our business into focus by relating it to a desired future	↔	**Present – Past** The present of our business is building on the learning of the past

Source: Based on Trompenaars, F. and Hampden-Turner, C. (1998) *Riding the Waves of Culture: Understanding cultural diversity in business*. London: Nicholas Brealy.

these dimensions, North Americans, and perhaps also the Dutch, score at one end of the scale (the universal truth), while the more one moves South, on both the American and European continents, the more one tends to move towards the particularistic view. The original decision not to serve wine at Disneyland Paris was probably based on the universal view of North Americans that wine (or alcohol in general) is bad, certainly in relation to children. As Trompenaars explains:

> 'universalist societies tend to feel that general rules and obligations are a strong source of moral reference. Universalists tend to follow the rules even when friends are involved and look for the one best way of dealing equally and fairly with all cases. They assume that the standards they hold here are the right ones and attempt to change the attitude of others to match. Particularist societies are those where particular circumstances are much more important than the rules. Bonds of particular relationships (family, friends) are stronger than any abstract rules and the response can be made according to the circumstances and the people involved.'

2 In an individualistic society, the primary orientation is towards the 'self'. In a collectivist society, the orientation is towards common goals and objectives. In individualistic societies, the fundamental belief is that individual freedom and responsibility should be encouraged. In collectivist societies, the fundamental belief is that individuals should be encouraged to work for consensus in the interest of the group. North Americans again would probably be put at the individualistic end of the scale, while many Far Eastern societies (Japanese, Koreans) would probably be at the other end.

3 This dimension is related to the extent one displays or is allowed to display emotions. This dimension rates societies from 'affective-neutral' at one end to 'affective-relationships' at the other. In affective-neutral societies, there is a fundamental belief that relationships should be governed by reason and not by emotions. 'We must control expression of our emotions so that we can consider issues objectively' is the unwritten rule. At the other end is the belief that we should 'be able to express whatever we think or feel openly and freely'. Again, in our North/Western world we tend to lean towards the affective-neutral end of the scale. In the South/Eastern world there is often more room for emotions.

4 This dimension is a bit more complicated and has to do with how deeply we become involved with others, distinguishing between specific and diffuse cultures. In specific-oriented cultures, the relationship a person has with somebody else is segregated and dependent on the 'task' or business dealing the person might have with that person. Private and professional relationships are strictly separated. In other countries, every life space and every level of personality tend to permeate all the others. Somewhat related to this dimension is the size of private space. How far do we let others penetrate our private space? Who is allowed to use our first name? When people visit our house, do we show them our bedroom? Generally, we believe that the North American's private space is smaller (i.e. public space is larger). However, the public space is compartmentalized (i.e. specific). In more Southern countries, the space is much more diffuse. In Belgium, there is perhaps a more restricted space, but it is perhaps more diffuse than the Nordic nations.

Based on this dimension, but also on the previous dimensions, is the differentiation between low-contact and high-contact cultures. In high-contact cultures people do not mind standing close to one another and engaging in frequent touching. People in low-contact cultures, on the other hand, prefer to stand at a distance and touch less.

5 A fifth dimension is related to the significance of status, or more accurately, the attitude towards status: 'Do you work for it or is it given?' In some societies, status is accorded to people on the basis of their actual achievements. In other societies, status is ascribed to them by virtue of age, gender, education or class. Trompenaars makes a distinction between achieved status and ascribed status. In the *achievement orientation*, people are appreciated and rewarded for the things they do and achieve, based on skill and knowledge. In the *ascription orientation*, people are respected for who they are, based on their experience and past record.

6 The final dimension is the way time is organized. This includes, first of all, the relative importance given to the past, present and future. In Figure 17.3[9] the importance of each of these three elements is expressed by the size of the circle symbolizing it. In the US, according to Trompenaars, the past is of relatively little importance; the future is what counts. This is in contrast to, for instance, France. Note the relative importance in Spain of the present, and the 'mañana' attitude symbolized by the lesser importance given to the future. A second element of this dimension is how people consider the past, present and future to be related. The view of time can be sequential, a series of passing events, or it can be synchronic, 'with past, present and future all interrelated'. The latter view means that both ideas about the future and memories of the past shape actions in the present.

Trompenaars' six dimensions help us to understand the fundamental assumptions in different cultures. However, it is important to exercise care in applying these dimensions. A first reason for caution is that, while there appears to be a broad consensus on the existence of cultural differences, the same consensus does not exist when it comes to the dimensions themselves. Geert Hofstede, another well-known researcher in this field, uses different dimensions.[10]

There is also a danger of stereotyping people. We tend to look at the extremes and extrapolate these extremes to the whole population. The real situation is much more like Figure 17.4, with a wide distribution within one population on a certain dimension and a

Figure 17.3 International views of the past, present and future

Source: Based on Trompenaars, F. (1998) *Riding the Waves of Culture: Understanding cultural diversity in business.* London: Nicholas Brealy.

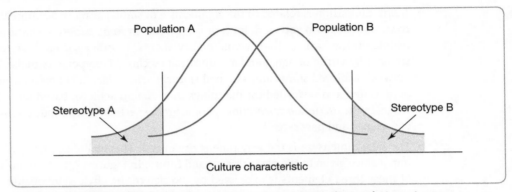

Figure 17.4 The relationship between cultural characteristics and stereotypes

great deal of overlap between various populations. It should also be noted that people will not always behave consistently according to one of the extreme positions. They fluctuate between various positions, depending on the situation at hand, and try to find a balance between the extremes.

Implication for service industries

As has been argued by many researchers, an appropriate and strong culture is a very important factor for success in service organizations. The 'customer service' culture at Walmart, symbolized by the 'ten-foot' rule, is an example of a strong culture. Organizational culture – that is, shared beliefs and values – is a way to 'control' people's behaviour. As we have already stated, the personnel's activities or behaviour are not always easy to prescribe and, therefore, contact personnel should be given more discretion and empowerment. The more the need to customize the service grows, the more this will apply. A service organization's management should perhaps devote more attention to culture than their colleagues in industrial organizations. Not only should they make sure that a strong culture is developed but they should also ensure that the right kind of culture exists – that is, the so-called *service culture*. In addition, they should be aware of the (ethnic) culture of both personnel and customers. Organizations, therefore, should not only look for a sufficient amount of culture-related consensus from the employees but also from the customers. The latter task is not easy for a service organization operating in an international environment.

Differences in ethnic cultures reflect the way customers perceive an otherwise identical service and, in particular, the servicescape. Serving wine (or not serving wine) in a family theme park will affect the perception of the service differently in France than in the US. The same is true for queueing and the extent to which queues are managed. A Belgian will react differently to a car salesman calling him by his first name during his first visit than an American will. A German will perhaps have difficulties sharing a table in a Japanese restaurant with total strangers. Students in certain parts of the world will react differently to being invited to participate in class discussions than in others. French and American employees will react differently to being told to take a shower every morning and change their underwear every day. Managing by objectives will be less effective in Asian countries than it is in the US, and so on. When we described the servicescape, we discussed how colour may play a determining role in how an environment is perceived; but a certain colour has a different meaning in different cultures. Yellow, for instance, is associated in China with royalty, in Greece with age, in Italy with prostitution and in Egypt with famine.

The examples described above are differences in behaviour or artefacts, but they are based on the fundamental assumptions we have explained. The decision not to serve wine in Disneyland Paris was perhaps an expression of the 'universalism' found in American culture, while, for the French, not having wine with dinner is a major quality mistake. They simply expect wine at the table. The acceptability of queueing is, without doubt, influenced by people's attitude towards time. Willingness to participate is influenced by the individualism-*versus*-collectivism dimension, or by the importance of hierarchy in a society. Standing close to the customer in front of you who is being served in a bank or public service is considered impolite in most Northern countries but not so in Middle Eastern countries. American cinemas keep the temperature in the theatre at 20 °C or below, so that people do not feel the body heat of their (strange) neighbour. Perhaps more important for services is the 'affective-neutral versus affective-relationships' dimension. The service culture, as described earlier, requires a much more affective type of relationship – a more 'feminine' society according to Hofstede – than is perhaps the norm in many more 'masculine' cultures.

Management implications for international service operations

When setting up international service operations, a company should be aware that there may be a conflict between corporate culture and the employees' ethnic culture. Such a conflict will not only prevent the company from developing a strong corporate culture but will influence the service concept, i.e. the product itself. A company should, therefore, examine its service concept and its service delivery system for cultural biases. Another implication relates to the conflict between corporate culture and the 'ethnic' culture of the customers. The same advice, as given in the previous points, can be offered here. The service concept and the service delivery system should be scrutinized to allow for cultural biases. It is clear that the Disney concept is very American, which is fine so long as it does not conflict with the fundamental values and underlying assumptions of the host country.

In the case of a conflict, the service concept and the service delivery system must be adapted. McDonald's serving beer in Belgium is a good example. The important question here, however, is how far a company can and should go in this adaptation process. There are some general core values or some company-specific values that cannot or should not be compromised. Doing so runs the risk of losing the essence of the service concept or sacrificing the fundamental characteristics of the service process (*see* Chapter 3). This may lead to the conclusion that certain services simply cannot be transferred unless we target a specific market segment that shares some of the original market's cultural characteristics. For instance, Marks & Spencer's decision to internationalize was fundamentally based on the existence of a British or Anglophile segment in foreign countries.

Internationalization strategies

When a service company decides to internationalize, it should understand that various strategies are possible. The best strategy, of course, depends on the objective the company is trying to achieve, but it also depends very much on the type of product, i.e. service.

Bartlett and Goshal[11] have developed a general framework that classifies various internationalization strategies and relates these strategies to various conditions. This framework is generally applicable to any type of industry, but it especially applies to service organizations (*see* Figure 17.5).[12]

There are two fundamental forces that one should take into account when considering an internationalization strategy: a force towards *global integration* and a force towards *local responsiveness*. The appropriate internationalization strategy will depend on the strength of these two forces, as indicated in Figure 17.5:[13]

● The force towards global integration has been described in previous sections of this chapter. This force refers to such factors as the presence of economies of scale, or opportunities to globally exploit certain assets, competencies and competitive advantages. The drivers towards globalization described earlier stimulate the move towards global integration or remove barriers to it. An increasing number of service organizations will be driven towards global integration as a result of this force. We are referring to industries such as airlines, film studios and electrical utilities.

● At the other end is the force towards local responsiveness. The more personalized and/or customized a service is, the more necessary it will be to adapt it to local needs. This is especially the case for services that are culture-dependent – for example, having a high language content, or involving local taste or traditional habits. Although there are, no doubt, some 'universal' theatre plays, most plays and actors will be local since they involve almost all the responsiveness factors mentioned. While there may be organizations that address universal educational needs, most educational systems will remain local as well. The need for local responsiveness may also result from a high level of government control. Governments often demand local content not only from companies manufacturing goods such as automobiles but also, for instance, in television and radio broadcasting.

Figure 17.5 A general framework of internationalization strategies

A global strategy

When the need for local responsiveness is low and the force towards global integration strong, companies will develop a purely *global strategy*. The characteristics of a global strategy are summarized in Table 17.2. The world is basically seen as one large market, which can and should be approached in a homogeneous way, or at least integrated across countries. The company's position in one country is evaluated not on its own merit but on its contribution to the global competitive position. There are few examples of service businesses using purely global strategies. Given the need for accessibility and the almost certain presence of interactions, there will always be some local content. However, international airlines such as British Airways, SIA, or KLM, fast-food restaurants such as McDonald's, and express package delivery services such as Federal Express come very close. The international business schools such as INSEAD or IMD also come close to this position. All of these types of service address a universal and homogeneous need and are very much scale-intensive.

Ikea,[14] the international retailer of furniture, follows a strategy that tends to be global. Country managers at Ikea assume control for day-to-day activities and are allowed some discretion in augmenting the basic range of Ikea products to meet local tastes. The responsibility for product development and purchasing lies with Ikea of Sweden, the original company that pioneered the 'blond' style of Nordic furniture and furnishings. The group's international headquarters in Denmark oversees investment in new markets and the refurbishment or expansion of existing stores. Ikea has strong centrally imposed formats and procedures. It has a single logistics system, funnelling the products from its bulk-buying operation into individual stores.

Table 17.2 Organizational models

	Global	International	Multi-domestic	Transnational
Dominant strategic capability	Global efficiency	Worldwide learning	Local responsiveness	Global efficiency, local responsiveness learning
Configuration of assets and capabilities	Centralized and globally scaled	Sources of core competencies centralized, others decentralized	Decentralized and nationally self-sufficient	Dispersed, interdependent and specialized
Role of international operations	Implementing parent company strategies	Adapting and leveraging parent company competencies	Sensing and exploiting local opportunities	Differentiated contributions of national units to integrated worldwide operations/supply chain
Development and diffusion of knowledge	Knowledge developed and retained at the centre	Knowledge developed at the centre and transferred to overseas operations	Knowledge developed and retained in each unit	Knowledge developed jointly and shared worldwide

Source: Bartlett, C. A. and Ghoshal, S. (1989) *Managing Across Borders*: *The transnational solution*, Random House Business Books. Reprinted by permission of Harvard Business School Press. From *Managing Across Borders: the transnational solution* by Bartlett, C. A. and Ghoshal, S., Boston, MA 1989. Copyright © 1989 by the Harvard Business School Publishing Corporation; all rights reserved.

A multi-domestic strategy

When the need for local responsiveness is high, on the other hand, and there is little drive towards global integration, the best internationalization strategy might be a *multi-domestic* one. This is actually a situation in which very few international companies will operate in the first place. While there are many international law firms that serve international companies, law services to individuals in most countries are very localized and few international 'chains' exist. The same is true today for health-care providers. These sectors are dominated by small local organizations. Even the big international law firms are usually much more domestic in nature. The characteristics of such a strategy are summarized in Table 17.2. If there is a headquarters, then control by the headquarters is very weak. The offices are staffed and managed by local people and form a loose confederation of very autonomous units. Each local unit contributes little more than profit, and at most prestige, to the whole.

A transnational strategy

In certain services, there is a simultaneous need for both local responsiveness and global integration. The service and the service delivery system must be adapted to local needs but, at the same time, there are important advantages to be gained from becoming bigger or from leveraging certain corporate assets. In this case, there is a need for an integrated network strategy or, what others call, a transnational strategy. Companies such as ISS – having acquired many small local service companies – have succeeded in moving from the multidomestic to the transnational situation. It has taken tremendous cultural changes in most local companies to achieve this. However, management of those companies has succeeded in highlighting the advantages of global integration: worldwide accessible expertise in many industries and professional management. Some companies are moving away from the global strategy position to the transnational position, in some cases, in order to be able to compete against strong local companies. McDonald's, for example, serves beer in Belgium and, in India, serves a vegetarian sandwich instead of a hamburger.

A good example of a company that appears to be following such a strategy is Toys 'R' Us, in contrast with Ikea's strategy, for instance. As described in the *Financial Times*:[15]

'The fickle nature of children's choices requires more latitude for local managers. Toy tastes vary significantly between different cultures. For example, Asian families like educational toys, while American children are heavily influenced by Saturday morning television programmes.'

Managers are given great latitude in the management of their business. Like Ikea, Toys 'R' Us has common store lay-outs and distribution procedures, but these are flexible to suit local markets. In Japan, some items are delivered directly to the stores, and the delivery of all items is more frequent than in the US, to take into account the limitation and cost of large warehouses in Japan. To keep in touch with local needs, the headquarters management of Toys 'R' Us travels frequently to its local stores. Mr Staley, President of the company's International Division is quoted as saying:

'We believe it's far better for our headquarters organisation to be able to meet on their own turf, dealing with their day-to-day problems, than to try to rationalise their business issues sitting here in Paramus, NJ.'

An 'international' strategy

Finally, there is the lower left quadrant of Figure 17.5. It is difficult to describe a strategy here. It may be that the *de facto* strategy of service organizations is such that they belong to this quadrant. This is an unstable situation. Companies in this position should seriously consider moving towards the right and being more locally responsive by adapting their service and service delivery system. By doing this, they may be able to protect themselves against foreign competitors who are following the global strategy. If this is impossible or unfeasible, then they should consider a move upwards towards the global strategy position. This means that they should carefully analyse their service delivery systems and look for elements that can be leveraged by exploiting them on an international scale.

Choosing the right strategy

The three strategies that we have described above (the fourth 'international' strategy is not considered a viable option) are broad generic orientations for a service company. However, this general framework should be applied to the various parts of the service and service delivery system at a more detailed level. For instance, it is possible to use a global strategy for the back office and a multi-domestic strategy for front-office activities. We have already mentioned that many service-based businesses need a local presence for their downstream activities because of the need for accessibility. Therefore, there is an opportunity to build local responsiveness into the local operations. The critical balance here is how much should be controlled by centrally designed operating procedures and/or by creating a common corporate culture, and how much leeway should be given to local offices, without sacrificing the 'integrity' of the service concept.

The applicability of each of the three strategies is very much dependent on the situation. It is clear, however, that, in certain service sectors, certain strategies are more applicable than in others. Lovelock and Yip,[16] for instance, make a distinction between people-processing, information-processing and possession-processing services. They state that global strategies are most appropriate for the latter two, more impersonal, types of service while, for the people-processing type of service, the multi-domestic or the transnational approach is more appropriate. Translated to the service classifications with which we are familiar, we could say that the more the service is of a maintenance or task interactive nature, the more a global strategy will be appropriate. In the case of services of a more personal-interactive nature, a multidomestic or transnational strategy will be more appropriate.

Conclusion

The view that services are by their very nature local and, therefore, cannot be internationalized is increasingly contradicted by what we see all around us. As a matter of fact, there are a number of reasons why services are becoming increasingly international. Service companies should, therefore, develop an internationalization strategy. The appropriate strategy depends on the particular situation and on the type of service that the company offers.

In this chapter, we have described the various strategies and the factors that determine the appropriate strategy. In developing an appropriate strategy, companies should give particular attention to potential cultural differences, since services are not culturally neutral. In designing the service and the service delivery system, companies should be careful to avoid conflicts between corporate culture and (implicit) cultural biases in both the service concept and the culture of the employees and customers. This chapter has described some useful dimensions that might help us understand and evaluate such potential conflicts.

Review and discussion questions

- Based on the description of the Walmart case at the beginning of the chapter, identify the drivers for internationalization in the retail sector. Why was Walmart in the end not successful? What would have been a better approach to enter the German/European market?

- Analyse the challenges and opportunities faced by the call-centre sector with respect to internationalization. See the report in *Financial Times* 'India learns language of customer service', *Financial Times*, 4 April 2001.

Suggested further reading

Hofstede, G. (1980) *Culture Consequences: International differences in work-related values*. Beverly Hills, CA: Sage Publications. A basic book on internationalization

Lovelock, C. H. and Yip, G. S. (1996) 'Developing global strategies for service businesses', *California Management Review*, Vol 38, No 2, Winter, pp. 64–86. This excellent study provides a framework for developing global strategies for service businesses. It integrates existing, separate frameworks on globalization and on service businesses and analyses which distinctive characteristics of service businesses affect globalization and which do not

Trompenaars, F. and Hampden-Turner, C. (1998) *Riding the Waves of Culture: Understanding cultural diversity in business*. London: Nicholas Brealy. Another basic book on internationalization

Notes and references

1 Tomkins, R. (1997) 'Walmart comes shopping in Europe', *Financial Times*, 21 December, p. 23
2 Gerrit, W. (2006) 'Why walmart decided to pack', *Financial Times*, 29 July
3 For an indication of the latest figures, see UNCTAD, *Handbook of Statistics*
4 Lovelock, C. H. and Yip, G. S. (1996) 'Developing global strategies for service businesses', *California Management Review*, Vol 38, No 2, Winter, pp. 64–86. *See also* Roberts, J. (1999) 'The internationalisation of business service firms: a stages approach', *The Service Industries Journal*, Vol 19, No 4, pp. 68–88
5 *See* Merchant, K. (2001) 'India learns language of customer service', *Financial Times*, 4 April, p. 11
6 Mead, M. (1978) *Culture and Commitment: The new relationships between the generations in the 1970s*. New York, NY: Columbia University Press
7 *Source*: Schein, E. (1985) *Organisational Culture and Leadership*. San Francisco, NY: Jossey-Bass Publishers
8 Readers who want to know more about this are referred to Trompenaars, F. and Hampden-Turner, C. (1998) *Riding the Waves of Culture: Understanding cultural diversity in business*. London: Nicholas Brealy
9 Ibid.
10 The four dimensions used by Hofstede are power distance, uncertainty avoidance, individualism, and masculinity. The main difference is that Hofstede limits his framework to work-related values: *Power distance* is the extent to which a society accepts that the power in institutions and organizations is distributed unequally. *Uncertainty avoidance* is the extent to which a society lacks tolerance for uncertainty and ambiguity. *Individualism* is the extent to which a society believes that people are supposed to take care of themselves and remain emotionally independent from groups, organizations and other collectivities. *Masculinity* is the extent to which 'masculine' or ego values of assertiveness, money and materials prevail

in a society rather than 'feminine' or social values of nurturing, quality of life, and people. For more information, *see* Hofstede, G. (1980) *Culture Consequences: International differences in work-related values*. Beverly Hills, CA: Sage Publications

11 Bartlett, C. A. and Ghoshal, S. (1989) *Managing Across Borders: The transnational solution*. London: Hutchinson Business Books

12 Note that service firms are internationalizing less than their manufacturing counterparts due to some of the complexities, outlined in this section. For a more recent empirical account, see Rugman, A. and Verbeke, A. (2008) 'A new perspective on the regional and global strategies of multinational services firms', *Management International Review*, Vol 48, No 4, pp. 397–411

13 Bartlett, C. A. and Ghoshal, S. (1989), op. cit.

14 Burt, T. and Tomkins, R. (1997) 'Case Study: Ikea and Toys "R" Us', *Financial Times*, 8 October

15 Ibid.

16 Lovelock, C. H. and Yip, G. S. (1996), op. cit.

Chapter 18

Servitization: or why services management is relevant for manufacturing environments

Steven Desmet • Roland Van Dierdonck • Bart Van Looy •
Paul Gemmel

'Many goods-dominant companies are intrigued by services because their traditional offerings are increasingly viewed as commodities by customers.'[1]

Objectives

By the end of this chapter, you should be able to discuss:

● what is meant by the notion of servitization

● how servitization develops in different stages

● why more and more manufacturing firms are opting for the servitization approach

● what the crucial prerequisites are for achieving servitization

Introduction

A survey held in 2002 among executives in Germany and Belgium indicated that over 90% of all manufacturing companies believe the further development of services is crucial for maintaining and improving their competitive position. This expectation did unfold. Recent data suggest that almost 60% of all manufacturing firms in Western economies offer services.[2] Moreover, the share of turnover stemming from services is far from trivial: recent research indicates that the average share of service sales has reached 31%[3] while, for some companies, this share exceeds 50%.

In the previous chapters of the book, we have identified the specific characteristics of services. This may have given the false impression that manufacturing goods and delivering services are so different that this book will only be relevant to companies classified as being in the tertiary or services sector of the economy. This is an outdated view.

Traditionally, manufacturing companies supplied goods, while service was seen as having only minor importance. This attitude has changed. Services have become important for manufacturing companies. More and more of these companies are offering an integrated package of products and services. Sandra Vandermerwe, one of the leading scholars on this topic, has called this movement 'the servitization of businesses'.[4]

[handwritten margin note: it can be used as an example]

This change affects the management of traditional manufacturing companies. The offering to the customer has to be redefined to include this 'bundle' concept. As a result, manufacturing businesses and service companies are no longer so very different, and each has something to teach the other.

In this chapter, we shall take a closer look at this change, describing the way in which servitization is evolving. We shall also examine some of the causes of this trend and some of the implications it has for a company's organization and its production processes.

From goods to services

Traditionally, the focus in manufacturing companies has been on making a good quality article. The objective has been to make a car that would take the customer from point A to point B, a lift that would go up and down, or a coffee machine that would make coffee. There is nothing wrong with this; we all want our cars to function smoothly or our coffee machines to make good coffee. Every manufacturer has to ensure that the goods – the substantive element of the product offering – work well. However, manufacturers have come to realize – often at the behest of customers – that the offering of a product is enhanced when it is complemented by services.

A classical form of customer service offered by manufacturing companies is after-sales service – the installation, maintenance and repair of goods sold. In so-called 'flexible factories', the notion of customer service also implies the introduction of breadth to the range of product offerings and the ability to customize the product to meet specific customer needs.

It is apparent, however, that customer services in this context are seen as 'services that accompany goods' – for example, initial configuration, acceptable delivery time, after-sales repairs, correct installation, etc.[5] Services are seen as an add-on or sometimes even as a necessary evil since, in the minds of most consumers or salespeople, an intervention after the sale is often associated with a defect in the product.

This notion of service can obviously be extended. Servitization goes beyond the traditional approach of providing 'additional' services. In the case of servitization, the offer is defined as a 'bundle' consisting of both goods and services. Servitization thus requires a different mindset:

> 'Management must break out of the mindset that considers manufacturing (or goods production) as separate from the service activities that make such products possible and effective.'[6]

Redefining 'products' will often mean taking a fresh look at customers' needs. Instead of trying to sell the item with the service as an add-on, we should address the problem that a particular product solves. This will often lead to the conclusion that the hardware is only part of the solution. Solutions are provided not merely by a good and some added-on

Figure 18.1 Goods and services: three stages of transition

Source: Van Dierdonck, R. (1993) 'Post-Lean Manufacturing: The importance of servitization'. Fourth International Forum on Technology Management. Berlin, October.

services but by means of a package that includes both goods and services. Both contribute to the fulfilment of customer needs.

Consider, for instance, the example of Schindler, the Swiss lift and escalator company. This company no longer sees itself as being in the business of manufacturing lifts and escalators but rather in the business of *ensuring the mobility of the occupants of a building*: 'Schindler develops, plans, produces, installs and services mobility solutions in accordance with customer requirements.'[7] This is done not only by designing, producing and installing the hardware but also by providing customers with simulation tools to determine how many lifts a building should have, given the traffic patterns and acceptable waiting times, and performing preventative maintenance to minimize down-time, or even to guarantee in a service-level agreement the up-time of the installations. This clearly required a change of mindset at a strategic level and a whole new kind of thinking about Schindler's product.

An examination of the different ways of defining the relationship between goods and services reveals three different approaches:

- considering yourself as a mere goods manufacturer and supplier;
- offering additional services; and
- embracing the notion of servitization.

Often these three different approaches follow an evolutionary process, as depicted in Figure 18.1.[8] A company may start with merely offering goods; it may then develop services as an add-on. The intrinsic value of services is then acknowledged in the following step.

Why servitization?

Why is it that manufacturing companies are becoming increasingly interested in giving their customers good service? Broadly speaking, there are two main reasons. First of all, most customers just want more service and are no longer satisfied with the good alone. They want the service that goes along with it – that is, the service that addresses the underlying needs. Second, offering a higher level of service than that of your competitors is a way of making your offering more attractive for your customers. It can differentiate you from your competitors.

Satisfying customer needs

Today's customers simply demand more services. They do not simply want to buy a computer or a car; they also want a guarantee that it works. They want ease of use, ease of repair, and a 24-hour information desk. This is not to say that the tangible element of the offering has become less important. Customers still want the same article, but they also want the services, so that they can get the most out of their purchase. Ultimately, it comes down to satisfying a need, which often implies more than the availability of products.

Redefining an offering as a bundle of services and goods may, therefore, meet customers' expectations. However, there is a danger of misunderstanding this approach or executing it poorly. Many suppliers simply add layer upon layer of services to their offerings without even knowing whether customers really want them, whether these services should be added on to the standard package or offered as an option, or even what the costs associated with these services are.[9] The notion of the service concept, discussed in Chapter 3, is as important to bundling as it is to 'pure' services.

Customers are also increasingly taking the so-called *life-cycle cost* into account. They are no longer looking at the purchase price alone but also at other costs incurred over the product's lifetime – for example, cost of use (fuel, parts and supplies, etc.) and maintenance. For many products, especially durable goods, the purchase price represents only a small fraction of the total life-cycle cost. The purchase price of an average car, for example, represents only about a quarter of the total cost. The remainder consists of fuel, maintenance, insurance and taxes. Providing good service to lower these additional costs can become an important aspect of competitive strategy. Mercedes-Benz recognized this and used it in advertising campaigns for their trucks. Customers were reminded that the price of a truck constituted only about 15% of the total average lifetime cost of the truck. The company's sales directors thus advised potential customers to calculate these additional costs – that is the costs 'in use' – taking into account Mercedes-Benz fuel-saving systems, lease or finance terms, and especially the availability of a broad range of vehicles, high quality production and efficient after-sales service before choosing a supplier.[10]

Exhibit 18.1 Colora: selling solutions[11]

Colora, a Belgian chain of franchisee-operated paint shops, provides a good example. Imagine yourself having to paint the living room of your new home. You go to the local do-it-yourself shop to buy paint and a brush, only to find hundreds of different types of paint. You look for someone to help you choose, but either you cannot find anybody or those you can find do not know anything about paint. Compare this with a typical Colora shop. It also has hundreds of different types of paint, but the employees are trained to help you. Based on the description of the type of wall in your living room, they advise you which is the best type of paint for your needs, or if that is not enough, they'll even come with you to your house to give information on the spot. Colora's management realizes that most customers entering a paint shop or DIY shop are not just looking for paint or a brush; instead, they are looking for help in solving a problem. Colora thus sells more than just products; it sells solutions to customer problems – solutions that consist not only of goods but also of a service, which together satisfy the needs of its customers. Hence, providing goods and services based on the sound technical knowledge of the employees are the key to Colora's success.

Seeking differentiation

Traditionally, competition between manufacturing firms has tended to focus on the goods themselves. A company gained customers or increased its sales because its goods were better than those of its competitors. Now, competition has shifted to another level, namely that of the product's service component. Many manufacturers only have limited competitive advantage in terms of their goods. Goods are sometimes easy to copy especially when patents offer insufficient protection against copying. Goods are becoming more and more alike in terms of their quality and performance. Manufacturers are finding it difficult to differentiate themselves from their competitors on the strength of the goods alone and, thus, have to find their source of differentiation elsewhere. Offering better service than the competition can result in an important competitive advantage.

The computer industry provides a well-known illustration of this trend. Competition, especially in the business-to-business market, is now less focused on speed, capacity or other qualities of the computer and more on the service offered – ease of use, after-sales service, etc. One of IBM's advertising slogans during 1985 was 'If everybody wants to have an IBM terminal, it is because IBM service is the best.' It is not that the tangible aspect of the offering is no longer important, but the fact that most manufacturers can make a high-quality, high-performance computer means that this does not differentiate anymore. It is as if the goods have become a 'qualifier', whereas the service offered has become the 'order winner'.[12] A good tangible product must be produced to even be in the running, but high margins are realized elsewhere. Focus has shifted from the core product towards the services because offering a mixture of goods and service components allows the company to differentiate and, hence, to create more satisfied and loyal customers. Satisfied customers are less eager to switch to the competition or less eager to do it themselves. By using services as a competitive tool, companies may also succeed in setting up barriers to entry to competitors and in creating switching costs.[13] Offering extended services can keep the competition away by making entry too costly and complex. Offering a bundle of services and goods also makes your competitive strength less transparent for competitors and hence more sustainable; an issue discussed in the chapter dealing with service strategy (*see* Chapter 16).

Making the transition

It is clear that the trend towards servitization offers companies many opportunities for differentiation. However, redefining the service and good offered and seeing its potential benefits are only half of the story. Realizing the benefits of servitization will require effort: for example, relevant information systems need to be put in place and an adequate organization should be installed, often including the development of appropriate skills.

Setting up customer information systems

In order to increase customer focus and thereby enhance customer service, a company has to know more about customers and their needs, and be able to act on that information.

ABB's Metrawatt division has adopted just such a strategy. The Metrawatt division has a computer database where all relevant data on each client is stored including key contacts, type of purchase, frequency of purchase and maintenance required. This information is used to schedule preventive maintenance, even if the client does not have a maintenance contract. The company can then contact its client before the client calls in distress. The same information is also used to forecast periods when maintenance activities will be heaviest as became apparent when discussing relationship marketing in Chapter 12.

Organizing the service delivery system

In the traditional view of services, customer service strategies had little impact on the production system. Customer service was viewed merely as a supportive and buffering sub-system to the production sub-system, and the customer as a potential disruptive factor. Direct customer contact was avoided because it reduced efficiency. Everything was done to insulate the production process from its surroundings.

However, when shifting from the production of goods to the production of goods and services as an integrated package (*see* Figure 18.1), the interaction between the customer and the production system increases, since an important characteristic of services is its (at least partially) simultaneous production and consumption (*see* Chapter 1). This certainly requires a big change in mentality from managers. A 1992 study,[14] consisting of a series of in-depth interviews with 80 senior managers and group discussions with 388 senior managers in 16 US-based multinational firms, reported that this increased interaction with the client was seen as one of the major difficulties in the servitization process. Adapting to *limita-tion* the dual role of the client as both customer and co-producer, and managing this increased participation, is thus seen as a serious challenge.

During the transition from being a manufacturing company to being a bundle-producing company, the customer should be made more visible not only in front-office activities but in the whole design–manufacturing support chain. What is needed is a form of open system with direct and accessible linkages between the factory and its internal and external customers.[15] 'The four walls of a factory no longer limit the domain of manufacturing', as Chase[16] puts it.

This has not only physical implications but also organizational consequences. The traditional breakdown into manufacturing, marketing and sales, product development, and field support divisions increasingly makes less sense. The vertical lines and structures should be replaced by horizontal lines including the interface between customers and suppliers. In particular, the interface between manufacturing and marketing and sales should be re-evaluated, since keeping the two functions separate will seriously hamper the fulfilment of customer needs. Manufacturing should not only be integrated upstream with, for instance, Research and Development but also downstream. This follows from the tighter and more direct coupling of customer needs with the organization's capabilities.

Note, in this respect, that coupling between 'product' and 'service' activities also becomes a managerial focus of attention. Indeed, one could argue that offering simultaneously products and services – within one and the same company – only makes sense if '1+1 equals 3', i.e. when synergies or spillovers between products and services can be achieved. If not, firms will in the end experience costs due to increased complexity and related coordination costs. While offering services that complement product activities definitely bear that potential, reality shows that companies have a hard time actually achieving these spillovers. This so-called 'Service Paradox'[17] – i.e. product companies not reaping the benefits from developing service activities – largely stems from the lack of enacted spillovers[18] (*see* Chapter 16). In order to ensure that these spillovers actually occur, a service value-oriented mindset is required as well as incentive arrangements that incorporate such spillovers.

Putting the right skills in place

As a result of servitization, more and more workers will have direct customer contact, which will require changes in employees' skills as well as their behaviour. Much more attention will need to be given to the interpersonal skills of customer-contact personnel. Factory personnel, in addition to possessing technical knowledge, must be adept at communication and sensitive to customer needs. The personnel should have a *service orientation* – that is, a helpful, thoughtful, considerate, and co-operative attitude.[19]

The simultaneous production and consumption of most services also means that customer-contact employees will often need to make instantaneous decisions in the absence of their supervisor, in the same way that field-service engineers spend most of their time in the company of the customer firm. Personnel empowerment should be increased to enable them to make decisions and to act in the customer's interest on the spot (*see* Chapter 11).

The virtual factory?

It is clear that servitization – that is, paying more attention to the service component of the product offering – may eventually lead to what has been called *the virtual factory*.[20] Generally speaking, a virtual factory is:

'a factory which attains its target of transforming materials and components into value for the customer by using resources outside the manufacturing function proper.'

Customers both possess, and are themselves, important resources and, therefore, should be included in the network of resources that a virtual factory controls. In addition, when the product is enhanced, the manufacturing organization should 'control', but not necessarily 'own', its various activities. ABB does not own its customers' spare-part warehouses but rather controls them.

In a number of cases, pure manufacturing is becoming less important to competition. As a consequence, we might see more and more manufacturing firms subcontracting the manufacturing component and concentrating on the various service activities downstream and upstream of the actual manufacturing activity. This may eventually lead to the virtual factory becoming a reality.

If the service component of the offering represents the core of the company's competitive advantage, then traditional manufacturing companies may ultimately subcontract the tangible part and concentrate themselves entirely on the service component. The example of E&J Gallo Winery, the largest wine producer and distributor in the US, shows that this fourth stage is not as improbable as we may think. Gallo outsourced the growing of specialized grapes for its wine:

'an activity many vintners consider the core of their business. Gallo devotes its resources and management attention to maintaining the legendary marketing and sales strength that give the company its volume advantages and to using the deep knowledge base its 31 per cent market share can provide to purchase grapes with the precise quality its wines require.'[21]

Another example pertains to IBM. Recall the 1985 slogan – 'If everybody wants to have an IBM terminal, it is because IBM service is the best.' Almost 20 years later, IBM sold its PC division to LENOVO (China). Consequently, parts of the product offering of IBM – on which it has built a layer of service activities – disappeared. This, however, did not prevent IBM from further growth, including growth in services, which currently contribute 39% to profits (before tax). Hardware products amount to 8%, while the remainder goes to software (44%) and financing services (9%).[22]

Exhibit 18.2 The development of ABB Services[23]

Asea Brown Boveri (ABB) provides an excellent example of a traditional manufacturing organization that came to recognize the importance of service and consequently broadened the definition of its offering.

ABB is one of the largest electrical engineering groups in the world. It was created on 1 January 1988 when Percy Barnevik, who at that time was Managing Director of the Swedish company Asea,[24] announced the merger of Asea with the Swiss firm Brown Boveri. Currently (2011), ABB is a $37 billion multinational company employing 134,000 people in 10 countries. More than half of ABB's activities take place in the European region, with around one-quarter in the Americas and a growing presence in the Asian Pacific.

Initially, in the 1950s and 1960s, Asea's service activities were not so explicitly organized. Service jobs were being done in the plants. Asea began to observe that 'these annoying warranty repair jobs' were disturbing work flow, planning and focus on production. The broken transformers and generators coming in through the back door were making it difficult to respect delivery deadlines and quality. Unforeseen urgent repair work was filling expensive production areas. Priorities were getting muddled and people were becoming disorganized, with the resulting delays creating unsatisfied customers. It became clear that 'service' needed another management and different behaviour, tools, customer approach, and methods from 'production'.

Changes came about in the 1970s and 1980s in part due to the ongoing expansion through acquisitions. Cost centres were transformed into profit centres: the total ABB organization was split up into 5000 profit centres. 'Service' became a separate business unit, a network of repair shops was installed, field engineers were sent to the customers, and the service offering was expanded through spare parts deliveries. This evolution implied first a shift in mindset; employees had to evolve from technical repairmen into entrepreneurs responsible for profits. However, the maintenance and repair activities offered were still mainly supportive and corrective and remained tied to ABB's products.

Things changed drastically in 1992–93 when ABB Service Worldwide was established to integrate the different local service organizations into a separate Business Area. ABB Service Worldwide belongs to the 'Industrial and Building Systems' business segment. This BA Service accounts for a $1.2 billion organization and now employs a total of 10,000 people in over 50 countries all over the world. ABB Service also developed its own mission statement:

> 'To foster customer success through service which is professional, close to the customer and comprehensive, and all from a single dedicated ABB Service organisation.'

Note that, in this statement, no reference is made to ABB *products*.

ABB Service visualized its service concept as a pyramid (Figure 18.2). Within this concept, the service market was divided into five market segments, from more generalized to extremely sophisticated maintenance services. Only upon closer inspection of this pyramid does it become clear that the notion of Full Service will eventually entail extending services beyond the add-ons to where the work of optimizing operations is done in partnerships with customers. The focus shifts from service on specific machines to proactive maintenance.

ABB Service proactively redefined its attitude from 'fix it when it breaks' to 'the worldwide expert in maintenance'. Even though ABB Service still services ABB products, it is now more and more directed to the huge open markets. Let us take a closer look at this pyramid:

- *General Service* denotes small repairs meaning largely standardized services. The main issue in this segment is cheap labour. Competition from independent local maintenance companies is very intense.

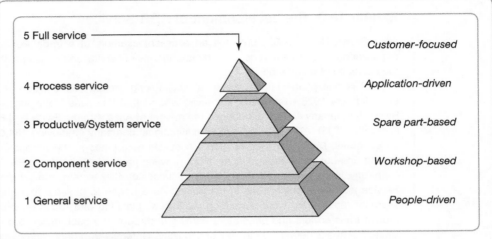

Figure 18.2 The ABB pyramid

- *Component Service* mainly involves the repair of products in an ABB Service workshop. This segment used to be 80% of ABB Service's business but by now it has dropped to less than 35%, mainly due to the products' improved reliability. The name of the game is good lay-outs, time-based management, throughput times, organization, etc.

Providing service in these first two segments does not differentiate ABB Service from competition, since they have become commodity services. If someone else is cheaper, ABB Service will lose market share:

- The third segment is *Product/System Service*: on-site repair of ABB equipment by specialists. Margins are higher, but this is still a case of services as an add-on. The critical success factor here is availability of spare parts.

- *Process Service* is mostly done by the plant operator. To perform this type of service, ABB Service must have specialists who know what petrochemical processes are, how cars are made, what quality steel means, at what speed paper leaves the machine, and so on. Here, the product loses focus; customers are demanding emphasis on their process. Although this segment is rather small, it is growing fast and margins tend to be higher. Moreover, service providers entrusted with these assignments hold key positions.

- Finally, *Full Service* is a strategic service 'package' where ABB Service partially or completely takes over the responsibility of its customer's maintenance function. Since maintenance activities are not core businesses for the customer, ABB Service can not only provide these functions better but also, in general, more cost-effectively than the customers. If ABB Service can expand the number of its Full Service contracts, it can develop the additional expertise and take advantage of economies of scale and scope. These contracts already account for $200 million in revenues per year in a business that did not exist three years ago. On top of that, these contracts generate at least $150 million additional service work and another $150 million pull-through of new ABB equipment.

This evolution towards Full Service again implies a change in mindset. This time, the relationship with customers has to be reconsidered, as illustrated in Figure 18.3.

In the 1980s, ASEA Service was still acting like a fire brigade – the customer would call only after a breakdown. As a result, ABB made money when the customer lost money. The new idea was to turn the relationship with the customer into a win-win situation (*see* Figure 18.3).

Figure 18.3 New view of customer service

With its Full-Service contracts, ABB Service is being paid for its expertise in optimizing a customer's processes. By providing guidance during the design and development stage, by offering preventive maintenance, and so on, ABB Service creates value for the customer, resulting in increased availability. Integral customer cost starts to correlate negatively with ABB Service profit; indeed, added value for customers goes hand in hand with ABB Service profit. Similarly, ABB Service gave a new competitive edge to Component Service with Total Motor Management Contracts. Here, ABB Service takes the long-term responsibility for the customer's motor park and guarantees their availability 24 hours a day, 365 days a year. This too is a win-win situation as both customers and ABB Service can aim for increased availability and optimize their profitability by doing so.

This focus on customer needs implies that ABB Service eventually will not only provide service on its own machinery but also on any piece of the customer's equipment. About 60% of all services are now performed on non-ABB products. Following this line of evolution, ABB Service's latest offering is named 'Global Service Agencies': service activities for manufacturers, who do not have their own worldwide after-sales service.

It is clear from this example that ABB Service's product has experienced a continuous evolution. Starting from a point where only limited attention was paid to service, it gradually extended its offering to include more and more services, such as training, 24-hour spare parts logistics, and a help desk. As ABB Service continues to move in the direction of more Full Service contracts and Global Service Agencies, it is clear that the definition of its 'business' is becoming much broader than the original one: from repairing electrical motors, to managing entire maintenance functions with or without ABB equipment (see Figure 18.4).

Figure 18.4 ABB Service redefined

onclusion

In this chapter we have seen that the traditional boundaries between manufacturing and service companies tend to blur, as manufacturing firms adopt more and more service components in their offerings – a trend which has been labelled servitization. This trend towards servitization presents itself as a three-stage process: from offering merely goods, to adding services and, finally, offering bundles of both tangible and intangible components.

The driving forces behind servitization are twofold. First, customers are asking for additional services as this will help to fulfil their own needs. Second, for manufacturing companies servitization implies the recognition that defensible competitive advantage usually derives from outstanding knowledge of customer needs, and linking these needs to human skills, logistical capabilities, knowledge bases and other assets and activities at various points on the value chain. This involves adding services to the offerings made to customers.

Finally, we have looked at some of the prerequisites for an efficient service delivery system: customer information systems, a well integrated service delivery system and, finally, the right competencies and skills.

Service management is, therefore, not only relevant to managers of service companies but also to managers of manufacturing companies. The trend towards increasing the service component of the offering will certainly continue. Manufacturing managers who fail to recognize this trend will be in for a rough ride in the coming years.

Review and discussion questions

- Do you think manufacturing companies can afford not to offer any services? Why? Why not? Do you see differences in this respect in relation to the type of industry?

- Do you think the reverse also holds true, i.e. should service companies start thinking about offering products as well? Why? Why not? Can you come up with examples?

- Product companies often try to differentiate themselves by offering services. Many struggle to make money at it.[25] This phenomenon is called the 'Service Paradox'. Why is it so difficult to make money in the service business?

Suggested further reading

Baines, T. S., Lightfoot, H. W., Benedettini, O. and Kay, J. M. (2009) 'The servitization of manufacturing: a literature review and reflection on future challenges', *Journal of Manufacturing Technology Management*, Vol 20, No 5, pp. 547–567

Chase, R. B. (1991) 'The service factory: a future vision', *International Journal of Service Industry Management*, Vol 2, No 3, pp. 60–70

Levitt, T. (1980) 'Marketing success through differentiation of anything', *Harvard Business Review*, May–June, pp. 83–91

Vandermerwe, S. and Rada, J. (1988) 'Servitization of businesses: Adding value by adding service', *European Management Journal*, Vol 6, No 4, pp. 314–324

Vandermerwe, S. (1993) *From Tin Soldiers to Russian Dolls*: *Creating added value through services*. Oxford: Butterworth-Heinemann

Notes and references

1 Brown, Stephen W. Professor of Marketing, Arizona State University in Ostrom, A., Bitner, M. J., Brown, Stephen W., Goul, Michael, Smith-Daniels, Vicky, Demirkan, Haluk and Rabinovich, Elliot (2010) 'Moving forward and making a difference: Research priorities for the science of service', *Journal of Service Research*, Vol 13, No 1, p. 7

2 Neely, A. (2008) 'Exploring the financial consequences of the servitization of manufacturing', *Operations Management Research*, No 1, pp. 103–118

3 Fang, E., Palmatier, R. W. and Steenkamp, J. B. E. M. (2008) 'Effect of service transition strategies on firm value', *Journal of Marketing*, No 72, pp. 1–14

4 Vandermerwe, S. and Rada, J. (1988) 'Servitization of businesses: Adding value by adding service', *European Management Journal*, Vol 6, No 4, pp. 314–324

5 Bowen, D., Siehl, C. and Schneider, B. (1989) 'A framework for analysing customer service orientations in manufacturing', *Academy of Management Review*, Vol 14, No 1, pp. 75–95

6 Quinn, J. B., Doorley, T. L. and Paquette, P. C. (1990) 'Beyond products: Service-based strategy', *Harvard Business Review*, Mar–Apr, pp. 58–68

7 http://www.schindler.com

8 Van Dierdonck, R. (1993) 'Post Lean Manufacturing: The importance of servitization'. Fourth International Forum on Technology Management. Berlin: October

9 Anderson, J. C. and Narus, J. A. (1995) 'Capturing the value of supplementary services', *Harvard Business Review*, Jan–Feb, pp. 75–83

10 Mathe, H. and Shapiro, R. D. (1993) *Integrating Service Strategy in the Manufacturing Company*. London: Chapman & Hall, p. 23

11 See: http://www.colora.be

12 A 'qualifier' is a quality your product must possess in order to even be considered by the customer. However, possessing such a quality will not give you any advantage over the competition. Only 'order winners' have that. For instance, a car with zero defects the first year is a qualifier, while one offering free air conditioning might be an order winner

13 Vandermerwe, S. and Rada, J. (1988), op. cit.

14 Martin, Jr., Claude, R. and Horne, D. A. (1992) 'Restructuring towards a service orientation: the strategic challenges', *International Journal of Service Industry Management*, Vol 3, No 1, pp. 25–38

15 Chase, R. B. (1991) 'The service factory: A future vision', *International Journal of Service Industry Management*, Vol 2, No 3, pp. 60–70

16 Ibid.

17 See Gebauer, H., Fleisch, E. and Friedli, T. (2005) 'Overcoming the service paradox in manufacturing companies', *European Management Journal*, No 23, pp. 14–26

18 Recent research by Visjnic and Van Looy (2011) illustrates this phenomenon when examining the performance of product-service divisions of a multinational equipment provider: Visjnic, I. and Van Looy, B. (2011) 'Can a product manufacturer become a successful service provider? In pursuit of a business model that fosters complementarity between product and service activities'. IESE Working Paper

19 Bowen, D. *et al.* (1989), op. cit.

20 De Meyer, A. (1992) 'Creating the Virtual Factory', INSEAD Research Report, December

21 Quinn, J. B. *et al.* (1990), op. cit.

22 IBM Annual Account, 2010

23 Based on an internal working document of ABB authored by J. Coene and B. Jonkers: 'Percy Barnevik's global crusade', *Business Week* (1993), 6 December, p. 59

24 On 1 January 1997, Göran Lindahl became President and CEO of ABB. Percy Barnevik continued as Chairman of the Board until 2002

25 Werner, Reinarts and Ulaga, Wolfgang (2008) 'How to sell services more profitably', *Harvard Business Review*, May, pp. 90–107

Technical notes

The following notes contain supplementary material of a more technical nature which should be used in conjunction with the text.

1 Analysing queuing systems in service environments
2 Simulation as a tool in designing services
3 How to manage complaints
4 Measuring customer satisfaction
5 Data envelopment analysis

Technical note 1

Analysing queuing systems in service environments

Paul Gemmel

This technical note should be read in conjunction with Chapter 10

Queuing systems and their characteristics

At many moments in our daily lives we wait for some type of service. At the supermarket, the post office, the bank, we join queues, waiting to be served. In services, queues are a mechanism to match supply with demand. Like inventories, queues are a kind of buffer, but instead of keeping products in stock, customers are kept waiting. Queues must be avoided; they benefit neither the customer nor the organization providing the service. 'Time spent queuing is time wasted forever.'[1] Let us examine the behaviour of queues more closely.

In the example of the supermarket, queues are formed when the time taken to serve a shopper at the check-out exceeds the time between two subsequent arrivals. In the same way, at a telephone call centre, queues are formed when the calls come in more quickly than they are handled. This is equally true of traffic jams and of doctors' surgeries. In other words, we can distinguish some common elements in the different queuing situations. There is a *server*, providing the service at a certain pace, on the one hand, and *customers*, arriving at a certain pace, on the other. In the case of the server, we speak of *the service delivery process* and in the case of the customer, of *the arrival process*. Queues are formed at the intersection of the arrival and the service delivery processes. The customer and his or her arrival process, the server and its service delivery process, and the resulting queues are the basic but common elements of every queuing situation. Recognizing these basic components means that queuing situations can be considered as a system and that analytical models can be developed to describe such a system. We term this '*queuing*' (or 'waiting-line') *theory*.

Arrival characteristics

Let us consider the example of the supermarket. After selecting their goods, clients arrive with their shopping trolleys at the check-outs. The time between two subsequent arrivals is the *interarrival time*. This interarrival time can be measured and an average can be calculated.

Table TN1.1 Arrival time, interarrival time and service time of 12 shoppers

Arrival	Time of arrival in minutes from time 0	Interarrival time	Service time
1	4	6	3
2	10	3	5
3	13	6	6
4	19	1	4
5	20	9	7
6	29	2	3
7	31	3	6
8	34	9	7
9	43	4	2
10	47	4	3
11	51	8	3
12	59	–	8
Total		55	58
Average		5	4.8

Table TN1.1 shows the registration of arrival times and interarrival times for 12 shoppers. The first shopper arrives 4 minutes after the opening of the supermarket. The second shopper arrives 10 minutes after the opening. There is a 6-minute time-lag between the first and second customer. This time-lag is the interarrival time. The average interarrival time for the 11 customers is equal to 5 minutes; this also means that one shopper arrives every 5 minutes, or 12 shoppers per hour. The indication of x number of customers per time period is called arrival rate l and is used to indicate the average arrival rate. It must be taken into account that the arrival process and thus the average interarrival time can be influenced by daily, weekly or even seasonal patterns. In a supermarket, Saturday is traditionally the busiest day of the week and Friday evening busier than the rest of the day.

The arrival of the shoppers in the supermarket cannot be scheduled and thus cannot be controlled. Scheduling patients in a hospital is one example of controlling the arrival pattern. Although most shoppers arrive alone, they may arrive in a group (e.g. a family). *Batching behaviour* can have an important impact on the performance of the queuing system. For instance, in many university restaurants, students arrive in large batches depending on what time courses finish.

Finally, the population from which arrivals are drawn can be infinite or finite. The calling population of a supermarket is *infinite* (or very large). A population is infinite when the probability of the arrival of the next customer is independent of the number of shoppers already present in the supermarket. If a small shop has only 10 regular customers, the chance that a customer will arrive is highly dependent on how many customers are already present in the shop (*finite*).

Server characteristics

Table TN1.1 also shows the time it takes to serve customers. In the example of the supermarket, serving encompasses the whole process of scanning goods, computing the bill, and placing the items in bags. The average service time in the example is 4.8 minutes. This means that on average one shopper is served every 4.8 minutes – 12.5 shoppers per hour. The service rate can vary among customers. For instance, Figure TN1.1 shows the relationship

Figure TN1.1 The relationship between method of payment and payment time in a supermarket

between method of payment and billing time. Certainly when a combination of vouchers and electronic funds transfer (EFT) is used, the billing time is significantly higher. Another characteristic of the service process is the number of servers available and whether servers are in a parallel or serial position. In a supermarket, servers are considered to be serial when the acts of scanning and registration are separated into two subsequent workstations.

Queue characteristics

In supermarkets, several check-outs are available for the shoppers. This also means that several queues are formed. In some other service organizations such as banks, there is only one queue for multiple servers. These are different examples of the organization of servers. In banks there is an ongoing discussion about how to organize queues. The multiple-server/ one-queue situation seems to work faster than the same number of servers each with its own queue. The former is also perceived as the most fair by customers and enhances the privacy of the service. On the other hand, with multiple-servers/multiple-queues, a company is able to differentiate services and assign more experienced servers to lines with more difficult transactions. Customers may be able to select their favourite server.

In any queuing situation, attention must be paid to the order in which customers are served (*queue discipline*). In the case of a single check-out, a '*first-in first-out*' (FIFO) system is used. When an additional counter is opened, this rule may be violated as shoppers who were last in the queue switch first to the newly opened counter. Impatient shoppers may switch queues (*jockeying*). If queues are exceedingly long, some customers may leave a queue before being served (*reneging*) or may decide not to join the queue (*balking*). The lower the value of the purchases in the shopper's trolley, the higher the chance that reneging or balking will take place. That is why express lanes are created for customers with only a limited number of items. When an express lane is used, different customers receive different priorities.

In summary, all queuing problems can be broken down, as shown in Table TN1.2.[2]

Linking arrival pattern, service pattern and queuing

The proportion of the arrival rate λ to the service rate M is the *average utilization* or occupancy of the server. We use the symbol σ. In our example of the supermarket, the average utilization of the check-out is 96%.

447

Table TN1.2 Different elements of a queuing system

1 *Arrival characteristics*
   1.1 Arrival rate or time between arrival statistics
   1.2 Controlled or uncontrolled
   1.3 Grouping (single or batch)
   1.4 Infinite or finite calling population
2 *Service characteristics*
   2.1 Service rate or service time/server
   2.2 Number of servers
      – one
      – multiple
      – serial
3 *Queue characteristics*
   3.1 Queue organization
      – one or more queues
      – queues with limited or unlimited capacity
   3.2 Queue discipline
   3.3 Queuing behaviour of customers
      – reneging
      – balking
      – no action

$$\sigma = \frac{\text{Arrival rate}}{\text{Service rate}} = \frac{12 \text{ shoppers per hour}}{12.5 \text{ shoppers per hour}} = 96\% \tag{1}$$

As we shall see next, the average utilization (σ) determines the length of the queues. In order to have a stable system, σ must be lower than 1.[3]

Queuing theory

As previously mentioned, analytical models have been developed to analyse queuing systems. Analytical models are always subject to, sometimes stringent, assumptions. In queuing theory the basic assumptions are summarized in an $a/b/c/d$ notation – that is, the so-called *Kendall notation* – where:

a = the distribution of the interarrival times
b = the distribution of the service times
c = the number of servers
d = the maximum number of customers in the queue

The M/M/1/∞ system

The M/M/1/∞ system is a queuing system where:

a = M = a negative exponential distribution of the interarrival times, indicated by M
b = M = a negative exponential distribution of the service time, indicated by M
c = 1 = one server
d = ∞ = an infinite queue capacity

Figure TN1.2 An example of the negative exponential distribution

A frequently used distribution in queuing modelling is the *negative exponential 'M' distribution* (*see* Figure TN1.2). An important property of the exponential distribution is that it is memoryless. This means that the time until the next event (arrival) does not depend on how much time has already elapsed since the last event (arrival).[4] Interarrival times can be modelled as a negative exponential distribution when the arrivals of customers in a service organization are independent of each other. For instance, emergencies in a hospital arrive independently of one another and their interarrival time can be modelled through a negative exponential distribution. In contrast, scheduled patients do not arrive independently of one another and in this case the exponential distribution cannot be used. Nonetheless, many service situations are memoryless.

An interesting characteristic of the exponential distribution is that it is a one-parameter distribution: mean and standard deviation are equal. It is also important to indicate that an exponential distribution of interarrival times means that the distribution of the number of arrivals per time period is a *Poisson distribution*. A Poisson distribution arises from the *Poisson process*. A Poisson process can be viewed in terms of its calling population (i.e. the group of potential customers). If the calling population is large (infinite), the probability that customers arrive independently is larger than in the case of a finite calling population, and the probability that a particular customer arrives during any small time interval is small and constant.[5] In this case, a Poisson probability distribution can be used.

For an $M/M/1/\infty$ queue system, it can be proved that the probability of having n customers in the system is equal to:[6]

$$P(n) = (1 - \sigma)\sigma^n$$

$$\text{with } n = 0, 1, 2 \tag{2}$$

In our example the chance that there are three shoppers in the system is:

$$P(3) = (1 - 0.96) \times (0.96)^3$$

$$P(3) = 0.035 \text{ or } 3.5\%$$

The mean ('expected') number of customers in the system is equal to:

$$L_s = \frac{\sigma}{1-\sigma}$$

$$L_s = \frac{0.96}{1-0.96} = 24 \tag{3}$$

The mean number of customers in the queue is equal to:

$$L_q = \frac{\sigma^2}{1-\sigma}$$

$$L_q = \frac{0.96^2}{1-0.96} = 23 \tag{4}$$

It is quite clear that in our example the queue is large (on average 23 customers per hour), mainly due to the high occupancy rate (96%). Assuming an occupancy rate of only 70%, the mean number of customers in the queue will be equal to an average of 1.6 using formula (4).

The expected time in the queue and time in the system are not uniquely defined by σ; they also depend on the arrival rate. In fact, there is an important relationship between the mean number of customers in the system (L_s) and the mean time in the system (W_s), and between the mean number of customers in queue (L_q) and the mean time in queue (W_q):

$$W_s = \frac{L_s}{\lambda} \tag{5}$$

$$W_q = \frac{L_q}{\lambda} \tag{6}$$

In our basic example (occupancy rate of 96%) this means that the mean time in the system is equal to two hours and that the mean time in the queue is equal to 1.9 hours:

$$W_s = \frac{24}{12} = 2 \text{ hours}$$

$$W_q = \frac{23}{12} = 1.91 \text{ hours}$$

This relationship between L_s (L_q) and respectively W_s (W_q) is the so-called *Little's Formula* and means that W_s and W_q are a direct function of the arrival rate $1/\lambda$ as the utilization σ is considered constant.

Other queuing systems

What happens if the average time between arrivals and the average service time are not negative exponentially distributed or if more than one server is available?

Queuing theory has developed some more advanced analytical solutions or approaches which take into account deviations from the M/M/1 queuing system. We refer readers who wish to use one of these models to the more specialized literature on queuing systems (*see* reference).

Suggested further reading

Hall, R. W. (1991) *Queuing Methods for Services and Manufacturing*. Englewood Cliffs, NJ: Prentice-Hall. This is a reference book on queuing. The different queuing models and the application of queuing in manufacturing and services are extensively discussed. Several strategies to avoid queuing or to reduce waiting lines are suggested

Notes and references

1 Hall, R. W. (1991) *Queuing Methods for Services and Manufacturing*. Englewood Cliffs, NJ: Prentice-Hall, p. 3
2 Partially based on Chisman, J. A. (1993) *Introduction to Simulation Modelling Using GPPS/PC*. Englewood Cliffs, NJ: Prentice-Hall, p. 9
3 A system is not stable if a queue continuously grows over time
4 Hall, R. W. (1991), op. cit., p. 61
5 Ibid., p. 54
6 Readers who wish to know how P(*n*) is calculated are referred to Appendix 1

Technical Note 2

Simulation as a tool in designing services

Paul Gemmel

This technical note should be read in conjunction with Chapter 10

Discrete-event simulation

In the supermarket example several checkouts (servers) are available. When customers arrive at the counters, some will choose the express lane because they have fewer than ten items in their trolley. Other shoppers will be jockeying from one queue to another. The service time for each customer is a function of the number of items purchased and the payment method used. It is not possible to approach this (more complex) queuing system analytically and to determine, for instance, the average waiting time using the formulas of queuing theory. In fact, pure M/M/1, M/M/n and M/G/1 queuing systems are relatively rare in daily life. When an analytical solution is not available, computer simulation can be used to evaluate the queuing system numerically.

Computer simulation models dealing with queuing problems in service environments are stochastic, time dependent, and discrete-event:

- In a stochastic model, the exact value of some variables cannot be estimated, but the probability of the occurrence of each possible value can be determined. For instance, the service time at a checkout is not known with certainty. Service time is in this case a stochastic variable and can be described by a distribution.

- In a queuing example, the passing of time is crucial. There is a sequence of events in time such as the arrival of the shopper at the supermarket, the checkout and the departure.

- In a discrete-event time model, time jumps from one event to another. If the first shopper arrives at 9.00 a.m. and the second shopper arrives at 9.05 a.m. and no other relevant event occurs between these two events, a discrete-event simulation model jumps in time from the arrival of the first customer to the arrival of the second customer. In other words, the simulation is event-driven.

In service organizations, there are many examples of problems which can be studied using such models. Discrete-event simulation is a necessary tool to compare and evaluate the design alternatives for a service process.[1] The building blocks of service design are the 'service', the facilities, the process and the interaction between the server and the customer. An example of the simulation of alternative service designs is to analyse the impact on the delivery performance of bank tellers when ATMs take over several kinds of banking transactions. Problems of service facility design which can be solved by simulation include, for instance, the question of how many checkouts the supermarket manager needs in order to keep checkout queues below five people each. A similar problem can be found in the banking sector. Service process design questions, for example, deal with the lift operations policy in a large building. An example of a design study which has an important impact on the interaction between the customer and the server is the study of the layout of a university student restaurant. Does the restaurant choose a continuous line layout or a free-flow layout? In each of the examples, waiting time is (partially) determined by how the service delivery is designed.

Components of discrete-event simulation models

In the example of the supermarket, the number of people in the queue (before each checkout) and the number of servers available are variables which tell something about the system state. Anything that occurs and that changes the state of the system is an event. The arrival of a shopper at the checkout or the departure of a client from the checkout are events because they change the state of the checkout from idle to busy and *vice versa*.

Each simulation model contains a timing routine and a time clock which allows jumps from one event to another. Note that the time increments between consecutive events are variable.[2] The scheduling of events at certain points in time drives the system. At the moment a shopper arrives at a checkout, a simulation programme immediately schedules the next event for this shopper – his or her departure. If no subsequent event is scheduled in the simulation logic with variable time increments, the system will shut down. Without the arrival of new shoppers, the dynamics of the supermarket will stop.

To obtain output from the simulation model, statistical counters must be defined. Statistical counters operationalize the performance measures which must be defined in order to design services which exceed customer expectations. Two kinds of counters are possible: *observation-based* and *time-integrated*. Average waiting time is an observation-based counter. It is the average of the 'observed' waiting time of each shopper. Time-integrated counters take into account how long a certain state lasts. For instance, the length of the queue is a state variable that changes over time. In order to measure the average length of the queue, it is necessary to know the length of time when one or more shoppers are queuing. A queue of three shoppers lasting 3 minutes has a larger impact on the average length of queue than a queue of three shoppers lasting 2 minutes. Using a report generator, the final value of the statistical counters can be presented in a mathematical or a graphical way.

As in any programme, it is necessary to initialize the system. This means, for instance, that the number of checkouts which are open at the beginning of the day is fixed.

Finally, all stochastic simulation models require random numbers. They therefore use a random-number generator which produces a stream of figures by chance so that the stochastic variables are not influenced in any way by past values.[3] This is because all discrete simulation modelling languages use the Monte Carlo approach for generating arrivals, service times, and other input variables.[4]

In summary, the most important components of a discrete-event stochastic and dynamic simulation model are:

1 variables which track the state of the system;

2 a list of events;

3 a mechanism (timing routine) to schedule events;

4 a time clock;

5 statistical counters;

6 a report generator;

7 an initialization routine; and finally

8 a random-number generator.

In order to show the concept of a random-number generator and to illustrate how the Monte Carlo approach works, we shall manually work out the supermarket case. Let us assume that there is a supermarket with one checkout. The interarrival and service-time distributions are described respectively in Tables TN2.1 and TN2.2. Random numbers can now be assigned to each distribution directly proportional to the respective probabilities in each frequency class. For instance, we assign random number '00' to the first frequency class to represent the event that the time between arrivals is zero seconds. In other words, if we draw a number from a two-digit uniform random number table (numbers ranging from 0 to 99 (*see* Table TN2.3)), we have one chance out of 100 (or a probability of 1%) of drawing one of these numbers. The numbers '01–40' represent a 40% chance of a time between arrival being 20 seconds (Table TN2.1). The same reasoning has been used for the service time distribution (Table TN2.2).

To generate arrivals, we shall start (randomly) in column 2 of Table TN2.3 and move down. The generation of service times will start in column 9. The first event is an arrival

Table TN2.1 Interarrival distribution

Time between arrivals	Probability	Cumulative probability	Random numbers
0 sec	0.01	0.01	00
20 sec	0.40	0.41	01–40
40 sec	0.30	0.71	41–70
60 sec	0.20	0.91	71–90
80 sec	0.09	1.00	91–99

Table TN2.2 Service-time distribution

Required service-time	Probability	Cumulative probability	Random numbers
20 sec	0.05	0.05	00–04
40 sec	0.55	0.60	05–59
60 sec	0.20	0.80	60–79
80 sec	0.15	0.95	80–94
100 sec	0.05	1.00	95–99

of a shopper. The random number of 92 (i.e. the first number in the second column of Table TN2.3) represents a time between arrivals of 80 seconds, since 92 lies between 91 and 99 (*see* Table TN2.1). Hence, the first shopper arrives at the counter 80 seconds after the opening of the doors. In order to determine the service time of this shopper, we pick the first number in column 9 of Table TN2.3. '41' lies between 05 and 59. This corresponds with a service time of 40 seconds. The second random number in column 2 of Table TN2.3 is 46. This means that the second shopper will arrive 40 seconds after the first one. The time on arrival is then 120 seconds (after opening the doors). Note that at this time the first shopper leaves the checkout, so there is no waiting time for the second shopper. Using the second random number '07' of column 9 in Table TN2.3, it can be deduced that the service time for this second shopper is 40 seconds. This procedure is repeated for a total of 10 shoppers in Table TN2.4.

The random number table is an essential component of Monte Carlo simulation. Random numbers cannot be reproduced (by definition), and so some mathematical models have been defined to imitate random behaviour. This explains the term 'pseudo-random number', used in simulation. The validity of the simulation results depends greatly on the quality of the pseudo-random number generator.[5]

Table TN2.3 A two-digit random number table

26	92	96	04	84	03	48	38	41	35
44	46	47	20	04	71	81	44	07	58
75	41	72	88	54	33	06	87	63	59
71	13	45	61	26	53	27	37	89	30
15	91	81	39	86	41	43	46	57	34
18	11	80	97	33	16	75	26	93	29
50	56	19	00	95	88	00	70	90	93
10	15	33	70	05	13	08	29	75	43
72	69	75	95	56	15	73	27	72	99
10	02	26	69	12	64	99	18	78	19

Table TN2.4 Monte Carlo simulation of the bank-teller problem

No.	TBA[a]	TOA[b]	ST[c]	WT[d]	Idle[e]	Queue[f]
× 1	80	80	40	0	80	0
× 2	40	120	40	0	0	0
× 3	40	160	60	0	0	0
× 4	20	180	80	40	0	1
× 5	80	260	40	40	0	1
× 6	20	280	80	60	0	2
× 7	40	320	80	100	0	2
× 8	20	340	60	160	0	2
× 9	40	380	60	180	0	3
× 10	20	400	60	220	0	4

[a] Time between arrivals
[b] Time on arrival
[c] Service time
[d] Waiting time
[e] Time during which server is idle
[f] The position in the queue that the arriving shopper takes

Tools for discrete-event simulation modelling

Generally, there are three categories of tools for discrete-event stochastic and dynamic simulation:[6] general programming languages, simulation languages and simulators.

Compared with the general programming languages, simulation languages and simulators have some specific built-in functions:[7]

1 a mechanism for advancing simulated time;

2 methods of scheduling events;

3 statistical counters;

4 methods of representing constrained resources;

5 a report generator;

6 debugging and error detection facilities;

7 random-number generators and related sets of tools;

8 a general framework for model creation.

While a programming code is still necessary in the case of simulation languages, this is no longer necessary for simulators. Simulators offer the user a number of building blocks which represent, for example, the arrival or the service process.

To select a specific tool, two important criteria have to be taken into account: flexibility offered and modelling effort.[8] The programming languages require more modelling effort than simulation languages because, for example, the timing mechanism (which is a normal feature of a simulation language) has to be modelled. The basic characteristic of a simulator is that it decreases the modelling effort. By using predefined constructs, the user is guided throughout the development of a simulation model. This decreases the flexibility to build in some specific or uncommon features. Most simulation software packages link the flexibility of a simulation language with the modelling efforts of a simulator. They work with different levels. On the first level, very aggregate building blocks are defined. This is the simulator level. On a lower level, a simulation language can be used. The interesting point is that these levels can be combined.

In selecting a simulation tool, other parameters such as price and the quality of the random-number generator must be considered. It should also be noted that some simulators are designed for specific applications.

There are more than 100 simulation languages and simulators on the market today. Examples of simulators are ARENA[9] and Entreprise Dynamics. We must stress that several of these simulators are typically made for a manufacturing situation. Our experience with ARENA in simulating service environments is positive. Moreover, ARENA combines a simulator and a simulation language (SIMAN).

Most simulators and simulation languages have a built-in module for animation of the computer model.[10] Animation is the use of a graphical interface on the computer to present entities and activities in a dynamic way. The advantage of animation is that it can be used to enhance the confidence in the model (*face validity*). At the same time, the danger of animation is that too much confidence is granted to the model without thorough statistical analysis. An example of animation of the supermarket example is shown in Figure TN2.1.

Figure TN2.1 Animation of the supermarket

Simulating the service encounter in a supermarket

As indicated before, simulation can be used to design service processes in order to improve the service encounter. In the supermarket example, the manager wondered whether the productivity of the clerks at the checkouts could be improved without decreasing the quality of the service encounter. Several productivity improvement strategies have been proposed, such as the use of a professional 'packer', the uncoupling of registering and billing where several scanning points are served by one cashier, the differentiation of a checkout, based on the payment method (for instance, only a few counters would accept EFT-payment). The supermarket manager wants to know whether the use of a professional packer will lead to a reduction of the throughput time at the checkout and consequently an increase in the potential throughput. The manager has observed that sometimes the process of scanning was blocked because the shopper could not bag the registered products fast enough.

In order to see whether a packer could make the difference, a simulation study is set up. The first step in the study is to define the system to be modelled. The components of the system, their interrelationship and the system's boundaries must be defined.

To reduce the complexity of the model, we limit the study to one standard checkout and one overflow counter which is opened and closed in a dynamic way in order to manage the queue at the standard checkout. Shoppers arrive at the checkout with their shopping trolley filled with food and/or non-food products. If the regular counter is busy, they will wait in the queue at the checkout. As soon as possible, a shopper places his or her products on the checkout. The scanning time is a function of the number of products. Then the shopper puts the products in the bag. The packing time is a function of the number of products, the kind of products and the experience of the shopper. After packing, the shopper pays and

457

the payment time is related to the payment method used. It may happen that the customer continues packing after paying. The clerk delays scanning the products of the next customer until the current shopper has left the checkout.

When defining the system, it is also important to indicate the performance measures to be used. In this case, we are interested in the throughput time of shoppers or the average throughput within some predetermined time period (for instance, 1 hour). The performance of only the standard checkout is registered.

To model the system, we also need some data on the arrival pattern of shoppers, the scanning time, the packing time, and the payment time. An experiment is set up. Over 8 hours, data on the different time components are collected in a situation as described above and in a situation with a professional packer. In the latter experiment, a student starts packing as soon as products are scanned. Meanwhile, the shopper can get his or her money ready for payment. No data are collected on the arrival pattern. It is decided to use a 'theoretical' Poisson distribution with an average number of arrivals per time unit which allows a continuous flow of customers at the checkout. If the queue at the regular checkout is longer than ten persons, the eleventh person is sent to the overflow counter. Table TN2.5 shows the results of these experiments. Note that the packing time decreases by 50% when a professional packer is used.

In the simulation study, we use the purchasing time, which is defined as the sum of scanning time, packing time and payment time. To be able to use the data in the simulation, we need to describe the distributions as in Table TN2.6. While it is possible to use the empirical distribution (as described in Table TN2.6) in the simulation model, we prefer to 'fit' an existing theoretical distribution (such as the normal distribution or the exponential distribution) to the empirical data. The main reason is that an empirical distribution is 'limited' to the observations, in this case for 8 hours in each experiment. It is highly probable that many different values are not caught by this empirical distribution. If we can prove that there is a high probability that the empirical distribution looks like a theoretical distribution, we have a greater certainty that all values are covered. Moreover, most of the theoretical distributions are pre-programmed in a simulation language or simulator so that it is sufficient to determine the relevant parameters of the distribution such as the mean and the standard deviation in the case of the normal distribution. Figure TN2.2 shows the fitting of the theoretical gamma distribution to the empirical distribution of purchasing time in the base case without professional packer. The Kolmogorov-Smirnov test as well as the chi-square test examine the goodness of fit of the gamma distribution to the empirical data. Most simulation languages

Table TN2.5 Summary statistics for different variables (in seconds) in the situation with and without packers

		Number of articles	Packing time	Payment time	Customer time*	Scanning time*	Purchasing time**
Without packers	Average	20	12	29	41	74	115
	Standard deviation	16	10	13	17	57	69
With packers	Average	21	5	29	34	65	99
	Standard deviation	18	6	17	20	51	65

*The average customer time is the sum of average packing time and the average payment time.
**The average purchasing time is the sum of the average customer time and the average scanning time.

Table TN2.6 Comparison of the frequency distribution of the variable purchasing time respectively in the situation with packer and without packer

Category (sec)	Frequency in the case without packer (%)	Frequency in the case with packer (%)
0–27	4	5
27–54	13	19
54–81	16	23
81–108	21	21
108–135	15	10
135–162	10	6
162–189	6	5
189–216	5	5
216–243	5	1
243–270	1	1
270–297	1	2
297–324	2	1
324–351	1	0
351–378	0	1
Total	100	100

or simulators have some input module which allows the user to fit theoretical distributions to the empirical data and to determine the parameters of the distributions. Figure TN2.3 shows the fitting of the log-normal distribution to the empirical distribution of purchasing time when a professional packer is used.[11]

Before going on, we must be sure that the previous data are adequate and precise and that the assumptions underlying the model are acceptable. Does the clerk wait until a shopper has left before continuing the scanning of the next customer's products? If this is not the case, what is the impact of this assumption on the results of the study? Is a gamma distribution a well-fitting distribution? If not, the results are not valid. This process is called *validation*. There are several ways to increase the validity of the model such as observing the real system or talking to experts.

Figure TN2.2 The fitting of a gamma distribution to the variable purchasing time (without a packer)

459

Figure TN2.3 The fitting of a log-normal distribution to the variable purchasing time (with a packer)

Once the model has been defined and validated, it must be translated to a computer program using one of the simulation tools which have been presented above. It is important that this translation is carried out accurately. Therefore, we need to carefully document the program and use techniques of structured programming. Once the program is finished, we must be able to check the path which is followed during the programming. Does the customer wait on a first-come-first-served basis? Does scanning precede packing? Animation can be helpful in studying this behaviour. In summary, we need to verify the program carefully.

In a next step, we make some pilot runs to further validate the model. At this point, we study the output of the pilot runs in the light of the goal of the simulation study and to verify whether the simulation output changes adequately if the input is changed. For instance, when the arrival pattern in the supermarket is such that the occupancy of the regular checkout is only 50%, the throughput must be much lower than in the case of 100% occupancy. The clerk has a lot of idle time in the 50% case.

If a similar 'real' system exists, the input/output of the simulation model can be compared with the input/output of the real system.

After validating and verifying, we start the production runs. There are two important decisions to make:

1 the number of times the simulation must run to deliver confident results; and

2 the length of the simulation run.

It is essential to be aware that each experiment must be replicated several times to obtain valid results. By sampling from a distribution (using the Monte Carlo method), random behaviour is introduced into the model. This means that the output of any single production run is not the exact value to be considered. It is probable that the results will lie within some confidence interval. Several replications are necessary to obtain a smaller confidence interval.

To determine the length of one simulation run and to analyse the output, it is important to make a distinction between different types of simulation:[12] the simulation of a terminating system or the simulation of a non-terminating (or steady-state) system. A *terminating system*

Table TN2.7 Results in terms of numbers of customers served by the clerk in an 8-hour day

Mean interarrival time	Without packer	With packer
50 seconds (occupancy rate of 100%)	317	353
200 seconds (occupancy rate of 50%)	177	176

is one with a clearly identifiable event beyond which no useful information can be obtained or with a time point at which the system is cleaned out. For instance, a supermarket closes at a given time; this is the moment at which the system is clearly cleaned out. In a *non-terminating system*, such an event does not exist. For instance, since hospital beds are continuously occupied, the start-up of a new hospital, when all beds are empty, is not representative of the working of the system. Therefore, the output collected during the start-up of the system must be excluded for further analysis.

Table TN2.7 shows the results of the simulation experiments. In each situation, we have run the simulation five times. Each run simulates an 8-hour workday. If there is no professional packer, the average throughput through the regular checkout is 317 customers during an 8-hour workday. The standard deviation is nine customers. With a professional packer, the mean throughput is 353 clients and a standard deviation of 10 clients.

We have repeated both experiments for a situation where the occupancy of the checkout is approximately 50%. In this case, both situations have a throughput of approximately 180 customers. This means that using a professional packer is only meaningful if the occupancy of the checkout is high.

The study concludes that using a professional packer leads to a significantly higher throughput in the case of high occupancy.

Conclusion

Simulation is a very powerful tool for solving operational or queuing problems in a service organization. It allows experimentation with new concepts or a new configuration without intervening in the real system. It is possible to answer many different 'what if' questions, as in the example of the supermarket. Nonetheless, simulation is not the panacea for every operational problem in services. Remember that 'garbage in' means 'garbage out'. When it is impossible to collect precise input data, the output data must be studied with a great deal of caution. In any case, no single simulation model gives exact results. That is the main weakness of simulation modelling as compared to queuing theory. Consequently, it is preferable to use the analytical model (if it can be applied).

The most important steps in performing a simulation study are:

1 defining and describing the system, its components, and its boundaries;

2 defining performance measures;

3 setting up an experimental design – i.e. describing the alternatives required to achieve better performance in the service design;

4 collecting and validating data for the input variables;

5 preparing the collected data for use in the simulation model;

6 validating the assumptions underlying the model;

7 translating the conceptual model into a computer program;

8 verifying the computer program;

9 making pilot runs to further validate the model;

10 making production runs;

11 analysing the output;

12 making a report.

This technical note shows that performing a simulation study is not easy. There are many booby traps which can completely compromise the results of the simulation study. For instance, it is essential to conduct multiple production runs for each experiment. Generally, the modelling stage is much more important than the programming stage. Before starting a simulation study, a serious amount of time must be invested in acquiring simulation and modelling skills. Selecting a good simulator can support this learning process in many ways. A good simulator is one which minimizes the modelling effort and maximizes the flexibility to adapt to a specific situation.

The current evolution in simulation tools allows individuals to simulate systems without being an expert in simulation. Furthermore, in order to design service delivery processes in such a way that they exceed customer expectations, several design alternatives must be considered, especially in a service environment which is characterized by high arrival and process uncertainty. Simulation is a practical tool which allows companies to perform such evaluations before deciding whether to commit large amounts of money to an untested design.

Suggested further reading

Chaharbaghi, K. (1990) 'Using simulation to solve design and operational problems', *International Journal of Operations and Production Management*, Vol 10, No 9, pp. 89–105. Different applications of simulation in changing processes are discussed. Some insights are given on how to select an appropriate simulation tool

McHaney, R. (1991) *Computer Simulation: A practical perspective*. San Diego, CA: Academic Press. This book is written for practitioners. It describes very clearly the different steps which must be performed in order to develop a simulation model

Notes and references

1 Ramaswany, R. (1996) *Design and Management of Service Processes*. Engineering Improvement Series. MA: Addison-Wesley

2 There are discrete-event simulation models with fixed time increments, although they are not so common

3 McHaney, R. (1991) *Computer Simulation: A practical perspective*. San Diego, CA: Academic Press, p. 92

4 Chisman, J. A. (1993) *Introduction to Simulation Modeling Using GPPS/PC*. Englewood Cliffs, NJ: Prentice-Hall, p. 27

5 For a discussion on the different methods of generating (pseudo-) random numbers, we refer to Kleijnen, J. P. C. and Van Groenendaal, W. (1992) *Simulation: A statistical perspective*. Chichester: John Wiley & Sons.

6 Chaharbaghi, K. (1990) 'Using simulation to solve design and operational problems', *International Journal of Operations and Production Management*, Vol 10, No 9, pp. 89–105.

7 McHaney, R. (1991), op. cit., p. 19

8 Chaharbaghi, K. (1990), op. cit.

9 Systems Modeling Corporation (1994) *Arena Getting Started Guide*

10 McHaney, R. (1991), op. cit., p. 27

11 A gamma distribution is characterized by a shape and a scale-parameter. The shape parameter is in this case 2.83 and the scale parameter is 40.49. This is the same as a mean purchasing time of 114.66 seconds and a standard deviation of 68.13 seconds. A log-normal distribution is characterized by a mean and standard deviation. In the example of Fig. TN2.3, the mean is 100.26 seconds and the standard deviation is 73.32 seconds

12 Thesen, A. and Travis, L. E. (1992) *Simulation for Decision Making*. St. Paul, MN: West Publishing Company, pp. 158–9; *see also* Law, A. M. and Kelton, W. D. (1991) *Simulation Modeling and Analysis*. New York, NY: McGraw-Hill, p. 527

How to manage complaints

Gino Van Ossel • Paul Gemmel

This technical note should be read in conjunction with Chapters 12 and 13

In this technical note we deal with the handling of complaints – that is, the setting up of a complaint management system. We shall discuss the advantages of lowering the complaint threshold and the importance of responding quickly and appropriately, before going on to discuss how a systematic complaint handling process should be set up. At the end we shall explore how complaints can be used to steer improvement projects and how they affect an organization's orientation towards customers.

Lowering the complaint threshold

The first step in complaint handling is to encourage dissatisfied customers to complain. If they do not complain, the service provider may not be aware of the existing dissatisfaction and consequently will have no opportunity for service recovery. Dissatisfied customers who do not complain may 'vote with their feet' and simply switch to another service provider. Several studies have revealed that the actual complaints are only the tip of the iceberg. Complaint submission rates in different studies are as low as 9%. One of the objectives of complaint management is therefore to maximize the number of complaints (while minimizing the number of actual service problems).

Whether or not customers who experience a problem complain, depends on a variety of factors:

- *The problem characteristics*. Customers are more likely to complain about severe problems and when the (potential) financial loss is significant. This is partly dependent on the type of, and involvement and experience with the product or service. The level of (un)articulated complaints also depends on whether the seller, the buyer or chance is to blame.

- *The customer characteristics*. Assertive and self-confident people, who are socially active, sensitive to declining product quality, and have positive prior experiences (mainly with other companies) are more likely to complain. Less important factors are socio-demographics, although the average complainer has a high income, is relatively young, well educated and has a high professional job status.

- *The expected redress.* Customers also balance the perceived trouble involved in complaining with the expected outcome. The complaint submission rate is much higher if customers know where and how to complain, if they believe the supplier to be responsive, and if they think the outcome will be worthwhile.

- *The height of the complaint threshold.* The level of the threshold consists of the sum of all perceived physical, emotional or monetary trouble (or encouragement) involved in formulating a complaint.

By improving the expected redress and lowering the threshold, service business should encourage the silent majority of dissatisfied customers to identify themselves. The most common ways to lower the threshold are:

1 communicating explicitly how the organization can be contacted; or
2 proactively inviting customers to complain if they have any problems.

Communicating how the organization can be contacted

Establishing a call centre that can be reached free of charge with a toll-free number is one option. Alternatives are customer complaint cards in hotel rooms or on the tables in restaurants. Personal visit complaints, signs directing customers to the complaint handling office and greeters who direct consumers and handle simple complaints in a store are also very effective.

Proactively inviting customers to react

Customers can also be asked proactively to react, whether or not they have any problems. Mercedes Belgium, for instance, in its customer satisfaction survey, asks customers explicitly whether they are experiencing any problems. To this end, it invites customers to fill out their names and contact information, if they wish Mercedes to contact them regarding a problem they have experienced or a question or concern they might have.

Similarly, Rank Xerox Belgium sent all its customers a card encouraging them to complain. Approximately 2.5% of the customers returned the card. About 80% of the responses were complaints which had not been made before. The remaining 20% were either existing complaints already known to Rank Xerox, or customers inquiring why they had received the card, as they were basically satisfied.

Soliciting complaints too explicitly may provoke dissatisfaction which would otherwise not exist. Sometimes managers are concerned that customers may become too demanding on trivial issues. In their opinion, the provocation of complaints about minor problems should be avoided at all costs. Since these problems are minor, non-complaining customers are seen as contented; once customers complain about these problems, they expect an appropriate reaction. If the complaint is not being dealt with properly, they will become more dissatisfied than if they had not complained in the first place. In short, managers believe that in the case of minor problems companies should 'let sleeping dogs lie'. There is no real empirical evidence to support the validity of this concern. The TARP studies indicate that a dissatisfied non-complainant is more loyal than a dissatisfied complainant who did not receive an appropriate response. On the other hand, however, a complainant who received an appropriate response became very loyal.[1]

This phenomenon is sometimes called *the frustration effect* – that is, expressing feelings increases satisfaction if the outcome is positive, but causes even more dissatisfaction if the outcome is negative.

There can be a downside to soliciting complaints. Focusing on negative issues can encourage a negative perception of the organization. Therefore, inviting customers to complain is often carried out more diplomatically. The complaint handling department is renamed 'customer service' to avoid the image of an unreliable organization that has to deal with numerous complaints. Similarly, complaint cards are often called suggestion or customer comment cards. A further tactic is for a company to provide customers with the opportunity not only to complain but also to praise.

Responding quickly

The key driver of satisfaction or dissatisfaction with complaint handling is the response time. A formal study indicated that only 8% of Germans are willing to wait for an answer for more than 1 week after filing a complaint.[2]

Satisfaction with complaint handling can therefore only be achieved through a quick response. Several elements help to accomplish this:

- anticipating complaints;
- empowering front-line staff;
- acknowledging the receipt of a complaint;
- routing complaints;
- prioritizing complaints.

Anticipation

When a service provider is aware of a problem that affects several customers in the same way, the organization can maximize its chances of service recovery by anticipating the complaints. The customer can be contacted before he or she contacts the company. This will not only permit a timely reaction, but will also involve the potentially non-complaining customers in the service recovery efforts.

Anticipation is particularly relevant and feasible in the following situations:

- *New services*. The likelihood of defects is much higher for new services than it is for existing ones. For instance, when the new Brussels air terminal was opened in 1995, the extremely sophisticated and fully automated luggage handling system was not compatible with the tags on luggage issued at certain other airports. As a consequence, these pieces of luggage were not automatically removed from the back-office conveyor belt but required manual intervention. Lead times of up to an hour were not uncommon. The operation could have anticipated these problems and, by doing so, could have avoided a large number of angry customers.

- *Recurring problems*. By tracking the nature and frequency of all complaints (see below), organizations can assess which problems merit a standardized approach. For instance, the airline industry is so often confronted with lost and/or damaged luggage that all operators have legally agreed upon a standard level of compensation.

- *Predictable problems.* A couple of years ago, we were to give a training seminar in Lithuania. We had booked a flight from Brussels to Copenhagen, where we would change airlines and board an SAS flight to Vilnius. Unfortunately, the Brussels–Copenhagen flight was delayed. At worst, we feared we would miss our connection and arrive 24 hours late for the seminar. At best, we hoped we would be able to change terminals and catch our flight, but it was extremely unlikely that our luggage would arrive in time. The cabin crew of our flight had warned SAS of our problems, however, and, much to our surprise, an SAS employee was waiting for us at the gate. He took us to a car on the tarmac, asked what our luggage looked like, and collected it from the airplane. He then drove us to our connecting flight, where the other passengers were already boarding. He made one telephone call, and put our luggage on the conveyor belt loading the airplane. Finally, he apologized for the fact that since it was too late to obtain a boarding pass for us, we would have to wait in the car until all the other passengers had boarded.

Empowering front-line staff

Empowerment is discussed in Chapter 11. Empowerment means providing service employees with enough autonomy to allow them to handle unforeseen problem situations such as complaints.

Acknowledging the receipt of a complaint

Although it is preferable to solve complaints immediately, sometimes finding a solution and deciding on the proper compensation may take a great deal of time. In those circumstances, it is vital to inform the customer that his complaint has been received and is being dealt with. Ideally, the confirmation specifies the name and telephone number of the person handling the complaint, and the deadline by which the final answer can be expected.

Advertising Age[3] ran an experiment in the US. Twenty-six car companies received an identical letter of complaint. Only two managed to respond within one week, 15 companies responded during the second week and seven companies did not respond at all. This result is supported by an experiment we witnessed in January 1996.

One of our students sent out decoy letters of complaint to 80 companies and monitored very carefully how the companies responded.[4] Figure TN3.1 gives an overview of the response delay. Note that after 6 weeks 29% of all companies had not responded at all and only one-third replied within 1 week. Contrast this with the experience of a Dutch friend of mine who sent a written complaint to the headquarters of the Dutch subsidiary of McDonald's, and received a response by telephone the following day. The call was made by the manager of the restaurant where the incident had occurred. After having been informed about what had actually happened, the manager asked whether the complainant would agree to accept vouchers for a free meal as compensation for the inconvenience. The vouchers arrived by post the following day.

The fastest way to respond is by telephone. In the research illustrated in Figure TN3.1, only 28% of the reactions were by telephone. Two-thirds of the reactions came by post, and 5% of the companies actually sent a sales representative. Interestingly, about one-third of

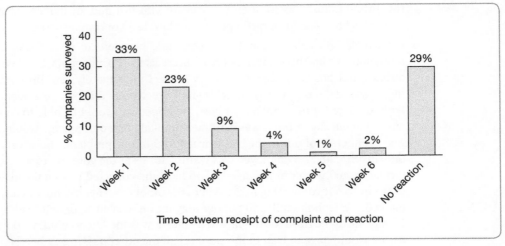

Figure TN3.1 Time taken for companies to react to complaints

the telephone reactions related to letters which did not contain the complainant's telephone number, indicating that some organizations had gone to the trouble of looking it up themselves.

Routing and prioritizing complaints

As a result of the simultaneity of production and consumption, complaints regarding services can be addressed to anyone at any level within the organization. Consequently, even if the organization empowers its front-line staff and tries to anticipate complaints as much as possible, the person receiving the complaint will not always be able to solve the problem. In those circumstances, much time can be lost transferring the complaint to the person or department which eventually has to handle it. Moreover, some complaints may merit a higher priority; the routing should therefore be different from one complaint to another.

In assessing whether a complaint should receive priority or not, the criterion should be the business at risk. This depends on the following factors:

- *Problem characteristics*. The more serious the problem is, the bigger the chances are that the customer will defect. Moreover, a customer who has experienced a serious problem is generally more demanding. Therefore, prioritizing may be justified.

- *Customer characteristics*. Key accounts represent more sales and profit than smaller customers. Consequently, complaints from important customers deserve preferential treatment.

- *Expected action by the complainer*. Customers put business at risk not only by defecting themselves, but also by creating negative word of mouth and/or by incurring costs. Often priority is given to complainers threatening to write letters to the press, to inform consumer organizations or to take the service provider to court.

In addition, it is very important to set up instructions about what to do when very serious complaints arise. Often the way they are handled will be outside the traditional complaint handling system. Some organizations instruct front-line employees to notify senior management.

The actual response

Complainers not only demand a quick response, they also expect proper redress. Customers judge the redress by three criteria:

- *The compensation*. The customer expects to be compensated for the problem he or she has experienced.
- *The sincerity*. The organization should care for the customer and the problem he or she has experienced. The customer wants to be taken seriously.
- *The follow-up*. Customer satisfaction with complaint handling can be increased by encouraging feedback from the customer afterwards.

The compensation

Granting the customer compensation requires balancing the costs and benefits of the compensation to the organization with the fairness of the compensation to the customer.

The costs and benefits to the organization

Organizations will grant compensation to retain the customer and to avoid negative word of mouth. The compensation should therefore always be smaller than the business at risk. Estimating the business at risk may require the assessment of the lifetime value of the complainant (*see* Chapter 12). Compensation can be higher for key accounts than for smaller customers.

To illustrate this issue, we can refer to the furniture store which receives a complaint concerning a scratch on a brand new leather couch. If the customer asks for a new couch, it is very unlikely that the same customer's future purchases will compensate the store for the cost of the new couch. The store will therefore not be inclined to give the customer a new couch, but will instead offer to repair the couch for the customer. In some circumstances, however, the company should replace the couch because it should also take the cost of negative word of mouth into account. This cost is admittedly much more difficult to assess.

The fairness to the customer

The complainer who is experiencing a problem wants to be compensated, and the compensation has to be perceived by the complainer as fair. Figure TN3.2 lists some types of compensation and the frequency of their use.[5]

Setting a fair compensation is not easy, particularly when the complaint is non-monetary. Moreover, in services, rework or repair is not always an option. For instance, if a meal is not satisfactory, a restaurant can offer to drop the bill, but what if the same problem occurs on board an airplane? Refunding the full fare would be overcompensating the passenger. What is a fair compensation?

In the case of minor complaints, companies may be tempted to offer mere apologies. However, doing so can be perceived as dishonest if it is not followed by a tangible outcome. The provision of symbolic compensations is therefore recommended for minor complaints.

For instance, a couple of years ago we sent a case study by mail to participants in a training seminar. Due to exceptional circumstances, the value of the stamps on the package

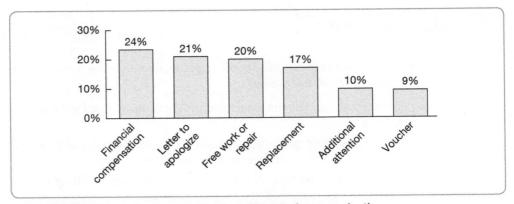

Figure TN3.2 Types of compensation used by service organizations

was insufficient, and so the participants had to pay a postage due fee of less than €1. We were afraid that our actually refunding the money would make things worse, as some people could have been offended because of the extremely low amount, and yet we wanted to go beyond a mere expression of apology. We eventually decided to create vouchers which looked like a huge stamp with a face value matching the penalty. On the final day, we distributed these to the participants, explaining that we wanted to compensate them for the inconvenience, and that they could exchange their vouchers for a free drink at the bar. The gesture was appreciated, as our customers understood that we had gone to some effort to make the vouchers. It is worth nothing that the customers were expecting to receive a free drink anyway, as they had already been invited to the farewell cocktail party on the first day of the programme weeks before the actual incident.

For more severe complaints, issuing vouchers which can be redeemed only by the service provider offers the advantage over a reimbursement that the customer has to make use of the company's services again in order to cash the voucher. Furthermore, the cost to the company of a voucher is usually lower than the actual reimbursement. Customers may find a financial compensation the fairest solution.

In judging the fairness of the compensation, it is also important to think of the inconvenience that the customer has suffered. If a customer's clothes are stained in a restaurant, paying only for the cost of dry-cleaning them does not make up for the time and effort invested in getting the clothes clean. Again, a token of apology – for instance, a complimentary drink – on top of the financial compensation, can work wonders.

If customers receive unequal compensation because of differences in business at risk, this may be perceived as unfair. Overall, customers believe they are being treated more fairly when they believe the provider is following company procedures, and that there are no special favours granted to specific customers.

A final consideration is that the compensation should not depend on whether the complaint is justified. If the customer perceives that the seller made a mistake, he or she wants to have compensation. The seller can try to convince the buyer that the seller is not responsible for the problem experienced, but when not successful, the dissatisfaction will remain. Again, balancing the costs and benefits to the organization should guide management's decision. Compensating for an unjustified complaint may result in retaining an otherwise lost customer.

▪ The sincerity

If a business operates with 0.1% defects, it means that one out of every 1000 customers will be confronted with a defect. That one customer, however, perceives that business and purchase as a 100% defect. The 0.1% defect statistic is not very convincing. That customer expects the company to deal with the particular problem with sincerity and empathy. This is not an easy endeavour. Each customer considers his or her problem to be unique and of the highest priority, whereas the complaint handler perceives it as a routine situation or even very exceptional and therefore negligible. Therefore, managing how the organization deals with complaining customers – whether in a specialized customer service department or by front-line employees – is an organizational issue.

Front-liners

Front-line employees should possess the social skills needed to deal with irate customers. These social skills are partly inborn and partly developed through training. Consequently, social skills will be a very important selection criterion when hiring front-line employees. The best way to further develop these skills is through simulated real-life situations and role playing. The airline KLM, for instance, organizes workshops around the world for its desk personnel to improve skills such as creativity and communication skills. A crew of actors simulate real-life situations that require creativity. This role play is recorded and afterwards discussed.

Specialized complaint handlers

Organizations that have to deal with many complaints set up specialized complaint handling cells, separate from front-line staff. The complaint handlers working in these cells should not only possess all the social skills mentioned above, but they also require additional technical skills. They should have a clear understanding of the organization as a whole, of the service delivered to the customer, and of the processes that exist within the entire service delivery system.

Complaint handling at Club Med, for instance, can involve requests for information to departments such as transport, marketing and sales, and local villages as well. Consequently, a broad understanding of Club Med's operations is required to answer complaints. At Club Med, this is achieved by job rotation.[6]

Job rotation is useful in general, as most complaint handlers suffer from burn-out after a few years, and develop a very negative image of the company. At British Airways, people are kept in the complaint handling department for a maximum of 2 years. A transfer to another department becomes inevitable to maintain the quality of complaint handling. Transferring complaint handlers after a few years to another department also increases the company's overall sensitivity to consumer problems. Replacing this staff is preferably done through in-company recruitment, because of the required knowledge of the business.

It is important to find a balance between technical and social skills. Case-based research in the Belgian tourist industry revealed that seven out of eight companies had staffed their complaint handling departments only with lawyers, indicating a defensive and argumentative attitude to complaint handling.[7]

Since service in complaint handling is of major importance and since complaint handling is very demanding, it can only be achieved by high-quality personnel. Therefore some organizations find treating complaint handling as a stepping stone to promotion a very effective means of attracting and ensuring high-quality staff.

471

Centralized versus decentralized receiving and handling

An organization cannot always control where complaints will be received, because it is the customer who makes that decision. However, the customer can be directed. Complaints can be received locally (in local agencies or stores), by front-office personnel, by customer service personnel, or centrally (in corporate offices) by the complaint handling office. Therefore, a major decision is whether to encourage customers to complain centrally or to the front-liners serving them. Equally important, the resolution of the customer's problems can also be entrusted to specialists in a central department or delegated to the front-line staff as much as possible.

Collecting complaints

Collecting complaints centrally offers more control. Logging, classifying and tracing the complaint handling is much easier. Furthermore, in the case of oral complaints, trusting the communication to specialists who are trained in dealing with irate customers can result in a better quality service. A central point of entry might also be helpful in lowering the complaint threshold. For instance, customers may be reluctant to drop a customer complaint card in a suggestion box inside a restaurant or shop, preferring to mail it to a central address. In addition, a central point of entry satisfies the desire of most customers to complain to a higher authority.

Organizations that are confronted with many complaints sometimes set up specialized customer service desks. This allows them to provide encouragement to customers to complain locally, while at the same time providing customers with complaint specialists.

Solving complaints

As already discussed, having specialists deal with complaints can offer the advantage of a broader view of the business and better technical skills. However, there are also major disadvantages. Often the 'specialists' have to call upon front-liners to explain the customer's background as well as to find out what really happened, which may cause unnecessary delays. In addition, having front-liners deal with complaints themselves makes them more aware of the importance of delivering quality service. There is thus good reason to divert the solving of complaints to the front-line staff, particularly for minor problems. If the complaints are serious, a central approach can be recommended. Another reason to centralize is if many complaints are very similar. This allows for a standardized approach resulting in economies of scale.

Consequently, there are four possible scenarios (*see* Figure TN3.3). In some cases, they can all occur within one organization, but usually one situation or a certain type of complaint handling is predominant.

The follow-up

Not all customers are very satisfied with the way complaints are handled. Therefore, after the compensation has been given to the customer, organizations can try to maximize the service recovery effort by adding some sort of follow-up. The customer can be informed about the service recovery. Furthermore, measuring the degree to which the customer is satisfied with the complaint handling will help to fine-tune the complaint handling process itself. The follow-up of complaints can be exhaustive or selective. Companies which receive a large number of complaints sometimes limit the follow-up to the most severe complaints

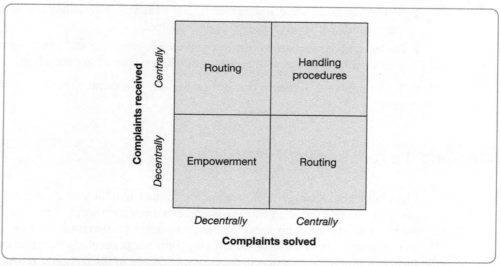

Figure TN3.3 Centralized and decentralized handling and receiving of complaints

or to complaints received centrally. There are a number of ways in which complaints can be followed up:

1 The first type of follow-up consists of calling up or writing to the customer afterwards to remind him or her of how the complaint was dealt with and what the actual compensation was. Reminding the customer can increase customer loyalty, particularly if the complaint was settled very quickly and/or if the compensation was perceived to be very fair. This type of follow-up should always attempt to ascertain whether everything is now according to the customer's wish. If it is, the customer is reminded of that fact. If not, the organization has a second chance at service recovery.

2 A more powerful alternative is to communicate to the customer that, partly based on his or her complaint, corrective actions have been taken to prevent the problem from recurring. Not only will this result in the greater involvement of the customer with the organization, it will also strengthen the image of an organization constantly trying to improve the quality of its service. It may yield both higher customer loyalty and positive word of mouth.

3 A final option is to measure the customer's satisfaction with the way his or her complaint has been handled. Again, dissatisfied customers will be identified, allowing a second attempt at service recovery. Furthermore, customers may perceive the measurement as an expression of the organization's concern for its customers and their complaints. This option is also interesting, as it allows for a comparison of the satisfaction regarding the complaint handling process with the overall customer satisfaction.

Designing a complaint handling system

Many service organizations handle complaints on an *ad hoc* basis. Whenever they receive a complaint, they find out more about the incident and handle the complaint, without following any explicit procedures. This approach has two main disadvantages:

1 Similar complaints may not receive similar treatment, which may lead to a perception of the organization as inconsistent or disorganized.

2 No learning takes place in terms of timeliness, efficiency and effectiveness of the complaint handling process. The organization keeps reinventing the wheel.

We recommend therefore that companies set up a comprehensive complaint handling system.

Tackling the root causes

Complaint management goes beyond the simple handling of individual complaints in order to retain dissatisfied customers and avoid negative word of mouth. The complaints should also inspire improvement projects in order to eliminate the root causes that led to the complaints in the first place. Complaints are particularly valuable as they relate to incidents which are so critical to the customer that he or she has gone to the trouble of filing a complaint. This explains why maximizing the number of complaints helps to minimize the number of problems.

Tackling the root causes involves expanding the remit of the complaint handling scheme, by three major steps:

● classifying the complaints by their nature;

● analysing the business at risk; and

● executing the improvement projects.

Building a customer-oriented organization

The final objective of any complaint management system is to build a customer-oriented organization. The way an organization deals with complainants is more symptomatic of its customer orientation: it actually strongly influences the company culture as it signals to all staff what priority top management attaches to customers and their concerns.

The organization's management system should therefore include the following complaint handling performance measures:

● number of complaints, possibly as a ratio to compliments, and/or limited to those centrally received;

● the speed of handling complaints, often measured as average number of days required and percentage of complaints taking more than X days;

● customer satisfaction with the complaint handling process;

● number of (successful) improvement projects resulting from complaint analysis.

By discussing the statistics during board meetings, by publishing them in the annual report or in internal magazines, and by portraying employees who deal with complaints in an outstanding fashion as employee of the month, complaint management will be taken more seriously throughout the organization.

By way of contrast to Exhibit TN3.1, an airline cabin attendant told us about how the management of her company reacted to the way she settled complaints. Although she was supposed to be empowered to compensate passengers for problems they experienced, she was very reluctant to do so. The main reason was that on the two previous occasions when she had issued a voucher, her manager had asked for an elaborate report on the exact circumstances of the incident. She had expected to be congratulated for serving the customer well, but ended up feeling that she had had to defend herself.

Exhibit TN3.1 Involving the entire company

A fine example of how this can be achieved is the way the complaint card was used by Hewlett-Packard in the Netherlands. All its customers received a yellow card stating:

'I give Hewlett Packard the yellow card because I am not satisfied. Please contact me.'

The card had to be returned to the attention of the general manager. Much to the surprise of both employees and customers, the members of the board actually took turns calling the complaining customers. Customers were surprised and delighted, and several of them immediately explained that the problem was not so important that the director had to get involved.

The impact on the employees was even more impressive. If complaints are so important that they merit senior management's time and attention, then certainly all staff should treat complaints as a priority.

Again, top management can offset these situations by monitoring the number of vouchers issued by each team. Teams issuing too few vouchers are either operating at zero defects (which is unlikely) or are too stringent in compensating passengers.

Conclusion

In this chapter we have also looked extensively at why complaints should be managed and how to manage them. Simultaneity and the importance of word-of-mouth advertising make complaint management of particular interest for services. Designing an adequate complaint management approach consists of lowering thresholds, responding quickly, giving a proper response and finally systematizing complaint handling. The ultimate goal of working on complaints is to create a more customer-oriented service company by tackling the root causes and improving services.

Suggested further reading

Stauss, Bernd and Seidel, Wolfgang (2004) *Complaint Management: The Heart of CRM.* Thomson South-Western, p. 310

Notes and references

1 TARP (1986) *Consumer Complaint Handling in America: An update study*. United States Office of Consumer Affairs

2 Meyer, A. and Dornach, F. (1995) *The German Customer Barometer: Quality and satisfaction*. German Marketing Association and German Post AG

3 Kauchak, T. (1991) 'A little service please!', *Advertising Age*, 21 January, S8–S10

4 Blontrok, V. (1996) *Klachtenbehandeling in België. Een empirisch onderzoek* (Complaint Handling in Belgium: An empirical investigation). Unpublished paper, De Vlerick School voor Management

5 Bourgeois, S. (1996) *Klachtenmanagement in de dienstensector* (Complaint management in the service sector). Unpublished final paper, University of Ghent, Faculty of Economics

6 Verhaeghe, K. (1996) *Klachtenbehandeling in diensten: een profielschets van enkele sectoren* (Complaint handling in services: a profile of some service sectors). Unpublished paper, De Vlerick School voor Management

7 Ibid.

Technical Note 4

Measuring customer satisfaction

Gino Van Ossel • Paul Gemmel

This technical note should be read in conjunction with Chapters 12 and Chapter 13

In this technical note, we give some important suggestions for managers when they want to develop systems to measure customer satisfaction. Measuring customer satisfaction (and acting upon the results of these measurements) benefits from having a benchmark. Other crucial considerations when setting up a customer satisfaction measurement system relate to determining whose satisfaction to measure, whose performance to take into account and how to collect customer satisfaction data.

Need for a benchmark

In order for a measure to have any impact, a reference point is required – a standard according to which an employee or company can judge performance, whether it is good or bad, better or worse. In other words, a benchmark is what is needed.

In customer satisfaction measurement, the most common benchmarks are:

- development over time;
- the different organizational units (for instance, branches, subsidiaries or business units);
- competition.

Evolution over time is the best indicator of whether an organization's customer focus efforts are paying off. Therefore, most customer satisfaction measurements assess the rate of improvement. Since comparisons are only possible if the measurement system is standardized over time, conceiving a customer satisfaction measurement system should be carried out with the utmost care. Indeed, adjusting the system regularly will hinder comparisons. This does not mean that temporary performance measures linked to improvement projects and/or individual or team performance cannot be used at certain points in time.

Quite often, a service organization operates multi-site facilities with different branches or service units at different places. This often makes it possible to carry out inter-organizational benchmarking. Measuring customer satisfaction across different service units is necessary to create peer pressure and internal competition, in order to create a willingness in all units to improve customer satisfaction.

In a competitive environment, outperforming competitors may yield more than simply achieving the highest possible performance. Therefore it is common to benchmark customer satisfaction scores against those of the competition, both in terms of the actual performance and in terms of the rate of improvement.

Whose satisfaction to measure?

This looks like an easy question to answer. Is it not the customer's satisfaction? This is the correct answer, but are we interested in *all* the customers, and who is 'the customer' anyway?

We have already explained that loyalty and referrals result from customer delight, while defections and negative word of mouth arise from dissatisfied customers. Consequently, in customer satisfaction surveys the focus should be on the percentage of dissatisfied and delighted customers, rather than on average satisfaction scores. The question remains as to whether the company should calculate these percentages for its average customer or for the customer representing the highest turnover, potential turnover or profit.

Key accounts or all customers?

If the Pareto principle applies and 20% of the customers account for 80% of company's sales and profits, delighting these 20% is far more important than delighting the other 80%. If a company surveys a representative sample of all its customers, however, the results will mainly reflect the satisfaction of that 80%, which accounts for only 20% of its business. This is one argument for a company surveying only its biggest customers. On the other hand, the biggest customers often receive to all intents and purposes the same service as the smaller ones.

In deciding which customers to survey, the following guidelines should be followed:

- *Percentage of delighted customers*. It is desirable to be able to calculate the percentage of delighted customers for key accounts separately from the other customers. The more important the key accounts are, the more special attention they should get. This may even necessitate a significant cash outlay to delight individual customers. Spending that money on key accounts will usually be more profitable than spending it on the average customer. Achieving customer delight among key accounts is the best defence against competitors. On the other hand, it is useful to monitor the overall percentage of delighted customers, as this percentage will indicate the company's potential for referrals. This is not an absolute necessity, however.

- *Percentage of dissatisfied customers*. The reasons for dissatisfaction are usually the same for large and small customers alike. Working on structurally improving the service process and offering will usually benefit all customers. However, since the large customers are limited in number, analysing only the (hopefully limited number of) dissatisfied key accounts may not provide a good insight into the root causes of customer dissatisfaction. That is why surveying all customers rather than only key accounts will probably offer more information on the areas for improvement. However, a single dissatisfied big customer poses a much bigger threat than a small one. It is thus desirable to calculate the percentage of dissatisfied key accounts separately from the overall dissatisfaction rate. Furthermore, and equally important, identifying dissatisfied customers is the first step in the service recovery process. The organization has to ensure that it can identify all key accounts which are dissatisfied.

Who is the actual customer?

A second question to be answered in an organizational buying situation is 'Who is the customer?' In business-to-business marketing, the familiar concept of the decision-making unit refers to all the individuals involved in the buying process. The company has to decide for which members of the decision-making unit they want to know the degree of satisfaction and dissatisfaction. These individuals can perform one or more of the following roles:

- *Users* – members of the organization who will use the product or service.
- *Initiators* – those who initiate the buying process.
- *Influencers* – those who affect the buying process, for instance by setting specifications (prescribers), providing information for evaluating alternatives.
- *Buyers* – those with the formal authority to select the vendors.
- *Deciders* – those who actually make the final decision on which vendor to choose.
- *Approvers* – those with the formal authority to veto the deciders.
- *Purchasers* – those who do the actual buying without having the formal power to decide anything.
- *Gatekeepers* – those who control the flow of information, particularly the stream of salespeople, mailings and sales material which targets the other members of the decision-making unit, thus indirectly influencing which vendors are selected.

As a general rule, it is obvious that the survey should focus in the first place on the members of the decision-making unit who have the biggest impact on the selection of the vendor. They will defect when dissatisfied and generate repeat business when delighted. However, in the long run, their satisfaction will also be affected by the satisfaction of the other members of the decision-making unit. Although it is dangerous to generalize, investing in their delight will usually not be profitable, but in the long run not preventing dissatisfaction may make the customer defect.

Whose performance to measure?

Another question to be answered before the details of a measuring instrument can be designed, is which organizational unit's performance should be assessed. Our recent studies have proven that the aggregate results for an organization as a whole do not generate actionable and relevant results. The smaller the unit of measurement, the richer the information will be; unfortunately, the effort and therefore cost are also proportionally greater.

In retail banking, for instance, it could be assumed that customer satisfaction with the bank's actual products (for instance, its savings account) would be the same across all branches, since these products are standardized within the bank. However, the service relating to the product is being delivered ('produced') at the branch level. Consequently, customer satisfaction may vary from one branch to another. In deciding which organizational unit's customer satisfaction will be measured, three elements should be taken into consideration:

- *The unit as seen by the customer*. The customer will only be able to judge a unit which he or she perceives as such.

- *The managerial unit.* Organizations aiming at improving their performance want to collect data for a manager and his staff. This managerial unit can be the organization as a whole (top management and all staff), the smallest unit possible (a crew leader and his crew), or something in between.

- *Costs.* As mentioned earlier, the smaller the unit for which we measure, the more expensive the survey becomes. However, we have come across several organizations that, mainly for cost reasons, calculated customer satisfaction scores only at the national level. These results turned out to be useless as they revealed nothing that could be used for improvement projects.

The compilation of statistics involves drawing a sample at the smallest level for which you want to make the analysis. Data can always be consolidated for a larger unit of measurement; it can never be broken down for sub-units.

How to collect customer satisfaction data

Once we have decided what we want to measure, for which organizational unit and with which customers, the final step in conceiving the customer satisfaction performance measure is deciding how to collect the data. As measuring customer satisfaction is simply a particular type of market research, the data collection methods are in many ways very similar. In this section we shall describe the basic elements of a system of data collection and shall highlight those details that are particular to a system of satisfaction measurement. We shall discuss the following areas:

- the communication method by which the data can be collected;
- the make-or-buy decision.

(For a more in-depth discussion of data collection and how to design the questions, you should consult the numerous excellent books on market research. *See* Suggested further reading at the end of Chapter 12.)

The communication method

Customers can be surveyed by telephone, by mail, in person or with a combination of the three. The main criteria for deciding on the communication method are:

- the nature and amount of information that has to be collected;
- control of the sample and supervision of the field work;
- response rates;
- time and cost considerations.

By telephone

The telephone is a very good means by which to collect a limited amount of relatively simple information quickly. This makes it a very good instrument for customer satisfaction performance measurement. However, it also has some disadvantages:

- Open-ended questions, inviting the customer to comment on how the organization might improve its service offering, usually result in short and rather superficial answers. We shall discuss later in this section how these questions are an important complement to the actual performance measure.

- The survey is never really anonymous. Even if the interviewer guarantees the respondent that the company will not know his or her personal opinions, the respondent knows that the interviewer by definition knows his or her identity. Obviously this is only a problem if anonymity is required.

Controlling the sample and field is also relatively easy by using Computer Assisted Telephone Interviewing (CATI). The telephone numbers are selected automatically by the computer and in case of non-response, the computer redials the number several times. Furthermore, if the call is answered, but the respondent is not present or does not have time at the moment, the interviewer can also instruct the computer to redial at another time. The questions and the possible answers are being displayed on a computer screen. The interviewer simply has to read them off and enter the respondent's answers into the computer. The computer automatically keeps track of the time a call takes and of the hit rate of each interviewer.

Problems related specifically to telephone interviews include:

1 Most people are not at home during office hours, which makes the method more expensive.

2 People do not like to be disturbed during their free time and may perceive it as an invasion of their privacy. This may not only result in a refusal to co-operate and consequently in a lower response rate, but it may even damage the customers' satisfaction.

3 Not all individuals have a telephone. In particular, elderly people, people with a low educational level and low-income families will be under-represented in the sample.

4 Different problems arise when surveying companies. It may take several calls before targeted respondents are present, assuming they are willing to answer the questions.

On the other hand, response rates are fairly high since only customers are being interviewed. Their interest in your product or service is usually relatively high. In our overall experience, the telephone is best used in a business-to-business context and is far less useful in assessing the customer satisfaction of individuals.

By mail

The major advantage of mail surveys is that it is possible to question all types of people at a relatively low cost. Compared to telephone surveys, it is not only possible to ask a larger number of questions but also more complex ones.

Promising anonymity and asking open-ended questions is perfectly feasible. Another advantage is that controlling the field is relatively easy. As field workers do not really intervene, except for entering the answers into the computer, the company has good control over the sample. Furthermore, standardized surveys being used over a long period of time can be processed automatically. Scanning becomes economically feasible if the number of questionnaires is high enough.

The major challenge is the response rate. Even when surveying one's own customers, response rates can be extremely low, particularly when surveying companies. The response rate is typically related to the effort that is required of the respondent and his or her involvement with the service and/or company. This effort largely depends on the length and complexity of the questionnaire. Enclosing a return envelope also lowers the effort required of the respondent. Affixing a stamp, or printing on the envelope that no stamp is needed, has a positive impact on the response rate, particularly when surveying individuals. An alternative to including a return envelope is to design the survey as a fax.

The involvement level with the service and/or company is always relatively high as the questionnaire is being sent only to customers; but not always high enough to trigger good response rates. One Belgian fast-food chain has received response rates of about 5%. Car distributors mailing their customers achieve response rates ranging from 25% to 50%. There are two main reasons for this variation:

1 It seems that more expensive makes achieve lower response rates than other makes. Possible explanations are that expensive cars are often company cars (resulting in a lower involvement) and that they are driven by business people who are busier and generally confronted with more surveys.

2 Response rates differ depending on the timing of the survey. Car distributors typically question their customers shortly after they have bought a car about the buying process and the delivery of the car. A couple of years later, they send out a second survey about the after-sales service.

A very important factor in increasing the involvement and consequently the response rate is the letter accompanying the questionnaire. The letter should state the objective of the survey, as well as identify the company undertaking it, and explain why and how the respondent will benefit from the survey and how much (or hopefully how little) time it will take.

If the company can manage to achieve an acceptable response rate by taking the above considerations into account, then sending out a survey by mail is the best option. Experience has shown that this is more often the case with individuals than with companies. Short questionnaires taking the form of a fax can yield high response rates with companies.

Finally, the nature of the service and the relationship with the service provider will also affect the response rate. Increasing the response rate is possible but very expensive. Announcing the survey in advance by mail or telephone and sending out reminders when people do not respond have proven their effectiveness. However, as customer satisfaction measurement is by nature ongoing, this option may prove to be too expensive.

In person

The most powerful data collection method is the personal interview. Lengthy surveys with complex questions, including open-ended questions, will trigger high response rates and elaborated answers. However, as customer satisfaction performance measurement typically uses relatively simple and concise questionnaires, this is largely a theoretical advantage. Given the disadvantage of their relatively high cost, true personal interviews are rarely used.

Personal interviews fall into four categories of location: interviews inside a service location, street interviews, interviews at a third party's location, and interviews at the respondent's home or office. Interviewing customers inside the service location is the only commonly used technique, as the high concentration of customers helps to keep costs under control. If the surveyor simply hands over the questionnaires and collects the answers afterwards, the cost is relatively low. If, on the other hand, the interviewer actually has to go through the questions with the customer, costs will increase, depending on the length of the interview and the response rate. In certain service industries this is a very common approach, particularly for individuals with low involvement. Its feasibility depends on the nature of the service. In a fast-food restaurant, for instance, this is often not a good option, as these customers by definition usually have little time to spare. Those who do have time to spare are not necessarily representative of the customer population. Surveying customers in this situation is only justified when the questionnaire is very short. An alternative in this situation is to hand out the questionnaire together with a return envelope reading 'postage paid'.

Certain service locations, such as trains or aeroplanes, are perfectly suited to questioning customers in person. Another example is a hotel chain which asks its guests in the evening if they would care to answer a limited number of questions while having breakfast the following morning. By announcing the interview in advance, very high response rates are achieved. This is the most common way to measure participants' customer satisfaction in management training programmes.

It should be clear that in all the above examples the interviewer's role is mostly to distribute a written survey in order to increase the response rate. The opportunity to ask a greater number of, or more complex questions, is rarely used.

An important disadvantage of this technique is that it is difficult to control the sample and the field. In aeroplanes, the cabin crew has to distribute and collect the surveys. If their evaluation hinges on the results of the survey, they may be tempted to manipulate the results. They can fill out some forms themselves, throw away forms with unfavourable answers, give the forms to different passengers, or simply look over the passengers shoulders in order to influence them. In shops or restaurants, the sample is unlikely to be random, unless the interviewers ask screening questions. Interviewers will always be inclined to select respondents who appeal to them – for example, people of the same age group.

Techniques other than interviewing inside the service location are rarely used for customer satisfaction performance measurement. Street interviews are a very inefficient sampling technique, as the percentage of targeted customers walking the street tends to be limited. Interviews at a third party's location (often the offices of a market research agency) or at the customer's location are extremely expensive. The customer has to be convinced to go to the third party's location, which typically results in high recruitment costs and low response rates. Interviewing at the respondent's home or office involves transportation costs for the interviewer.

These methods do offer important opportunities for more qualitative and unstructured or semi-structured surveys (*see* below). However, for quantitative customer satisfaction performance measurement, which does not go beyond simple and concise questionnaires, these techniques are far too expensive.

Combining different media

While discussing the personal interview techniques, we indicated that the interviewer's role can be limited to distributing and/or collecting written questionnaires. This could be considered as combining different data collection methods. Other more advanced combinations are also possible. For instance, companies have experimented with calling respondents to notify them in advance that a written survey was going to be sent to them. The response rates can increase significantly, but unfortunately this is an expensive solution.

Rank Xerox is using the reverse combination. It mails a questionnaire to the respondents, explaining that they will be called to assist the company in answering the questions. The actual data collection is done by telephone, but the respondent can see and read the questions and alternative answers. Rank Xerox has chosen this method because it allows the company to combine the length of a written survey with the higher response rate of telephone interviews in a business-to-business context.

Response rates

When discussing the issue of response rates, managers always express their concern about whether the participants in the survey are representative of the whole population. In other words, they wonder if the outcome would have been different if the people who did not respond had done so. Their concern is only partly justified. In fact, it is necessary to distinguish between the *representativeness* and the *stability* of the measurement.

Customer satisfaction measurement is rarely representative if the response rate is not close to 100%. As we explained earlier, the more involved people are, the more they tend to participate in a survey. By definition, the dissatisfied and the delighted are more involved than the somewhat satisfied, who are 'indifferent' vis-à-vis the service and its provider. Consequently, it is safe to assume that the dissatisfied and the delighted are over-represented among those who respond. Therefore the answer to the managers' concern has to be: 'yes', the people who do not respond will probably give a different opinion from those who do. This means that it is dangerous to treat the results of such a measurement as absolute fact. Stating that the customer satisfaction score of a company is 8.2 on a scale of 10 denies the simple fact that the score would almost certainly have been different had the response rate been different. Similarly, comparing scores across companies should be carried out with the utmost care. Even if the wording and the scale of the questions are identical, differences in response rates can account for differences in calculated scores.

Of course, measuring customer satisfaction by telephone may yield high response rates, so that representativeness can be obtained, but without these high response rates there can be no true representativeness.

In their concern for representativeness, managers often overlook the true objective of performance measurement. As we explained at the beginning of this chapter, performance measures can only be interpreted if they are compared to a benchmark. Therefore the stability of the measurement is more important than its representativeness. Stability means that the same results would be obtained if the survey were duplicated. Sending out the same survey to a different sample should give the same result. The issue should not be whether or not there is a measurement error, but whether or not the measurement error is constant.

Decentralized service organizations therefore have to monitor whether the response rates are the same across all organizational units. A retail bank, for instance, does not simply report the results of its measurement for each branch, but also its response rates. Typically these will be about the same for all branches. Any exceptions to this rule are studied with the utmost care, because differing response rates are usually a symptom of some underlying phenomenon. Similarly, in comparing results over time or across competitors, stable response rates are an indication of a stable measurement error. Consequently, benchmarking the results is justified, which is ultimately the objective of the performance measurement.

In our experience the true challenge is not to obtain representative or stable results. Neither is it to convince the managers directly involved in the satisfaction measurement, or those responsible for organizational units performing well, that representativeness is less of an issue than obtaining stable results. Managers responsible for organizational units which do not perform well will always question the representativeness and validity of the measurement tool, and will remain blind to their own inability to meet their customers' expectations. This is particularly tragic as it is precisely these managers who would benefit most from the measurement, as their opportunities for improvement are the greatest. The challenge lies in making these managers see the opportunities for improvement in their unit. The greater the importance attached to the customer satisfaction performance measure when evaluating managers, the more the representativeness will be contested. By linking the appraisal to the performance measure, managers are offered only two alternatives: they can either leave the organization or give up their resistance and focus on improving their performance.

The make-or-buy decision

In conceiving and executing customer satisfaction surveys, a company has to decide whether to make use of a market research agency or not. Unless the company has its own market research specialists, using outside help is desirable. Even if those in-house specialists are available, however, the peculiarities of satisfaction may justify hiring outside consultants. However, selecting an outside consultant is not easy. Even excellent market research agencies do not necessarily have the required skills to construct customer satisfaction surveys.

Not all market research agencies are experts in ongoing research in general, and in satisfaction measurement in particular. For ongoing research, the distinction between conceiving and executing the survey is extremely important.

Conceiving versus executing the survey

Conceiving an ongoing survey requires brainpower, while executing an ongoing survey (including analysis) is largely operational. Therefore, any request for a quote from a market research agency should stress the distinction between these two elements.

The company must also demand copyright over the survey and the questionnaire. This will give it the flexibility to hire another agency to execute the survey if this is necessary, or even to execute it itself.

In the conception stage, in-depth knowledge of the ongoing research in general and of customer satisfaction measurement in particular, is essential. If in-house research specialists are available, the hired outsiders should be able to demonstrate great expertise in customer satisfaction measurement.

In the executional stage, however, efficiency is important. We have come across companies who were paying an agency a fortune to simply repeat the same research over and over again. The agency could virtually process the survey automatically, but was still charging for its brainpower. Moreover, the contract stated very clearly that the agency was the intellectual owner of the survey, so that the company was bound to that agency.

It should be clear that conceiving the survey with the help of outside experts will not automatically result in excellent surveys. On the other hand, executing the survey can be handled by any good field agency, since mail, telephone or written customer surveys require limited field control and are relatively easy to sample. Cost considerations are important here.

Ad hoc versus ongoing research and customer satisfaction measurement

In *ad hoc research*, a specific management problem is translated into a series of research questions. For the in-depth study of that management problem, a custom-made research design is developed. That particular design is usually executed only once. Both the field and the analysis are unique and will probably not be duplicated again. As a result, the cost implications of each question are more or less limited. Furthermore, it is almost impossible to detach the conception from the execution (particularly the analysis) of the research.

In its most typical form, the *ad hoc* research consists of two stages. The first or qualitative stage aims at inventorying all possible views and aspects of the research questions. The second or quantitative stage sums up all those views and aspects and comes up with a representative answer.

Ongoing research, however, is different in many respects. The survey has to be executed several times and often over a very long period of time. This has many consequences:

- From a budgetary point of view, the execution and analysis stage is much more important in ongoing research than it is in *ad hoc* research. Since the same research will be executed several times, the total field work is much greater. Consequently, with ongoing research, the cost of the field work is more carefully planned during the conception stage. This usually results in relatively short surveys which can be processed as automatically as possible. Sometimes the survey is designed for CATI and sometimes the written surveys can be scanned into a computer.

- The analysis itself is also standardized. The same calculations are performed so that the bare facts and figures are also generated automatically. Interpreting the facts and figures is also much easier as a learning effect occurs.

- Finally, the questionnaire itself should be generic enough to be useful over a relatively long period of time.

Furthermore, customer satisfaction measurement is ongoing research of a very specific nature. It is important to reiterate the need for unbalanced scales, the issue of which organizational unit to measure, and the importance of the percentage of dissatisfied and delighted customers rather than the average satisfaction score.

Suggested further reading

Hayes, B. E. (2008) *Measuring Customer Satisfaction and Loyalty: Survey design, use and statistical analysis methods* (3rd edn), Milwaukee, WI: ASQ Quality Press

Technical note 5

Data envelopment analysis
Paul Gemmel

This technical note should be read in conjunction with Chapter 13

Several techniques are available for relative efficiency benchmarking of service units. The most basic technique is the ratio-analysis, where the ratio of one output to one input is compared between several units. In the case of the example of bank branches, efficiency is defined as:

$$\text{Efficiency (branch 1)} = \frac{\text{Output}}{\text{Input}}$$

So, the relative efficiency of branch 1 is the result of the comparison of the efficiency of branch 1 to the efficiency of another branch (e.g. branch 2):

$$\text{Relative efficiency} = \frac{\text{Efficiency (branch 1)}}{\text{Efficiency (branch 2)}}$$

If branch 2 is a best practice (i.e. in this case branch 2 produces more output with the same amount of input than branch 1), branch 2 forms the frontier for branch 1 and the frontier efficiency of branch 1 is determined. Depending on how much shape is imposed on the frontier, a distinction is made between non-parametric and parametric frontiers. Non-parametric approaches, such as DEA, do not impose any particular functional form that presupposes the shape of the frontier.

Using DEA, a best-practice function is empirically built from observed inputs and outputs. Linear programming is used to derive this best practice function. The objective is to maximize a service unit's efficiency – expressed as a ratio of outputs to inputs – by comparing a particular unit's efficiency with the performance of a group of similar units delivering the same service. Some of the units are evaluated as 100% efficient as compared to the other units. These 100% efficient units are said to lie on the efficient production frontier. Other units have an efficiency rating of less than 100% and are considered to be relatively inefficient. DEA further indicates how an inefficient service unit can improve its performance. By identifying a reference set of efficient service units for each inefficient unit, one can determine how the amount of some of the input factors must be reduced to attain the same level of output in an efficient way. In this way, the efficient production frontier represents a standard of performance that the units not on the efficient frontier could try to achieve. In other words, the efficient frontier envelopes (encloses) all the data points. This is the origin of the term 'data envelopment analysis' (DEA).

The most basic DEA model was developed by Charnes, Cooper and Rhodes (CCR) in 1978.[1]

The CCR model allows that each unit adopts a set of weights which shows it in the most favourable light in comparison to the other units. Suppose that there are k branches j involved in the study. Each branch uses different amounts of n inputs to produce m outputs. For each branch j, y_{rj} and x_{ij} indicate respectively the observed amount of output r and input i. The efficiency of a target unit j_0 can be described in the following algebraic model (adapted from Charnes et al., 1994[2]):

$$\text{Max } E_0 = \frac{\sum_{r=1}^{m} u_r y_{rj_0}}{\sum_{i=1}^{n} v_i x_{ij_0}} \tag{1}$$

$$\text{Subject to } \frac{\sum_{r=1}^{m} u_r y_{rj}}{\sum v_i x_{ij}} \leq 1 \text{ for each unit } j = 1, 2, 3, \ldots, k$$

$$\text{and} \quad u_i \geq \varepsilon \text{ for } r = 1, 2, \ldots, m$$
$$v_i \geq \varepsilon \text{ for } i = 1, 2, \ldots, n$$
$$x_{ij} \geq 0, \, y_{ij} \geq 0$$

The above model (1) is a fractional model trying to look for a set of weights (u_r, v_i) which gives the target unit j_0 the highest possible efficiency rating. 'Highest possible' means that when these same weights are used in the other units $j, j = 1, 2, \ldots, k$, the efficiency ratings of the other units cannot be higher than 1. Furthermore all input and output weights need to be greater or equal to an infinitismal small value ε. This guarantees that each input and output variable is included in the model. Nonetheless the positive value ε is so small that it cannot disturb any solution involving only real numbers.

Because it is not always possible to solve non-linear fractional models such as stated in (1), Charnes and Cooper propose to convert it into a linear non-fractional model that can be solved with linear programming (adapted from Charnes et al., 1994):[3]

$$\text{Max } \omega_0 = \sum_{r=1}^{m} u_r y_{rj_0} \tag{2}$$

$$\text{Subject to } \sum_{i=1}^{n} v_i x_{ij_0} = 1$$

$$\sum_{r=1}^{m} u_r y_{rj} - \sum v_i x_{ij} \leq 0; \text{ for } j = 1, 2, \ldots, k$$
$$u_r \geq \varepsilon \text{ for } r = 1, 2, \ldots, m$$
$$v_i \geq \varepsilon \text{ for } i = 1, 2, \ldots, n$$
$$x_{ij} \geq 0, \, y_{rj} \geq 0$$

Because model (2) is a typical linear programming model, there exists also a dual problem formulation (adapted from Charnes et al., 1994):

$$\text{Min } z_0 = \theta - \varepsilon \left(\sum_{r=1}^{m} S_{rj_0}^{+} + \sum_{i=1}^{n} S_{rj_0}^{-} \right) \tag{3}$$

$$\text{Subject to} \sum_{j=1}^{k} \lambda_j y_{rj} - S_{rj_0}^+ = y_{rj_0}; \; r = 1, 2, \ldots, m$$

$$\sum_{j=1}^{k} \lambda_j x_{ij} + S_{ij_0}^- = \theta_{j_0} x_{ij_0}$$

$$\lambda_j \geq 0; \; j = 1, 2, \ldots, k$$

$$S_{rj_0}^+ \geq 0; \; r = 1, 2, \ldots, m$$

$$S_{ij_0}^- \geq 0; \; i = 1, 2, \ldots, n$$

In this dual model (3), $S_{rj_0}^+$ and $S_{ij_0}^-$ denotes slack variables and λ_j are intensity weights defining the linear combination of best practices to be compared with branch j_0. The primal model (2) is referred to as the multiplier form, while the dual problem (3) is referred to as the envelopment form. The duality theorem of linear programming can be used to guarantee that $z_0^* = \varpi_0^*$ where the superscript* denotes an optimal value with intensity weight. The optimal value of the intensity weight is based on the composition of a hypothetical efficient branch with output and input so that the composite branch level has input levels that do not exceed those of branch j, and output levels that are at least as high as those of branch j_0. The optimal value yields an efficiency rating that measures the distance that j_0 lies from the frontier. Thus j_0 is efficient if and only if $z_0^* = \varpi_0^* = 0$. j_0 is not efficient if any component of the slack variables in the optimal solution is not zero. The values of these nonzero components identify the sources and amounts of inefficiency in the corresponding outputs and inputs.[4] The variable indicates how all inputs of branch j_0 must be proportionally reduced in order to become efficient. When the focus in the model is on the maximal movement toward the frontier through proportional reduction of inputs, we speak about an input oriented CCR model. It is also possible to focus on maximal movement via proportional augmentation of outputs. In this case, we speak about an output-orientation.

Suggested further reading

Sherman, D. A. (2006) *Service Productivity Management: Improving Service Performance using Data Envelopment Analysis (DEA)*. Springer Science + Business Media, LCC. This book is a reference work for Data Envelopment Analysis and its application as a benchmarking technique in services

Notes and references

1 Charnes, A., Cooper, W. and Rhodes, E. (1978) 'Measuring the efficiency of decision making units', *European Journal of Operational Research*, Vol 2, pp. 429–444

2 Charnes, A., Cooper, W., Lewin, A. Y. and Seiford, L. M. (eds) (1994) *Data Envelopment Analysis: Theory, methlodogy and application*. Kluwer Academic Publishers

3 In transforming the fractional programming model (1) into a linear programming model (2), μ_r is set equal to tu_r and $n = tv_i$, where $t^{-1} = \sum_i v_i x_{ij_0}$

4 Charnes, A. *et al.* (1994), op. cit., p. 26

The state probability (P(*n*))

The probability of having *n* customers in the system is called the state probability P(*n*). To find the state probability P(*n*), it is necessary to formulate and solve a set of balance equations that equate the rate at which transitions occur into the state to the rate at which transitions occur out of the state. The rate into a certain state must be equal to the rate out of this state to reach a situation of steady state. A situation of steady state is necessary to solve a M/M/1/∞ queuing system analytically. In setting up these balance equations it is important to remember that only one customer can arrive at a time and that only one customer at a time can leave the server. The transition rate into P(2) (the probability of having two customers in the system) can be obtained either by multiplying the probability that there is one customer in the system P(1) with the arrival rate λ or by multiplying the probability that there are three customers in the system P(3) and that one customer is leaving after being served. The transition rate out of the state P(2) is the consequence of an arrival or a departure. Balancing the transition in and out of the state P(2) leads to the following equation:

$$\lambda P(2) + \mu P(2) = \lambda P(1) + \mu P(3)$$

If we repeat the previous reasoning for different states, we obtain the following set of balance equations:

State

0      $\mu P(1) = \lambda P(0)$

1      $\lambda P(0) + \mu P(2) = \lambda P(1) + \mu P(1)$

2      $\lambda P(1) + \mu P(3) = \lambda P(2) + \mu P(2)$

. . .   . . .

n $\lambda P(n-1) + \mu P(n+1) = \lambda P(n) + \lambda P(n)$

It is easy to transform the above set equations to the following set:

State

0      $\mu P(1) = \lambda P(0)$

1      $\mu P(2) = \lambda P(1)$

2      $\mu P(3) = \lambda P(2)$

. . .   . . .

n $\mu P(n+1) = \lambda P(n)$

This gives the following general relationship between two state probabilities:

$$P(n) + \lambda/\mu P(n-1) = \rho P(n-1)$$

When this relationship is worked through until the single state probability P(0) is reached, this gives:

$$P(n) = \rho^n P(0)$$

To determine P(0), another characteristic of a proper probability distribution is used, i.e. that the sum of the state probabilities must be 1:

$$\sum_{n=0}^{\infty} \rho^n P(0) = 1$$

This is the sum of a geometric series. Using the standard equation for the sum of a geometric series, we can write:

$$P(0)\frac{1}{1-P} = 1$$

or

$$P(0) = 1 - \rho \text{ with } \rho < 1$$

This results in:

$$P(n) = (1 - \rho)\rho^n \text{ with } \rho < 1.$$

Index

Page references to Figures or Tables will be in *italics*